A HISTORY

OF

MUSIC IN SCOTLAND

Da Capo Press Music Reprint Series

GENERAL EDITOR

FREDERICK FREEDMAN

VASSAR COLLEGE

A HISTORY

OF

MUSIC IN SCOTLAND

BY HENRY GEORGE FARMER

𝄢 DA CAPO PRESS · NEW YORK · 1970

A Da Capo Press Reprint Edition

This Da Capo Press edition of Henry George Farmer's *A History of Music in Scotland* is an unabridged republication of the first edition published in London in 1947. It is reprinted by special arrangement with Edition Peters.

Library of Congress Catalog Card Number 70-100613

SBN 306-71865-0

Published by Da Capo Press
A Division of Plenum Publishing Corporation
227 West 17th Street
New York, N.Y. 10011

Manufactured in the United States of America

A History of
Music in Scotland

PLATE I

SIR EDWARD BONKILL (*ca.* 1476)
Provost: Collegiate Church of Holy Trinity, Edinburgh.
Palace of Holyroodhouse

To
Janey C. Drysdale

A HISTORY
OF
MUSIC IN SCOTLAND

by

HENRY GEORGE FARMER,
Ph.D., D.Litt.
Cramb Lecturer in Music (1933), University of Glasgow.

" Of all the arts beneath the heaven
That man has found or God has given,
None draws the soul so sweet away
As music's melting, mystic lay."
—James Hogg.

HINRICHSEN EDITION LIMITED
25 *Museum Street, London, W.C.1*

PRINTED BY ROBERT STOCKWELL, LONDON, S.E.I.

CONTENTS

PLATES

PREFACE

" De quoi diable se mêle-t-il ? "

SOME of my readers may be surprised to find me dealing with a *History of Music in Scotland* after more than thirty years spent in another field, but the truth is that this subject claimed my interest before I became absorbed in Oriental Studies. As a student of, and a prizeman in, Scottish History under the late Sir Robert Sangster Rait[1], Historiographer Royal for Scotland, who urged me to devote myself to a history of music in Scotland, I could not easily neglect a subject that was so near to my heart. Yet it is clear that complete fruition has come late in a life that has been devoted almost wholly to Oriental music. Not that I have completely ignored the music of Scotland. Reference to some of my writings will prove otherwise[2]. Therein I have treated of specific periods and subjects, but in the present work I have attempted to tell the complete story of music in Scotland for the first time, and in doing so I have redeemed a promise made so many years ago to my old teacher.

As in most pioneer work, this undertaking has necessitated rough spadework being done, the soil being upturned and the brushwood uprooted, often in what may be considered a ruthless fashion. Yet such treatment is inevitable in all clearances. How this is done and what is laid bare may offend some timorous souls, although, by the same token, it may gratify others, in so far as their political, social, religious, or æsthetic convictions sway them. Obviously it would have been much easier to have taken the smooth path or

---

[1] He was Professor of Scottish History (1913-30) and later Principal (1930-36) at the University of Glasgow.

[2] "Music in Mediaeval Scotland " (*Proceedings of the Royal Philosophical Society of Glasgow*, 1926-7): ditto (*Proceedings of the Musical Association*, 1929-30): " An Old Scottish Violin Tutor " (*Proceedings of the Society of Antiquaries of Scotland*, 1930-31): " The Scots Guards Band," " Scots Duty : The Old Drum and Fife Calls of Scottish Regiments," " The Scots March " (*Journal of the Society for Army Historical Research*, 1944, 1946, 1947): " Concerts in 18th Century Scotland " (*Proceedings of the Royal Philosophical Society of Glasgow*, 1944-45: " An Historic March " (*Music and Letters*, 1945): " The Glen Collection of Musical Instruments " (*The Art Review*, 1945): " Music in 18th Century Scotland " (*Scottish Art and Letters*, 1946).

old furrow, satisfying suave convention or pandering to perfervid nationalism, but I have preferred the rough road with its attendant inconveniences.

In this attitude I recall the words of George Bernard Shaw at a lecture which I attended as a youth, when he vindicated his frank and often brusque methods on the ground that progress often depended on this approach. He pointed out how remarkable it was that, in an apparently crowded bus, with standing room only, if one in the latter category deliberately trod on the toes of someone who was rather too comfortably seated, how readily the requisite repose was found for the culprit's torso. In a similar way a candid or even a blunt word or two often produces accommodation in a question which had previously not found a hearing. Plain speaking never did any harm, as even the Christian Fathers recognized, for let us remember that urbanity and gravity do not always spell wisdom and verity, nor does acquiescence to current opinions make for true righteousness. In any case I do not offer these explanations as an apology. Rather would I say that they are a vindication of my attitude.

Of the particular form of my book and the precise subjects discussed, a word or two seems desirable by way of explanation. The music of every age is determined by the particular form of society in which it is given expression. Because of this it is necessary that we should know the structure of this society if we wish to understand its music. That is why I have treated my subject as if it were a part of social history, since all music is primarily a phase of social life, however much æsthetes may think otherwise. Yet the general run of historians of music have preferred to treat music *per se*, as if every reader were a political historian and sociologist knowing the *raison d'être* for each particular type of music. Such readers are few and far between, and because of this I have sought to show music in Scotland as an integral part of the general social structure, in the cottage as well as the castle, at the market place or fair as at the theatre, concert, or church, with the wandering vagabond minstrel as with the liveried urban musician.

A nation's music is not made up of symphony concerts or what superior people call classical music. Only the merest fraction of the population can appreciate such things. The vast majority, the working class, have neither the leisure nor peace of mind that are so requisite for the appreciation of this higher domain of the art. Their interest is held by a music not so complex or factitious, an art less cunning and dexterous, something that is more homely and intelligible to them. This is especially true of Scotland, and more so of the Lowlands which is, as Ruskin once said, " of all districts of the inhabited world, pre-eminently the singing country," and so, a history of music in Scotland which does not take the Scots songs into the fullest account is unthinkable. I make no apology here, or elsewhere, for using the adjective "Scots," despite Ritson's sneer at the word as " a national barbarism."

Some years ago, J. A. Kappey, a German musician for almost half a century resident in England, was abashed at the snobbishness of the English in matters musical. In that land he saw " the music of the people . . . passed over with almost contemptuous indifference," as if they were ashamed of it. This is true even of Scotland in some respects, and this aloofness, not to say affectation, is not confined to music. Highbrows, for example, may sniff at what they term " industrial art," such as those superb railings which surround the Glasgow School of Art, although they issued from the imaginative genius of a Charles Rennie Mackintosh, but it is such things that have an influence on the spiritual life of a nation more sublime than the most superb canvases. Of course, this is realized by more discreet thinkers and art critics today, and it is no uncommon thing to see Dr. T. J. Honeyman of Glasgow begin a lecture on art appreciation with a spoon or flagon in his hand rather than a much prized *objet d'art*. And so you will find the simple song of the folk, the uncouth skirl of the pipe, and the hoiden swing of the reel given due recognition in these pages. As Carlyle says—"Go deep enough, there is music everywhere."

I have to acknowledge that the frontispiece, taken from a triptych in the Palace of Holyroodhouse, is reproduced by gracious permission of H.M. The King. For other reproductions we are indebted to the courtesy of the British Museum, the National Library of Scotland, the University of Edinburgh, and the Fitzwilliam Museum, Cambridge.

Lastly, it is necessary for me to offer my respectful thanks to several friends and helpers. To F. G. Rendall of the British Museum I am indebted for several favours, not the least of which are the dates of much modern Scottish music. For information gained through correspondence and conversation I have to express my thanks to Professor J. D. Mackie, C.B.E., Professor of Scottish History in the University of Glasgow. In a similar way I owe thanks to Dr. Harry M. Willsher, whose store of knowledge of pre-Reformation music in Scotland is a veritable mine. Tribute is likewise due to Janey C. Drysdale, the sister of Learmont Drysdale, the Scottish composer, since much out-of-the-way information has come through her kindly hands. Gratitude for loans, favours, and information must also be paid to librarians and university officials, and among them: Dr. W. R. Cunningham (Glasgow University Librarian), Dr. L. W. Sharp (Edinburgh University Librarian), W. Beattie (National Library of Scotland), Professor S. T. M. Newman (Edinburgh University), W. Y. Baldry, O.B.E., Charles P. Finlayson (Edinburgh University Library), R. G. Cant (St. Andrews University), Dr. Millar Patrick, John Dunlop (Mitchell Library, Glasgow), J. Duncan Dundas (Dundee Public Library), Marcus K. Milne (Aberdeen Public Library), R. Buchart (Edinburgh Public Library), as well as Jean M. Allan and Phyllis Hamilton of the latter institution. Finally, I have to express my indebtedness to Wilson Steel and Dr. James Robson of Glasgow University, who have so materially relieved me of much of the tedium of proof reading, whilst, as a *coda*, I must pay tribute to Max Hinrichsen for his enthusiastic support of this book, which is only one of the many benefactions which he has bestowed in his endeavours to advance British music.

Glasgow, 1947 HENRY GEORGE FARMER

INTRODUCTION

" From the mere knowledge of the facts of history, there is little profit for either soul or mind ; but the facts become alive and fruitful, when they are seen in the light of an animating tendency. ' We are what you were ; we shall be what you are ', ran the patriotic hymn of the Spartans ; and the words imply what we must consider the highest lesson to be derived from the study of our national history—the sense of debt to the past and of duty to the future."—*P. Hume Brown.*

" Now, instead of going on denying that we are an unmusical nation, let us do our utmost to prove that we are a musical nation."
—*Sir Alexander C. Mackenzie.*

. . . .

In choosing these " aizles " from the hearths of a Scottish historian and a Scottish musician, I do so that they may perhaps kindle a flame anew in the hearts of those in Scotland, as well as in England, who would fain cherish the music of their own land rather than follow the mutable many who decry everything in music that does not come from the Continent. Secondly, these *dicta* serve as vigilant outposts in this raid into a territory that has not hitherto been completely probed, an undertaking which, I hope, may clear the way to a better understanding of the history of music in Scotland, and a more just appreciation of the reasons for her scant contribution to the creative side of the art since the Reformation.

I believe that Scotland has too long been judged unfairly in her attitude to music. Much of it comes from irresponsible people such as those who point to the bagpipe of Caledonia " stern and wild " as her ideal in music. It may be an excellent joke to those who know no better, but it so happens that this pipe is one of Scotland's treasures since it is a folk instrument, and as such is cherished by her people just as the *piffero* is in Italy or the *cornemuse* is in France. Strange to say it is only the English who, not possessing a folk instrument themselves, cry " sour grapes." Other nations are more perspicuous over the music of the Scots, Germany especially, as such a book as Dr. Nelly Diem's *Beiträge zur Geschichte der schottischen Musik im XVII Jahrhundert* (1919) amply reveals. Sheer ignorance is often the cause of the English attitude, so palpably plain in Davey's *History of English Music*

(1895), as we shall have occasion to point out, but what excuse is there for the statement of Frank Kidson in his article in *Grove's Dictionary of Music* (1940) where he says :[1]

> " There are many early entries in royal and other accounts showing that musical performances were frequent, but there is nothing to show that these performances were of native music ; the contrary seems to be the case, and that English, French, or other fashionable compositions were rendered."

The facts are that there is not the slightest justification for this observation, and even if there were, surely the same could be said of other countries, including England ? In the 17th century indeed, when Scotland was beginning to emerge from what Matthew Arnold called " the prison of Puritanism," we read that at the court of Holyrood there could be heard " old Scottish music, vocal and instrumental," as well as English and other music.

Scotland, as these pages will tell, has had a troublous political history. In the early Celtic days, so far as can be discerned, she possessed a culture comparable to that of England, and even centuries later, in spite of Norman and English ravages, she could still boast of a fairly equable position in music with her southern neighbour from the 12th to the 16th century. Yet her principal towns, the very nurseries of her cultural life, were much too near the brutal, raiding, English borderers, to be able to build up sequential centres of refinement. England, on the other hand, was more auspiciously situated, with her capital and most of her great towns hundreds of miles outwith the prey of counter raiding by the Scots.

When the Reformation came, Scotland's particular doctrinal views in this great movement retarded her from any higher flights in music than a bare and frigid psalmody, and yet even within the narrow bounds of this almost despised phase of musical expression, she produced one feature in her own polymetred psalter that was immensely superior to that of any other country. Following this constricted Calvinistic *régime* even greater troubles afflicted her when, rather than cede one iota of her doctrinal or political convictions,

---

[1] Vol. iv., p. 696.

Scotland unsheathed the sword in their defence, with consequential unsettlement and devastation in the land for a century or more. When, after the mid-18th century, Scotland was able to emerge from her tribulations with a modicum of social tranquility and a new spiritual freedom, her classical traditions in music, such as existed in Carver, Johnson, and Douglas of the 16th century, could only be viewed mistily over a gap of two centuries, with the result that she had to begin *de novo* in the creative sphere of music, and was compelled to look to mentors in England, Germany and Italy. Is it any wonder that the late Sir Richard Terry once said at a lecture which I gave on " Music in Mediaeval Scotland " before the [Royal] Musical Association, that Scotland seems always to be " cleaning the slate " in her music.[1]

Yet without the slightest knowledge of the works of her great composers of the Golden Age, Scotland began to make her way, with toddling footsteps at first, in the 18th century, showing almost as great an appreciation of the art in its highest forms as did its more favourably situated neighbour, England. In this century her composers—Macklean, Oswald, McGibbon, Erskine, Foulis, and Reid, a mere handful it is true, began to show that, given the opportunity, this land could still make worthy offerings at the shrine of St. Cecilia. Alas, the effort petered out, as we shall see at length, and the 19th century opened silently on the creative side. Save for the church music of Robert A. Smith and the dramatic and orchestral works of John Thomson, who died all too soon, there is little to record of the first half-century, while the work of Alexander Ewing, which followed, never saw the light of day. In the second half-century, however, there arose the star of Alexander C. Mackenzie, who was one of the pioneers of the Renascence of British music, and it was the prostyle of his work that actually gave birth to the Scottish National School of composers in Hamish MacCunn, Learmont Drysdale, John B. McEwen, William Wallace and Charles Macpherson.

---

[1] *Proceedings of the Musical Association*, 56th Session (1929-30), p. 83.

Even the 20th century displays in Frederick Lamond the famous pianist, and in Hugh S. Roberton with the Orpheus Choir, that even more than national recognition has been won by Scots. Further, it reveals in its more recent composers, Robert E. Bryson, William B. Moonie, James Friskin, Riddle Hunter, Francis George Scott, Eric Chisholm, Ian Whyte, and Cedric Thorpe Davie, that Scotland may yet stand, at least in the approaches, where she did when Giraldus Cambrensis penned his flattering line about Scotland's pre-eminence in music, eight hundred years ago. I say " may yet stand," however, with much uneasiness, because Scotland gives but scant acknowledgment to her sons in music, for it is the same today as it was two centuries ago when Oswald and others were forced to find shelter in England. Even in the last century it was Germany that gave recognition to Mackenzie, as the composer has so poignantly written on one of his scores. Today the music of Learmont Drysdale is heard in Moscow and in Australia, but rarely is it performed in Scotland, whilst an Eric Chisholm finds that it is a distant land, South Africa, that honours him with a university Professorship in Music. As Dr. Vaughan Williams has said in his frank and outspoken *National Music* (1934) : " The business of finding a nation's soul is a long and slow one at the best, and a great many prophets must be slain in the course of it. Perhaps when we have slain enough prophets, future generations will begin to build their tombs."

PLATE II

From Iona, Dupplin & Capprington.

CELTIC INSTRUMENTS

1. Cithara & Chorus. 2. Harp. 3. Horn.

PLATE III

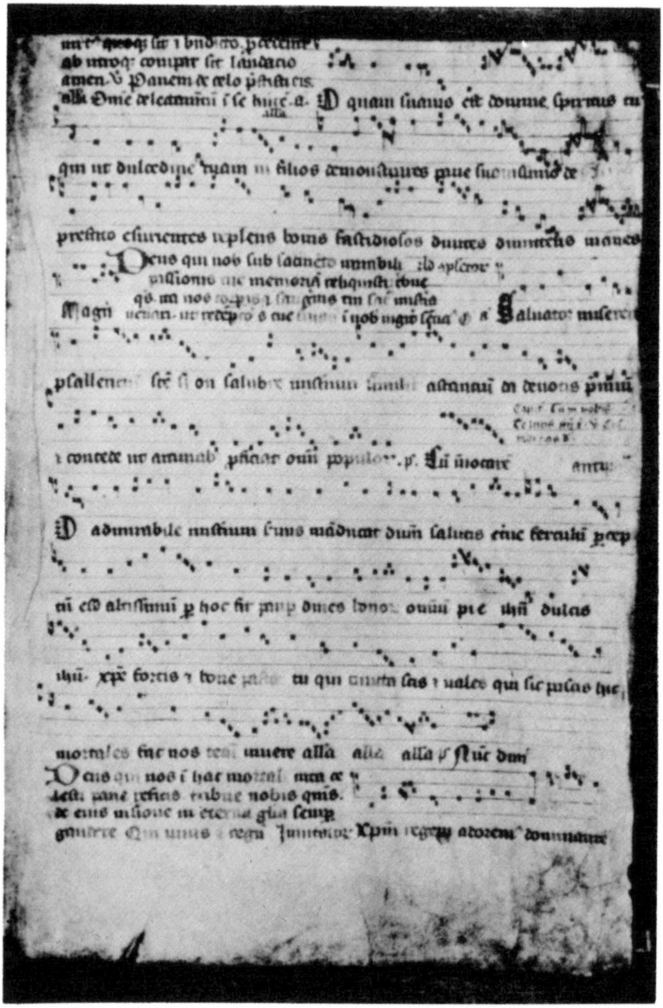

Edinburgh University Library.

EARLY SCOTTISH CHURCH MUSIC
Inchcolm Priory MS. (ca. 1340).

PART I

THE CELTIC PERIOD

" It is not correct to separate and contrast the music of Ireland and that of Scotland as if they belonged to two different races. They are in reality an emanation direct from the heart of one Celtic people."
P. W. JOYCE : *A Social History of Ancient Ireland.*

IN my early brochure, *Music in Mediæval Scotland* (1930),* I said that the Celtic period need not detain us long because we do not possess sufficient data for a comprehensive survey. That statement is still true in substance, but since those were the days of the *fons et origo* of Scottish music, we cannot afford to gloss this period in a similar way when wider scope is afforded our pen. More especially are we compelled to indulge in more ample treatment because in no other part of the British Isles have old Celtic customs survived with such persistence as in Scotland. In Wales, for example, a land far more homogeneous and more fervidly national, we do not find a tithe of such relics from the cultural past, for the simple reason that it lost its political independence, although not its language, rather early. Nor can Ireland, the very fount of Celtic culture, despite its cry of *sinn fein,* boast of much on the musical side from its ancient glorious past, since alien occupation was even more thorough, and when a revival of this art of yore came with the emancipation of yesterday, most of its bardic musical lore was lost beyond recovery.

It may be true that the Goidels or Gaels of Ireland and Scotland (or rather North Britain at that period) were, and are, different from the Brythones or Cymri of England and later Wales, but they were of the same Celtic stock, speaking variants of the same language and, so far as can be discerned, indulging in the same type and practice of music, or, at any rate, they had much in common. So far as Scotland is concerned we know very little for certain of its early music save the brief reference to it in the tales of St. Columba and other meagre sources, as well as the scant archæological finds and monuments. Yet in view of the close

---

* Written in 1922.

political and cultural links between Ireland and Scotland at this
time, we may assume that the music of the " Land of Song " hinted
at in *Tara's Halls* was little distinctive from that of the " North
Countrie, a nation famed for song," which Beattie praised in *The
Minstrel*.

The connection in music between the two countries lasted until
comparatively recent years, a link which could scarcely have been
otherwise, since the Irish of the days which I have termed the Celtic
period were the apostles of culture and learning in western Europe
itself. Indeed, so teeming was the Irish missionary movement that
St. Bernard likened it to a flood. Irish musicians, both theorists and
practitioners, were in demand not only in Britain but on the
Continent. In the 7th Century, St. Foillan and St. Ultan, Irishmen
both, were teaching psalmody at Nivelles in Brabant, whilst in the
9th century, Maengal was music master at St. Gall, a monastery
founded by Irish monks, where among his greatest pupils was the
egregious Notker Balbulus. Even William of Malmesbury testifies
that St. Dunstan (d. 988) of Glastonbury studied the theory of
music under Irish teachers, and probably the *ars citharizandi*, in
which the saint delighted, was taught him by some Irish *clairsair*
or harpist. The learned Sophus Bugge (*Bidrag til den aeldste
Skaldedigtnings Historie*) says that Scaldic poetry began after the
Viking raids on Britain and Ireland under the influence of the Irish
file (poet).

CHAPTER 1

PAGAN AND EARLY CHRISTIAN DAYS.

" Bardi etiam facta virorum illustrium, heroics composita versibus
cum dulcibus lyrae modulis, cantitarunt."
                                        AMMIANUS MARCELLINUS.

One must be wary of the old extravagant notion that the so-called
Caledonians of early Scotland were " barbarians." That opinion
has long been laid aside by responsible historians. The tale of
Dio Cassius (d. *ca.* 235) about the " naked and shoeless " polyga-
mous people of this region who lived on " nuts," save when pursued
into the forests when they subsisted on " bark and roots," is due to
the fancy of an ignorant soldiery or romancing chroniclers, and is

on all fours with Strabo's description of the Irish as cannibals. Fortunately we have archaeological remains that furnish us with sufficiently cogent data to enable us to label such stories as arrant nonsense. As Dr. W. Douglas Simpson and his painstaking predecessors have shown, these early inhabitants of Scotland " were possessed of a high degree of practical and artistic knowledge . . . evidenced in the beautiful brooches, rings, . . . armlets, . . . all wrought in bronze, sometimes finely enamelled in various colours." As their music was never written down, nor was that of the ancient Irish, Britons, or Romans for that matter, we cannot assay its value in a like manner. Indeed, if they could have committed their music by notation to parchment, it would perhaps have scarcely defied the hand of Father Time so triumphantly as the more durable metal and pottery.

One naturally asks,—" Who were these early inhabitants of Scotland to whom the Romans refer ? " This we cannot answer with any degree of certainty, but many indications point to their being Celts. Somewhere about the 5th century A.D. we can speak with more assurance, for at that time we know of four differently named peoples in Scotland,—the Picts in the north, the Scots in the west-centre, the Britons in the south-west, and the Angles in the south-east. Of the Picts we know little or nothing racially or culturally, although if we can trust their art remains, we should be inclined to count them as Celts. Their territory stretched as far south on one coast as the Firth of Forth, and on the other to Mallaig. Of the Scots of Dalriada, i.e. modern Argyll, we have considerable information. These people were immigrants from the north of Ireland, then known as Scotland, a country where music and poetry, as well as learning in general, cultivated by a highly skilled professional class, were cherished. Much the same enthusiasm was shown to the arts by the Britons of Strathclyde who were linked culturally with their fellow Celts in Cumbria and Wales. These people may have belonged to a later Celtic invasion which drove the earlier Goidels westward and northward. The Angles of Bernicia were still later invaders, and they, in their turn, pushed the Britons to the west. It is evident therefore that the prevailing culture in

Scotland for five or six hundred years at least was dominantly Celtic.

As I have said, it is difficult, for lack of specific data, to give any details of this Celtic culture *in Scotland* at this period, although some vague hints come from Irish sources. The poems for example picture Scotland as the home of learning and culture. Of course it has to be recognized that the Scots of Dalriada were their own kith and kin, and distance always lends enchantment. We read, for instance, of a certain Neitha the son of Adhna, the court poet of the King of Ulster, Conchobar MacNessa (1st Cent. A.D.) who, " after finishing his education at home, passed into Scotland to add to his learning and knowledge of the world in the schools there." In which part of Scotland he studied we are not told, but at his return we learn that " he set out from Cenn Tire [Kintyre]." The saga of his contemporary, the Ulster champion Cuchulaind, tells that when the hero reached the western isles [of Scotland] he found the stringed instrument known as the *timpan* or *tiompan* in use.

Whether in Gaelic or Cymric regions, all learning and culture were in the hands of a privileged class. The pagan Celtic druids were the soothsayers who, like their Oriental forerunners (as in the Hebrew prophets), placed considerable reliance on the chant in their sacred office. *Cantus* is the word that Julius Caesar uses in his *Gallic Wars* when he tells of the druidic chants of the Gauls which, he says, were not committed to writing, but were passed on [to novices] *viva voce*. This word *cantus* tells its own story from the very cradle of human culture, since our own word " enchantment " is derived from it, just as " charm " comes from *carmen* (= song). Celtic religion was basically pantheistic, and the learned O'Curry has given from the ancient *Book of Leinster* an exquisite archaic hymn, an invocation to nature, perhaps the earliest of its kind. Carmichael has shown (*Carmina Gadelica*) that survivals of these pagan chants are still to be heard in Scotland. This pantheism may well explain the longing for the music of nature,—the voices of the wind, the waves, the rain, the trees, and the birds, which saturates Celtic lore, just as it permeates later Irish and Scottish writers, and peeps out in Marsden and Burns. This alone explains the reason why the druidic chant was unwritten. Being a panneustic possession, i.e. given by the inspiration of nature, one dared not commit it to a notation for vulgar edification lest it should lose its potency. Every phase of pagan Celtic life reeks of anthropomorphism. The Elysium of the Celt was the abode of music. Here the very swaying of the branches of the trees gave forth the most divine music, as we read in the story of the illness of Cuchulaind. Even the very stones gave music in Celtic lore and one recalls how the Celtic maiden tries to allure Oisin to the Land of Youth, where " harpers shall delight you with their sweet music," as we read in the *Voyage of Bran.*

In secular life, if one can use this word of a stage of society in which the cult determined everything, there were chants for almost every phase of human activity, and some still subsist in the rationalized toil songs of the Scottish Highlands. Originally these were cult chants, i.e. enchantments, for such were the milking song, the sower's song, the boatman's song, the smithy song, all of which had their origin in the belief that nature could be allured or induced to help by the chant's persuasion. Later, under the pressure of secularization, man found that this erstwhile cult chant had a practical value in that the rhythm of the song (*né* chant) not only relieved the monotony of toil but disciplined it. Thus it became an invaluable asset in regulating the milkmaid's pull, the seedsman's cast, the oarsman's stroke, the smith's swing. Even the animals were influenced, and Carmichael tells us that today in the Highlands, cows " will not give their milk without them [the toil songs]."

What the cult chants and toil songs were like in their pristine state we cannot properly judge. Probably they were of the same structure and character as those which we hear in purely pastoral and agricultural communities in the Near East today, where they consist of a simple melody with a compass of four or five notes. The particular vocal character of the Celtic chant and song was a crooning (*cronan*) seemingly. Just as Micah (i, 8) says,—" I will wail and howl," so one can imagine a Celtic seer saying,—" I will croon." One recalls that the name of the musician who visited St. Columba, as recorded by St. Adamnan, was Cronan the Bard. This crooning, we are told, was a particular glottal production used in the cult chant for augury and invocation, and in the more secular eulogy and elegy. Thus it dominated the keen (*caoin*) and the panegyric (*aidbse* or *cepoc*). The keen or funeral chant, originally devised to affect the spirit of the dead, still survives, retaining much of its early pagan character. The panegyric was called the *aidbse* in Ireland, and it was this that was sung to St. Columba at Drumceat by his encomiast Dallam Fergall the bardic chief. We know from the glosses on the *Amra of St. Columcille* that what was called *aidbse* in Ireland was termed *cepoc* (*cepog*) in Scotland. O'Curry held the view that the *caoin* was simply a degenerate form of the *aidbse*, yet it seems more likely that the *aidbse* was actually a later artistic development of the *caoin*.

CHAPTER 2

THE MUSICIANS.

" The Ireland men, fra quhum the Scottis first discendit."
BELLENDEN-BOECE : *Chronicles of Scotland.*

As already stressed, it is to Ireland, the cradle of Celtic music, that we must perforce turn for a panoramic view of this art in Celtic lands. Here, music was part and parcel of life itself, a statement borne out by the story of Adam and Eve in the *Saltair na Rann* (*ca.* 1000), where we are told that when the first pair were banished from Paradise they were without food, raiment, shelter, and *music* for a whole year, a circumstance which proves that the art was considered one of the absolute necessities of life in ancient Ireland. Indeed, it not only found ample expression in almost every phase of this life but, if we can believe St. Adamnan (d. *ca.* 704), of life in the world to come as well, which was itself a pagan conceit as we know from the epic of Cuchulaind.

Music, both in the theoretical and practical sphere, was in the hands of the *ollamh* (" learned man," originally " seer "). If the latter specialized in history and genealogy he was called a *seana-chaidh*. If his *forte* were poetry, song, and literature, his title was *file*. We know that the latter not only composed verse and music, but sang and played his compositions, generally to the accompaniment of a rote (*cruit*) or harp (*clairseach*), as did his druidic forerunners, of whose rote (*lyra*) playing both Diodorus Siculus (1st cent. B.C.) and Ammianus Marcellinus (d. *ca.* 400) tell us. That the *seanachaidh* chanted the traditions and lineage of the people when he performed, there is presumptive evidence. Indeed, what better mnemonic aid could there be than assonance and melody? This *ollamh* class continued to occupy a relatively high position in both pagan and Christian times. O'Flaherty shows that the musician, poet, and historian were part of the retinue of the ancient kings and chiefs of Ireland, a custom which lasted until the time of Brian Boru (d. 1014) at least, although sometimes, as O'Curry points out, one *ollamh* combined all these functions. Not only did these officers receive a regular stipend, but they had land gifted them, a practice which continued for centuries in Scotland.

In addition to this learned and cultured class there was the poet-musician of the more popular type. This was the *bard*, whose talents found an outlet among the people at large. He stood in relation to the *file* as the modern entertainer does to the *Mus. Doc.* The custom therefore of labelling all who followed the craft of music as bards, a word used as early as Diodorus Siculus, does not seem to be admissible, at least so far as Ireland is concerned. As the *Brehon Laws* (iv, 361) aptly put it,—" A *bard* is one without lawful learning but his own intellect." Again, as the *Book of Rights* (183) says,—" It is not the right of a *bard*, but the right of a *file*, to know each king and his right."

Then there were other types of entertainers who passed under the generic title of *druth*, and it is interesting to note, especially in view of the later proscription of the minstrel class in general, that even in pagan times, as we know from the *Senchus Mor*, the *druth* was under anathema and practically denied civil rights in Ireland. The origin of and reason for this *infamia* are not quite clear. In ancient Rome, at the time of Julius Caesar and Augustus, actors (*scenici*) were denied civil rights, but not musicians (*thymetrici*). Yet in spite of disabilities, the *druth* in Ireland was encouraged throughout the land, for he was not only the purveyor of song and dance, but he was the great disseminator of news.

How much of this Irish art and practice of music in the secular

sphere obtained in Scotland is not easy to apprehend, the reason
being that in the matter of documents Scotland stands in relation to
Ireland as an arid desert to a fertile valley. All that is vouchsafed us
is to be found in the life of St. Columba, a line or so in the doubtful
Vita Kentigerni, and the monumental remains, to which philo-
logy, with a little latitude, adds a pinch. Yet we can surely believe
that the pagan Irish forerunners of the Christian Columban emi-
gration to Scotland took, at least, a modicum of the Irish art and
craft of music with them. This could not have been otherwise
because the *ollamh*, whether a *file* or a *seanachaidh*, was indispensable
to the social polity. The former was the seer, and the latter was the
history maker, and music was a necessary adjunct to the *file's* pro-
gnostications, just as it was the means whereby the *seanachaidh*
memorized his data.

St. Adamnan's *Life of St. Columba* contains a glimpse of Colum's
interest in secular music as well as his zeal in its religious purpose.
St. Columba was born in the " Land of Song " in the year 521, and
studied literature and music under a Christian *file* named Gemman
at Clonard in Leinster. The saint's addiction to the bardic and
felic art was probably due to his early training, and when he left
Ireland for Scotland in the year 563 he made reference in his
" Farewell " poem to his native land, " where birds sing so sweetly "
and " where clerics sing like birds." The story of Cronan the Bard,
given by St. Adamnan, reveals, to some extent, the saint's concern
for music and song. The bard had just departed when some of
St. Columba's fellow monks said to him,—" How was it that thou
did'st not call upon Cronan the Bard, when he was going away from
us, for some song to be musically rendered after the manner of his
art ?" His partiality for bards is also illustrated by his conduct at
the Convention of Drumceat in 577 when the supression or discip-
lining of the bardic order was under consideration. St. Columba
pleaded for toleration, pointing out the supreme service which the
order had rendered to poetry and music. The result was that only
a severer discipline was imposed on the bards. It was by reason of
this timely defence of bardism by the saint that Dallam Fergall,
the bardic chief, composed a piece (*aidbse*) in St. Columba's honour

which he sang to the assembly. The saint must have displayed some signs of pleasure at the flattery, because he was at once rebuked by his kinsman Baithan for this. St. Columba thereupon hushed the bardic pæanist with the admonition,—" Praise only the dead."

That an advanced stage of culture was to be found among the upper classes in Scotland at this period is even dilated upon in Irish literature. When Prince Cano the son of Gartnan, a contemporary of St. Columba, fled from Scotland to Ireland (*ca.* 620), we are told of his courtiers and their rich habiliments and costly weapons and of their ladies in their torques of burnished gold and diadems and brooches of a like richness, with cloaks bordered with silver, and smocks interwoven with a thread of gold. Further, their attendants carried that stringed instrument known as the *timpan* or *tiompan* which, in this instance, had a body of bronze. All this was but a resounding echo of the arts of Ireland itself, of a culture which had no peer in western Europe. One imagines that the great centres of Celtic life in Scotland, from Lewis to Kintyre in the west which St. Moluag and St. Maelrubha had converted, and from Loch Ness to the Forth and Clyde where St. Drostan, St. Curitan, and St. Kentigern had laboured for the church, resounded with the music of the Gaels only.

In the south-west corner of the land were the Britons of Strathclyde. Being Celts, although of another stirps, they possessed a musical culture little different possibly from the Scots of Dalriada. Cymric music must have been deeply influenced by that of Ireland for there was constant intercourse between the two countries from the third to the eleventh century. Irish music seems to have been the basis of the progress made in the days of Howel Dda (d. 950), and from that date until 1095, Irish annals testify to the exodus of Irish harpers to Wales, whilst it was at the Eisteddfod of Caerwys about the year 1078 that Irish musicians, together with the native bards, reorganized Welsh music. Perhaps the Arthurian romance came from the Cymric bard. Giraldus Cambrensis and Thomas the author of *Tristan*, both of the 12th century, speak of a *famosus fabulator* called Bledhericus or Breri who belonged to this class. That the Cymric music of Strathclyde was little different from that of Ireland seems to be evident from the story in the *Vita Kentigerni* which tells of a minstrel *(joculator)* sent by an Irish king to the court of Radanach, King of Strathclyde, where he delighted everyone by his performances on the *cithara* and *timpanum* which, it would appear, were the Latin names for the Gaelic *cruit* and *timpan* or *tiompan*.

In Bernicia, which was situated in the south-east, there were strangers, speaking a different tongue and possessing another culture. The Scots looked upon this *Sassenach* land and polity with suspicion at first, although later the Gael and Teuton got on well together. Actually the people were not Saxons but Angles, for the *litora saxonica* was on the south coast of England. In Bernicia we find the *scop* and *gleeman* who were the Anglian counterparts of the Celtic *file* and *druth*, i.e. the urban and peregrine musician, and they favoured the same instruments in the rote and harp.

We see these musicians in precisely the same predicament as with the Celts, at the hall of the chief, the camp fire, and the humble cottage, singing the heroic chant or the *wassail* song, and always to favoured treatment from high and low alike. With them, music was probably not so elevated an art as with the Celts at the era of the invasion, but time soon remedied that, and before long harp playing was considered by the Angles to be a necessary accomplishment for all and sundry even before such a thing was possible in Celtic lands. With them also the periodic festivals, which prevail in all agricultural and pastoral stages of society, showed great development. Many of these took root in Celtic Scotland, and we must remember that music and the festival were causally interdependent.

Thus we see that throughout the entire land, which we now know as Scotland, both instrumental and vocal music were in the ascendant although, for certain reasons, the *druth* of the Gaels and the *clerwr* of the Cymri, who were the peregrine musicians, were looked upon with grave suspicion by church and state, possibly by reason of the free and independent life which they led. In Scotland we find decrees (if genuine) against this class rather early. Kenneth MacAlpin (844-59) is said to have made laws " for the commoun wele of the Scottis," one of which reads in Bellenden's version of Boece (d. *ca.* 1536) thus : " All vagabonds, fools, bards, obscene wits, and idle persons shall be burnt on the cheek and scourged through the town." It is sad to see the bard and jester lumped in this way with vagabonds in Scotland, a land famed for its freedom, but it would seem that the state was afraid of their political influence, whilst the church was especially jealous of their suasion. Note in one of the decrees of the Council of Clovesco (Glasgow ?) in 747 (*can.* 12) how the church was scared of the influence of secular poetry. It was ever thus, although Sarah Bernhardt once rebuked an offensive cleric who was condemning the stage by reminding him that people in the same line of business ought not to fall out. Two centuries later, a harsher law against musicians and their fellow entertainers is said to have been made by Macbeth (1044-57), the wording of which has much significance. It runs : " Fools, minstrels, bards, and all such idle people, unless they be specially licensed by the king, shall be compelled to seek some craft to earn their living. If they refuse, they shall be drawn like horses in the plough and harrow." These two laws, whose genuineness is questionable, are anterior to anything of a like character in England.

CHAPTER 3

THE INSTRUMENTS.

" The two renowned sons of Milesius,
Who conquered both Erinn and Albain ;
With them came
A comely poet (*file*) and a gifted rote player (*cruitire*)."
Saltair na Caisel (*ca.* 900)

The instruments of music used in Ireland were perhaps more varied and more numerous than in any other Celtic land. Here, the rote and harp were the outstanding art instruments and, as Ruskin says, " the harp is the true ancient instrument of Scotland as well as Ireland." The former had long been favoured by continental Celts, as we know from Diodorus Siculus and Ammianus Marcellinus.

The Irish name for the rote was *cruit*, and legend dates it back to Fomorian days before the Firbolg and Milesian invasions. The designs on the monuments at Castledermot (8th Cent.), Ullard (9th Cent.), and Clonmacnoise (10th Cent.), reveal the *cruit* as a type known for millenia in the Orient.   In Scotland the rote was also called the *cruit* and we see it figured later at Iona on St. Martin's Cross (13th Cent.).

The trigonal harp was the *clairseach*, a name of unusual pagan interest, since the very name tells us that its body was made of wood, upon which birds (so loved by the Irish) once chirped when it was a tree branch.   To be sure the very wood absorbed their delightful music.   One recalls that the Anglo-Saxon name for the harp was *glee-beam* i.e. " music-wood."   Seemingly the *clairseach* was of later adoption by the Irish, possibly from the English, as Canon Galpin has surmised, and as Gerbert's St. Blasius MS. (12th Cent.) suggests.   We see the instrument on the Monasterboice crosses (10th Cent.).   In Scotland, where it is generally written *clarsech*, there are several representations on the monuments, the most notable examples being at Auldbar in Forfarshire (9th Cent.), at Nigg in Ross-shire (10th Cent.), and at Dupplin in Perthshire (11th Cent.).   On the Dupplin stone the harper is seated on a throne, which reminds one of the " throned bard " (*bardd cadeiriog*) mentioned in the Welsh Laws of Howel Dda (10th Cent.).

Next we have the *timpan* or *tiompan*.   Its identity is not too clearly defined.   Some claim it to have been a stringed instrument having from three to eight strings, and played with either bow, plectrum, or fingers.   O'Curry says quite definitely that the performer used a " wand furnished with hair " i.e. a bow, although he gives another passage which indicates the finger-nail as the implement of sounding. According to Cormac's *Glossary*, the instrument had a frame of willow wood with brass strings, and we have already seen a reference to a frame of bronze for the *timpan* or *tiompan*.   In the *Agallamh na Seanorach* the treble strings of the *timpan* were of silver and those of the bass of white bronze, whilst the tuning pins were of gold. That it was a stringed instrument is strengthened by the life of St. Dunstan (d. 988), a pupil of Irish monks, who used to wile his mind by playing *in timphano*, and we can scarcely imagine this instrument to have been a drum (*timpanum*).   Aelfric (d. *ca*. 1020) translated *tympanum* by *hearpe*. Canon Galpin suggests that it was a psaltery, and the use of the term *symphonia* in Cormac's *Glossary*, in relation to the music of the *timpan*, certainly bears out the similitude. We read of a *cimphan* in Scotland during the Anglo-Norman period, but this may have been the hurdy-gurdy known as the *sumphion*. Yet we have to bear in mind that Giraldus Cambrensis (d. *c.* 1220) lists the *cithara* and *timpanum* of the Irish and Scots, a circumstance which has led many writers to suggest that the latter was a membranophone. At any rate, the *cruit, clairseach,* and *timpan* were the art and ceremonial instruments of the Irish and Scots, being invariably found in the hands of musicians of high standing. All three instruments were furnished with metal strings.

Among wind instruments there was the reedpipe called the *buinne* in Ireland, one type having a hornlike terminal end similar to the Phrygian *aulos* and the modern Scottish *stockhorn*. It was an instrument known generically later as the *piob*, a word of Anglo-Saxon pedigree. Stone carvings at Durrow (11th Cent.) reveal this instrument. That the double pipe was known in Roman times is evidenced by the *tibiae pares* delineated on the Bridgeness legionary tablet. The bagpipe was termed the *tinne* in Ireland, whilst the recorder or beaked flute was the *cuisle*, which was also its name in Scotland, and is pure Anglo-Saxon. Indeed, the word *cuisle* seems also to have covered the bagpipe in Ireland, as it did much later in Scotland. The trumpet was called *stoc* or *sturgan*, whilst the horn was the *corn*, although there were several varieties and names. We read of the *buinnire* and *cornaire*, i.e. piper and horner, at festivals, whilst bagpipers and trumpeters were attached to the entourage of kings and chiefs in Ireland, not merely for state display but for the circumstance and clamour of war. There are innumerable specimens of bronze horns in the Dublin Museum.

CHAPTER 4

THE CHURCH.

" What was the style and character of the music of the Celtic Church ? To this enquiry, unfortunately, no answer can be given beyond the negative one, that it was not the Roman chaunt in its Gregorian, nor probably any other form."

WARREN : *Liturgy and Ritual of the Celtic Church.*

The reason why the above statement is made must be due to the fact that not a solitary neume or note of music from the Celtic Church has been preserved. From the 13th century however, there is in the British Museum (*Add.* 36929), a part of a psalter for three voices in neumes written in an Irish hand by one Cormac. Yet in spite of the lack of this, or of any other confirmatory documents, the learned Mabillon and the scholarly O'Conor have discussed this question of the music of the Celtic Church at some length, and have concluded that its chant was not even Occidental. Its origin, they say, was Oriental, and this eastern *usus*, we are informed, was introduced into Britain and Ireland in the 5th Century, and carried from the latter country into Scotland in the 6th Century. That the music was alien to Roman *usus* is highly probable since the liturgy itself most certainly was. Reference to the *Book of Deer* (12th Cent.), the *Vita S. Margaretae* (12th Cent.), where we read of the " barbarous rites " of the Celtic Church, and in the *Breviarum Aberdonensis*, which refers to the " rites of the primeval church," may support this view.

If no actual music of the Celtic Church has been spared by the hand of decaying time, at least the words of a few hymns have come down to us, although even these are, with one exception, of Irish provenance. Some of these hymns, attributed to saints of the 6th and 7th Centuries, are to be seen in the *Antiphonary of Bangor* (7th Cent.), the *Second Vision of St. Adamnan* (7th Cent.), the *Book of Mulling* (9th Cent.), and the Irish *Liber Hymnorum* (11th Cent.), as well as in some Continental codices (11th Cent.). These hymns of the Celtic Church are extremely interesting, for some of them contain what seem to be old pagan ideas in a Christian dress. Indeed Eleanor Hull has very forcibly demonstrated that the heathenish character of some of these ancient Celtic hymns is perhaps a survival of pagan usage. In fact, under the new Christian dispensation, these hymns were actually used as charms and incantations as of old, the loricas especially. We observe in the lorica attributed to

St. Columba that God is addressed as " King of the White Sun," whilst Christ is sought as " My Druid." Indeed, it is not too much to suggest that the characteristic tonsure of the Celtic clergy, over which the Roman Church created so much pother, may have been an old pagan tonsure. Clearly, the main drift of all this evidence of survivals is, that what is discernible in the outward visible sign of the mere words may surely show itself in the inward spiritual grace, i.e. in the music. In other words I suspect that some of the chants may have been a residue of pagan vocal incantations.

In the 5th Century the term *decantare* is used of the introduction of the liturgy of the Celtic Church into Ireland. In the next century, Gildas speaks of the " ecclesiastical melodies " in Celtic England, and of the youth of the land praising God in singing. In Scotland, St. Adamnan shows that both psalms and hymns were used in the offices of the church. St. Columba himself wrote a *Liber Hymnorum* and St. Gregory is said to have sent him a similar volume of hymns for the various services of the week. We still possess the hymn *Altus Prosator*, attributed to St. Columba.

St. Columba's musical activities at Iona are given prominence by St. Adamnan. The latter credited the saintly Colum with a wonderful larynx. He says, " The voice of the blessed man in chanting the psalms . . . was sometimes heard for four furlongs, . . . sometimes even eight furlongs." When on his famous mission of conversion in Pictland he was chanting the 44th Psalm as he approached the castle of King Brude. The pagan priests, afraid of his influence, endeavoured to keep the saint at a distance but, " in a wonderful manner his voice was at that moment so lifted up in the air, like some dreadful thunder, that both king and people were affrighted." Thus in the simple narration of St. Adamnan we have the old pagan notion of the magic of music in a Christian setting. A similar story had been told of St. Patrick at Guth-Ard, where his powerful voice paralysed the pagan worshippers and overthrew their idol. It is but the story of the rival magicians, Jewish and Egyptian, at the court of Pharaoh (*Exodus*, vii) all over again.

The Psalms of David were St. Columba's greatest joy. Indeed, his first embarrassment in Ireland as a young man was caused by his copying a psalter of St. Finian without permission. In the old Irish *Life of Columba* we are told that the saint " slept not at all, except for the time that his disciple Diarmid chanted three chapters of the *Beatus*. After that he rose up and made lamentation and hand-clapping [an old pagan practice], . . . After that he sang the hundred and fifty psalms until morning." Even when his days were almost numbered he was transcribing a psalter, having reached the 34th Psalm, and when his brethren bore him to his last resting place, it was to the solemn chanting of psalms that they performed the sacred obsequies. When the news of this irreparable loss to Scotland and Ireland reached the ears of the Ulster bard Dallam Fergall, he indited that line in his elegy on the departed saint which afterwards became proverbial among Gaelic-speaking peoples :

> " A *cruit* (rote) without a *ceis* (tuning pin.)
> A church without an Abbot."

The simile was most apt, for the tuning pins of the rote, around which each string was wound, determined, by its tightening or slackening, the pitch and concord of the instrument. Without the tuning pin (*ceis*), all was anomaly and dissonance, hence the metaphor of the bard of bards.

Of the later musical offices of the Celtic Church we are able to speak with a little more certainty. The scholarly Dr. Bernard, in editing the Irish *Liber Hymnorum*, has shown very reasonably that the presence of the *Magnificat, Benedictus, Te Deum*, etc., in the early documents, suggests *prima facie* that they were " used in choir," whilst we know that the *Gloria in Excelsis* was " sung " because a gloss tells us so. Warren gives his opinion without any reserve that " the services of the Celtic Church, both at the altar and in the choir, were choral." Whether any instrumental music accompanied the services we have no definite knowledge, but it might very well have been the case.

John Gunn (*Historical Enquiry Respecting . . . the Harp*) said that " from the middle of the sixth century . . . until the end of the twelfth century, the superior clergy were generally performers on the harp." I do not know his authority for this statement, but it is certainly a reasonable assumption. The Irish clergy, as Joyce points out, took great delight in the rote (although he too calls it the harp), and were wont to carry their *cruit* with them on their missionary wanderings. We read of this in the lives of the Irish saints, and it is a circumstance for comment by the later Giraldus Cambrensis (d. *c.* 1220) who mentions that the *cruit* (*cithara*) of the goodly St. Kievan (d. 618) of Glendalough was still venerated as a precious relic even in his day. That St. Columba himself, and his successors at Iona, led the singing with rote in hand, is not improbable, and the same might be said of Ireland and Northumbria. We know that the abbot of York wrote to St. Boniface (d. 754) in Germany asking him to send a player " on that kind of instrument which we call a *rotta*," i.e. a *cruit*. At the same time this story seems to be that mentioned in the year 764 when an abbot of Northumbria named Gutberchtus wrote to Lullus, a Continental bishop asking for a *citharista* able to play a *rotta* which he possessed. The 8th century Durham manuscript, said to be Bede's, displays the rote and horn in a scene of church praise, and similar Anglo-Saxon manuscripts in the British Museum are equally explicit and illuminating regarding this practice of instrumental music in Anglo-Saxon church praise. Indeed, if the contention of Mabillon, O'Conor and Warren is correct, that the music of the Celtic Church is of Oriental foundation, then it is only natural that we should expect such instrumental music, since the Byzantine and other Near-Eastern churches used the *kithara*, *aulos*, and *cymbals*, all of which found sanction in the fact that David and his companions were supposed to have used the rote (*kinnor*), pipe ('*ugab*), and cymbals (*mziltayim*). Of course, the very word *psalm*, derived from the Greek *psalmos* (" a song sung to a stringed instrument "), gives a plain and unmistakable clue. Even as late as Aelred (d.1166) the English churches were using pipes and cymbals as well as organs.

As to the structure of the music of the Celtic Church this was, as in the secular sphere, purely homophonic, as we shall see presently. Of its precise character one can only hazard conjectures. If, as it is believed, the music was of Oriental origin, then we may reasonably assume that it was highly melismatic, and that in the singing of psalms and hymns, and especially in the *Alleluiah*, the fullest decorative licence would be permitted. Thus would be rendered those definitely Ephesine thanksgivings in the Scottish *Book of Deer* and the Irish *Book of Dimma*.

CHAPTER 5

THE MUSIC.

" What music might have been heard in the Celtic portions of the British Isles at this period is debatable.   Literary references show that from very early times music occupied a position of great importance in Celtic life and was practised by a highly trained bardic profession."
GUSTAVE REESE : *Music in the Middle Ages.*

Celtic music of pagan and early Christian times was monodic or homophonic, despite claims to the contrary.   Dr. Ernest Walker has stated in his valuable *History of Music in England* that the Irish were apparently the first in the field with " free *organum*." basing his argument on the passage in the *Divisio Naturae* of Johannes Scotus (d. *ca.* 877) but, as I fully demonstrated in 1930 (*Historical Facts for the Arabian Musical Influence*), this belief in *organum* being alluded to in this passage is simply a myth copied for centuries by one writer after another who, for the most part, had never consulted the passage or, if they had, did not comprehend it.   At most Johannes Scotus only refers to *symphonia*, i.e. magadizing.

The zealous, though provocative Irish writer, P. W. Joyce, likewise cajoled himself at first to believe that " the ancient Irish must have used harmony," and gave the famous passage in the *Topographia Hibernica* of Giraldus Cambrensis (d. *c.* 1220) as his authority, although it is quite obvious that one can hardly speak of the " ancient Irish " at the close of the 12th century.   At the same time Joyce was forced to admit that even the relative musico-technical terms in old Irish, on which he partly staked his claim, simply meant " singing or playing together."

Added to these assumptions was the one advanced by the late Dr. W. H. Grattan Flood, with whom I had more than one duel, that the passage in St. Adamnan's *Life of St. Columba* proved that the Irish " sang canticles in counterpoint."   Reference to the original Latin shows that there is not an iota of justification for this assertion.   Thus one is impelled to state that this supposition, as well as those which precede it, may well be disregarded, since the most that we can allow the Irish at this period, and similarly the Scots, is that they could only have used *symphonia*.

The Gaelic words which Joyce posited as proof of his contention do not in any way constitute evidence for the use of harmony in our connotations of the term, but rather strengthens the claim for magadizing in *symphonia*. The word *comseinne* for example must mean " playing or singing together." One other word which Joyce translated as " harmony " is *cuibdius*, yet when the old Irish writers say that " David added *binnius* and *cuibdius* to the Psalms," it is far more likely that it means that "melody and metre [=rhythm] " were added by the reputed psalmist.

It might be thought that this old Celtic music, being monodic or homophonic, could not be so developed or interesting as harmonic or polyphonic music. The truth is that, fundamentally, the same principles obtain in both. If, for example, one sings or plays C E G in succession, the aesthetic reaction and result is much about the same as if these three notes were vocalized or instrumentalized simultaneously. Yet I suppose that we must admit that homophony is a more fleeting and quiescent art than that which we know as harmony or polyphony, and certainly its beauty is not so easy of appreciation because, outside of the Roman Church, one cannot get the requisite atmosphere for its direct apprehension.

I have already spoken of the glottal crooning (*cronan*) as a characteristic of one phase of Celtic song, but perhaps a more artistic feature of felic and bardic music was the decoration or ornamentation of the melodic outline which, as those who are conversant with Gaelic music will know, has persisted into quite modern times. This art, probably a relic of Oriental practice, was somewhat akin to that melismatic decoration in plainsong. Indeed, when I recall the *fioritura* that I heard from Irish singers in the days of my youth, I can imagine that the earlier device of festooning the melody must have been far more florid than that which we know today as *melismata*. We see this feeling for decoration in other aspects of Celtic life.

If we let our gaze fall on that inimitable craftsmanship in the Irish Tara Brooch and the superb penmanship of the *Book of Kells*, or in a lesser way, that of the Scottish Monymusk reliquary and the *Book of Deer*, the conceit flashes to one's mind that this filigree and figuration is precisely what we *hear* in Celtic music. The similitude is not so wayward after all, as the Viennese Hanslick showed us many years ago in his writings on aesthetics, because although music is primarily an emotional product, abstract emotions are analagous to abstract ideas. We see it more convincingly in the Orient where the delightfully intricate arabesque in Saracenic art finds a like expression in Arabian music in the so-called " gloss " or, as the Arabs call it, *tahsin* (" adornment "). Strange to say the Gaelic word *caoin* (" keen ") actually came to signify " beautiful, polished."

The Celts have ever had a genius for imagery and embellishment which reveals itself in the byways as well as the highways. One sees it in quite another sphere, in those eerie and airy stories of the *bean-side* (banshee) and the *leprecaun* which, leaving the average Anglo-Saxon unmoved, rouse the Celt to a high emotional pitch. These fairy imaginings are simply another kind of decoration, this time of social life rather than of music or the industrial arts. They are adornments which make the humdrum theme of mere existence a little more interesting and perhaps more tolerable.

PART II

THE ANGLO-NORMAN PERIOD. (1124-1424).

" King Malcolme [1057-93] . . . maid ane buke callit *Regeam Maiestatem*, contenand the lawis how his realm suld be governit, and quhat importance salbe gevin to his Chancellar, Marscheall, Chalmerlane, Iustice, Thesaurar, Secretar, Register, Compttrollair, and all vther officis of his houss."

BELLENDEN-BOECE : *Chronicles of Scotland* (1527).

HOWEVER unwilling one may be to intrude politics into a work of this kind, it has to be admitted that it is hardly possible to avoid such an encroachment if we are to appreciate properly the cultural conditions which are so often bound up with the body politic. Like a good shoe that pinches, sheer necessity compels us to tolerate it. At any rate, it is by this means that we are able to co-ordinate our material even though, here and there, we may create *concordia discors*.

We have seen that there were " four nations " in Scotland,— the Picts, the Scots, the Britons, and the Angles. In the year 844, Kenneth MacAlpin, King of the Scots, became King of the Picts as well, and from that moment the two kingdoms became as one. After a century and three quarters another and even more pregnant absorption took place when Malcolm II, King of the Scots, became ruler of the Angles of Bernicia, having utterly defeated them at Carham in 1018. This gave further consolidation to the kingdom, in that the intermarriage of the Scottish royal family with that of the British of Strathclyde brought the crown of the latter to the house of Malcolm II. By all these events Scottish rule and Celtic custom were later extended to the Tees in the east and to the Derwent in the west, and it was by these means that the land which we now know as Scotland first received its name. The circumstance had an important influence on Scotland culturally.

No nation can boast of being " pure and simple," either racially or culturally. Indeed, it is just as well that it is so, since most of what we owe to progress and civilisation is due to racial mixture and to the impinging of one culture on another. Until the 11th century, one may safely say that the culture of Scotland was, generally speaking, Celtic, but with the appearance of Malcolm Canmore

(1057-93) on the Scottish throne, we can discern a definite tendency to the adoption of southern manners and customs, although it must be understood that this statement only applies to the Lowlands, which was the locus of the king and the nobility who supported him. Much of this *ad meridiem* gaze was directed, not towards Anglian Bernicia, but to the very hub of English culture in the south. Malcolm himself had spent fourteen years at the Saxon court of Edward the Confessor where he had found refuge from the murdering sword of his uncle Macbeth (d. 1057). Further, his second spouse, Margaret, was the grand-daughter of Edmund Ironside (d. 1006) the valiant Saxon king. At the Norman Conquest, Margaret, together with her mother, brother and sister, found sanctuary at Malcolm's court, and it was the daughter of Malcolm and Margaret, " the good Queen Maud," who married Henry I of England. She proved to be so fond of music and so profusely generous to musicians and poets, that she is said to have expended all her revenues upon them.

Under Malcolm and Margaret the Scottish court and church became deeply influenced by English, and even Norman ideas, for quite apart from encouraging the English, the king gave land and benefice to many a dissident Norman knight and cleric, much to the chagrin of his own people. As we can grasp from the Bellenden-Boece quotation at the threshold of this chapter, the English system of lordly feudal officials at court became the fashion, together with the introduction of " other officers of his house," which latter, we may confidently assume, included court minstrels. Of course, these Anglo-Norman ideas were not exactly novel, since something of the sort already existed in Celtic polity, but what was new was the feudal basis which was now beginning to be established. In the church, much the same kind of thing happened as we shall observe presently.

Family connections between the Scottish and English courts grew apace in succeeding years until the time of the first interregnum. Alexander I (1106-24) married Sybilla a daughter of Henry I of England, and his charters were addressed to " Scots and English," like those of his predecessor Edgar (1097-1107). David I (1124-53) spent his youth at the court of Henry I and he married a daughter of the Earl of Northumbria. Malcolm IV (1153-65) served Henry II during the war with France (1159-60) and was knighted by him. William the Lion (1165-1214) also served under the banner of Henry II in Normandy (1166) and all his daughters married English barons. Alexander II (1214-49) married Joan, daughter of John of England, whilst Alexander III (1249-86) married (firstly) Margaret, a daughter of Henry III of England. Much of this association helped to consolidate those English and Anglo-Norman practices which were being regularly established or unconsciously adopted since the time of Malcolm Canmore.

Although the rationale of the southern governance asserted itself from the time of David I, another cultural flow, this time French, also began to be felt. Whilst David I, was still heir to the throne he had established at Selkirk a colony of French Benedictines from the Abbey of Tiron. In 1118, canons regular from Beauvais were brought to Jedburgh, and in 1147, a third importation, this time Augustines from Aroise near Arras were implanted at Cambuskenneth. These influxes are worth noting because, as we shall see later, French music became predominant in the Scottish church, to its great glory. Indeed, it is significant that some of the king's charters were addressed to " Galwegians, *French*, and Angles," as well as Scots, which reveals perhaps the first buds which later flowered into the " Auld Alliance " between Scotland and France. From the time of Alexander II, when a military pact with France was made, the Gallic influence began to show itself more clearly in Scotland, which his marriage with Marie de Courcy must have encouraged. His son, Alexander III, took Yolande, a daughter of Robert Comte de Dreux, as his second wife, and he married his son to a daughter of the Comte de Flandre.

At the same time it must be understood that what applied to the Lowlands, and every line of the above spells that, was quite alien to the Highlands. Here the powerful lords were quite independent, although many a king sought to bring them to heel. These territorial chiefs did not need to claim the right of " pit and gallows " from any crowned head, since it had been their inalienable privilege from time immemorial. This state of affairs continued, more or less, until the death of Robert III (1406), as such episodes as the Wolf of Badenoch, the Clan Chattan, and Red Harlaw testify. From the vestiges that survive in the records of the troublous times it is palpable enough that the use and wont of daily life in the Highlands was still the outlook of the Celt. Since Gaelic alone was on the Highlander's tongue we can reasonably assume that the song retained its Celtic lilt, and the same can be asserted of the dance. Of this persistence there can be little doubt because the Celtic strain was still asserting itself in the period of the Golden Age (1424-1560) and even later, as we shall have occasion to see in fuller detail.

CHAPTER 1

THE COURT AND NOBILITY.

" Bifor the king he sat adoun
　And tok his *harpe* so miri of soun,
　And trempreth his *harp* as he wele can,
　And blisseful notes he ther gan.
　　　　　　Orfeo and Heurodis (14th century).

" Thair talk that tyme is table honorable
　Befoir lordingis and ladeis amiable
　Is oft *singing* and sawis of solace
　Quhair *melody* is the mirthful maistrace."
　　　　　　Cockelbie's Sow (15th century).

It is frequently urged that history is too often a mere chronicle of kings and courts, a procedure which is so artificial that it frequently conveys quite a wrong perspective. Whilst this objection is valid enough, the fact remains that in the Middle Ages the records of kings and courts are generally our only indices. Further, we cannot neglect the classes any more than a trigonometrical surveyor dare spurn high altitudes for his basic planning if just results are the aim. In any case, both high and low are to receive equal attention in this survey, and if one begins with the court and castle it is because it is here that we see the art resources at their best.

As in Celtic times, the king and nobility had their musicians who, in spite of such names as minstrel (*ministrallus*) mime (*mimus*), jester (*joculator*), and player (*histrio*), all followed the art of music but with these added accomplishments. These were new names to Scotland and they came with the Anglo-Norman fashions. Before long they completely ousted the old Gaelic titles of *file*, *bard*, and *druth*, at least in the Lowlands. The name *bard* certainly persisted, but because he retained so much of the old technique, which the new dispensation would consider uncouth and pagan, his calling fell into disrepute. On the other hand, one office from old Celtic days did flourish, the *seanachaidh*, of whom we read at the coronation of Malcolm Canmore (1058) and of Alexander III (1249), where he could still be found, dressed in a robe of red, chanting the king's genealogy.

Court minstrels were much in evidence during the whole of this period. From references to them in the state papers we know that they were definitely officers of the royal household, possibly under the control of the " King's harper." This officer seems to have held a position somewhat analogous to the English *joculator regis*, of whom we read so early as *Domesday Book* (1085-6). The king's harper was doubtless a privileged artist who sang and played in the privy chamber, as we observe in *Orfeo and Heurodis*, whilst the subordinate minstrels in ordinary attended to the more domestic needs of the royal household in matters musical, not merely when occasions of church and state demanded, but when feasting, sport, and pastimes were afoot. There were trumpeters, horners, and drummers for state and martial display, as well as pipers handling shawm, bagpipe, and recorder, who were indispensable for outdoor music in general. Then there were others who discoursed music of more delicate facture, i.e. rote and harp players, fiddlers of all kinds, psaltrists, lutars, and others. The vernacular literature of the 14th century is eloquent in praise of the *harpe*, *fethill*, *lute*, *gitterne*, *rybybe*, *horne*, *tabour*, *trompe*, and *crowd*.

Although it was the king's minstrels who were at the Battle of the Standard (1138), it is not until the following century that we get definite information concerning them. When Alexander III

(d. 1286) was in London paying homage to Edward I in 1278, his court minstrels were with him, since we know of payments being made to Elyas the " King of Scotland's harper," two of his trumpeters, and two of his minstrels, as well as to four other Scottish minstrels. In this same year a *menestrallo Regis Scociae* is found at Durham Priory. When this king married Yolande Countess de Montfort in 1285, Fordun mentions *multi modis organis musicis* at the ceremony. Elyas le Harpur, above mentioned, comes into greater prominence in 1296, at the close of the regal career of John Balliol. Seemingly, Elyas had been deprived of his lands by Edward I, who was then in a conquering mood in Scotland, but in this year the English king issued a writ to the sheriffs of Perth and Fife which restored to this harper the lands previously held by him. This is one of the many instances of the survival of the old Celtic custom of gifting land to court musicians.

At this particular period there was no *de facto* King of Scotland, and it is not improbable, since musicians were ever fickle, that Elyas had accepted temporary service with the new master. At any rate, Edward's own man, Adam the King's harper, was at that moment out of favour with the English king by reason of a charge of reset against " his boy." Nor was Elyas the only harper as a land-owner at this time, since we find Ughtred le Harpour of Lanark-shire and John le Harpur of Saltoun having their land restored to them in 1296. In this selfsame year, probably under precisely the same circumstances, there were taken those instruments of sub-mission extorted by the English king from the Scottish nobility and landowners recorded in the Ragman Roll. These documents reveal that many more favoured minstrels were holding lands. Herein we have the rigmarole (a word derived from " ragman-roll ") of homage made in severalty by the last two harpers (?) mentioned, as well as by Robert le Harpur of Ayrshire, Rogier le Harpur of Berwick, and William le Harpur, the seal of the latter displaying what would appear to be a harp. Other surnames of the period, e.g. Nichul Bard and Patrick Trumpator, reveal the craft or pro-fession of the owner, or that of a near progenitor, whilst quite a dozen of the seals of the Ragman Rolls carry a buglehorn as a crest.

Whilst Edward I was wintering in Scotland during the second interregnum there is a payment in 1303-4 to a certain " King's piper " named John of Kinghorn. Actually he is dubbed *fistulari regis*, a title which could cover a player on the shawm, recorder, or bagpipe. He too may have been a renegade like Elyas, faithless to party and principle in piping for the English king. Yet one must allow that *force majeur* and the prospect of " siller " are sovereign persuaders. In any case, Elyas and John were not alone in this alienation, since we read of five Scottish harpers (*citharisti Scocie*) playing for the puissant overlord in 1303-4 between Durie and Sanford, although they only collected 5s for their obsequious harping. Then in August 1304, divers minstrels of Perth, performing on the fiddle (*vidula*), psaltery (*cimphan*), and other instruments, tinkled sweet melody for the conqueror, whilst three Scottish trumpeters, Nigello Beymer, Andree de Clydesdale, and Gilberto Bride, served him from Sterling to Yetholm.

Yet the days of independence were nigh, and with the advent of the valiant Robert the Bruce (1306-29), who won Scottish freedom from the English yoke at Bannockburn, a new era dawned. Needless to say, his life was too busy militarily to permit of much attention to court minstrelsy, although at the end of his days, for the Christmas festivities of 1328, we read of a fiddler (*viellario*) getting 20s, whilst thrice that amount is disbursed among minstrels. At the nuptials of his son Prince David at Berwick in July 1328, the minstrels were rewarded by £66 odd, whilst the King of England's minstrels, who probably accompanied the bride Johanna, the sister of Edward III, also received handsome gifts at Dumbarton. That harpers were still in high favour at court is evident from a grant of land being made to a certain Thomas Citharista.

The Bruce's son and successor, David II (1329-71) made several similar grants, to wit,—to Patrick Citharist of Carrick, Ade Chichariste of Forfar, and Nicholas Chicharist of Linlithgow. As these were " forfaultries," they may be taken as testimony of royal munificance and appreciation of the minstrel class. In 1330, the state papers record instruments being purchased for the king's mimes, and tell of £30 paid to minstrels at his coronation in 1331, although twelve thousand golden florins were spent on the anointing oil. Despite the Papal unction, David's life was a tragedy. Taken prisoner by the English at Neville's Cross (1346) he spent eleven years in captivity. Small wonder that we have so little news to impart about court music save a few scattered entries. In 1335-6 a *histrio* (minstrel) of the Scottish king's household was performing at Durham Priory, and a John Harpour of the household of John of Stirling is found there in 1357. Then we have mention of payments to pipers in 1362, a line about a Johannes Trumpour in 1365-6, and a payment of 40s to the " King of Scotland's harper " in 1370. That miming still prevailed may be seen from the Exchequer Rolls where " the stage-players at Inchmurdoch " get £10 in 1366, whilst a " minstrel " and " other players " have 30s between them.

The remaining reigns, those of Robert II (1371-90) and Robert III (1390-1406), need not detain us long since there is but a mere pittance to offer. In the reign of the former we read of forfeited lands in Haddington being assigned to Thomas Citharist, whilst in 1371 there is mention of Sir John Foulerton of Ayrshire receiving lands called " Harperland " in the Barony of Kyle, obviously held originally by some favoured royal minstrel of the class already noticed. In 1377 there are payments to court minstrels, and we read of Thomas Acressan as a " King's minstrel." Another regal minstrel was Thomas de Folehope or Fulhop who received a salary as such from 1390 to 1406, whilst a certain Bergus (more likely Fergus) was another court musician in 1399-1400. The latter might very well be the William Fergus who, with Roger Harpour, were playing at Durham Priory in 1376-7. In 1394-5 a " Rotour de Scocia," probably a player on the rote, was also performing there.

The chief officers of state, the great barons, and high ecclesiastics, also had their minstrelsy, which was generally on the same plan as that of the court but, in virtue of feudal etiquette, not so imposing. In 1325, the state papers refer to the " Harpour of the Steward of Scotland " being released from prison in London. This " steward " was Walter Stewart (d. 1326), the father of Robert II. One remem-

bers the lines in *Orfeo and Heurodis* (14th Cent.), picturing the
castle minstrels :—

> " In the castel the steward sat atte mete,
> And mani lording was bi him sete,
> Ther were *trompours* and *tabourers*,
> *Harpours* fele and *crouders*,
> Miche melody thei maked alle, . . .
> And Orfeo sat stille in the halle
> And herkneth."

Music at meals seem to have been the rule with " lordings " as
we read in the *Buke of the Howlate* :—

> " At the myddis of the meit,
> in come the menstralis."

Considering the times, it was a fairly sumptuous display in minstrelsy, and many a Scottish castle today still shows the corbels of the
rafters which supported the minstrel's gallery at the end of the
great hall, and in one or two instances, the gallery itself.

On the whole it can be safely averred that the court and castle
minstrels of Scotland during the Anglo-Norman period were quite
as imposing, in numbers certainly, as those of England, a circumstance of no mean importance when one takes into account the wide
disparity between the two countries in wealth. It is true that
Scotland could not claim such an array of minstrels as those present
at the knighting of the heir apparent of England in 1306, but there
was at least one Scottish minstrel present on this brilliant occasion,
when " Le Roy Capenny " with " Le Roy de Champaigne " top
the minstrel roll. The former was probably the " King Caupenny
of Scotland " who is mentioned by Chappell under the year 1290.
Other Scottish minstrels travelled abroad, doubtless *via* France, and
in the Spanish state papers we have an entry that the court minstrels
of Robert II (1371-90) were received at the Spanish court. What
new ideas in music did these minstrels bring back to Scotland ?
Were the *Portingall, Naverne,* and *Arragone,* those dances mentioned
in *Cockelbie's Sow* (15th Cent.) among them ?

CHAPTER 2

THE PEOPLE.

" A maistir swynhird swanky
And his cousing Copyn Cull
Fowll of bellis fulfull
Led the dance and began
Play us *Joly lemmane*
. . . .
Sum *Be yon wodsyd* singis
Sum *Lait lait in evinnyngis*."

Cockelbie's Sow (15th cent.).

Apart from the traditional folk music, i.e. the old Celtic toil songs and the simple ditties of the homestead, which were part of life itself in the Highlands, and what were their equivalents in the Lowlands, the only other music was that heard at festival time, prompted by the church, the feast, and the revels, much of which was of an exotic character because of the wandering minstrel who now traversed the land from one end to the other, although it may be doubted whether the Anglo-Norman type of performer penetrated into the fastnesses of the north. In Celtic times we have seen that the roving musician existed in the *druth* who stood in relation to the *file-bard* in much the same way as the Welsh *clerwr* did to the *teuluwr*, or the Anglo-Saxon *gleeman* to the *scop*. One was the carefree peregrinator and the other the more respectable urban minstrel. By this time men of all classes had taken to " the road " under the guise of minstrelsy, for the roving life had attracted quite a crowd who yearned for release from the shackles of inherited usage. This attitude of mind which had expression not only in the minstrel's outlook on life and manner of existence, but found an outlet in their free views on government and religion, which were chanted in many a ditty and bandied in an occasional sly jest, as we see being done by the French *jongleur* Rutebeuf (13th Cent.).

One must realize that there was no regular theatre as we know it today, and even books, i.e. manuscripts, were rare. Even so, there were few who could read. It need not therefore be a matter for wonder that the minstrel class had such popularity. Their very dress and mien commanded attention. Gaudy raiment and flat shoes, shaven faces and cropped hair were not merely the mark of the craft, but were an added attraction, for the quaintness itself allured the crowd, the mutable many. What they had to play and sing was primarily what their audiences were interested in, yet what they *said* and *did* was probably of equal attraction, and it was this latter which gave them not only popularity but much influence, for there is nothing like the widely versed and travelled man in weaning people from their insular prejudices. Indeed, it was on this particular point that the state and church fell foul of the minstrel. To flutter the hearts of the lasses with the love tale of *Troilus and Cressida*, to conjure the fancy of the lads in the exciting recital of *Robin Hood and Maid Marion*, or to thrill both with jig and hornpipe, all of which were common to both England and Scotland, was harmless enough, but a couplet which asked, " When Adam delved and Eve span, who was then the gentleman ?", or a *jongleur* line which ran, " Hell await thee Rome," was interpreted as red revolution and rank heresy. The result was that many a minstrel paid dearly for his loose tongue, as did poor Till Eulenspiegel many years later, whose moods and deeds have been so diversely portrayed in tone by Richard Strauss.

As was only to be expected, the minstrel, unless he was under the protection of court, castle, priory, or burgh, was denied the law of the land and the rites of the church, and, if we can accept the decree of Macbeth (d. 1058), was actually subjected to the branding iron and scourge when the sheriff's hands were laid on him. It was much the same elsewhere. In Ireland, under the parliament of Lionel Duke of Clarence (*c.* 1327), it was made a penal offence to harbour " Irish minstrels, rhymers, and newstellers." A similar edict was issued in Wales against the minstrel class in 1402.

The clergy, in their turn, frowned on those ditties which parodied the most sacred formulas of the church, whilst they naturally winced at the minstrel's invective against Papal hypocrisy and corruption. Yet he did no more than the Englishman Walter Mapes (d. *c.* 1108), or the later Scottish Wedderburn (16th Cent.). Indeed, he could say with the former in his own defence,

> " When I see evil men in their riches delighting,
> How can I help a satire inditing ?"

The church answered the minstrel and his kin by denying them the rites of the church, pronouncing him a " lecher " and his spouse a " wanton." In the face of this can we wonder that the old Gaelic name of *druth*, which once simply meant " an itinerant minstrel " now came to equate with " lewd " and " harlot." Yet these labels of opprobrium were affixed by a class which, in company with Scotland's kings, were notorious for their immoralities and broods of illegitimates. Meanwhile it is quite exhilarating to see the minstrel's rejoinder, as in *Aucassin et Nicolette*, which was one of the pieces of his *répertoire*. The hero is threatened with hell's fire if he takes a mistress. The menace troubles him but little since this is the destination, he says, of all the harpers and minstrels, *as well as kings*. And then there is that other minstrel tale of the musician who went to hell where he and St. Peter (who belonged to the other establishment) played dice, the stakes being the souls of men. But St. Peter won so many souls for paradise that no further minstrels were admitted to hell for the future. One can imagine how these sallies were appreciated by the boisterous crowd at the fair and even by the more restrained gentry in the castle hall.

To bring these people to discipline it is alleged that it was made a condition of lawful minstrelsy that he who vended it had to be " specially licensed by the king." Of what this consisted we do not know, but it could not apply to the minstrel at court, castle, priory, or burgh, because his status was already secured. Nor can we believe that the peregrine folk were granted individual licenses. Possibly it was the absence of a guild or fraternity of minstrels in Scotland, which elsewhere controlled and disciplined its members, that brought about the severe repressive laws against minstrels in this country. It is certainly passing strange that whilst associations of minstrels existed in England and on the Continent there is no trace of any such organisation in Scotland, not even after the rise of craft guilds in the 15th century.

The *locus* of popular minstrelsy was the market place, the village green, the wayside shrine, or the cross roads, but the greatest occasion was the " fair." usually on the days of church festivals.

It was generally held in the precincts of the church which brought people together from far and near. Whilst bartering and selling were going on at one end of the fair, the minstrels had their corner in another spot where song, melody, and dance were in full swing. Travelling round the country one must naturally expect to find English and even foreign minstrels in these troupes. Indeed, I have suggested elsewhere that it is highly probable that it was the minstrel class that contributed considerably to that "triumph of English speech and civilisation " that took place in Scotland at this period. At the Norman Conquest, the old Anglo-Saxon *scop* and *gleeman* had to lie low, for the conquerors had no stomach for those defiant songs which gloried in the deeds of Hereward, and we can well imagine that many took refuge in Scotland just as their rulers did. Generally, the erstwhile *scop* and *gleeman*, mixing with the new minstrel groups, became, as E. K. Chambers observes, " the natural focus and mouthpiece of popular discontent."

I have already said (*Music in Mediaeval Scotland*) that the wandering minstrel, touring through different lands, brought new forms and styles of music, sometimes to the accompaniment of exotic instruments which they had picked up abroad. " The whole aspect of music changed with these wandering folk, and here we have the real starting-point of the folk-song and folk-dance in the recreative sense. The people at large for the first time became participators in general culture. The forms of music were certainly affected. The old bard of court and castle, and the precentor of abbey and monastery, bound everywhere by a strict conservatism, had kept musical art at a standstill. With the wealth of fresh ideas in melody, rhythm, and form, that must have swept the country, it was inevitable that the more serious forms of the art were influenced. It was no longer the bardic and church song that obtained, but compositions of a more varied nature such as have come down to us in ballad literature," like the simple *cantus* made on the death of Alexander III (1286), as preserved in the *Orygynale Cronykill of Scotland* by Wyntoun (d. *c.* 1420)—

> " This falhyd fra he deyed suddanly,
> This sang wes made off hym for thi."

Or the song made by the Scots at Berwick (1296) as handed down
in a Harleian manuscript which runs,

> " Wend Kyng Edewarde with his lange shankes,
>   To have gete Berwyke al our unthankes,

Or that made, as Fabyan (d. 1513) tells, about Bannockburn (1314),

> " Maydens of Englonde, sore maye ye morne,
>   For your lemmans ye have loste at Bannockisborne,
>   With heve a lowe."

which was sung " in the carols of the maidens and mynstrelles of
Scotland " for many a decade, and even quoted by the English
Marlowe (d. 1593) long after. Barbour (d. 1395) says likewise,

> " For quhasa likis, thai may heir
>   Young wemen, quhen thai will play,
>   Syng it e-mang thame ilke day."

Then there were long narrative poems like *Sir Tristrem* (14th Cent.)
which were sung and not merely recited.

All that has preceded in this account of the music of the people
obviously concerns the Lowlands of Scotland. What obtained in
the Highlands can only be conjectured. It is recorded in Irish
annals that Randall, the Lord of Arran (*ca.* 1180), had both *stuic*
(*stoc*) and *sturgan*, i.e. trumpets, in his military music. In the next
century we read of an Irish *file* Muireadhach Albanach, i.e. Murdock
or Muirhead the Scot, being in Scotland. He served the Ulster
kings. His name was still green in Scotland when the *Book of
Lismore* (1512-26) was penned. Another such poet-minstrel was
Gilla-Brighde Albanach, i.e. Gilbert the Scot. O'Curry tells us
that he received his name, as did the previously mentioned, because
he spent " so much of his time in that country," for Scotland
" came within his professional province as much as any part of
Ireland."

If we dare appeal to Cymric testimony in the matter of the wide
appreciation of music among the common people, we can cite
Giraldus Cambrensis to show that about 1188 the rote or harp
(*cithara*) was freely used. " Every family " he says, " is here well
skilled in the knowledge of that instrument." When he turns to
praise the music of Scotland, there seems to be every reason to
suppose that he is speaking of the Highlands rather than of the

Lowlands. ˴ this passage, as we have seen, the Irish are given the palm over ι Welsh by reason of the " faultless artistry " and the " subtlety oι ιeir modulations," but Scotland, says Giraldus, outshone her teacher Ireland in this respect. That the connection with Ireland in music still continued is established by many proofs. One, from an Irish source, tells us that when Mulrony MacCarroll, the blind Irish harper was slain by Sir John Bermingham in 1328, he was lamented as " the chief minstrel of *Ireland and Scotland*." About the year 1078, Gryffith ap Cynan, a King of Wales, invited Irish musicians to an Eisteddfod in his country where they assisted in the reform of the instrumental music of the Welsh. If the musical connection between Ireland and Wales was so close in these days as to occasion such an event, how much greater is the likelihood that the musical bond between Ireland and Scotland was even more intimate, especially since their people were of the same race.

CHAPTER 3

THE INSTRUMENTS.

" *Harpe* and *fethill* both thay fande,
Getterne and als so the *sawtrye* ;
Lutte, and *rybybe*, bothe gangande,
And all manere of mynstralsye."
Thomas of Ersyldoune (14th cent.).

" Ther were *trompours* and *tabourers*,
Harpours fele and *crouders*."
Orfeo and Heurodis (14th cent.).

At the opening of the Anglo-Norman era we are greeted by the valuable testimony of Giraldus Cambrensis concerning Celtic instruments of music in the last quarter of the 12th century. We read in his *Topographia Hibernica* that the Irish used only two [art] instruments, the *cithara* and *timpanum*, the Scots had three, the *cithara*, *timpanum*, and *chorus* ; the Welsh three, the *cithara*, *tibia*, and *chorus*. By the *cithara*, Gerald Barry possibly includes both the rote and the harp. The former was the Gaelic *cruit*, of which we have many representations on Irish crosses as we have seen. In Scotland we have an example on the St. Martin's cross at Iona

(14th cent.), in which one side of the instrument is curvilinear rather than rectangular, a feature displayed on the earlier Irish Durrow Cross (11th cent.). In Wales it was written *crwth*, which was Anglicized into *croud* or *crowd*, and time came when the bow was applied to it, a central fingerboard being added to the instrument itself. Whether the *crouders* in *Orfeo and Heurodis* plucked or bowed their instruments we shall never know. We have difficulty in recognizing the precise genus of the instrument of the *harpours* to which Orfeo " herkneth " in the castle hall. Possibly it was the Lowland harp with gut strings rather than the Highland *clarsech* (Irish *clairseach*) whose strings were of metal. The *timpan* or *tiompan* is forgotten by the poets, possibly because they were of Lowland breed, and this instrument nestled more comfortably in the Highlands where we have evidence of its existence at this time. The *clarsech* or/and Lowland harp, with a curved fore pillar, may be seen in St. Oran's Chapel and the Cathedral at Iona (13th cent.) and better still in the chapel at Keills, Argyllshire (14th cent.).

The other old Celtic instrument of Giraldus is the *chorus*. In this I prefer to recognize the early type of bagpipe, i.e. a simple wind-bag, or other wind-chest, with an inflation pipe and a drone (or chanter). The *chorus* of the pseudo-Jerome *Hieronymus ad Dardanum* letter was such an instrument, and St. Nicholas of Lyra (14th cent.) says, " *chorus* . . . gallice *chevrette.*" Iconographic examples are not plentiful but Gerbert's *De cantu et musica sacra* shows an early design, whilst a closely related instrument may be seen in Scotland on the St. Martin's Cross at Iona (13th cent.) which I have also shown in my *Music in Mediaeval Scotland*. Again the poets are blissfully ignorant of its existence, although some of those " pipers " in the state papers may have handled it.

Ere many decades had passed in this era, a new world of instruments had dawned. This was due to the peregrine minstrels to a large extent. Coming from many lands, even Moors from Spain, these wanderers introduced all sorts of fresh instruments, or at least new models, as well as novelties in technique. It was the returning Crusaders who were also responsible for some of these exotic instruments that they had found with the Saracens and

Moors, and among them were the rebec, the fiddle, the lute, the psaltery, and the gittern. The rebec, i.e. the Scottish *rybybe*, was derived from the Arabian *rabāb*, and we see its form, pearshaped with a vaulted back, the lower part of the belly being of parchment, in the 12th century in Europe. Jerome of Moravia (13th cent.), who was himself acquainted with Arabian music theorists, says that it was mounted with three strings. For centuries the European rebec retained its Oriental features.

The fiddle was the instrument known as the *geige* in Germany. We can almost trace its passage from the East in the Oriental *ghichak*, the Slavonic *gega*, the Russian *guiga*, the old Norse *gigja*, to its German name. Unlike the rebec, which was vault-chested, the fiddle was flat-chested. In Scotland, as in England, it was called *fethill* or fiddle after the Latin *vidula*, although among the Latin races the middle consonant was elided.

Of equal importance were the lute and gittern which like the two instruments just mentioned, were vault-chested and flat-chested respectively. The lute was like the modern mandoline in shape but larger, with the peg-box turned at a right angle to the neck. Similar to its classical Arabian model, it had four to five gut strings at this time, and was played with a plectrum. The psaltery or *sawtrye* was already known in Europe in a rectangular form, but the new Oriental instrument which came into use had two fresh shapes, (1) a trapezoid, and (2) a truncated triangle. All these neoteric contrivances caught both eye and ear by reason of the strange shape and fresh tone colour.

Even in the domain of wind instruments there were a few novelties from the East. The most important of these was the long cylindrical bore *trump* or *tromp* whose shrill piercing blast was much more penetrating than the hoarse bray of the earlier conical bore horns. Then there were the characteristic Saracenic pulsatile instruments in the double-headed cylindrical drum called the *tabour*, the bowlshaped kettledrum or *naker*, and the tambourine dubbed the *timbrel*. Almost all of these instruments were used by the minstrels whether at court, castle, burgh, or on " the road," those of the wind and percussion groups being specially favoured in open-air music.

Although there are few iconographical examples in Scottish manuscripts or industrial art, it is hardly likely that they differed much
from those so well figured and described in Galpin's *Old English
Instruments of Music.*

In church music it was the organ that held sway, as in England.
William Dauney, the early historian of Scottish Music (1838),
once suggested that the organ was introduced into churches in
Scotland in the 12th century because, as he argued, " it is not easy
to imagine that a monarch like David I (1124-53), who did so much
towards the erection of churches and monasteries, should have
omitted to furnish some of the former with . . . the most important
adjunct to the solemn magnificence of Catholic ritual." It is quite
evident from Fordun (d. *c.* 1384) that on the occasion of the removal
of the remains of the saintly Queen Margaret from the outer church
to the high altar at Dunfermline in June 1250, the organ accompanied
the chanting of the choir in procession. What was the practice at
Dunfermline might very well have been followed at other abbeys.
It is true that the musical service of the Roman Church did not, and
does not, call for any music other than that of the human voice, the
" living psaltery " as Eusebius says, but the general rule of the
church at this time, despite the opinions of the Church Fathers,
and even more modern purists, was the use of the organ in church
praise. Aeldred (d. 1166), in England, complained of the " sound
of the organs, the noise of the cymbals and other musical instruments," a condemnation which, conceivably, could include Scotland,
for Aeldred had been at the court of David I as a young man, and
was a missionary to the Picts of Galloway in 1164.

CHAPTER 4

THE CHURCH.

" The ancient music of the Church of Scotland was plain, easy
and simple, like that of the primitive Christians."
MACKENZIE : *Writers of the Scots Nation.*

Although Gregorian Song had been introduced into England
in the 7th century, it is extremely doubtful whether it found complete
acceptance in Scotland until the following century, and concerning

this we read in Mansi's *Sacrorum conciliorum . . . collectio* (bk. 15) in which the Council of Clovesco (Glasgow ?) of 747 decreed that in " the celebration of the masses, the manner of chanting shall be performed in one way only, viz., according to the rule that we have received *in writing* from the Roman Church." As we have no documents showing neumes earlier than the 9th century in the Occident, this is perhaps one of the first direct references to neumatic writing, although, obviously, it must have been used earlier.

In the 11th century York claimed the ecclesiastical superiority over Scotland and we may assume that York *usus* was observed there at this time. If that view be accepted, it is probable that the cursive musical notation which accompanies the antiphone for St. Nicholas in the *Liber Sancti Cuthberti* in the Sidney Sussex College MS. may be taken as a sample of what was practised in the Lowland churches of Scotland at this time. The Sarum *usus* was probably the common rule in Scotland by the 12th Century, although in its adoption by Glasgow Cathedral (1147-64) there were certain reservations. In the 13th Century we find the Sarum use in the *Sprouston Breviary*, *Hyrdmanniston Breviary*, and the *Pontificale Ecclesiae S. Andreae*. In the first two documents the Scottish saints in the calendar have been added by a later hand, a circumstance which seems to point to an English origin, although the former contains the rhymed office of St. Kentigern. The present writer once possessed a portion of a service book of the Scottish Church, dated by the British Museum and the late Professor J. S. Phillimore (Glasgow) as the 11th-12th Century, which contained a part of the office of St. Kentigern. The earliest specimen of Scottish Church music that has been located dates from the 14th Century (Priory of Inchcolm).

By this time, in place of the old monastic rule of the Celtic Church, and in conformity with Anglo-Norman feudal notions, Scotland was divided into dioceses under bishops, and an ecclesiastical constitution was instituted which followed, with but slight modification, that of the English Church. Here and there however, the *ancien régime* lingered with the so-called Culdees, who continued to use an office " after their own fashion," until the reign of David I (1124-53). It was this king who finally brought the church in

Scotland into ecclesiastical conformity, and it is to him that we owe the famous abbeys of Selkirk, Jedburgh, Holyrood, Kelso, Melrose, Newbattle, Dundrennan, Cambuskenneth, and Dryburgh, whose spacious choirs, now alas in ruins, were once the conservatories of the music of the Scottish church.

The organisation of church music in Scotland was little different from that of England. Naturally, it is in the cathedral, the bishop's seat, that we see it at its peak, possibly because it usually housed secular canons. In the statutes of Elgin Cathedral (1212 and 1236) and St. Machar's Aberdeen (1256) we are furnished with precise particulars of the standing and duties of those connected with the choir. Of the four *principales personae* of the chapter of canons, the second and third rank were the precentor (*cantor*) and chancellor (*cancellarius*). They sat at the west end of the choir, the precentor in the extreme north stall, facing the dean of the chapter, and the chancellor next to the latter. Dowden (*Mediaeval Church in Scotland*) says that " the reasons for this arrangement are not stated, but it obviously enabled these four officials to supervise the behaviour of the whole body of clerks and boys while the service of the Canonical Hours was being sung."

The duties of these two dignitaries are clearly set forth in the early statutes. It was the responsibility of the precentor " to regulate the music used in the services of the church, to admit to office the boys who took part in the services, to see to their instruction and discipline, and to appoint the teacher in the song-school." The chancellor had to see " that the service books had been correctly transcribed " and " the singers and readers told off weekly for the several services." At this early period we cannot always be certain of the actual numbers constituting the choir, but at Aberdeen (1256) there were thirteen canons, at Brechin (1372) there were eleven, at Moray eight, and at Ross (1235) as few as four. In addition there were the choir-boys but, unlike England, where they were employed in great numbers, they do not seem to have been used so lavishly, since six, four and two, are the numbers mentioned at this period. Yet we need not elevate the brow of disdain at paucity, since even a quartet of voices may express an art more exquisitely than the most ample choir.

The office of the canons and the discipline connected therewith reveal some interesting features on the musical side. When a canon did not personally fill his office in the choir he was compelled to supply a substitute, hence this deputy was called a vicar-choral, although in one instance the vicarious requirement was the supply of six choir-boys. This deputy system was widely prevalent, although this does not mean that music was of secondary importance in the church. Sometimes a canon was unable, either vocally or musically, to fulfil his office, but there was also the canon who, because his prebend was a parish church, had to give whole or part attention to his charge. Actually, the church took the greatest care that its music was given as much attention as anything else. " Before appointment " says Dowden, the vicars " were subjected to a careful examination as to whether they knew how ' to read and sing ' (*an sciat legere et cantare*), i.e. as one may presume, to interpret the musical notation of the Gregorian plain-song, and to render it vocally. If they passed this examination successfully, they were subjected to a year's probation that they might learn the three service-books that contained the music of the choir services, viz. the Psalter, the Hymnary, and the Antiphonary," as we know from the Aberdeen statutes of 1256. In addition, a rigid discipline ensured a strict attention to duty and excellence of performance, both of which came under review weekly at the chapter meeting. Fines and corporal punishment were meeted out for neglect or defect, and at Aberdeen we read of fines for singing out of tune. Absence was sometimes met by the culprit having to sing the whole psalter, which might, of course, mean the Seven Penitential Psalms. At other times a whipping was added to the latter correction, whilst the stoppage of food was another penalty. Nor were the choir-boys exempt, and many a chorister was whipped for absence, for a third offence of which he was expelled.

In the process of time the vicars-choral became almost an independent corporation (*collegium*) within the church, holding land and goods for the body itself, all of which tended to heighten and improve the functional art of the choir. Indeed, when Dowden says that "the vicars of the choir played a very important part in the actual life of the cathedral communities," one feels inclined to add that they contributed a great deal to musical culture in Scotland. The song-schools, directed by the precentor or sub-precentor (the latter office itself showing its musical importance), taught the youth reading and the elements of music, from the 13th century at least, although, as Hume Brown says, "it was mostly those who wished to be monks or priests."

CHAPTER 5

THE MUSIC.

"Of the actual state of National Music in Scotland prior to the 15th Century, authentic history affords no distinct traces, although it appears that both poetry and music were highly esteemed in the south and east of Scotland, and on the English Border, as far back, at least, as the 13th Century."

GEORGE F. GRAHAM : *The Songs of Scotland* (1848).

During the first millennium of the Christian era, western Europe knew nothing of harmony as we connote this term. All music, whether secular or religious, was homophonic. Certainly the melody was often doubled at the octave by magadizing, which was an art known as *symphonia*, fully described by early theorists. When the fourth and fifth, and later the third, were admitted in a like manner, a decided advance was apparent, and this new artifice was named *organum*. Despite Arabic clues, it is not unlikely that the first prompting among Occidental peoples for this diversion, for such it must have been primarily, came from Britain, and one of the hints in this detection is the illusive passage in the *Topographia Hibernica* (*c.* 1185) of Giraldus Cambrensis. It deals with the harp-playing of the Irish and seems to point to the simultaneous use of fourth and fifths. Much clearer and more precise is the passage in the same writer's *Itinerarium Cambriae*, where he says that the Welsh "do not sing in unison like the people of other lands, but sing in different parts." He also observes that the people of North Britain, "beyond the Humber," use "a similar kind of harmony . . . singing only in parts, one . . . in the bass, the other . . . in the treble." Giraldus hints that this novelty was due to Scandinavian influence, on which account some writers urge that Scandinavia was the *point de départ* of this novelty, to which proof they bring forward the 13th century Upsala manuscript which shows the use of parallel thirds throughout. Against this there is the earlier evidence of the 12th century Cornish manuscript in the Bodleian Library, whilst reference to the so-called *Anonymous* IV manuscript (*c.* 1273-80), where the use of thirds is said to be used mostly in the "[Celtic] west of England," seems to strengthen the British claim.

Indeed there appears to be no reason why Ireland and Scotland should not have some slight share in this innovation. Giraldus himself bears witness that the Irish harpers were " incomparably more skilful than those of any other nation " that he had seen. That is transcendence indeed, yet when he appends the further conclusion that " in the opinion of many, Scotland not only equalled Ireland her teacher in music, but has prevailed over and surpassed her, so that they look to that country [Scotland] as the fountain of this art," one naturally asks in which domain of this Orphean delight was it that Scotland excelled ? Perhaps it was only on the practical instrumental side that Giraldus speaks, but even this implies practical theory, and nothing could be simpler than the practice of *organum* on the *clarsech* (Celtic harp) with the due observance of the B flat (*semper tamen ab B*), as Giraldus says. In addition we have vague hints and some small proof of progress in both the theoretical and creative spheres of music in Scotland.

History furnishes us with the names of two Scots from this period who are claimed to have contributed to the discipline of music, and I use the term *disciplina* in the strictly classical connotation. The first was the Scottish born Aaron, the abbot of St. Martin's at Cologne (*fl.* 992-1052). He is credited with having introduced the Gregorian evensong into Germany. Our particular interest in him is his authorship of two books on music, *De utilitate cantus vocalis et de modo cantandi atque psallendi*, and another, *De regulis tonorum et symphoniarum*. The first of these titles shows that playing a stringed instrument was not considered sinful or even undignified in Germany, although a church council of 679, and a capitulary of 789 were against such things. The second work seems to have dealt with the eight ecclesiastical tones upon which Gregorian song was based. Neither of these books has been preserved, which is to be deplored, more especially because the section on "playing" in the first named would be a most precious find for musicologists.

More important as a theorist, if we can trust the annalists, is a certain Simon Tailler, said to have been born in Scotland in the reign of William the Lion (1165-1214) and to have flourished there with some degree of fame at Dunblane in the mid-13th century. Having finished his early studies in his native land he went to Paris where he entered the Dominican order. Here, says Mackenzie (*Writers of the Scots Nation*), " he applied himself to the study of theology and mathematics, but more particularly to that part of mathematics, which treats of sounds and harmony, which we call music." About the year 1256 he returned to Scotland with other Dominicans and settled at Dunblane where he gained some distinction as a reformer of church music. " At the time of our author's [Tailler's] arrival in Scotland " says Mackenzie, " the music of the churches was altogether rude and barbarous, upon which he made a proposal to the bishops and clergy, for reforming both their vocal and instrumental music. They, knowing him to be a very great master in that science, very willingly complied with his proposal, and he was so successful, that George Newton, in his *History of the Bishops of Dunblane*, says that, in a few years, he brought them to such perfection, that Scotland might have contended with Rome for musicians. . . . What reformations our author made in it, cannot be well known, since all his works are now lost for aught that we know. . . . Dempster [*Historia Ecclesiastica*, 1627] says, that George Newton says, . . . that his books of music were masterpieces in their kind, and that he was thought to have been as skilled in that science as Guido Aretinus." The four books which both Dempster and Tanner attribute to Simon Tailler are, *De cantu ecclesiastico corrigendo* [*reformando* in

Tanner], *De tenore musicali, Tetrachordorum,* and *Pentachordorum.*
Whether these works were " masterpieces " or not we cannot
judge since we can no longer scan them. Perhaps the reforming
zeal of the mid-16th century consigned them to the rubbish heap or
vandal flames when that " goodly " building, as Archbishop Laud
called Dunblane Abbey, fell into the hands of the reformers. One
thing is certain, any man who could devote a book each to discussing
the tetrachord and pentachord was no ordinary mortal.

In the creative and appreciative sphere of music we can speak
with better and more certain knowledge since the music written
or used in Scotland at this period, as exemplified in the Wolfenbüttel
MS. (677), confirms the high position reached by church music in
this country which Dempster avers was brought about by Tailler.
Yet the problem is a highly controversial one. In the history of
Mediaeval music the contribution of the British school, which
blossomed into florescence in Renaissance polyphony, was truly
immense. Even the Germans, who rarely acknowledge cultural
debts to others, have laid particular stress upon this merit. Most
of these however, from Haberl (in *Bausteine zur Musikgeschichte,*
1885) to Lederer (*Über Heimat und Ursprung der mehrstimmigen
Tonkunst,* 1906), have based their appraisement on Dunstable
(d. 1453), being quite oblivious to the more abundant testimony
of the much earlier Wolfenbüttel MS. (677). This " monument
of English polyphony," as it has been called, has since (1932) been
given in facsimile by Dr. J. H. Baxter, the Professor of Ecclesiastical
History in the University of St. Andrews, whilst its contents have
been carefully examined (1932-3) by Professor Jacques Handschin
of the University of Basle, and by (1938) the Rev. Dom. Anselm
Hughes.

It so happens that this Wolfenbüttel manuscript has a domestic
claim upon us because it originally belonged to the *Monasterium
S. Andreae in Scocia* in the 14th century, but in the year 1553 it
was acquired in a rather suspicious way by the eminent theologian
Flacius Illyricus, that " writhing serpent " whom Melanchthon
once flayed. Subsequently (1597), this precious manuscript found
its way to the Wolfenbüttel Library. What is more, we know the

very names of the men who were responsible, directly or indirectly, for the "acquisition." Not only did the manuscript originally belong to St. Andrews but it is now considered a probability that it was either written *at* or *for* St. Andrews. An authority of such eminence as Professor Handschin says that "the manuscript as such might have been written *at* St. Andrews," or that it "was written *for* the community of St. Andrews." Gustave Reese gives the opinion that it "seems to have been written in Scotland," with a hint, "very likely at St. Andrews." What strengthens these assumptions are some of the contents. Fascicle 3 contains two responsories for St. Andrews Day, *Vir perfectus* and *Vir iste*, both of which have been partly reproduced by Professor Handschin and Dom. Anselm Hughes. Other items in the earlier portion of the manuscript reveal a species of composition "so far only represented in insular [i.e. British] sources." Among them is a three part *organum* entitled *Haec dies*, which I have twice produced in Glasgow (1936, 1942). It has been partly transcribed by Professor Handschin.

More striking examples of undeniable British composition are to be seen in fascicle 11, which is made up of two part writing for Mary Masses (tropes for the *Kyrie, Gloria, Sanctus* and *Agnus Dei*), Alleluias and Sequences, Offertories, etc. G. M. Dreves, in his *Analecta* (xxi), clearly demonstrates that the words and themes are of English origin, and although Professor Handschin once thought that the music might have proceeded from St. Andrews, his later judgment has led him to pronounce that the items in fascicle 11 "more likely . . . came from elsewhere in England or Scotland, and were only made use of at St. Andrews." This admission allows us to assume that at St. Andrews in the 14th century, this book, containing the best church music of the day, was used in what became (1472) the Metropolitan see of Scotland. Further, since it contains, besides the above mentioned works of undoubted British facture, the compositions of Perotinus Magnus and Leoninus, the famous masters of the Notre Dame school (12th cent.), it reveals the high conception of church music held by Scotland in these days. This was a period when books were not acquired as they are today for show and display as rarities, but for practical use.

How much the theory of music found mention in the literature of the period is apparent from more than one example. In the Asloan version of *Orpheus and Erudices* we read,—

> " Thar' leryt he tonys proporcionate
> As *duplere triplere* and *emetricus*
> *Enoleus* and eike the *quadruplat*
> *Epodyus* richt hard and curiouss
> And of thir' sex swet & deliciouss
> Richt consona[n]t five hevinly sym[ph]onis
> Componit ar' as clerkis can devyss.
> First *diatasseron* full sweit I wiss
> And *diapason* symple & duplate
> And *diapente* componit with a diss
> This makis five of thre multiplicat
> This mery musik & mellifluate
> Complete & full with novmeris od & evyn
> It causit be the moving of the hevin."

Of course the whole world had been moving forward apace culturally, and even before Giraldus wrote about part singing, free *organum* was being developed in the Paris Notre Dame School, where two (hence *discant*), and occasionally three and four part *organum*, was being composed as we have seen in what has immediately preceded. Seemingly France was in the van in music in these days, and that is why her influence was felt in Scotland, due, it would seem, to political issues, perhaps to those ecclesiastics brought from France by David I (d. 1153) and later clerics such as the Valliscaulians at Ardchattan, whose spacious architectural choir may still be admired, as well as the Cluniacs at Paisley and elsewhere. One result of the development of free *organum* was the necessity for mensural regulation and discipline to permit the varying parts to be performed *together*. Thus rhythmic modes were born, the device being prompted by, if not actually borrowed from Arabian models, as I have frequently shown. Again we find that the most important authorities on this new device were of English blood, and so too were the leading composers, and it was these latter who appear to have wrested supremacy from their Gallic neighbours in the domain of music. What part Scotland took in the adoption of the new *musica mensurata* we have no record, but she was probably affected quite early since we know that from the year 1212, Scotland was in close touch with English cathedrals and was adopting some of their customs.

As for secular music, I confess that I cannot apprehend why George F. Graham should have been so dubious of history furnishing us with distinct traces of national music. As I have attempted to envisage in the chapter devoted to the music of the people, there was the popular song in Scotland as well as the toil song, just as there were in Ireland and England. Indeed, it was the former which handed down the only " authentic history " that we wot of in those early days, for I would sooner trust the minstrel's interpretation of the events of history than I would the monkish chronicler or courtly annalist. In importance, secular music might be said to occupy the littoral or fringe of the art itself. Not that minstrelsy did not contribute its iota to the progress of the higher forms of music, because it did, since the varied dance measures were to infuse something new into music, for rhythm has rightly been called the fecundator of music. Yet minstrelsy in the earlier years of this period was still monodic for the greater part. One can scarcely believe that even the early court minstrels had any written music before them. Their *répertoire* was not wide and its extension was a matter of contact with other performers with the consequential borrowing *viva voce* and by rote of each others " specialities," as a modern theatrical variety artist would say. One frequently reads of court minstrels going or being sent abroad to visit " minstrel schools." Possibly the monotony of their *répertoires* was more than kingly and courtly ears could stand.

This does not mean that secular music was not ever notated. On the contrary it was, but it probably came from the hands of clerics. Indeed there is much to be said for the guess of old Sir John Hawkins that all of this music came from them. Actual examples of minstrel composition have survived. Gennrich (*Grundiss einer Formenlehre des mittelalterlichen Liedes*) has given us words and music of the *Audigier, dit Raimberge* from *Le Jeu de Robin et Marion* of Adam de la Halle (d. *c.* 1288), whilst the melody of the verse of the *chante-fable* known as *Aucassin et Nicolette* also exists. Coming nearer home, perhaps even Scotland itself, there are other specimens. The song *In Rama sonat gemitus* in the Scottish Wolfenbüttel MS. (677), which originally belonged to St. Andrews, might conceivably have come from Scotland. It is true that this piece concerns Thomas à Becket (d. 1170), and that it was written in his day, possibly by an Englishman, but it was known in Scotland and could therefore be looked upon as a type which was considered to be the best of its kind in those days. There were also definitely English songs that were notated, as in the St. Godrich example, *Crist and Sainte Marie* in the British Museum, and in the strongly vernacular *Mirie it is while sumer ilast* (13th cent.). Scotia was not outwith the ken of St. Godrich, since the Yorkshire saint once averred that King Malcolm III of Scotland and Thomas à Becket were more pleasing to God than any other men although, as the late Professor Hume Brown once remarked, " we may wonder how the saint came to know this."

The music of the folk in Scotland (and anywhere else for that matter), in those days, could not have been other than artless, in the strict etymological significance of the term. Indeed even today, the real music of the folk, when it can be found, is frequently more than unsophisticated, it is positively rude and inelegant, and quite unlike the Kennedy Fraser *corpus* of Hebridean song. Scott seems to have got to the core of things in *Marmion* :

> " Then came the merry masquers in,
> And carols roared with blythesome din ;
> If unmelodious was the song,
> It was a hearty note and strong."

As for the words of the songs, we actually know nothing of them, although the titles of many " ane hie ruf sang " (*Peblis to the Play*) of the succeeding period, as in *Cockelbie's Sow*, reveal something a little less modest than the conventional carol, and the people do not change their habits overnight. Even in the 19th century, the indecorum of the Scottish song was still troubling editors as it did, strange as it may seem, even Burns in the previous century. In any case, the song ruled everywhere, " for tonge es chefe of mynstralsye " as Thomas of Ersyldoune has said.

This was the pristine age of Scotland's arts as appears in the
vigorous verse of Thomas of Ersyldoune, Huchoun, Barbour,
Wyntoun, and Blind Harry. From these days came likewise the
significant mural at Inchcolm Abbey, and another at Cullen House,
the paintings in the Abbot's house at Arbroath, and in the tower
of Dunkeld Cathedral. It was the same in music and " all manere
of mynstralsye," for so attractive were its practitioners that they
were beckoned to a foreign court. Even a Welshman, Giraldus
Cambrensis, could laud its pre-eminence in music above his own
country. Dempster, in spite of all the reveries for which he
has been blamed, considered that the church musicians vied
with those of the Holy See at Rome, whilst the music of the church
itself was derived from, or was based on that of the finest masters
of the Notre Dame school, which was the pinnacle in those days.
Thus equipped, Scotland entered the most brilliant period of
her musical history, the Golden Age.

PART III

THE GOLDEN AGE (1424-1560).

" Dyvyne service incressitt with grete honour and cerymonis, and
decoritt with crafty musik and organiis, quhilkis was nocht usit afoir
his tyme. Finalie, the Scottis incressitt sa profundlye in every kynde
of musik and playing that thai war of na less craft and erudicioun
than Inglismen, howbeit thai excell maist in the samyn."

BELLENDEN-BOECE : *Chronicles of Scotland.*

THIS laudation of the reign of James I comes from the pen of
one, Boece (d. *c.* 1536) who, though known to be a credulous, if
not an unveracious historian, had earned the praise of Erasmus
and the friendship of Elphinstone. Since he wrote a century after
the events of his commendation, one naturally asks what was the
authority for this approbation ? It is true that contemporary 15th
century historians allow the highest praise to James I for his
abilities in music, and Bishop John Lesley (d. 1596), who was
once master of the Aberdeen Sang School, said of him,—*praeter
quam enim musicae omnis generis.* He was famed especially as an
instrumentalist, but all this, in itself, does not permit us to allow
parity in music between Scotland and England at this period, as
the above statement suggests. This was the era of England's
acknowledged world supremacy in the art, as such names as
Dunstable and Power prove in composition, and Gulielmus
Monachus and Hothby display in " erudition." Perhaps Boece
was judging from the state of music in his day, such as he experienced
at Aberdeen when he was a canon under the celebrated Elphinstone,
an opinion which Bellenden (d. *c.* 1587) might well have felt was
valid enough from what he knew of music in Glasgow, where he
was precentor at the cathedral.

That the Boece-Bellenden encomium was deserved of Scotland
in their day there cannot be much doubt, as we shall have occasion
to stress, but it could hardly have been true of the opening of the
15th century. Scotland was then only beginning to take her place
in the world of culture, for her " Golden Age " was only at its
dawn. The causes of the abounding radiance were manifold. As
elsewhere, the feudal notions of the state were fast disintegrating,

whilst the very dogmas of the church were being challenged. All this was due to a new spirit, the Renaissance, that " glorious contagion " as Walter Pater calls it, which was sweeping through western Europe, breaking down the old intellectual and cultural barriers. Pagan learning and art, i.e. the classical heritage of ancient Greece, which had once been considered a useless study and a sinful occupation, were now assiduously examined and copied. Works on Greek science and philosophy, hitherto only known in translations from the Arabic, such as those of Michael Scot, began to be read in their original tongue and in newly translated versions. Scotland's first universities, St. Andrews (1412), Glasgow (1451), and Aberdeen (1495), had opened, or were soon to open, their doors. Scotland's first printers (1507) were beginning to multiply those treasures of knowledge which were to materially assist in the great social, intellectual, and cultural awakening. The arts too were profoundly affected by this resuscitation, and their refining influence was in itself a contributory factor in the new era that dawned. Even in trade and commerce there was a new spirit abroad. Scotland had established merchant and craft guilds, whilst two at least of the " seven seas " carried her argosies. One has but to scan the lines of two strangers who visited her shores, Aeneas Sylvius (1435) and Pedro de Ayala (1498), to see what happened in half a century.

How Scotland received the new spirit is too long a story, but we can touch upon the *via media* that brought her the new outlook upon music. Those lands nearest her geographically, commercially, ecclesiastically, and politically, were her natural prompters. With England, despite family connection between the two royal houses, Scotland was athwart for most of the period, mainly owing to her " auld alliance " with France, who egged her in this perversity. Yet at the opening of this era there was, fortunately, little strain between them. James I (1424-37) had been educated in England, and had been taught music there. Further, he had married Joan Beaufort, his " milk-white dove," as he caressingly called her, the daughter of the Earl of Somerset. The English were even encouraged at his court, and their manners and customs were widely adopted. If music rose to such heights in Scotland as her historians aver, then we may surely attribute some of this to English tutelage. Unfortunately, for lack of documents, precise details are denied us, but we imagine that if, to use the words of Bellenden-Boece, James I " brocht oute of Ingland and Flanderis ingenious men of sindry craftis to instruct his pepill," musicians can safely be counted among these " ingenious men," for the king himself was a keen musician, and one might hazard a guess that his Chapel Royal would have echoed some of the solemn strains that he had once heard performed by Henry V's *plena cantoribus ampla capella*. English influences certainly asserted themselves very prominently when James III (1460-88) ascended the throne. His patronage of the English musician Dr. William Rogers, and his plan for the endowment of the Chapel Royal as a music school, mark the epoch. James IV (1488-1513), who married Margaret Tudor, the eldest daughter of Henry VII, brought further cultural ties between the two countries. With her came many English minstrels, and one might ask what Sassenach subtleties in the art did these people bring to the minstrelsy of the " North Countrie ?"

Flanders was linked with Scotland by commercial ties, and this land also played its part in influencing the music of Scotland. The Netherlands School of composition was already swaying the world of music, and Scotland, like the rest, was sitting at her feet, as the solitary Scottish book which has been preserved on the didactics of music so completely proves. For practical instrumental instruction, Flanders was also the place for tutelage. In 1473, a certain Heroun, " clerk of the chapel," received money for his passage to the " scholis," seemingly in Flanders. We find a lutar of the court being sent there to " lerne his craft " in the same year. Another lutar journeyed to Bruges this year, whilst a further entry tells of a court minstrel receiving a gift whilst there. In the next year we read of the king's " litill lutar " being sent to the latter city, and in 1512 a " Flemys lutar," with so good a Scots name as Rankine, as well as " foure scolaris menstralis," all from the court, were in Flanders. It is worthy of note however, that there was some give and take between the two countries, since there is a record of three " joueurs de hautbois et sachottes [sacbuts ?] . . . venant d'Écosse " being employed at Malines in 1504-5. The fact that James II (1437-60) married a daughter of the Duke of Guelderland in 1449 may have strengthened ties with Flanders.

It has been said that " all roads lead to Rome." At this time this was as true in the ecclesiastical sense as it had been in the classical. Yet Italy had nothing to offer in the higher realms of music comparable with France, England, and Flanders. In the purely ecclesiastical sphere, Italy leaned to a strictly conservative outlook at this time, although in the secular field she was beginning to make her influence felt. Her instrumentalists seem to have attracted universal attention since we find them at foreign courts. In England, quite a crowd could be found, and even in Scotland there are repeated entries in the accounts of the court about " Italien menstrales " during the first half of the 16th century. Indeed there was a whole family by the name of Drummonth [Drummond], some six of them, who were Italians, and well favoured at court. Whether there was any requital by Italy in respect of favours to Scottish musicians in that land we have no knowledge, but in the *Frottole* of Petrucci (1466-1539) there are five works by a Paulus *Scottus*. Incidentally it might be mentioned that Petrucci handed over his Venetian printing press to Amadeo *Scotti*, whilst two other famous music printers and musicians of Italy at this time were Ottaviano *Scotto* and Girolamo *Scotto*. It is to the Italian Ferrerius, who was in Scotland in the year 1529, that we are indebted for information about the music school planned for Scotland by James III, whilst a later Italian writer, Tassoni (d. 1635), was sufficiently conversant with Scottish music to mention it in reference to the madrigalist Carlo Gesualdo (d. 1613).

Although England and Flanders were the founts in the higher realms of music for the greater part of the " Golden Age," it has to be acknowledged that, towards the close of the period, i.e. the last half-century, the influence of France was dominant in the lighter vein of the art. This was by reason of that " weill keipit ancient aliance " between the two countries which the reigns of James V and Mary helped to consolidate. Both of the wives of James V, Madeleine de Valois (1537) and Marie de Lorraine (1538), were French, and the Duke of Albany, who was acknowledged " Governor of Scotland " (1515-24) during the minority of James V, was born and educated in France. Indeed he was said to be more French than Scots. The daughter of James, Mary Queen of Scots, resided in France for thirteen years (1548-61) and married the Dauphin of France (1558) who became François II (1559-60). During a great part of this period the queen-mother, Marie de Lorraine, acted as Regent. From this alone we see that throughout the first half of the 16th century, France was the predominating influence in Scotland, and it reflected itself in music.

For centuries there had been a large number of Scots in France, not merely as soldiers, a fact so well known, but as scholars, for many a cadet of the best of Scotland's families sought his intellectual fortune in this land. Some, like George Buchanan (d. 1582), who taught Montaigne, even held professorships there. Indeed, the founding of Balliol College at Oxford (1282) was scarcely of such moment to Scotland as the establishment of the Scots College in Paris (1326). When Scotland raised her first university at St. Andrews (1412), it was France that gave the model. When she published her first book, its imprint carried clear proof of its founder. Wherever we look, in the schools, in law, in literature, in architecture, and in the fine arts, France looms pre-eminently in Scotland. That music was influenced may be taken for granted.

French minstrels were much esteemed at court. In 1505 a " Franch *quhissalar* " is found there, and in 1508 a " French *fithelar* " and his son are paid off when going homeward. In 1512-13 there are many of these " Franchemen " engaged in minstrelsy at court. When James V was in France for nearly nine months in 1536-7, we see his favours to *trumpettis, howboyis, sifleris,* and *cornatis* of the King of France and the Queen of Navarre. When he came home, the *howboy* (hautbois) soon became the fashion instead of the noisy *shawm*, whilst its bass, the *curtall*, i.e. the French *courtaud*, also became the fashion. The *cornett* had been recognized since 1503, but in 1550 there are payments to " certane Franchemen that playit on the *cornettis*." One very definite Gallic touch is the adoption of *violaris* instead of *fiddlaris*. Among these violars was Jakkis Collumbell, obviously a Frenchman.

In the dance, an art so intimately bound up with music, the French convention found ample expression. We have already seen in the old *Cockelbie's Sow* (15th cent.) how, among the old Scottish dance tunes, there peeps out such strangers as the *Orliance* (Orléanaise) and *Naverne* (Navernais), and in a work entitled *The Boke Named the Governour* (1546), the writer, enumerating the older English dances says, " In stede of these we have nowe *Base daunces, bargenettes, pavyons, turgions*," whose very labels bespeak their origin, just as do the Scottish *paspay* (passepied), *sincopas* (cinq pas), *brawl* (branle), and *galyert* (gaillarde). One recalls how the country folk in *Christis Kirk on the Grene*, throw aside the old tunes and cry to the minstrel to " blaw up a *brawl* of France." The craze for these terpsichorean fancies lasted well beyond the end of this period, and so it is quite clear that in both the lighter forms of music and in the dance, Scotland owed a great deal to France. In the very nature of things, the debt could not be repaid in like for like, although Scotland did furnish Charles VII (1422-61) of France with a court minstrel in John Fary, and Henry IV (1589-1610) with two favourite lutars in James and Charles Hedington, whilst we learn from Tabouret's *Orchésographie* (1589) that the *branles d'Escosse* were " the rage " of the day, and they already had a place in the *Danseries* (1564) of Jean d'Etrée.

And what was there to be heard of Scotland's own music, the old Celtic art ? Just as we have seen in Anglo-Norman times, Irish musicians were still finding a welcome in the Highlands and were even received at court. That the native music of the two countries was still considered as one and the same art, finds frequent expression. In the *Annals of the Four Masters* we read that about 1451, when Margaret the wife of O'Conor of Offaly gave a banquet of honour, she invited the poets and musicians of *Ireland* and *Scotland*. We are told in the *Buke of the Howlate* (*c*. 1450) of a " bard owt of Irland " who knew about the

" schenachy " and the " clarschach," whilst we read in the *Book of Lismore* (1512-26) that " Cas Corach, the son of Caincinde, . . . [was] the best musician of *Erinn* or *Alba*," which once more illustrates the one type of musical culture in these lands.

Many a Highland and Irish harper (*clarsair*) played at court in those days, especially when James IV sat on the throne, for he was possibly the last of Scotland's rulers to speak Gaelic. Here we see the " ersch *clarschar* " (1492) or " Ireland *clarscha* " (1502) " clawing " his strings, evidently to everyone's delight. Whether Ireland is always implied is doubtful. At any rate, one cannot be too sure of the implication unless we read of " a harper on the *clarscha* " and " the Ireland *clarscha* " in the same passage. Even then we have to be wary since so late as 1691, Robert Kirk (*Secret Commonwealth*) speaks of the " northern Scottish and Athole men " as " Irishmen," by which he must mean Erse or Gaelic-tongued Scots. Thus, in spite of English, Flemish, Italian, and French influence on music in Scotland during the " Golden Age," the old strain of Celtic music not only persisted in the Highlands, but found expression in the Lowlands, even to the king's court.

CHAPTER 1

THE COURT AND NOBILITY.

" All thus our ladye thai lofe, with lylting and lift,
Menstralis and musicians, mor than I mene may :"
RICHARD HOLLAND : *Buke of the Howlate* (*ca.* 1450).

Although Mrs. Malaprop has warned us that " comparisons is oderous," one feels that it is often necessary to indulge in relative estimates if we are to assess values properly. In 1460-61, according to the Lord Chamberlain's Accounts, the musicians of the English court numbered twenty-five in all, probably thirteen instrumentalists and twelve others, if we take a leaf out of the *Liber niger domus Regis*. A century later, i.e. in 1546, it comprised thirty-one musicians, besides eighteen trumpeters and thirteen singers, not counting twenty-one more in the Chapel Royal. Against such an array as this, Scotland could not hope to compete.

In the first place she could not afford it, and in the second there was no need for it. The courts of the Scottish kings and queens were conducted on much simpler lines, and that was why Pius II, when he came to Scotland as Aeneas Sylvius in 1435, could say that the palaces of the Scottish king were not even so well furnished as the houses of rich merchants on the Continent. The king's chief abode was Stirling Castle, and we know what it was like in those days, as we do the other royal palaces. All were less pretentious than similar edifices in England. Indeed, the Chapel Royal at Stirling had a thatched roof which, in 1583, was not proof from " weitt or rane." Even the space allotted to the choir was what a Scot would call " scrimpit." So when we find that the minstrels of the Scottish court and the choir of the Chapel Royal are not so imposing as those of England, we can understand why. For all that, what the Scots had was ample enough, by which I mean that it fulfilled the needs.

Yet although not numerically so impressive as that of its southern neighbour, Scottish court minstrelsy was probably kept at a relatively high standard for the simple reason that all its rulers, from James I to Mary, with one exception, were not only appassioned of music, but were skilled performers. James I (1424-37)[1] has been claimed as highly proficient in music. Bower (d. 1449), his contemporary, says that he could play on the harp (*lyra*), psaltery, organ, reedpipe or shawm (*tibia*), recorder (*fistula*), trumpet, and even the bagpipe (*choro*) and drum. To mention precise accomplishments, he touched the harp like Orpheus according to Bower and Maior, and was " richt crafty in playing baith of the lute and harp " in the words of Bellenden. Nor need the Sassenach snigger at his handling the bagpipe, if that is what the *choro* was, since even Nero was a *utricularius*, if we can believe Suetonius. Unfortunately the Lord High Treasurer's Accounts do not go back so far as his reign and precise information concerning court minstrels is sparse, but during Albany's governorship we read of a Patrick of Carrick in 1414, who is glossed as a *tubicen*.

---

[1]· He began to reign in 1406 but he did not ascend the throne until 1424.

Perhaps he was related to the Johannes Trumpour, *alias* John Turnbull, who was Carrick Herald in 1365-6. That heralds were often trumpeters at this time is vouched by numerous authorities including Froissart. Miming, which was closely dependant on music, is better recorded. In 1434, there is payment to the King's players under a " written mandate," and two years later £18 is paid for mere expenses for players from Bruges. Under James II, (1437-60), the mimes have excellent patronage.

Military matters were far too pressing for the latter king to pay attention to court minstrelsy, but in 1438 we notice that a *tuba* called " a trump " was procured for the queen, Marie of Guelderland. Two of the " King's mimes and minstrels," Marco Trumpet and Ade Rede, are mentioned in 1446, and the following year there is a Flemish touch (cf. Marie of Guelderland) in an entry for three trumpets from Johannes de Vansking, whilst Bu_an le Trumpet is entered in 1452. Trumpets were evidently in great demand, first because they were the insignia of royalty, and secondly because war was in the ascendant, as the charred walls of Inverness, Dunbar, Alnwick, Dumfries, Warkworth, Roxburgh, and Inverkip testified at this particular date. It is as well that this deliberate register of burning and carnage in one short reign should be duly noted, because similar happenings had been going on for a century or more, to the detriment of social well-being and general culture. It is no wonder that Boece pours out the vials of his wrath against these slaughterings and holocausts, when he saw, as he particularly points out, how the arts and crafts had especially suffered. Still, the king's trumpets often sounded in heralding the arts of peace, and so their place in the king's minstrelsy is worthy of attention. In 1474 the trumpeters of James III wore blue gowns and black doublets and hose. In 1494, the hose was red, but then, the royal livery of James IV was red and yellow. Six trumpeters seems to have been the norm in 1503, although we find four in 1502, and five in 1505.

Turning to the more serene music of the privy chamber, or the more jocund tones of the minstrel gallery, we see much that is interesting. James III (1460-88) had his grandfather's delight in music, and drew to his court all who cherished the art. Alas we have but scant information about court minstrelsy during his reign, because the High Treasurer's Accounts are denied us. One lutar at least is known by name, John Broun. Much more is registered in the reign of James IV (1488-1513). He had a penchant for " Inglis *pyparis* " (1489, 1491), perhaps a mere political gesture, since it was the more sedate Lowland harp, the Highland *clarsech*, the lute, and the *fithel*, that usually enticed his ears. Young, the Somerset Herald says that, on the king's wedding day, the bride-groom entertained the bride, Margaret Tudor, by performing on the *clarychordes* and lute, which pleased her " verey much." Seemingly the queen brought some English minstrels with her to the Scottish court. According to the Lord High Treasurer's Accounts, eight English minstrels were remunerated to the extent of £56 in the nuptial year. These may have been the musicians mentioned in the English Lord Chamberlain's Accounts, although nine are specified here, " five trumpeters and two shakbotters [sackbut players]," whose instruments were draped with bannerols, as well as two other minstrels, Gabriel and Kenner, the latter being, possibly, " Krennar, the quenis lutar," mentioned in 1505. We learn that the " Quenis four menstralis " [from England] remained, from which we may assume that the others went home, including the " Erle of Oxfurdis tua menstrales " who came north at the same time and received £5-12-0 for their services.

At the court of James IV, harpers were particularly encouraged, James Mylsoun (1496-1502), an " Inglis harpar " (1502), Sowles the harper, Alexander, as well as Henry Philp and Bragman (1506). Naturally the Highland *clarsech* appealed to the Gaelic-speaking king and in consequence we read of Martin *Clareshaw* and another " ersche *clareschaw* " in 1490, Pate Harpar, *clarscha* (1503), " Odenelis (Ireland man) harper " (1512), and others. Lutars were the next to receive royal approval. The ordinary lutars seem to have had 14s. a quarter. Some of them are named, Wardlaw, Lindores, Rankine, Robert Rudman, Adam Dikeson, Robert Hay, John Ledebetar, Craig, and Gray Steil who was called " soutar lutar " i.e. the " shoemaker lutar." Specially bountied performers, such as Krennar the queen's lutar, received £3-6-8 for the half year (1505), and a certain Jacob, of whom there are entries from 1489 until 1503, when he pawned his lute, received twice as much as the ordinary lutars, i.e. 28s. a quarter. I have remarked about James IV's colours for his minstrels' livery, yet it would appear that his queen chose different hues since the accounts tell us of coats of " rede and grene " lined with " blak gray " for her " twa luter men " (1505).

The accounts deal with fiddlers (*fydlaris*) at court quite early (1490-1533), but we cannot be absolutely sure whether they bowed violins or rebecs. In 1503, three are mentioned, Adam Boyd, Bennet, and Jame Widderspune. This completes the stringed instrumentalists at court, for I imagine that the " pare of *monicordis* " which John Hert brought " fra Abirdene to Strivelin " in 1497, was for the personal use of the king, just as was the *regal*.

Players on the wood-wind and other " lowd menstrales " (1503) were more generally used in the open air, for example when the " Mons Meg " cannon was taken to the castle gate. Whether they handled *schawm* (shawm), *recordour* (beaked flute), *quhissel* (whistle), or *dron* (bagpipe), they were usually written down as pipers (*pyparis*), and so, as previously mentioned, one cannot be certain which instrument they piped. What is especially interesting is the occasional mention of the " common pipers " of Aberdeen or Edinburgh being given audition at court, which doubtless refers to the town pipers. There were four " Italian *schawmiris* " attached to the court in 1505, together with their youthful assistants (*childer*), sometimes dubbed " yong *piparis* " or " yong *scameris*." Yet the piper and the shawmer may have been considered different, as we know from a reference to " ane *pipar* " who " playit with the *schamis* " (1507). Drummers, some of whom played with the wood-wind as well as with the trumpets, were usually termed *tabronars*. There were four of these at court at this period, Ansle, Guilliam, Portuous, and Quhynbore (1504), as well as a " More," i.e. a Moor (1505). Later (1520-33) there appears to have been only one, although in 1542, two became the rule.

Whilst we read occasionally of a "king's sangster," such as Nicolas Aberncthy in 1512 at £20 a year, vocalists, apart from those in the Chapel Royal, do not seem to have been employed regularly until the very close of this period. We find the singer more generally on the casual list, which included all sorts, from the strolling players like "Wantones and her twa marrowes" who amused James IV in 1508, and the "crukit vicar of Dumfreise" who sang at court in 1507, to "Wilyeam, sangster of Lithgow" who gave the king a "sang bwke" in 1489. On one occasion we know that the old romance *Gray Steil* was sung to the king, of which the very words have been preserved, and these, together with the poems of David Lyndsay, which we know were set to music, give us some idea of the words at least which constituted the more refined vocal music of these days. Nor can we omit mention of Harry the Minstrel, for Blind Harry appeared at court with harpers and fiddlers in 1490-91. Dunbar (d. *c.* 1520) salutes him in his *Lament for the Makaris*, and Maior (d. 1550) praises his *William Wallace*, which, in itself, is a typical minstrel's song-story.

James V (1513) being a minor at his father's death, the Duke of Albany took charge of the realm as "Lord Governour," and much of the expenditure on minstrelsy stands in his name, both French and Italian minstrels being specially favoured. We know from David Lyndsay that he was a poet, but whether he wrote *Christis Kirk on the Grene*, *The Gaberlunzie Man*, and *The Jolly Beggar*, there is no certain proof. Thomas Wood, writing in 1566, says that "James the Fifth, who was a musician himself, . . . had a singular good ear, and could sing that [which] he had never seen before, but his voice was 'rawky' and harsh." His favourite instrument was the lute, and in 1526, when he assumed regal authority, he began his rule by ordering an instrument through William Galbraith for £2, and five years later acquired another at £2-10-0. Again in 1538, John Barbour paid £2-16-0 for a lute for him. These were goodly sums at this time, seeing that Henry VII, with a more affluent purse, only parted with 13s. 4d. for a lute for his daughter Mary. James seems to have diligently practised the instrument, since his expenses for strings were considerable. He sent specially to Edinburgh for these guts in 1531, and had Glasgow combed for more in 1533. Four dozen strings in this latter year cost 24s., but later he got into the habit of buying ten or twelve dozen at a time. It was possibly for his consort that Thomas Mulliner, the master of the choir of St. Pauls, London, composed the *Queene of Scottes gallyard* (c. 1540), seemingly for the gittern.

One might reasonably conclude that the king's passion for the lute would enhance the position of the court lutars, who previously had been consistently patronized. Strange to say they do not appear in the general lists, a case of professional jealousy perhaps. In their stead it was *fidlars* who flourished, a certain Cabroch (1530-33) being a favourite. Yet if the latter's name or nickname has any significance, he might have been but an easy performer, as *cabhruich* means " worthless." After James' return from France in 1537 with the daughter of Francis I as his bride, the king turned his back on mere fiddlers, and affected *violars* playing their instruments at the knee. Four of these became the rule, possibly a choir, as in France, and £23-7-0 was expended on their livery. Up to the end of his reign, four *violars* were maintained on the establishment.

On the wind instrument side, he favoured the recorder, and the smaller flute known as the *quhissel*, the two brothers Thomsoun being employed together with " Antonis' boys " (1532-35). These had their place in state and martial music for when the king went to France for his bride in 1536 he took " four *trumpetouris*, four *tabernaris*, and three *quhislaris* " (fifers) with him to reinforce his kingly dignity, all dressed up in his father's colours of red and yellow. In 1539-42 there were still the four who sounded " the *trumpettis* of weir [war]," for which they received £20.

In the reign of Mary (1542-67) we know little concerning the court minstrels until after the Reformation. At her accession there were fifteen minstrels at court, five of whom were Italians. In the year that she went to France (1548) for her long stay, we read of payments made to " *vyolaris*," of which there were four in 1542, sa well as to others including Stewyn a *tabronar*, Cunynghame a *lwtar*, and a *harpar*, all for the entertainment of " my Lorde Governour," the Earl of Arran. On the 1550 lists are " certane Franchemen that playit on the *cornettis*." This drummer named Stewyn or Steven is to appear during the Reformation under rather unusual circumstances. Mary herself was quite an accomplished musician, as Chalmers has shown in his life of the unfortunate queen. Brantôme, who could speak from actual knowledge, says that her voice was " très douce et très bonne," and that she sang well. Of her lute playing he considered that she had a solid touch. In addition she played the virginal, an instrument on which, as Sir James Melville tells us in his *Memoirs*, she " occasionally recreated herself." Asked by the termagant Queen Elizabeth how her rival Queen Mary played on this instrument, the tactful Sir James was compelled to reply, " reasonably [well] for a queen."

The total muster of Scottish court minstrels at this period was never very high in comparison with that of the English court. At the latter, in 1525-6, there were eighteen minstrels and eighteen trumpeters, who were paid £6-10-4 each *per annum*, which constituted the highest fee paid to favoured artists in Scotland, and three times as much as the ordinary minstrel was paid there twenty years earlier, although values between the two countries were not at *par*. In 1511, the Scottish court had fourteen minstrels, *including trumpeters*, whose gowns, doublets, and hose cost £6-10-0 per performer. In 1513, just before Flodden, there were only eleven on the permanent roll and they received £4-7-6 per annum. Some however, had better salaries, as in 1515, when six of them (five Italians and one Scot named George Forest) had £78-15-0 between them, whilst the liveries of five of them cost £65. In 1542 there were fifteen liveried minstrels, four *veolis*, four *trumpettis*, two *taburnerris*, and five " *Italianis*."

As in the previous centuries, the great barons who were among the *pares*, as well as the lesser fry, and the higher clergy, possessed minstrels, generally one or two. We read of the *clarsair* to the Earl of Argyll (1503,1506), the Laird of Balnagownis' harper (1502), the Thane of Calder's harper (1502), the Countess of Crawford's harper (1503) and lutar (1505), Lord Semphill's harper (1504), the Lord of Ruthven's lutar (1505), " Maklanis [Maclaine's] *clarscha* " (1506), Lord Fleming's *tabronar*, Lord Hamilton's *tabronar* (1506-7). Nor were the clergy backward in this respect since there are entries of the Bishop of Ross' harper (1502), the Bishop of Caithness' harper (1503), and his lutar (1502), the Bishop of Moray's lutar (1505, who also had a *tabronar* (1506), and the " Ald Prior of Quhitherne's " *clarsair* (1507).

So it is quite evident that, on the whole, the court, castle, palace, and priory, were well provided with minstrelsy in the " Golden Age." To its professors, this class was notoriously lavish in its gifts and liberal with its honours, although the regular stipend may have been rather low. But gifts to the minstrel class had been the recognized practice for five centuries at least. How generously they were treated is well illustrated in the law of 1471 which denied the wearing of silk to anyone save " knichtes, *minstrelles*, and heraulds," as well as the landed gentry. Those who dared defy the law were amerced in a fine of £20, and their silken cloak, doublet, or hose forfeited for the benefit of these same minstrels and heralds. Of course, these particular minstrels were those who served the " upper ten." Those who discoursed minstrelsy for the people at large were not so fortunate.

Needless to point out, the court was ever regaling itself from the days of James I with mumming, masques, and dancing, all of which necessitated both vocal and instrumental music. John Young tells of the English actors who came to the court of James IV. " After dinner a morality was played by the said Master Inglishe and his companions, in the presence of the King and Queen, and then dances were danced." It will be remembered that William Dunbar (*c.* 1460-*c.* 1520), the " Rhymer of Scotland," limns himself in the courtly dancing—

> " Than cam in Dunbar the Mackar ;
> On all the flure thair was nane frackar,
> And thair he daunset the Dirrye-dantoun :
> He hoppet lyk a pillie wantoun ; "

Unfortunately, not a solitary line has been spared to us about the individual accomplishments of any of these favoured minstrels, save those who gained repute abroad who, we imagine, must have possessed outstanding talent to have received this recognition. Yet we need not conclude from this that none was worthy of mention, because even in England, where its history of music has been more cared for, not a single name of a performer of eminence has come down to us from this period. Why then, it may be asked, these long lists of Scottish court minstrels ? The answer is simple enough. If for no other reason that these lists show that the owners of these names were Scots for the greater part, the proceeding is fully justified, because it is just as well that we should understand that in spite of frequent alien infiltrations the Scottish performers still seem to have held their own.

Strange to say, there were a few people within the church who looked askance at this court minstrelsy, and were more intolerant than the later Reformers. One of these, so often quoted in these pages, was John Bellenden, erstwhile precentor at Glasgow Cathedral, and ultimately Rector of Glasgow University. He shows his venom in no uncertain fashion. To him the courtly *menstralis* were anathema, and rulers who had a taste for such music were the most depraved *tyrannis* and *monstouris*. Only the " warlike trumpet " would he allow those of high estate. Listen to these lines—

> " Schaw now quhat kynd of soundis musicall
> Is maist semand to vailyeand cheveleris.
> As thondrand blast of trumpat bellicall
> The spretis of men to hardy curage steris,
> So syngyng, fydlyng, and piping not efferis
> For men of honour nor of hye estate.
> Becaus it spoutis swete venome in thair eris
> And makis thair myndis al effeminate."

CHAPTER 2

THE PEOPLE.

" Gif there be onie that makis them fuiles [jesters], and ar bairdes [bards], or uthers sik like rinnares about, and gif onie sik be fundin, that they be put in the king's waird, or in his irons for their trespasses, als lang as they hauve onie gudes of their awin to liue upon—that their eares be nailed to the trone [pillory], or till ane uther tree, and their eare cutted off, and banished the cuntrie—and gif thereafter they be funden again, that they behanged."

Act of Parliament, 1449.

This *praeludium* throws a spot light on the social conditions and policy of this troublous period. As it stands, clear and stark, this act looks truly savage, but when kings and nobles were committing open murder, what less barbarous laws could one expect. Factions were loose in the land, with kings against nobles, and nobles against kings, a law until themselves, yet the " powers that be " knew full well the influence of the minstrel class in pleading rival causes. England realized this in the songs of the earlier John Ball (1381) and had learned the lesson. When the Welsh became restive, we know from the act of 1402 that they were forbidden to encourage or maintain minstrels or rhymers who, said the act, were " partly cause of the insurrection and rebellion now in Wales." Yet in Scotland at this turbulent time no attempt was made to revive the repressive laws against the wandering minstrels in general. What was enacted, as seen above, was directed against a particular type, to wit, " any that make themselves fools and are *bards*, or other such runners about." The law only applied to the vagrant class, " sornares, *bardis*, maisterfull beggaris and fenyeit fulys," as the later act of 1457 says, for there is ample evidence that the better type of wandering minstrel was permitted to go " scot free." From the *Buke of the Howlate* and *Cockelbie's Sow* it is quite patent that the *bard* had fallen from his high estate. Indeed it seems clear enough that the *bard* and *minstrel* were poles asunder musically and socially by this time. The bard was the lineal descendant of the old pagan seer-poet-musician, and Hollinshed (d. *c.* 1580) blamed him for " dreaming fables " which later became current as " assured histories." As late as Martine (*Reliquiae Divi Andreae*) the *bard* was still given to the " making of mystical rhymes, and to magic and necromancy." As the church probably had a hand in the acts of 1449 and 1457, it is no wonder that such laws were passed, for the clergy would view the *bards* as their professional rivals in ultramundane affairs.

The minstrel proper, who was of Anglo-Norman introduction, had by this time developed mainly into an instrumentalist pure and simple, and as such was still welcomed everywhere. Indeed we see the strolling class under invitation to the king's court. James IV (1488-1513) could call to his privy chamber (1508) a certain " Wantones [a female minstrel] and her twa marrowes [partners] that sang with hir," and patronize a " *barde* wife callit Agnes Carkhill " (1512). This music loving monarch evidently had no animus against the peregrine minstrel, whether a " rinner about " or not. What a joyous day it was to the town and country folk when a troupe of these wandering minstrels came at fair time to their permitted stance in the market place or village green, bringing music and dance of a kind that was new to their ears, for local music, with its narrow repertory of tunes, must have sorely tried tempers. One recalls how William Dunbar (d. *c.* 1520) complains of the monotonous strains of the Edinburgh pipers—

> "Your commone menstralis hes no tone,
> Bot *Now the day dawis* and *Into Joun.*"

The former may be identical with *The ioly day now dawis* mentioned by Gavin Douglas (d. 1522) in his *Virgil*. Fair time was the occasion when the people at large made revelry, as we read in *Cockelbie's Sow*—

> " And all the menstrallis attonis [at once]
> Blew up and playit for the nonis."

If Chaucer's miller could blow his bagpipe well, so could Will Swane " the meikle miller man " in *Peblis to the Play* (15th cent)—

> " Giff I sall dance, have doune, lat se
> Blaw up the bagpypr than."

What Gavin Douglas says in his *Virgil* would probably reflect contemporary practice—

" Some sang *ring-sangs*, *dancis*, *ledis* and *roundis*,
With vocis schil, quhil all the dale resoundis ;
Quhareto thay walk into thare *karoling*,
For armourus layis dois all the rochis ring ;
Ane sang, *The schip salis ouer the salt fame*.
Some other sings, *I will be blyith and licht*,
My hert is lent apoun sae gudly wicht."

These song titles are legion in the vernacular literature of this period. Some occur as early as *Peblis to the Play* (early 15th cent.), where we have the refined and sentimental *Thair sal be mirth at our meting*, and the more rollicking and plebeian *Thair fure ane man to the holt*. In *Cockelbie's Sow* (15th cent.) there is as replete a list of dance tunes and songs as in any modern music-seller's catalogue, and their many titles are verifiable elsewhere, such as *Twysbank* (*When Tayis Bank*), *Trolly Lolly* (*Trolly Lolly Leman Dou*), and *Lulalow lute cok*. David Lyndsay in his *Complaynt of the Papynago* (1529) gives a tune named *Gynkertoun* (Dancer Town) that was evidently " all the rage." In Wedderburn's *Complainte of Scotlande* (1549) the author tells how the shepherds sang " sueit melodius sangis . . . of antiquite," and then he lists the titles of no less than thirty-five songs of both Scottish and English origin, most of which were doubtless well known at this date, and many, certainly, are traceable in other works. One is almost forced to conclude that all these songs, at least their melodies, were traditional, and were sung by high and low alike. Indeed, in these days it is unlikely that were any poets of the standing of Henryson, Douglas, Dunbar, and others who would, as Robert Chambers points out (*Songs of Scotland Prior to Burns*), have indited anything " strictly of the nature of songs. Such men never thought of composing songs, that is, lyrical compositions to be sung to music by the people." This aloofness was soon to change.

The cities and towns, for the greater part, had their minstrels, and in 1545, when a certain John Tulledig was appointed as a town minstrel, he had to play with another two in *three parts*. Yet whilst they are usually termed the " toun minstrellis " they were but pipers and drummers generally, although the humbler towns contented themselves with the drum only. The chief duties of these minstrels were related to public announcements. By pipers it does not always mean bagpipers because in many instances it meant players of the shawm, as at Ayr and Kilwinning (1505-6). They were clothed and salaried out of the rates, fines, taxes, or common good, and they wore a special livery displaying the town's colours or coat of arms. It was not unusual to find one or other of these town minstrels parading early morning and late evening through the whole town, a proceeding which was on all fours with what we read of English waits. Proclamation at the " mercat cross " had to be made by " *touk o' swesch*," i.e. beat of drum, and this instrument with the pipes were always to the fore at parades, pageants, and processions. At festival time their services were of the utmost importance to the success of pageantry. When Queen Margaret, the wife of the musical king James IV, visited Aberdeen in 1511, Gavin Dunbar portrayed the event in *The Quenis Reception at Aberdein*, in which he describes the display from the time that the " fair procession mett hir at the Port," where there could be heard " the sound of menstrallis blawin to the sky." Then he delineates the pageant, seemingly of the Nativity, and how the " four and twentie madinis," clad in green, of marvellous beauty, played on *timberallis* (timbrels) and were " syngang rycht sweitlie."

Plays and pageants are frequently mentioned in the burgh records at festival time, especially at Corpus Christi, which was a moveable feast, and at Candlemas (2nd February). Once again we use Aberdeen for our purpose. Here the master of ceremonies who produced such plays and pageants was called the Abbot of Unreason or Abbot of Bon-Accord, the counterpart of the English Lord of Misrule. We find him at the granite city from 1440 until the Reformation, which put an end to such " vanities." He also flourished at Linlithgow (1501), Leith (1504), the King's Court (1504), Haddington (1537), and Peebles (1555). The characters, and often the expense of the production, of the plays and pageants were furnished by the craft guilds. At Aberdeen we see such displays as Halyblude (a Passion Play) at Corpus Christi, and the Nativity at Candlemas, beside other representations, which featured Robin Hood, Little John, and Queen of the May. Minstrels obviously played a considerable part in these displays, especially in processional duties, which would, no doubt, come within the orbit of the town minstrels. Yet there were other minstrels who were required for incidental music, and as there was no craft guild of minstrels in these days, for musicians in Scotland were as yet not " crafty " enough to organize, as were the tailors, skinners, and others, minstrels had to be hired for these pageants, and on one occasion at least in Aberdeen (1442) it was the Baxters' (Bakers') Guild which was responsible for providing the minstrels.

Whilst these displays were the people's efforts at plays, it must be remembered that there were also the professional players, who had been encouraged since the robust days of James IV. In 1488 we read an item of expenditure, " To the King himself to play in Perth £20-7-0. Next year Patrick Johnson and his fellow actors played before the King at Dundee. English comedians performed at the court of James IV in 1503, and Sir James Lyndsay was his master of revels. It was the stage, as we shall see, that played a prominent part in the anti-Roman propaganda just prior to the Reformation, a contribution which the Reformers soon forgot when their otherwise sober judgment was marred by a narrow and bigoted puritanism. The stage was indissolubly connected with music and so they had to share their sorrows together.

Yet whilst town minstrelsy continued to be a feature of civic life until the eighteenth century, the wandering minstrel class began to die out. Eventually the growth of the printing press and the appearance of the chap-book narrowed the field of the minstrel's activity to instrumental work, and in Scotland the new era ushered in by the Reformation made his calling profitless. It was the same with the strolling player. On the countryside he could attract an audience but in the towns, where the settled professional devoted more serious attention to the histrionic art, he could not compete. In the next century, as we shall see, when more enactments were to operate against the wandering minstrel, there was little left to the better type by way of livelihood. Those who were sufficiently adaptable in the handling of pipe, fife, trumpet or drum found refuge in soldiering, where men with glib tongue and personality, as well as deft musicianship, were needed for such employment.

That a fair number of the middle and upper classes were seriously interested in music was due to the existence of schools of music, more generally known as the Sang Schools. Their foundation goes back to the 14th century at least, the year 1370 being supposed to be the earliest date of the Aberdeen school. At the opening of the 15th century, documents concerning them become more plentiful and we know of the Brechin school in 1429. The Sang School was part of the church's educational system although, in many instances, the town also had part control, as it had in other church affairs, as we see at St. Andrews in 1447, and at Aberdeen in 1532, where it dismissed the cathedral choir. Primarily the Sang School was for the musical education of priests and choristers. Every priest, so as to be able to perform the offices of the church, had to have, at least, a modicum of knowledge of music, whilst precentors and choristers were expected to be adepts and therefore needed a systematic training. There were also outsiders who received benefit from the curriculum of the Sang Schools and, as Livingston says, " it looks as if a considerable number had taken advantage of them," for, in addition to music, there was taught reading, writing, and arithmetic, and probably reading in the vernacular, not forgetting " manners and virtue."

In pre-Reformation days we know of Sang Schools at Aberdeen, St. Andrews, Glasgow, Brechin, Edinburgh, Elgin, Restalrig, and other places. Not a few of their Masters rose to higher positions, notably " Sir " John Lesley (1527-96). He was appointed Master of the Aberdeen Sang School in 1554. He was then a prebendary of the choir of the cathedral, but in this year the town council decreed that he was " to have the organs and Sang School for instruction of the minds of the good bairns," for which he was paid £20 a year. He afterwards became Bishop of Ross (1565) and a well known author. Whilst in England on behalf of Mary Queen of Scots he was held a prisoner (1571-73) and thus became acquainted with the famous English composer Christopher Tye, whose music was not unknown in Scotland in those days since

the David Melville MS. in the British Museum contains his
Ascendo [*ad Patrem*] for five voices.

It is the existence of the Sang Schools that not only explains the
high quality of church music produced in Scotland at this period,
but it gives the *raison d'être*. The explanation is that the schools
turned out not merely producers of the commodity but consumers
also. David Lyndsay (d. *c.* 1555) hints that these people were
competent in part-singing. Of course, the latter, being of the
middle and upper classes, would be in the minority, but they were
powerful as well as appreciative patrons, and their views carried
weight. Not that this church music was completely beyond the
appreciation of the people at large, since I have long held the view
that the latter took part actively or passively in this music, for it
is conceivable that a familiar *cantus firmus* was used, not so much
in obedience to church discipline, as the need of a well known
tune for the congregation to participate, if not vocally at least
spiritually, in praise or devotion. Indeed, this must have been
the primary urge when composers used a secular melody for the
cantus firmus, for in this the people could detect and follow something that was definite and familiar in the polyphonic crowd of
notes which would bring heart and voice into one spirit.

CHAPTER 3

THE INSTRUMENTS:

> " The *psaltery*, the *sytholis*, the soft *sytharist*,
> The *croude* and the *monycordis*, the *gittyrnis* gay ;
> The *rote*, and the *recordour*, the *rivupe*, the *rist*,
> The *trumpe* and the *talburn*, the *tympane* but tray ;
> The *lilt pipe* and the *lute*, the *fydill* in fist,
> The *dulset*, the *dulsacordis*, the *schalme* of Assay ;
> The amyable *organis* usir full oft ;
> *Claryonis* lowde knellis,
> *Portativis* and *bellis*,
> *Cymbaclanis* [*cymbaelanis*] in the cellis,
> That soundis so soft."
> RICHARD HOLLAND : *Buke of the Howlate* (*ca.* 1450).

The originality of some of these lines of Holland are suspect.
How could an author who spent most of this life in the Highlands,

and whose *beau ideal* was the " Scots-speaking Gael," possibly omit
mention of the harp ?   Gavin Douglas (d. 1522) found a place for it,
as did his predecessors, in another list of instruments,

> " On *croud, lute, harp,* with mony gudlie spring ;
> *Schalmes, clariounes, portatives,* hard I ring,
> *Monycord, organe, tympane,* and *cymbell,*
> *Sytholl, psalterie,* and voices sweet as bell."

The hiatus of Holland is almost unbelievable when we consider that
James I (1404-37) himself had such fame as an harpist.   Indeed
there is abundant proof that the Highland and Lowland harps were
both prime favourites at this period.   Yet truth to tell, Holland
actually knew of the harp, as those evasive lines beginning, " The
schenachy, the *clarschach* " very pointedly illustrate.   The second
reason for believing that some of this passage is second-hand in
structure is the inclusion of the " *schalme* of Assay," an instrument
which only has existence in the " *muse* d' Aussay " of Guillaume de
Machaut (d. 1377).

Although generically, both the Highland *clarsech* and the Lowland
harp belonged to the same family, there were marked differences
between them.   Maior (1521) shows that the *clarsech* had brass
wires instead of gut.   Another dissimilarity was that the sound-
chest of the *clarsech* was covered with leather.   The instrument was
greatly in vogue during the 15th and 16th centuries, not merely in
the Highlands, but at the king's court, and in such Lowland towns
as Ayr, Dumbarton, Wigton, Glenluce, and Dumfries.   One
particular characteristic was that the performer plucked the wire
strings with his fingernails which were grown very long for this
purpose.

The Lowland harp was probably the instrument which James I
and his royal successors favoured.   Unlike the preceding, it was
mounted with gut strings in which respect this was its chief claim
for superiority over the *clarsech* in its mellow tone.   There is a
good representation of the harp in the hands of David in the *Culross
Psalter* (*c.* 1470) as well as a rather rude one at the beginning of the
Chronicon Jacobi Primi Regis (mid-15th cent.) published by the
Maitland Club, but more important is the famous *clarsech* called the
Lamond harp, which has come down to us, if we can accept the

date, 1464, which is claimed for it. At any rate, it cannot be later than the first half of the 16th century. John Faed, the Scottish painter, has shown a harpist in a dark corner of his picture of James I and his associates but unfortunately it is not the Highland *clarsech*.

Since Douglas mentions the *rote* we can only assume that the old Celtic *cruit* was still to the fore as a plucked cithara, although this is the solitary reference to it. The *psaltery* of Holland and Douglas was of the triangular type mentioned already, known specifically on the Continent as the " stromento di porco," which shape we see in the sculptured figure at Melrose Abbey (15th cent.) where it is bi-cordal and furnished with sound-holes. In performance the strings were plucked by the fingers or *plectra*. The *dulset* and *dulsacordis* may have been similar instruments, but played with small hammers instead of *plectra*, i.e. they were dulcimers. This latter instrument, furnished with mechanical hammers and a keyboard was known as the *manichord*, which was the *monychord* of Holland and Douglas. Somewhat similar was the *clavicord* or *claricord*, and one recalls that it was the *clarychordes* on which James IV played to his bride on his nuptial night in 1503.

Being a keyboard instrument a simple modulation to another such keyed device, the organ, seems called for. From the time of James I (d. 1437) the " amiable *organ* " was heard everywhere in the churches in Scotland. Bower (1447) says that this monarch *introduced* the organ into this country, whereas he ought to have said, as Dauney suggests, " organs of improved construction." One cannot deal with its mechanism here, but in an inventory of the organs at the Chapel Royal at Stirling in 1505, we are told that there were " three pairs of organs, one of them of wood, the other two of tin or lead [pipes]," which, I imagine, refers to separate pipe and reed organs. If that is so, their construction was far behind that of Flanders and Germany. As a frontispiece to my *Music in Mediaeval Scotland* (1930) I gave a reproduction of one of the wings of a triptych at Holyrood House at Edinburgh which displays an organ of the 15th century. Apparently this painting originally belonged to the Collegiate Church of Holy Trinity at Edinburgh, erected by the widow of James II, Marie of Guelderland, in 1462. The central figure is Sir Edward Bonkil, the first provost of the college, who is said to have visited Flanders to have this painting done at the hands of the famous Hugo van der Goes (1435-82). Of far greater interest is the organ itself which would perhaps represent the actual instrument used at Holy Trinity. In comparison with the large and more elaborate organs used on the Continent, the instrument is small and unpretentious, but it would serve the needs of the choir of Holy Trinity which comprised a provost, eight prebendaries, and two choir-boys. Clement Antrobus Harris, writing in 1920 about this picture, said that " it is obvious that Provost Bonkil must have taken with him much local material " when he went to Flanders for this picture, and possibly the organ design was included in this local colour. Three rows of pipes are suggested, the front row showing eighteen pipes.

Costs are always interesting. In 1511 a certain Gilleam, " makar of the King's *organis* " was paid £8-4-0 for " goat skins and parchment for the bellows, nails and sprigs of iron, glue, paper, . . . ," all for an organ. At the palace at Holyrood there was quite a spate of expenditure on organs. A pair of organs for the King's Chapel there in 1537 cost £66-13-4. Another supplied in 1542 for the same is put down at £60. Both instruments were supplied by a William Calderwood. In 1551, David Melville of Leith received £36 for a " pare of organes " for the same place.

The small portable organ, the *portative* of Holland and Douglas was more generally known as the *regal*. It was a small reed organ, and we see it admirably delineated in the sculptures at Melrose Abbey (15th cent.). It continually crops up in the state papers, because the king took it about with him on his journeys. In 1494 it had to be taken to Stirling, and then from Stirling to Edinburgh in 1497. The instrument was at Inverness in 1502, because one named John Goldsmyth received 7s 8d for a case " to turs [carry] the *organis* in." Four years later the same man had the same job at Eskdale at the other end of the country.

Instruments of the lute, guitar, and citole groups were quite fashionable, as we see from Holland and Douglas. The two first named had been favoured since the previous century, and it was the former which seems to have finally ousted the *clarsech* and Lowland harp from their foremost place, mainly by reason of their simpler handling and control. This lute still retained its Oriental features and shape, and was the favourite of almost all Scotland's rulers from James I to Mary. It was played with a plectrum, as we see from the sculptured example given by Dalyell (*Musical Memoirs*, pl. xxxiv). Another fine graven specimen at Cowthally Castle (15th cent.) shows four strings. A lute bought for James IV in 1496 only cost 6s 8d, although those purchased for James V were more expensive, since one named William Galbraith paid 40s. in 1526 for one, and 50s. in 1531 for another. We read of a fourth lute picked up in Glasgow " with a case and a dozen of strings " for 40s. Strings were fairly costly as we read in 1533, " ane dozen luyt stringis . . . 6s." and this continued to be the price for a long time. One of the songs in Wedderburn's *Complaint of Scotland* (1549) is entitled, *Bille vil thou cum by a lute*. The jovial lines in *Christes Kirk on the Grene* tell us about—

> " Tam Lutar was their minstrel meet
> Gude Lord how he could *laus*."

The guitar, the " *gittyrn* gay " of Holland, was different from the lute in many respects. It had a flat sound-chest like the fiddle, and indeed it could be called a plucked fiddle, for such nomenclature obtained in Spain where the two types of instrument were called the *vihuela de penola* and *vihuela de arco*. The *sythol* of the poets was the instrument known in England as the *citole*. It was pear-shaped and vault-chested, but its head was straight, not turned back at a right angle like the lute. There is a sculptured example at Roslyn Castle (15th cent.). Both the *gittyrn* and the *sythol* seem to have had four strings and, like the lute, was played with the fingers or a plectrum.

The bowed instruments were still the crowd, rebec, fiddle, and viol, all of which, save the last named, had been in use for two centuries at least. The *croude* or *croud* is not mentioned anywhere else save in Holland and Douglas, and we have no pictorial representation of it in Scotland. Still, we imagine it to have been the same instrument mentioned in the last part, where we saw that it was the older rote i.e. the Celtic *cruit* with a central finger-board added and played with a bow. Neither does the rebec appear in the literary references of the early period although perhaps the term *fithel* might have covered it. Yet iconography shows that it was quite distinct from the fiddle as we know this instrument today. It was the old *rybybe* of Thomas of Ersyldoune, and it is to be seen in the stone figure at Melrose Abbey (15th cent.) where, although badly weathered, one can still discern its Oriental features in the pear-shaped structure and the leathern band running under-neath the bridge so as to protect the parchment belly. At Roslyn Chapel (15th cent.) it may be seen in its later form without this band, and perhaps with an entire wooden belly. A carved wood panel at the National Museum of Antiquities (KL 38) probably represents a later specimen of this instrument. The rebec still had three strings.

The fiddle proper, so often mentioned in the state papers, was not of the shape of the rebec. It was flat-chested like the guitar, and had incurvatures at its sides. A design, taken from a Dun-fermline Abbey MS. (14th cent.), shows this "*fydill* in fist" as Holland writes, and it has been reproduced by Dalyell (*Musical Memoirs*, pl. xxx), where it shows two strings. Brantôme, in his *Dames Illustres*, speaks of those "wretched fiddles" (*méschants violons*) with which the Scots serenaded Mary Queen of Scots in 1560, but by this time they were probably the four stringed in-struments that we know today although not of such delicate facture.

The *viol* is not mentioned by the poets quoted for the simple reason that it had not made its *début* in Scotland in their day. James V seems to have adopted the instrument when he returned from France after his nuptials. Here he had found the instrument being used in various sizes, two treble viols, a tenor, and a bass, and from four being employed at the Scottish court we imagine that such a choir was used. Like the lute, the *viol* was fretted on the fingerboard. It is highly probable that all these *viols* were mounted with four strings at this period. In Scotland they were quite costly. In 1535 there is payment to Richard Hume an " Inglis-manne " of £20 for " stuffe " [material] necessary to " mak violis to the kingis grace." To this there had to be added the cost of making. Hume, in spite of the above qualification, is quite a Scottish name, and we imagine that Richard was the first of that long line of violin makers in Scotland—Urquhart, Kennedy, Ruddi-man, and Matthew Hardie, who so worthily enriched the craft.

Among the wood-wind instruments were the recorder, shawm, and bagpipe. The *recordour* of Holland was a beaked flute, and from the German Virdung (1511) we know that it was made in various sizes, three, in his day, comprising a set or choir. Whether the latter was adopted in Scotland we have no knowledge, but from the inventories of Henry VIII, we see that such was the practice in England, and we imagine that Scotland was not far behind. In a sculpture at Roslyn Chapel (15th cent.) we can see a one-handed type of recorder, the one generally used in the combination known as " tabor and pipe," or even more popularly as " dub and whistle." The *quhissel* was the Swiss fife, recently adopted from France which, with the Swiss side drum, i.e. the *swash talburn*, gave brilliance to martial music.

The shawm was an instrument of the modern oboe class but the conical bore body of the instrument was wider and the reed was larger. Further, the reed was taken completely into the mouth, and not held by the lips as today. The result was that the tone of the instrument resembled that of the bagpipe. The *schalme*, as Douglas calls it, may be seen in the Roslyn Chapel sculptures, where the acoustical vent holes at the bell end of the body are clearly discernible. Early in the 16th century, the shawm was practically superseded by the *hautbois* or *howboy* as it was called in Scotland, although not infrequently we see both the " *chalmes* and *howboyis* " playing together. The tenor or bass to the latter was the *courtal*.

What the *lilt pipe* was that Holland mentions can only be guessed. Perhaps it was a cylindrical reed-pipe of the clarionet type. Such an instrument would be the " pipe maid of ane gait horne " mentioned in Wedderburn's *Complainte of Scotland* (1549). This reed-pipe, with its up-turned " goat horn " bell would be identical with the 18th century Lowland *stockhorn*. They were all rustic instruments of the *floyt* (flute) and *pype* (pipe) class of which we read in the rollicking *Cockelbie's Sow*, some of which were made of a " borit bourtre " (bored eldertree).

In the bagpipe group there was the simple " pipe maid of ane bleddir and of ane reid " mentioned by Wedderburn (1549). It was probably identical with the ancient *chorus*. Then there was the bagpipe with chanter and drone. We read of Nicolas Gray (1505) and Jamie (1507) who played " on the drone," and again (1506) of a " piper with the drone." There are two excellent delineations of the instrument with a chanter and two drones at Roslyn Chapel, and a much disfigured one at Melrose Abbey, both of the 15th century. " Pipers " crowd into the documents of the period, but one has to be wary of the term because it often covers players on the shawm and recorder. It is only when we have such unmistakable entries as a " dron " or " drone pipe," that we can be sure of our ground. The bagpipe was a great favourite with the people at large in both civil and military life. W. F. Skene, the eminent Scottish historian and author of *The Highlanders of Scotland* (1837), places the introduction of the bagpipe into Scotland at quite a late date, which is clearly quite untenable in view of iconographical and documentary evidence to the contrary. That it was in use during the Anglo-Norman period there cannot be much doubt. It is true that Buchanan, writing before 1579, states on the authority of Donald Monro (*Westerne Isles of Scotland*, 1549) that " the bagpipe was substituted for the trumpet by the western islanders." Obviously the crucial question is *when* was it substituted ; this substitution must have taken place before 1549 since the Earl of Argyll's Highlanders who were ravaging the Lowlands were being encouraged by *cornemeuses*, as Beague says in his *Histoire de la Guerre d'Écosse* (1556). In any case, whatever the date of the " substitution " may be, the circumstance can only refer to the adoption of the instrument for warlike purposes by the " western islanders."

Then there were instruments with cupped mouthpieces among

which the *cornett* takes first place. This was originally a natural horn with finger holes, but by this time it was made in wood and in various sizes. Bugles, trumps, trumpets, clarions, and horns, were instruments of the martial throng. The horn had long been favoured in warfare by the Scots and their methods of using it so as to unsettle their enemies was commented on by Froissart. William Stewart (d. *c.* 1550) says, " *Buglis* blawand hiddeous." It was replaced by the more penetrating *trump* and its diminutive the *trumpet*. The *clarion*, if we are to accept Horman (1529), was " wounde in and out with a ho[o]pe," i.e. it was a wreathed trumpet. Douglas speaks of the " *claryonis* lowde knellis." The *draucht trumpet*, mentioned (1505-68) among the court trumpeters, was the sackbut.

Lastly comes the percussion and concussion group. Holland's *talburn* was but the earlier *tabour*, which was a cylindrical drum with two heads. Once more we must look to Roslyn Chapel for its form. From the opening of the period under review *tabroners* or *taberners* are in evidence in the peaceful music of the court and castle, in the civic needs of town life, and in the " pomp and circumstance of glorious war." Yet the particular military type was a much larger instrument and was called the *swash* or *swasche talburn*, i.e. the Swiss drum, and this was played in a tilted vertical position, whereas the ordinary minstrel's *talburn* was played in a horizontal fashion. The *tympane* was, of course, the kettledrum. The phrase " *tympane* but tray " has puzzled the commentators, but surely the two latter words must be the French *batterie*, and that the phrase means the " tympane beating."

Bells (*bellis*) and cymbals (*cymbaelanis*), introduced by Holland and Douglas into their poems, are too well known to require further remark, although the " *cymbaelanis* in the cellis " of Holland do not refer to the hand clashing cymbals that we know, but to the tiny metal plates which jingle in their compartments (" cells ") on the rim of the timbrel. Here we include the *ribupe* (*rivupe*) or Jaw's Harp, a folk instrument, which seems to have derived its name from the French *rebube* (=guimbarde) of which we read in Le

Loyer, *Histoire des Spectres* (1605). Under the name of *trump* it appears in the *Complainte of Scotland* (1549).

When one considers this formidable array of instruments of music used in Scotland at this period it can be readily understood why historians write so grandiloquently of the music, for these were the tools of those who discoursed the art. Nor was it left to a professional class to be adepts on them, for both the rulers and the gentry vied with each other in proficiency in the instrumental art during most of the Golden Age.

CHAPTER 4

THE CHURCH

" Not only were the clergy to be versed in the Gregorian or plain-song, but in some cases they were also to be learned ' in discant and pricket sang ', the harmony and counterpoint of the day."

DOWDEN : *Mediaeval Church in Scotland.*

In the previous chapter it has been shown how the choral organisation of the cathedral and other churches functioned. In the period under review (1424-1560) we have a fair list of cathedral precentors preserved for us at Aberdeen, Dunkeld, Ross, Brechin, Caithness, Moray, Glasgow, and even Lismore, together with those of other ecclesiastical institutions, and it was these precentors who were nominally responsible for the music of the church, the only art music which existed in these days. As already pointed out, not all of them were actually cantors. Some, who were not singers, provided deputies. Others held the post as a sinecure, as did John Duncanson the precentor of Glasgow (1523) who was most of his time in Rome, or John Thornton the precentor of Moray (1544) who was officiating as a canon at Glasgow. In point of fact the statutes in the cathedral only compelled six months residence. Of course the office, when it was a lucrative one, would probably be filled in most cases by the nepotic, sycophantic, or simoniac. Alexander Gordon, who was precentor of Moray, became Bishop of Aberdeen (1514) at the behest of his kinsman the Earl of Huntly, just as Archbishop Gavin Dunbar gifted the precentorship of Glasgow (1537) to Archibald Dunbar, one of his " ane ilk." Simony was openly practised, as in the instance of the aforesaid precentor John Duncanson, whilst William Meldrum, who " bought " the bishopric of Brechin in 1488, had the effrontery to absorb the post, or at least the tiends, of the precentorship as well in 1505.

In spite of all this the music of the church was well cared for, not by the money-grubbers, but by the music-grubbers who, without lucrative preferments, placed their art and their religion first. Their name is legion in Scottish church history. Among them were those Dunkeld notables signalized by Alexander Myln (1514), to wit, John Stephan (" sublime in music theory and organ playing "), James Lawder the chaplain of Abernyte (" well learned in music ") William Martyn (" a master of music "), and Thomas Bettoun of Muklere (" theorist "). Then there were John Malison of Aberdeen, of whom Boece (d. c. 1536) speaks in high praise, Alexander Paterson of the Chapel Royal commended by Robert Richard of Cambuskenneth (1530), and Alexander Smithe of St. Andrews lauded by Sir James Melville. Not a note of their music, nor a line of their writings has been preserved, the Reformers took good care of that, so we have to content ourselves with mere names. Yet the music of the few that did actually escape the reforming holocaust, including the works of Johnson, Douglas, Carver, and Angus, provides eloquent testimony to the greatness of Scottish church music during the Golden Age.

In the general choral organisation of the cathedrals many interesting sidelights illumine the scene. At Glasgow during the first half of the 15th century, one canon who held a prebend had to supply six choir-boys instead of one vicar-choral as his deputy. This was beneficial to music since six choir-boys were certainly better than one full-time vicar-choral or a half-time canon. In 1480 there seems to have been some difficulty in the city of St. Mungo in obtaining vicars-choral for the £5 annual stipend that was paid. The result was that the remuneration was doubled, i.e. £10 a year was offered. The official resolution covering the increase says that it was due to the church's desire to contribute further " to the praise of Almighty God and the increase of divine worship."

Whatever the reason, we may be sure that the more liberal stipend attracted a better class of singer, for it was even higher than what was paid to the king's minstrels.

In Aberdeen, as shown by Elphinstone's *Constitution* of 1506, the choir had been increased since 1437. It now mustered twenty vicars-choral at £10 a year, the choir boys getting £2-13-4. Eleven choir-boys were stipulated in the new foundation, but only six appear on the register. The Vicars-choral were provided with a decent habit, which probably meant, as in the previous century, a cape of black fur, in addition to the usual surplice and cope.

One recalls the amusing lines about the cock in the *Buke of the Howlate* (*c*. 1450) :—

> " The cok in his cleir' cape that crawis and cryiss
> Was chosyn chantour full cheif in the cannonry."

At Elgin, i.e. Moray, in 1489, things were not so rosy. Here there were seventeen vicars-choral who received from 5 to 10 marks, although there was a doubtful benefit in that they could only be dismissed at four months notice. At Kirkwall, as reconstituted by Bishop Reid in 1514, one of the last of its kind before the Reformation, we see an organist and six choir-boys.

In the collegiate churches and the monasteries the music was in more favourable and disciplined hands. By the mid-16th century there were about forty of the former and almost as many of the latter. In the collegiate foundations the vicars-choral were compelled to attend to their offices personally. No substitute *ad libitum*, nor deputies under the six months rule were permitted here as in the cathedrals. Indeed, when Marie of Guelderland founded Holy Trinity collegiate church at Edinburgh (1462) she made it a condition of appointment that fifteen days absence rendered the position vacant *ipso facto*. James Kennedy, the Archbishop of St. Andrews, also made it a provision that its priests as well as the choir, should be versed in plain-song and harmony (discant).

In 1487, that music-loving monarch James III raised the dignity of the church at Restalrig to that of a collegiate order, on which occasion one of the nine prebendaries had to be skilled, not only in Gregorian song, but in harmony (*discantus*) and organ playing, and also to teach in the " sang school." At St. Mary and St. Anne (c. 1528) in Glasgow, there were eight prebendaries, one to be expert in playing the organ, and three choir-boys " skilled in singing, in letters, and science." This church also had a sang school. In St. Nicolas at Aberdeen, collegiate church music was probably at its best. It was made a collegiate church in 1441, when the city itself provided " song-books for our choir " among other gifts. In 1491 it was ordained that no person should be accepted into the college unless he was conversant with plain-song, and could sing the antiphons, responses, versicles, epistles, gospels, masses, etc. In 1517, at Crail, there were seven prebendaries and choir-boys, and five years later a rule reads that one of the former had to be skilled in organ playing, plain-song, harmony (*discantus*), and *precantus*. Here it was the duty of the first prebendary to instruct the choir-boys " in plain-song, harmony, and *precantus*." At Peebles in 1444, even at the parish church, they were particular that " no man shall be engaged unless he can sing plain song sufficiently well to help God's service in the choir, and if it happens that one is engaged who cannot sing, he shall be removed by the Dean and have no fee." In 1543 it became a collegiate church, when it was furnished with twelve prebendaries and ten choir-boys.

Quite a different atmosphere pervaded the monasteries. Places like Dunfermline, Melrose, Kinloss and Cupar, which were famous for their monastic libraries, were also reputed as centres of culture in the 16th century. Here there was a hush, a quietude, which the cathedrals could not secure. Within these walls there was no absolute need to conform to the service demanded outside and so, despite the austerity of monastic discipline, music could be studied with greater zeal, and works of more ornate and elaborate facture produced " for the greater glory of God." Boece (d. 1536) says that the priory of St. Andrews was always celebrated for its music, whilst singing formed one of the exercises of the students. Hard by, at the College of St. Leonards (1512), those admitted had to be sufficiently instructed in Gregorian song.

Per contra, the severity of cloistered life seems to have compelled, at least once in pre-Reformation times, a somewhat similar austere outlook on music, a view which insisted on the utmost simplicity in the art, and such a doctrine was enunciated at Cambuskenneth in 1530 by a canon there named Robert Ricard in his *Commentary on the Rule of St. Augustine*. Ricard had lived among the Augustinians at Paris and he based his argument for the simplicity of church music on St. Augustine's *Confessions*, without reference to *De civitate Dei* or *De musica*. It is true that the great saint warns us in his *Confessions* that one may be tempted to hearken to entrancing music rather than to sublime and sacred words, but does he not also say in *De musica* that " Music is the science of modulating *well* " (*Musica est scientia bene modulandi*) ? Surely, if the exigency of social life is *well doing* (*Vos autem, fratres, nolite deficere benefacientes*, II, Thes., iii, 13), why not in music also, especially when it is to the glory of God (*ad ornandum locum sanctificationis Meae*, Isaiah, lx, 13) ? Still, here is the complaint of the worthy canon of Cambuskenneth.

Firstly he strongly condemns the tendency of display in church music and censures those singers who desire to " show off " their abilities so as to win applause. St. Ambrose, he says, did the same thing at Milan when he introduced Ambrosian song to please the multitude. This is wrong, he continues, because its aim is to satisfy carnal desires rather than spiritual needs, and so he urges that nothing should be done in music save that which is consistent with the statutes of our forefathers. He then speaks of those who had introduced new masses composed after their own conceits, and complains that much valuable time is wasted in Scotland and England in singing a single mass, when this time could be better spent on the sacred text. And so he begs for a return to the plain and simple Gregorian song, such as he heard in Paris at Notre Dame and at the Chapel Royal at Stirling where, under Alexander Paterson, " one syllable is made intelligible with one note." What the immediate result was of this attack on the prevailing music of the church we have no record, save that the book *On Singing the Mass* by the above mentioned Paterson and the Abbot of Inchcolm appears to have been on similar lines. That the later reformers took a leaf out of Ricard's book is scarcely likely, since the stern view of music which they adopted was prompted directly by Calvin and his school. Yet it is worth noting that such opinions on church praise had already been enunciated in Scotland *before* the Reformation.

Finally there is the musical activity of the Chapel Royal at Stirling to be discussed. Here one sees precisely how the king himself looked upon the organisation and structure of church music. James III (1460-88) was the real musical benefactor of this institution which had been founded so far back as 1120. Among the court favourites of this headstrong though artistic king, who were the cause of so much political trouble to the country, was an Englishman Sir William Rogers (d.1482). Ferrerius, the continuator of Boece, speaks of Rogers as " *rarissimus musicus ex Anglia.*" He had been sent with others to Scotland by Edward IV to negotiate a twenty years' peace between the two countries, and had remained there as the Scottish king's favourite, presumably by reason of his musical abilities. It has been generally accepted that James III had planned his Chapel Royal as a music conservatory under the direction, or at least the guidance, of Rogers. Pitscottie says later that there was appointed a dean, archdean, treasurer, subdean, chanter, subchanter, and all kinds of other offices pertaining to a college. The staff was doubled, one half was to accompany the King wherever he went, " to sing and play for him and hold him merry " ; the other half to remain at home " to sing and pray for him and his successors." How far James III proceeded with this design we have no definite record, for Rogers was one of the two courtiers seized and hanged by the dissident nobility at Lauder Bridge (1482). Yet Ferrerius has placed it on record that he had met several worthy people in 1529 who claimed that they had studied at the *schola* of Rogers.

In the year 1501, James IV essayed to partly homologate his father's plans and made the Chapel Royal a collegiate church. To it he appointed a dean, subdean, sacristan, 16 canons, and as many trained prebends, and 6 trained or "fit to be trained" choir-boys. We know their stipends. The dean and subdean received 500 and 240 marks respectively, one canon (probably the precentor) had £100, seven other canons 100 marks each, seven more canons at £20 each, whilst the choir-boys had 90 marks. The following year the precentor was officially recognized. It is interesting to note that James Beaton, who had been precentor of Caithness, i.e. of Dornoch, in 1497, became dean of the Chapel Royal in 1508, and later Archbishop of St. Andrews. Maior (d.1550), the historian, who has devoted a line or two to music in his famous work, was treasurer of the Chapel Royal.

In the year 1505 an inventory of the chapel tells us of a few items of musical interest. First, there was a table on which was depicted Christ with two angels carrying *musical instruments*. Secondly it was recorded that there were " Three pairs of organs, one of wood and two of tin or lead [pipes]." Thirdly there were a number of precious books and manuscripts. Among these were four large manuscript antiphonaries of parchment with large gilt capitals ; three manuscript graduals of parchment ; an old manuscript gradual of parchment given to the king by the deceased abbot of St. Columba ; two manuscript volumes of parchment with notes in *faburdone ;* ten manuscript processionals of parchment written and notated by the pen ; as well as numerous missals and breviaries, both manuscript and printed.

Nor was the Chapel Royal the only establishment well endowed with a permanent music library, and I say permanent because it is doubtful whether much of the contemporary compositions of men like Carver, Johnson, or Douglas, would be found in the repertories, if I may use the word in this connection. The library of Glasgow Cathedral in 1432, which was a fairly rich collection, and included manuscripts " illuminated in gold " or " well illuminated," there were ten graduals, seven antiphonaries (four marked as ' missing '), five processionals, and so on. Dowden, in remarking on the small number of books in this cathedral for the choir service of the canonical hours, explains this under the not uncommon regulation

which " required the vicars-choral to be able to say the service by
heart." At Aberdeen, at the same period, there was a similar
plenitude of music books. When the College of St. Salvator opened
its doors at St. Andrews (1450), among the books of the choir
that were catalogued were " ane gret prykkyt sang buk and tua
smallar of pryllyt sengyn," which are still in existence, one at St.
Andrews and two at Wolfenbüttel. Under the impulsion of Bishop
Elphinstone of Aberdeen, a man " fond of music," the *Breviary
of Aberdeen* was printed (1509-10), and from an act of the Privy
Council it would seem that other works for the service, " after our
own Scottish use," were planned to be printed, whilst all books of
the Sarum use were forbidden.

How far the organ was used in the church seems to have been
a matter of doubt among earlier writers such as Dalyell and Livingston, to be repeated by David Hay Fleming, although there is not
the slightest reason for uncertainty. The Bellenden-Boece account
of the benefactions of James I (1424-46), that divine service was
" decorated with crafty music and organs " answers for the opening
of this period, whilst *The Buke of the Howlate* (*c*.1450) continues
the affirmation. At St. Nicolas' Church at Aberdeen there was an
organ in 1437, and in 1485 the city was taxed for a new instrument.
In 1505 there were three organs at the Chapel Royal, and since £7
were spent on repairs in the following year one imagines that they
were not new, more especially when another £8 4s. 0d. is charged
for further repairs in 1511. That there was more than one performer
is evident from *organeris* (organists) being paid in 1513. John
Cumyng was playing the organ at the Aberdeen (St. Nicolas')
sang school in 1518. In 1527 Aberdeen gave sanction to Gilbert
Robertson to pass to the schools to learn the organ. Other sang
schools had organists, for example at Ayr (1538) where Robert
Paterson held office, and at Glasgow where John Painter officiated.
If they were employed in the sang schools they *must* have been playing
in the cathedrals and collegiate churches to which the schools were
attached, of which we have abundance of proof, as in the case of a
fine performer like John Stephan at Dunkeld Cathedral (1514) and

the player at the Restalrig collegiate church (1487). We find one
also at the Priory of Inchmahone which granted its organist a pension
in 1548. Even the parish kirk at Linlithgow in 1546 had an organist,
Thomas Mwstard, who had some fame upon the *organis*. Thus we
see that in every type of ecclesiastical institution in Scotland at this
period, the " amiable organs," praised by Richard Holland, could
be heard.

CHAPTER 5

THE MUSIC.

" *Proportionis* fine with sound celestiall,
Duplat, triplat, diatesserial,
Sequi altera, and *decupla* resortis
Diapason of mony sindrie sortis.

. . . .

In *modulatioun* hard I play and sing
Faburdoun, priksang, discant, countering,
Cant organe, figuratioun, and *gemmell* ;"
GAVIN DOUGLAS : *Palice of Honour (ca.* 1501).

In dealing with the influence of discussion on progress, Walter
Bagehot pointed out in his *Physics and Politics* that there are periods
in history when great ideas are " in the air," when poetry, science,
and architecture, far removed as they are at first sight from such
an influence as discussion, are suddenly started onward. We see
precisely the same thing in music, an art which, at " first sight,"
is even further asunder from the influence of discussion. Actually,
the spoken or written word is not necessary in the arts. It is the
deed itself that matters, for it is not a question of what is right or
wrong, which is the ambit proper of discussion, but rather what is
acceptable to the eye and ear. It may be true that the pen is mightier
than the sword, but in the arts the deed is more potent than the pen.
The accomplished fact is certainly more provocative than the
argument, as in the realism of a Courbet or a Richard Strauss,
or perhaps what is more convincing still, the *par le fait* doctrine
of modern anarchism. At the period of the Renaissance we have
in music ample evidence of the persuasion of the *thing done*, irrespective of any preceding or accompanying *apologia*.

As we have seen in the last chapter, France was the Parnassian height in music, yet there was no apology or justification for the new ideas in the *organum* and *conductus* of the Notre Dame School, or the novel motets and cantilenas of the later Guillaume de Machaut and his kind. What takes the place of discussion is what the French call " l'éducation de l'oreille." If the ear is pleased, it accepts what it hears. If it is not pleased, then it rejects it until inurement breaks down the repulsion. We are told by Calderwood (*d*.1650) that when James I (1424-37) came to the Scottish throne " he brought into divine service a *new kind of chaunting and musick* wherein he was expert himself." Further, he says, " they placed a great part of religion in *curious singing* in these days." The term " curious" was the word used by the later reformers to indicate polyphonic music, and we see their fear of it in the dedication to Este's *Whole Booke of Psalmes* (1592) where " curiositie is shunned." Unfortunately we are not aware precisely what kind of " curious " music it was that James I introduced, but we do know that by the beginning of the 15th century England had wrested the lead in music from the French schools, and that her new *discant, gemmell,* and *faburdoun,* to use the terms of Gavin Douglas, were influencing other people far beyond Albion's shores. The apostle of this English School was John Dunstable (d.1453) and with him there " began a new epoch of musical history " (Adler, *Handbuch der Musikgeschichte*). Once again there is no *argument* in favour of this " new [English] art," as Tinctoris (d.1511) the Fleming calls it. Everything made its way, not by discussion, but by " l'éducation de l'oreille." Since James I spent eighteen years (1406-24) in England, where he was educated and taught music, we may surely conclude that some of the " curious " music that he introduced into Scotland was of Dunstable's school.

That English influence was still felt in the following century we may deduce from the use of the name of Robert Fayrfax (d.1521), called by Anthony à Wood " the prime musician of the [English] nation." A hint of this composer's sway in Scotland is made by Thomas Wood, the Vicar of St. Andrews who, in 1566, lamenting

the parlous state into which music had fallen in Scotland, said, " If
Dr. Fa[y]rfax were alive in this country he would be condemned
and perish for lack of maintenance." True, the passage itself
merely shows the veneration in which Fayrfax was held by the
editor of the Scottish *St. Andrews Psalter* (1566), but this esteem,
coupled with the fact that Fayrfax is one of the " authorities "
in the only Scottish theoretical treatise of the period that has been
preserved, almost suggests some influence. At the same time, the
works of Carver, Johnson, and Douglas, which are to be described
presently, are in some respects in advance of what has appeared
in print from the hand of Fayrfax.

So far as can be judged from examples of the work of Fayrfax
that have been available, he was thoroughly English in his craftsmanship, and owed little or nothing to the later Flemish School which
was then dominating Europe. Strange to say, it is this school
which is the main authority of the Scottish didactic work on music
of the 16th century just mentioned. It is entitled, *The Art of
Music collecit out of all Ancient Doctoris of Music (ca.1540)*, a work
which the present writer hopes to publish in its entirety. Originally
there were two volumes, but only the second of these has been preserved, and it is now in the British Museum. Its material is divided
into three books. The first begins, *Quhat is Mensural Music,* and
comprises fifteen chapters. The authorities quoted are, Ornithoparcus (*fl.*1517), Gafori (d.1522), Tinctoris (d.1511), Jacobi Fabri
(*fl.*1514), Wollick (*fl.*1501), Johannes de Muris (14th cent.), and a
writer quoted by Ornithoparcus named Erasmus Lapicida (15th cent.)
Among the musical examples are twenty-five canons, one being by
Josquin des Près (d. 1521). The second book begins, *Music
Mensurall,* and has five chapters on counterpoint, with examples of
harmony in 3, 4, and 5 parts, rules for *countering* and *faburdon*, with
numerous examples including the 4 part *O Lux, Beata Trinitas* of
Fayrfax, with the plain-song in the tenor, a typical Scottish pro-
ceeding, even down to the 1635 Psalter. The third book, *On
Proportion*, is unfinished.

On the purely philosophical side of music, and this was ever the field in which the Scots have been prominent, there was James Bassantin (d. 1568) who was born in the palmy days of James IV. He was primarily interested in mathematics and astronomy which subject he pursued at his home at Bassendean in Berwickshire. Even after his death his works still commanded interest as evidenced by *Astronomia Jacobi Bassantini Scoti, opus absolutissimum* . . . (Geneva, 1559). About 1560 he published (?) a work in French and Latin on the Platonic theory of music entitled *Musica secundum Platonem*.

The British Museum treatise mentioned above indicates the type of book which appealed to those in cathedral, collegiate church, and monastery in Scotland, who were interested in the higher domain of music theory. Of these, quite apart from the composers known to us, there must have been quite a goodly number, since Dunkeld alone could boast of four such enthusiasts at this time, John Stephan, James Lawder, Thomas Bettoun, and William Martyn. Indeed, the lines of Gavin Douglas which sound the opening fanfare to this chapter, written when he was Provost of the collegiate church of St. Giles, might very well reflect his own, or his colleagues proficiency in the art. We have seen what was demanded of precentors, vicars-choral, and even priests, in the chapter which deals with the organisation of music within the church, and even if but a modicum of theoretical knowledge was required of them in the general run, we may be sure that those who sat in organ loft or taught in the Sang School would, of necessity, have had to delve deeper. Added to this we have the radiant testimony of the music itself which has been spared to us. In this we have a precious legacy in that it fills, not merely a gap in the creative work in Scotland during the Golden Age, but it helps perhaps to cover a short period in *British* music twixt the Fayrfax (d.1521)—Taverner (d.1545) group and the mid-century composers, Shepherd (d. *c.*1563), Tye (d. 1572), Whyte (d. 1575), and Tallis (d. 1585). " There were giants in the earth in those days," and three of them can be found in Scotland, Robert Carver of Scone, Robert Johnson of Duns, and Robert Douglas of Dunkeld, although the history of music has taken scant heed of them, save in the instance of Johnson, whose name has been cared for by reason of his English connection, and because perhaps the English are more appreciative of such things.

Robert Carver was born in 1491 and was a canon at Scone Abbey in 1513, which is the date of one of his compositions there. Another of his works is dated 1546, and between these dates is the only other news that we have of him, and this is when he was a signatory to a document in 1544. He was practically unknown until recent years when the late J. A. Fuller-Maitland brought his name into prominence, although he was not the first to discover him. Carver was first signalized in the old *Dictionary of Music* (1824) compiled by John S. Sainsbury, which made reference to a Robertus Carbor, " one of the oldest known composers of sacred music in Scotland " whose " mass of . . . the twelfth [sic] century is extant." When I looked through the music manuscripts now in the National Library of Scotland I found that this Carbor was in reality a certain Robert Carbor, Carlbor, or Carver, *alias* Arnat or Arval, whose compositions were to be found in a manuscript (5/1/15) labelled *Antiphoniarum*, which, by the way, it is not. Yet it was Fuller-Maitland who did the pioneer work in editing and publishing the first of Carver's works when he issued the motet *O bone Jesu* in 1926, and made frequent reference to the composer later, as in his book *A Door-keeper of Music*. Then came the Rev. Father A. Long of Westminster Cathedral who scored other works of this great Scottish master, and these are quite numerous, although they still remain in manuscript.

Fuller-Maitland says that the *Antiphoniarum* contains " a round dozen masses and 30 motets, with 6 settings of *Magnificat*," and two of *Salve regina*. The earliest mass would appear to be the one on the theme *Dum sacrum,* the antiphon for St. Michael's Day, which was composed in 1513. It is for 10 voices (2 trebles, 2 altos, 3 tenors, and 3 basses) and is of considerable length. Father Long says that it is solid rather than brilliant—and no doubt very gratifying to young Carver who was barely twenty-two years old.

Of greater moment is the mass on the well-known melody *L'homme armé*, a *cantus firmus* which had already been used by Dufay (d.1474) and Josquin des Près (d.1521). England, which was not particularly interested in secular melodies for this purpose, does not seem to have used this melody, a circumstance which might show that Scotland was not so much influenced by England at this time as by France and Flanders. At the same time, Carver used an English folk-song, *The Western Wynde*, in a *Kyrie*, seemingly before Taverner, Tye, and Shepherd, the only English composers of importance to borrow this secular theme for a religious purpose.

As Father Long has pointed out, Carver was a man who painted on a large canvas and used to the full the ample resources of his monastery. This is patent from his *O bone Jesu*, a work, in its *tutti* sense, for 19 voices, i.e. 4 trebles, 2 altos, 10 tenors, and 3 basses. Of this work Fuller-Maitland says, " The skill with which the 19 parts are handled, the composer's sense of melodic beauty, and, perhaps more than all, his command of sonorous effect, are far in advance of his time. . . . The sequence of harmonies is surprisingly rich and varied." I do not wonder that Father Long has said that Carver must have ranked with the great composers of Europe, . . . contemporary with Taverner, Merbecke, Tye and Mundy in England, with Lassus on the Continent, . . . in the full vigour of his genius when Palestrina was born. In spite of all these encomia he is neglected in Scotland and possibly the only occasion that his *O bone Jesu* has been performed there for four hundred years was when the present writer produced it in Glasgow in 1934. Yet his memory is cared for elsewhere. As the late Sir Henry Hadow wrote a few years ago, " Further works of Robert Carver are now finding their way into the choir books of Westminster Cathedral and of other places where they sing. We are in process of restoring to its dignity the reputation of this great forgotten Master." Just so, but there is no such redemption so far *in Scotland* !

Robert Johnson of Duns has, perhaps, a wider appeal than the preceding composer because we have his secular as well as his church compositions, although we may have but scant details of his life. Thomas Wood, writing 1566-78, says that he was " ane Scottis priest borne in Dunse " in Berwickshire, the birthplace of the more distinguished Duns Scotus, the *doctor subtilis* and polemic adversary of St. Thomas Aquinas. Beyond this, nothing is known of his early life. This great composer must have been born at the close of the 15th century and doubtless entered the church. In one place in his *Psalter* (1562-66) Thomas Wood had originally attributed Johnson's *Domine in virtute tua* to " ane Inglisheman, and, as I have heard, he was blind when he set it." This he cancelled and substituted, " This was set in Ingland be ane Scottis preist baneist." In a later copy (*c*.1575-78) of the psalter, Wood wrote that it was " set in Ingland be ane Scottis preist being deletit to have beine ane heretyke fled thair lang before Reformation. Thomas Hutson's fader, now wyth the king kent him." To *delate* in Scotland is to summon before an Ecclesiastical Court, but whether Johnson accepted the call and was *banished* in consequence, or whether he *fled* rather than face the inquisitors, is not clear. The Act of 1525 against Lutheran and similar doctrines, and the burning of Patrick Hamilton, another priest and composer, as a heretic in 1528, were clear warnings, and either or both events may have driven Johnson from Scotland, although I can find no charge against any person of his name, yet a certain Andrew Johnson was convicted before the Renfrew sheriffs in 1536. At any rate, Johnson would have had to keep his heresy under a soft pedal in England because Henry VIII was burning Lutherans as late as 1540. The Thomas Hutson (Hudson) mentioned who *knew* Johnson " weill " was, at that time (1566), a Scottish court musician, and later (1586) became Master of the Chapel Royal. He came from England and it was probably here that he knew Johnson. Further, since he speaks in the past tense, it would appear that Johnson was then (1566) dead.

In England Johnson's career is equally difficult to trace. If the song in Wynkyn de Worde's song-book of 1530 is Johnson's, then he was in England before that date. He is said to have been a chaplain to Anne Boleyn (d.1536), and his beautiful madrigal *Defyled*

is my name, h   ̫een called, although not with complete proof,
a " Complaint ؟ Ằnne Boleyn." John Baldwin of Windsor, a
later member of the English Chapel Royal who copied some of
his works, says that Johnson was a " priest of Windsor," and
presumably he could speak with authority. One of Johnson's
compositions at Christ Church, Oxford, certainly names him as a
" peticanon of Windsor."

Johnson has rightly been called " the most considerable composer
born in Scotland until comparatively recent times " (Grove,
Dictionary of Music), and on this account his works deserve something
more than a mere schedule. Of his pre-Reformation compositions
his *Ave Dei Patris* for 5 voices stands at the peak with a superb
dignity and grandeur. Dr. Ernest Walker says that it is " finely
austere and more expressive than the bulk of his work." Next I
would place his *Domine in virtute tua* for 5 voices which, from its
frequent occurrence in early manuscripts, must have been high in
favour. The late Dr. W. Gillies Whittaker and Harold Thomson
edited a " performing version " of it at my request. Then comes
Sabbatum Maria Magdalene for 5 voices, which Burney wisely
inserted in his *History of Music* (1776), contrasting it with Taverner's
work and naming Johnson as " greatly his superior." For 4 voices are
his *Deus misereatur nostri, Gaude Maria virgo,* as is his setting of
Dum transisset Sabbatum, whilst *Laudes Deo* and *Dicant nunc Judei*
are for two voices. Other works of a like nature are only preserved
in instrumental arrangements, possibly of the post Reformation
period, such as *Ave plena gratia, Ave Dei Patris* (another setting),
Benedicam Domino, all for lute, organ, or virginal. Four viols is a
setting of *Deus misereatur nostri,* whilst two pieces for organ or
virginal entitled *In nomine* might conceivably have been for a like
combination. Then there are three items for five viols entitled
A knelle, Gaude virgo, and *In nomine,* of which the first has been
edited by Peter Warlock and André Mangeot.

Definitely post-Reformation compositions are his anthem *O happie
man,* as well as an English version of *Benedicam Domino* as " O Lord,
with all my heart." More important still are the three solid but

musicianly prayers, *Relieve us O Lord, O eternal God,* and *I gave you a new commaundement* which were published in Day's *Certaine notes* (1560). Of his secular vocal works is that delightful madrigal *Defyled is my name* which Hawkins gave a place in his *History of Music* (1776), at the same time giving a specimen of his skill in canon on the plain-song *O lux, Beata Trinitas.* Other songs are the emotional *Com palefaced death, Elisa . . . is ye fayrest quene,* and perhaps the boisterous *Ty the mar[e], tomboy,* the latter having particular Scottish interest since the words are credited to William Kethe, one of the versifiers of the 1561 and 1562 English psalters and the Scottish one of 1564. In the *Fitzwilliam Virginal Book* there are three very intricate *almans* by Johnson, with his *pavan* " sett by Giles Farnaby."

Of the actual position of Johnson in the music of the first half of the 16th century, opinions differ. Burney (1776), although not always a reliable critic, labels Johnson " a learned musician " who " was one of the first of our church composers who disposed his parts with intelligence and design." Burney must therefore have considered Johnson's work to have been earlier than that of Shepherd, Tye, Whyte, and Tallis, which it doubtless was. Dr. Ernest Walker places Tye, Whyte, and Tallis among the " great geniuses," and relegates Johnson, together with Shepherd, Thorne, and Parsons, to the rank of " lesser men." On the other hand, Rockstro included him with Tye and Shepherd and their predecessors Fayrfax and Taverner. The late Sir Richard Terry, who told me that he had scored all of Johnson's works, took another point of view. " If you take Scottish counterpoint of the early 16th century " he says, " as you find it in Robert Johnson, it is flowing, it is skilful, it is effortless, it is convincing, it achieves real distinction." This is praise unstinted as he gestures it with one hand. With the other hand however, he rather conditions his benison when he insists that " Robert Johnson can hardly be termed a typical Scottish composer " because " the traces of English influence are very strong." " Looking carefully through his music " he continues, " you might almost imagine it to have been written by the Englishman John

Shepherd. The fluency of Johnson's counterpoint and the general lay-out of his motets is strikingly like Shepherd, and is distinctly English in character." Yet as I see the problem, Johnson was earlier than Shepherd, and seemingly Burney held the same view. That being so, might not one say, *per contra*, that " Shepherd's counterpoint and the general lay-out of his motets are strikingly like Johnson ?" I would not go so far as to add " and distinctly *Scottish* in character," to complete the argument, because it seems to me that, to a great extent, both English and Scottish composers were speaking, shall we say, a common tongue in music, drawing from a common British fount, depending upon a common musical tradition of the church. At the same time, Johnson might have been, as Burney says, one of the first to give symmetry to part writing.

Patrick Hamilton (1504-28) was another composer of the period, although we know of but one of his works and even that by name only. He was the second son of Sir Patrick Hamilton, and was educated at Paris and Louvain, where he possibly first imbibed Lutheran doctrines. Returning to Scotland he entered St. Andrews University in 1523, where he became influenced by the atmosphere of music which pervaded the oldest of Scotland's universities, whilst in its St. Leonard's College the art was a *sine qua non*. Here he appears to have become the precentor, and Alexander Alesius tells us that " he composed a mass for 9 voices for the office of the missal which begins, *Benedicant Dominum omnes angeli ejus*, and superintended its execution in the cathedral as precentor of the choir." In 1527, the Archbishop of St. Andrews, David Beaton, ordered that Hamilton should be seized and interrogated as a heretic, but he managed to escape to Germany. Here he met Luther, Tyndale, and Fryth, and it was the latter who translated his *Loci communes* into English. His zeal for the reformed religion meant that he was lost to music for ever. He returned to Scotland where he was arrested, tried, convicted, and burnt at the stake in 1528. Of his solitary known composition, beyond what Alesius has recorded no information is available. Yet his opinions prevailed, and it was said that the " reek [smoke] of Patrick Hamilton infected all that it blew on." In this same year another musician was seized for heresy at Oxford. This was Taverner, but he was more fortunate than Hamilton because, in his case, " the Cardinal for his musick excused him, saying that he was but a musician."

The next composer was Robert Douglas or Dowglass, but once more we lack biographical details. All that we know is contained in the *Antiphonarium Ecclesie Dunkeldensis* of the early 16th century in the Library of the University of Edinburgh, which contains the inscription, " Robert Dowglass with my hand at the pen William Fische." Herein may be found " anthems, chiefly in honour of the B.V.M. followed by the music for the Ordinary of the Mass, *Kyrie, Gloria, Credo, Sanctus, Benedictus,* and *Agnus Dei.*" Many of his works have been scored by Father L. Long of Westminster Cathedral, and one of these, broadcast by him in 1935, was a mass of more than ordinary interest, for it is a work finely organized and powerfully moving. In the opinion of Father Long it is as good as some of that time and better than others. Another of Douglas' works with which I am familiar, and which I performed in 1936, is his motet from "The Song of Songs" (vi) *Descendi in hortum* for 5 voices. It is majestic, massive music, but sensibly poetic withal, as we see in the opening descending passage. No wonder that Father Long has called Douglas an imaginative craftsman.

Perhaps the most outstanding Scottish organist of his day was John Fethy or Futhie. He seems to have been the same John Fethy who, in 1498, was granted a licence to go abroad. He did not return until 1531, when we find him master of the Sang School at Dundee. Thomas Wood, writing in 1592, says that he was " the first Organeist that ever brought in Scotland the curious new fingering and playing on organs,—and it is mair nor threscore yeiris since he com hame." In 1544 he became organist at St. Nicolas' Church, Aberdeen, and master of the Sang School, at £20 per annum. In 1551, he went as master of the Edinburgh Sang School, where we find an entry of him being paid 24/- for " tonying [tuning] of the organis."

What the special accomplishment was that he introduced into Scotland in 1531 is not so patent as it would seem to be. Was this " new fingering " the use of all the digits, or merely the employment of the thumb ? Amerbach of Leipsic shows in his *Orgel und Instrument-tablatur* (1571) that three fingers only were used, and that the thumb of the right hand was never, and that of the left, rarely employed. If one only knew where Fethy sojourned whilst abroad (and some Continental church must have such a record) it might be possible to posit an explanation. Van der Goes' delineation of the organ in the Provost Bonkill painting reveals a keyboard eminently suitable for such a fingering with all the digits. As a composer, we only have the prayer preserved by Wood in the 1562-66 Psalter, entitled *O God Abufe*, in four parts. It is a worthy production, since both the words and the music (" bayth letter and not ") came from his pen.

David Peebles, Pables, or Peblis (d.1579) was originally one of the conventual brethren of the Abbey of St. Andrews and, according to Thomas Wood, writing in 1562-66, " ane of the principall mussitians in all this land in his tyme." He set the canticle *Si quis diligit me* in 4 parts about the year 1530, but in 1547, " a lytill before Pinky," a fifth part was added by a novice, Francy[s] Heagy, who was his disciple, which Wood thought he accomplished " verray weell." At the Reformation, Peebles still remained at St. Andrews, where he was favoured on account of his skill in music by the Prior, who was Lord James Stewart. Certain St. Andrews' Priory documents quoted by David Hay Fleming, show us that Peebles was in residence there in January 1565-6. Again in April 1571 he and his wife, Katherine Kynneir, had a house and land there. In this latter document he is mentioned as one of the foundation members (*fundatis membris*) of the priory. We shall see him presently in the Reformation period when he was engaged in harmonizing the psalms, hymns and canticles. Wood calls him " ane honorable and singulare cunning man," and the canticle mentioned above certainly reveals this latter.

These are all the names and works of Scotland's famed musicians that have come down to us from the " Golden Age." They are but a handful it is true, if we compare the total with the dozen or more men of similar radiance, and a crowd of lesser lights, who show themselves with distinction in England. Indeed, one might feel inclined to depreciate Scotland's contribution to music in those days which I have called the " Golden Age," yet the cause of this paucity is not hard to explain for, as Davey says in his *History of English Music* (1895), " the compositions of the old Scottish school—from James I onwards—perished largely in the general confusion and devastation " at the Reformation. It would however have been nearer the mark had Davey said " almost wholly " instead of " largely." Johnson's works were saved because he had settled in England, but what would have happened to them had he remained in Scotland we know from the history of the Reformation there. The compositions of Carver and Douglas can only have been spared to us by a mere stroke of good fortune, since the Reformers destroyed almost everything on which they laid their vandal hands.

PART IV

THE REFORMATION

(1560-1603)

> "[In 1559], where they found in their way any kirks or chapells, incontinent, they purged them, breking down the altars and idols in all places where they come. And so praising God continually, in singing of psalmes and spirituall songs, they rejoiced that the Lord wrought thus happily with them."
>
> *Historie of the Estate of Scotland.*

WE are not directly concerned with the causes of the Reformation, whether " politike, ecclesiastical, or oeconomical," as the Scottish psaltrists would divide human interests, although some such reference to these things must inevitably creep in. Primarily, all that calls for notice in these pages is the effect of this momentous event on music and general culture in Scotland. The Reformation had long been seething. James Resby (1407) and Paul Crawar (1433) had already gone to the stake for the doctrines of Wycliffe. By 1525 an Act had been specially devised to meet the new Lutheran heresy, and an early victim (1528) was the precentor and composer of St. Andrews, Patrick Hamilton. John Knox himself tells of another musician, a singer at the Chapel Royal, named Richard Carmichaell, who leaned to the new doctrines and was accused of heresy before the Dean of the Chapel. Yet his offence was not a doctrinal one. He had merely said in his sleep, " The Devil take away the priests, for they are a greedy pack." This seems to have taken place about 1530-36, and Knox avers that this young *singar* from Fifeshire was compelled " to burn his bill," i.e. recant his heresy. Yet the records of the Privy Seal reveal that his shoulders carried a heavier punishment, since so late as March 1539, the said Richard, having been " abjured of heresy," had his escheated goods returned to him. Even after the first flush of the Reformation, another court minstrel, Sandy Steven, a professed Romanist, was playing with even more dangerous fire, since Knox records that this *tabronar* stated " that he would give no more credit to the

New Testament, than to a tale of Robin Hood, except it were confirmed by the doctors of the church," which was Higher Criticism before its time. By the " Fifties," the Reformation was already under way, and many precentors and priests of the old church had gone over to the Reformers, including John Angus. Until this period, the stake had been the sole arbiter between the Church and the Reformers, and the fire was not slaked. It was not until George Wishart was brought to the cruel flames that the Reformers unsheathed the sword in the slaying of " the carnal Cardinal " David Beaton in retaliation (1546).

As of old, popular song revealed its potency as a weapon in a popular cause, and with many a well aimed shaft pierced the armour of the old church. The authorities realized immediately the danger of this form of attack and met it by edict. First, in 1549, the provincial council of Linlithgow threatened all who were found in possession of *aliquos libros rythmorum seu cantilenarum vulgarum scandalosa ecclesiasticorum* with dire penalties. Then Parliament took a hand and passed an Act in 1551 prohibiting " any books, ballads, songs," either in Latin or English, without Royal license. Meanwhile the orgy of war and riot had begun, and from the year 1545, when the state papers first tell of the English party burning abbeys, down to the grand assault of the Reformers in 1559, the " rascal multitude," to use the words of John Knox, was destroying or sacking cathedrals, collegiate churches, and monasteries throughout the length and breadth of the land. One only needs to read the accounts of the Reformers themselves to appreciate the ruin and devastation that followed in the wake of the subversion in which music suffered so deeply.

 No wonder Sir John Graham Dalyell, in his *Musical Memoirs* (1849), poured out his contempt on that " fanatical zeal which sated its wrath on inanimate objects " during the Reformation, on vestments, altars, memorials, chalices, organs, *service books* and *music*, as well as the very walls, all destroyed or overthrown. As the Rev. Father Long pointed out in a broadcast a few years ago (1935) on pre-Reformation church music in Scotland—Vestments and images can be replaced, but musical works so destroyed are gone for ever. How much was *spulzied* (to use an appropriate Scots word) in this direction will never be known. We are told what happened, for example, at Scone Abbey, where Carver had not long before composed his motet, *O bone Jesu*, and Knox himself is the narrator. It was destroyed by a mob from Perth. " Some of the poor [of Perth] in hope of spoil, and some of Dundee, . . . passed up to the same Abbey of Scone. . . . And so was that Abbey and Palace appointed for sacking, in doing thereof they took no long deliberation, but committed the whole to the mercy of fire." As for the abbey at Dunkeld, that perhaps housed the creator of *Descendi in hortum*, Robert Douglas, we read that those " Lords of the Congregation," Argyll and Ruthven, ordered the Lairds of the district to go to Dunkeld Abbey and " take down the whole images thereof, and bring forth to the kirkyard, and burn them openly. And similarly cast down the altars, and purge the kirk of all kinds of monuments of idolatry, . . . and you will do us singular pleasure." One can well imagine what little chance music books had of being spared the tender mercies of a mob in blind fury, for not only were these things excellent tinder for the flames, but they belonged to such as were " dedicated to superstition " which was specially marked out for destruction.

We know from the report of the Governor of Berwick of the " burnings of images and mass-books " at St. Andrews in 1559. At Lindores Abbey, as we read in Laing's *Knox*, the " idolatrous vestments and mass-books " were committed to the flames, and we can imagine that the " Popish stuff," as Saddler reports in the state papers, that served as fuel when the abbeys of Paisley, Kilwinning and Dunfermline were despoiled, included mass-books. In 1560 it was reported that Arran and Stewart had burned " all the books and mass-cloths " found at Dalhousie Castle. The inventory of Queen Mary's books made in 1569 reveals six " massbooks," probably salved by her from Holyrood Chapel. Later we find the Regent Morton burning " mass-cloths and books " at Haddington. And these things took place *after* the victory.

Spottiswood (d. 1639), the Archbishop of St. Andrews, tells us that the "registers of the church and *bibliothèques* were cast into the fire," and Robert Keith (d. 1757), the Bishop of Fife, who drew from another Spottiswood version, says, "*Bibliothecks* destroyed, the volumes of the Fathers, councils, and other books of humane learning, with the registers of the church, cast into the streets, afterwards gathered in heaps, and consumed with fire." All this has been openly admitted and defended by later historians. David Hay Fleming (*The Reformation in Scotland*) boldly avows and assents. "It may be frankly acknowledged" he says, "that the Scottish Reformers heartily approved and encouraged the destruction of altars, images, and *service books*; and in this they were by no means singular. They were only following the example which had been set in several of the continental countries, and also in England. There is no evidence, however, that they exported and sold as the English did. . .". Lovers of art may have good cause to regret the loss of priceless treasures, *but the Reformers would have been culpable had they, on that score, spared.* . . . When immortal souls are in the balance with works of art, no Christian can hesitate as to which should be preferred." Whatever religious justification there may be for this vandalism, to urge mitigation because others had committed the offence seems to be of doubtful validity, whilst to plead lenience on the ground that the destruction of the offending article was better than selling it "as the English did," cannot be allowed for the simple reason that the Scots also sold the "Papistic stuff," as we shall see when dealing with instruments of music.

Even when service books and original manuscript music did escape the bonfires they were not safe. Printing had reduced the importance of manuscripts as such, and few of the "rabble multitude" could discriminate between ordinary graduals or antiphonaries, and sole exemplars of masses and motets. So far as the crowd was concerned, parchment brought them *siller*, and in these days booksellers were on the look-out for this material for strengthening book covers. To the pilferer, parchment was parchment, irrespective of what was written thereon, and just as we see the palimpsest of Cicero's *De Republica* being used elsewhere for St. Augustine *On the Psalms,* so the musical fragments from an old Scottish Church Service Book may be found supporting the binding of a Dundee Protocol Book of 1575, still preserved in that city.

By 1560 the more violent scenes of ruthless destruction were past, and the outward visible sign of the Reformation showed triumph, although its inward spiritual grace was not particularly manifest. The " Confession of Faith " was ratified by Parliament, and at the end of the year the first General Assembly held its session, a body that was to rule Scotland for many a year to come. That being so, the Reformed Church was able to assume even greater power than that wielded by the Roman Church, and this revealed itself in its attitude towards music, not merely within the church itself, but in the wider sphere of social life. In this course the General Assembly stood unchallenged, save for the stand made by James VI, called " the wisest fool in Christendom," who was sufficiently sapient to curb the " Popes of Edinburgh " in their interference with secular affairs, but was unforgiveably sappy when he essayed to intervene in religious matters. That this period was a disastrous one for music in Scotland is universally admitted. For nearly two hundred years the land was impotent. As James C. Dibdin (*The Musical Educator,* v, 169) has said, " The Reformation wave swept away all inborn love of art : sculpture, painting, music (save for the droning Kirk psalm), architecture, and everything artistic became a dead language in the nation."

CHAPTER 1

THE COURT AND GENTRY.

"He [the King] is weill myndit as he hes already begun, that the said art [of music] salbe restorit partlie agane within this realme be providing sic personis as hes some entres in the art, and will gif thair mynd and labouris thairto to the prebendareis and chappellenries of the Collegis and Kirkis that wer foundit and erectit of auld to be served be musicianis."

Anno 1586 (*Bannatyne Club*).

Even in these days of plain and stern manners we see from the above that James VI was still particularly concerned that the music of the Royal collegiate churches should be maintained as in the old days. Like his mother, he always had a considerable attachment to music. Mary (1542-67) was only seven days old when she was called to the throne. Still in her swaddling clothes, she was "crowned" the next year. As the Earl of Arran and Marie of Lorraine the Queen Mother were Regents, the court music was their music. As she grew up she became enamoured of the art, much as her father would doubtless have wished. Naturally the Chapel Royal attracted her special attention. This, as an institution, had been transferred from Stirling to Holyrood, the old fabric being deserted meanwhile. In both places, through Mary's efforts, "the organs and ornaments . . . were preserved when those in cathedrals and other churches were wrecked and ruined," as the Rev. Charles Rogers tells us in his *History of the Chapel Royal.* This however did not prevent the spoilation of service books and their like which were the very symbols of Papistry, as the Roman service was termed. We have seen how fairly extensive was the collection of music and service books in the Chapel Royal in 1505, but the inventory of 1561-62 revealed that all that remained was a "Mass book of parchment, with a noted Antiphonale of parchment." What had become of that precious old gradual of the Abbot of St. Columba? Where were those other music books with gilt capitals illuminated perhaps by Sir Thomas Galbraith?

Mary, as the politic Randolphe has so benignly expressed it, was "troubled for the preservation of her silly Mass." He adds that her musicians would not accommodate her in this. They probably had good reason for their reluctance since he himself has told us of the " sport " that happened previously when " her Grace's devout chaplains would . . . have sung high Mass." On this occasion the gallant Argyll and Stewart " so disturbed the choir, that some, both priests and clerks, left their places with broken heads and bloody ears." However, Mary managed to secure a little of her own way in these matters and later (1562-65) she and her personal domestics were permitted to hear Mass. At Sterling, in April 1565, so Randolphe reports, " there was never in any time of most Popery than was this Easter, . . . at her High Mass." More daring was the ceremonial at the baptism of her son, afterwards James VI, in 1566. At the sacrament itself the choir of the Chapel Royal at Sterling " sang appropriate airs, accompanied by the organs." The General Assembly was shocked at the Papistic display, and the Countess of Argyll was ordered to make public repentance at the Chapel for her share in the event. Between the palace and the chapel, clarions and other instruments sounded the joyous tidings and, after a great banquet, there was " dancing and playing in abundance." Thereafter, for a whole week, there was more music and masques under the direction of the chief court minstrel, John Hume who, for the occasion, wore " a hat and [sic] velvet bonnet, rapier and belt," and received for himself and his assessors, £177 odd.

Hume was also the principal of the three lutars at the court. One of the latter was John Adesone, who was also a *valet de chambre*, receiving £24 a year for these offices. The court violars were five, John Feldie, Moreis Dow, William Hay, John Dow, and John Hay, all of them Scots seemingly, who were paid £10 a year *plus* perquisites. So many as seven violars appear on the lists (1560-63) but later, until 1570, there were only four. Among the wood-wind players were James Heron and James Ramsay, and in 1563-64 the latter had a salary of £59 odd. Other court minstrels were Jakis Dow and Alexander Feldie. All of these were clad in a special livery consisting of coats and hose of white taffety, with red and white for bonnets. Vocalists were also on the pay roll, and in 1565 we read of clothes and Paris hats for five *sangsters*. In addition there were trumpeters and drummers who fulfilled the needs of functional music. Among the former was Julius Drummond the grandson of Julian Drummond who fell as trumpeter under the Queen's standard at Pinkie (1547). The Drummonds belonged to the old Italian family of court minstrels.

That singers of the court were also valets we know from the *Memoirs of Sir James Melville* :—" Now there came here in company with the ambassador of Savoy, one David Riccio of the country of Piedmont, who was a merry fellow, and a good musician. Her majesty had three valets of her chamber who sung three parts, and wanted a bass to sing the fourth part. Therefore they told her majesty of this man, as one fit to make the fourth in concert. Thus he was [in 1561] drawn in to sing sometimes with the rest ; and afterwards when her French secretary retired himself to France [1564], this David obtained the said office." Rizzio was certainly more favoured than the other valet-minstrels by way of salary and emoluments, since in January, 1562, he is shown receiving £50 " by a precept," and in 1564, his salary was £80, paid quarterly.

Although Lord Herries (d. 1583) refers to Rizzio as a " musician " who became a " Secretary of State," we see from the above that he was not even one of the regular court minstrels save by courtesy. The legend that has grown up about him being one of the founders of Scots music, seems to have begun with Melville, Birrel and Irwin who spoke of Rizzio as being a " good musician," " well skilled in . . . music," and a " great musician " respectively, and the notion was developed in *crescendo* until William Thomson (*Orpheus Caledonius*) and James Oswald (*Scots Tunes*) attributed compositions to him, a fathering which deserves to rank with another paternity, that related by Osborne in his *Traditionall Memoyres*, which avers that James VI was " David the Fiddler's son." James Beattie (*Essays on Poetry and Music*) gave a more cogent reason for the Rizzio myth when he said that the latter was more probably the first to " collect " these old Scottish tunes.

Rizzio was slaughtered outside Mary's chamber in 1566. His brother Joseph who is claimed to have been concerned in Darnley's death, took David's place as French secretary and musician, but fled to England the following year.

On the whole, despite the new puritanic *régime*, secular music at the court went on its way with little interference. There was pin pricking occasionally, as might be expected. The state papers tell us (1562) that " Mr. Knox is so hard that much of their dancing is laid aside." This was probably quite a salutary discipline for Mary since her over indulgence in these terpsichorean revels made her ill in 1563. In addition to this the Queen was impolitic if not foolish in this direction. A ball at Holyrood was in progress when the news arrived of the massacre of Protestants at Vassy in 1562, but whilst the ill tidings shocked the people at large Mary, unabashed, if not secretly pleased, continued the revelry. When Knox denounced her the following Sunday for " dancing like the Philistines for the pleasure taken in the destruction of God's people," he had good reason. On the other hand she was probably sadly harassed by the stern faced folk for, as Robert Aytoun the poet says in his *Bothwell*,

> " Was but the sound of laughter heard
> Or tinkling of the lute,
> . . . .
> Would Knox with unction tell
> The vengeance that in days of old
> Had fallen on Jezebel."

Forced to abdicate in 1567, Mary was delivered over to England where she was detained as a prisoner until she was beheaded in 1587, an event which, incidentally, gave rise to a few legends, e.g., certain music supposed to have been performed at her execution and said to be preserved at Oxford (*The Book of the Bishop's Castle*, 1888, p.74), and the madrigal *The Noble famous Queene*, attributed to Byrd, in the British Museum (*Add.* 29401) which, on the evidence of the words themselves, must rather have been in memory of Mary of England. During the imprisonment of Mary Queen of Scots, one of her most faithful servitors was a court minstrel, " John, the musician who played the base violin," who took messages to the Queen from her Scottish supporters, as we know from the state papers.

When her son, James VI (1567-1603), came to the Scottish throne, Regents took control until he came of age. He had four violars assigned him, Thomas Hudsoun, Robert Hudsoun, James Hudsoun, and William Hudsoun, quite a close family arrangement it would seem, and there were good reasons for this. Although most of the preceding court minstrels had been Scots, as their very names trumpeted, the new comers were English, and we imagine that the appointments had a political import. Obviously England could not permit the gall of that mischievous " Auld Alliance " with France to interfere any more with the peace between England and Scotland, more especially since the latter's king was the possible heir presumptive to the English throne. Thomas Hudsoun was chief violar, but he was much more. His nickname " Meikle " tells us that he was towering physically, and even intellectually and musically he seems to have been outstanding. He was the translator of the *Historie of Judith* (1584) from the French of Du Bartas, a work probably prompted by his royal master who had a *penchant* for this author, as his *Essayes of a Prentise in the Divine Art of Poesie* (1584) discloses. That Thomas Hudsoun was appointed Master of the Chapel Royal in 1586 may point to outstanding musical qualifications. Of Robert Hudsoun we read in the state papers, whilst James of that ilk was a friend of Alexander Montgomery the poet (d. *c.*1610).

Despite the assertions of the English historians of music, Burney and Hawkins, that James VI was, " either from nature or education," not able " to receive any pleasure from music," and that " he did not understand or love music," this monarch's whole life is redolent of his affection for and protection of this art. Burney, who was a friend of such good Scottish musicians as James Oswald and General John Reid, ought to have known better. How was it that he was not aware that " rare " Ben Jonson had told James VI, who had criticised the poetry of Sir Philip Sidney, that his teacher George Buchanan had corrupted the King's ear when young, when

he " learned him to *sing* verses when he should have read them."
When only in his fifteenth year (1580) James specially ordered " two
pair of virginals " from London, and his servitor James Lawder,
specifically states that they were obtained at " His Highness'
direction and command." In 1596, we read of another personal
touch in an entry which records £32 being paid " by his Majesty's
special direction, *out of his mouth*, to four English violars in Holyrood
House." In the next chapter we shall have occasion to observe
this king's particular attitude towards music whilst in England as
James I, in the face of which it makes it more difficult to understand the attitude of Burney and Hawkins for which there is not
the slightest justification.

The Chapel Royal, which hitherto had escaped drastic reorganisa-
tion at the hands of the Reformers, now received special attention
under an Act of 1571. This ordered that the said Chapel should
be " purged of all monuments of idolatry or other things whatsomever dedicated to superstition," and it empowered the Earl of
Mar in the " searching and seeking of all monumental vessels,
vestments . . . apparelling whatsomever which were within the said
Chapel " and do likewise with them. One may safely assume that
the organs, service books, and music, which had been spared in
previous purgings, now made their final exit, as the Rev. Charles
Rogers has assumed in his history of the establishment. That some
vestiges remained, or had been revived, is apparent seventeen years
later, for in 1586, when Thomas Hudsoun was appointed " Master
of his Majesty's Chapel Royal," he was commissioned to " *search
and try the old foundation*, and all superstition and idolatry being
abolished, to follow and embrace the form, so far as it agrees with
God's word and religion presently professed within the realm."
In this appointment he also had charge of the King's " other
chantorie colleges," as the " College Kirk of Restalrig," and the
above instrument reveals the King's solicitude for this musical
college which had been founded, as he says, " for entertaining and
maintaining of the art of music," and the " support and sustentation
of such persons as professed the said science." This document

avers that the emoluments of the foundation had been diverted into the hands of people unskilled in the art, and he proposed that the revenues be now devoted to " qualified persons." In 1592, Parliament ratified what had been already laid down in 1586 concerning the Chapel Royal, and two years later another Act further secured it as a " musical institution."

When Prince Henry was born in 1594, James VI looked forward to a grand ceremonial at the baptism in the Chapel Royal. In view of this he ordered the razing of the old structure at Sterling and the building of a more commodious edifice in its place, which he personally superintended. Herein, according to the *True Reportarie* (1594), which describes the baptismal ceremony, " the provost and prebends of the Chapel Royal did sing the 21st psalm of David, according to the art of music, to the great delectation of the noble auditory." By the phrase " art of music " one may suppose that it was not the plain psalmody of the conventicle that was heard, but rather a fully harmonized form, which seems apparent from what followed. At the subsequent banquet, the most elaborate masques and music were presented which must have gladdened the eyes and ears of those who could recall the days of yore. Here was seen " Arion . . . [who] played upon his harp," and there was " music in green holly (*holyne*) oboes " in " fine [? five] parts." After this were heard " viols, with voices in *plain* counterpoint," and the singing of Latin hexameters which had been specially composed for the occasion. Then were the ears delighted by " a still noise of recorders and flutes " and, as a conclusion of the first part of the entertainment, " a general *consort* of the best instruments " was presented. Finally, " there was sung, with most delicate dulce voices, and sweet harmonies, in seven parts, the 128th Psalm, with fourteen voices." It was the first and last great ceremony in the new Chapel Royal of Stirling, and ere long the building was allowed to fall into neglect, for Holyrood had now come to house the Chapel Royal as an institution.

By this time the secular musicians at court, i.e. those previously called minstrels, were considered part of the Chapel Royal, e.g.

PLATE IV

Roslyn Chapel, Melrose Abbey, Cowthally Castle.

MEDIAEVAL INSTRUMENTS (15TH CENTURY)

1. Psaltery.   2. Lute.   3. Rebec.   4. Regal.   5. Shawm.
6. Tabor & Pipe.

PLATE V

MASS IN F (1513) BY ROBERT CARVER
Scone MS. (16th Century).

when William Chalmer was appointed "luter" to the Chapel Royal, Holyrood, in 1601. Here the court minstrelsy was as much in evidence as ever, for whatever straight and narrow path the people at large were expected to tread in this respect, those of the regal, purple circle at court had a wide road all to themselves with no hindrance. Not that the Church was in agreement with this latitude, since more than once was it at pains to rail at the "sins of our princes," and especially at those offences in "His Majesty's House," laying special emphasis on dancing and other frivolities of the Queen. Indeed, "God's silly vassal," as Andrew Melville called James VI to his face, was never quite free to please himself in his musical likes and dislikes until he found himself in the coronation chair at Westminster on the 25th of July, 1603.

CHAPTER 2

THE PEOPLE

" Thus with violence shall that great city Babylon be thrown down, and shall be found no more at all. And the voice of harpers, and musicians, and of pipers, and trumpeters, shall be heard no more at all in thee." *The Revelation : XVIII*, 21-22.

One must understand that these lines, which are on the threshold above, were taken in their literal significance by the more pious in those days. Those harpers of the classes and those pipers of the masses were things to be abhorred, and the stricter Reformers would have the same obliteration as in Babylon. In justice to the latter it must be stated that their attitude towards music in general was not new. Most of the Christian Fathers from Clement of Alexandria (d. *c.*220) to St. Augustine (d. 430) had set their eyes and ears against it. The Jewish *amoraim* in the *Talmud*, and the Arabian ' *ulamā* ' in the books on *fiqh*, held precisely the same views when they placed " wine, woman, and song " in the same category among the forbidden pleasures. Yet the world had moved since those beleaguered days. The Renaissance had brought about the abandonment of the old formulas, ideas, and standards in most things, and the result was reflected everywhere. A new freedom had been born, and mankind grasped it with both hands. The contemporary vernacular poetry shows that music and dancing did not necessarily mean drunkenness and licentiousness. It was the same with the visual arts. Painting and sculpture could reveal life and nature so vividly as to preach a new humanism more eloquent even than those " sermons in stone " of which Ruskin wrote.

Into this world the Reformers came, but in railing at " the whore of Babylon " and her " purple and scarlet " they revealed, in such phrases as these, their innermost souls, a revelation of *The Revelation*. The senses had to be curbed. In the church, all decoration and display, the use of organs and the indulgence in florid music became *anathema* in consequence. Whatever the church's apologists may claim to the contrary, this was the kernel of Calvin's message (Sermon : 1 *Samuel* xviii) but, although the Genevan master does not express it, you cannot have, in a Puritan dispensation, one ethic within the church walls and another without, and this was what the Scottish Reformers realized as plainly as did the Christian Fathers and the purists of Jewry and Islam. In their own light the teaching was perfectly logical. Whether it was politic is another matter.

When the Reformers banned all music from the church save a plain and, as some say, a soulless psalmody, they killed an art of which the old church had been the mainstay in its highest expression for centuries. Not content with this, the new presbyters set themselves to determine, outside of the kirk, in what form of music, if any, the people at large might indulge. Robert Chambers is not always a reliable historian but he often uttered some palpable truths. In his *Songs of Scotland Prior to Burns* he has a passage that is worthy of quotation. He says, " The long era of the religious struggle brings before us but one fact in respect to our national minstrelsy—namely, that it was looked upon as a thing low, clandestine, and sinful : the clergy treated it as simply one of the bad habits of the people." Indeed, although it is not stated in so many words, any kind of music that *in itself* roused emotion was considered improper, if not sinful. With the psalm it was different. It was the word, not the music that mattered. As Baird the Huguenot historian says, " The psalm is our epic." The music that accompanied the words was looked upon as the mere vehicle for the discipline of congregational utterance. By Act of Parliament (1579) every gentleman and yeoman was compelled to possess a psalm book " under pains contained in the said Act," and the following year an edict went forth to pursue all those who transgressed in this particular. In Edinburgh they made sure by forcing everyone to take their psalm books to the Presbytery clerk who authenticated possession by entering their names therein, thus " eschewing of all fraud," an odd testimony to the efficacy of the new moral world that had dawned. A " searcher " was actually appointed who could walk into each household at will. That he did so and found culprits is evident from the Privy Council Records. Yet he and his coajutors did not have it all their own way, for in 1582 one of these searchers sought a decree against the very sheriffs-depute of Fife for not helping him in the exercise of his duty. It is quite clear from such proceedings that the people were being dragooned under the new *régime*, and one can appreciate the attitude of W. S. Provand in his Hastie Lecture (1914) when he stigmatizes the church's discipline at this hour as " a terrible engine of oppression."

Outside the kirk, discipline was just as stringent, since a regular *Pestapo* pried into the private lives of the congregation so as to detect those " evil livers " who, among other things forbidden them, would listen to instrumental music or indulge in what were considered indecent songs. Women were charged at Aberdeen (1574) with singing " filthy songs " on Yule Day and Sunday evenings, but what the " filth " was we are not told. At Errol (1593) we know that mere " caroling " was considered " fornication," and so, perhaps, the preceding " filth " was a mere love ballad. " Lewd songs," by the way, were one of Calvin's *bêtes noires*, but in this also we do not know the words which were considered objectionable, and perhaps if we did, that song *Verdurette* might turn out to be quite harmless.

Dancing, and more especially promiscuous dancing, was considered an unhallowed diversion in the eyes of the Reformers, despite *Psalm* XXX. 11, although in this instance the versifiers took precious care to render the Hebrew word *mahol* as " cheerful voice " instead of " dance." The acute Pulleyn knew better in *Psalm* CXLIX. 3. How differently that philosophic hand writes in *Ecclesiastes* III, where we are told that there was a season for everything under heaven, " a time to weep and a time to laugh ; a time to mourn and a time to dance." The far seeing author of that rare French book *Orchésographie* (1589) thought that the dance was an absolute necessity in social polity because one could see the physical fitness of a partner in marriage, and he even said that the kiss demanded at the close of a set revealed, from the breath, the state of a person's health. Yet the Reformers would have had no patience with eugenic or hygienic reasons for the dance. The portion of those who indulged in such was the flame of hell. One recalls the scene in Scott's *Heart of Midlothian* where Effie Deans had dared to mention a *dance*. " Dance," said her irate father, " dance said ye ? I daur ye, limmers [strumpets] that ye are to name such a word at my door-cheek." That is a fair example of what this sour and dour *régime* brought to the life of the Scottish people in one aspect alone.

·Under the old church, Sunday was free to all to enjoy themselves on the one toilless day of the week, after they had fulfilled their religious obligations at the church. The Reformers changed this although they found it no easy a regulation to enforce. As might be expected, the main victims of Presbyterian tyranny were the masses. The one instrument that provoked the people to joy and the kirk to rage was the bagpipe. At a St. Andrews Kirk Session (1570) three pipers were admonished " to keep the Sabbath holy, and to attend sermon on Wednesday." Further, they were " to abstain from playing on the streets after supper or during the night," which, in this particular, was certainly a most wholesome discipline. At Glasgow (1594) the Presbytery forbade a piper from playing on Sundays " from the sun rising till the sun goes to." In 1581, the people working at the trenches at Leith came into the town when finished with pipes playing and flags flying, which the kirk considered "offensive" and "dissolute." Two pipers in the same town were forced to bend the penitent knee and promise to abstain from playing on a Sunday (1591-93). Another pair (1595-96) added dancing to the heinous crime of piping on a Sunday and were suitably punished. A third, at Braid, bound himself "never to profane the Sabbath day in playing with his pipes." The list of miscreants might go on *ad nauseam*. The King, James VI, was not troubled in this matter, for he was almost a law unto himself, and so when he attended Dalkeith Church, he had a couple of pipers skirling in front of him, an offence almost as criminal as that of those Franciscan friars, about whom Knox complains, who had pipers in their procession with a new St. Giles image in 1556. Yet, notwithstanding the penalties, pipes found lungs to inflate them, and ears to listen. One of the special customs in Scotland was the piper at weddings, which was probably hoary with antiquity. The kirk tried by every means in its power to forbid his presence. The pipe meant joy and a St. Andrews Kirk Session of 1570 was most perturbed about the "minstrelsy and harlotry" which were "a great abuse" at weddings.

ı Apart from the bagpiper, whether urban or "on the road," there was little other "music for the people" on the instrumental side, since further Acts of Parliament had denuded the towns of the strolling minstrels. In 1560, Edinburgh gave notice to "all vagabonds, fiddlers, pipers," and others who were without masters or houses within the town, to depart "furth the same" under pain of burning the cheek. Another Act, nineteen years later, adjudged "all minstrels, singers, and tale-tellers" as "idle beggars," unless they were attached to Lords of Parliament or great burghs as their "common minstrels." If otherwise, and they were apprehended and convicted, it meant "scourging" or being "burned through the ear with a hot iron." Not content with her previous edicts anent minstrels, Auld Reekie issued another in 1587 which included "common *sangsters*," especially those who sang "bawdy and filthy *sangs.*" Such things were forbidden the common people's ears, although His Majesty King James VI, as Sir Anthony Weldon tells us in his indecorous *Court and Character of King James* (1650), had his own special court jester " to sing bawdy songs and tell bawdy tales."

In the cities and towns little change had come to official minstrelsy although, since the new *régime* did not favour junketing, minstrelsy was strictly confined to what was requisite for burghal parades and proclamations. The town *tabronar* or *suescher*, i.e. the drummer, still had to announce by tuck of drum, all official pronouce-ments, and this was even resorted to by the church when kirk sessions were announced and were sitting. Bells, as Dalyell assures us, took over the drum's duty later. One of the main duties of the town minstrels was to rouse the inhabitants and again send them to rest. At Lanark (1581) the minstrels had to " *gang* through the town with the drum (*swys*) morn and even," but if it was wet, " when the drum may not *gang*," then the pipe had to do the job. In Aberdeen (1566) the " Town Swescher " had six marks a year for playing " in time of war as peace, and sport and play." We see these fellows in almost every phase of civic public life, from the fun at " riding the marches " to the more depressing ceremony of fixing some unfortunate in the stocks.

, Beyond this official music there was little to be heard. Plays and pageants, which always provided sumptuous minstrelsy, had been suppressed by Act of Parliament since 1555, when it was ordained that " in all time coming, no manner of person be chosen Robin Hood nor Little John, Abbot of Unreason, Queens of May, nor otherwise," under the penalty of £10. Further, if " any women or others " were found " about Summer trees singing," they were to be put in the stocks. By 1562, attempts were made in Aberdeen to evade this, and the city bellman was haled with others before the magistrates on this account. Again in 1565 other citizens were charged with having disobeyed the proclamation against making " any convention, with drum (*taburne*) playing, or pipe, or fiddle, or have ensigns, to convene the Queen's lieges, in choosing of Robin Hood, Little John, ..." The culprits were disfranchised. In 1567, Edinburgh tried and sentenced to death a certain James Gilliam for playing Robin Hood. Fearing the rage of the populace, John Knox pleaded with the magistrates to stay proceedings, but they would not budge. A riot ensued when the tolbooth was broken into and the " felon " released, much to the chagrin of the authorities. At Perth, in 1577, the records of the Kirk Sessions lament that the whole town had been " dishonoured " by certain of its inhabitants giving " a *Corpus Christi* play " that was " idolatrous and superstitious." That was in the July of this year. By the December, not to be tamed by the fiats of any Kirk Session, the Baxters (Bakers) presented the play of St. Obert, their patron saint, in which a band of musicians took part, as was usual. The promoters were sent to prison to cool their heels.

Yet the condemnation of these mystery and morality plays was by no means universal in the land. At St. Andrews, in 1574, the Kirk Session permitted the Minister of Balmerino, with due censorship safeguards, to play " the comedy mentioned in St. Luke's Evangel " that was called " The Forlorn Son," although this same year the General Assembly had interdicted " comedies and tragedies made of the canonical scriptures," permitting only such " other profane plays " that were not scriptural. In truth, the Church did not, at first, possibly from fear of the people, know its own mind from one year to another on this question. When it did arrive at some degree of fixity it was a rigid opposition to everything connected with the stage.

The mysteries and moralities were considered to be relics of Romanism because of their connections with saints and church festivals. Further, the mere pageantry and jollification of these things cut the sober faced and sanctimoniously minded to the quick. The suppression of these pageants was a blow at the professional stage, which was its cousin-german, and yet it was James Wedderburn's tragedy *Johne the Baptist*, and David Lyndsay's *Satyre of the Thrie Estatis* that sounded the first stirring *reveillé* for the Reformation. It is said that the number of playhouses in the 16th century was so great that they were complained of as a nuisance, and the Reformers soon played their part in their suppression. An example of the wary attitude of the Church in its first approach is to be seen at Perth where the Kirk Session in 1589, showed its grace to a travelling company of players by giving permission conditionally that " no swearing, banning nor no scurrility shall be spoken " and, forestalling the Lord Chamberlain of today, that " nothing shall be added to what is in the register of the play itself." Soon however, the Church was in complete mastery, and in Glasgow in 1595, a Kirk Session ordered the town drummer to forbid " all people from going to Rutherglen to see the vain plays on Sundays." In Edinburgh in 1593 and 1599, the King himself opposed the clergy who were prohibiting congregations from attending " profane comedies." He had issued the permit to these players and so he forced the Kirk to rescind its prohibition. The four Kirk Sessions of the capital had published an ordinance which denounced " the unruly and immodest behaviour of the stage-players " and threatened pains and penalties on all who witnessed their performances. When challenged by the Privy Council they climbed down, saying that they had been misled by " sinister and wrongous reports " and would now allow " their flocks to fairly enjoy the benefits of his Majesty's liberty." That so much attention has here been devoted to the stage has been necessary since this art was not only bound up with minstrelsy, often merely as its handmaid it may be admitted, but because the stage provided the widest public field for the use of vocal and instrumental music.

Rich and poor were supposed to fare alike in all this forbiddance, for it was said officially (1566) that there was to be " no partiality in discipline and censure," but actually the classes were, in the nature of things, more fortunate. Closeted safely in the privacy of court, college, and castle, they were fairly secure from, although probably indifferent to, the stealthy, sober faced folk prying into other people's affairs. That is why, during the whole of this militant period of the Reformation, we still find that instrumental music was used by the classes without stint. As to the royal court, we have already dealt with its privileged position, but much the same was to be found elsewhere.

At the same time, even where instrumental music was indulged in by the upper and middle classes, much was done privily in these days. James Melville has shown in his *Diary* that music, both vocal and instrumental, was part of his daily college life, and of others, at St. Andrews. Under the year 1574 he writes, " I loved singing and playing on instruments passing well, and would gladly spend time where the exercise thereof was within the College ; for two or three of our condisciples played intently (*fellon*) well on the virginals, and another on the lute and gittern. Our Regent had also the spinet (*pinalds*) in his chamber." Under the year 1579 he shows that the same delight existed in the west. He says, " Far greater and sweeter [music] had I in Glasgow of a gentleman's house in the town, who entertained most expert singers and players, and brought up all his children therein." Yet Melville unbosoms himself with this confession (1574),—" It was the great mercy of my God that kept me from any great progress in singing and playing on instruments ; for if I had attained to any reasonable measure therein, I had never done good otherways."

A similar attitude of mind may be discerned in Alexander Hume (d. 1609) the poet, who wrote some spiritual songs which may be found in his *Hymnes or Sacred Songs* (1599). In one of these occur the lines,

> " Even on my jolie *Lute*, by night,
> And trimling trible string,
> I sall with all my minde and might,
> Thy glorie gladlie sing."

These lines have often led me to wonder whether Hume had in mind that beautiful song with lute accompaniment by his fellow Scot, Robert Johnson, *O Lorde with all my harte and mynde* (*Benedicam Domino*). Hume, although a minister of the Reformed Church, was a keen musician, and we know from his will that he still possessed a lute and another " musical instrument." Yet he was unrepentantly averse to instrumental music in church, and specially condemns the organ among the corruptions of the Church of England.

At the militant phase of the Reformation, when the Roman edifices and institutions were being overthrown, it was only natural that the Sang Schools suffered material damage. Despite the grandiose schemes proposed in the *First Book of Discipline* (1560) for education in general, little was done. It was, perhaps, not the fault of the church, since much of the likely revenue for such plans had gone into the pockets of the nobility, who held grimly to their spoils. With the Sang Schools in particular, there were other reasons for their temporary decay. Since the choir-boys of the cathedrals and collegiate churches were no longer needed, there was obviously no use in keeping Sang Schools for the training of " hired singers " so detested by the Reformers. Further, there was less money for the upkeep of such, and there was even petty interference from the church. At Aberdeen in 1574 John Cumyng, Master of the Sang School, was admonished for allowing the scholars to have holiday (*play*) on those days " dedicated to superstition in papistry," and he was told that in future he had to keep the scholars " at their lessons " on such days. In some places, the authorities were quite indifferent towards these institutions. At Glasgow, the Sang School was supported out of the " Common Good " fund, but in 1588, when the pestilence caused heavy charges against the fund, the Sang School was suppressed. Although we know that it was functioning again in 1592, this temporary attitude towards these schools tells its own tale. In other places however, liberal ideas prevailed. At Ayr, for example, the Master of the Sang School not only taught his scholars how to sing but also how " to play on the spinet."

The Masters had a rather precarious time in the stormy days of 1559-60. At Aberdeen and Edinburgh, probably the two most important Sang Schools in Scotland, the institutions were despoiled. John Black (d. 1587) had been Master of the Sang School of *Bon Accord* since 1556, but he lost his post in 1560, and was not re-appointed until the refurbishing days of the " Seventies." Edward Henryson (d. 1579), Master of the Sang School of " Auld Reekie," suffered likewise at the spoliation of 1560. In

1574, by the mercy of the church's dire need at that time, he was appointed " Uptaker of the Psalms " at St. Giles, where he had been, in pre-Reformation days (1542-51), a Prebendary ! In spite of the austerity of life demanded from those connected officially with the Reformed Church, Henryson appears to have still indulged in instrumental music at his home and, seemingly, his family also, since his testament (will) mentions " a pair of *monycords* " left to his son.

In pre-Reformation days, the title " Sir " had been given to the masters of the Sang School, as well as to organists, precentors, and others. It was purely an honorific and ecclesiastic label, but under the new *régime* it was dropped, and plain " Mr." took its place, although here and there the name " Doctor " (in its pristine sense of Teacher) was used, together with " Musicianer," to designate these people. Later, the Doctor in the Sang School was the assistant to the Master.

We shall see later how the church was forced to modify its narrow views regarding music in the church since, as time went on, its attitude towards the Sang Schools soon bore proof of its folly. Having " spulzied " this training-ground of music, there were now no musicians in the land to be had. The only hope of remedy was the re-establishment of the Sang Schools, and in this need the Regent Morton and James VI came to music's aid, although one can scarcely believe that either of these individuals took this step solely at the behest, or in the interest, of the Reformed Church. And so in the year 1579, a most important statute was passed for encouragement of Sang Schools. "For instruction of the youth in the art of music and singing, which is almost decayed, or shall shortly decay, without timeous remedy be provided, our Sovereign Lord, with advice of his Three Estates of this present parliament, requests the provost, baillies, council, and community of the most special burghs of this realm, and of the patrons and provosts of the colleges, where Sang Schools are founded, to erect and set up a Sang School, with a Master sufficient and able for instruction of the youth in the said science of music, as they will answer to his

Highness upon the peril of their foundations, and in performing of his Highness' request do unto his Majesty acceptable good pleasure." There are not many lands in Western Europe that can boast of so politic a piece of legislation as this Act of James VI, and Scotland can lay it as flattering unction to her soul, although the Church itself stultified what might have accrued beneficially from it. It is true that some advantages came to both to the religious and secular art from this re-organisation, but the hand of the Church was too heavy to allow of a general renascence. Alexander Hume of Logie, himself a musician and a minister, as we have seen, reveals the mind of one who might be taken as an extreme Liberal on the question at issue, and yet his *Hymnes or Sacred Songs* (1599) reveal a puritan of the most confirmed type. Here is what he says, " In Princes' courts, in the houses of great men, and at the assemblies of young men and young damsels, the chief pastime is to sing profane sonnets and vain ballads of love, or to rehearse some fabulous *faites* of Palmerine, Amadis, or other suchlike reveries, and such as either have the art or vain poetic, of force they must show themselves vain followers of the dissolute ethnic poets, both in phrase and substance, or else they shall be had in no reputaunce. Alas ! for pity, is this the right use for a Christian's talent ?"

Miles Coverdale (d. 1569), in England, was of a similar kidney for, instead of ballads and work-a-day songs, he would have had the people singing psalms all day. He actually looked forward to the minstrels themselves following this lead and with almost unbelievable naïvete pictured carters and ploughmen, as well as women at their spinning wheels, indulging in psalmody. With such music he really believed that "they should be better occupied than with *Hey non nony, Hey troly loly*, and such like fantasies."

The Puritan objection to the blithesome song and love ballad reveals a vain, unmoral attitude to life. The very titles of the Scottish love songs in *The Gude and Godlie Ballaties* (1567) show their lofty and serious purpose, *For lufe of one I mak my mone right secreitlie, My lufe murnis for me, Tell me now and in quhat wyse how that I suld my lyfe forga,* or *Downe by yone river I ran.*

What could possibly be wrong with *Rycht sorelie musing in my mynde* or *The wind blawis cauld furius and bauld*. They may be called " profane " in that they are not sacred in the Christian sense, but they breathe of that spirit that will outlast all creeds. We see more of these profane things in the Bannatyne MS. (1568) in such as *The wowing of Jock and Jenny* and *The ballat of guid fallowis*, and in those mentioned in *Newes from Scotland* (1591), where *Commer goe ye before* and *The silly bit chicken* suggest a different vein. Some of these Scottish songs went far afield. *Tak your auld cloak about ye* possibly adorns Shakespeare's *Othello*, whilst *O Bothwell Banks thou blumest fair* was heard in distant Palestine, as we know from Verstegan's *Restitution of Decayed Intelligence* (1605), and all without corrupting the morals of either the English or the Arabs. Many protested against this narrow bigotry and among them the old lawyer Sir Richard Maitland (d. 1586), who longed for the old times when there was merry-making,—" blitheness, dancing, singing, game, and play."

As the Scottish historian Thomas Faulds Henderson has so well expressed it in his *James the First and Sixth* (1904), " The most dangerous element of Puritanism was its narrow intolerance—its determination to foist on the nation a rudely fanatical and cast-iron system of morals and manners, which left almost no scope, not merely for harmless recreation, but for the free exercise of man's higher intelligence, *and for the noble enjoyment of art*." James VI had himself said in his *Basilikon Doron* (1599) that the Reformed clergy were more arrogant and intolerant than those of the church they were supposed to have reformed, whilst by insisting on the supremacy of the church over the state the Presbyter was no better than the Priest. Not that James was a paragon in this respect since, not being content with his temporal greatness, he deluded himself into a belief of a spiritual supremacy. " Kings," he fervently believed, " are the word of God called Gods, . . . and so adorned and furnished with some sparks of the Divinity." The English, with their usual forbearance, forgave him that conceit, but they sent his son to the block for attempting to put it into practice.

CHAPTER 3

THE INSTRUMENTS.

" *Organs* and *Regals* thair did carpe
With thair gay goldin gilttering strings,
Thair was the *Hautbois* and the *Harpe*
Playing maist sweit and pleasant springs ;
And some on *Lutis* did play and sing,
Of instruments the onely king.

Viols and *Virginals* were heir
With *Githornis* maist jucundious,
Trumpets and *Timbrels* maid gret beir,
With instruments melodious ;
The *Seister* and the *Sumphion*,
With *Clarche Pipe* and *Clarion*."

Burel : *The Queenis . . . Entry* (1590).

Almost everywhere in wide, western Europe, was this a period
of the utmost importance in the domain of instruments of music.
Playing had now been exalted to a position equal to, if not higher
than singing.   From the craftsman's point of view this was long
overdue.   Formerly, singing enjoyed a halo under the church's
protection, but the rise of craft guilds to power, plus the *Zeitgeist*
that was sweeping through German speaking lands, soon brought
different values, and playing, which demanded a longer apprentice-
ment than singing, came into its own.   The very implements of
the player now called for special notice and attention.   In 1511,
a German priest named Virdung had issued a treasured book,
Musica getutscht, i.e. " Music Germanized," which was eagerly
read by the multitude, for earlier works had been in Latin.   Herein,
instruments were not merely described but they were shown in
woodcuts.   Then came an even more useful book by a Lutheran
precentor named Martin Agricola entitled *Musica Instrumentalis*
(1528), which ran into five editions.   In these books it was demonstrated what instruments were like physically, and they also revealed
how to play them, which was more than could be learned in the
Middle Ages unless one happened to be apprenticed to a member
of a minstrel guild.   What is more, this new outlook on instruments
of music came from Protestant Germany, where the art and practice

had risen to even greater heights than in pre-Reformation days. In England and Scotland however, it was different. To some extent this was because of the narrow path which the Reformation took in these lands, especially in the latter, where instrumental music was discountenanced, to use no stronger word.

Since the *organ* and *regal* are the first instruments lauded by Burel in his pæan, they receive priority here. We have already observed the attitude of the Reformers to the organ. Everywhere the instruments in cathedrals, collegiate churches, monasteries, and parish churches were " assailed by the populace," as the Rev. Charles Rogers tells us, and where they were not " broken up," they were abolished. The Rev. Dr. James Begg also avers that they " were mostly destroyed," those of the Chapel Royal excepted. This is probably why Burel gives the instrument a place, since it was a royal occasion of which he speaks. Yet at the outset one is naturally querulous of those " gay golden glittering strings " which he mentions in connection with the *organ* and *regal*. " Strings " of pulsatile usage could not be a structural part of these instruments, and yet, to what does the allusion apply ? Possibly the word *carpe* supplies a clue. Does it hint at the cords or bands by which the *regal* was carried and supported ? If so, the insinuation is that these " gay glittering " cords appealed as much to the eye in their harmonious colours as the concordant sounds of the pipes did to the ear.

Next, and likewise a keyed instrument, was the *virginal*. This had already outclassed the *clavicord* and *monycord*, of which we have read in the previous part. In the *virginal* the strings were " plucked " by means of levered quills, whereas in the *clavicord* and *monycord* the strings were " struck " by levered tangents. The former was a much more effective instrument for several reasons, but chiefly because, when struck, the strings were free to vibrate, whilst in the latter, when the tangents struck the strings, the very impact deadened the sound. Mary Queen of Scots played " reasonably [well] for a Queen " upon the *virginal*, as we are informed by Sir James Melville. It is this latter also who tells us that his fellow students at St. Andrews played " intently (*fellon*) well " on it. The *spinet* or rectangular instrument was also popular in Scotland at this period although Melville calls it the *pinalds*. In those days there was no music of Scottish origin for these instruments, although Robert Johnson, the priest who had fled to England " lang before the Reformation," was already delighting the Sassenach with some intricate pavans, still extant, for the *virginal*.

Among the stringed instruments we must give place to the *harp*. Whether Burel's instrument was the Highland *clarsech* or the Lowland species we know not, but the harp that adorns the borders of the illuminated pages of Wood's psalter (1562-66), with a straight front pillar, might very well be outwith either type, since it is shown with nine strings, i.e. giving perhaps the diatonic scale with the major and minor thirds. Actual specimens that have come down to us from this period, the Lamont and the Queen Mary harps, are quite different. The former, with thirty-two strings, is said to date from 1464, but rather a century later would be a nearer date. The latter, with twenty-nine strings (later augmented to thirty) is probably 16th century. Both of these instruments are preserved in the National Museum of Antiquities in Edinburgh, with casts in replica at the Art Galleries and Museum in Glasgow. By the 16th century the harp was beginning to fall into neglect in the Lowlands where the lute and viol had challenged its supremacy. It does not appear at court except, if rumour can be trusted, in the hands of Mary Queen of Scots. Yet it was in firm repute in the Highlands, as we know from Buchanan (1565). Here the chieftains still maintained their feudal hereditary *clarsair*.

The fingerboard stringed instruments of the period were the *lute, gittern, pandore,* and *mandore*. The *lute* had been the chief instrument of this group for a century or more, and Burel recognizes it as " of instruments the only king." According to Brantôme and Melville, the *lute* was played by Mary Queen of Scots, and Melville says that it was in the hands of the students at St. Andrews. We have four instruments of the lute class delineated by Wood in his psalter (1562-66), all of which retain the ancient Oriental outline

PLATE VI

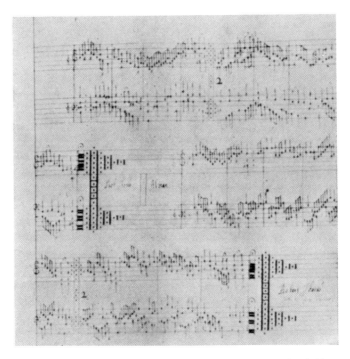

Fitzwilliam Museum, Cambridge.

TWO ALMANS BY ROBERT JOHNSON (d. 1562)
Fitzwilliam Virginal (17th Century).

PLATE VII

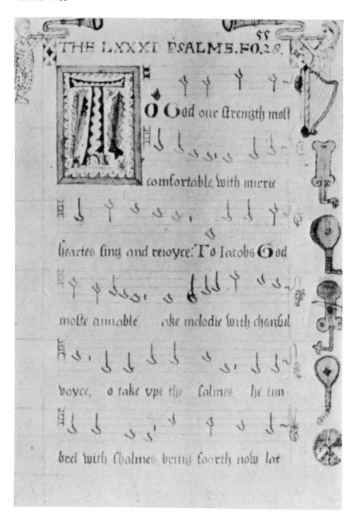

PSALM LXXXI arr. by JOHN BUCHAN
Wood's MS. Psalter (1562-66).

and mien. The first that occurs in the psalter's margin is a four string *lute* with its characteristic bridge-tailpiece or string-holder. The second instrument, with a smaller and hemispherical sound-chest, is probably a *pandore*. This also has four strings. The fourth instrument in the margin of the opposite page of the psalter might conceivably be the *mandore*, since its strings are not attached to a string-holder on the belly of the instrument, but seemingly to small pins underneath the bottom. All three instruments have convex sound-chests.

The " jocund " *githorn* of Burel was the same as Holland's *gittyrn* " gay " of the preceding century, and the similarity of the honorific adjective is passing strange. It had a flat sound-chest with incurvatures at the side like the modern *guitar*, which is its linear and lineal descendant. Again we read that the *githorn* was among the instruments of the students at St. Andrews in 1574. In the Donaldson Collection at the Royal College of Music in London there is a *guitar* which " is said " to have belonged to Mary Queen of Scots. The instrument itself reveals French workmanship although this does not necessarily exclude the Scottish queen's ownership of it. The *gittern*, *gittyrn*, or *githorn* also had four strings, as we know from Anthony Holbourne's *Cittharne School* (1597).

Next come the bowed or rubbed instruments, the *rebec*, *fiddle*, *viol*, and *symphony*, the first three being played with a bow. That the *rebec* was still favoured seems proved by Brantôme's reference to it in the rejoicings at Mary's arrival at Holyrood from France in 1561, when he tells of an " aubade de méschants *violons* et petits *rebecs* " with psalm singing. From his phrases, " mal accordez " and " Hé ! quelle musique," he was certainly not pleased with the result. Calderwood (d. 1650), the church's historian, being a good Presbyterian, does not mention instruments on this occasion, contenting himself with reference to " music " and " musicians," with which, he says, the Queen was " well pleased." A few weeks later, after another short absence from the capital, there was more rejoicing at the Queen's return, and this time, in the midst of pageantry, she was presented with a " Psalme Buik," at which gift we imagine she was not " well pleased." Both *violins* and *rebecs* must have been as common as psalm books in these days since Brantôme says of them that " there is no scarcity in this country."

We see the *violin* of the period, with its old cumbersome bow, in the hands of Rizzio in Lord Seafort's portrait of the favoured Italian musician-valet. *Viols*, in sizes of treble, tenor, and bass, seem to have been used at court, or at least *four* violars are provided, and we know from the Rizzio incident how particular Mary was over the complete four parts. When James VI was received by the Edinburgh magistrates in 1579, there were *four* violars employed, and both these and the *sangsters* received 30s. for their services. There is a delineation of a *bass viol* with four (?) strings and an unusual lute-like peg-box turned at right angle in Wood's psalter (1562-66). Nor were makers wanted in Scotland since two names at least have come down to us,—Rose (1598) and Smith (1633).

The last of the rubbed instruments is the *symphony*. This is the *sumphion* mentioned by Burel. It was a refined hurdy-gurdy, a stringed instrument shaped and furnished like a viol but played with a rosined wheel which rubbed the strings, the various notes being obtained, not by finger stopping, but by levered tangents. It was of ancient origin and very popular with strolling players hence its name *lyra mendicorum* or *lyra rustica*. We find a *symphioun* mentioned in the Edinburgh Burgh Records of 1582.

Then come that large family of wind instruments. The flute section was represented by the *recorder*, *flute*, and *whistle*. As we have seen, the *recorder* was a *flûts à bec*, not the transverse flute that we know to-day, yet at the concert at Stirling Castle when the son of James VI was baptized in 1594 the account distinctly mentions " *recoders* and *fluts*," although another entry concerning the same event speaks of a *flute recorder*. A smaller type of flute was the *whistle* or rather the *quhisil* in " auld Scots." Being shriller in sound, it was eminently suitable for military and burgh service, and at Edinburgh in 1559, a *quhisler* had 6s. 8d. for playing the " watch " at night. At the capital also we find the *quhyssil* and *trumpet* together in 1565. By this time the whistle had become known as the *fyfe*.

The *shawm* was still in use, although it had, more generally, been superseded by the *hautbois*, a much more delicately toned instrument. Sometimes we see them in use together, but Burel only specifies the *hautbois*. Mary Queen of Scots rewarded an *howbois* player and a trumpeter with ten crowns in 1562. These two instruments came to be looked upon as complementary and we find them thus at Prince Henry's baptism in 1594. What Burel's *clarche pipe* was like can only be guessed. May be was an early form of reed-pipe like our clarionet, which could easily be called a *clarus pipe*, i.e. a " clear-sounding pipe." It might even have been the *stockhorn*. One imagines that the tenor shawn or hautbois, which was known as the *curtall*, was still in use, although it is not actually mentioned at this period.

The *bagpipe* continued to be the favourite instrument of the people, as we know from the kirk's frown at its too frequent use in merrymaking. Its structure seems to have remained the same, with one or two drones and the chanter, and was recognized as a definitely martial instrument. It was probably used at Belrinnes (1594), and from Alexander Hume's reference to it in the Bannatyne MS, " On Heiland pipes, Scottes, and Hybernicke," we might suppose that two different kinds were in use in 1598. Moneypennie, in his *Certain Curious Matters Concerning Scotland* (1597), says that with the Highlanders, " in place of a drum they use a bagpipe."

Instruments with a cup mouthpiece, such as the *trumpet* and *clarion*, both praised by Burel, were used by the army and burgh, as well as at court. The *cornett* is not mentioned, although it must have been in use since we find it flourishing as late as 1696. According to Horman (1529) the ordinary *trumpet* was the short instrument with a straight tube. The old *trump*, which had a long straight tube, had been made more portable by two devices. One was by fashioning the tube into bends of snake-like curves as exemplified in the drawings in Wood's psalter (1562-66). The other, as Horman tells us, was by bending the tube upon itself, as in the modern fashion, which instrument was called the *clarion*. The Jaws Harp, likewise called the *trump*, was a great favourite with the folk. Geillis Duncan played upon it at the witches saturnalia at North Berwick in 1590, and repeated the performance before James VI, as we read in *Newes from Scotland* (1591).

Like the trumpeters, the drummers, generally called *tabronars* or *suescheris* at this time, were still to the fore in military and burghal service. Both the *tabron* or *talburn*, also called *suesch* or *swash*, were side-drums in those days, very little different in shape from what they are today. Six *tabrons* were used in 1560 at the opening of Parliament, but in 1565, for the same ceremony, the instrument is dubbed a *swash*. This latter name had come from the military men who had adopted the martial instruments of the Swiss infantry, hence the *tibia Helvetica* and the *swache talburn*. The *timbrels*, which Burel says " made great noise (*birr*)," were usually tambourines, but here perhaps, the poet refers to *tabrons* which would, more commonly, accompany trumpets.

CHAPTER 4

THE CHURCH.

" Notwithstanding of this travell I have taken [in editing my book],
I cannot understand bot musike sall perish in this land alutterlye."
Thomas Wood : *Psalter* (1562-66).

In speaking of the Reformation, Heine once urged that the art of Michel Angelo and Titian were " much more fundamental theses than those which the German monk [Luther] nailed to the church door of Wittenberg." It may be so, since the crowd were never much impressed by theses. Indeed, one feels inclined to believe that the unanimous *dicta* of the Protestant reformers that the church's vocal praise should come from the people rather than from the priesthood was of far greater moment in the reforming movement than either Luther's theses or the appeal to the humanizing visual arts. You can always command success if you appeal to the crowd's emotions, and the sure and certain way is to allow the fullest scope to *their* voices, as community singing completely proves. When the church transferred vocal praise from the vicars-choral to the congregation they flattered the peoples vanity and secured their attention.

There was not however, complete unanimity among the Reformers as to what form the crowd's vocal praise should take when the word went forth,—" Let the people sing." There were two schools, (1) The Lutherans who, whilst favouring congregational praise, retained much of the Roman service, but in the vernacular : and (2) The Calvinists, who, at first, would have nothing to do with the " Papistic stuff " as the old service was called, and eschewed even the plainest harmony in the psalms which alone were retained in church music. Of course, Luther was a musician, and that is why England, France, and Germany retained, to their eternal glory, so much of the musical service of the old church. In Scotland, unfortunately, the views of Calvin became the norm, to the utter neglect of this older music.

We have already seen that the early Christian Fathers, and even a few of the later churchmen of England and Scotland, were averse to instrumental and polyphonic music within the church. The first English Protestant, Wycliffe (d. 1384), railed against " descant, countre note and organs . . . that stirreth vain men to dauncing more than mourning." Yet some of the new reformers were more pointed in their views, in most cases because polyphonic music was beyond their ken, or perhaps their opposition was simply temperamental. Zwingli (d. 1531), for example, was quite contemptuous when he said that " the roaring in the churches, scarce understood by the priests themselves, is a foolish and vain abuse, and a most pernicious hindrance to piety." Erasmus (d. 1536) was cruelly derisive. To him it was " a tedious and capricious kind of music, . . . a tumultuous noise of different voices, . . . for the keeping up thereof whole choirs of boys are maintained at great expence, . . . a thing that is pestiferous." Calvin (d. 1564), whose views counted most in Scotland, was equally against this so-called artificial music and was averse to so simple an artistic device as harmony. In his introduction to the Genevan psalter (1543) he speaks at length on what was to be musically admissible as church praise. " It should always be seen to " he says, " that the [church] song should not be light and frivolous, but that it have weight and majesty, . . . [for] there is a great difference between the music that is employed for the enjoyment of men at table, and in their houses, and the psalms they sing in church in the presence of God and the angels." On this account Calvin urges that the music of church praise should be " simply constructed." Plainer still are his views on instrumental music in the service of the church. " It would be simply a ridiculous imitation of Papistry to decorate churches and to believe that it is offering God nobler service by using organs and other amusements of that kind." Thus says Calvin in his sermon on I *Samuel*, xviii. A note on Calvin's attitude towards music, as reported by Zwingli, is contained in a British Museum MS. (*Sloane*, 1021).

Almost everywhere, because of such affirmations, there was a protest against instrumental music in the first flush of the Reformation.   In Geneva there is some evidence of this forbiddance, although not in Germany. The Lower House of Convocation in England considered the playing of organs in churches a " foolish vanity," and so late as 1586 a pamphlet spoke of organs as a fashion of " Antichrist the Pope," but here the animus soon faded away. In Scotland it was different. Yet since the authoritative doctrinal books of the Reformation in Scotland do not actually mention instrumental music, it has been thought that, fundamentally, there was no objection to this kind of music. David Hay Fleming says, " Neither in the *Book of Common Order*, nor in the *Book of Discipline*, nor in the *Confession of Faith*, is there any direct reference to instrumental music. The reason probably is that there were comparatively few organs in the English Church in Edward the Sixth's time, and fewer still in Scotland before the Reformation." So far as these doctrinal works are concerned, his statement is true enough, but neither is there any reference to vestments in these books. If we have no *words* from the church about such things its *deeds* sufficiently demonstrate its attitude towards the " kist o' whistles " and " Roman ragges," as the organ and vestments were so charitably dubbed. Even Fleming admits that " from several casual record references it appears that the few [organs] which were in Scotland were cast out of the churches : and apparently there was no desire to have them restored."

In the year 1560-61, the Edinburgh Dean of Guild reported £6 as the result of a sale of " three bellows of the organs," although he made a much better bargain for a cross and two chalices. In 1574, the organ at Aberdeen was ordered " to be removed out of the kirk " with all " expedition," and it was decreed that the profit derived from its sale should be put " to the use and support of the poor." It was a Calvinistic echo, for such had been proposed at Geneva when the organ of Rive was to be sold for the same purpose. Not all the organs in Scotland were destroyed or sold, because there is a Privy Council enquiry concerning church property in 1576, when *organs* are mentioned, their whereabouts being duly attested, although they were not in use. Incidentally, the supression of organs did not affect the Chapel Royal at Stirling or Holyrood as we have seen, and so early in the Reforming days as 1562, Mary was having her organ at Holyrood repaired.

The attitude of the Reformers towards polyphony was due to Scotland following Calvin rather than Luther. The result was a plain homophonic psalmody, whilst that which was really " weighty and majestic," to use Calvin's words, in the polyphonic music of the old church was considered mere vanity and expunged from the service. It is no wonder that the Protestant apologist for psalmody, the Rev. Dr. Neil Livingston, calls the period that followed " the ' dark age of church music in Scotland." Nor was it certain at the outset that even a homophonic and unadorned psalmody was to be admitted. In Whittingham's preface to *The Forme of Prayers . . . in the English Congregation at Geneva* (1566) we read that there were two kinds of prayer, one with words only, and another " with songs joined thereto," but the latter he says, was " called by many into doubt *whether it may be used in a reformed church*."

What psalms were used during the early period of reform in Scotland, and to what *tunes* they were sung, provide an interesting interlude.

In the mid-" Forties," certain psalms and spiritual songs in the vernacular were certainly being sung both openly and secretly in Scotland. These had been compiled by the brothers Wedderburn, James, John and Robert. Calderwood (d. 1650) says of John, who had heard both Luther and Melanchthon, that he translated " many of Luther's *dytements* into Scottish metre, and the Psalms of David. He turned many bawdy songs and rhymes in Godly rhymes." Robert is said to have edited his brother's work and supplied the appropriate tunes. This production was *The Compendious Book of Psalms and Spiritual Songs*, commonly known as *The Gude and Godlie Ballatis*, a work which must have been known prior to January 1545-46, although the earliest edition that we possess was issued in 1567. *The Gude and Godlie Ballatis* was never formally sanctioned by the Church, for it contained many things which the latter Reformers did not countenance, including Christmas carols, to say nothing of some " indelicate and gross " ballads, as Dr. Thomas McCrie calls them, for whilst a few might have snickered at the lines,

> " God send to everie priest ane wyfe,
> And everie nunne a man."

the Church, as a body, would certainly have shunned such wholesome bluntness.

The tunes for the psalms were not indicated, save in one instance, but some of those of the ballads came from secular sources, and among them such popular tunes as *Johne cum kis me now*, *For our Gud man*, *With Huntis up*, and others. Popular airs to religious words had been frequent in early days as the *cantus planus* in the Mass, and the Reformers in France were already adopting a similar device to catch the people's ears. It was the same in England, and Shakespeare, whose eye and ear nothing escaped, duly noted this in *A Winter's Tale*, where in the " songmen " he espies " one Puritan amongst them, and he sings psalms to hornpipes." Indeed, when the Wedderburns wrote the lines,—

> " Preistis, change your *tone*,
>   And sing into your mother tung
>   *Inglis* Psalmes, . . . "

the change of *tune*, for that was what *tone* meant, was a plain hint
that a *lilt* was preferable to a *stilt*. The sole reign of *The Gude
and Godlie Ballatis* was not long (*c*.1542-50), because the psalm
books of Genevan, i.e. Calvinistic tradition, soon became the rule.
Had the first response to the Reformation in Scotland, which was
Lutheran, held its ground, the lamentable history of its music might
have been different.

The next source of vocal praise for the Reformers (*c*.1550-57)
was probably the English *Al suche Psalmes of David* (1549) of
Sternhold and Hopkins. There then followed, it would seem, the
use of the *One and Fiftie Psalmes* (1556) and Wood's psalter of
1562-66 tells us that the Genevan *Foure Score and Seven Psalmes*
(1561) came next for adoption, the *tunes* of which Wood borrowed.
This was superseded by the first Scottish psalter, *The Forme of
Prayers* (1564), in which the mere tunes of the psalms were given,
and this feature became the rule in all subsequent Scottish psalters
until 1625, when Scotland issued her first partly harmonized psalter.

Dr. Neil Livingston, the painstaking editor of, and the best
authority on the 1635 psalter, has tried to explain the reason why
" the Church left the musical element [the harmony] uncared for "
in this way. He says that " it might have been to reduce the price
of psalm books, or because a lower sense of the importance of
regulating the music was entertained ; but there is ground to suspect
that it was partly from deference to parties in England with whom
they anticipated permanent union, but those views in this matter
tended to extremes." Yet the latter excuse could scarcely have
been the explanation since the English psalter, *The Whole Psalmes
in Foure Partes* (1563), had already been printed. Nor can we
believe that " expense " was the reason. The history of the attitude
of the Reformation in Scotland towards music proves, without the
least shadow of doubt, that no music other than the " plain tune "
was to be allowed, and even that was to be vocal. In France, this
solemn adherence to the tune alone, which was in accord with

Calvin's " simply constructed " and " undecorate " psalmody, had long been dropped, for Goudimel had already (1551) set Marot's psalms in 3, 4, and 5 parts, and the same was happening in Germany, where the whole Lutheran service was thus set.

In England, a land which Scotland had hoped to bring into a common policy in this respect, it was urged by the Commissioners of Edward VI that the singing should be " clear," and disapproval was enunciated of " quavering operose music which is called figured." In Pierce's *Vindication* however, it is made palpably clear why " plain singing " was preferred. It was claimed that the " kind of singing used in Cathedrals is so curious and difficult that *it is beyond the capacity of the people*." This latter then, was the crux of the situation, and it was thus that Scotland judged the problem as seen by Neil Livingston. Fortunately for England, this attitude was the minority opinion and it found little acceptance, and so this country escaped what Dr. Ernest Walker has called " this ruinous artistic calamity," and was soon pusuing her old path in cultivating the best church music. Here the finest musicians of the day were contributing to the church service, and in Day's *Certaine Notes* (1560) and the *Mornyng and Evenyng Prayer* (1565), the Scottish composer, Robert Johnson of Duns, driven from his own land, was displaying his wondrous gifts in four part writing for *English* congregations. In Scotland it was different, at least officially.

It might be argued that the Scottish Reformers could not do otherwise than adhere to the mere " tune " in psalmody because, having destroyed the old music, banished the old professional choir and organists, and reduced the Sang Schools to impotence where they were not already suppressed, the Reformed Church could not help itself. Yet this is not the whole truth, for there were still a few of those professionals of the choir of days of old who, for sheer subsistence, had accepted service in the Reformed Church, and were available if the musical needs of the latter demanded. Obviously, they were not wanted, because all vocal praise had to come from the body of the kirk, and such an idea as " hired " or

unhired " professionals " was, to the Presbyteries, a thing "pestiferous." As the *Book of Common Order* tells us, it was for the people
to " sing a Psalm all together, in a *plain* tune." This had been the
traditional custom of the Reformers as we know from the *Brieff
Discours off the Troubles Begonne at Franckford* (1554), wherein it
was agreed that the people should " sing a psalm in metre in a
plain tune, as was, and is accustomed in the French, Dutch, Italian,
Spanish, and *Scottish* churches." Still, as *plain* as it was, we are
not told the results, especially in Scotland. Perhaps it is best
left to the musical imagination. At any rate, only the " Minister,
Exhorter, and Reader " were compelled to have a psalm book
according to what the General Assembly ordained in December 1564.
How the congregation fared without it is not recorded. No wonder
W. S. Provand, in his Hastie Lecture (1914) on *Puritanism in the
Scottish Church* (1923) avers that " musical culture seems to have
been at a very low ebb, for it is provided that the Psalms are to be
sung *when possible.*" Indeed this latter is clear from the *First
Book of Discipline* (1560) where we read,—" In some churches
Psalms may be conveniently sung, *in others they cannot.*"

What we do know is that the " people " were not a success at
first, and they were enjoined to " exercise themselves in the Psalms "
so as to be proficient when they came to church, as the above book
reveals. Yet even this injunction did not make for the promised
land in psalmody, as we see these same Reformers, tongue in cheek
probably, being compelled eventually to hire the same professionals,
whom they had once spurned, to help them out of their musical
troubles. These were appointed " Takers up of the Psalms," as
they are dubbed in the *Second Book of Discipline* (1561), a proceeding
perilously akin to a Popish practice. Even this saving grace did
not suffice since it was soon necessary for the " up-taker " to be
assisted by others who were appointed by the Kirk Session. This
is what happened in Glasgow in 1587 where it was ordered that
" Mr. William Struthers, teacher of music, shall sing in the High
Kirk . . . and appoint *four men to sit beside him.*" This looks as
though they were there to assist in singing, more especially when

in the next year (1588) it was ordered " that the *sangsters* in town sing with Mr. Struthers on Sunday."

In spite therefore of what we read in the English psalter of 1556, which the Scots adopted at first, where the Papists are sneered at for " hiring men " to sing " curious music of a wanton sort," we see that the Reformers themselves were compelled to fall back on the system of employing professionals, and among them probably a few confident souls, lately vicars-choral who, for sheer artistic joy rather than religious conviction probably, were only too glad to accept office which would enable them to salvage something from the wreckage of reforming zeal. It was these people who formed a rallying point of musical culture within the Reformed Church, prompted by ideals of a most praiseworthy nature. Of this movement we have the evidence of Thomas Wood and his psalter (1562-66), which will be dealt with later.

That something more than psalm singing found acceptance through this urge, although possibly not under official sanction, might be argued from the inclusion of spiritual songs in Wood's manuscript psalter. These also show themselves in the printed psalter of 1571, where the settings of *The Ten Commandments*, the *Nunc Dimittis*, and *The Lord's Prayer* have a place. The 1575 psalter adds the *Second Lamentation*, *Veni Creator*, and a doxology. These continued, more or less, in later psalters of this period but, as Dr. Neil Livingston points out, " there seems to be good ground for the conclusion that they were only used for private purposes." It is certain that whilst psalm singing is featured in the literature of the period, there is no mention of these spiritual songs.

So long as the old vicars-choral, and the choir-boys who had by now grown up, were available, there was still some part-singing to be heard on *extra mural* occasions, as we know from the account of John Durie's return to Edinburgh in 1582, when a psalm *in four parts* is expressly mentioned as being sung. Within the Church itself the rule was " the *tune* and nothing but the *tune*," although other opinions prevail on this point. It was stated authoritatively on the radio (12th Nov. 1935) that "part-singing soon came into general use, and for a time it appears to have been fairly general." The truth is that part-singing was not officially recognized until 1625, and one can scarcely consider sixty-five years after the Reformation as "soon." Secondly, that part-singing was "fairly general," we have but little evidence even in 1635. The best historian of psalmody in Scotland, Neil Livingston, is more guarded in his utterances on this question, although they vary. He says, "There is no reason to think that the practice of part-singing was discouraged by the Church, or neglected by congregation." Later however, he is not so confident of this opinion and admits that "the amount of part-singing ... may have been chiefly by individuals dispersed among their fellow worshippers." Lastly he confesses that "it is not likely that the project of providing harmony was formally sanctioned by the church authorities, but leading men may have given their approval privately."

Two things are certain, (1) That a plain homophony continued to be the norm in the church itself until 1625, when the first harmonized Common Tunes appeared. This was in accordance with the rubric of the *Order of Geneva*,—"The people sing a Psalm all together in a *plain tune*." (2) That part-singing was actually discouraged by the church is partly suggested by the Perth Kirk Session of 1583 where we read that John Swinton was ordered "to keep [to] the tenor [the melody] in singing the psalm." Further, outside of the Chapel Royal, there is not the slightest evidence of part-singing *in the church* at this period. There was, it is true, the manuscript psalter of Thomas Wood which dates from 1562-66, with later additions, but there is no mention of it ever having found usage during this period, and Wood's own lamentation that music would perish in Scotland was doubtless prompted by the Church's open neglect of his harmonized psalter. That the words as well as the music itself were under strict censorship is evident from the close eye kept on John Buchan the composer. In the year 1596, whilst he was Master of the Sang School and Reader at the New Kirk in Glasgow, he seems to have given offence in this respect. It was therefore ordered that " there be nothing read or sung . . . but that which is contained in the word of God."

Thus the music of the Kirk in Scotland went on its doleful way. Even Thomas Wood, the leader of the movement in support of good music in the church, eventually realized the hopelessness of the struggle against the fiats of the Reformers and the general apathy of the people. His piteous cry in the quotation at the head of this chapter reveals the state of affairs that had come to Scotland, the land that had produced Robert Johnson of Duns, Robert Carver of Scone, and Robert Douglas of Dunkeld.

CHAPTER 5

THE MUSIC.

" I have said . . . that Musik will pereishe, and this buke will shaw you sum resons quhy : We se be experiance that craft nor scyence is not learnit bot to the end he [that learns] may leive be it quhen he has the craft or scyence : and if Dr. Fa[y]rfax wer alyve in this cuntry he wald be contemnit, and pereise for layk of mentinance : and sa of neid force it [Musik] man dikeay."

Thomas Wood : *Psalter* (1562-66).

It is just as well that the reader should have this further lament from the painstaking Vicar of St. Andrews, because this chapter will show that these fears that music would perish in Scotland came to be realized. In spite of all his " travail," and the labours of his coadjutors, the Reformers turned a deaf ear to his harmonized psalter and spurned his spiritual songs and hymns. As for the men who were doubtless willing to compose and arrange music for the Reformed church, men like John Angus, Andrew Blackhall, David Peebles, John Buchan, Andrew Kemp, John Black, John Fethy, and other musicians, not the slightest gesture was made by the church towards them in this respect.

Just imagine so great an event in Scottish history (as these days would have deemed it) as the nuptials of James VI being denied recognition by the art of music. It was reserved for a German, Abraham Praetorius, *in Germany*, to contribute an *Harmonia Gratulatoria Nuptiis* for six voices. The fame of Scotland's great literator George Buchanan was worldwide, and his polished Latin has not been surpassed by any modern. Yet nobody in Scotland rose to the occasion of setting his graceful verses of the psalms to music. Once again it was a German, Statius Olthoff (d. 1629), a precentor at Rostock, who made four-part settings of them in his *Psalmorum Davidis paraphrasis poetica Georgii Buchanani Scoti: Argumentis ac melodiis explicata atque illustrata* (Frankfort, 1585). The reason for the neglect is easily explained. By this time there were scarcely any of the old school of composers left in Scotland, and even those who had survived were either past the urge or, through lack of encouragement, were no longer interested. This was the situation to which Scotland had been brought by the Reformers, for they had " killed the goose that laid the golden egg " in music, since the Roman Church, with all its faults, did support this art in its highest forms. Obviously, the latter did not encourage it for its own sake, but rather for the glory of the church. Still, music benefited, just as did architecture and the arts in general. Unfortunately, in their urge to remove what was evil in the old church, the Reformers swept away much that was good, including its music, although this " reform " was already a settled policy. As the apologist of Reformation psalmody, Dr. Neil Livingston, has testified, this " reform " was not " the result of blind impulse or weak compliance, but of *enlightened preference and conscientious conviction*."

The Rev. James W. Macmeeken (*Scottish Metrical Psalms*) says that " the Scottish Reformers made Congregational Psalmody a stated portion of public worship," and officially the only music of the Reformed Church of this era, was that contained in the Scottish psalters from 1564 to the close of the century. That of 1564 was the one called *The Forme of Prayers . . . with the Whole Psalmes of David in English meter*, in which the *plain* tune only was given to the psalms in accordance with Genevan procedure. Each psalm was assigned a tune considered " proper " to it, and later these came to be called Proper Tunes. With five or six exceptions, all these tunes can be traced to Anglo-Genevan (1556, 1558, 1561),

English (1561, 1562), and French (1551, 1557) psalters, as well as two other minor sources. That being so, it might be said that there cannot be anything particularly Scottish about the music of this psalter. Such a deduction would not be strictly correct because it is highly probable that some of the Anglo-Genevan examples are of Scottish origin, and certainly the music of the Psalms LXVI, LXXX, CXVI, CXL and CXLV, have prior claim to Scottish parentage.

Of course the English also borrowed from this fount in their psalter, but the latter contains only forty-five psalm and eighteen hymn tunes, whereas the Scottish psalter has one hundred and five tunes for its psalms alone. This is not the only difference between the music of the two psalters, since the versification in the Scottish production, having such wide and venturesome metrical settings, produced a most varied rhythmical structure to the tunes, which gave the Scottish psalter a superiority over the English. Nor must we omit to mention the three Scottish versifiers, William Kethe, Robert Pont, and John Craig who, between them, supplied forty-six out of the one hundred and fifty psalms.

The late Sir Richard Terry has explained the musical disparity between the two psalters thus :—" The greater metrical variety in the Scottish Psalter naturally gave the composers [or rather the arrangers mainly] of the tunes greater scope. But even when they were confined to Ballad Metre they shook off its monotony in rather bolder, or at any rate more forthwith fashion, than their English contemporaries. Where the latter fought metrical monotony with subtle *contrapuntal* devices, the Scotsmen got their variety by melodic means " (*A Forgotten Psalter*). Again, quoting the same authority, we read elsewhere :—" The Scottish Psalter . . . sets an example which all subsequent psalters (especially the English ones) would have done well to follow. The English psalters are characterized by the monotonous preponderance of Ballad Metre. In the Scottish Psalter you find as much variety and freedom as in the German chorales. After you have eliminated the ordinary metres (L.M., S.M., and C.M.), there still remain thirty-five varieties in the Scottish Psalter" (Preface to Farmer's *Music in Mediaeval Scotland*).

This laudation concerns the official, plain and naked homophony of the Scottish psalter, for harmony, i.e. music in parts, was disallowed within the church, although, in its very earliest years, the introduction of harmony seems to have got the merest footing at St. Andrews, the Chapel Royal, and perhaps elsewhere. It came about, as already hinted, through a handful of enthusiasts, belonging musically to the *ancien régime*, who longed for a return to the polyphony of the old service, something like that which obtained in the English church. Foremost among these music lovers were Lord James Stewart and Thomas Wood or Wode, and it was the latter who, during the years 1562-66, collected material for his book of psalms, canticles and hymns in 4 and 5 parts, one of the most precious of the documents that have come down to us from the militant days of the Reformation.

Lord James Stewart (d. 1570) was educated at the University of St. Andrews, within whose musical precincts he first evinced a love for music. As a minor (1538) he had been appointed Prior of St. Andrews, but at the Reformation (1559) he embraced the new faith. After a few years he came to realize the serious plight of music under the Reformed Church and secured the services of one of his canons, David Peebles, to set or re-arrange the plain music of the Genevan psalter in four parts. The whole story is told by Thomas Wood, whose name has so often been mentioned in these pages.

David Laing, the earliest writer on the Wood psalter, thought that Wood had previously " acted as Reader in one or other of the churches in Fife " before he went to St. Andrews. At the earliest fixed date (1562) that we know of Wood, he held a church post at St. Andrews, and later (1566) was at Dunbar. In 1575 he was given the vicarage at St. Andrews. Of his later career we know but little save the dates of his alterations and additions, in his own hand, to his psalter. Wood tells us that he had been gathering the musical material for his harmonized book of psalms, canticles and hymns since 1562, but was persuaded, in this year, to stay his hand awhile, as " the whole psalms were [already] printed at Geneva and were to come home shortly." When the Genevan book, the *Foure Score and Seven Psalmes* (1561), did " come home," Wood took the music of each of the psalms noted therein in the *plain melody*, and, in pursuance of Lord James Stewart's plan, proceeded to have them harmonized. We have seen that the latter had already commissioned David Peebles to do this work, but he seems to have been rather apathetic, probably because he was only a Reformer for sheer subsistence sake, and had as little interest in its music as its doctrines. At this juncture however Thomas Wood arrived in St. Andrews and, although not a composer but simply a passionate lover of music, he took the matter in hand from Peebles. How he went to work is well described in a note written in 1570, after the murder of his patron Lord James Stewart, then the Earl of Moray, at whose obsequies we imagine, Wood would have been present, since Knox preached the sermon and Buchanan contributed the epitaph. Here are Wood's words in modern English : " I have thought good to make it known who set the three parts to and agreeable to the Tenor, or common part of the Psalm book. The Mass and Papistical service abolished, and the preaching of the Evangel established here, into St. Andrews, My Lord James (who after was Earl of Moray and Regent) being at the Reformation, Prior of St. Andrews, causes one of his Canons, to name David Peebles, being one of the chief musicians into this land, to set three parts to the Tenor. And my Lord commanded the said David to leave the *curiosity* of music, and so make *plain* and *dulce*, and so he has done. But the said David was not earnest : But I being come to this Town, to remain, I was ever requesting and soliciting till they were all set. And the Canticles (like as *Veni Creator*, the *Song of Ambrose*, the *Song of Mary*, etc.) I oft did write to Master Andrew Blackhall, to John Angus. And some Andrew Kemp set. So I noted Tenors, and sent some to Mussel-burgh and some to Dunfermline, and so [they] were done. God grant we use them all to his glory. . . . To a great man that has but a reasonable grip of music, these five books were worthy of their weight in gold." Thus came into existence Wood's historic *Psalter* (1562-66), a work which owes nothing to the English *Whole Psalmes in Foure Parts* (1563) in the psalm setting, nor in the canticles and hymns to any borrowings from the Genevan psalter of 1561 which, by the way, only recognized in this latter *The Ten Commandments, The Lord's Prayer*, and the *Song of Simeon*, although most of the canticles and hymns themselves were approved in the English psalter of 1562.

Wood's first editing of his collection was completed by December 1566, but he made many additions, and even duplicate copies, at later dates (1569, 1570, 1578, etc.). The tenor, treble and bass parts of this psalter in holograph, together with duplicates of the first and last, are preserved at the National Library of Scotland. The contra tenor part, of later date (after 1578), with still later material in another hand (after 1604), is to be found in the British Museum. The " fifth book," so called by Wood himself, and dated 1569, is at Trinity College, Dublin. This latter volume contains, in Wood's own words, " Songs of four and five parts, meet and apt for musicians to recreate their spirits."

The Scottish composers and arrangers who contributed to Wood's collection were, David Peebles, John Angus, Andrew Kemp, John Buchan, Andrew Blackhall, and John Fethy. All of the psalms with two exceptions which were undertaken by John Buchan, were the work of David Peebles. The canticles, motets, and anthems (=voluntaries), were contributed by Kemp, Angus, Peebles, Blackhall and Fethy, most of them, so it would seem, being their compositions. Many anonymous works find a place in Wood's collection as well as those of two defunct masters of the old Scottish school, Robert Johnson and Robert Douglas. The contemporary compositions and arrangements shall be dealt with under each of the above composers and arrangers.

Nor was the good " Vicar of Sanctandrous " unmindful of the secular art. One might recall what he wrote in the Dublin supplementary volume when adding songs to the psalms. These he recommended, as one educated under the *ancien régime* naturally would, as a solace when people found themselves " overcome with heaviness, or any kind of sadness, not only musicians, but also even to the ignorant of a gentle nature, hearing shall be comforted, and be merry with us." And so Wood added his mite in this coin to his collection, wherein we find Tallis' *When shall my sorrowful sighing slack,* Orlando di Lasso's *Susanne un jour,* as well as some anonymous items, *O parsi sparsi, Ecco d' oro l' eta,* and " ane mirry sang " called *Un jour,* all of which he said was " singular gude musike."

The Wood psalter contains numerous errors, yet apart from these, the work as a whole, reveals a fairly high standard in spite of " consecutives " and a few other crude and forbidden things which may shock pedants and sticklers for propriety today. Of course, so far as the psalms and some other works are concerned, it must be understood that it was *commanded* that the work should be " plain and dulce," but in some instances the work shows that, given a modicum of freedom, these musicians of the erstwhile Roman Church could still write music that was interesting. Since neither Wood's psalter, nor its composers and arrangers (with one incorrect exception) have been noticed in Grove's *Dictionary of Music and Musicians* (1940), nor is there much better to be said of Eitner's *Quellen-Lexikon der Musiker* (1904), or the *Dictionary of National Biography,* some fuller account of the individual works of these musicians seems appropriate.

David Peebles, Pables or Peblis (d. 1579), of whom we have read in the previous chapter as " one of the principal musicians in all this land," was responsible for almost all the settings of the psalms in Wood's collection. He also composed the motet in four parts, *Quam multi Domine sunt,* written for " My Lord Marche," of which there are contra tenor copies in the British Museum, one being dated 1579.

John Buchan or Bughen, might have been, according to Dr. Neil Livingston, the son of Andrew Buchan who held the " parsonage of Dalmellington," a prebend of the Chapel Royal, who died about 1583. We know from a lengthy testimonial accorded John Buchan, Master of the Sang School at Haddington from 1583 to 1592, that he had " used his office and cure with all dexterity without offence or slander offered by him or against him." In the latter year however, this " most honest, quiet, and sober " man went in charge of the Sang School in Glasgow. In 1596, the Glasgow Presbytery ordered John Buchan, who was its " Reader " at the New Kirk, not to sing or read anything that was not contained in " the Word of God." He was still Master of the Sang School there in 1608. The two known psalms which he set for Thomas Wood were, *O God that is Lord*, and *Blessed art thou that fearest God*.

John Angus (*c*.1515-96) was one of the conventual brethren of the Abbey of Dunfermline. Wood speaks of him affectionately as " good Angus, good and *meike* John Angus." He was the precentor at the abbey in 1543, but soon after this he joined the Reformers, and so must have been one of the very apostles of the movement, being thereafter given one of the livings attached to the Chapel Royal at Stirling, although he still seems to have had connection with Dunfermline since Wood speaks of sending to this town when he was editing the canticles, seemingly to Angus He was certainly attached to a living there in 1584 because James VI granted a pension of £10 that year to John Angus, " Coventual brother of the said Abbay " and seven others of " his lovit daylie oratouris " of this establishment. Angus set and composed many hymns and canticles for Wood's collection, *The Song of the Thre Childring* (" O all ye workes of God "), *The Song of Zacharias* (" The onlye Lord of Israell "), *The Sang of the Blessit Virgin* (" My soule doth magnifie the Lord "), *The Sang of Simeon callit ' Nunc Dimitis '* (" O Lord, because my heart's desire "), *The Simboll or Creide of Athanasius* (" What man, soever he be "), *The Ten Commands* (" Attend my people "), *The Sang of Simeon* (" Now suffer me, O Lord "), *The Lord's Prayer*, *The XII Articles of our Belieff*, and *Da pacem Domine*.

Andrew Blackhall, Blakhall or Blakehall (1536?-1609) was, before the Reformation, " one of the conventual brethren of the Abbey of Holyroodhouse," but in 1567 was minister at Ormiston, where we read of him being subject to a censure at the hands of the General Assembly in that year. In 1574 he was transferred to Musselburgh where he remained until his death in 1609. According to the inscription placed on his tombstone, Blackhall was seventy-three when he died, hence his birth was fixed at 1536, but since he claimed assistance in 1593 on account of his *advanced age*, which at this reckoning would only be fifty-seven, it seems highly probable that his age at death in 1609 was ninety-three, *not* seventy-three, which would make the year of his birth 1516. Of his settings and compositions for Wood's collection are, *The humble Sute of a Synnar* (" O Lord, of whom I do depend "), *Robber Wisdome* (" Preserve us Lord "), *Voluntarie* (" Of mercye and of judgemente bothe "), and another *Voluntarie* or anthem (" Blessed art thou "). This latter was written at " the earnest sute of L[ord] Morto[n] " who presented it (" in propyne to the King ") to James VI. It is dated 1566, 1567 and 1569 in the various manuscripts. The first *Voluntarie* was " set and sent by Blakhall to my L[ord] Mar at his first marriage with my L[ord] of Angus's Sister." Both of these works are admirable, and reveal a constructive faculty of the highest order. Alas, Blackhall's progeny do not seem to have followed in his footsteps, as we read in 1627 that his son Andrew had disposed of the pension held in behoof of the " musick schoole " at Musselburgh which, in consequence, was then destitute.

Andrew Kemp or Kempt is not so well known biographically. In 1555 he appears to have been at the Sang School at Dundee, and in the " Sixties " was at a similar institution at St. Andrews, which we know was still flourishing in the stormy days of 1560. During 1570-73 he was Master of the Aberdeen Sang School. His *Te Deum* in the Wood collection has been placed first among the " Certain Godly Songs, perfectly set in four parts, and singular good music." Here also are to be found his *Veni Creator spiritus* (" Cum, Holy Ghost") which is of outstanding grace, *The Complaint of ane Sinner* (" Where righteousness doth say "), and the anthem *Have mercy God*, written at the " desyre of gude Maister Gudeman."

Who this latter was we do not know, but we read of a Christopher Guidman who was " Reader " of the church at Ayr in 1559 at £20 a year. Dr. Harry M. Willsher, who discovered about forty settings of the psalms by Kemp among the Panmure manuscripts a few years ago, informs me that they are worth all Peebles' settings put together.

John Black or Blak (d. 1587) was a pupil of John Fethy at Aberdeen under whom he served in 1546, and succeeded to the mastership of the Sang School there in 1556, in addition to being chaplain of the choir in the parish church. At the Reformation (1559) he petitioned the town council to be allowed a place in the choir of St. Nicolas. As the Sang School was despoiled in 1560 he lost his post there as Master but, in 1570, the town council, seeing that there was " no exercise of music used in the said school, . . . these divers years begone," and that John Black was " presently absent the realm," appointed Andrew Kemp as Master of the Sang School. About 1575, Black was again back in his old position as Master of the Sang School, receiving £14 13s. 8d. for two terms. Later he was being paid a pension of twenty marks a year for his "good and continual service in the choir of the parish church " and for " learning and instruction of the *bairns* " in the Sang School. We have no actual record of his compositions in the Wood collection, but Edward Millar, the compiler of the 1635 psalter, counts him among the " primest musicians that ever this kingdom had " who originally contributed to the setting, composing, or harmonizing of the music included in his psalter. In the secular field, more certain indications of his hand are discernible. These are to be found in the David Melville MS. (after 1604) in the British Museum which, although only a bass part of a larger work in four and five parts, is supplemented elsewhere in the William Stirling (=Leyden) MS. at Edinburgh (1639) where the treble to these particular items is given. In the first of these we have such titles as *Sir John Black* and *Blak maior* for items which are instrumental quartets, as well as *Musick fyne* and *Lytill blak*, included among madrigals. These numbers would seem to equate with the melodies of *Black called my delight*, *Black Major*, *Black called fyne musick*, and *Lytill Black*, found in the latter manuscript.

Another of the "primest musicians" mentioned by Edward Millar is a certain Smith. He is probably identical with Alexander Smithe who, says James Melville, was "trained up among the monks of the Abbey" of St. Andrews. In 1560 he was assistant teacher at the Sang School there, and in 1574, as "servant to the Primarius of our College," as Melville relates, taught him "the gamme, plain-song, and many of the trebles of the psalms." William Skene or Skein was another musician of this period. He succeeded John Anderson as Master of the Aberdeen Sang School in 1589, and in 1596 was receiving £86 for two terms. In the following year he was also required to be "uptaking of the psalm" in the kirk for an additional ten marks. He died in 1598. In the David Melville MS. in the British Museum are three or four pavans, two of which are entitled *James Lauder's pavan* and *Maister William Skein's pavan*, which might very well have been composed by these individuals. James Lauder is mentioned in the burgh records of Edinburgh in 1552-53, when he was a prebendary of their choir. On this occasion he was granted permission "to pass *furth* of the realm to the parts of England and France . . . to get better erudition in music and playing." Seemingly he must have acquired this more perfect art, sufficient at any rate, to pen his pavan. He was probably the same James Lawder who purchased two pairs of *virginals* for James VI in 1580.

Notwithstanding the knitted brows of the sanctimonious, the *pavan, gaillard, brawl,* and *buffon* were much in favour at court and among the gentry, and for these dances music was necessary. Although no names of composers of instrumental music for dance and other forms have been preserved from this century in Scotland, the need of fresh instrumental music for special occasions, such as the baptism of Prince Henry in 1594, must have produced native composers, for there were no others, whilst in the realm of the dance we can be fairly certain that the vogue of the French dances would compel many a composition from Scottish pens, as evidenced by the few already indicated. That the French dance forms were generally popular earlier in the century is shown by Alexander Barclay (d. *c.* 1552), who came from "beyond the cold river of

Tweede," in his *Introduction to Write and Pronounce Frenche* (1521), wherein is to be found " the maner of dauncynge . . . after the use of Fraunce." The dances themselves are listed in Wedderburn's *Complainte of Scotlande* (1549).

Of the song, vernacular and otherwise, there is also the fullest evidence of its vitality, if mere titles are of any account, as we see from the above *Complainte of Scotlande* ana *The Gude and Godlie Ballatis* (1567). Yet the merest iota of the actual music has survived, and even this dates from the 17th century but, considering Scotland's general unproductiveness in music in the early years following the trek of James VI to the south, this music might very well be identical with what was used in the 16th century. It is true that it is sometimes difficult to fit the 16th century texts to the 17th century music, but that is due to the alteration of the melodic outline to suit the instrumental exigencies of the lute or mandore for which they were arranged. Of what might be termed the vernacular songs in the 16th century, and by that we mean those of putative Scottish origin, one might count such songs as, *If care do cause men crie*, *My heartie service to yow* (" The Pleugh Song "), *All sones of Adam* (a Christmas carol), *Trip and gow hey* (a Christmas medley), *O lustie Maie* (mentioned in *The Complainte of Scotlande*), and *Intill a mirthful May morning* (given in *The Gude and Godlie Ballatis*). More important are those composed to the words of the Scottish poets Alexander Scott (*fl.* 1550) and Alexander Montgomery (d. *ca.* 1610), viz., *How should my feeble body fure* (Scott), *When as the Greeks did enterprise* (Montgomery, *cf.* title), *Lyk as the dumb Solsequium* (Montgomery), *Even death behold I breath* (Montgomery), and *Away vaine world* (Montgomery) which the poet himself says goes to the tune of *Sall I let hir goe*. Who composed the music to these songs is not recorded. Some might have been set to popular airs that had the vitality of centuries, as Montgomery had done in the last song named. Others may have been adopted from English sources, but all those mentioned above are not traceable elsewhere, and there is no reason therefore why Scotland should not be given the benefit of the doubt.

The works of the known composers and arrangers mentioned in this chapter constitute the entire creative musical output of the Reformation period (1560-1603) in Scotland, although in sorry truth, almost every composer belonged by education to the old *régime*. Yet in spite of this training, their compositions, settings, and arrangements, do not reach the level of the works of their predecessors, Johnson, Carver and Douglas. The explanation of this is plain and palpable enough. The new dispensation had set its eyes, ears and hearts against that " curious " music of the old church, for this was their name for harmony, counterpoint or canon. The deliberate instruction given by Lord James Stewart to David Peebles, when he was commissioned to harmonize the psalms, was to " leave the *curiosity* of music " alone, and to concentrate on making his arrangements " *plain* and dulce." Even the court violars in 1594 were conditioned to " plain counterpoint." This direction clearly reveals the temper of the age, although even the plainest and dulcet harmonies were themselves suspect by the church militant, which the Reformed Church most certainly was at this period. Why the Reformers took this stand has been fully explained, although the whole procedure presents a strange anomaly. The versifiers of the psalms were permitted every possible license and latitude in their treatment of the words, even to prolixity and periphrasis, yet no such freedom was allowed to those who furnished the music. If it were permissible to the versifier to embellish his lines by assonance and imagery, one naturally asks why the composer or arranger could not have been accorded equal privilege to enrich the melody with harmony or counterpoint ? Facts are stubborn *chiels*, as Burns once said, and it might as well be admitted that from the last quarter of the 16th century to the beginning of the 18th century, Scotland did not produce a solitary known composer, and this in a land which, from the late 12th century to the mid-16th century, had held a fairly reputable position in music. Is it any wonder that Dr. Ernest Walker, in his *History of Music in England* (1907), could write that " from that day [the Reformation] to this, Scottish church music has, apart from psalm tunes, been *an absolute desert*."

PART V

THE SEVENTEENTH CENTURY

(1603-1707)

" Owing to the long quarrels between the Scottish Kings and their subjects, the country could not make so much progress as it otherwise might have been."

P. HUME BROWN : *History of Scotland.*

THIS is the period between the Two Unions, since it begins with the day of the Union of the Crowns of Scotland and England, and ends with that of the Union of the two Parliaments. Much benefit accrued from the Union of the Crowns, and whatever happened in music to the contrary in the north cannot be laid to the blame of either the union or to the Crown, but to the people of Scotland themselves. This is made palpably clear in this century in Scotland's persistent Puritanic outlook in church music. Once again let it be understood that the position as we see it is not what either Calderwood or Laud thought doctrinally in this matter, but rather what St. Cecilia would have considered proper. And so, the question of religion apart, whether Presbyterian or Episcopalian, Scotland's rejection of the higher cultural life in church music meant a denial of employment to skilled professional musicians as organists and choirmasters. In England, professional musicians had a beneficent church whose bounties guaranteed them at least a basic subsistence. In the service of this church they could satiate themselves as composers and instrumentalists either for the glory of God or personal emolument, to which benefits could be added a wide and not unprofitable secular field. In Scotland, under Presbyterianism, a far different outlook prevailed. Professionalism in music was not wanted within the church for, as the best authority on the subject, the Rev. Neil Livingston, has said, the current opinion was that not only did vocal expression suffice, but that even " singing as a religious instrument is to be trusted only when it appears in the very *humblest* style of performance." This meant that laymen, often from the artisan class, became leaders of psalmody which was not only homophonic, but as plain and unadorned as possible. Outside the church the new *régime* frowned viciously at the stage, the most important public vehicle for secular music, whether vocal or instrumental. This meant that the Presbyterian Church obstructed the two main avenues for the professional musician in Scotland.

When James VI of Scotland became James I of England, he found that music, both as an art and a science, were in a highly flourishing state in his new home. The " King's Musick " counted such eminent musicians as Dr. John Bull, Dr. Nathniel Giles and Dr. Orlando Gibbons on its pay roll. Their doctorates were won at and conferred by Universities, and were not doled out as mere courtesy titles to all and sundry by the Church as in Scotland. The king saw that his English Chapel Royal was the chief nursery of music in the English kingdom, a fact which made him particularly intent on having his Scottish Chapel Royal equally as nourishing. In the English cathedrals and principal churches he realized how the greatest of the country's musicians were contributing to the glories of the Anglican service. Is it a matter for wonder that James saw in Episcopacy a coefficient, not only in the betterment of music, but also in the security (" No Bishop, No King ") of his doctrine of Divine Right!

We have seen that James was interested in music in the days of his youth, and in England he had far greater opportunities of enjoying it. Even foreigners relished the King's affection for the art, as Abraham Praetorius had already learned, and now a certain Sydrach Rahel dedicated some interesting canons to the new king, including one, *Vivat Jacobus primus*. One of James' first acts, in 1604, was to grant a charter of incorporation to the Company of Musicians of Westminster for " the good and faithful service which his said musicians had done and performed unto him." Indeed, he took special care that his two sons, Prince Henry and Prince Charles, were instructed in the art, and both appear to have been taught the *viola da gamba* by the famous John Cooper (Coperario). It was Prince Henry who, in the year 1610, revived and rectified "the March of this our English Nation" which was in danger of being lost and utterly forgotten. Would that he had been as solicitous of *The Scots March*, the identity of which has been the cause of so much discussion, as I have shown elsewhere (*Papers on Military Music*). Music, and what was attendant upon it, seems to have filled the court of James, and a few musical items from court masques, written and composed by Ben Jonson and Thomas Campion, have been preserved in contemporary Scottish lute books. When Prince Henry died in 1613, it was Campion and Cooper who wrote and composed the memorial *Songs of Mourning* which, exquisite gems as they are, have passed into the night of oblivion, just as the madrigal, *Faire Brittan Ile*, composed probably by Byrd, written for the same sad event, has been forgotten. Music lost an enthusiastic patron in the passing of Prince Henry.

James VI had long toyed with Episcopacy for Scotland. The Black Acts had made him "Head of the Church," and the creation of bishops had been agreed. By 1606 he had managed to coerce Parliament into passing an Act which gave him further powers in this direction, and when James made a journey north in 1617, the preparations that were made for his stay led the Scots to become mightily suspicious that "the [Roman Catholic] Mass would surely follow." How far music reflected the coming changes must be left to be discussed in its proper place in dealing with the court. The next year, by threats and bribes, the king secured the Five Articles of Perth. Its clauses established Episcopacy and the Anglican service but, so far as the latter is concerned, it still remained merely as part of the clauses of the Act, and never found acceptance save perhaps within the walls of the Chapel Royal in Scotland, and even here, as we shall see, it had fallen into desuetude by 1625, the year of James' death.

His successor, Charles I (1625-45), was not a Scot in spirit like his father, except in the trying days of his final troubles. As we have seen, he was educated in music, and John Playford, in his *Introduction to the Skill of Music* (1672) says that Charles was "not behind any of his predecessors in the love and promotion of this science, especially in the service of Almighty God, and with much zeal he would hear reverently performed, and often appointed, the service and anthems himself, . . . being by his knowledge in music a competent judge therein : and would play his part exactly well on the bass viol, especially of those incomparable fancies of Mr. Coperario to the organ." When Charles was a prince, Campion dedicated to him his *New Way of making Fowre parts in Counterpoint* (1613), a work which was a pioneer one in the domain of didactics. Henry Playford's *Harmonia Sacra* (1688) contains Henry Purcell's delightful setting, to Charles' own words, *Close thine eyes and sleep secure.*

Charles continued to have the services of Nathaniel Giles and Orlando Gibbons in his English Chapel Royal and at Westminster. On the more domestic side he favoured Nicolas Laniere who was Master of the King's Music, together with such famous composers and performers as Robert Johnson *secundus*, Thomas Ford, Alfonso Ferrabosco, and Richard Deering. Among his state trumpeters were two who had accompanied his father to England in 1603, John and Robert Ramsey. As John Playford has vouched, the king took the deepest interest in the English Chapel Royal where he insisted on services every day, " both morning and evening with solemn music like a collegiate church." It was this affection for the Anglican service that probably had some influence on him in his plans for forcing Episcopacy on Scotland, an undertaking which eventually brought such disastrous results to himself.

The King's first step in this direction is to be seen in his letters of May 1627 to the Privy Council regarding the Chapel Royal in Scotland. From then onwards to 1637, his anxiety that this establishment should be on the lines of his Chapel Royal in England became increasingly apparent, not merely in the partial adoption of the Anglican service within its walls, but in such close details as having cornetts and sackbuts to play with the organ. The coronation service of 1633 showed the Scottish people the precise trend of affairs and, so far as music was concerned, it is not improbable that little opposition would have displayed itself, for there was certainly a growing interest in better music within the Reformed Church as shown by the 1625 and 1635 psalters. Unfortunately there were other innovations which impinged on more cherished Presbyterian doctrines. Charles had authorized the English Archbishop Laud to prepare a new Liturgy or Service Book for Scotland which, music apart, the Scots considered Papistic, and in May 1637, when the new liturgy was ordered to come into force in Edinburgh, there was a riot. The result is well known. By February 1638 the National Covenant was being signed by thousands, and soon a free Parliament and an unfettered General Assembly were demanded. The sword was unsheathed to compel obedience to the law, but Scotland was prepared to face this and to fight for these freedoms. Soon, England was to throw her weight into the scale against the King, for she, in her turn, had found it necessary to demand political justice. The end came in January 1649 at Whitehall, when Charles I paid for his folly with his head.

Yet neither of his two successors seem to have learned much from their father's experience. One of the early Acts of Charles II (1660-85) was to re-establish episcopacy in Scotland, and a cruel struggle between the Government and the Covenanters ensued. The Pentland Rising, Drumclog, Bothwell Brig', the Cameronians, are names that stand out in the days of slaughter and persecution that followed. His brother, James VII (1685-88) was no better. He planned to re-establish Roman Catholicism but, unlike his father, he moved more swiftly to his doom. In the fall of 1686 he began his schemes with structural alterations in the Chapel Royal in Edinburgh so as to make it more suitable for the Roman service. The following year brought the appointment of a musical staff for the establishment, which was to be a conventual church. He then centred his attention on the Abbey Church, and by February 1687, as the *Historical Notices* of Lord Fountainhall has it, " Litanies and masses are said in the Abbey, by the Popish Priests." Riots followed in Edinburgh. In England there was equal unrest, and before long the " Glorious Revolution " was well under way. The

Protestant House of Orange was approached, and William of Orange set sail for England when, thanks to a " Protestant wind," so 'tis said, he landed on these shores. James fled from Whitehall, and on that very day another " Protestant wind " blew an Edinburgh crowd in a riotous mood into the Abbey Church which not only despoiled it of its Papistic trappings, including its organ, but committed irreparable vandalic destruction.

The reigns of William and Mary (1688-1702) and Anne (1702-14) do not interest us so far as music in Scotland is concerned. Presbyterianism was re-established in Scotland in 1690, but the event had no effect on the music of the church, except to its further neglect. As we shall see in the section devoted to the subject, church music in Scotland had, by this time, fallen to its lowest ebb. Rous' psalter *without music* came in 1650, when the greatest of the Scottish psalters, that of 1635, fell into complete disuse together with its predecessors. The Sang Schools, one by one, sickened and died in the smaller towns, even those established under Royal protection, whilst those in the larger towns showed no more than a fitful existence. Secular music certainly flourished, but among the middle and upper classes it was mostly but a reflected art from other climes, England and Italy. Among the people of the countryside and the artisan class, the old vernacular songs and the traditional dances still brought joy, although here and there even these were losing their hold. One proof of this latter may be seen in the cancellation of the three vernacular songs in the last edition of Forbes' *Cantus* (1682). Strange to say, where the vernacular song and dance did gain ground was in England. The seeds of this cult for Scottish music were planted by that " beggarly rabble of Scots," those " Caledonian boars," to use some of the courteous contemporary expressions, who accompanied James VI to England in 1603 and later. Before the end of the century the popularity of the " Scottish tune " and " Scotch song " became almost a craze with the Sassenach, as both the sheet music and music books of the London publishers amply testify. Yet Scots were accepted even further afield, as in France, although here they probably came from seeds sown earlier in the days of the " Auld Alliance." There was a singer named Dun who sang and danced in Molière's *Pastorale comique*. His son Jean, a baritone, took the part of Hidraot in Lully's *Armide* (1688). His two daughters and a son, the latter also named Jean were attached to the Opera House as singers in 1742, and this Jean is shown as a pensioner in the *Calendrier des Théâtres* as late as 1772.

CHAPTER 1

THE COURT.

" The quhilk first fundatioun being so advysedlie set doun, hes nevertheles beine within thir few yearis transgressit be the inopportune inquyring of unqualifeit persones to be presentit to the places of the said chappell [royal] being . . . altogidder voyde and ignorant of ony knawledge . . . of musick . . . And now, it being his maiesties . . . will, mynd, and intentioun . . . to have . . . persones qualefeit in musick and able to attend and serve his hienes within the said chapell. . . ."

Privy Seal Register, 18th Feb., 1605.

After 1603, there was no court in Scotland and, as a result, there was no court music. The court itself followed James I (which was his new title) to England, the " Land of Promise " as he called it in contradistinction to his " wandering above forty years in a wilderness and barren soil," i.e. Scotland. From this point of view the latter country was well rid of him, for these very sentiments were soon to show a *crescendo*, much to the English tax-payers' regret, as we see the king spending as much on jewelry in one year in the " Land of Promise " as he received in his total income in the " Wilderness." Still, the English court minstrelsy benefited by his lavish disbursements at the people's expense.

What accompanied James from Scotland in the way of music and musicians is not at present traceable, although it may have been considerable. It was only natural that the King would surround himself with his " ain folk," just as William of Orange did with Dutchmen, and the Hanoverians with Germans. James' entourage were those " Scottish beggars " whom Guy Fawkes wanted to

" blow back to their native mountains." Besides the *élite* of the habit of Thomas Erskine, James Hay, Robert Ker or Carr, and others, there was a goodly crowd of lesser lights, and one may be fairly sure that a few journeyed who could give James and his minions a good Scots *sang* or *tone* which they could relish, just as he had his own jesters, David Droman and Archee Armstrong, because their pawky and bawdy wit was more to his palate than the humour retailed by the existing court fools.   Yet the fact remains that, at present, details of these Scottish musicians in England at this period are thinly scattered, although one strongly suspects that the two well known composers, Henry Youll (*fl.* 1608) and Tobias Hume (d. 1645) were cradled north of the Tweed.

It is certain that six of the Scottish court trumpeters journeyed to London with their king.   They were William Ramsey, Robert Dromond or Dromane, Nicholas Wadoll or Woddall, Archibald Sym, John Ramsey and Robert Ramsey.   Dromane, like the court fool of this name, belonged to the old Italian family of court minstrels who had entered Royal service in Scotland as far back as 1500. The Ramsey family was even larger than what is recorded above, and Robert Jr. was still drawing a pension in 1684.   What became of the Hudsoun or Hudson family of court musicians, with whom James was particularly intimate, is not quite certain.   There is no trace of them in the lists of the " King's Musick " in England, although some of them may conceivably have been given other and more profitable domestic posts. ᐧ In the reign of Charles II, two of the English court musicians were George Hudson (d. 1681) a lutanist, and Richard or Robert Hudson (d. 1682) a violinist, both of whom seem to have belonged to that ilk, whilst decendants flourished in the King's Music in the 18th and early 19th centuries. But to return to Scotland.

All that was kept going of the Scottish court at Holyrood, so far as music is concerned, was a skeleton staff at the Chapel Royal. Snugly throned in England, James had little interest in, or use for, this distant and less pretentious establishment in the north save, of course, its revenues which, of late years, had been almost wholly secularized. We see the King's attitude towards it in three document of 1605. A certain John Gib, a groom of the Privy Chamber when the King was a child, had been appointed a prebendary of the Chapel Royal as far back as 1586. In 1605 however, Gib was made factor and receiver of the whole revenues of this establishment of which we read in a lengthy document which serves, in part, to garnish the threshold of this chapter on " The Court." Then there was William Chalmer who had been appointed " luther " to the Chapel Royal in 1601, but in 1605, since there was no need for such a post, he was given other revenues from a " living " and lands of the Chapel Royal amounting to £50 a year for " gude, trew and thankfull service." In the same year, one named Symeoun Ramsay was appointed other revenues from the said Chapel " for his better sustentation and entertainment at the schools, and to encourage him to continue in the study of letters and exercise music."

All these acts of the King, notwithstanding his insistence on his predecessors and his own desires " for advancing the liberal science of music," were considered by Parliament in quite another light. They saw in the Chapel Royal a national institution, and they resented the King's free handed gifting of lands and benefices from this source, more especially to his favourites. The argument between the two parties lasted for many years, although Parliament passed an Act which provided that the Chapel Royal " shall not, nor may not, in any time coming be lawfully possessed *but by the ordinary members only of the said Chapel Royal* astricted to serve His Majesty and his successors in Music and other Godly and lawful exercise agreeable to the foundation and not repugnant to the true religion presently professed within this realm." Further, they took the patronage out of the hands of the king, and to this Act of 1606 James VI was compelled to give his sanction.

From the year 1612 we get some information about the musicians at the establishment. We read that the service appointed to be read in the Chapel Royal had for a " long time been intermittent in default of a Dean and Master to whom it chiefly belongs to provide prebendaries and men skillful in music for service in the said Chapel."

As a result, a certain minister of Ayr, William Birnie (1563-1619), who had for " a long time resolved to restore the ancient dignity of our Chapel Royal," was appointed Dean and Master, in which he was directed to choose prebendaries who were " skillful in music." We have no precise details of what music the service consisted in these days but, in view of the Act of 1606, we imagine that nothing "repugnant to the true religion" in *music* would have been permitted, and this would have meant a plain Presbyterian psalmody.

By 1617 however, there were many changes in the Chapel itself. The plain furnishings of Presbyterian worship had given way to costly sculptured and ornamental display more in accordance with Anglican ideas. Not only were the stalls of the prebendaries and choir-boys more suitably adorned and enhanced, but Thomas Dallam, the famous English organ-builder, supplied an organ with " twenty angels " as part of the ornamentation, which had been constructed under the august eye of the " English Palladio " Inigo Jones. All this was understandable. James had been fifteen years in London and had become used to and enamoured of both its music and its church service. That was the reason why, as the old *History and Life of King James the Sext* has it, " the Kingis palise was reformit . . . [and] his chappel-royal was decorit with *organs*, and uther temporal policie." Indeed, Secretary Lake's letter to Sir Dudley Carleton specifically states that the King wished to " set up his [Holyrood] chapel in like manner of service " to that of London.

When James arrived in Edinburgh and heard the new service in the Chapel Royal he must have felt extremely gratified. Of the services in May, August and December, the great protagonist of Presbyterianism, Calderwood (d. 1650), makes his terse entries anent " the English service, . . . playing of organs, and singing of men and boys, both before and after anthem." John Row *secundus* (d. 1646) gravely describes the scene where there were " brave organs put, and choristers appointed to sing, and the English service ordained to be said daily; wherein many, for novelty, came to see and hear what such things could be; but seeing nothing but profanity, abusing of the service of God, and taking his name in vain, they came never again."

It seems perfectly clear that the people at large did not relish the innovations, and Bishop Cowper who, as Dean of the Chapel, had taken over complete control from Birnie, now complained of damage to the organs. He suggested (1617) that the organs had been " too commonly visited [? usited] . . . that the spokes that raise the bellows had been somewhat unskillfully used by ignorant people." One strongly suspects that the said bellows had, more likely, been " visited " and skillfully *misused* by overzealous Presbyterians. Yet a ribald Englishman, reputed to be the scandalizing Sir Anthony Weldon, who came with the Royal train, thought that whilst the populace was furious with all the Papistic pomp and display, and did " threaten to pull them down soon after his [the King's] departure, and to make them a burnt-offering," he presaged, with delicate wit, that " the organs . . . will find mercy, because they say there is some affinity between them and the bagpipe." Thus we read in *Batavia, or the Hollander Displayed* (1686). Yet despite all rumours nothing violent happened although, after the King's return, things were allowed to drift in the matter of the Anglican service.

Bishop Cowper was followed as Dean in 1619 by Andrew Lamb, formerly Bishop of Brechin. He was succeeded in 1621 by Adam Bellenden, Bishop of Dunblane, but affairs went from bad to worse as one might expect from mere ecclesiastics. By about the year 1623, the music of the Chapel Royal was in a decrepit state. According to a document entitled *Church Affaires from the yeire of God* 1610 *to the yeire* 1625, in the Sir James Balfour Collection, it appears that out of 16 canons, 9 prebends, and six choir-boys, a total of thirty-one, *only seven were in attendance*, so that " only *they* sing the Common Tune of a psalm, and, being so few, are scarce known." The whole trouble was inadequate stipends rather than disagreement on doctrine, and we know that there were fourteen people whose salaries totalled £67. Yet the King did nothing to remedy the lamentable state of affairs.

When James had been gathered to his fathers, his successor, Charles I (1625-45), took more interest in the Chapel Royal in Scotland and, once more, the special excitation was due to the urge to force Episcopacy upon Scotland. As with his father, the first sign of his concern in its establishment was in the furnishings, and it was ordered that "the seats of the prebendaries or singing men should be distinguished from others of the Nobility, Council and Session." This was in 1627. Seemingly it was considered outrageous that mere musicians should be seated in a like manner to their betters. The next year we read of a very worthy man in charge of the music at the Chapel by the name of Edward Kellie. He had been a " servitor " to George Hay of Dupplin, afterwards Earl of Kinnoul, but in this year Kellie was appointed as a Prebendary and " ordinar musician " to the Chapel Royal. Two years later, he was promoted to Director of Music of this establishment. He was most zealous in his efforts to revive the ancient glories of the Chapel, even to maintaining an " expert organist, singing men, and boys," out of his own stipend. In 1631 he detailed at length to Charles I all that he had done in furtherance of his ideals. He had been responsible for the music at the coronation ceremony, and whilst in London he had made " twelve great books, gilded, and twelve small ones, with an organ book," wherein was written " the said psalms, services and anthems." He deposed all " insufficient persons " in the Chapel Royal, replacing them by those " more qualified." Further, he " carried home [to Scotland] an organist, and two men for playing on cornetts and sackbuts, and two boys for singing divisions in the *versus*," all of which he said were " most exquisite in their several faculties." In his own chamber at Holyrood, he says that he had " provided and set up an organ, two flutes, two pandores, with viols and other instruments, with all sorts of English, French, Dutch, Spanish, Latin, Italian, and *old Scotch music*, vocal and instrumental." Here, rehearsals were held twice weekly. As for the service at the Chapel Royal we get a glimpse of this also from Kellie's report. He says, " There is sung before the sermon a full anthem, and after sermon an anthem alone in *versus* with the organ." According to the *Historical Collections* of John Rushworth (d. 1690), Charles ordered " that there be prayers twice a day with the Choir, as well in our absence as otherwise, according to the *English liturgy*," The whole coronation service of 1633 proved the truth of this. Edward Millar, another excellent musician, succeeded Kellie in 1635, and we shall have to deal with his activities elsewhere.

Yet precisely the same state of affairs existed in the Chapel as in the days of his father, i.e. inadequate stipends of those who contributed the music. Even before the English liturgy was ordered, Archbishop Laud himself had petitioned the King saying that their case " deserved a great deal of commiseration." The King paid no heed and when at last Laud's liturgy was ordered to be introduced in May 1637, the King certainly did not have the sympathy of even the musicians of the Chapel Royal. Further, Scotland as a whole repudiated the new Anglican Service Book. Cheated of his hopes and dreams, Charles still essayed a brave front, thinking that, so far as the Chapel Royal stood, he could maintain the *status quo*. He ordered as follows, " You are to give direction that the same service be used in our Chapel-Royal, that was before the enjoining of the Service-book. . . . For the organs in the Abbey Church, we leave them to your discretion when to be used, and to advertize me of your opinion." Whether these organs were ever used again we have no knowledge. According to the Spalding *Memorials* we find that not only were " the glorious organs of the Chapel Royal, violently (*maisterfullie*) broken down, and no service used there, but the whole chaplains, choristers and musicians discharged, and the costly organs destroyed and [rendered] useless (*unusefull*)." Actually they were not *all* destroyed, as we read in the minutes of the Holyrood Kirk Sessions (1643) of " the organ which was taken down, and put into the aisle, now lying idle, mothing and consuming; yea, moreover, the same being *an unprofitable instrument, scandalous to our profession,* whether the same might not be sold for a tolerable price, and the money given unto the poor."

Yet this was not the end of music in the Chapel Royal. Following the troubles engendered by the events of 1637, the revenues became secularized once more, but with the accession of Charles II (1660-85) hopes were again raised for Episcopacy. When in exile and begging for the throne, Charles had sworn to uphold the Covenant and the Presbyterian Church, but before he left Breda at the Restoration, he consented to re-establish Episcopacy, and Robert Leighton, Principal of the University of Edinburgh was appointed Dean of the Chapel Royal and Bishop of Dunblane (1660-68), but was succeeded in both of these offices by James Ramsay (1668-89). Charles then proceeded with structural alterations at Holyrood and proposed to house the Chapel Royal in the Abbey Church. What happened musically in the establishment we know but little, but if it were to have been on the same lines as that which obtained in his Chapel Royal in England he would scarcely have got very far with the scheme. In England his " Twenty-four Violins " were playing *ritornelli* between pauses in the anthems at the Chapel, which was " better suiting a tavern or playhouse than a church " as the sedate Evelyn records.

It was not until James VII (1685-88) assumed the purple that any real attempt was made at a revival of music at the Chapel Royal in Scotland. When he was Duke of York, he spent some time in 1682 at Holyrood Palace, where he and the Duchess made great show in reviving the old regal grandeur in patronizing music, plays, balls and other entertainments, but there was no outstanding music, such as they had been used to in England. There does not seem to have been anyone capable or sufficiently bold enough to produce a congratulatory ode to mark any of the days of his stay in the Scottish capital. Yet so soon as James had set his foot on London soil than Henry Purcell, saluted him with a welcome home piece, *What shall be done in behalfe of the Man*, and already there was a popular song, *Jockey away Man: Scotland's Good Wishes to His Royal Highness* (1682). Unfortunately, when he came to the throne, he had, what were to him, more important aims. James, as we have seen, was bent on making the Chapel Royal the foraging ground in his scheme to Romanize Scotland, and in 1687 he appointed persons " for the service of the music employed for the use of our Chapel in our Palace of Holyrood," to which end the Privy Council allowed a mere token £100 a year. The Chapel was now to be a conventual church, and a Canon of St. Géneviève, Paris, was actually appointed Abbot. Trouble soon began to brew, in spite of the acquiescence of the time servers on Privy Council and the Town Council to his views. Here, many " gauds " (ornaments) had been introduced as well as a large and magnificent organ. Lord Fountainhall (d. 1722) reports in his *Historical Notices* that in February 1688 there were litanies and masses being said by " Popish Priests " in the Abbey Church. The end was nigh. In December, the same " rascal multitude " that annoyed Knox in his day, but now more mellifluously called " ane rable of all sorts," invaded the Abbey Church in angry mood, with the inevitable result. Six months later, as we learn from the Leven and Melville Papers (*Bannatyne Club*), it was reported that the entire building had been seriously despoiled.

CHAPTER 2

THE PEOPLE.

" What soul can be so sick, that by thy songs
(Attired in sweetness) sweetly is not driven
Quite to forget earth's turmoils, spites and wrongs
And lift a reverent eye and thought to heaven ? "
WILLIAM DRUMMOND of Hawthornden (d. 1649).

It was almost impossible to enforce complete discipline under the Presbyterian " new morality." The rein was intended for all and sundry, but only the latter were brought under its taut stress. In the old days, there was much more freedom among the people at large, and the new dispensation could not easily brush aside the customs of yore. Among these were the church festivals, the " fair days," of which we have but a token today. These holidays meant rest and recreation to the toiling multitude, and, in the latter, music, and its erstwhile concomitant, dancing, played their part. Yet the church, bent upon obliterating the memory of Papistic festivals, abolished what they conveniently could of these, but with no compensating advantages, save when James VI, gave a holiday on August 1st as a thanksgiving for his delivery from the alleged Gowrie Conspiracy (1600). On this new holiday, " after preaching and thanksgiving " had been attended to, everyone was allowed to spend the rest of the day " in lawful and honest gladness, and accompany their magistrates through the town in singing psalms and praising God." The suppression of the old festival holidays was resented even by the schools, as we have seen in the previous century, and another such riot occurred at Aberdeen in 1612, where the scholars " rose against their masters, seized the Sang School, and held it by force of arms for three days."

The petty interferences with the peoples pleasures still continued. Carols and Yule songs were considered evil. At Aberdeen in 1605, the people were forbidden to sing *any songs* at the New Year, and we read of the same again in 1612, although they were called " idolatrous songs " on this occasion. Another sore thorn in the Presbyterian flesh was the *lyke-waik* of Pagan Celtic times, which had wisely been allowed by the Roman Church with reasonable safeguards. This, with the wedding celebration and the festivity at a birth, invariably brought music. The Reformed Church could not stomach the Pagan dances, clapping of hands, and *darges* (dirges) at *lyke-waiks*, and forbade their use. It was the same with the hoary practice of music and the dance at weddings and births, at both of which the church frowned, the reason being, (1) they engendered immorality, and (2) they were relics of the Pagan and Papistic past. How much instrumental music was *anathema* to the strict Presbyterians is well evidenced in *The Booke of the Universall Kirk*. In the days of the Roman Church, a bagpipe or other instrument of wind music, might even be seen heading a church or religious procession, just as we have mentioned in 1556, when a church gathering was led to St. Giles, Edinburgh, by a piper. When the Reformation had been brought about, the people naturally saw no harm in such a procedure, and in 1575, at Dumfries, the people actually " brought a Reader of their own [to the Kirk] with *tabroun* and *whistle*, and caused him to read the prayers." The upshot of this unseemly practice was a complaint to the General Assembly, as we read in the book mentioned above. The new dispensation was well answered by a certain David Wemys in 1599 when he was called before the St. Andrews Kirk Session for being present at a dance. He replied that " he never saw dancing stopped before " and added that " the custom was kept in Raderny ere any of the [Kirk] Session were born." He was locked up in the church steeple for his sins.

In view of their carefree attitude, bagpipers were disliked by the Kirk, more especially because the bagpipe was the popular muse. As Patrick Macdonald, himself a minister, says in his *Collection of Highland Vocal Airs* (1784), the great Highland pipe was " for war, for marriage, for funeral processions, and for other great occasions," whilst the smaller bagpipe was for " dancing tunes." But the Kirk would not permit the pipe for such purposes. At Stirling in 1648, according to the orders of the Kirk Session, no more than fifteen persons, and *no pipers*, were allowed at weddings. It was the same at Edinburgh the following year where it was ordered that there " be no pypers at brydels." Needless to say, the Kirk was powerless to enforce this rule completely since we know from Morier's *Short Account of Scotland* (1679) that the bagpipe was " the chief delight at marriages," and that the guests went home to the " ravishing " skirl of the pipes, to make the further jollification and dance on the green. Yet the Holy Willies had their way in many instances. At Holyrood Kirk Session in 1653, we read that a woman was haled before the authorities for dancing, but pleaded in extenuation that English soldiers had " brought over a pipe with them." In 1628, the Presbytery of Lanark spoke of " the insolence of men and women in foot-racing, dancing, and playing *Barla Breks* on the Sunday," and in 1649 the General Assembly inhibited dancing in general and referred " the censorship . . . to the care and diligence of Presbyters." When *piping* took place on a Sunday it was considered atrocious, and we read in 1606 of Richard Watson of Leith being threatened with censure for such conduct, whilst James Clark, in 1624, was fined 20s. for having a " piper playing into his house in time of sermon upon his Lord the Sabbath."   At Perth, in 1623, a man was charged for playing the " great pipe," and at Lanark in 1625, six people were arraigned " for fetching home a May-pole, and dancing about the same upon Pasch Sunday."   Once again, in this same town, in 1660, pipers and promiscuous dancing were forbidden. We also read that no person shall " suffer any pipes to play at their houses or yards in time coming under the pain of 40s. each person."   Nor were the people the only sinners.   In 1688, one of the elect, Thomas Heriot, a minister of Dalkeith, was accused of " dancing about a bonfire publicly in the streets, with *pipe* and *drum*, and drinking a health upon his knees."

Pipers had a bad name with the Church in those days, of which *infamia* the Presbyterian opponents of the Episcopalian James Sharp, Archbishop of St. Andrews, took full advantage.   Sharp had the good fortune to have a bagpiper as his grandfather, and his scurrilous critics sneered that it was a pity that the grandchild was not a *piper* instead of a *prelate*, which was jocund alliteration but unchristian charity.   They suggested that if Sharp still had his grandsire's pipes he could " gift them to some *landwart* church to save the expense of a pair of organs."

Yet we sometimes see the peoples' appreciation of the piper, as in the case of Robert Sempill (d. *c.*1665) who wrote " The Life and Death of Habbie Simpson, Piper of Kilbarchan " (*c.*1640), in which we read that " There's nane in Scotland plays sae weel, since we lost Habbie Simpson."   In these lines too we find that the old song *The day it daws* was as popular as ever.   Habbie Simpson's effigy still stands in front of the parish church at Kilbarchan, and the words of *Maggie Lauder* will ever enshrine his memory.

Equally odious and hateful to the Presbyterian conscience was the stage, an institution closely linked, socially and professionally, to music.   In 1624 the Glasgow Kirk Session intimated that all

" resetters of comedians " would be severely punished, i.e. nobody was to give shelter to those of the motley and tinsel. Yet the church could not wholly bar the people from these harmless pleasures, and so they appealed to the civil law in 1670, when the magistrates of Glasgow interdicted " strolling players from running through the streets, and from performing plays in private houses." Indeed the pious but pecuniary city of St. Mungo was possibly more virulent against the stage than any other town in Scotland, although the sanctimonious crews who ran the towns were all much of the same mind.

Despite scourgings and burnings, stocks and prison, the wandering musician seems still to have found a meagre living in the land, although his orbit was but the hamlet and village, since the repressive parliamentary acts and burghal laws had made the towns inaccessible. Fletcher of Saltoun (d. 1717), in his *Two Discourses concerning the Affairs of Scotland* (1689) computes this " loose and disorderly crowd in Scotland," including strolling players and musicians, at 100,000. He speaks of them as an unspeakable oppression to the country, yet the more sympathetic and acute Dauney, in his *Ancient Scottish Melodies* (1838), well answers this " Scotch gentleman . . . with a stern, sour look," as his fellow Scot, Gilbert Burnet, has described him. Dauney astutely observes that these unfortunates were but " the wretched offspring of a political system which provided for the interest of certain privileged orders, to the entire neglect of the great mass of the community, and reared up the pride and the personal aggrandisement of the one upon the misery and degradation of the other." All that a supine government could do to meet the situation at this period was to pass fresh acts of oppression even more vile than what had preceded. These latter were, in all conscience, bad enough, but the crowning infamy came in that which was enacted in the 16th year of the reign of Charles II, in which " excellent overtures are set down for the punishment of vagabonds," which included the wandering minstrels, so excellent indeed that *death* was now the punishment for a *second* offence. It may be recalled that it was

Sir George Mackenzie (d. 1691), more familiarly known in Scotland as " Bluidy Mackenzie," who was so prominent in this merciful legislation.

Denied the innocent fun of the strolling player or the dance-tune of the wandering fiddler, all that the townfolk of the lower class could hope to listen to was what the town musicians supplied, and this had little changed. The instrumentation of these bands varied in the several towns, bagpipers, shawmers, hautboists, fifers, trumpeters or drummers, although we usually find the last named in company with one or more of the others. Glasgow however, then as practical and businesslike as today, was content with drummers only. The town musicians still continued to be paid and clothed by the town itself and were employed in all kinds of duties. Generally they were expected to play through the town twice daily, very much in the same way as army musicians did at *reveillé* and *retreat*, and for almost the same reasons. They were present on all ceremonial occasions, being attendant on the provost and baillies, not only to add display to the function, for they wore an official garb in harmony with the robes of the foregoing, but more particularly because their music was part of the town's insignia and meant " authority." Indeed this music invariably preceded and succeeded official announcements so as to imprint the legality of the proceedings as it were. In some instances a town had its official music, as did the trade and merchant guilds, a stave or two of which has come down to us as in the *Perth Glovers' March*.

The usual combination was bagpipe or other pipe (shawm) and drum. This is what we find at Dundee in 1607 although on account of expense they were temporarily abolished in 1687. Strangely enough, we read in 1685 that the impost on *malt* at Dundee contributed to the upkeep of both *drummers* and *ministers*, a rather derogatory coupling and a most unpuritanic enactment. Yet in the most talked-of city of Bon Accord, i.e. Aberdeen, the piper was dismissed in 1630 as the City Fathers considered his music " an uncivil form to be used within such a famous burgh."

On the other hand, Pèrth, whose people were roused by the bagpipe at so early an hour as 5 a.m., thought that its music was " inexpressibly soothing and delightful."

In addition to these official musicians there were a few instrumentalists who managed to make a living in the various towns. Although not attached to noble or burghal service, as demanded by parliamentary acts and burghal laws, they seem to have been tolerated so long as they resided in the town. Court cases and kirk sessions, as well as burgh records, give plenty of evidence of their existence at this period which is, in itself, conclusive proof that professional performers on the violin, virginal, hautboy and flute, must have been in fair demand, in defiance of the strict Presbyterian outlook that visualized such things as the hand of the Anti-Christ. In that amusing squib, *Vox Borealis, or the Northerne Discovery* (1641), we get a sidelight on the puritan point of view where the Episcopalian is likened to " a Fiddler and a Fool " who *sing* " Scots jigs in a jeering manner at the Covenanters." Yet respectability must have been the badge of some of this class since Patrick Burnie (b. *c.*1635), apparently famed as a " fiddler," had his portrait painted by Aikman (1682-1731). Burnie is the reputed author and composer of *The Auld Man's Mare's Dead.*

Towards the close of the century, social pressure compelled the authorities to give nodding approval to dancing, and dancing masters soon made their appearance. Even sanctimonious Glasgow was one of the first to appoint an official dancing master but, he was " to teach at seasonable hours, keep no balls, and . . . shall so order his teaching that there shall be no promiscuous dancing of young men and young women together." This was in 1699. Even when private dancing masters appeared they had to be approved by the licensing authority. In Edinburgh we read of a Master of the Revels who claimed to have authority in 1694 over all kinds of music making, and even games and sports, to see that " nothing immoral or indecent " was allowed. A judgment in this year however, went against him, when his jurisdiction was interpreted to cover only music in theatres. The dancing master, with kit or fiddle in hand, now became part and parcel of social life and, what is more, was often looked upon as the town's *entrepreneur* when instrumental music was required, and he was also the main support when concerts first showed their timorous heads in Scotland.

Even from the beginning of the century the dance was persisted in notwithstanding the attitude of the church. The country folk and the artisan class indulged in the *hornpipe*, *jig*, *reel*, *lilt* and *spring* to their heart's content, whilst the middle and upper class had in addition their more sedate *pavan*, *courant*, *brawl*, *alman* and other exotic dances, the music of which has been preserved for us from the time of the Rowallan lute MS. (1612-28) to that of the Leyden MS. (*ca.* 1692). They will be treated at length in the section devoted to the music itself.

Vocally, the people could supply their own music, and if it was not permissible to sing those Pagan and Romanist yule songs, or " bawdy " or " filthy " songs (as the church termed some possibly harmless amorous ballads), there was a wide field elsewhere. The Skene (1615-35), Stralloch (1627-29), Stirling (1639), Guthrie (1675-80), Blaikie (1683-92) and Leyden (*c.*1692) manuscripts, as well as Forbes' *Cantus* (1666), give song titles which show that a few songs came from the masses. The period also reveals a revival of the old appeal to secular melodies in spiritual songs, a custom which had been one of the bulwarks of reforming days. The *Gude and Godlie Ballatis* (1567, 1568) of the Wedderburn family had been re-issued in 1578, 1590, 1600 and 1621, the later editions being more ample versions, " with augmentations of sundry good and godly ballads not contained in the first edition." There was no real sanction of the church for these productions, but the fact that the publishers proceeded without hindrance seems to imply tacit agreement. Indeed, many of the songs would have been quite acceptable in church praise, although others could not possibly have been admitted. That the music was considered good seems tolerably certain from the fact that this type of song has a place in the William McKinnoune MS. (dated 1657), where we have

John come kiss me now as " ane excellent catch for any psalm,"
and in Forbes' *Cantus* (1666). Probably the clergy, as Dauney
suggests, found it necessary to allow such things to the people
so as to " unite religious edification with their musical recreations,"
although this could only have been an afterthought. Alexander
Montgomery's book *The Mindes Melodie : Contayning certayne
Psalmes . . . applyed to a new pleasant Tune* (1605) also shows the
general trend of thought.

Towards the close of the century a clergyman named William
Geddes became especially enamoured of the secular song for this
purpose, seeing no reason, as some profane wit even earlier than
Wesley has expressed it, why the Devil should have all the good
tunes. At the same time, Geddes, in his *Saints' Recreation* (1683),
which contains these songs, takes a rather different view of the
problem, or at least gives another reason for his action. He
suggested that many of the secular airs that were current in his
day had been " surreptitiously borrowed " from church melodies,
and these latter he wanted to " bring back to the right owner."
Knowing that many of his cloth would object to these profane
melodies being used to sacred words, he imagined them saying
that " these airs or tunes were sung heretofore with amorous
sonnets, wherein were (may be) some bawdy-like or obscene-like
expressions." But Geddes had his counterblast to such criticism
and claimed that " many of our airs or tunes are made by good
angels, but the letters or lines of our songs by devils." Among
the tunes that he had in mind were, *The bonny broom, I'll never
leave thee, We'll all go pull the hadder* [*heather*] and such like.
One can imagine that his endeavours found approval among the
people at large, since it was but a continuance of an old custom.

As we shall see presently, in dealing with " The Church," there
was a definite falling off of interest in official psalmody, i.e. that
which was practised within the church. Yet strangely enough,
there was a lively appreciation of psalm tunes outside the church,
since we find these tunes included in general collections of instrumental music as in the Rowallan MSS., the William Stirling MS.,

and the Kinloch virginal MS., which chiefly include ballad airs, marches and dance music. In other words, psalm tunes were now looked upon as part of the general fund of music, and one can guess that, set for a chest of viols, they would in many instances make quite pleasurable music. John Forbes of Aberdeen, in his *Cantus* (1662 *et seq*), planned his "Songs and Fancies, to Three, Four, or Five Parts " as being " apt for Voices and Viols," and his title page depicted a psalm singer on one side and a lutanist on the other.

In these days, Aberdeen was, after Edinburgh, the musical centre of Scotland, and Forbes considered it not only "the sanctuary of the Sciences, the manse of the Muses, and nursery of all the Arts," but a place whose other " fine endowments hath almost overspread whole Europe," in proof of which he shows " the great confluence of all sorts of persons from each part of the same, who of design have come (much like that of the Queen of Sheba) to hear the sweet cheerful Psalms, and heavenly melody of famous Bon-Accord." Here it would seem that psalm-singing had become quite a secular performance by this period and took the place of our community singing, the psalm itself being merely the vehicle for expression, just as the mass songs on folk themes are in Russia today.

In the purely secular field of vocal music, as illustrated by the contents of Forbes' *Cantus* (1662) there does not appear to be an item which could be counted as being from the songs of the people. Forbes' patrons must have noticed the omission because in his second edition (1666) he remedied this by adding three items which clearly appealed to wider tastes. These were, *My heartly [heartie] service to you* (" The Pleugh Song "), *All sones of Adam* and *Trip and go hey*, which, said the late Prof. Sanford Terry, showed " distinctively national or local flavor." The remainder of the songs in Forbes' books, if we include the last edition (1682) show a catholic taste, as we shall see. The lute, mandore and viols books of these days, as reflected in the Rowallan, Straloch, Stirling, Skene, Guthrie, Blaikie and Leyden MSS., in addition to the several Dalhousie MSS. for virginal, gittern, lute and violin, show the wide appreciation of secular music.

Despite the measures of interference with the rough and ready open air music of the people, no attempt was made at curbing the indoor musical pleasures of the middle class. For one thing, the fiery zeal of the reforming days in this direction had petered out. Indeed at the opening of the century the Sang Schools, which were almost the preserves of the middle class, were in a flourishing way. These, with the Grammar Schools and Writing Schools, constituted the chief educational facilities prior to entering the Universities. Many excellent and conscientious men were functioning as Masters in the Sang Schools. Aberdeen may be taken as an example, although admittedly the best. Here Patrick Davidson was Master (1603-36) and he is said to have studied in Italy. He was succeeded by another worthy man, Andrew Melville (1636-40), to be followed by Thomas Davidson (1640-75), who was better known for his help in Forbes' *Cantus* (1662 *et seq.*). After him came the more celebrated Louis de France (1675-82). Those who later held the post were not so eminent, although one of the masters of Aberdeen's other Sang School, St. Machars, had some small celebrity. This was William Hay, afterwards Bishop of Moray, who was precentor and master of the Sang School in the " Fifties " of this century.

The position of music in relation to other subjects that were taught is made clear in the school at Newbottle in 1626, where the kirk session ordered that scholars were to pay 10s. quarterly for learning to read and write " Scots," and for music 6s. 8d.

Whilst the church was neglecting, when it was not condemning, instrumental music, the Sang Schools were encouraging it. True, their main duty was to teach the elements of music, sufficient to be able to read the Proper and Common Tunes, but there arose in this century such a desire for proficiency in instrumental music that the Sang Schools were persuaded to add this to the curriculum in some towns. So early as 1603, the Sang School at Elgin had already adopted this line. The Master at Haddington in 1610 taught the virginal, lute and gittern, as well as singing, and as late as 1677 he was to instruct "men as well as children . . . to sing

music and play upon musical instruments." When John Mow
(d. 1647) was appointed to Dundee Sang School in 1609, he brought
a pair of virginals on stipulation with him. At Leith in 1613,
the town insisted on an instrumentalist as Master. Yet they were
all badly paid in the smaller towns. Although Dundee could pay
£250 (which included rent money), Inverness could only afford £36
(without rent allowance), whilst Elgin furnished £230, but the
Master had charge of the English School as well for this stipend.
In 1626, Glasgow had to forbid other singers in the town from
teaching singing, before it could obtain a Master for its Sang School.

This last item reveals the approaching decay of the Sang Schools.
After the re-establishment made by James VI in 1579, things
went well with these institutions, and this continued into the next
century. Then we find that the Masters, owing to lack of official
or outside support, were being appointed Uptakers, Raisers or
Precentors, and even Readers of the parish churches so as to
implement their meagre stipends. The mere fear of Episcopacy
and the Anglican service, had its deadening effect on music after
the events of 1637. The Sang Schools languished and fell into
neglect in many places. In Glasgow, it was admitted that the
Music School was " altogether decayed within this said borough,"
and plans for its restoration were laid, at which time it was stated
that the Master was to teach both vocal and instrumental music.
In 1627 it was found at Musselburgh that the funds for the upkeep
of the Music School endowed by James VI had actually been
disposed to someone else. At another place, where there once
existed a provision for a Music School, there was at this date no
funds for its maintenance.

As we have seen in the century that has passed, some of the
great divines were privily fond of music, but afraid that it would
lead them astray. This was the attitude of James Melville and
Alexander Hume in Reformation days. In the 17th century John
Livinstone, in his *Autobiography*, admits that there were " two
recreations I was *in danger* to be taken with." One was " *singing
in a consort of musick*, wherein I had some little skill, and took

great delight; but it was *thirty-six years* since I used it." What a confession ! He tells also of Principal Robert Boyd of Glasgow " who would call me and some other three or four, and lay down books before us, and have us sing sets of music." William Guthrie was another of that type. Dunlop, his biographer, says that Guthrie took " great pleasure in music, in the *theory and practice of which* he had a more than ordinary dexterity." In the *Panmure Manuscript* (*c.* 1632), the notes on the theory of music were made by the Rev. Robert Edwardes, Minister of Murroes, Forfarshire. All these references attest the fact that all the clergy were not such " dour bodies " as externals would lead us to believe.

Of course the existence of music books for the lute, mandore, gittern, violin, *viola da gamba* and virginal among the leisured classes, in addition to the fairly widespread use of the instruments as we shall see presently, do not in themselves reflect the musical culture of the people in general, but since so many of the songs and tunes have a distinctly " popular " *flair*, we may justly assume that some at least were possibly bosomed by the " people " first. Yet it was only in the nature of things that the best music was in the hands of the leisured classes, whether the nobility or the rich bourgeoisie, and it is to them that we owe the birth of the concert in Scotland.

England was probably the first among European nations to establish what we know today as concerts, the earliest being given by John Banister in London in 1672, but Scotland was not slow in following this lead. When the Duke of York held his revels in the tennis court at Holyrood Palace in 1682, music was one of the special features. Rogers, in his *Social History of Scotland*, says that the Duke created " a taste for operatic music," but adds that such things were " condemned by the Church and denounced by the multitude." According to Dr. D. Fraser Harris (*Saint Cecilia's Hall*), the " concerts seem to have been given . . . in the tennis-court, then under the ducal ' set.' " Twelve years later, as Chambers (*Domestic Annals of Scotland*) tells us, " a man named Beck, with some associates, had now (1694) erected a concert of music." This concert was held on the 10th January and was the first of its kind in Scotland. A more conspicuous landmark on the terrene of concerts in Scotland is that of 1695, when Henry Crumbden, a German, "long the Orpheus of the musical school of Edinburgh," arranged and conducted the famous St. Cecilia's Day concert of that year. About thirty performers took part, including nineteen gentlemen of " first rank and fashion " and eleven " masters of music " who were professionals. William Tytler (1711-92) has left a full account of this concert (*Transactions of the Society of Antiquaries of Scotland*, 1792). Among the more outstanding of the nobility who performed on this occasion was Robert, Lord Colville of Ochiltree (d. 1728) who is said to have " understood counterpoint well." Daniel Defoe (d. 1731) gives him a line in his *Caledonia*,—" The God of Musick joyns when Colville plays." Even the professionals claim passing notice if only because of their progeny. Matthew McGibbon, who played the oboe, was the father of William McGibbon the violinist and composer, whilst Daniel Thomson, trumpet, and his son William, violinist, both performed on this occasion, the latter being the well known compiler of the *Orpheus Caledonius* (1725).

CHAPTER 3

THE INSTRUMENTS

" Go take up the Psalmes,
The *timbrel* and *shalmes* :
Bring foorth now let see,
The *harp* full of pleasure,
With *viols* in measure,
That well can agree."

PONT : *Psalm* LXXXI.

Seeing that half a century had passed since the days of storm and stress in the Reformation struggle, one is compelled to ask how the 17th century Reformers, when singing this fine stirring psalm as paraphrased by one of the stalwarts in the fight, still managed to square their views in condemnation of the instrumental praise of God with these very pointed lines of the psalmist? It is of some importance because this dislike of instrumental music in worship was still in full vigour, a proceeding which, although lofty from the Puritan ideal, was calamitous to music in Scotland. In England, on the contrary, in spite of a short Puritan reaction that was bent on destroying or removing instruments, this was a period of great importance for the organ.

By this time the organ had developed out of all semblance to the instrument that had existed in the previous century, as we know from many sources. In England, the Dallam, Harris, and Smith (Schmidt) families had become famous organ builders, and it was the first named who constructed the organ for the Chapel Royal at Holyrood in 1617. We have no specification of it, although there is an account of Dallam's organ built for King's College, Cambridge, with which the Holyrood instrument would most likely be comparable. Yet we have the authority of Devon's *Issues of the Exchequer* (1836) that this latter was a " fair, large, and very serviceable double organ " and that it cost £300. We do know also that it was fashioned under the supervision of the famous Inigo Jones, which control, probably, only covered externals. Under Charles I this organ continued to be used at the Chapel Royal, and his Scottish Master of Music, Edward Kellie, installed another organ in the privy chamber of the palace itself in 1630-31. At the turmoil created by Laud's Liturgy in 1637, and the general outcry against the Anglican service, the organs, for there was more than one as was customary, were banned from the Chapel. It is said that they were destroyed, but so late as 1643, one of them was still lying derelict in the aisle. When James VII tried to re-establish the Roman Church in Scotland, a " large and beautiful organ " was installed in the Abbey Church, but it was demolished, says Maitland (*History of Edinburgh*), by the " giddy multitude " in 1688. It was almost a half century before Scotland heard an organ again in any place of worship. That the organ was in private use elsewhere in this century is shown in *The Glamis Book* (S.H.S.) and in Innes' *Sketches of Early Scottish History*.

Virginals and *spinets* were still the rage in Scotland among the well-to-do. Dalyell mentions two virginal makers in Edinburgh in 1653 and 1659 named John Davidson and Alexander Adam. At Aberdeen, a John Davidson, probably the same man, had to substantiate his claim as an expert virginal maker before the Town Council would permit him to establish himself there. This delicately-toned instrument (and does not Edmund Spenser name it " mildness virginal ") attracted everyone, low and high. In 1610, the master of the Sang School at Haddington was teaching the instrument to the *bairns*, and at Holyrood Palace " a pair of virginals to play upon " is registered in 1625. We also find the instrument up in the Highlands of Sutherlandshire under the pliant fingers of a *laird's* daughter in 1653-54, and so far south as Ayrshire, at Kilmaurs, the infant daughter of the Earl of Glencairn (d. 1644) had a diminutive instrument made specially for her tiny hands. Even at the close of the century (1694), an inventory of a house of the Earl of Airth and Monteith on the islet of Tanna reveals " a pair of virginals " in the hall. Contemporary virginal music is preserved in the Panmure, Kinloch, and Lady Jean Campbell manuscripts, as indicated by Dr. Harry M. Willsher. In the English *Elizabeth Rogers Virginal Book* (1656) are *The Scots' Marche*, *A Scotts Tuen*, and the *Glorye of the North*. As for the instrument itself, a beautiful virginal, once belonging to Lady Mary Stewart, Countess of Mar, and cousin of Mary Queen of Scots, was once in the possession of the late Sheriff Erskine Murray. Boswell, in his *Journal*, records (1773) having heard " several tunes on a spinet [i.e. a triangular form of the virginal] which, though made so long ago as 1667, was still very well toned."

Music for fingerboard stringed instruments, i.e. the lute, mandore, and the like, is fairly plentiful at this era, and among the relics are the Rowallan (1612-28), Skene (1615-35), and Straloch (1627-29) manuscripts, of which only the Skene book has been edited and published. By this time the *lute* had become a specially favoured instrument, and William Drummond of Hawthornden (d. 1649) sang in its praise. In England, choirs of lutes, i.e. of various size and pitch, were in use. At a masque given for the nuptials of Lord Hay in 1607 there were three lutes used, two *mean* lutes [possibly treble and tenor] and a *bass* lute. At another masque, when James VI's Queen and his daughter Princess Elizabeth performed, twelve lutes of different sizes doubtless, were being sounded. An inventory of the effects of the King's favourite, the Earl of Somerset, the erstwhile James Ker or Carr, reveals a lute.

In Scotland, the instrument was mounted with four, five, or six strings, and the title-page of Forbes' *Cantus* (1662 *et seq.*) reveals a four-stringed type. With *diapason* strings at the side there would be many more strings, and probably the lute of the Rowallan MS. would be strung,—D F A *diapason*, with D G B e a, on the *finger-board*. In the Straloch MS. the *Queen's Almone* is stated to have been " played on a fourteen cord lute."

Closely allied to the lute were the *mandore*, *pandore*, and *gittern*. The *mandore*, as we have seen, was a kind of treble lute mounted with four strings. Seemingly, the Skene MS. was written for this instrument, and it contains rules for " tuning the *mandwr* to the old tune [*accordatura*] of the lutt," from which we know that the lute formerly had four strings. The *pandore* was originally a long-necked instrument of the lute class, but by this time it was a flat-chested, large sized gittern, with incurvatures at the sides and mounted with 10, 12, or 14 strings fixed bicordally. Kellie, the Master of the Chapel Royal at Holyrood, when furnishing the palace musically in 1630-31, supplied two *pandores*. We know much about the instrument generally from Thomas Robinson's *School of Musicke* (1603). Its meaner brother was the *gittern* but, unlike the lute and mandore, it had wire strings, as Mace tells us in his *Musick's Monument* (1676), although the lower strings were of gut covered or " wreathed " with wire, as Lord Bacon describes them. It must have had wide approval in Scotland among both the masses and classes, since we find a master of the Haddington Sang School teaching it in 1610 to the *bairns* of the people at large, whilst music for it, in the Panmure MS., as Dr. Willsher informs me, gives proof of its popularity with the leisured folk.

Nor can we forget the *harp*, although this national instrument had already been pushed aside by the lute, mandore, gittern, and viol. It was however, still cherished in the Highlands, as William Kirk tells us in his *Secret Commonwealth*, wherein we read of " our northern Scottish and Athol men " being " much addicted to and delighted with *harps*." That was in 1691. A letter to Robert Wodrow in 1700 also mentions that the music of the people about Inverlochy and Inverness-shire included playing on the *clarsech* or Highland harp. Among the " Upper Ten " a harper was still attached to a household as part of feudal dignity, in precisely the same way as in Ireland as Barnaby Rich shows (*New Description of Ireland*, 1610). Indeed, harpers from Ireland were frequent in Scotland. Rory *dall* O'Cahan spent most of his life there (1601-50), and left his imprint in the many *puirts* (ports), notably *Rory dall's port* in the Straloch MS. (1627-29) which Burns used later for *Ae fond kiss*. With those who went south to the " Promised Land " with James VI in 1603 and after, the *clarsech* still found acceptance, since in the inventory of the belongings of Robert Ker or Carr, afterwards Earl of Somerset under the accolade of James, we find " two Irish harps." These were doubtless Scottish harps, but they still carried the name of their original provenance—" *ersch clarsechis*." By this time the shape of the Scottish harp had undergone a considerable change. The front pillar was higher and the top of it had now an ornamental scroll. It may be seen in the cuts on the title-pages of the 1611 and 1633 psalters, as well as elsewhere, notably the Urquhart (Cromarty) coat of arms dated 1651 in the National Museum of Antiquities, Edinburgh. These particular features were passed on in the next century and they are reflected in the Irish Bunworth harp (John Kelly, 1734). John Gunn (*An Historical Enquiry*) tells of a Roderick Morison, " one of the last native Highland harpers," who composed the *port* called *Suipar chiurn na Leod* " about 1650," and a certain John Garve Maclean, " an excellent performer on the harp," who flourished even earlier. He was in the service of the Macleans of Coll.

Viols and *fiddles* were as much to the fore as ever, and we have a continual reference to their manipulators from 1604 when we read of " Andrew Peddy, fiddler," to 1710 when " David Hood, Linlithgow " is mentioned as a similar executant. Doubtless a " chest " of viols, i.e. a quartet of two trebles, a tenor, and a bass, was the rule in these days in Scotland. These are prescribed in Playford's *Introduction to the Skill of Musick*. *Viols* were among the instruments ordered for Holyrood House in 1630-31 for the delectation of Charles I, and we read of " four violars " being engaged for the coronation solemnities of Charles II at Edinburgh in 1660. That viols were popular is evident from the penalties inflicted by the Town Council of Glasgow in 1691 on persons passing through the city with viols and other instruments to the scandal of the burgh. Music for viols in Scotland is not plentiful. The Scottish David Melville MS. (17th cent.) contained pieces for a string quartet, probably viols, some of the music being of Scottish origin. Then there is the Guthrie MS. and the Leyden MS. which, being in tablature, reveals that the *accordatura* was $\underline{D} \ \underline{G} \ D \ G \ B \ d$ and $\underline{D} \ \underline{G} \ D \ G \ B\flat \ d$. The Blaikie MS. has similar features. When Forbes issued his *Cantus : Songs and Fancies* (1662, 1666, 1682), he said that his work would be in three, four, or five parts, " apt for voices and viols," and so must have been catering for a commonly instrumented combination. Whether Tobias Hume (d. 1645) was Scottish born or not, it is interesting to note that he issued a work—*Poeticall Musicke . . . for Two Basse Viols* (1607).

The *flute* and *recorder* seem to have been the one and same instrument at this period, and it was a *flûte à bec*. Two *flutes* were introduced by Kellie with other instruments for the privy chamber in Holyrood Palace in 1630-31, and at one of the first known public concerts in Edinburgh in 1695 there were six flutes, and their performers are named. There are a few manuscripts of flute music in the British Museum containing two jolly and characteristic " Scotch Tunes " for two flutes, and other solo " Scotch Tunes," genuine or otherwise, set by Purcell, Leveridge, Finger, and Sadler. The *quhisel* (whistle) was the common transverse fife, which was used in the army and civil life with the side drum as an excellent enlivenment of the march. Indeed, Sir James Turner (d. 1686), the eminent Scottish soldier, preferred the *Almain whistle*, as he called it, to the *bagpipe*.

Although we have seen in the previous century that the *hautbois* had taken the place of the more primitive *shawm*, both were still in use because the tone of each was distinctive. We read of the Edinburgh Town Council having five *chalmes* and *howboyes* in 1607, although by 1694 and 1696, *hoyeboyes* only are employed. The *courtall* was the tenor of this family, and the bass was provided by the *double curtle* which Edinburgh had in its town waits in 1696, when Malcolm McGibbon played it. He and John Monroe, hautboist, were considered " compleat masters " as players. *Hoboys* were also used by dragoons and regiments of foot in Scotland.

More martial still, at least in Scotland, was the *bagpipe*. Sir James Turner, possibly owing to having been inured to other marching music whilst serving abroad, would not (1683) tolerate the bagpipe in the service. Most other Scots had different views. Lord Lothian, writing to Lord Ancrum in 1641, said,—" We are well provided of *pypers ;* I have one for every company ; and I think they are as good as drummers." The Scots abroad in Holland (1629) had three per company at 12 Rix dollars a month each, i.e. about £3. Many of the towns had the bagpipe, and the household piper still found a place among the domestics of the gentry, as we read of the " piper to the laird of Buchanan " in 1604. It was also the joy of the people at large, as the Kirk Session Records often reveal, for the skirl of the pipe meant merriment. One other instrument of the people was the Jaws harp. In Martin's *Voyage to St. Kilda* (1697) we are told that " the *Jewish Harp* [*Jews Harp*= *Jaws Harp*] or Trump, is all the music they have."

Instruments with cupped mouthpieces were not many,—the *cornett, horn, trumpet* and *sackbut*. The first and last of these were often used together, not only in processions, but in church and chamber music. *Cornetts* and *sackbuts* were part of the " King's Musick " in London when Charles I reigned there in days of splendour. They were used in the Chapel Royal, and in 1630-31,

Kellie, his Master of Music in the Scottish Chapel Royal, carried to the latter "two men for playing on *cornets* and *sakbuts*." The *cornett* was also to be found among the Edinburgh town musicians in 1679. The *horn* was no longer an instrument of the martial throng, but was reserved for the chase and hunt alone. The *trumpet* still maintained its pre-eminence for signals and fanfares in military and ceremonial affairs. All regiments of horse had the *trumpet*, as the Articles of War for the Scottish Army of 1641 show. Town councils also employed trumpeters for their displays and we see this in Edinburgh as late as 1649. Even the nobility had them. Patrick Earl of Orkney in 1615 had three trumpeters who sounded before the first course at dinner and after grace. That state trumpeters still held office in Scotland is evident from Charles the First's orders calling on the Privy Council and others to attend divine worship in the Chapel Royal in 1629 " by sound of *trumpett*." In 1681, these state trumpeters were still demanding their " due and accustomed allowance " from newly elected Lords of Parliament for services rendered. Contemporary Scottish iconography has much interest for the trumpet. Sometimes we see the time-honoured straight *trumpet* tube, and at others the wreathed *clarion* tube that we know to-day. We have examples delineated in the Funeral of the Marquis of Huntly (1636), and the Funeral of John, Duke of Rothes (1681), as well as elsewhere. The latter reveals a feature of unusual interest in that it depicts both the *open* and the *close* trumpet, the latter being the *muted* instrument. This accessory is very rarely delineated, and one of the few occasions that it has been shown is in Sieur de Gaya's *Traité des Armes* (1678).

Lastly come drums. When we saw the *tabron* or *talburn* lately it was a side drum, linked almost exclusively with military and cere-monial usage, an employment with which it continued during the 17th century and was more generally called the *drum*. In Scottish regiments of dragoons and foot, two drummers were attached to each company, whilst *kettledrums* had a place with regiments of horse, as in the case of the Scottish Life Guards at Holyrood in 1665. On the authority of Gordon of Rothiemay (*History of Scottish Affairs*) we know that the Scottish drummers were beating " taptoes, reveilles and marches," and among the latter, the *Scottish March*, the *Irish March*, and the *English March*. The town side drums of Edinburgh (temp. Charles II) and Aberdeen (17th cent.) are still preserved in these cities, whilst two similar drums of Covenanting times are in private hands.

And so, despite the neglect and even condemnation of instrumental music by the church, this phase of the art flourished everywhere in Scotland. When we note that it was even encouraged by the Sang Schools we can be sure that interest was widespread. Trade in instruments is also a fair index to their popularity, because duty had to be paid on those that were imported, and there must have been a fair amount of business in this line for the authorities to trouble about an impost. The ledgers of Andrew Haliburton show that a pair of *virginals* was taxed at £20, a *lute* at £10, a *viol* at £4, and a gross of *whistles* at 12s. 5d.

CHAPTER 4

THE CHURCH

" While, in England, the change of religion did not produce any great immediate alteration in the music of the Church, in this country [Scotland], there can be no doubt, that the annihilation of the great choral establishments, the exclusion of organs and other instruments from the service, and the severe simplicity of the style of psalmody introduced by the rigid disciples of Calvin and Knox, had a considerable effect in checking the progress of the art."

DAUNEY : *Ancient Scottish Melodies* (1838).

Officially and unofficially, the Kirk gave neither approval nor countenance to the organ, choir, or part-singing. This was the attitude of the militant days of the Reformation in Scotland which we have just passed, and it continued, with but a slight *decrescendo*, during the period under contribution. Even with Pont's rousing *Psalm LXXXI*, and the more pointed praise of *Psalm CL* ringing in their ears, the Reformers were still opposed to instrumental music in church praise. The " Popes of Edinburgh," as the General Assembly was dubbed by its opponents, would probably say of the music of the psalmists, as Calvin did, that in the time of the Law the Jews were in their childhood, Of course the Presbyterian Scots, being grown up, knew better. Some of the most revered Presbyterian divines of the period make their position regarding instrumental music quite clear. Samuel Rutherfurd (d. 1661) had no liking for the " droning of organs," as he states in his *Divine Right of Church Government* (1646). David Calderwood (d. 1650) is openly contemptuous and places the Romanist prelate who " loveth carnal and curious music " in the organ, lute, and cittern, in opposition to the Reformed pastor, who " loveth no music in the house of God but such as edifieth," i.e. the human voice. In Charles Mouat's MS. (1661) in Glasgow University Library entitled *A Breefe Refutation*, it is laid down that " musical instruments are not to be used in God's worship." Certainly, as we have seen, the organ was in use at the Chapel Royal, and Charles wanted organs erected in all the cathedrals and principal churches in Scotland, but the church was quite refractory to such a proposal, and in 1638 the General Assembly registered open defiance against instruments of music in public worship. In 1644, in a letter to the Assembly at Westminster, the General Assembly said,—" We were greatly refreshed to hear by letters from our Commissioners . . . of . . . the great organs at St. Pauls and St. Peters taken down."

As for choirs, it must be pointed out that the opinion of the late Sir Richard Terry that the Presbyterian Church employed expert choirs at this date is, to say the least, an exaggeration. In his chatty book, *A Forgotten Psalter* (1929), he says,—" As is well known, the choirs in those days were manned by skilled singers who (like all other Mediaeval guilds) jealously guarded the mysteries of their craft." Actually what is " well known " of " those days " is that choirs in the Scottish church were non-existent, for the simple reason that they were considered a Papistic relic as has been fully demonstrated. Contemporary documents (1560-1625) make this quite clear. Where there *was* singing in the church (and it was not universal) it was in the *congregation* only. The justification for this practice was quite valid, as the late Dr. Neil Livingston pointed out,—

> " With whatever defects the church singing of Scotland has been chargeable in later times, it has all along continued to be, with few exceptions, *congregational*. The rival method of conducting praise is that in which a select number sing. . . . It would be too much to deny that it is possible to obtain devotional edification by this method, and it may be admitted that such power as music adds to language is thereby more fully developed. But if music pass much beyond the ability of the hearer to join with it vocally . . . it is very apt to be listened to *simply as a performance*."

From this particular point of view one can apprehend the aim of the church and appreciate its fear. Indeed, precisely the same argument could be urged against preaching and *a fortiori*. Knox and his fellows were not a whit less rhetoricians than Tertullian and his Patristic circle. Not all of the Reformers were given to the plain evangelical sermon and homely vernacular. Many who wrote their sermons indulged in the elegant expression and revelled in the decorative style, often artificially pompous. Although Scotland did not produce a Jeremy Taylor, many of her divines spoke and penned the graceful and polished line, the grandiose rhythm, the felicitous illustration, studying what should be tersely expressed and what elaborately expounded. How indeed could it be otherwise ? We are but human, whether preacher or congregation, and eloquence moves the utterer, just as it appeals to the listener, emotionally, but, to apply the words of Livingston, "is not preaching likewise very apt to be listened to simply as a performance ? ".

That church singing in Scotland was performed by the congregation and not by a choir up to 1625 there cannot be any doubt. In earlier documents we read such phrases as the *people* " sing a psalm together," " The *people* shall sing," " The *assembly* shall be dismissed after *they* have sung." There is not a solitary mention of a choir " in those days," as Terry thought. In 1561, " uptakers," later called " raisers," and soon to be dubbed " precentors," were admitted, but they merely gave the " tone " and led *congregational* praise. By 1587, we have seen what looks suspiciously like hired men creeping into the singing, which may be thought to be the seeds of a choir, but actually they were only there to strengthen *congregational singing*. That there was a dearth of good singers is well illustrated in James Melville's *Diary*, where he tells of the Laird of Doune who, in 1570, out of charity, had entertained a blind man. Finding him possessed of a " singular good voice," he was appointed " Doctor " of the Sang School, to teach " the whole psalms in metre, with the tones thereof, and sing them in the kirk." As for part-singing in the church, there is some slight evidence that it was even forbidden. It is true that the Chapel Royal, which was a law unto itself, had a choir and most likely used the harmonized psalter which only circulated in manuscript, but a choir and part-singing *were not used in the ordinary church*.

The music of the printed psalters from 1564 to 1621 was purely homophonic, i.e. only the melody was given. Obviously the church would not sanction a harmonized version at this time, and since no person other than the official printer was permitted to issue any psalm book, or even " bring hither the same out of other countries," there was little chance of an outside music lover placing a printed harmonized psalter on the market.

In 1611, many of the Proper Tunes were suppressed and three fresh English tunes were inserted, but these liberties were rectified in the 1615 psalter issued by Andro Hart. In this work, in addition to the Proper Tunes, a new feature appeared in what was known as Common Tunes. These, as the late Sir Richard Terry once pointed out, were a " concession to *congregations* who might boggle at the complex rhythms of the Proper Tunes." They were all in common metre, and could be utilized for any similarly metred psalm. Some such expedient seems to have existed earlier, since the 1565 psalter had a tune called *Old Common* which, although " proper " for *Psalm* CVIII, was considered " common " to any psalm of a like metre. Between 1602 and 1615, two other " proper " tunes came to be used as " common," viz., *London* and *English*. When the 1615 psalter appeared, twelve Common Tunes found a place in the economy of psalming, and since things were not too rosy in the church musically, their advent was a blessing to the congregation which was in dire need of simpler metres and rhythms. These Common Tunes, repeated in the Edinburgh 1625 psalter, were:—*Olde Common, London, English, Dundie, Stilt, Dukes, Dumfermeling, Martyrs, Kinges, French, Abbay,* and *Glasgow.* Of these, if prior date of publication is to be the rule (save in *Olde Common*), the first five must be considered English. By the same token, the last seven are of Scottish origin, which judgment, by the way, was delivered by Ravenscroft in his *Whole Booke of Psalmes* so far back as 1621, and no evidence since that date has invalidated this decision.

The growing muster roll of Common Tunes did not end with the Apostolic twelve. The Aberdeen psalter of 1625, where they were harmonized, gave fifteen, which was still the norm in 1633 psalter where they are also harmonized. In that of 1634, and in the more famous harmonized psalter of 1635, there are *thirty-one* Common Tunes. Incidentally, this rising numeric *crescendo* in the Common Tunes is, in itself, an index to the dwindling musical skill of the congregation. When the original Proper Tunes were fixed for the psalms, the congregations still had seated in their midst the residue of the erstwhile vicars-choral and choir-boys of the old *régime.* These skilled singers and readers could make a good job of the intricate rhythmic Proper Tunes and, in spite of the absence of part-singing which was then *anathema,* it must have been a joy to have heard *Psalm* CXXI, or even the richer *Psalm* LXXXI from such a body. But a half-century had elapsed since those days, and the old professionals who once had psalmed *in the congregation* had gone. What was left was the congregation only. Need one say more ? These people were unable to cope with the more intricate Proper Tunes and the emergence of the Common Tunes was the result. In this way the people were able to jog along comfortably in what Dauney has called " a simple and naked psalmody." Such conditions could not for ever obtain sufferance from those who yearned for something more elevating, impressive, and emotional. Some, perhaps those who from their secular indulgence in music (although much of this was naturally screened for respectability sake), saw a better type of church music being indulged in elsewhere, and what this was we shall see.

When the Episcopal movement first raised its head in Scotland in 1606 *et seq.*, the imposing Anglican service found little response save among the privileged classes. With the masses, while the doctrinal and ceremonial aspects of Episcopacy were repellent, there was one thing in which a few could have had sympathy, and that was its music. First of all there was the attraction of part-singing. This was something in which many reformers indulged outside the church, and they would fain see it practised inside. Then there were those hymns and anthems which they found quite agreeable even to reformed worship, more especially since they added variety to the conventional psalmody. Finally, the contrapuntal devices used in the Anglican service were really intriguing to the real musician. This is how Scotland would feel the impingement of the southern art. In the year 1617, the Privy Seal Records note that " the English service was begun in the Chapel Royal, with the singing of choristers, surplices, and playing on organs." It was all very Papistic to the narrower Presbyterian mind, but the innovation held sway for a quarter of a century, long enough for the more liberal minded of the reforming church to become familiar with, if not somewhat enamoured of, some features at least of the music of the Anglican service. The first fruits of this influence was the printing of the Common Tunes of the psalter in four-part harmony. This feature showed itself quite early, possibly before 1625, because the Raban Aberdeen psalter of 1625 has these Common Tunes harmonized.

In 1635 the greatest of all the Scottish psalters was published. This was Edward Millar's complete harmonized psalter, which had been compiled in 1626, as we shall see presently. It included both the Common and the Proper Tunes, which were set with much greater freedom than the previous " note against note " principle of harmony. More audacious was the appearance of some highly contrapuntal " Tunes in Reports " which, displaying that " curious " art so redolent of Roman and Anglican services, must have shocked the more conservative clergy. Livingston says that it can hardly be doubted that the Tunes in Reports were used in the Chapel Royal where Edward Millar, the editor, was in control. That the printing of the psalter was done with a *verso* page on the left side printed upright, and a *recto* page on the right side printed upside down, shows that a regular choir in rows facing each other, reading from the same book, was visualized.

Already some sort of musical organisation in the Reformed churches had been showing itself. In 1621, " the Master of the Sang School *and his bairns* " were sitting in the church at Stirling to assist in psalm singing. These *bairns* were doubtless his scholars at the Sang School, and their appearance in this way would suggest an attempt at a choir, although no more than trebles and altos could be counted on with this material. By this time, it may be mentioned, Masters of the Sang Schools were generally expected to be Precentors or Readers in the churches, a circumstance which points to the indifference with which both the civic and church authorities looked upon both these offices, although primarily it was the lack of funds which prompted one man for two posts as a remedy. The whole system was bad in both principle and practice since it led to the decay of the Sang Schools and the deterioration of music in the church. In any case, the attempt of Charles I to force Episcopacy upon Scotland stemmed any hope of betterment or any likelihood of the peaceful penetration of a higher Anglican form of music within Presbyterian precincts.

At the same time the General Assembly had long considered the advisability of having a new psalter, especially one that would be less difficult to the congregation. Charles I considered that a version made by his father, James VI, ought to be chosen. The General Assembly was not to be forced or cajoled into its acceptance, and the famous *Reasons against the Reception* (1634), written probably by Calderwood, expressed many truths and half-truths. The new metres, it was thought, " served to make people *glaik*." More practical, from a point of view of self-preservation, was the criticism that " if psalms be removed *other things might follow*." To our mind, the most cogent argument against acceptance was that (a) " Sundry musicians of the best skill . . . have set down Common and Proper Tunes to the whole psalms according to the *diverse forms of the metre*." (b) " Both pastors and people by long custom, are so acquainted with the psalms and the tunes thereof." Charles I, with those Divine Right theories turning his head, thought otherwise and, as Row says, insisted that King James' version be " received and sung in all the kirks in Scotland."

The troublous times that followed the attempts at enforcing Episcopacy brought about the neglect of even plain psalmody in some places. Psalters without music now became the rule. From 1564 to 1625, nine out of the ten psalters, of which we have information, contained the music. From 1625 to 1644, out of *thirty* psalters, of which we have copies today, only *six* contain music, a circumstance fraught with significance. Of course it could be argued that since most of the churches only used the more usual twelve Common Tunes, which were learned *viva voce*, there was no need for the luxury of psalm books with music. Indeed psalm-singing seems to have actually disappeared for a time. We certainly read this startling note in Nicol's *Diary* (*sub anno* 1653), " In the year of God 1645, the reading of Chapters in the Kirk, by the Common reader, and *singing of psalms were discharged*, and in the place thereof came the lectures. . . . This did not content the people because there was no reading of Chapters *nor singing of psalms* on the Sabbath Day ; wherefore ministers thought it good to *restore the wonted custom of singing of psalms*, . . . This began in October, 1653." Whether this practice of omitting the psalms obtained generally we cannot say, but in 1650 the congregation was singing psalms in Glasgow Cathedral.

In this year, 1650, a new psalter, known as the Authorized Version, was ordered to be used by the General Assembly. As the bibliographer of Scottish psalmody, William Cowan (*Early Scottish Psalm-Tune Books*), has said: "This book was issued not only *without tunes, but without any directions whatever as to suitable music.* The result of this neglect on the part of the Church authorities was that the cultivation of Church music in Scotland fell to a very low ebb." Much trouble and care had been expended on the authorized version so far as the paraphrase and metre were concerned, but nothing was done about the music. That was forgotten, or else it was not considered of sufficient importance. So with the publication of the 1650 psalter the pristine period of the Scottish psalter drew to an inglorious close.

What follows in the history of the music of the Scottish psalter to the end of this era is of little consequence. As the Rev. James W. Macmeeken says, in paraphrasing Neil Livingston, the Church ceased to protect her music. "A depreciated estimate of the place and power of music in religion began to prevail," he says, " occasioned, among other causes, by the recoil from the pressure of . . . the Episcopal movement which ended in 1637. A jealousy of, and aversion to, every indication of an interest in the external elements of worship, seem to have been thus engendered. The old psalm books, with the music, became increasingly scarce; the Sang Schools became extinct, and the fallacy laid hold on the Scottish mind that it matters not about the quality of the musical material or its execution if the heart be rightly exercised."

It was in this wise that Scotland lost " the fixed connection between psalm and tune." How miserably the Church failed in this direction has been well summed up by Neil Livingston himself. Nor will he allow blame to be thrown on the shoulders of the precentors who, after the fall of the Sang Schools, were obviously inefficient. His words, which cannot be glossed over, are these: "Confessions of Faith, Catechisms and other guides, were formed for the assistance of ministers, teachers, &c., but the poor precentors were left to grope in the dark, and discover the principles of their art as best they might. *Not a page seems to have been furnished for their instruction for one hundred and fifty years.*"

Church music in the Highlands and its seeming influence on the Lowlands deserves treatment. It does not appear to be generally recognized that the Highlands were never fully reformed. Indeed, it was here that the core of resistance by the Church of Rome settled itself, strengthening its barriers as late as 1709, when the Society for the Propagation of the Gospel (such is the alleged excuse for its being) was founded. It was not until 1659 that the Synod of Argyll introduced a Gaelic First Fifty of the Psalms of David (*An Ceud Chaogad do Shalmaibh Dhaibhidh*). The music was the plain, homophonic kind that we have seen in the Lowland psalters, yet when Mainzer was collecting materials for his *Gaelic Psalm Tunes of Rossshire* (Edin., 1844) he found an intricate, melismatic treatment of the simple melodies of *Dundee*, *Stilt*, and other tunes, so persistent, that he half suggested that it was a relic of pre-Reformation days. This may be true enough, and the " quaverings " of the later singers in the Presbyterian Church up to about 1760 may even be an offshoot of a Roman practice. So long as there was part-singing, as there was in the larger towns immediately after the Reformation, such *fioritura* was quite unlikely to be indulged in, but in the country parishes, and above all in the Highlands, the bald psalm tunes, sung homophonically, lent themselves to decoration, just as some of the priests of the old church had indulged in embellishments to the service chant. Further, we must remember that, after the Reformation, many a chorister of the old church found himself a member of the new congregation, willingly or otherwise, and it would only be natural that, when part singing was neglected, he would fall back on *fioritura*, a style of singing that he had heard in the old days.

On the other hand there is quite an acceptable explanation of this florid decoration in the psalm tunes to be found elsewhere. Highland music, i.e. Gaelic music, more especially in the recitative, and other unrhythmic types, is very embellished. People who were used to such floridity in the toil or social songs of everyday life would naturally give expression to it in church singing, as it was a recognized accomplishment. In addition, there is the likelihood that the Gaelic language itself demanded a variation from the strict reading of the tune of the psalm book. The preface to the 1659 Gaelic psalter makes this palpable enough, since it expresses a fear that the new book will be " despised " because it requires the psalms to be put into " a kind of metre that is foreign to, and not agreeing with the Gaelic language." This factor alone could have created additional notes, although perhaps the original prompting for grace notes, and the almost *glissando* effects that were introduced, were due to the unsubduable decorative art of the Highland singer. And since all decoration is infectious, it would be certainly catching to the Lowlander, and so his " quavering " became part of his psalm singing, which he probably considered to be a spiritual outpouring, as much so as the ejaculative *Hallelujah* elsewhere.

CHAPTER 5

THE MUSIC

" In the seventeenth century the notes of the minstrel were intermittent, the voice of philosophy was silent."
REV. CHARLES ROGERS : *Social Life in Scotland.*

Under the political and religious conditions of this century, and what was leavened by them—the social conditions, how could anything else have been expected than what we read above ? Nor need the Scottish historian have halted at minstrelsy and philosophy, since the whole field of *belles lettres* is likewise a wilderness. Only in the sciences is there any output that marks the era—a giant like Napier of Merchiston (d. 1617), who can rank with Copernicus, Kepler, and Galileo ; Archibald Pitcairne (d. 1713) probably the first physician of his age ; Robert Morrison (d. 1683) the botanist who added to the laurels of Oxford ; and David Gregory (d. 1708) the Savilian professor who graced the same university. Yet they are but a handful. In music, there was but one name, John Abell (d. 1724), and he gained his fame *outwith* Scotland, to use the appropriate Scots word.

This was a period which, in its apprentice years, measures the attitude of the Church towards music at its best or worst, according to the reader's point of approach. During the previous strictly

Reformation era, in spite of the burning zeal of its protagonists, the period was rather one of tentation, in which one can clearly discern how warily the Church trod the course of illapse and relapse. With the dawn of the 17th century, however, it was able to judge more definitely how the wind was blowing and could thus set its course on more rigid lines. By the year 1603, which was forty years since the triumph, the old skilled composers, organists, vicars-choral, and choir-boys of the Church of Rome had gone, and nobody had taken their places since these vocations were redundant. In the secular world, the disapprobation of vocal and instrumental music by the stricter Presbyterians, however ineffectual it may have been with the amateurs of the privileged classes, led to the diminution of professional musicians. Since the stage was barred, the professional lost another most advantageous field both as composer and performer, and that is why I have stressed the special importance of the Church's attitude towards the stage. Added to this was the close and narrow monopoly of printing. It is true that the presses were busy enough at music until 1644, but the platens were for psalm books. How different was the situation in England, where nearly two hundred books of purely secular music alone had been printed before 1600. Even in the 17th century, Scotland only issued one book of secular music, and this was Forbes' *Cantus* of 1662, with two later editions in 1666 and 1682.

These circumstances indicate why, in the creative sphere of music, 17th century Scotland has little or nothing to show, since the church spurned music and the stage was non-existent. The only professional musician of any standing was the Master of the Sang School, and his creative work, where he was capable of such, was conditioned by his office, which he held from the church or burgh, who ran their affairs hand in fist together. It may be allowed, if we take the script as evidence, that these masters sometimes taught " the airt of musick " in the Sang School, but we know that this more generally meant an elementary instruction in psalmody, as dozens of Kirk Session Records amply prove. The extent of the didactics of the Sang School is well illustrated by

Forbes' *Cantus* (1662 *et seq.*) which is derived from John Playford and Thomas Morley, Englishmen both.

One imagines that the English theorists were the main source of instruction for the few insignificant composers who did appear in Scotland during the century. A few Scots abroad, writing in Latin, were interested in music theory, but only as a part of the *quadrivium*, and these were almost mediaeval in their outlook. Examples may be seen in *Hugonis Sempelii Craigbaitaei Scoti de Mathematicis Disciplinis* (Antwerp, 1635), and *Alpharabii vetustissimi Aristotelis interpretis . . . studio et opera Guilielmi Camerarii, Scoti, Fintraei* (Paris, 1638). John Napier, unlike John Wallis, has left nothing on the subject. Strangely enough one finds interest in the question being displayed by amateurs. One, in the Panmure MS. (*c.*1622), written by a clergyman, Robert Edwardes, is, so Dr. Harry Willsher informs me, " mostly derived from *De musica* of Aretino," i.e. Guido of Arezzo (d. 11th cent.). Another, by a certain William McKinnoune *(fl.* 1657) writes on *rudimenta musicae* in *An Musick Book* in manuscript at Aberdeen University. On the whole, after taking into consideration all the circumstances, it is a wonder that Scotland even produced the mere trifles that we do see in musical didactics.

In the creative domain of music it seems only proper that church music should have first consideration because, seeing that the Presbyterian Church was now in full control in every sphere, this might be considered the period *par excellence* for the expression of its music. It will be recalled that the first deviation from the authorized homophonic psalmody came with the Raban Aberdeen psalter of 1625. In this we see, for the first time, a setting of the Common Tunes, fifteen of them, in four-part harmony, which would appear to have been a prompting from Anglican circles. The 1629 psalter of Raban also gave these harmonized Common Tunes, as well as the words of the General Confession from the *Anglican* Book of Common Prayer, an addition which, although purely temporary, has some general cultural significance for the period. In the 1633 psalter of Raban we get additional Common

Tunes harmonized, but with the so-called " Church part " of *Montrosse* and *Bon Accord* in the " Trebble " instead of the usual Tenor, which may have been an Anglican influence, and one must also observe that the prose psalms are here borrowed from James I authorized version of the Bible. From a musical point of approach this 1633 psalter has a distinctive feature in that the two Common Tunes mentioned above, *Montrosse* and *Bon Accord*, are not in the conventional " note against note " treatment, but display " curiosity" in setting which had so unsettled the consciences of earlier Reformers. Here we see much greater freedom of part writing than was expected in Common Tunes, and they actually agree with *Psalms* XXI and XII of the Psalms " in Reports " as found in the 1635 psalter.

One is prompted to enquire who was responsible for these settings in the Aberdeen psalters of Raban ? There is a psalter indicated by Livingston (prior to 1629) which carries an imprint :—*The Common Tunes in foure parts, in more perfect forme than ever heere-to-fore : Together with the Tunes of the whole psalmes, diligently revised and amended, by the most expert Musicians in Aberdene."* It would seem that this must be identical with the 1625 psalter mentioned by Joseph Robertson (*Book of Bon Accord*) and the imperfect copies at Glasgow and the Bodleian. Two individuals can be fitted into this picture of Aberdeen's " expert musicians," viz. Patrick Davidson and Andrew Melville. The former was Master of Aberdeen's Sang School from 1607 to 1635, and the Rev. Gideon Guthrie (1663-1732), as quoted in C. E. Guthrie Wright's *Gideon Guthrie* (1900), speaks of him as " an exquisite musician, bred in Italy." Andrew Melville was his assistant in this school and married his daughter. In 1636 he succeeded Davidson as Master, a position which he held until 1640, when his brother-in-law, Thomas Davidson (d. 1675), was appointed Master. Gideon Guthrie, who married Melville's granddaughter, writes that Melville " refined the Musick at Aberdeen, composed the Common Tunes, and prickt all the other music . . . assisted by his father in Law." The Melvilles may have come from the Midlothian and were, perhaps, connected with that David Melville of Leith who, in 1551, supplied Mary Queen of Scots with a " pare of organes " at £36. Indeed, the Common Tunes made their homophonic *début* in Andro Hart's Edinburgh psalter of 1615, and Andrew Melville might conceivably have been the actual composer of the seven which are claimed to be of Scottish facture.   On the other hand, the use of the term " composed " by Guthrie need not be taken in its modern connotation, but rather in its more general application meaning " arranged " or " harmonized."   The late Professor C. Sanford Terry would have us believe, *per contra* (*Musical Quarterly*, xxii), that " prickt " meant " harmonized."   This seems unlikely. To have " prickt the music " simply meant to have " written the music," and this is quite clear from the above quotation, since whilst Melville " prickt " all the other music, i.e. the Proper Tunes which were unharmonized, he " composed " the Common Tunes, which were harmonized.   " Pricked " certainly meant no more in the 18th century, as we know from Burns and from James Thomson's *Collection of Best Church Tunes* (Edin., 1778).

In comparison with the psalmody of the composers and arrangers of the English school, e.g. in Ravenscroft's *Booke of Psalmes* (1621), the 1633 Scottish psalter does not take a negligible place.   There may be many things in the music at which twentieth century musicians may feel inclined to shrug the shoulders, but such casualties were not confined to Scotland.   In two of the 1633 ex- amples, however, *Montrosse* and *Bon Accord*, we see what the Scottish composer was capable of if the Church had been a little more liberal in its views about this much-maligned " curiosity " in music. Yet it was the same in music as in social polity, since both could cry with some justice, *An the Kirk wad let me be*, to quote the song of a few decades later.

Yet the greatest triumph in this respect, and one of which the Church of Scotland ought to be proud, was the production of Andro Hart's *Psalmes of David* (Edinburgh, 1635), edited by Edward Millar, a work which deserves more than passing notice here, although Dr. Neil Livingston's monumental study of this book in

1864 is the primary source of information on the subject. In this psalter we see the music divided, for the first time, into Proper Tunes, Common Tunes, and Tunes in Reports. The Proper Tunes, as the title indicates, were those assigned as " proper " to individual psalms, a practice dating from the first Scottish psalter of 1564. The Common Tunes, still unharmonized, made their first appearance, as we have seen, in 1615, and were intended for those congregations which were not such adepts in the intricacies of the more difficult rhythms of the Proper Tunes. The Tunes in Reports, i.e., tunes in " imitation," as Playford has explained in his *Introduction to the Skill of Musick* (1655), were, in some instances, elaborate contrapuntal settings of the psalms. Not all however were of the strict " imitation " genus, but they were sufficiently " curious " to the Presbyterian mind to be categoried as such. Edward Millar, the editor, says that they were composed " for the further delight of qualified persons in the said art," although not, as Sir Richard Terry thought, because the *choirs* " might not relish the total abolition of the contrapuntal music to which they had been accustomed." The truth is that *choirs* did not exist generally, and probably the one in the Chapel Royal alone was " accustomed " to such luxuries as " Reports," although even here it is doubtful whether there was a soul who could remember the contrapuntal days of the old church, except what had been preserved by Thomas Wood in his psalter of 1562-66. At any rate, Livingston himself is quite abashed that they should have appeared *at all* in the 1635 psalter and puts this down to Edward Millar's connection with the Chapel Royal. " Whether," he says, " they would have been permitted before 1600 may well be questioned." It is not improbable that this " curious " music was borne in mind in 1637 when the revolt against Episcopacy and the Anglican service began. Two of these Tunes in Reports (xii and xxi) are to be found in the 1633 psalter among the Common Tunes where they are named *Bon Accord* and *Montrosse* respectively.

The editor of this psalter signed himself E.M., which letters were undoubtedly the initials of the Edward Millar mentioned above. Millar took his A.M. degree at Edinburgh University in 1624, and

he has been identified with one of the same name who lived in
Blackfriars' Wynd in Edinburgh in 1627, where he is entered as one
who " teaches bairns." In the previous year he appears to have
been acquainted with James Pont, a younger son of Robert Pont,
one of the original versifiers of the old Scottish psalms. The *Book
of Psalmes* (Edinburgh, 1615) belonging to James Pont, with personal
family details entered in the Kalendar, is in the possession of Cosmo
Gordon, London, and bound up with it, in manuscript, is the music
of the psalms in the holograph of Edward Millar. It contains the
settings in four-part harmony of seventy-five out of the one hundred
and five Proper Tunes as well as sixteen Common Tunes, i.e.,
Culross, Cheshire, St. Johnstoun (=*Elgin*), and *Bon Accord* being
added to the hitherto orthodox twelve. What is particularly precious
is the name and date which ends Psalm CL, and these read, " Ed.
Millar, 2 Aprile, 1626," in an elaborate monographic signature.

In 1635, Charles I appointed Millar, by reason of " his experience
and skill in the art of music," to succeed Edward Kellie as Director
of Music at the Chapel Royal in Holyrood, and here he began to put
the final touches on his work for a complete harmonized setting of
the psalms for the Scottish Church, of which, as we have seen from
the above, he had laid positive foundations nearly ten years before.
His position at the Chapel Royal and the assured patronage of
Charles I doubtless emboldened him to include the elaborate
settings in the " Tunes on Reports," some of which one might,
despite his protests, accept as Millar's own work, just as the additional Psalm CXXIV is most likely his, since we find it in his manuscript of 1626, where it alone occurs. All this " curious " music
would be obviously pleasing to his new master Charles I, whose
ears had been attuned to the works of Orlando Gibbons and
Nathaniel Giles.

It is not clear how much of the psalm settings in the 1635 psalter
are Millar's own. In his salute " To the Gentle Reader " he
protests that he has but " poor talents " although he had spent
" much time, travail, and expenses " upon his work. What his
motives were, are set down thus,—" Chiefly God's glory, the ad-

vancement of this Art, the saving of pains to teachers thereof, the incitation of others to greater acts of this kind, the earnest desire of some well affected . . . " and so on, but especially by reason of an abuse which he observed "*in all churches*, where sundry Trebles, Basses, and Counters set by diverse authors, being sung upon one, and the same Tenor, do discordantly rub upon each other, offending both musical, and rude ears . . . ". From these lines it is quite apparent that, by this time, *part-singing* must have become fairly well established in the larger towns in addition to the Chapel Royal, and we have seen that the Common Tunes in harmony had been published since 1625. Millar himself disclaims any credit save editing. His words are :—" I acknowledge sincerely the *whole compositions of the parts* to belong to the primest Musicians that ever this kingdom had, as Dean John Angus, Blackhall, Smith, Peebles, Sharp, Black, Buchan, and others famous for their skill in this kind. I would be most unwilling to wrong such shining-lights of this art, by obscuring their names, and arrogating anything to myself, which anyways might derogate from them." In spite of this disclaimer, Millar's work on the psalter was considerable, although he will take no praise. " The first copies of these parts " he says, " were doubtless right set down by these skilful authors, but have been wronged and vitiated by unskilful copiers thereof, as all things are injured by time : And herein consisted a part of my pains, that collecting all the sets I could find on the psalms, after painful trial thereof, I selected the best for this work, according to my simple judgment." That is quite true, but when we compare the psalms set by Peebles and Buchan in Wood's psalter of 1562-66 with those in Millar's psalter of 1635, the differences are so great, and so many, that one can only conlude that Millar, or someone earlier, had re-harmonized a goodly few of the psalms. Indeed, there is a marked improvement in what Millar issued in 1635 when compared with what he put forth in 1626 in manuscript for James Pont's psalter.

All of the " primest musicians," of whom he speaks above, with one exception perhaps, belonged to the old pre-Reformation Church originally. On that account we can understand their skill in music which Millar emphasises, although, save in the Tunes in Reports, the composers all worked with circumspection, lest their music might appear too " curious " in the eyes of the Reformers. The one composer who may not have been pre-Reformation is Sharp. Nothing is found about him in the usual sources, but in the Scottish David Melville MS. in the British Museum there is a Sharp's *Miserere*, and possibly an *Agnus Dei*, preserved in a bass part, whose very titles might, however, suggest a pre-Reformation date.

Of the quality of the work in Millar's psalter of 1635 one can give the opinion of the late Sir Richard Terry who made a lengthy study of the subject, as his racy book—*A Forgotten Psalter* (1929), his remarks in my own *Music in Mediaeval Scotland* (1930), and above all in his precious edition of *The Scottish Psalter of* 1635 (1935), so patently reveal. In his Introduction to my brochure, which is practically a reproduction of his remarks at my lecture before the *Musical Association* (56th Session), Sir Richard adopted, probably because the occasion demanded it, a belligerent attitude, and stated categorically, of the psalter that " the counterpoint is decrepit to a degree." By 1935 however, some spark of commiseration had lit his soul, or at least he was not so bellicose. Having arranged all the psalms for modern usage, he had, by this time, a fuller knowledge of them, and he gave this opinion : " Although the melodies of the Scottish psalter are virile and satisfying, the part-writing of them does not come up to the standard of polish which one finds in the Psalters of Ravenscroft, Este, Alison, and their contemporaries. The troublous times of its appearance no doubt account for this."

There may be much truth in these strictures although, as I pointed out to him at the time, most of the original Scottish composers and arrangers :—Peebles, Angus, Blackhall, Buchan, and Black, had made their original contributions *seventy years* before 1635, and that the Englishmen with those work he compares that in the Scottish psalter, were *not* their contemporaries, as the English psalters are dated,—Est (1592), Alison (1599), and Ravenscroft (1621). During the interim, England had bosomed Whyte, Parsons, and Byrd, who were treading fresh paths in music, all of which revealed new territory. Even Daman's harmonized psalter of 1579 would have been an unfair comparison. If one country must be pitted against another, the only resource is Day's *The Whole Psalmes in Foure Partes* (1563), and even then a Scot, Robert Johnson, might have had a hand in that. Whether the 1635 Scottish psalter can be said to " come up to the standard of polish," as reflected by Est, Alison, and Ravenscroft, as Sir Richard avers, is purely a matter of opinion. One thing is certain, and that is that not one of these English psalters have anything approaching the standard of the Scottish " Tunes in Reports."

At any rate, even accepting the period (1635) to which Sir Richard had assigned the music, it was certainly a " troublous " one for music in Scotland, as he admits, for the simple reason that the Reformation had stemmed two generations of likely composers. Yet in his earlier book, *A Forgotten Psalter* (1929), Sir Richard was more sympathetic. Here he enunciated the view that, in this psalter, Scotland had " produced a highly effective art-work, which compares more favourably with similar work produced in other countries," which statement, presumably, excepts England. He was certainly on the right lines when he said that considering how Scotland " had for centuries been torn by internal feuds, the wonder is that she found any time at all to cultivate the arts."

Sir Richard also had a word of praise for the Tunes in Reports, and rightly so, for they are the worthiest things in the 1635 Psalter. I quote from his criticisms thus :

" Their counterpoint may lack the grace of Scotland's greatest polyphonist,—Robert Johnson, . . . but when rendered by human voices and not played upon a pianoforte it is anything but unvocal."

" The unabashed employment of ' forbidden consecutives,' and the stark exposure of bare fifths no doubt *looks* crude to academic eyes, but it does not *sound* crude to anyone who is able to think of music in other terms than those of the pianoforte."

As for those " clashes between natural and sharpened notes," which are characteristic of the period, he points, in extenuation, if not triumph, to that " most ravishing example " in Byrd's *Ave Verum*. In 1936, when the Scottish B.B.C. broadcast, with my annotations, the Psalms xvii and cxvi in " Reports " from the 1635 Psalter, the late Dr. W. Gillies Whittaker said that they were worthy of Byrd.

Before bidding adieu to the music of this old psalter of 1635, the last music of the truly Reformed Church, a word about the origin of the melodies would not be out of place. In dealing with its progenitor, the 1564 psalter, it was said that most of the Proper Tunes were of alien origin, although some of those ascribed to Anglo-Genevan sources might very well have been Scottish in view of what was stated categorically in the *Brieff Discours off the Troubles begonne at Franckford* (1554). Further, five at least of these melodies have a not unreasonable claim to be considered Scottish. To sum up Scotland's contribution to the " tunes " from the psalter of 1564 to that of 1635, it would appear that out of 118 Proper Tunes, Scotland can claim at least 9, whilst of the 31 Common Tunes and 8 Tunes in Reports, she can possibly assert rightful ownership to 24 and 3 respectively. As for the harmonizing and setting, from what material there is at hand to justify an opinion, it can be stated that these proceeded from Scottish hands. One thing is certain, and that is that they are different from what we find in the English psalters, although in some cases they are admittedly of inferior value. In one instance, the *Monros* tune, the bass is identical with that found in Est's psalter, but the inner parts do not agree.

Secular music in Scotland was differently placed almost everywhere. Yet, in spite of an unlimited freedom of expression in form and treatment, the outlook was quite conservative. Vocal music was confined to the ballad in which every verse followed precisely the same music. In the madrigal, for obvious reasons, there was greater development. The instrumental sphere was often but a rehash of the vocal repertory, although dance forms predominated. If England was behind the Continent in this respect, Scotland lagged still further in the rear of her southern neighbour. If the old Chapel Royal music library which Master Edward Kellie provided in 1628 had only survived, we might have been able to say much about that " old Scotch music," both vocal and instrumental, which had its place on its shelves with that of England, France, Holland, Spain, and Italy.

The clearest indices to the type of secular music which appealed to the classes are to be found in the several Scottish lute, mandore, gittern, virginal, viol, and vocal manuscripts of the 17th century. We see much that is purely Scottish in the Rowallan lute MS. (1612-28), which includes such items as *Ane Scottis Dance* and another *For kissing for clapping*, the latter " set to the lute by Mr. Mure." Sir William Mure (d. 1657) was not merely a musician, but a poet and a versifier of the psalms, proofs of which additional accomplishments are still preserved. The pages of the Rowallan vocal MS. (*c.*1631) are crowded with examples from the English madrigalists, a circumstance due to those of the Scottish nobility who had been at James the First's court in London, and this influence grew in a rapid *crescendo*. The Skene mandore MS. (*c.* 1615-35), in its 114 items, still retains some of the vernacular music, although a fair half would appear to come from elsewhere. Again the influence of the London court flaunts itself in several masque tunes. The Straloch lute MS. (1627-29) follows much on the same lines as the preceding, but it is all good tuneful music. English influence is predominant in the William Stirling MS. (=Leyden vocal MS., 1639), although a few of John Black's trifles find a place here. In the Guthrie (1675-80), Blaikie (1683, 1692), and Leyden lyra-viol (*c.*1692) MSS., quite half of the contents of each is of Scottish provenance although they but consist of dance measures. The Dalhousie MSS. of this century, which have been examined by Dr. Harry M. Willsher, also reveal English court influence, e.g., in a book of airs for two violins by Nicola Matteis (*fl.* 1672-96) and some dances by John Jenkins (d. 1678). The

Kinloch MS. in the same collection contains original music for the virginal, including a piece written after the style of Byrd's *Battel* which William Kinloch, the composer, entitles the *Battle of Pavia.* That all these manuscripts, together with the David Melville (*after* 1604), Panmure (*c.* 1622 *et seq.*), Dublin Supplement to Wood (1600-50), Louis de France (*c.* 1682), and John Squyer (1696-1701) MSS., and the famous Forbes' *Cantus* (1662-1682), show a very similar structure, proves that the repertory was fairly consistent throughout Scotland.

The David Melville MS. (*after* 1604) in the British Museum is of outstanding interest. Every page of this work carries the name of David Melville, and since it is in a contemporary hand we may reasonably suppose that he was the owner and transcriber of the volume, although the late Augustus Hughes-Hughes, the author of the *Catalogue of Manuscript Music in the British Museum,* suggests that possibly some of the works are by Melville himself. Unfortunately, only the bass part of this rather important work has been preserved, although the treble and counter tenor of some of the items are to be found in other contemporary Scottish music books. Out of eighteen Latin motets, four are by Tye, Robert Johnson, and Sharp, the remaining being untraceable in printed sources. There are over a hundred madrigals, in which Morley, Byrd, Tallis, and Est figure, in addition to some Italians—Mosto and Giovanelli, but there are some thirty songs in English whose titles are not found elsewhere, although two seem to be by John Black, who has been mentioned already. More interesting are some five-part compositions, perhaps for viols, ten in all, including *James Lauder's* and *Maister William Skein's pavans,* as well as a *Sir William Keithis pavan and galliard.*

Another Scottish music manuscript, entitled *Ane Buik of Roundells* (1612), said to be written by the same David Melville, was published by the Roxburghe Club (1916), and edited by the late [Sir] Granville Bantock and H. Orsmond Anderton. The main contents were derived from Ravenscroft's *Pammelia* and *Deuteromelia* (1609), although one item, No. 95, has been attributed to James Melville

(1556-1614) the Reformer, a brother of the preceding. It ought to be mentioned that there was another David Melville, the Aberdeen publisher of the *Psalmes* and the brother of Andrew Melville, Master of the Sang School. Lady Dorothea Ruggles-Brise possesses a contemporary music manuscript bearing the signatures of Robert and Gilbert Melville, who seem to have been the nephews of this David Melville.

The first book of secular music printed in Scotland was Forbes' so-called *Cantus* (1662), a work which, as the late Professor C. Sanford Terry said, registers " Aberdeen's reaction from the Puritan tyranny." Hitherto the city of Bon Accord " could have claimed," to use Forbes' words, to have been " that famous ornament of vocal and instrumental music," but alas, the Reformation robbed her of this fame. We know little of Forbes biographically. In 1656 he was merely called a " Stationer," but with the appearance of his *Cantus* he and his son John were appointed the official printers to Aberdeen. The full title of his music book is, *Cantus, Songs and Fancies, To Thre, Foure, or Five Partes, both apt for Voices and Viols. With a briefe Introduction of Musick, As is taught in the Musick-Schole of Aberdene by T. D. Mr. of Musick.* It is usually called Forbes' *Cantus,* and for convenience sake I do likewise, although the late C. Sanford Terry speaks of this as a " miscalled " title. It is true that the title-page refers to other parts besides the *cantus* part, from which it might be assumed that Forbes intended to issue these other parts. There is no evidence that he ever published these latter, and yet his two later editions (1666, 1682) still carried the title *Cantus.* That the other parts were available in manuscript we know from several sources. Did Forbes hire these other parts in manuscript to the general public, in the same way that manuscript full scores can be hired nowadays where only the parts and a short score of certain works have been printed? In any case, after the 1662 edition, one can only assume that Forbes continued to use the title *Cantus,* not in the treble part sense, but rather in its purer classical meaning as " Music," " Song." Forbes died in 1675.

Almost the whole of the preliminary matter shows how much Forbes was dependent on England for his information. This could not be helped since it was a pioneer work in Scotland, as the Reformation had retarded the earlier appearance of secular music. His dedicatory verses reveal his knowledge of Christopher Tye's *Actes of the Apostles* (1553), whilst the prose discloses his dependence on John Playford's *Brief Introduction to the Skill of Musick* (1658). Even the " briefe Introduction of Musick," by T.D., i.e. Thomas Davidson, is borrowed from Thomas Morley's *Plaine and Easie Introduction to Practicall Musicke* (1597). From the first (1662) to the last (1682) edition of the *Cantus* there was included the very acme of the work of the English madrigalian school, derived from Morley's *First Booke of Ballets* (1595) and such works that followed up to the time of John Playford's *Musical Companion* (1673), including the publications of John Dowland, John Bartlett, Richard Alison, Henry Youll, Robert Jones, William Byrd, Thomas Ravenscroft, Michael Est, and Thomas Campion. In all these, only the melody and the words were given, but in the 1682 issue of the *Cantus*, a number of works in three parts were included. These were six songs by Gastoldi, extracted mainly from Playford's *Select Musicall Ayres* (1643), and seven English songs by Henry Lawes, Simon Ives, William Webb, John Playford, Jeremy Saville, and John Wilson. In all, Forbes' *Cantus* contains seventy-seven items, of which fifty are to be traced in English publications. The remaining twenty-seven may be of Scottish origin, and almost all of them occur in the earlier music manuscripts of Scotland.

Towards the close of the century there was a sudden spurt towards the greater appreciation of the music of Continental masters, the Italians especially. We have already seen how quite a swarm of the latter occupy pages in the David Melville MS. (after 1604), and that Forbes' *Cantus* (1682) contains not a few. Yet England was even more fully occupied with and influenced by the Italian school as we know from the *Harmonia Sacra* (1693), where the supreme gifts of Purcell are likened to " Corelli's genius to Bassani's joined." In Scotland, at the St. Cecilia's Day concert of 1695, we also see this appreciation, which shows the perspicacity of the musical circle of Edinburgh. Here we have programmed the orchestral sonatas of

Corelli, Bassani, Torelli, Pepusch, Finger, and Barrett, as well as an overture by Clerk, the latter, perhaps, to be identified with Hugh Clerk, a Scot, of whom later.

Then there was that music which was not so imposing in character or treatment. It will have been observed by the student that most of the songs that have come down to us are of serious countenance in both words and music. Indeed, as the editor of the 1879 reprint of Forbes' *Cantus* (1682) remarks,—" even where the words call for mirth there is no response from the music," save perhaps in the glee *Now in the Month of Maying*. Yet we must remember that these were grey and sombre Covenanting times, " killing time " for many. As odd as it may seem, the only ray of brightness in notated themes was in the secular tunes to religious words. Still one feels that the jolly and the indecorous song had expression in these days, although little or nothing has been preserved. Such items from English sources called "Scottish Songs " as well as the more genuine *Jockie drunken bable, Bony roaring Willie,* or *Johne Devisonns Pint of Win,* belong to the species that I have in mind, whilst the slightly later *Geld him Lasses* is even more pertinent.

Neither can the dance forms be ignored, for it was these that produced the more extensive rhythmic variety in these days, and it was in their measures that the great composers, Byrd, Robert Johnson, Bull and Farnaby, wrote much of their music. Among the Scottish national dance forms of the 17th century were the *hornpipe, jig, reel* and *lilt*. The *hornpipe* or *sean triubhas* may have been a relic of an old Celtic dance. In Playford's *Apollo's Banquet* (1687) there is a *New Scotch Hornpipe*. There is a *horn-pyp* in the Leyden MS. (*c.*1692), whilst an Englishman, Edward Sadler, composed a *Scotch hornpipe* in 1693 (British Museum MS. *Add.* 22098). Scotland was also acquainted with the English variety, since *A Lankishire hornpipe* appears in the Guthrie MS. (*c.*1675-80), which might have been Scottish (=Lanarkshire). We also know what the Scottish *jig* was like at this period since we have *Binny's jigg* and *Hopton's jigg* in the Blaikie MS. (1683, 1692), and another in the Leyden MS. From English sources we have a *Gigue* (*Scotch*) in the British Museum (*Add.* 15118). Of course the English had long been acquainted with the Scottish jig, and Morley, in his *Plaine and Easie Introduction to Practicall Musicke* (1597) shows that it was something unique. " I dare boldly affirm that, look which is he who thinketh himself the best discanter of all his neighbours, enjoin him to make but a *Scottish jygge*, he will grossly err in the true nature and quality of it." Shakespeare appreciated this jig, as we know from *Much Ado about Nothing* (*c.*1600), where he makes Beatrice say :—" Wooing, wedding, and repenting, is as a *Scotch jig*, a measure and a cinque pace ; the first suit is hot and hasty, like a *Scotch jig*, and full as fantastical."

We read of the *reel* at the extraordinary trial of witches (1591) with which James VI was acquainted. Here, it was averred " Geilles Duncan did go before them playing a *reill*." Its character may be seen in *To dance about the Baillzeis dubb* in the Skene MS. (*c.*1615-35), and *The bony brow* and *New Hilland ladie* in the Leyden MS., although none is called a reel there. A slower dance was what was then known as the *lilt*, of which many examples exist in the above named Scottish manuscripts, notably in the Skene MS., in both triple and quadruple time. In the earlier Rowallan lute MS. is one named *Gypsyes lilt*, which leads us to the reminiscence of those Egyptians that " dansit before the King [James V] in Halyrud House," the same ruler who favoured, in 1540, Johnne Faw, " Lord and erle of Litill Egipt," whose name must have prompted the later famous tune of *Johny Faa, or the Gipsie Laddie* (cf. *British Minstrel*, 1844). Perhaps it was these people of Yetholm, or those " Saracens or Gipsies " that were in Galloway a century earlier, who were responsible for the Morris dance.

The *Morris dance* was known quite early, and it runs into a line or two of *Christis Kirk on the Grene* (15th cent.) where " Auld Lychtfute " did " op the Moreiss danss." In the Skene MS. there is *Ane alman Moreiss*, i.e. a German Morris dance, in common time. According to the above poem in which it is called

" counterfeited Franss," it would seem to have been borrowed from Scotland's Gallic partner. Those who know Scott's *Fair Maid of Perth* will remember the description of the Morris dancers at the door of Simon the Glover. To-day, the Glover's Incorporation of Perth still displays the bell furnishings worn by the Morris dancers when Charles I was greeted by the town in 1633.

One other national dance deserves mention here, the *strathspey*. Although not mentioned under this name at this period, it would seem that the instrumental pieces that go by the name of *port* (*puirt*) in the Skene and Stralloch MSS., which have the precise characteristics of this dance, may be recognised as its progenitor. The familiar " snap " ♪. ♩ quite unknown in the 17th century, occurs in a much simpler figure as ♫ ♩ as in *Port Ballangowne* and other *ports* of the century, whilst in *Apollo's Banquet* (1690), it displays itself in " The Scotch-man's Dance." This dance, together with those just noticed, was indulged in by the classes with as much verve and relish as by the masses, although the former could count many other dance measures in its repertory, mostly of Continental origin.

France, as we have seen already, was the determining factor in polite society in Scotland, and her trippings with " the light fantastic toe " were in Gallic measures. The Skene and Stralloch MSS. are replete with music for the *pavan, gaillard, brawl, buffon, courant, cinque pas, saraband, alman, bergomask, pantalon,* and *canary*. Many of these bear the names of royal, noble, or other eminent patrons, e.g., the *Queen's Almone, Horreis [Herries] Galyiard,* and *My Lord Hay's Currand*. Not all of this *music* could have been of exotic origin since it is most likely that many were of Scottish facture, especially those that carry the names of patrons from the " Three Estates," just as those reels and strathspeys of the fiddlers of the 18th and 19th centuries were dedicated by hundreds to the same classes. It is all quite rhythmic and melodious stuff, most of it not traceable elsewhere which, in itself, rather favours the above conclusion of its indigenous production. Only a handful has been spared to us in parts. Nor can we afford to ignore the music of those who " went a sodjering," when the pipe, fife, and drum cadence in the march lightened many a weary mile. During the 17th century there were several marches of Scottish provenance whose dates are even earlier than those assigned them. Among these are *The Scot's Marche* (c. 1656), *General Leslie's March* (1652), *The Highlanders' March* (1666), *Montrose's March* (1666), *Monk's March* (1675-80), *Mackay's March* and *The Boyne a New Jocks' March* (1694-5). Most of these marches were for fifes and drums or hoboys and drums, which were the official instruments in the army. Probably the bagpipe took a turn with some of this music, although the pipe had its own individual creations apart from marches. Still we cannot be too sure of some of the 17th century dating of this pipe music. In any case, we must recognize that these were the days of the re-awakening of interest in *ceòl mór*, i.e. the art music of the pipe. Indeed it has been called " the great MacCrimmon age," and MacCrimmon is a name that commands authority north of the Tweed when *piobaireachd* is afoot. This family were hereditary pipers to the Macleods of Skye, and there was a MacCrimmon there in 1540. The first, however, who was famed as a piper, says Grattan Flood, was Donald [? Finlay], who was followed by his grandson, Donald *mór* (*fl.* 1600-35), and he was succeeded " by Patrick *og* (*fl.* 1680-1720), and he by Malcolm (*fl.* 1743) and Donald *bán* (*fl.* 1745), and the latter by John *dubh* (c. 1731-1822), the last of this celebrated race of pipers."

The music of the Scottish lute and mandore books, in which much of the above appears, is generally of simple construction. Of course, being what one might term popular music, it was, for this reason, of an unsophisticated structure. On the other hand, *The Scottish Hunts-upe* of 1616, in the British Museum (*Eg.* 2046) is one that will test the executive ability of even the adept. Most of the chordal settings in Scottish lute music are in skeleton, probably because much was left to the ingenuity of the lutanist, as the *accordatura* or tuning simplified most of the progressions. At the same time there was an interest in the classics for the lute in Scotland, since the works of the great Gaultier family of France, possibly Denis, are to be found in the Dalhousie MSS., as Dr. Harry M. Willsher has shown.

From what has preceded we see that 17th century Scotland produced no great composer on her own soil. It is true that we have a formidable list of the " primest musicians " in the land given by Millar in his 1635 psalter, but these, with probably one exception, belonged actually or culturally to the pre-Reformation period. The only Scottish composer of any note was John Abell (1650-1724), and he gained his fame outside the land of his birth, as did so many of his compatriots in the 18th, 19th and 20th centuries. *Grove's Dictionary of Music* says, on what authority I know not, that he was born in London. Sir Samuel Forbes of Foveran (1653-1717), in a *Description of Aberdeenshire* (1716-17) says :—" Music here is much in vogue, and many citizens sing charmingly. The well known Abel was a native of this place, and his kindred are known by the name of Eball ; and, it is said, there are other [of the family] as good as he." Abell may have had his first training at the Aberdeen Sang School under Thomas Davidson, although we first know of him at the Chapel Royal of England in 1679, in which service he remained until 1688. Meanwhile he was sent to Italy to study, and on his return in 1682 he was lauded by Evelyn. After the Revolution he was abroad for some years where he seems to have gained fame as an excellent singer and lutanist. From a portion of a letter in the British Museum (K.2, g.15) dated 17th October, 1699, we learn that from July 12th to October 17th, 1695 [*sic*], Abell was at Zell, Hanover, Berlin, Brunswick, and Loo. In spite of being a Romanist and " very poor," he seems to have been appreciated, although a certain Cresset calls him " the harmonious vagabond Abell," and says that " he maintains the character of the *Vertuosa Canaglia.*" Nor can Cresset omit to mention that " his Catholicity does not hinder him from singing Victoria for us." He was back in England in 1700 when Congreve said of him that " he certainly sings beyond all creatures upon earth." He was the composer of two books of vocal music:—

A Collection of Songs in Several Languages (1701) and *A Collection of Songs in English* (1701). These were followed by *A Choice Collection of Italian Ayres* (1703). He is only known to have visited the north on two occasions. Of the first of these we know from a claim made for his Italian Airs that they were " Sung to the Nobility and Gentry in the North of England." Of the second visit we have the evidence of a concert which he gave in " Fair Edina " under the patronage of the Duke of Argyll in 1706. Of his interest in the Scottish muse there seems to be some suggestion from contributions to *A Collection of . . . Scotch Songs* (1740) which I have not seen, although in his earlier years a Scots song could be found in his repertory, as in 1680, when he sang *Katherine Ogie* at a concert at the Stationers' Hall, London.

Finally, a word may be spared for England's interest in Scottish music at this period. We have already noted in the 16th century that Morley in England had paid his tribute just as Thoinot Arbeau had given his appreciation in France, and the *Écossaise* was a general favourite on the Continent, as well as in England, by the 17th century, whilst in Sweden that strange *Skottska* must originally have been cradled under Caledonian skies. When James VI made London his home, he surrounded himself with his " ain folk," and with these people the " braid Scots sang " from their own musicians was more eagerly listened to than the polished English ballad. At first its alien character was the subject of Sassenach jest, and even so late as Shadwell's play *The Scowerers* (1691) we read of " a *Scotch song*, more hideous and barbarous than an *Irish cronan*." Yet the English came to relish this music and Dryden, in his edition of Chaucer's poems (1700), is actually quite tolerant, and in comparing Chaucer's verse with that of Lydgate and Gower, says :—" There is the rude sweetness of a *Scotch tune* in it, which is natural and pleasing, though not perfect." By this time, however, as Alexander Campbell says, " an inundation of Scotch songs, so called, appears to have poured upon the town [London] by Tom D'Urfey and his Grub Street brethren." Yet this was only an extension of the craze for " Scotch music " that had become almost a cult, of which John Hilton's Scotch catch beginning " Pratty Naun " and *A Northern Catch* in *Catch that Catch Can* (1658) is perhaps the earliest example.

Such well-known composers and arrangers as Henry Purcell, John and Henry Playford, as well as lesser lights in Jeremiah Clarke, Akeroyd, Richard Beveridge, and others, were playing up to the demand, and when the genuine article was exhausted they factured the " in the Scottish manner " commodity with considerable profit to themselves. John Playford in his *Dancing Master* (1650-61, *et seq.*) and *Musick's Delight* (1666), and Henry Playford in *Wit and Mirth, or Pills to Purge Melancholy* (1698), gave a foretaste to this Scottish speciality, which soon grew to wider bounds. Indeed, Henry Playford, in his *Original Scotch Tunes* (1701), had learned that albums of Scottish music were a money-making concern. Nor can we forget church music since Thomas Ravenscroft in his *Booke of Psalmes* (1621) acknowledges the debt to Scottish psalmody. Scottish dances were even in demand. Milton's clever nephew, Edward Phillips (d. *c.* 1696), reveals that the " North-country dance " was being favoured in England. " I warrant," he says, " it will please the ladies better than all your French whisks and frisks."

Thus closed the 17th century for music in Scotland, a period which, in spite of all tribulations, was not quite inglorious. Certainly there was little or nothing in the serious creative field, but the deep affection for music was kept going in certain quarters as of old, although the uninformed historian of music may think otherwise. An example of the latter may be descried in Henry Davey, and here is what he says : " Probably music was little cultivated in Scotland ; it is mentioned in 1669 that there was not one musician in Glasgow. Letters in the Duke of Argyll's MSS., written in 1667, mentions a song, *Auld Lang Syne*." This foolish statement was not made by a foreigner who might have been excused for such a passage, but by an Englishman who wrote a much quoted *History of English Music* (1895). Had he probed a little deeper before he penned those lines he might have written differently, as did Dr. Nelly Diem in her *Beiträge zur Geschichte der Scottischen Musik im XVII. Jahrhundert* (1919). And yet Davey himself, ever solicitous about the erection of Aunt Sallies, once asked of another phase of musical activity :—" Why have the Puritans been so foully belied ? " Mainly, says Davey, " because the popular imagination takes a salient point, and is apt to look at that distinguishing mark *only*." Just so. As Davey says of the lies about the Puritans, so we say of his statement regarding Scottish music :—" Possibly the exaggeration and slander will be once more repeated," since once it appears in print, " it is almost impossible to get it corrected." On the other hand perhaps one ought to treat Davey's affirmation in the pawky Scots way as a " blithesome frolic," as James Thomson would say, and repel it by pointing out that the English historian was quite in error about the lack of *musicians* in Glasgow at this time since the burgh records show that there were two *drummers* !

PART VI

THE EIGHTEENTH CENTURY

" The years that closed the seventeenth and ushered in the eighteenth century were years full of too much political fermentation to afford the necessary tranquillity for the growth of any very generally shared artistic life in the Scottish capital."

D. FRASER HARRIS : *St. Cecilia's Hall* (1911).

THESE prefatory remarks express the commonly accepted opinion of writers on music in Scotland, as in *Grove's Dictionary of Music* (1940, ii, 143), and they are given prominence on that account. Obviously the "' fermentation," as Harris calls it, was mainly the affairs leading up to 1715 which, with the events of 1745, even so acute a critic as H. Sandiford Turner (*Dunedin Magazine*, 1915) considered " a serious drawback to the artistic progress of the nation." In sober truth it was nothing of the sort, as anyone who cares to plumb the shallows of these statements can readily test for themselves. On the contrary, Scotland, in the 18th century, was perspicuously triumphant in every phase of her artistic, literary and intellectual life, which had been roused by a broadening humanistic outlook on life following a loosening of the fetters of a narrow religious intolerance. Indeed it was this century that actually produced a renascence of culture in the land.

By far too much stress has been laid on the social and political unrest of the period. It is true that the dawning skies of the century reflected an erubescent hue that forebode trouble, but the storm that broke in 1715 and reverberated until 1745 actually enriched and fecundated the soil. Instead of halting artistic progress, the "troublesome times " acted as a stimulus, since the people sought music as a solace from their woes, and the national song actually became a vehicle of spiritual outpouring, as much so as the old psalms had been in days of yore. Still, it is just as well that we should know exactly what there was besides the " Fifteen " and "Forty-Five," which have so often and so sedulously been laid at Scotland's door, because it enables us to understand the artistic conditions that were dependent in many ways upon the political.

Although a whole century had elapsed since the Union of the Crowns of Scotland and England there was no concord of hearts between the two peoples. Indeed, when Anne came to the throne (1702), the Scots and English were still as athwart and estranged as ever, and at this time the tension between them was at breaking point. The Scots had good reasons for dissatisfaction if not hatred. The memories of the massacre of Glencoe (1692) and the tragedy of the Darien scheme (1698) still rankled in the souls of most Scots, whether they were for or against the new queen. They came to realize that Scotland was treated as of no political consequence, save in the commercial sphere where, so as to preserve the trading interests of the English, she was looked upon as a serious competitor and was, by law, denied traffic with the American colonies. Her unimportance in English eyes was made palpable in the English Act of Settlement (1701) which determined the succession to the throne without the slighest reference to the wishes of Scotland, who answered it by passing her own Act of Security (1704), so as to protect her religious and secular freedom. Tempers ran high and acts of violence were perpetrated on both sides. A peaceable solution was found in the Union of Parliaments (1707) which, although ratified by the Scottish Parliament, did not express the majority opinion of the people at large.

Whilst the Union has since proved its political value, many, more especially in the Highlands, thought it of little consequence if not inimical to Scotland, as the risings of 1715 and 1745 so tragically proved. These two events, although prompted by the highest motives, caused great bitterness in England, and the very name Scotland became anathema south of the Tweed. Unfortunately the English did not discriminate between the Highlands and the Lowlands, and every Scot was eyed askance almost as an outlaw. What he had to expect from Londoners can be read in *Roderick Random*, whilst, for the basest of political ends, the lampoons of Swift, the letters of Junius, and the pen of the notorious Wilkes fanned the flames of passion against North Britain. An interesting sidelight is reflected in the original John Murray of book publishing fame.

When he started in London in 1768 he wisely trimmed his sails to the hostile winds by the elision of Mac from his patronymic.

In comparison with her great neighbour, Scotland was a poor country materially, but with a spiritual abundance that had to find expression somewhere, and England was the saucer that caught the cream that overflowed. We see it in David Hume, Tobias Smollett, David Mallet, James Thomson, and Thomas Campbell, all of whom earned their livings south of the border. It was precisely the same urge that took the musicians William Thomson, William McGibbon, James Oswald, and Robert Bremner to London. The two latter saw their fellow countrymen, W. Boag, Peter Fraser, David and John Rutherford, and possibly John Simpson, flourishing in the metropolis as music publishers, and the former, being skilled musicians in addition, imagined that they could do better still, and did. It was only human that much clannishness prevailed among the Scots in London, a circumstance which the mercenary press made a pet theme, ignoring the fact that it was the enmity of the English which created the sodality. It may be true that the Duchess of Hamilton was the means of William Thomson's favour at court, and that the Earl of Bute was responsible for much of Oswald's success, but patronage was part and parcel of everyday life in art and literature, and the Scottish aristocracy in England were in the forefront of both. It was the Earl of Abercorn who was mainly responsible for the Academy of Antient Music (*c.* 1710) in London, and the Duke of Queensberry and the Earl of Stair were among the sponsors of its Royal Academy of Music (1719), whilst the Earl of Eglinton and the Marquis of Lorne were foundation members of the London Catch Club (1761). In 1790, when the Edinburgh Fund for Decayed Musicians was started, the letter of appeal made the point that " the greater part of the Scottish nobility are supporters of the Musical Fund in London." That the clannishness had its good points is evident from the society known as the " Temple of Apollo," of which Frank Kidson has written (*Musical Antiquary*, ii), which seems to have comprised Thomas Erskine the Sixth Earl of Kellie, Captain (afterwards General) John Reid, James Oswald, and Dr.

Burney, an outsider, although perhaps a Scot by race. They published a number of musical works of unusual interest. England owes a debt of gratitude to the previously mentioned Scottish music publishers, not only for their excellent printing, as in the case of Oswald and Bremner, but also because of their enterprise in introducing so many new works to the public, some in score. The pity was that there was not the field for their energy under Caledonian skies, for even at the date of Oswald's departure (1741), Scotland's musical renascence had not asserted itself to any fullness, as Ramsay's biting line in the *Scots Magazine* reveals at the loss of Oswald :

> "London alas ! which aye has been our bane,
> To which our very loss is certain gain."

It was not until the turn of the half-century that music publishing in Scotland became a paying proposition as we shall see. Meanwhile we must return to Scotland.

A country's art and culture are determined everywhere by social forces, just as much as a plant is healthy or otherwise in relation to the nature of its soil. Thus the state of music in 18th century Scotland can only be understood by reference to the prevailing economy in social and political affairs, although one must not unduly emphasize fractions as integers, as I have shown at the opening to this chapter. In the previous century it was of some slight moment who held regal sway, and what the tastes and politics of the court were, for we must admit that the later Stuarts, with all their faults, did interest themselves in the arts, whether (according to the reader's point of view) it was for good or evil. Yet those days went out in what has been termed " the Glorious Revolution," and now (1714) the Hanoverians were on the throne, but since their personal interest in Scotland, and Scotland's interest in them, were at zero, there is obviously no need to deal with kings as in previous chapters where, even so, they were merely used as pointers. Not that the early Hanoverians brought no benefits to music, because they did. It was at their behest or favour that so many Germans, or German-tongued foreigners, came to England, and the overflow, of the kidney of Lampe, Schetky, and the Reinagle and other families, drifted into

Scotland, much to its profit musically. Yet there were other factors pressing upon cultural activities.

When the Reformation identified the beautiful with the good, it bred an attitude of mind that was disastrous to the arts in Scotland. To teach that the most rapturous spiritual delight was to be sought in the plain and simple in all things was, perhaps, æsthetically admissible, if the Reformers ever bothered about æsthetics, but to insist that that which was florid and decorative was monstrously evil was a doctrine that curbed the cravings of the people for a music which was as deeply spiritual as any religious devotion. Thanks to reason, humanity has always been able to save itself from such calamities because, sooner or later, the great God Pan, with his alluring notes, calls man back to the bounteous inheritance that mother earth has provided for her children. The call to this freedom was heard in Scotland in the days on whose threshold we are entering and, as a result, the old severe, puritanical outlook on life began to lose its final hold. The doctrine was clinched in the intellectual sphere when Francis Hutcheson in his *Inquiry Concerning Beauty* (1725) dared to separate ethics and æsthetics by reviving the study of the beautiful, whereas his philosophical predecessors had considered it beneath their dignity to consider the emotional.

Scotland's material progress had much to do with this movement towards intellectual and cultural unrestraint. In the first half of the century, industry and commerce had developed to a comparatively enormous extent, and towns began to grow apace in size and wealth as a result. The second half of the century—the age of machinery—hastened this material prosperity, and there was the inevitable trek from the country to the town by those who desired to participate in the new life, a movement which gave greater vitality to the national songs. All this benefited both the classes and the masses. There were better houses, finer clothes, and more money, but, above all else, it brought the individual units of the masses into closer contact than before, and a wider social and intellectual horizon became visible. One cannot however, shut an eye to the evils of the industrial revolution, but at least it brought people together in their joys as well as their sorrows, and music often became a balm in the latter, for it was equally available to the workman as the merchant, to the ploughman as the landlord. Captain Topham, speaking of society in 1774-5 in his *Letters from Edinburgh*, marvels at " the degree of attachment which is shown to music " in Scotland, but Burns shows how even the agricultural worker pored over songs when " driving his cart or walking to labour." Indeed, the bard himself says that they were " daily sung . . . by the common people." Many of the music books and music sheets of the second half of this century that have passed through my hands show that they were once the treasured property of humble folk as well as lordly aristocrat in Scotland.

The advertisements in the periodical press are a fair index of what interested the people at large in the realm of music. All possessed a glottis, if they only knew how to coax it, but it depended on the station in life whether one had a harpsichord or a flute, and even then the depth of the purse determined whether it was " organized or plain," as the advertiser classed these wares. Further, it was often social need that prompted the kind of instrument in use. The guitar was favoured by the " Upper Ten," because its technique confined it to the stately minuet of the classes. The violin was favoured by the masses more especially because it was eminently suitable for the more boisterous reel and strathspey. The difference in public requirements can be noted in Edinburgh and Glasgow. In the patrician capital the music for harpsichord and pianoforte was in demand, whereas in the industrialized city of the west greater sales came from what was arranged for violin, flute, or fife. In Dunbar's *Social Life* is a letter from Lady Thunderton (1710) in which a lady says,—" I can . . . play on treble and gambo viol, virginal and minicords." That the national song was in particular demand is evident from the general advertisements, and more so since it was a social factor.

As the Rev. Charles Rogers points out in his *Social Life in Scotland*, it is remarkable how men, who hitherto only assembled to concert measures against a despotic government, now met for social pastime and literary recreation in clubs. If the classes had their eclectic literary groups, the masses had their free-and-easy debating clubs, but both had two things in common—the song and the " flowing bowl." It was from such convivial gatherings, which at first only encouraged the simple song, that the later concerts sprang. Indeed, the early concerts in Edinburgh, Aberdeen, and Glasgow, wore their swaddling clothes in the friendly tavern. To the older Presbyterian eye, this was as it should be, with " wine, woman, and song " lumped together as wiles of Satan. Nor was Scotland any different from other countries in this respect, as we see precisely the same tavern evolution of the public performance of music in London. Given the song as an essential for conviviality, it only needed a party urge to make the national song the desideratum. The song, in its turn, became the *note sensible* for something more satisfying musically, hence the concerted piece. If the *concerto* or *cantata* were sufficiently attractive for the club, why not extend the benefit to outside friends ? It was thus that the concert began, but always with the members themselves being the chief participators. Indeed, there were as yet few professional musicians available in Scotland.

It was not until the turn of the half-century that the professional musician could claim reliance on his art and craft for absolute support, and much of this was due to the fact that shelter was afforded a few organists and choirmasters by the Episcopal Church, whilst the theatres enabled other classes of instrumentalists to earn a not inconsiderable salary in their bands. Of course, teaching, the concert, and the dance, slightly embellished the earnings of the latter but, even then, the cream of engagements went, in the first two classes of " gigs," to the Italians and Germans—at least in Edinburgh, where they ruled the roost. On the whole it would seem that the people were beginning to feel that they preferred to make their own music than have it made for them by others. Quite apart from the instrumental music societies of the leisured and merchant classes, which will be dealt with separately in treating of the amateur societies and the concerts, there were vocal music clubs. These, although at first cultivated by the aristocracy, soon became popular with the masses. The Vocal Music Club (1770) and the Sacred Music Institution (1798) both founded in Glasgow, showed the more general trend of interest. It was to the Edinburgh Catch Club (1771), an aristocratic affair, that James Sibbald dedicated his *Collection of Catches, Canons, Glees* . . . (Edin., 1780), an important work in four volumes which was later reissued in London by Longman and Broderip, and again by Clementi and Co., a borrowing that is worth noting. Thomas Erskine, the composer, was the leading spirit in this club, and his cousin, the Lord Advocate, Henry Erskine, has left some interesting verses concerning its activities, showing, incidentally, that the members worshipped at another shrine in addition to that of St. Cecilia.

In Glasgow, John Bain's *Vocal Musician* (1774), which consisted of arrangements of songs in two, three, and four parts, was popular. The Glasgow clubs divided their interest between psalms, hymns, glees, and catches, and many publications catered for such a mixture of taste, as in Allan Houston's *Collection of Church Tunes,* . . . *Canons and Catches* (1799). Indeed, in a copy of Finlay and McLachlan's *Precentor* (1776), in Glasgow University Library, there is bound up at the end a number of songs, two of which have such titles as " Love, thy godhead I adore " and " Let us love and drink our liquor," which seems to show that " Wine, woman, and [religious] song " went together in some instances with unblushing ease.

Whenever we turn our gaze during this century we see the art and craft of music slowly, but surely, progressing in the land. The upper class took music in their stride as part of their educational curriculum, whilst the bourgeoise merchant and professional classes vied with the former for competency in the art. As for the masses, so far as can be judged, it was their one great pleasure, especially in the national song, which grew to unprecedented favour with them, outstripping even the attraction of the dance tunes. Burns reveals what happened at the " simple frugal social meeting at Mossgiel," where " among other entertainments, each did his or her best at singing." Whilst church music fell into desuetude, the secular usage of the psalms, that had previously found acceptance, began to give way to the catch and glee. The birth of the concert and the wider appreciation of orchestral music in the cities gave greater scope to native performers and composers. The latter were but a handful it is true, but the few that emerged could stand shoulder to shoulder with many of those in England, and even with some in France and Germany. Finally, the broadening interest in music is evidenced by the many music printing presses that flourished in the capital, whilst the demand for music books and sheet music, even prompted the Englishman John Watlen to settle in Scotland as a publisher.

In the Highlands, still the promptuary of Celtic culture in spite of the repressions of 1715 and 1745, much of the old musical life persisted. As Burns has pictured,—" the wandering minstrels, harpers and pipers, used to go frequently errant through the wilds both of Scotland and Ireland," a contingency which enhanced the older art. The *céilidh* had its homely attraction for the folk in general, and Patrick Macdonald has preserved many an old melody in his *Highland Vocal Airs* (1784). Indeed some people, like John Macculloch in his *Description of the Western Islands*, aver that many Lowland airs are simply older Highland melodies altered. It seems quite true that the inordinate elevation of the strathspey in the Lowlands from the end of the first quarter of the century was due to the trek or displacement of many of the Highlanders southward after 1715. The form was long known before this, certainly in the early 17th century as I have shown, although not under this name, and the new designation reveals the place from whence the revivification came — the valley of the Spey, " so famous in Scottish music," as Burns reminds us. Thomas Newete says in his *Tour* (1791) that its first musical exponents were the Browns of Kincardine and the Cummings of Freuchie or Castle Grant. Incidentally, it ought to be remarked that the choreographical intricacies of Highland dances of the period can best be studied in Peacock's *Sketches Relative to the History and Theory*, *but more especially to the Practice of Dancing* (Aberdeen, 1805). The " Immortal Bard " himself illumines the conservative attitude of the Highlands in the days of his northern tour (1787) when he describes an evening at a Highland house. " Our dancing," he says, " was none of the French or English insipid formal movements ; the ladies sang Scotch songs like angels, at intervals ; then we flew at *Bab at the Bowster, Tullochgorum, Loch Erroch-side,* etc. [in the dance] like midges sporting in the mottie sun."

The traditional wind instrument of the Highland folk, the bagpipe, was still to the fore. W. H. Grattan Flood, the historian of Irish music, thought that the Highland instrument " almost disappeared for a time," but the only evidence of this is the remark of Dr. Johnson who said, in reference *only* to Mull and Skye, that it was then (1773) falling into oblivion. Yet if the competitive array of pipers at the festivals held in Edinburgh from 1783 onwards may be taken as an indication, the instrument was well in favour elsewhere. According to the loquacious lexicographer, the principal families in the Highlands still kept their pipers and that a " college of pipers " was in existence. Shaw, in his *History of the Province of Moray* (1775), says the same of the eastern Highlands. Whether a " college," in the accepted sense of the word, ever existed is extremely doubtful, but a *collegium,* in the old functional meaning, i.e. a guild or body of performers, must have had its place in the social economy of Highland life. Johnson shows that the MacCrimmons of Skye were still a power in the land, and that fame in piping had also come to the Rankins, the pipers of the Macleans of Coll. The MacArthurs of Mull, the pipers of the Macdonalds of the Isles, were likewise among the elect as pipers, which is the testimony of Pennant.

CHAPTER 1

THE PEOPLE

"That I for poor old Scotland's sake
Some useful plan or book could make
Or sing a sang at least."

ROBERT BURNS.

No history of a country's music can afford to ignore the traditional vocal melodies and dance measures of the people. More especially is this a requirement in Scotland, where they have ever been cherished, not only by reason of the national urge, but more so because they are, and have always been, a social necessity, a condition which is practically non-existent in England. Scottish writers and poets have generally paid their meed to the momentum of the old Scots songs and dances in the nation's material and spiritual progress. True, most of the former are of Lowland brew, but they are not a whit the worse for that, since what issued from the Lowlands can be counted as the very salt of Scottish culture.

Robert Chambers (*Songs of Scotland Prior to Burns*) rightly judges the renascence of the national song as concomitant with the country's emancipation from the religious struggle. He says:—
" When Scotland herself began, after the Revolution, to rise above her religious troubles, and to pay some attention to secular matters, the upper class, and especially that section of it which inclined to Episcopacy and Jacobitism became also aware that their country possessed an inheritance of some value in her popular songs and melodies." Yet the trouble was that most of this lore was only on the lips and not before the eyes, for at the dawn of the 18th century, strange as it may seem, there was no printed secular music that came from a Scottish press, save Forbes' *Cantus* (1662, 1666, 1682) and we have seen what a modicum of Scottish song that book showed. Indeed save for the guidance of a few manuscripts, most of the old airs were passed on *viva voce* or by rote, and in Scotland, if anyone wanted printed secular music, Scottish or otherwise, it was to England that one sent for it. Here, during the first quarter of the century, could be found sheet music of such

items as *Katherine Ogie, Thro' the Wood Laddie, The Bush aboun Traquair, Tweedside,* and the like, together with as many " Scotch Songs " as the uninitiated were tempted to buy of the type that the Englishmen Akeroyd and Leveridge composed, much of which was re-issued later by Walsh in his *Collection of Original Scotch Songs* (Lond., *c*.1732). Of course the genuine article, despite Chappell's opinion to the contrary, could be found in Henry Playford's *Original Scotch Tunes* (Lond., 1701), as well as in Walsh's *The Merry Musician* (Lond., 1716, *et seq.*), although in the latter we must ignore the attributions to James V of Scotland and David Rizzio.

That the national song was as popular as ever in Scotland is evident from Ramsay's early poem *To the Music Club* (1721) right down to the days of " the immortal bard," whose confession that " the collection of songs was my *vade mecum* " is irrefutable testimony to the ways of the common people. Yet, sad to relate, it was from England that the first notable collection of Scottish songs with music came, when a Scot in London, William Thomson, put forth the *Orpheus Caledonius* (Lond., 1725). It consisted of fifty of " the best Scotch Songs set to music." In 1733, a second edition was issued with an added second volume which also comprised fifty songs. The venture, in spite of the benefits conferred, heaped coals of critical fire on the editor's head. Allan Ramsay was annoyed that Thomson had borrowed words from his *Tea-Table Miscellany* (1724) without a line of acknowledgment, a fact that he made public in the 1734 (10th edition) issue of the latter work. Hawkins, the English music historian, also growled that " the editor was not a musician, but a tradesman," and gave the opinion that " the collection is accordingly injudicious and incorrect." Despite this condemnation which, from the point of view of unlicensed pilfering and poor accompaniments, may have been quite legitimate, Thomson's work is a veritable signpost in the history of the national song of Scotland, since it has registered what is more truly the melodic outline of many a Scottish song, with which others have tampered.

Thomson belonged to Edinburgh, where his father, Daniel, had been a professional musician, playing the trumpet at the 1695 St. Cecilia's Concert, and a state trumpeter since 1705. William was a vocalist and harpsichordist who, as a boy, had also performed at the St. Cecilia's Concert. In the early " Twenties " he was already in London, where he was favoured at Court for his Scots songs, and Burney records a benefit concert for him in the metropolis in 1722. All the songs in his 1725 volume, and most of those in that of 1733, would have been vocally familiar to Thomson, and they may perhaps have comprised his repertory. They would have been learned, probably *viva voce*, by him as a youth in Edinburgh, and for that reason the Scots songs in the *Orpheus Caledonius* stand apart from those which had appeared in other English collections and sheet issues in London.

Although Scotland herself had previously sensed the need for a collection of her national songs, it was Thomson's contribution that provoked a greater keenness. Allan Ramsay had already whetted the public taste in his *Scots Songs* (1718, 1719), but even more so in his *Tea-Table Miscellany* (1724), but there was no music to them. Ramsay did what Burns was to accomplish later in supplying new words to old tunes in several instances and he mentioned *which tunes*. In the year 1726, Ramsay remedied this defect when, under the editorship of Alexander Stuart, there was issued the *Musick for Allan Ramsay's Collection of Scots Songs*, a work which is now almost as rare as the *Tea-Table Miscellany* (1724) itself. Alexander Campbell (*Albyn's Anthology*) rightly says that Stuart was " the first on record who harmonized and adapted Scottish melody to vocal poetry," if we add the works " in Scotland." The work of Stuart, with Lorenzo Bocchi's twelve sonatas and a Scots cantata (Edin., 1726), and Thomas Bruce's *The Common Tunes* (Edin., 1726) which included several ballads, was the first secular music published in Scotland since the 1688 edition of Forbes' *Cantus*. Ramsay's work must have had a phenomenal reception, with an early exhaustion of the stock, but others soon stepped in to supply the want. Adam Craig (d. 1741) of Edinburgh submitted his *Collection of the Choicest Scots Tunes*

(Edin., 1730), whilst Alexander Munro issued his *Collection of the Best Scots Tunes* (Paris, 1732). Yet these were instrumental collections. Alexander Campbell, like Hawkins, espied in Munro's melodies an attempt to " accommodate them to the Italian style," but adds,—" would to Heaven this had been the only instance." Craig may have also been a composer since the " Catalogue of Musick " of Robert Lord Colville, dated 1728, has one of the lots marked as " Mr. Adam Craig's Works, in one book, folio, MS." Of Munro, little is known, unless he can be identified with the Munro, Monro, or Monroe (although this latter may have been George Monro), found contributing to *The Merry Musician* (1716 *et seq.*), *The Musical Miscellany* (1729-31), *The Muses Delight* (1754), and *Apollo's Cabinet* (1756). There was a musician named Munro in Edinburgh in 1743.

Then came the first of James Oswald's many productions of this genre in his *Curious Collection of Scots Tunes* (Edin., 1740), the second of which, known as *A Collection of Curious Scots Tunes* (Lond., *c.*1742), raised the ire of many later critics because the editor attributed certain works to David Riz[zi]o. About the same time was issued the first book of his more famous *Caledonian Pocket Companion* (Lond., 1745-59). Fortunately for Oswald's reputation he has been ably defended by John Glen in his *Early Scottish Melodies* (1900), although he omitted to whisper the not unlikely probability, enunciated by James Beattie, that Rizzio may have been the first to *collect* these old tunes, a circumstance which could easily have been the cause of Oswald's error, and even that of others, since the Rizzio attribution was earlier than Oswald's day. William Thomson, in 1725, had already fathered seven airs upon Rizzio, although he withdrew this paternity in 1733. Still, Watts' *Musical Miscellany* (1729-31), Sadler's *Muses Delight* (1754), Peacock's *Fifty Favourite Scotch Airs* (1762), and John Clark's *Flores Musicae* (1773), the two latter published in Scotland, all implicitly credited Rizzio as a composer, but they have not been subjected to the innuendo and abuse that have been the portion of poor Oswald, which began with mere joking in the *Scots Magazine* of 1741.

In the same year as Oswald's second book there appeared William McGibbon's *Collection of Scots Tunes* (Edin., 1742), followed by a second and third collection in 1746 and 1755. These are excellent works, for the editor was, like Oswald, a fine musician, as we shall see presently. Yet unlike the latter, McGibbon preserved much more of the pristine character of the old airs. Alexander Campbell was not pleased. He thought that " like every thing of the same kind that comes through the hands of professed musicians," it savoured " strongly of pedantic garnish." Seemingly he considered that McGibbon was of German tutelage since he says that the Italian influence " did less harm to our Scottish melodies than the exquisitely refined taste of the *modern* German school." Of course the modern German school had not been born in McGibbon's day and, as I have said elsewhere, the latter was actually influenced by England. The later George Thomson, himself an editor of Scots songs, and pardonably jealous of all other editors, frowned on Oswald's arrangements because he saw them " decked . . . out with embellishments in order to display the skill of the singer." The amazing thing about Oswald's obvious " graces," is that Campbell considered that Oswald was " among the very few to whom we can trace the authenticity of our national melodies," and this, we must presume, in spite of him being a professed " musician " and his " graces." The truth is that by this time the Italian influence was undoubtedly pervading even the national song, and vocal and instrumental graces, the *acciaccatura* and *appoggiatura*, were " the rage." We see at an Edinburgh concert in 1755 the following item,—" *Tweedside*, newly set in the Italian manner (for the sake of variety) by Signor Pasquali." Not that these embellishments were accepted everywhere. In 1759 the directors of the Aberdeen concerts instructed their Leader to play his part " in a more Simple and less Ornamental taste than he has hitherto been accustom'd." Indeed, an Italian, Francesco Barsanti, then resident in the capital, entered the lists in competition with the early native editors in the issue of *A Collection of Old Scots Tunes* (Edin., 1742), probably at the prompting of his dedicatee, Lady Erskine. Yet it is a commendable work, as one might reasonably expect from a composer of his ability, and there is actually a minimum of embellishment in his work, which is far different from the efforts of his fellow countrymen later. It was this Italian festooning that raised the ire of Charles Dibdin when he came north and heard those " beautiful simple and plaintive melodies . . . mutilated and destroyed " (*Observations on a Tour in England and Scotland*, 1801). Watlen, the English publisher who had settled in Edinburgh, tried to rid us of the Umbrian conceits in his *Complete Collection of Scots Songs* (Edin., 1796), wherein they were set, " plain and simple, without being Italianized in the least," but the smart set in the capital, doting on the Tenducci, Urbani and Corri fraternity, would have none of Watlen's pristine purity.

Since there was now a plenitude of collections on the market, a publishing lull in this direction resulted and nothing fresh appeared for fifteen years in Scotland save the issues of McGibbon already mentioned. In 1757 however, Robert Bremner set the ball rolling afresh with his *Thirty Scots Songs*, in which it was acknowledged that the music was " taken from the most genuine Sets extant " and " the Words from Allan Ramsay." A second volume was published the same year. In 1759 he issued the *Songs in the Gentle Shepherd* and *A Curious Collection of Scots Tunes*, as well as reproductions of the collections of Adam Craig and McGibbon which appeared after he had settled in London in 1762. Neil Stewart, in 1761, produced newly engraved editions of McGibbon, another *Collection of Scots Songs* (*c.* 1780), and a re-issue (1770) of Bremner's *Thirty Scots Songs* with an added third volume (*c.* 1795). Concerning the latter, Alexander Campbell has a sly reference to the " dropping base " employed as being more pleasurable to a person of " unsophisticated taste " than " a more measured harmony in which the subtilties of chromatic trick are commingled." It reminds one of William Tytler's affection (1780) for this " dropping base," which seems to have been infectious since even Burns caught it, as we see in a letter to

George Thomson (1794). Meanwhile Francis Peacock published his *Fifty Favourite Scotch Airs* (Aberdeen, 1762), Alexander Reinagle his *Collection of the most Favourite Scots Tunes* (Glasg., 1782), and Patrick Macdonald his *Collection of Highland Vocal Airs* (Edin., 1784), the latter being the first attempt to collect Highland music. Strangely enough, there had been an earlier publication *Ais-eiridh na sean chanan Albannaich*, by Alexander Macdonald, published in 1751, but in this work many songs were directed to be sung to Lowland airs, an instruction which later raised the ire of Alexander Campbell, who added :—" as if there did not exist Highland and Hebridean melodies in abundance, and better suited to Celtic vocal poetry than Low Country tunes."

The most favoured of all the collections was *The Scots Musical Museum* (Edin., 1787-1803) issued by James Johnson. It comprised eventually six volumes and contained some 600 songs, although not all Scottish. Robert Burns lent his magic pen to Johnson's venture and it was Stephen Clarke and his son who were responsible for editing the music. As we know from Burns' letters to Candlish and Skinner, the original project was for " our native songs," with " the words and music . . . done by Scotchmen," although an earlier scheme distinctly mentioned " Scots, English, and Irish songs." Eventually English songs were included, a proceeding which gave the contentious but frequently uncritical William Chappell the opportunity to belittle the " *Scots* Musical Museum," in spite of the clear explanation made in the preface anent this title. The later George Thomson, of whom we shall speak presently, was also unduly censorious of the *Museum*, and complained about the inclusion of " tawdry songs " which he " would be ashamed to publish." Thus he wrote in 1821, when he saw that the *Museum* was still selling as well, if not better, than his own *Select Collection*. By 1838 he had shed his jealousy and confessed that he was " far from insensible of the merit of a work in which there was so much of Burns." The plain truth is that these " tawdry songs " which, he said, were only fit for " topers," ex-pressed the unvarnished tastes and habits of the Scots, to which

his " select " collection was quite alien. That the old Reid
Professor of Music, John Thomson, and his assessor, Finlay
Dun, had a good word for Johnson's *Museum* in their *Vocal
Melodies of Scotland* (Edin., 1836) is of some import.

George Thomson tells us that it was Domenica Corri's singing
of the old Scots songs that urged him to collect them and to supply
accompaniments " worthy of their merit," and yet, strangely
enough, he does not breathe a word about Domenico Corri's
famous publication, *A New and Complete Collection of the Most
Favourite Scots Songs . . . with Proper Graces and Ornaments
peculiar to their Character* (Edin., 1783), a work which won great
popularity and was open to much criticism by reason of what could
have been termed " improper " graces which were never " peculiar
to their character." Seemingly, Thomson preferred to vent his
spleen on another Italian editor, Pietro Urbani, whose *Selection of
Scots Songs . . . Improved with Simple and Adapted Graces*
(Edin., 1792-1804) he considered " a water-gruel collection." In
spite of the graces, Urbani's contribution was a highly meritorious
piece of work which was, in addition, scored for strings. Burns,
who thought that Urbani sang " delightfully," but was " conceited," contributed to the third volume of the Italian's *Scots
Songs*. Still, with the very best motives, his petty criticism of
his predecessors and fellow workers notwithstanding, George
Thomson planned *A Select Collection of Original Scotish Airs*
(Edin., 1793-1841), the undertaking of a half-century, in which he
had the greatest of living composers as arrangers,—Pleyel,
Kotzeluch, Haydn, Beethoven, Weber, and Hummel, and had to
pay the penalty for it, although the kindly Burns foretold that
" fame " would be Thomson's reward before " the illustrious jury
of the SONS AND DAUGHTERS OF TASTE—all of whom
poesy can please or music charm." The facts are, as Thomson's
own biographer, J. Cuthbert Hadden, has admitted in his sympathetic *George Thomson : The Friend of Burns* (1898), that the
arrangements " failed nevertheless in the great majority of instances
to catch the characteristic style of the music." With all his faults,

Plate VIII

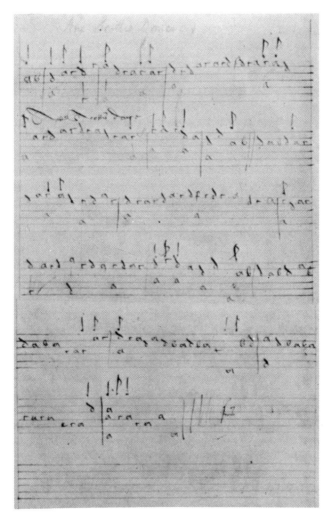

Ane Scottis Dance
Rowallan Lute MS. (1612-28).

PLATE IX

THOMAS ALEXANDER ERSKINE (1732-81)
Sixth Earl of Kellie.

George Thomson (1757-1851) deserves our praise as an "Old Mortality" of Scottish music. As a young man he had played at the old Edinburgh Musical Society Concerts, and later was one of the celebrities of "Auld Reekie," being limned in Crombie's *Men of Modern Athens.*

Such were the foremost collections of national song that issued from Scotland in such abundance. Yet England, too, was still holding affectionately to the Scots *sangs.* The *Aria di Camera . . . a Choice Collection of Scotch, Irish and Welsh Airs* (c. 1730), in which a certain Alexander Urquhart of Edinburgh edited the first mentioned, was the forerunner of general collections published in England which later included Walsh's *British Musical Miscellany* (1734) and Simpson's *Calliope* (c. 1746). Longman and Broderip issued three sets of *Scotch Songs* (Lond., c. 1782) of a poor class, seemingly collections based on plates of earlier sheet music. More important was William Napier's specialized *Selection of the most Favourite Scots Songs* (1790-94). the first volume containing arrangements by Samuel Arnold, William Shield, and two others, whilst a second volume came from the hands of the great Haydn. Napier (c. 1740-1825) had been a violinist at the Edinburgh Canongate Theatre, and later became a member of George the Third's Private Band, but gout having afflicted his hands, was compelled to take to music publishing. Joseph Dale also issued a set of three volumes which carried the title :—*Dale's Collection of Sixty Favourite Scotch Songs . . . with a Thorough Bass carefully revised, taken from the Original Manuscripts of the Most Celebrated Authors and Composers* (Lond., c. 1795), a title which is probably as veracious as is the *Sonatas on Scottish Airs* by Pleyel(?) that he published.

From what has preceded, one need not necessarily assume that the popularity of the national song was due solely to a biased political urge. Obviously this did have its share in the preference, but there was also a genuine feeling that the "auld Scots sangs" were better than others, and their very dissemblance from the latter was a theme of justification with many of the older appraisers of the Scots songs. Further, the vernacular settings of Ramsay and Burns contributed to the higher and persistent esteem. Indeed, much might be written of which of the old Scots songs have stayed the course by reason of the witchery of the lines of Ramsay and the "Immortal Bard," and which of the ballads have persisted through the fascination of the airs themselves. It may be rank heresy to postulate such a theorem, but what of Principal John C. Shairp (1819-85) who stated :—" Instead of saying that Burns created Scottish song, it would be truer to say that Scottish song created Burns." In any case, that something beyond a narrow nationalism claimed the souls of the people at large is evident from the general collection of songs which issued from the Scottish presses, as in John Bain's *Vocal Musician . . . Select Scots and English Songs* (Glasg., 1774), J. Brown's *Musical Miscellany* (Perth, 1786), David Sime's *Edinburgh Musical Miscellany* (Edin., 1792-3), James Sibbald's *Vocal Magazine* (Edin., 1797-9) and Alexander Adam's *Musical Repository* (Glasg., 1799).

Dance music in the national melody and rhythm challenged the national song for general acceptance. Since the opening of the century, dancing was openly recognized, and most of the larger towns had their dancing masters who were appointed or approved by the Town Council. From the James Thomson (1702), Agnes Hume (1704), and Margaret Sinkler (1710) manuscripts we have a fair idea of the measures which allured the feet in those days—the refined minuet and the boisterous reel. The earliest of the national tunes in print—Adam Craig's *Collection* (*c*.1730), as well as James Oswald's and William McGibbon's collections, reveal much dance music. Bremner's *Collection of Scots Reels and Country Dances* (Edin., 1757-61) with a second set (Edin., 1768), seem to have been the first books confined to these measures, of which there was soon to be a glut in the works of Neil Stewart (1761), Joshua Campbell (1778), Alexander McGlashan (1780), Angus Cumming (1780), Robert Ross (1780), James Aird (1782) and Niel (1784), and Nathaniel Gow (1797), all of which contained, wholly or partly, the old dance tunes either in prototype or ectype.

That something more than the reel and strathspey also continued
to be favoured is evident from Oswald's *Collection of Minuets* (1737),
the Gillespie MS. (1768), Joshua Campbell's *Newest and Best Reels
and Minuets* (1779), McGlashan's *Scots Measures, Hornpipes, Jigs,
Allemands, Cotillons* (1781), and John Riddell's *Scots Reels, Minuets*,
etc. (1782), although some of these were original compositions.
But the Scots more generally preferred the lively measures,

> " Nae cotillon brent new frae France,
> But hornpipes, jigs, strathspeys and reels
> Put life and mettle in their heels."

England, as with the songs, caught the infection of Scottish
dances, just as it had contracted it in the previous century. The
publications of Oswald, McGibbon, and Bremner, so persistently
re-issued in London, reveal their popularity, as do such independent
works as Walsh's *Caledonian Dances* (*c.* 1730), as well as the books
of Cooke (*c.* 1738) and John Johnson (*c.* 1748) with the same title,
together with Thompson's *Caledonian Muse* (*c.* 1789), W. Campbell's *Country Dances and Cotillions* (*c.* 1790), Duncan Macintyre's
Slow Airs, Reels, and Strathspeys (1795), and Napier's *Dances and
Strathspeys* (*c.* 1798), all issued for the " light fantastic toe " of
London. So we can afford to ignore the statement in Lily Grove's
chatty volume on *Dancing* (1895) that Scots reels and jigs were
introduced into London by Jane Duchess of Gordon in 1815. As
we see above, they were known and danced in the great metropolis
long before that, even at Almack's, founded by William Almack in
1764. This was only natural since Almack himself was a Scot who
is said to have changed his name from Macall, possibly for the same
reason as others did, to escape opposition. Yet most people seem to
have known of his origin and the gossiping Guy Williams, writing
to the eccentric George Selwyn, refers to " Almack's Scotch face
in a bag wig."

The literators were equally solicitous in paying compliments
to the national music in its historic role. The first seriously to
plough the field was David Herd (1732-1810), who published his
Ancient and Modern Scottish Songs (1769, 1776), which Frank

Kidson rightly considers a "trustworthy account of traditional Scots song," a work accomplished in the days when documents were not so abundantly available in research work. Then came William Tytler (1711-92), who contributed *A Dissertation on Scottish Music* to Arnot's *History of Edinburgh* (1779), which re-appeared in his *Poetical Remains of James the First* (1783), in the *Transactions of the Society of Antiquaries of Scotland* (1790), and in Napier's *Scots Songs* (1790). In the *Transactions* also appeared his paper *On the Fashionable Amusements and Entertainments in Edinburgh in the last Century, with a Plan of a grand Concert of Music on St. Cecilia's Day,* 1695. Tytler collected a little that was relative to music from the old Scottish historians but, although a perfervid admirer of the national song, he was quite uncritical. At the same time, John Glen's attitude towards him on the question of the diatonic scale is mere fastidiousness. Like most of his contemporaries, Beattie, Gregory, and other Scottish *illuminati*, Tytler was enamoured of the Italian school.

More important was the contribution of Joseph Ritson (1752-1803), the acrimonious English antiquary who so unmercifully assailed both Warton and Percy for their work on the ancient songs. Yet he was much more subdued in his volume on *Scottish Songs* (1794), and even spoke with commendation, although not without condescension, of his predecessors in the field. Probably much of his mellowness was due to the fact that he was not so much at ease on Scottish as he was on English territory, and there was always the possibility that there might be a counterblast from men of the type of John Leyden who would "thraw his neck." Ritson's work on Scottish songs certainly clarified many points, and his prefatory "Historical Essay" cannot be neglected by those interested in the question, although it comes from an alien hand. At the same time, the many manuscripts which have come to light since his day have conditioned some of his strictures.

Lastly, there was Alexander Campbell (1764-1824), the friend and music preceptor of Sir Walter Scott, whose *Introduction to the History of Poetry in Scotland . . . Together with a Conversation on*

Scottish Song (1798) deserves its place in the literature of the subject, although the author is better remembered by his *Albyn's Anthology* (1816-18). Campbell may not have been a musician of great ability, and he was certainly never among the *arrivés*, but he possessed a fine critical sense. As a composer and arranger he will have consideration elsewhere. Like many of his craft he died in extreme poverty.

From what has preceded we are able to assess how fervid was the appreciation of the national muse in 18th century Scotland, which was deepened, as I have attempted to show earlier, by the events of 1715 and 1745. Indeed, Scotland's affection and fascination for her homely song and dance quite outweighs any claim by sister lands— England, Ireland, or Wales—in their respective country's devotion to its national music. How then can it be averred that the Scots, as a people, are unmusical? The culture of a nation, as Wagner said, is determined, not by the expression of the privileged few, but by the response of the folkdom (*Volksheit*), and if it is the people, as he argues, who are the conditioning force in art, then Scotland in the 18th century had all that was requisite for the renascence of music in the land.

CHAPTER 2

THE CHURCH

" Congregational singing was, during the progress of the eighteenth century [in Scotland], performed roughly. The music ordinarily lacked melody."
        Rev. Dr. Charles Rogers : *Social Life in Scotland.*

Whatever vitality the music of the people, as expressed in the national song and dance, showed in this century, the music within the Presbyterian Church in Scotland was in a truly lamentable state. There were still no organs and no choirs. The General Assembly must have realized how bad the congregational singing was, because in 1706 it sought to remedy this by appeal to family psalm singing, just as it had tried in 1560. It urged the promotion of " scriptural songs in private families," for the church thought that if the youth were brought up to such things at home all would be well at church. In 1713 it was recommended to the presbyteries that they " have such schoolmasters chosen as are capable of teaching the Common Tunes." The order was repeated to schoolmasters in 1746 " to instruct the youth in singing Common Tunes," but again it was all to little purpose since the authorities would not learn from past experience, and would still not tolerate the professional musician in their midst. In addition, the Sang School, whose master had functioned as precentor here and there, was now moribund, yet rather than admit the professional the church preferred to nurture the amateur as precentor who, even so, as the Rev. Charles Rogers says, " long continued to be underpaid." An advertisement in the *Glasgow Courier* in April, 1786, illumines the state of affairs. A schoolmaster was required at Cathcart Parish who understood music and was able to " officiate as precentor at the kirk." By May there was *one* applicant. The great protagonist of the old psalmody, and one who invariably spoke his mind, the Rev. Neil Livingston, ruthlessly tears aside the veil in his criticism of the attitude of the church. " There has been no end of jokes and sneers " at the expense of these old precentors, " but the fault lay in reality with the Church." " It was expected," he continues, " that men employed in handicraft occupations and possessing only the common elements of education were . . . to discriminate the shades of sentiment in different psalms, and fix upon felicitous adaptations of tunes." Yet a few of these precentors were outstanding men. One was Thomas Neill (*c.* 1730-1800) of the Old Church, Edinburgh. He was a fine *basso* and his features may be seen in Kay's *Edinburgh Portraits* (1837).

Some of the most amazing enactments were passed by the General Assembly which stultified previous orders. In 1746, for example, the old practice of the precentor repeating each line before singing it was stopped, and this in face of the glaring fact that " the majority of every congregation were unable to read," and even those who could were handicapped by the scarcity of psalters. Some parishes rebelled, especially in Ayrshire, where they continued to read the line as of old. The psalters themselves testify to the state of affairs. As the bibliographer of Scottish psalmody, the late William Cowan says (*Publications of the Edinburgh Bibliographical Society*, xii), the issues of psalms books were " few and far between." The general indifference which this latter reflects, had set in after the adoption of Rous' musicless revised psalter of 1650, and even Cowan was unable to trace more than *three* psalters with music during the second half of the centennial period covered by the preceding chapter (1602-1707), although actually there were more. These three were all from the old centre of musical activity, the house of John Forbes of Aberdeen and dated 1666, 1671 and 1706. The first of these contained the twelve Common Tunes *plus* the tunes of *Bon Accord* and *Psalm* XXV, all arranged in four parts. The other two issues may be considered as second and third editions. With the dawn of the century under treatment, interest in psalters still continued to be negligible. In 1700 there appeared *A Collection of Psalm Tunes in Four Parts* (Glasg.) by William Brown. In 1714 and 1720 two more psalters came from Aberdeen which were no more than a fourth and fifth edition of the preceding issues of the house of Forbes. They are called *The Twelve Tunes*, but whilst *Bon Accord* is added to the Common Tunes, *Psalm* XXV is subtracted. However, they contained an elementary introduction to music " as taught by the Master of the Musick School of Aberdeen," which was but a breeze from the past.

A wider scope reveals itself in *A Collection of Psalm Tunes* (Dumfries, 1723), which contains the twelve Common Tunes as in the Aberdeen psalters, as well as a *New Town Tune*, all in four parts, with *Psalm* CXIX in two parts, and the Proper Tunes of *Psalms* CXXXVI and XXV in melody only. More remarkable was *The Common Tunes* : or *Scotland's Church Music Made Plain* (Edin., 1726 *et seq.*) by Thomas Bruce. Here is to be found an excellent introduction to music, whilst the tunes are in four parts, to which are added some ballads :—*Joy to the Person, Shepherd did you see* [= *Shepherd saw thou not*], both century old songs, as well as *Coridon arise,* and the *Christchurch Bells.* Once again we must note the significance of this inclusion of ballads in psalm books, which we have already seen in the previous century, since it shows that psalm-singing was still a secular pastime as well as a religious devotion and bespeaks as much for music as for piety. Then came *A Short and Useful Psalmody . . . Used in the Churches of Scotland and England* (Edin., 1742), by James Dallas. It had eighteen psalm tunes of the old type with the addition of a *Te Deum,* two anthems, some English hymns, and Byrd's *Non nobis Domine,* all of which go to show, as Cowan presumes, that this psalter was " mainly intended for use in the Episcopalian congregations."

Equally important was a psalter (title unknown) issued by James Chalmers (d. 1764) in Aberdeen (1749), to which was added " Observations concerning the Tunes and the Manner of singing them." It contained twenty-three tunes in two parts, tenor (melody) and bass. There were twelve Common Tunes, three Proper Tunes, as well as others, mainly English, including *St. Ann, St. Paul, St. Mary, Lichfield, Bristol,* and *Southwell,* although *St. Paul* has been claimed for Andrew Tait the Scottish Episcopal organist, in spite of Mainzer (*Standard Psalmody of Scotland*) who ascribes it to William Tate. In 1753, *A New and Correct Set of Church Tunes . . . Collected by Andrew Tait* (Aberdeen), was a newly edited version (called " The Third Edition ") of the preceding.

The period of crux in Presbyterian congregational psalmody had now been reached when a small minority was urging reform. The Episcopal Church, as small, poor, and persecuted as it may have been, was pursuing a far different path with organists, choirs, and good music, and we can see from the above-mentioned psalters of Dallas, Chalmers, and Tait, that the influence of the Episcopal Church was being felt. The latter had much wider opportunities. Apart from the Anglican service itself, there were anthems and hymns, which many of the Presbyterian Church thought might profitably be introduced into their church, as we know from John Craig of the New Kirk, Glasgow (1763). Of course, so far back as

Zachary Boyd, scriptural songs had been introduced (1647-48], and the older Thomas Wood, in his manuscript psalter of 1562-66, had included them. *Spiritual Songs, or Holy Songs* (Edin., 1686) had also been issued at the behest of " John Gibson, Merchant in Glasgow."

We have seen that scriptural songs had been recommended in 1707, and in 1745-47 proposals for paraphrases began to take shape. Yet by the " Sixties " the scheme was still in abeyance. The church's procrastination was noted in several quarters and one protest came from Glasgow in *A Persuasive to the Enlargement of Psalmody . . . By a Minister of the Church of Scotland* (Glasg., 1763). The protester was actually the Rev. John Craig of the New Kirk, Glasgow. It was addressed to the General Assembly and urged that it should " revive and prosecute the scheme about Scripture Songs," which looks as though the scheme had been shelved. It was not until 1781 that the paraphrases were published. There was the usual opposition to the introduction of the latter as savouring of " Prelatic leaning," and at Corstorphine a considerable part of the congregation seceded, whilst at Mauchline the paraphrases were not accepted until so late as 1805.

As for psalmody itself, a general effort at its improvement came in the mid-century. Aberdeen seems to have led the way in 1753, when part-singing became more the fashion. It was introduced by a soldier, Thomas Channon, of the 20th Foot, then under Lt.-Col. Wolfe, afterwards the famous General. This regiment was at Aberdeen in 1753, and Channon began his new teaching in the parish of Monymusk. One of his settings in four parts, said to be autograph, is a psalm tune named *Monymusk*, found in the Glasgow University Library. His success was immediate and it spread to neighbouring parishes. The result was that a number of ministers of the Synod applied to Lieut.-General Bland for Channon's discharge from the army, the details of which, together with a synopsis of the teaching, is contained in the *Scots Magazine* (1754-56), which admits that at this time " Church music . . . had undergone degeneracy and corruption " in the land. From what we know of his aims, Channon was just the man for the job.   He suggested "The proper teaching of melody, and the introduction of harmony . . . Choosing the best old tunes previously known in Scotland, composing new ones, and collecting others from the best authors. . . . Teaching the tune or sound truly and plain without quavering or any kind of affectation. . . . Teaching them the proper time. . . . As to harmony . . . in different parts, this was in use in the country at the time of the Reformation, and long afterwards."

The musical evangelist was soon to meet with bitter opposition as his gospel was preached and practised in the town of " Bon Accord," which should have been, unless we belie history, the very tabernacle of good music.   In April 1754, a correspondent of the *Scots Magazine* complains that " a new-fangled profanation of the Sabbath was introduced by singing the psalms at Church with a herd-boy's whistle, . . . which gives great offence to many serious Christians, which led to the innovation of singing music in parts by trained choristers, set apart by themselves in a loft or corner of the church, begun by a profane heretic above a thousand years ago." The Kirk Session was compelled to take heed of such profanations, and in the following January, just after a grand public performance had been given to demonstrate the value of the new teaching, it announced the unanimous finding that the new tunes " should not be introduced into public worship ; and they appoint their precentors to sing only, in all time coming, the twelve church tunes commonly sung in churches in Scotland, and printed in parts." The Session said that the innovations had occasioned such disturbances, " that the 1745 was but a jest to it."   Indeed, one of Channon's henchmen, Gideon Duncan, who dubbed himself " Teacher of the New Singing in the College of Old Aberdeen," was haled before the magistrates " for interrupting the clerk in reading out the line, raising a noise, and making a tumult " at Old Aberdeen.   Gideon evidently would not, as did his namesake in *Judges* vii, hide his light within a pitcher, and for this he was fined £50 or two years imprisonment.   Alas ! he became a pervert and anti-Channonite, publishing a brochure entitled the *True Presby-*

terian : or a Brief Account of the New Singing . . . (1755), which
is a perfect gem of its kind. The singing in three parts, which
Gideon once thought quite proper when he was a Channonite, was
now malison to his ears. The new singing, he said, " appears like,
and really is, three different Tunes, the one not the least resembling
the other when sung separately ; which must of necessity create
utter confusion through the whole Kirk." Gideon was but a humble
weaver originally, and whilst he once had tolerated the plain
" note against note " harmony, the use of counterpoint, in the
modern usage of the term, was now an abomination to him. The
pitchpipe also brought forth execration from the " True Presbyterian," which shows that the instrument was a novelty in Scotland.
This seems to be borne out by Thomas Moore in his *Psalm-Singer's
Compleat Tutor* (1751), where it is fully described for what I believe
to be the first time. Here it is stated that it " generally contains
about ten or twelve notes . . . which are marked on a piece of
wood which is made to fit the tube." Two late 18th Century specimens may be seen in the Glasgow Art Galleries and Museum.

In Edinburgh, the attempt to lift church music out of the rut
of mediocrity met with more success. Here, in 1755, an Anglican,
Cornforth Gilson, a chorister from Durham Cathedral, was engaged
by the Town Council to teach music, and his *Lessons on the Practice
of Singing, with an addition of the church tunes, in four parts, and a
Collection of Hymns, Canons, Airs, and Catches* . . . (Edin., 1759),
reveals his catholic tastes. We shall read more of him. That
opinions were broadening everywhere is evident from Bremner's
issue of Hintz's *Choice Collection of Psalm and Hymn Tunes for
the Citra or Guittar* (*c.* 1760), which reveals the use of sacred airs
in secular recreation. By 1757, the old Sang School being defunct,
at least eight schools (= classes) had been opened in the Capital
for instruction in music, primarily church music. Yet Edinburgh
had already taken a hand in the issue of a new psalter when Robert
Bremner published his *Collection of the Best Church Tunes, in Four
Parts* (Edin., 1756) which, he says, was issued by " Order of
. . . the Committee for improving Church Music in the City of

Edinburgh." It was practically identical with the addenda to his *Rudiments of Music . . . to which is added a Collection of the Best Church Tunes, Canons and Anthems* (Edin., 1756, 1762, Lond., 1763). In editing the old tunes, Bremner leaned to the conservative side, and published them "just as they are set and as they were sung in the days of John Knox, when Church music appears to have been more regularly performed *than it has been among us for many years past* [?]." He would not alter one note, for the simple reason that the music "had certainly been composed by the very great masters," the "fullness and grandeur" of whose harmonies made them "far preferable to most modern compositions of this kind." He included six anthems, four canons, and the Anglican *Venite, Te Deum, Benedictus, Jubilate, Magnificat, Nunc Dimittis,* etc., which titles speak for themselves.

In the west, Glasgow was even more speedily at reform, and it beat Edinburgh Town Council by two days when it engaged Thomas Moore (d. *c.*1792), also an Anglican, to open a "free school . . . to encourage and promote the improvement of church music." He was the precentor at Blackfriars Church, and his *Psalm-Singer's Pocket Companion, containing . . . English Psalm Tunes, suited to the different metres in the Scotch version of the Psalms . . . set in Three and Four Parts . . .* (Glasg., 1756), was a favoured textbook at the time, yet out of thirty tunes, only eight are from the old 1635 Common Tunes. Moore, like Bremner, fell in with the conservative view of maintaining the old Scottish and other settings in the psalms, and in his *Psalm-Singer's Delightful Pocket Companion* (Glasg., 1762) he vents his wrath against those "conceited novices and pirating quacks" who, by altering the harmonies, "endeavour to make themselves famed for their skill in this science." The truth is that Moore had a grudge against John Girvin, the precentor at the Tron Church Glasgow (1761-2), who had just issued *A New Collection of Tunes* (Glasg., 1761), in which he had dared to use his own settings. For this crime, the amiable Thomas Moore pilloried his professional rival, who he called "Mr. Marmusic," with the above mentioned protests.

Girvin must have given further umbrage to his critic by his later book, *The Vocal Musician* (Edin., 1763), which dealt with the " Grounds of Music " and " the Manner of Teaching Vocal Music." It contains a few quaint notions, one being :—" Give tunes in a flat key to words on a grave or dull subject, and on the contrary tunes in a sharp key to cheerful subjects." The book also shows, to Girvin's disapproval, that " men sing the Trebles, and women Tenors, where such parts are sung," This practice was only just dying out when Robert A. Smith published his *Devotional Music* (1810).

Another of these innovators was John Holden, who is said to have composed the tune *Glasgow*. He was precentor at the University Chapel Glasgow, and we know of him from 1757, when he was made a Glasgow burgess. Calling himself *Philarmonikos*, he published *A Collection of Church-Music* (Glasg., 1766) in which he essayed to " exemplify some new discoveries in the scale of music." His interest in this seems to have been kindled by a work entitled *A Preliminary Discourse . . . shewing the Perfection and Harmony of Sounds* (Westminster, 1726) by William Jackson of London. He uses twenty-two psalm tunes, which only include two of the old Scottish Common Tunes, and two anthems, yet in none of these does he strike a new note that can be said to have been worth the pother. The old settings of the 1635 psalter may be old fashioned but they certainly show more vitality than those of Holden, whilst his alteration of the bass of Worgan's anthem (*Psalm* XCII) was not an improvement. On the other hand, if the *Ten Pieces for the Organ* (*c.* 1785) by Philo Armonica came from his pen, one might allow that Holden was capable of something better. Two other books deserving mention are James Thomson's *Rudiments of Music : To which is added A Collection of the best Church Tunes, Hymns, Canons, and Anthems* (Edin., 1778, 1793, 1796), the last edition having catches added—a definite sign of the times—and Robert Gilmour's *The Psalm-Singer's Assistant . . . The Most Approved Psalm and Hymn Tunes* (Paisley, 1793). Even in the country districts there was to be found in circulation

The Elements of Music, wherein the fundamental principles of that science are explained . . . To which is annexed a Collection of the Best Church Music . . . with a view to the improvement of Church Music in Scotland (Aberdeen, 1787). The author was a William Taas, an intinerant teacher of psalmody who roamed through Banffshire.

From this date we clearly discern the more rapid infiltration of English tunes for the psalms and hymns in the Presbyterian Church of Scotland. In *The Psalms of David . . . with Twenty-three Select Psalm-Tunes*, issued by Alexander Adam (Glasg., 1773), only *two* are from the old Common Tunes, and all of them are given *in melody only*. This was a most obvious decline from the admirable standard set by William Brown in his *Collection of Psalm Tunes in Four Parts* (Glasg., 1700). The editor justifies his position by saying :—" Foreign churches may affect and captivate the senses, but the modest simplicity of *our* vocal praises is better calculated to promote real devotion." Thus, at a stroke, Glasgow was brought back to the ideal of 1560. Fortunately, this specious argument had but little effect in this direction, although the fashion for Anglican tunes became increasingly apparent. In *The Precentor . . .* (Glasg., 1776) of Finlay and McLachlan (d. 1791), out of thirty-four tunes for the psalms, only nine are from the old Scottish psalter. Worse still was the position in the east. In *A Collection of the Most Approved Church Tunes now used in the Church of Scotland* (Edin., *c.* 1790) by Archibald Walker, there are thirty-five psalm tunes, of which but seven are borrowed from the old source. This book reveals that psalm-singing as a secular recreation still flourished, since it includes ten Scottish and other songs, together with seven catches for three voices. Even the Methodist Church in Scotland, which had no monuments from the past, could look with favour on at least two of the old Scottish Presbyterian Common Tunes, as we know from *A Select Collection of Psalm and Hymn Tunes* (Glasg., 1793) by Henry Boyd, who was precentor at the Methodist Chapel, John Street, Glasgow. Some heretical outsiders, such as the Glassites or Sandemanians, were trekking back to old camping grounds musically, since they were using popular ballads for their hymn tunes. This we see in *Christian Songs . . . Versified for the Help of the Memory* (Dundee, 1775, 5th edit.), where *Roslin Castle, Comin' thro' the Broom, She Rose and Let Me In, Gilderoy, Bonny Jean, Tweedside, Birks of Invermay, Yellow-haired Laddie, Gaberlunzie Man, Flowers of the Forest,* and *Gala Water* are used as hymn tunes, to say nothing of the more modern *Black Ey'd Susan.*

In the country districts, the old tunes of the Scottish psalter persisted. Here the Anglican influence would be inconsiderable, although in 1713, the bigoted Wodrow says in a letter to Cotter Mather that " the English service is setting up in all corners of the church." As we know from Burns, the old tunes were among the household gods :—

> " Perhaps *Dundee's* wild warbling measures rise,
> Or plaintive *Martyrs*, worthy of the name."

Elgin also was counted among "the sweetest far of Scotia's holy lays" in *The Cottar's Saturday Night.* Yet the neglect of the old sources soon became fairly general. " Ultimately," as the Rev. Dr. Neil Livingston says, " Scotland seems to have become chiefly dependent upon England for its supply of music ; only some half dozen of its old Psalter tunes being retained, and nine-tenths of its precentors, it may be affirmed, being entirely ignorant that such a work ever existed." Presbyterian music had become as contemptible and pitiful as it was mean and trashy. We know what Burns thought of Presbyterian architecture, and one might equitably apply the same argument, *mutatis mutandis*, to its music—" What a poor, pimping business is a Presbyterian place of worship ! dirty, narrow and squalid : stuck in a corner of old Popish grandeur such as Linlithgow, and much more Melrose ! Ceremony and show, if judiciously thrown in, absolutely necessary for the bulk of mankind, both in religion and civil matters." That such a state of things had come to pass in its music was highly discreditable to a Church which was for ever displaying sanctimonious concern for its Reformation martyrs. We shall see in the 19th century that even outsiders began to wonder why it was that Scotland had rejected her old church tunes, and they probably concluded, as Calderwood did two centuries earlier over another change in the psalter, that the people rightly deserved to be called " light headed Scots."

Meanwhile the best traditions of church music were being upheld by the Episcopal Church of Scotland, whose organists and choirs were partakers in the more advanced musical life of the land. There were quite a number of rather outstanding personalities as dissenting organists, although they were not all Scots. A Ferdinand Shoneman was organist at St. Andrews chapel at Banff in 1737 according to Macklean's *Twelve Solos . . . for a Violin.* He was doubtless the father of Charles F. Sheniman who lived in Edinburgh in the " Seventies," and was the composer of the estimable *Four Sonatas for the Harpsichord . . .* (Edin., *c.* 1780). At St. Paul's Aberdeen, Andrew Tait was organist, and we read of him there in 1737 in Macklean's *Twelve Solos.* In 1748 he was cashier and organist for the newly formed " Musical Society " there and edited Chalmer's *New and Correct Set of Church Tunes* (1753). Dr. Johnson has a kindly paragraph about him in his *Journey* (1775) when he speaks of " an excellent organ well played by Mr. Tait." He appears to have died in 1783.

His successor at St. Paul's and the Musical Society was John Ross (1764-1837). Although born in Northumbria, he was of Scottish parentage, and the greater part of his huge output of compositions and arrangements were in the Scottish idiom. His abilities are best revealed in his *Six Concertos for Pianoforte and Orchestra* and his sets of *Sonatas for Pianoforte,* all of which rise above the ordinary of his day. Another very able organist, also an Englishman, was Dr. Musgrave Heighington (*c.* 1680-1764), and he was in charge (1756-64) at Dundee. In Scotland his name is kept fresh by the church tune *Heighington.* His songs had some vogue at Vauxhall and other gardens, and some appeared in Simpson's *Calliope* (1737-46). Another Dundee organist was William Speight (*fl.* 1782), possibly Heighington's successor.

PLATE X

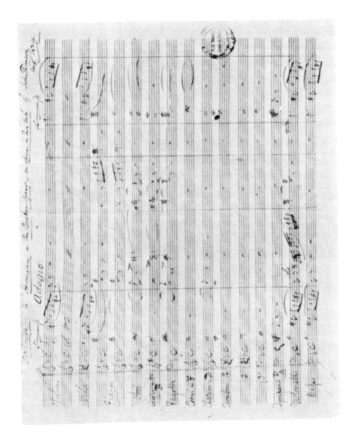

Reid School of Music. Edinburgh.

OVERTURE TO THE OPERA "HERMANN" (1834)
by JOHN THOMSON (1805-41).

Autograph

PLATE XI

From "The Baillie," Glasgow
SIR ALEXANDER C. MACKENZIE (1847-1935)
Principal: Royal Academy of Music (1888-1924).

The Episcopal organists in the south were equally sedulous. At Edinburgh a Signore Pescatore was " organist of Mr. Grant's Chapel " in 1750, and the chapel in the Cowgate had another Northumbrian, Stephen Clarke (d. 1797), who had been organist there since about 1764. As we know from the poet's correspondence, he was the friend of Burns, and harmonized the airs for Johnson's *Scots Musical Museum* (1787-1803). He composed but little, although his talents in this direction were not inconsiderable, judging by his *Six Sonatas for the Harpsichord . . . [and] Violin* (*c.* 1790). Alexander Campbell considered that Clarke was " the first organist of his day north of the Tweed," although George F. Graham dubbed him " but a mediocre musician," which is not true. He was succeeded at this chapel by his son William (*c.* 1780-1820). He was born in Edinburgh, and it was from his pen that the harmonies of Johnson's later volumes came. Then there was Alexander Campbell (1764-1824) who was organist at the non-juring chapel, Nicholson Street, Edinburgh, of whom we shall read later. Glasgow claimed an organist in John Fergus (d. *c.* 1820), who came from Huntly, Aberdeenshire, and was the first organist at St. Andrew's Episcopal Chapel Glasgow, from 1775. He was one of the outstanding musicians in the West, as we shall see presently. His son, also called John (1767-1825), was organist at the Roman Catholic Chapel in Clyde Street, and he called himself " Junior " in 1781.

All these Episcopal, Dissenting and Roman Catholic organists were actually the leaders of musical activity in their respective towns, and the concerts in Aberdeen, Dundee, Edinburgh, and Glasgow, owe much in their formative years to Tait, Ross, Heighington, Pescatore, Clarke Senr., and Fergus. Pescatore himself gave organ recitals in a garden near Holyrood in 1757. Some of the concerts of Fergus at Glasgow were given in the Episcopal Chapel, as were those of John Thomson (d. 1837) in St. George's Chapel, Edinburgh. The latter was the composer of *Three Sonatas* (Edin., *c.*1785) which are quite interesting. Yet whilst all this musical itacvity was displaying itself in Episcopal Scotland, the humble precentors of the Presbyterian Church were dumb, although there were signs that presaged a change.

What was expedient in the Anglican witchery was the trained choir, and this notion was to find favour eventually within the Presbyterian Church, although it must be understood that this was not so much at the wish of the church itself as the pressure of the congregation. Vocal societies and catch clubs, which began to flourish in the " Seventies," were fostering the love of part-singing, and this naturally gave a fillip to the encouragement of church choirs, since congregational singing was rather uncouth. Holden (1766), at the University, speaks of " loud " singing being universal and " most intolerable." Boyd (1793), a Methodist precentor, also censures the " bawling." James Beattie (1760-1803) gives a perfectly frank criticism in his tract *On the Improvement of Psalmody in Scotland* (1778). He assures congregations that " it is not necessary that every Christian should join in " singing the psalms. His reason was quite obvious since he says : " I would earnestly entreat those who sing ill, not to sing at all, at least in the church." Church choirs made no great development in Scotland until the 19th century and even then not before the mid-century, when organs dared to make themselves heard in " Whistlin' Kirks," as churches which employed them were contemptuously called.

Beattie was not opposed to the organ in worship. " The reasonableness of using Instrumental Musick in churches " he says, " might be proved, from Scripture ; from the general practice of Christians ; from the constitution of the human mind ; and from the very nature of the human voice, and of musical sound. But I need not enter upon the proof ; as, in this country at least, the practice can never become universal. For though the Assembly were to authorise it, I doubt whether there are sixty parishes in Scotland, that could afford the expence of an organ, and an organist."

CHAPTER III

THE INSTRUMENTS

" The Beaus and Belles were gone, the Concert o'er,
And *Kelly's* sprightly strains were heard no more.
Thro' the deserted room, dead silence reigned,
And still and dumb each tuneful string remained,
When, from the case in which a *Fiddle* lay,
Arose a voice that said, or seemed to say,
' *Basses*, and *Tenors*, *Kettledrums* and *Flutes*,
Trumpets and *Horns*, *Fiddles* and *Flagelutes*,
From you that solemn groan to you that squeak,
Patient attend, and hear a brother speak.' "
    HENRY ERSKINE : *The Musical Instruments* (C. 1770).

The proposal in the confounding voices of the instruments in the fable above was the election of a king. Yet it was none of these that secured the place, since the purple went to the humble pitchpipe who sounded but one note to attune all others. It is a pretty conceit, and the moral is palpable enough. The author was the Hon. Henry Erskine (1746-1817), the Lord Advocate for Scotland, and it was probably written in the days when he was a playing member of the musical society at St. Cecilia's Hall, Edinburgh, where his more musically distinguished cousin, Thomas Erskine, the 6th Earl of Kellie, was its shining light. The latter's brother, the Hon. Andrew Erskine (d. 1793), was also a prominent member.

By this time the craft of instrument making in Scotland had been steadily advancing, and the advertisements in the newspapers continually indicate the progress in both the manufacture and the importation of instruments. For example, Robert Bremner of Edinburgh advertised in 1754 that he " sells all sorts of musical instruments, viz., Bass violins, Harpsichords, and Spinets, German Flutes in ivory, ebony, or fine wood, Common Flutes [Recorders] of all sizes, French Horns, Bagpipes, Pitch-pipes, and Tabors, and all other sorts of wind instruments." A trade card from the other side of Scotland, that of James Aird, Jr., of Glasgow (*c.* 1780), tells us that he vends " Violins, German and Common Flutes, Fifes, Spinets, Hautboys, Pianofortes, French Horns, Clarionets." That some of these came from England would appear from an advertisement of Neil Stewart of Edinburgh in 1759, which says,—" Lately arrived from London and brought down from the best makers a large assortment of . . . musical instruments." Before long this latter firm had become instrument makers themselves and advertised that they "*make* all kinds of Harpsichords, Piano Fortes, Spinets, Guitars, etc., which they sell 25% cheaper than any *importer*." At the same time they also offered imported instruments for sale.

Although we sometimes read of the organ in private use in Scotland, as in the case of Lord Colville of Ochiltree among the aristocracy, and Thomas Macpherson the Edinburgh flautist, I do not imagine that it was in common domestic use, and I do not recall any pictorial representation of it at this date from Scottish sources, although the frontispiece to the *Compleat Tutor for the Harpsichord or Spinnet* (Lond., c. 1755) probably displays the instrument which would be supplied to Scotland, as there were no professional organ builders in the North Country in those days. At the same time, there were a few individuals who tried their 'prentice hands at the job. Three organs were made by the famous James Watt (d. 1819), one of which (dated 1762) is preserved in the Glasgow Art Galleries and Museum. Another such instrument was that used by the Aberdeen philosopher James Beattie (d. 1803), which had been built for him by his son James Hay (d. 1790) and his friend Dr. Laing in the year 1778. In the churches during this century it was only used by the Episcopalians, and latterly by the Roman Catholics.

Chambers (*Traditions of Edinburgh*, 1825) said that the first organ in the Episcopal Church in Scotland was erected in a chapel in Edinburgh in 1747. There were several before this date. So early as about 1730, as we know from *Letters . . . from the North* (Lond., 1753), an organ was being played at the Episcopal Chapel in Aberdeen. After this we read of the instrument at similar places at Banff (1737), Edinburgh (1747), Dundee (1756), and Glasgow (1775). Many of the concert halls were equipped with the instrument, as at Aberdeen (1752), Edinburgh (1753), and Glasgow (1780). The instrument at St. Cecilia's Hall, Edinburgh, erected in 1762, was, at the dissolution of the Musical Society in 1798, installed in the Assembly Rooms, George Square.

In 1757 an organ was used at the Edinburgh Theatre to accompany a *scena* in " the Romish form," and in this same year more organs infiltrated from England. We read in the *Courant* (25th Oct., 1757) which, quoting from a Newcastle journal, says : " By a master of a ship just arrived at Shields we are assured that seven fine organs are gone from London to Edinburgh, . . . two of which are for the city, and the other five for west-country kirks." They were, of course, for the Episcopalians or others, and not for the Church of Scotland, to whom the instrument was still *anathema*.

We get little information in the way of specifications, but an organ offered for sale in a house in the Cowgate, Edinburgh, in 1710, was " a fine cabinet organ," whilst another, in 1747, was described as " of concert pitch." James Ray, in his *Compleat History of the Rebellion* (1749), speaks (1745-46) of the instrument in St. Paul's Episcopal Chapel as " a neat organ," and the one made by Snetzler of London for the Aberdeen Musical Society in 1752, at a cost of £46, was described as a " bureau organ," which was " in the shape of a chest of drawers and desk." Snetzler also built in 1774 the organ still used at St. Paul's Episcopal Church, Edinburgh. The organ at the Cowgate Chapel, Edinburgh, was also a Snetzler, and later went into the possession of St. Andrews Chapel, Glasgow. In 1774 the organ at St. Andrews Chapel, Edinburgh, was offered for sale, when it was described as having eight stops and 484 pipes, of which 460 were of metal. Another organ at the same sale, which originally cost £120, was made by " the celebrated Mr. Thornbackle of London." The organ of the Sacred Music Institution, installed at the Trades Hall, Glasgow, in 1797, was made by Donaldson of York.

One other keyboard instrument which deserved mention is the *celestina*, in which the sound was produced by a rosined band of silk or other material rubbing the strings as in the old *symphony* or *hurdy-gurdy*. It had the appearance of a harpsichord and had been invented by Adam Walker in 1772. In 1779 it was introduced into Scotland at a concert at the Theatre Royal, Edinburgh, when, as the *Evening Courant* announced,—" Mr. Corri will play a new-invented instrument by Dr. Walker, called the *Celestino*, being the only one in this country."

The *monycord*, *virginal* and *spinet* had been practically superseded in Scotland by the *harpsichord* early in the 18th century. Indeed the first named, as the *minicords*, occurs so late as 1710, and the latter is mentioned in the account of the 1695 concert. Yet here and there the virginal still lingered. That the instrument still had its admirers may be deduced from the first issue of Pasquali's *Thorough-bass made Easy* (Edin., 1757) which, as quoted by Dalyell, was for " spinet, harpsichord, or virginal," although the last named instrument was cancelled on subsequent title-pages. My own copy of this work, dated 1757, only mentions the harpsichord. The persistence of the spinet is equally evident, since James Ray, in his *Compleat History of the Rebellion . . . in 1745* (1749), speaking of Inverness, says,—" It is noted for its handsome women . . . many of them are taught Musick (as the Spinet) and Dancing." So late as 1783, a music-seller advertised in the *Glasgow Mercury* that he sells spinets in the ordinary course of business with harpischords. The frontispiece of the *Musick for Allan Ramsay's Collection of Scots Songs* (1726) shows us precisely what the keyboard instrument was like in Scotland although the maker's name is glaringly " Fenton " of London.

Apart from the above, early reference to the *harpsichord* is made in Adam Craig's *Collection of the Choicest Scots Tunes arranged for the Harpsichord or Spinnet* (Edin., 1730). In this city the instrument is frequently described. " A single key harpsichord " by " the famous Thomas Fenton " is mentioned in 1748. In 1769, an " exceedingly fine double harpischord, by Rucker," is specified, which would probably be an instrument by a scion of the famous Flemish makers, Ruckers. " A single harpsichord, with three stops and a pedal, which takes off an unison and an octave, so plays more conveniently than a double harpsichord," is noted in 1774. In this year a Scot named Samuel Gillespy invented a new quill principle for the harpsichord. Scotland seems to have had a fair number of makers. John Glen (1833-1904) once possessed a spinet made by Christian Shean, Edinburgh, of whom we know in 1761 when he lived in Bull's Close, and called himself a "Harpsichord and Spinet Maker," but by 1794 had developed into a "Pianoforte Maker." Other makers were John Smith, Richard Livingstone, William Luid, James Logan, and Richard Horsburgh.

Yet the *pianoforte* itself had already made its appearance in Edinburgh. Thomas Somerville (1741-1830) says that it was introduced " after 1760," which statement seems to agree with the earlier printed music in Scotland for the instrument is found in Tenducci's *Collection of Lessons for the Harpsichord or Piano and Forte* (Edin., 1768). A Miss Marshall performed on the pianoforte at a concert in St. Mary's Chapel, Edinburgh, and at one in Leith, in 1774. Two years after, Domenico Corri played a concerto on a " great pianoforte . . . the only one of the kind in the country." Again in 1778, Corri was advertised to use at St. Cecilia's Hall, Edinburgh, " a pianoforte never seen here before of the kind." Although this specious placarding savours much of what we see in modern variety entertainment advertisements, there may have been a grain of truth in these announcements. Yet the question arises :— " What was the novelty ? " Could it have been that the 1774 instrument was the patent grand pianoforte of Americus Backers, who had been aided in his work by the Scotsman John Broadwood and his assistant Robert Stoddart ?

John Broadwood (1732-1812), who was a native of Cockburnspath, Berwickshire, joined Shudi the harpsichord maker of London in the year 1761, and from 1782 was the sole proprietor of the celebrated firm of Shudi and Broadwood. The latter began producing his noted square pianofortes on Zumpe's model in 1773, but in 1780 he produced his own original designs and, discarding the old wrest-plank and tuning pins of the clavichord system, he patented in 1783 a new instrument which became a pattern to later manufacturers. These and subsequent inventions were universally adopted. Several of Broadwood's productions may be seen at the Glasgow Art Galleries and Museum, notably one of 1786.

Scottish dealers soon took advantage of the novel contrivances and designs and the newspaper advertisements frequently stress the importance of these. We read, for instance, in the *Glasgow Mercury* (5-12-1787),—" Double and single harpsichords, with or without patent swells, and different stops : Grand pianofortes, patent ditto, organised and plain ditto, of different constructions and sizes." The " grand pianofortes " would probably refer to Stoddart's models, whilst the " patent ditto " would possibly mean Broadwood's 1783 patent.

Save perhaps in the Highlands, the old *clarsech* or harp was becoming neglected. John Gunn (*Historical Enquiry*) gives 1734 as the approximate date of disuse. He says that Murdoch Macdonald " appears to have been the last native harper of the Highlands of Scotland." It is claimed that he was a pupil of Rory *dall*, but this could not have been Rory *dall* O'Cahan. He then entered the service of the Macleans of Coll as their *clarsair*, and was functioning as such in 1734. He retired to Mull, where he died. Still, the most famous Irish harpers were welcomed even in the Lowlands, just as Rory *dall* O'Cahan had been fêted there in the previous century. Both Denis Hempson (1696-1807) and Ecklin O'Cahan (fl. 1773) performed in Scotland, which shows that ears there were still attuned to the *clarsech's* delightfully quiescent tones. The former played before the Pretender in Edinburgh, and the latter is alluded to by Boswell in his *Tour in the Hebrides*. Speaking of the late 18th century, Thomas Somerville (1741-1830) says :—" Instruction in music and drawing was confined to young ladies of high rank . . . Instruments then in use were the *harp* and spinet, chiefly the latter." The harp mentioned here was scarcely the *clarsech* but rather the more modern harp. Curiously enough, it was an Italian named Passerini who, in 1752, seems to have tried to resuscitate interest in the harp in Edinburgh, although even in this instance it was not the *clarsech*. At the Musical Society's concerts he was announced to play " for the first time, on a new instrument called David's Harp." At the last concert of the year the performer's name was given as Meyer, from which we suspect that this was Philipp Meyer, who played the modern harp.

Whilst the *viol* family continued to be favoured elsewhere, side by side with the violin group, it had but an uncertain existence in Scotland. The *viola da gamba* or *bass viol* probably held the field longest. We certainly have evidence of it being taught in Haddington in 1728, and Oswald's *Curious Collection of Scots Tunes* (1740) still specified the bass viol. In 1752 a modified tenor viol appears to have had some attention in Scotland. We read at a concert at St. Mary's Chapel, Edinburgh, in that year, that Passerini would play on the " violin or *viole d'amour*," the latter being termed " a new instrument." It was probably the *viole d'amour* with five double strings and sub-fingerboard sympathetic strings. Another viol that was resuscitated in Scotland was the *cither viol* with five double strings. It was called the *psalter* or *psaltery* in Scotland, and it appears to have been first featured by Pasquali at a concert in Edinburgh in 1754, although the *salterio*, which Signor Carusi played at a concert in 1750 in St. Mary's Chapel, may have been this instrument. The psalter was claimed, in 1762, to be " unequalled for delicacy and sweetness." At the Leith Assembly Rooms in 1785 a quartet of " Scots music " included a psalter. A Glasgow sale in 1786 named " one psaltery," whilst three years later John Banks played a solo on the instrument at a concert in this city.

What mainly contributed to the disuse of the viol was the growing popularity of the violin family whose four strings, tuned in fifths, contributed to an easier mastery of its technique. Since the days of Charles II, the violin had insinuated itself upon most music lovers, especially by reason of the tone of the fine instruments which issued from the workshops of the Italian masters,--Gasparo, Maggini, Amati, Stradivari, and Guarneri. The Scots were evidently excellent connoisseurs since we find the very best of the Cremona school in their hands, much of the demand being due to the Italian professionals who were being flattered at that time in Edinburgh. One of the things which annoyed the Englishman Captain Topham when he was in Edinburgh (1774-75) was to find " respectable characters " among the Scots, " disputing the merits of an Italian fiddle." In 1708 " two Cremona violins . . . and a parcel of fine music books " were offered for sale in " Fair Edina." Pasquali, who settled in this land in 1752, had " some Cremona " and other violins for sale. Stabilini, who led the concerts in Edinburgh, possessed a Guarneri, whilst Niel Gow boasted of a Gasparo da Salo.

By this time, however, Scotland herself was producing fine craftsmen in violin making who followed in the footsteps of their illustrious forerunner and fellow Scot, Thomas Urquhart, of the previous century. The first to make a name for himself was Alexander Kennedy (1695-1785), who also settled in London, and became the founder of a family of violin makers, among whom were his son John (d. 1816) and a grandson Thomas (d. c. 1870). Then came Joseph Ruddiman (1730-1810) of Aberdeen. His early violins, like those of Kennedy, were on the Stainer model, which shows that Scotland could appreciate the bold work of the German master. Later (1780) Ruddiman followed Stradivari with his own special features. Honeyman (*Scottish Violin Makers*) says,—" Everything about Ruddiman's work shows the touch of the true artist." John Dickson (b. c. 1725) of Stirling, was an even earlier maker who took Amati as his pattern. He also went to London and then to Cambridge, where his work is known from 1750 until 1760.

Cathune Adams of Garmouth, Elginshire, was another good Amati copyist who flourished 1775-1805. A better workman was John Blair of Edinburgh, whose instruments are dated 1790-1820. In him, as Honeyman says, we see the " practised hand of an artistic and expert maker," on the Stradivari model. He is also to be praised as the master of one who has been dubbed " the Scottish Stradivari," Matthew Hardie of Edinburgh (1755-1826). Sandys and Forster, in their *History of the Violin*, say that Hardie " could execute first-class work," and they praise the " great power of tone " of his violins, violas, and 'cellos. For the recipe of his varnish, see Peter Davidson's *The Violin* (Glasg., 1871). Hardie may be said to have founded a Scottish school in his pupils, notably his son Thomas (d. 1858), who has been pictured by Charles Reade as

" Thomas Harvey " in his *Christie Johnstone* (1853). Honeyman states that John Dodd (1752-1839), the famous bow maker, was born in Stirling, but Fleming (*Fiddle Fancier's Guide*), himself a Scot, makes no such claim for " the English Tourte." It is to Tourte and Dodd that we owe the modern bow, and it was the former who introduced the screw principle, which seems to have been fairly new to Scotland in 1788, since the *Glasgow Mercury* for that year advertises " screwed bows " as a speciality.

Among the novelties of the century in Scotland was the adoption of a doubly-strung violin, and the late W. H. Cole of Glasgow possessed such an instrument. This was put forward in a work entitled *Melody the Soul of Music* (Glasgow, 1798), published anonymously, the actual author being a Glasgow bookseller and minor poet, Alexander Molleson. The author suggested that the tone of the instrument could be enriched by stringing the violin in pairs, each of the added strings being tuned an *octave lower* than the parent string. Of course, there was nothing novel in the suggestion, since the cither viol or psalter was already equipped with double strings, although these were in unison.

The old Scottish method of holding and tuning the violin have some interest. Those who remember Raeburn's portrait of Niel Gow (d. 1807) will recall that he holds the violin with his chin on the *right* side of the tail-piece, although the modern method, with the chin on the *left* side, was already in vogue elsewhere, as we know from M. l'Abbé's *Principes du Violon* (c. 1760). Yet Scotland was not the only land that persisted in the old way, since Paine still advocated this method in his *Treatise on the Violin* (1825). Another feature of Scottish violin playing was that instead of holding the violin horizontally, the head was lowered so as to enable the left elbow to rest on the hip. We see this in the frontispiece to *Musick for Allan Ramsay's Collection of Scots Songs* (1726) and in David Allan's picture *The Penny Wedding* (1795). The special Scottish *accordatura* for dance fiddlers is quite intriguing. Many of the strathspeys and reels are difficult to play, but they were simplified by altering the tuning. Two examples of simplified

" scordatura," as it was called, may be seen in *Grigs Pipes*, a reel, where the strings were tuned to A E a c♯, whilst for *Black Jock* and *My ain kind dearie* the tuning was A E a e. (*See* my paper in *Proceedings of the Society of Antiquaries of Scotland*, 1930-31.)

As I have mentioned elsewhere, if the harpsichord belonged to the " upper ten," the violin was supported by the " people," not only because of its moderate cost, but more especially since it was eminently suitable for dance music, and in this latter art there emerged another instrument of the fidicinal type. This was the *kit*, which was almost wholly used by the Dancing Master. It was a narrow-chested instrument, about half the width of the violin, sometimes even a third, these dimensions making the instrument more portable, even for carrying in a large inside overcoat pocket, hence the name *pochette*. A *kit* of this period, which once belonged to John Hall of Ayr (d. 1862), may be seen in the Glasgow Art Galleries and Museum. It was purchased by me many years ago, together with his manuscripts, now in Glasgow University Library. The *kit* bears the label of " James Aird, junr., Gibson's Wynd, Glasgow," and the date must be 1780, or earlier, since Aird moved to a new address in that year. What is equally interesting is that the instrument reposes in its old rectangular mahogany case.

Side by side with the growing popularity of the violin, its congeners, the viola or tenor, the violoncello, and the double bass, also came into the limelight. That a solitary tenor was admitted in the 1695 concert, shows that the instrument had not yet found a permanency in the orchestra. In the " Sixties," Thomas Erskine the sixth Earl of Kellie was writing specially for the viola in his orchestral scores. At the 1695 concert, both " violincellos and *viol de gambos* " are mentioned in Tytler's list of the orchestra, but the original document of James Chrystie only mentions " basses." The violoncello was certainly known in Edinburgh in 1720 because when Lorenzo Bocchi arrived in this city in this year, he was heralded as " the second master of the violoncello in Europe." When the 'cello definitely took the place of the *viola da gamba* we do not know. It may have been in the " Forties." At any rate, Oswald's *Curious Collection of Scots Tunes* (1740) specifies the bass viol (= *viola da gamba*), whereas William McGibbon's *Collection of Scots Tunes* (1742) and Barsanti's *Collection of Old Scots Tunes* (1742) includes the violoncello. Arnot, in his *History of Edinburgh* (1779), neglects to include the violoncello in his instrumentation of the " Musical Society " and only mentions " a double or *contra* base." Yet this must be an oversight, since there is plenty of evidence of violoncellos in this orchestra at this period. Bremner, in 1754, advertises " bass violins."

By this time, the violoncello as an accompaniment to the violin had become the mainstay of dance music in Scotland, and the innumerable collections of reels and strathspeys that were published during the second half of the 18th century show how closely in consort these two instruments were. We see them side by side rather later in Sir David Wilkie's picture *The Penny Wedding* (1818), a scene which typifies the people's music in those days. John Gunn (1765-*c.*1824) published *The Theory and Practice of Fingering the Violoncello* (Lond., 1793, 2nd ed., 1795) and an *Essay, Theoretical and Practical, on the application of Harmony, Thorough-bass, and Modulation to the Violoncello* (Edin., 1801).

What service the *lute* family performed during this century is not too apparent. Alexander Fergusson (*Henry Erskine*, 1882), on the authority of Erskine's son, the twelfth Earl of Buchan (d. 1857), mentions that Christian Fullerton, Erskine's wife, " played well on the lute." Yet the precise instrument may have been the English guitar, which is what we see in her lap in George Willison's portrait of her (*c.* 1772). The long-necked *archlute* was also still favoured in Scotland, and we see in the hands of Lady Mary Coke in her portrait by Allan Ramsay (d. 1784) in which the spinet is also shown. I possess a copy of Broderip's and Wilkinson's *New and Complete Instructions for the Lute* (Lond., *c.* 1805) which once belonged to William Goold, a music teacher of Glasgow, which shows that the instrument was certainly in vogue even as late as this.

The *guitar* seems to have overtaken the lute and, like it, was an instrument of the classes rather than the masses, as the frontispiece to Bremner's *Instruction for the Guitar* (Edin., 1758, Lond., *c.* 1762) so amiably reveals. It is also figured in the pages of Corri's *Select Collection of the Most Admired Songs* (Edin., c.1779). Although James Oswald published *The Pocket Companion for the Guittar : Containing . . . Italian . . . and Scots Songs* (Lond., *c.* 1755), Bremner's guitar tutor was probably the earliest of its kind in English, and he himself says that the guitar was " but lately introduced into Britain." The craze came from Italy, but the instrument was rightly called the " English guitar " since it was practically identical with the old cittern, as we know from John Playford, which had fallen into disuse a half century earlier. Dalyell assures us that this English guitar " long continued in repute in Scotland," and that its practice " was a regular branch of female accomplishment." Frank Kidson looked upon it as " the feminine substitute for the German flute." Corri's picture of the instrument presents it with five double strings. On the other hand, the guitar in the lap of Mrs. Henry Erskine (Christian Fullerton) in Willison's portrait (*c.* 1772) has twelve tuning pegs, eleven of which are visible (Fergusson's *Henry Erskine*, 1882), and Preston's arrangement was an *accordatura* of C E G c e g, the two lower strings being single, and the four others double, although Longman's and Broderip's *Compleat Instruction for the Guitar* (Lond., 1780) makes all the strings double. That the instrument found acceptance well into the 19th century is apparent from the fact that almost every piece of sheet music published in Scotland from about 1780 to 1810 had appended an arrangement for the " guittar," and even Bremner's *Songs in the Gentle Shepherd* (1759) was issued specially for this instrument.

The Spanish guitar was also to be found in Scotland in the 18th century, although in England, according to *Grove's Dictionary of Music and Musicians* (1940), it did not make its appearance until 1813-15. It was known in England so early as the *Musical Entertainer* (Lond., 1737-38) of George Bickham. In Scotland, Joshua

Campbell of Glasgow was teaching it in 1762, and we see the instrument in the hands of Lady Caroline, Fourth Marchioness of Lothian, in her portrait painted by Allan Ramsay (d. 1784), now in the National Gallery of Scotland. Unlike the pear-shaped English guitar, the Spanish type had a contour somewhat similar to that of the violin but with the belly and back quite flat. Another dissimilarity from the former was that there was no bridge, the strings, which were five, being fastened to a combined bridge-tailpiece as in the lute.

The instrument which ran the violin very close in popularity was the flute. During the first two decades of the century this was the recorder, also called the English flute, or the common flute. Alexander Baillie's *Airs for the Flute* (Edin., 1735) was for this instrument, the " flute a beque," as he calls it. That it was still used in choirs, i.e. various sizes, is evident from a Bremner announcement in 1754, and that it had admirers so late as 1781 is to be seen from an advertisement of James Aird of Glasgow, which refers to the " German flute, fife, and common flute." It was the German flute which eventually ousted the recorder or common flute. According to Tytler, it was Sir Gilbert Elliot, afterwards Lord Justice Clerk, who introduced the German flute into Scotland in 1725, he having learned the instrument in France. It soon became the rage. Adam Craig's *Collection of Choicest Scots Tunes* (Edin., 1730) is for the " Voice, Violin, or German Flute," a subscription which continued on most title pages till the close of the century, and rarely was sheet music issued without an arrangement being added at the foot for this instrument. At first the German flute had but one lever key, that of D sharp, but by the close of the century the six-keyed flute was in use. In 1788, James Aird, Jr., of Glasgow, advertised " German flutes, mounted with ivory and silver keys or plain. Regimental or common fifes." Thomas Macpherson was the most outstanding Scottish flautist in the second half of the century.

John Gunn (1765-*c*.1824) of Edinburgh published *The Art of Playing the German-Flute on New Principles* (Lond., 1793), a work which W. S. Rockstro considered to be " a noteworthy effort on the part of a clever musician to teach the flute on scientific principles." Gunn also wrote *The School of the German Flute* (Lond., 1794). The *fife* was in general use in the drum and fife bands of Scottish regiments, whilst in the numerous volunteer and fencible associations raised during the Napoleonic era it was an especial favourite. Even in the homes of the people the fife became as popular as the flute, since the cost of the former was only half that of the latter.

The *flageolet*, which is one of the recorder *genus*, was known in Scotland so early as 1708, in which year we have a record of a maker in Edinburgh named James Lilly. If we can trust the poem of Henry Erskine, the flageolet, which he calls *flagelute*, for the sake of assonance perhaps, was used by the Edinburgh Musical Society. According to Dalyell, this is not unlikely, although the instrument described by the latter was actually a bass recorder, three feet nine inches long with one key. When Dalyell saw this instrument, it was in the possession of Gilbert Innes of Stow, and he was of opinion that it " probably belonged to the Musical Society," although he confesses that he had only heard of but two in Scotland.

The *hautboy* had been considerably improved since last we viewed the instrument, and after the mid-century an octave key had been added. It had been the mainstay of the military bands where, with the bassoon, a choir of these double reed instruments, was in common use. An Edinburgh advertisement of 1708 reads :— " James Lilly . . . Con's Close, turns flutes and *hautboyes* in ivory and hard-wood." We see the hautboy in the orchestras of the concerts and the theatres in 18th century Scotland. Johann C. Fischer (d. 1800), the famous performer on the instrument, may have resided, or have frequently performed, in Scotland in the " Eighties " of this century, since one of this name was much in evidence in the land at this time. He is the " Vischer " to whom Beattie refers. Scotland's own superb artist on the hautboy was Thomas Fraser (*c.*1760-1825), whose playing of *Hey, tuttie taitie*, said Burns, " often filled my eyes with tears." The *bassoon*, according to Dalyell, was introduced into Scotland in the year

1696, and during the succeeding century we not only find it in the orchestras and regimental bands, but also with the Edinburgh waits where, with two hautboys, it continued to give delight when the burghal players did their rounds in " serenading the inhabitants." The *clarionet* had, by the mid-century, reduced the importance of the hautboy. This also had been developed in the military band and gradually assumed a place in the orchestra. It seems to have been heard for the first time in Scotland at the Edinburgh Assembly Rooms in 1755, when Messrs. Charles from London performed select pieces on the instrument. The *stockhorn* was still flourishing as we know from Ramsay's *Gentle Shepherd* (1725), where we read,— " When I begin to tune my *stock and horn*," and from many delightful title-page vignettes of this century. Nor was it confined merely to a shepherd's delight, since Charles Sharpe of Hoddam, that " brother-cat gut " of Burns, played *The Ewe-milking's Bonnie* to its reedy tones.

The *bagpipe*, naturally, was the popular favourite, in spite of what Grattan Flood says to the contrary, as I have shown. The old Scottish regiments of the British Army still retained their pipers although they were not officially provided by the Army Estimates. When the newer regiments were raised towards the close of the century, these too had their pipers, and it was its usage by the army that doubtless increased its popularity. Of makers at this period the most outstanding was Hugh Robertson (*c.* 1730-1822) of Castle Hill, Edinburgh, whose daughter continued the craft in the 19th century. Specimens from this period are plentiful. Two outstanding examples are at the West Highland Museum, Fort William, and at the Castle Museum, Edinburgh, which are said to date from 1687 and 1698 respectively, but both are probably early 18th century. A famous piper who could vie with a Mac-Crimmon, a Rankin, or a Charles MacArthur, was George Syme (*c.*1700-*c.*1790), who is portrayed in Kay's *Portraits*. Angus MacArthur of that ilk was another piper of celebrity, although the manuscript of his *piobaireachds*, as recorded by his pupil, now in the National Library of Scotland, is not 18th century as the catalogue states, but early 19th century. Peter McGregor (d. 1824) and Allan Cameron (d. 1833) were two other pipers who deserve mention. In the border counties the bellows or Lowland pipe was favoured, and one famous executant was Thomas Anderson of Kelso. Stenhouse says that his father and grandfather, who lived at the close of the 17th century, were " esteemed good performers." In Edinburgh, T. Campbell was teaching the Irish pipe. Curiously enough the old *Jaws Harp*, the erstwhile *ripube* or *trump*, whose " twingle-twangle " so thrilled Burns, was still in favour as a folk instrument, as David Wilkie has shown in his delightful picture *The Jew's Harp*. We read of it at Dingwall in 1741, whilst Pennant found it with the Highlanders in 1769, as did Stoddart in Lochaber in 1799-1800.

Among the brazen throated instruments which found acceptance in the 18th century were the trumpet, French horn, and trombone. The *trumpet* had retained its old lineaments and found a place in orchestras at both the concerts and theatres, as well as in the regimental bands. The band of the Company of Archers had trumpets with their oboes in 1726. Only one was used at the 1695 Edinburgh orchestral concert, but later two became the rule In the army, as in the Scots Greys, trumpets had taken the place of drums in dragoons in 1764, not only for signalling purposes but as a component part of the regimental band. The *French Horn* had similarly kept its earlier form and, like the trumpet, was non-chromatic, being restricted to the harmonics of the tube. The Royal Company of Archers had the French horn (*cor de chasse*) in its band in 1732, and the Scots Greys had two in 1777. In the orchestra it was used in pairs and, with the trumpet, was usually given special mention on the programmes, where it would be said that an item was " accompanied by French horns." Thomas Erskine, the leading Scottish composer of the period, always scored for two horns, and two were generally found among the hired professionals at the concerts in Edinburgh, Aberdeen, and Glasgow. The *trombone*, the erstwhile sackbut, had fallen into neglect in these islands, as we know from the difficulty in finding performers for the Handel Commemoration of 1784. Once again, it was the military band, in whose ranks it was first revived, that first demonstrated the value of the instrument, although it did not find a permanent place in orchestras until the following century.

Finally comes the percussion and concussion group, of which the *kettledrums* take first place. These constituted a regular feature of the orchestras at Edinburgh and Aberdeen from the mid-century onwards, and the instruments were also to be found, although not officially provided for, as an accompaniment to the trumpeter bands in the cavalry. The *side drum* was still favoured by the burghs for the " town minstrel " in Scotland, and even so late as 1790, the town clerk of Greenock, with a merry twinkle in his eye, advertised for a town drummer at a " fair salary," intimating that " those who incline to stand *trial*, will appear in the *court*-hall " on such-and-such a date. Only for this purpose, and as a signal and marching instrument in foot and dragoon regiments, was the instrument used in these days. At the turn of the mid-century however, a craze for Turkish instruments became rampant among the military authorities, and in this exuberance there appeared the *bass drum, cymbals, triangle*, and the bells known as the *jingling johnnie*, all of which became the high lights in musico-military display in Scottish and other regiments. The width of the bass drum of those days was sometimes double its diameter, whereas nowadays the diameter is usually double the width of the instrument. An old Edinburgh bass drum (*c.* 1794), which once enlivened the march of the Royal Edinburgh Highland Volunteers, is preserved by Messrs. J. & R. Glen, Edinburgh, whilst a jingling johnnie belonging to the Scots Guards may be seen at the Castle Museum and others are preserved in the University Music Room of that city. Soon these Turkish instruments came to be used by orchestras, more especially after Mozart and Beethoven had given them approval. Even in the home, ladies took themselves to the tambourine and triangle, as accompaniments to the pianoforte, as we know from the works of J. B. Cramer and Muzio Clementi. In Edinburgh, a Thomas Crichton advertised himself as a " Teacher of the Tambarine " (*see* his *Six New Tunes, Strathspeys,* etc., issued by Gow and Shepherd). These instruments were actually introduced into the mechanism of the pianoforte, in which they were sounded by pedal action.

CHAPTER IV

THE PUBLISHERS

" The press of Scotland suffered under a most mischievous system of license and monopoly during a long period. . . . The harassing of printers and publishers was of course fatal to the production of musical works. . . . It is therefore not to be wondered at that printers were not ready to risk fine, confiscation of plant, or imprisonment over works which might not even pay the cost of production."

KIDSON : *British Music Publishers* (1900).

What Kidson avers actually relates to the 16th and 17th centuries, although in principle the same fears existed even later, as we know from Kincaid's action in 1770 to enforce his " privilege." Even at the close of the 17th century, when there was an increasing demand for secular music, nobody in Scotland was willing to supply the need, not even the pirate publishers of psalm books. It is not improbable that the latter were afraid lest the church might be offended. When the trade in secular music first arose in Scotland it was as an inconsequential brook, discerned in one or two engravers like Cooper and Baillie, making but little current. Then it showed itself in a larger, though still somewhat languid stream of printers, as in Bremner and Neil Stewart, without gathering any perceptible momentum. When as a river it reached the last quarter of the century, we see its waters flowing briskly and in volume, finally to almost overflow its banks in a fair spate of public demand.

It will be remembered that, apart from the *Cantus* of Forbes (1662, 1666, 1682), there was no printed secular music in Scotland up to the close of the first quarter of the 18th century, but in the year 1726 there were three historic publications. The first was a work by Signor Lorenzo Bocchi, containing twelve sonatas for different instruments and a Scots Cantata, the words of the latter being by Allan Ramsay. No copy of this work is extant, but such is the substance of an advertisement in the *Caledonian Mercury* (22-2-1726). The second was the *Musick for Allan Ramsay's Collection of the Scots Songs*, which was edited by Alexander Stuart. The third was *The Common Tunes* (Edin., 1726) arranged by Thomas Bruce, which was a psalm book with some ballads added. It was a poorly engraved book. The second of these publications was of some moment since it was engraved by Richard Cooper who, if Kidson's guess is correct that " no doubt he kept a shop for the sale of music," may be considered the father of music publishing in Scotland. It was this excellent engraver who also cut the plates and vended the prints of the works of Craig (1730), Oswald (1734), Macklean (1737), and McGibbon (1740, 1742, 1746, 1755). One of his pupils or workmen was the famous engraver Sir Robert Strange (1721-92). Alexander Baillie was another early engraver of Edinburgh, although we only seem to have his *Airs for the Flute* (1735) and Barsanti's *Collection of Old Scots Tunes* (1742). James Reid and Thomas Phinn were two other engravers who produced good workmanship, which may be seen in Bremner's and Neil Stewart's publications of the " Fifties " and " Sixties."

However, the first real music-seller in the capital was the versatile Robert Bremner (1720-89) who, by 1754, was already installed in business at Blackfriars Wynd. From his first publication, *The Rudiments of Music* (1756), to his last in Edinburgh, *The Harpsichord or Spinnet Miscellany* (1761), he was busy re-issuing the Scottish music collections of Ramsay (1757, 1759), McGibbon (1759), and Craig (1759), together with much original music and didactical works, all of which helped to excite Scotland's reawakened interest in music. Alas, " Auld Reekie " did not make a response that was commensurate with Bremner's enthusiasm and he, like Oswald and others, went to London in 1761, leaving his Edinburgh shop in the charge of a manager, John Brysson. In the greater metropolis he launched out in greater freedom, publishing the orchestral, chamber, and operatic music of the leading composers, Abel, Arne, Avison, J. C. Bach, Barbella, Boccherini, Corelli, Giardini, Gossec, Guglielmi, Haydn, Jomelli, Mozart, Pergolesi, Piccini, Pugnani, Sacchini,

Stamitz, and others, including his Edinburgh friend Schetky and his fellow countrymen Erskine and Reid. I make this roll-call because most of this music filtered into Scotland through his branch shop. After his death, John Preston bought his stock and plates, and in reprinting from the latter referred to Bremner's publications as " not only the most extensive, but the most valuable list of work ever exhibited in this kindgom." Frank Kidson (*British Music Publishers*, 1900) says : " Bremner's publications are always distinguished for excellent engraving and printing." Even his work in Scotland had a character that was " so neat and clean, and in a style peculiarly his own."

At Bremner's death (1759), his Edinburgh manager, John Brysson, seems to have taken over the business for himself at the back of the Cross Well, and this he directed with success until 1820. His printing is admirable, and well exemplified in his excellently produced *Six Duetts . . . for Two Violins* by Pleyel, from the burin of Alexander McIntosh, the *Eighteen Airs . . . (c.* 1790) of George Jenkins, and many other works. His sheet music issues were enormous.

Yet the man who actually took Bremner's place in Edinburgh as the leading Scottish music-seller was Neil Stewart, of whom we first read at the Exchange, High Street, in 1759, and later at other addresses. His shop became the centre for Scottish national music since he published or re-issued the works of McGibbon (1761), McLean (*c.* 1772), Daniel Dow (*c.* 1775), Alexander McGlashan (1780), Marshall (1781), Niel Gow (*c.* 1795), and the Ramsay-Bremner *Thirty Songs* (*c.* 1795). All of these works, as well as his numerous issues of the compositions of Schetky, reveal the very best work in printing, James Johnson having " graved " almost all of it.

James Johnson (1753-1811) was the best known of the music engravers at this time, and his work is known from 1772, although he does not seem to have registered in business until 1775-76. As Kidson says, "a list of his work, could it be compiled, would be almost a complete bibliography of Scottish music during its most interesting period." His *Scots Musical Museum* (1787-1803), which brought him into contact with Burns, seems to have led him into music selling as well, and this he carried on in the Lawnmarket as James Johnson & Co., from 1788 until his death in 1811.

One of the many recurrent tragedies in the musical profession is the composer or performer burning his fingers at music publishing, and Domenico Corri, Nathaniel Gow, and Pietro Urbani are contemporary examples in Edinburgh. In the year 1772 there was published in Edinburgh the *Six Canzones for Two Voices and Bass and Guitar*, composed by Domenico Corri. The event seems to have been the beginning of Corri's unfortunate business career. His failure as an impresario at the Theatre Royal, which caused his sequestration, then led to the use of his son's name, since we read of John Corri as a publisher of *A Select Collection of the Most Admired Songs* (Edin., *c.* 1779). In the following year the business was known as Corri and Sutherland. When his partner James Sutherland died in 1790, Domenico betook himself to London where, after 1792, he linked arms with his son-in-law, Dussek, and traded as Corri, Dussek & Co. The Edinburgh shop was carried on as Corri & Co., seemingly under his brother Natale (1765-1822). The Edinburgh firm did a flourishing trade and had two shops at 37 North Bridge Street and 8 South St. Andrew Street, both working in conjunction with the London firm. Between them they published a considerable amount of music by Haydn, Pleyel, Dussek, and Corri, as well as much that was of purely Scottish appeal and the trivial stuff in popular balladry. The two firms in London and Edinburgh toppled over financially in 1801 and soon came to an end, although Natale Corri established himself independently at the head of Leith Walk.

Pietro Urbani (1749-1816), who was well known in Edinburgh and Glasgow as a composer and teacher, went into business with a partner in 1795 as Urbani and Liston at 10 Princes Street, Edinburgh, but beyond publishing the later works of Urbani and some sheet music, they were but general music sellers. Urbani, who had lost heavily in attempting to revive Handel's oratorios, soon found further unsuccess in the music trade, and had to seek his fortune elsewhere. His business failed about 1808-09, and he died in Dublin in 1816 absolutely destitute.

The Gow family also lost money in the music trade. Nathaniel Gow (1763-1831) went into partnership with another musician, William Shepherd (c.1760-1812), as Gow and Shepherd at 41 Bridge Street, Edinburgh, in 1796. After the death of the latter in 1812, trade slackened and Gow sold out. Yet in 1818 he was back at the counter at 60 Princes Street as Nathaniel Gow and Son, the latter being Neil, Jr. (c. 1795-1823). When his son died he sought another partner, and the firm was known as Gow and Galbraith, but bankruptcy came in 1827. Even before Nathaniel took to business, his two brothers, John (1764-1826) and Andrew (1760-1803), had set up in the music trade in London, which firm worked in conjunction with Nathaniel in Scotland. The publications of both houses consisted almost entirely of dance music and the compositions and arrangements of the Gow family. At the same time a little of the more serious music favoured in London came north bearing the labels of John and Andrew Gow.

Other Edinburgh music sellers and publishers were of little consequence. Laurence Ding (d. c.1801) had a place in Parliament Square, and was known for the *Songster's Favourite* (c.1784), the *Anacreontic Museum*, and a reprint of Bremner's *Curious Collection of Scots Tunes*. James Sibbald (c.1747-1803) was a bookseller who issued a *Collection of Catches, Canons, Glees . . .* (1780), which became an outstanding success, as well as some sheet music. Robert Ross (d. 1808), who was a professional musician, famed for his *Choice Collection of Scots Reels* (1780), had a shop at the back of the Fountain and later at the historic Carrubber's Close. John Watlen, an Englishman employed by Corri & Co. from 1785, opened a music selling and publishing shop in North Bridge Street in 1792. Here he issued a great quantity of music, including much of Scottish interest, such as his *Complete Collection of Scots Songs* (1796). He failed in business and settled in London.

In Glasgow, James Aird (d. 1795), appears to have been one of the earliest of the music sellers and publishers. In 1778 he was at the Candleriggs; later (1779) New Street and elsewhere. His *Selection of Scotch, English, Irish and Foreign Airs* (1782), which ran into six volumes, was very popular. There was an A. McGoun a music seller in the Stockwell in 1783, and in Argyle Street in 1790, whilst an Archibald McGoun, Jr., probably his son, was flourishing at the latter address in 1801, when their *Favourite Collection of Scots Tunes*, the *Repository of Scots and Irish Airs*, *Strathspey Reels*, and other books had a large sale. All of these Glasgow publishers issued a quantity of sheet music. Perth had two music sellers and publishers,—J. Brown, who produced Ramsay's *Gentle Shepherd* with music (1786), and the *Musical Miscellany . . . Scots, English, and Irish Songs* (1786), and J. Anderson who published *Anderson's Pocket Companion of . . . Highland Strathspeys, Country Dances*, and *Anderson's Flute Companion* (*c.* 1775, *et seq.*).

I have not dealt with the Scots as music publishers in London, although a great quantity of music with their imprints was to be found in Scottish homes, including Rutherford's *Country Dances* (1750-76), Oswald's many publications, the works of Bremner by the score, Campbell's *Country Dances*, Boag's sheet music of Scots songs, and many of Napier's excellent issues. In addition there were the publications of Birchall, John Johnson, Longman, William Randall, John Simpson, Straight & Skillern, Peter Thompson and his family, John Walsh, and Daniel Wright. In this way much serious (although sometimes quite indifferent) music came north where it was vended with good and proper Scottish acumen with the retailer's stamp thereon, or even by covering the English imprints with Scottish labels. In other instances the certainty of its Scottish currency was proved by the owner's name.

From what has preceded it might appear that the music publishing fraternity in Scotland does not look very imposing against that of England. Yet the conditions were very different in the two countries, and in view of the size of the Scottish capital and the fact that England had a start of two centuries, the output of its music publishers may be considered to have been equal to the occasion.

From most of the presses there came a fair amount of music of the higher class, and generally in a more expensive book form which, as publications, were certainly as good as anything that issued from London.

Save where there was an assured sale, publishers in Scotland would not risk accepting unknown works, and even the native composers of serious music,—Erskine, Oswald, McGibbon, Macklean, Reid, Foulis, Fergus, and others—had to " pay the piper," or resort to guarantor purchasers. Patronage was the order of the day here as elsewhere, as almost all the Scottish dedicatory pages reveal, and the many " List of Subscribers " amply confirm. Even in the field of national dance music, to the eye of the publisher it was only the traditional tunes that would have a safe sale, and so the composer of new strathspeys or reels who sought publication had to doff his bonnet to the privileged laird or the opulent merchant, for which reason almost every new item was a " Lord-So-and-So's Reel " or a " Miss So-and-So's Strathspey." This method of approach not only secured purchasers but, when the composer or editor was a performer, it also provoked likely performing engagements. This explains why we occasionally see the same tune issued later under a different name, as it sometimes happened that the previous dedicatee did not come up to the propitious expectations of the dedicator.

The biggest sales were made in sheet music, the foremost attraction being the national songs, and most of the Edinburgh and Glasgow music publishers specialized in this. If there was a greater demand for this commodity, the publisher could scarcely be blamed in catering for such needs. The next sheet music in popularity was " the rage " song of star vocalists who, appearing in the motley and tinsel, were featuring such ephemera in the ballad and comic operas. The fame of some of these artistes may not have persisted, but in those days their names conjured " siller " into the till of the music shops. Among these " stars " whose names sold a song were Mrs. Billington, Maria Dickons, Anna Crouch, Mrs. Jordan, Mrs. Jackson, Mrs. Wrighton, Miss Catley, and Miss Thornton, whilst among the gentlemen were Tenducci, Incledon, Michael Kelly, Gilson, Moss, and others, as well as those who appeared at the concerts such as Urbani, Corri, Wilson, and the rest. It is not difficult to appreciate the reason for the demand for this type of music. Most people invested in this ephemeral balladry because they were hypnotized by an unconscious conceit, imagining, when they sang a ballad that they had heard rendered by one of these stars, that they were actually giving a similar interpretation. It is the same to-day. Still, thanks to the growing musical consciousness of Scotland, there was also a genuine craving for good music, from that of Handel, Haydn, Pleyel and Mozart to that of the more acceptable Dussek, Hummel, Gelinek, and Kotzwara, all of which was supplied by Scottish presses, although a great deal more came from the London shops of Bremner, Corri, and Gow, as well as purely English firms, as I have already shown.

Present-day collections in libraries of 18th century Scottish printed music, whether published in Scotland or in England, deserve to be specified. Perhaps the finest collection is that known as the Wighton Collection at Dundee Public Library, the gift of Andrew J. Wighton (1802-66). It contains many rare items. Unfortunately there is no catalogue, only a very unsatisfactory hand-list. Second to this is the Glen Collection in the National Library of Scotland, Edinburgh, presented by Lady Dorothea Ruggles-Brise. The catalogue, Glen's own slips, needs revision, many of the items being undated. Next in import is that of the British Museum, although so far as works published since the Copyright Act of 1842, their collection stands first. Then comes Glasgow University Library which contains two collections, the Euing Musical Library and the Scottish Music Collection, both containing items not to be found elsewhere. The latter collection is especially rich in early sheet music, which has been card indexed. The catalogue (1878) of the former has been gravely criticised by several bibliographers. The Mitchell Library, Glasgow, also contains some rare and scarce items, mainly in the Kidson Collection, whilst the catalogue of the original Kidson Collection, made up of Kidson's own slips, is worthy of attention.

CHAPTER 5

THE THEATRE

" Some comedians have lately come to the bounds of the Presbytery
and do act within the precincts of the Abbey, to the great offence of
many by trespassing upon morality and those rules of modesty and
chastity which our holy religion obligeth all its professors to a strict
observance of, therefore the Presbytery recommends to all their
members to use all *proper and prudent methods* to discourage same."
Presbytery of Edinburgh, March, 1715.

The theatre has a threefold claim to notice in the history of music
in Scotland. Firstly, on account of the Italian and ballad operas,
as well as other musical productions which were staged ; secondly,
because it gave more regular employment to instrumentalists and
vocalists, which enhanced the professional art ; and thirdly, by
reason of the fact that the theatre could not have functioned but for
music in the mid-18th century in Scotland, because of the opposition
of the Church.

At the dawn of this period, the Church of Scotland was still
bitterly antagonistic to the stage and, in spite of its pretence of
" proper and prudent methods " to combat its influence, was prepared to descend to the lowest depths of calumny and victimisation
to gain its ends. One of the leading protagonists of the stage in
Scotland was the poet Allan Ramsay (d. 1758). So early as 1718 we
know of his interest in the Musical Club of Edinburgh as expressed
in *Edinburgh's Address to the Country*. The following year he was
writing the prologue to a play, in which he poked delightful fun at
the long-faced gentry who " in pulpits thump and rair " against the
stage :

" But let them tauk : in spite of ilk endeavour,
We'll cherish wit, and scorn their fead or favour."

Yet it was not until 1725 that he began to take a practical interest
when he wrote *The Gentle Shepherd ; A Scots Pastoral Comedy*,
interspersed with old Scots songs, a work which Edmund Gosse
considered " the most vertebrate and interesting bucolic drama
produced in Great Britain." Indeed, there are good reasons for
believing that Ramsay's pastoral was the actual prompting for the
English ballad opera craze which began with *The Beggar's Opera*

(1728) of Gay and Rich in London. What strengthens this credence is Ramsay's connection with a certain Mr. Gordon and a Signor Lorenzo Bocchi. The *Edinburgh Courant* (12-7-1720) announces that these two latter individuals had arrived in Edinburgh with plans for " consorts." In 1722 Gordon gave a concert in Glasgow, and immediately afterwards he issued " Proposals for the improvement of music in Scotland, together with a most reasonable and easy scheme for establishing a *pastoral opera* in Edinburgh." In 1726, as we know from the *Caledonian Mercury* (22-2-1726), Bocchi was in close touch with Ramsay, when he set music to one of the latter's songs, probably *Blate Jonny*. From this it is quite evident that ballad opera was already visualized in Scotland even before *The Gentle Shepherd* (1725) and *The Beggar's Opera* (1728), and that it was Gordon probably who originally gave Ramsay the notion.

In the year of *The Gentle Shepherd*, Anthony Aston and his company had dared to produce " abominable stage plays " in the capital, and the following year Ramsay wrote a prologue for the " blythsome Tony," who was entertaining Fair Edina " with medley, merry song, and comic scene," as Ramsay penned. The Town Council, backed up or pushed by the Church, then forbade Aston from submitting any plays, and in November 1727 the pulpits were furious in their denunciation of " stage plays." Fortunately, an appeal to the Court of Session, reversed the magistrates' interdict, much to the chagrin of the unctuous Rev. Robert Wodrow, who shed crocodile tears at the magistrates' unsuccess " against those seminaries of idleness, looseness, and sin." Ramsay himself published a restrained counterblast to the bigots' calumnies about the " dangerous infection of the theatre " in a tract entitled *Some Few Hints in Defence of Dramatic Entertainments* (1727). Still, the stage had a hard time of it, and in 1729 the " Scots Company of Comedians," denied a living, were forced to quit, leaving their debts behind them, as the *Edinburgh Courant* smirkingly remarked.

In 1731, an English company was playing to packed audiences in Edinburgh, and again the meddling and mischievous Wodrow bemoaned the circumstance as " a dreadful corruption of our youth,

and an eyelet to prodigality and vanity." Still the drama flourished
in Scotland, and the ballad operas, Ramsay's *The Gentle Shepherd*,
Gay's *The Beggar's Opera*, and Coffey's *The Devil to Pay*, were
equally successful. Yet the Church was powerful enough to
intervene here and there. In 1736 Ramsay attempted to re-open
the theatre in Carrubber's Close, Edinburgh, and in his prologue
pilloried the clergy who,—

> " From their gloomy thoughts, and want of sense,
>   Think what diverts the mind, gives Heaven offence."

Unfortunately the Church and the bigots had their hands strengthened by the Act of 1737, which declared that " every person who
should, for hire or reward, act or cause to be acted, any play, or other
entertainment of the stage, without the special license and authority
mentioned in the said Act, should be deemed a rogue and vagabond,
and for every such offence should forfeit the sum of £50 sterling."
Not content with this weapon, the vilest of pamphleteering was
indulged in by the clergy, in which actors and actresses were dubbed
" the most profligate wretches and vilest vermin that hell ever
vomited out : . . . the filth and garbage of the earth, the scum and
stain of human nature, the excrement and refuse of all mankind."
The Edinburgh magistrates, armed by the law, and strengthened
by the plaudits of the illiberal fanatics, swooped down on Ramsay,
and the Carrubber's Close Theatre, which he had re-fitted " at vast
expense," was closed the following year. What a difference from
London. Here *The Beggar's Opera* had made " Rich gay, and Gay
rich," but in the land of the " unco' guid," Allan Ramsay was driven
to the verge of bankruptcy. He petitioned Duncan Forbes, Lord
President of the Session, in verse, and asked,—

> " Shall London have its houses twa,
>   And we be doom'd to 've nane ava ?
>
> . . . .
> Wherefore, my Lords, I humbly pray
> Our lads may be allowed to play,
> At least till new-house debts be paid off,
> The cause that I'm the maist afraid of."

Needless to say, no heed was paid to the pleading of the gifted
and worthy Ramsay who, a saddened but wiser man, retired to his

books and verse-making to retrieve his shattered fortune. As for those " pious, prudent, and learned ministers, whose praise is in all the churches," as the Presbytery itself described its militant anti-stage members, they were jubilant at the victory, more especially since the stage was silent for two years. When, in 1739, some players had the audacity to offer Shakespeare's *Macbeth* in Ramsay's old theatre, the Presbytery ordered a prosecution *in its name*, whilst some hired scribbler in the obsequious *Caledonian Mercury* promised to tell its readers how the players " acted " in the dock.

Still, the bigots did not have it all their own way. The persecuted began to find friends, as they usually do, and further, public taste was changing. Before long a plan was laid to evade the law and to thwart the Church. It will be remembered that since the year 1694, when William Maclean's appeal to the Court of Session to prevent concerts was dismissed, there had been no interference with this class of entertainment. Concerts could be given for " reward " without a special licence, but not a stage play. It was this aspect of the law that prompted those who were interested in the stage to see how the authorities could be defied, and soon after the Ramsay affair we find that the erstwhile " Playhouse " had become a " Concert Hall," and in 1742 there was announced " A Concert of Vocal and Instrumental Musick, after which [will be performed] *She wou'd and she wou'd not*," the latter being a play. There was no " reward " sought in presenting the " play," so there was no illegality. What was paid for was the " concert." This state of affairs continued for over twenty years, and by that time the " stage-play " was established. It was under such stealthy circumstances that Handel's *Acis and Galatea* and Lampe's *The Dragon of Wantley* were performed in 1751.

Of course the Church was fully aware of what was going on, but it was quite impotent of legal resort. What was more, the classes and masses had grown more liberally minded, and the fiats of Presbyteries were not of such consequence as they had been. To this embarrassment the Church put on a bold face and, in an *Admonition and Exhortation* of January 1757, the Edinburgh Presbytery told its flock how it had become " particularly affected with the unprecedented countenance given of late to the Playhouse." It boasted how, in the past, when " the players, . . . being so audacious as to continue to act in defiance of the law, the Presbytery did *at their own charge* prosecute them before the Court of Session and prevailed in the process. The players were fined in terms of law ; and warrants being issued for apprehending them, they fled from justice. But others came in their place, who since that time have attempted to elude the law, by changing the name of the *playhouse* into that of *Concert Hall.*" The Presbytery's " exhortation " only influenced the minority of their flock. In 1767 the theatre was legally established and the fiats of the clergy became of no account save to the bigoted few.

This was the era of the ballad opera and its kin, a form of entertainment to which the legitimate stage alone could do justice. It was this new craze that drove the Italian opera from the English boards, although this latter had never gained sustenance in Scotland, and all the praises that were sung in this land anent the Italian art concerned the music itself, not the stage presentation. For the ballad opera, Edinburgh, and even a few of the other towns, rose to the occasion. As we have seen, Ramsay's *The Gentle Shepherd* (1725) was the likely prompting, and this delightful pastoral was a great favourite in Scotland, with Coffey's *The Devil to Pay* (1733) running it close in public estimation. It was this latter, as *Der Teufel ist los,* which gave rise to the *Singspiel* in Germany. Yet neither of these was as popular north of the Tweed as Gay's *The Beggar's Opera* (1728), which was constantly in the repertories, and in 1750, Mrs. Storer, who had sung the part of Polly at Covent Garden in 1747, played the *rôle* in Edinburgh. Other ballad operas which found their public were Carey's *Cephalus and Procris* (1734), *Harlequin Skeleton* (1745), Arne's " opera of operas " *Tom Thumb the Great* (1751), Lampe's *The Dragon of Wantley* (1751), as well as the more serious *Acis and Galatea* (1751) of Handel, which was a real pastoral opera. Another of the *opera seria* type was John C. Smith's *The Tempest* (1756).

In 1763 a season of Italian opera was presented when Pergolesi's *La Serva Padrona* and similar works were performed, the score of the former having previously (*c.* 1760) been published by Oswald in London. Yet this was but a flash in the pan, since the general public, Gallio like, " cared for none of these things," and demanded the old fare when, among the more outstanding productions, *Love in a Village* (1765) and Arne's *Comus* and *Thomas and Sally* (1769) were staged. The former was an evergreen in these palmy days, and one production (1793) had the famous Elizabeth Billington as Rosetta, whilst another (1794) featured Maria Dickons in the *rôle*, with the great Incledon as Young Meadows. Oswald contributed an item to a later edition of this work. Another noteworthy piece was Arne's opera *Artaxerxes* (1769), which is unaccountably ignored by Dibdin (*Annals of the Edinburgh Stage*). For the Edinburgh production of this year, three Scots songs were introduced. These were *Braes of Bellenden*, *Roslin Castle*, and *Lochaber no More*, to which the poet Robert Fergusson had written words. Tenducci, as Grosart assures us, was a friend of Fergusson, and he sang these songs in the *rôle* of Arbaces. The music of the opera is to be seen in a rare issue of this year made by Martin and Wotherspoon, Edinburgh. Others of the ballad opera type were Colley Cibber's *Damon and Phillida* (1768), *The Royal Shepherd* (1769) with Tenducci, Dibdin's *The Waterman* (1777), *Lionel and Clarissa* (1794) in which [Michael] Kelly and Anna Crouch appeared, and *Sans Souci* (1799). Then followed Arnold's *Harlequin Dr Faustus* (1778), *Castle of Andalusia* (1782), and *Inkle and Yarico* (1798), with Shield's *Rosina* (1784), and Mazzinghi's *A Day in Turkey* (1792). In many of these works Scottish airs were introduced, and in *Rosina* there were two, not counting the finale to the overture, which was a march tune for the oboe " to imitate the bagpipe," with bassoons for the drone. John Glen was of opinion that Shield added this later, probably for the Edinburgh performance. The tune would appear to be based on an earlier strathspey, *The Miller's Daughter*, published by both McGlashan and Cumming in 1780, and later to be immortalized by Burns in *Auld Lang Syne*.

Ballad operas with Scottish airs created a *furore* in London, as evidenced by Mitchell's *The Highland Fair*, which consisted " wholly of Scotch tunes," and Cibber's *Pattie and Peggy*, an adaptation of Ramsay's *The Gentle Shepherd*. Yet neither of these operas, strange to say, found a place on the Scottish stage. Perhaps the producers thought it too much " like carrying coal to Newcastle," or else they may have been afraid of the dialect since almost all the players in Scotland were English, and the mother of Charles Kirkpatrick Sharpe said that " people were in convulsions of laughter at the bad Scotch pronounced " by them in *The Gentle Shepherd*. The only other ballad opera of a Scottish character was Shirrefs' *Jamie and Bess* (1787), in which the composer himself took part in 1797, but on this occasion it was performed by " natives of Edinburgh," Robert Mackintosh conducting. The few Scottish composers that there were in this century ignored the stage, although the Italians in the country filled the gap, as we see in Urbani's *The Siege of Gibraltar* (1785) and Domenico Corri's *The Wives Revenged* (1778) in Edinburgh, and Dasti's *Britannia's Triumph* (1780) in Glasgow. Scottish composers appear to have been more interested in serious music, but a few had their songs introduced into plays, as Oswald did when he composed the song " When Damon Languished " for Garrick in *The Gamester*.

All these ballad operas, and even the more serious operas, have now been forgotten, save perhaps *The Beggar's Opera*, which has been revived of recent years for precisely the same musical mentality for which it catered two hundred years ago. Yet these ephemera satisfied the public taste in those days, not only of Scotland, but of England and Ireland as well. Naturally, those who frequented the ballad opera were not such perfervid music lovers as those who attended the concerts, and it would seem that the former were attracted more by the play than the music. At the same time, the demand for music at the theatre meant that a fairly sized orchestra had to be maintained. In Edinburgh, in 1750, a harpsichord was added, for the first time, to other instruments in the orchestral pit, when the management announced that " the orchestra will be enlarged." Indeed the importance of the orchestra is evident from a letter of a producer to the management in this year, in which he assures the latter that he had secured " all the musick of *Romeo and Juliet*, *Merchant of Venice*, *Tempest*, etc."

At the Canongate Theatre in 1758 the orchestra comprised eight instrumentalists, five of whom played the violin, tenor, bass, and horn, the other three being, probably, another horn, harpsichord and hautboy. Their wages, according to their importance, ranged from 2s. to 6s. a night. In 1763, for the Italian Opera Season, it was placarded that " the band of music will consist of the very best *hands* the managers can procure, and the orchestra enlarged accordingly." Seemingly the musicians were considered artisans! Still, even the player in *Maggie Lauder* was a piper " to trade." In this year, this theatre orchestra went on strike by reason of wages having been unpaid as far back as 1756. It is the first recorded musicians' strike, as I have pointed out in detail elsewhere (*The Musicians' Journal*, Oct., 1931). When Dibdin came north with his *Sans Souci* entertainment in 1799, he seems to have been able to dispense with an orchestra since the *Courant* (2-5-1799) tells us that the accompaniments were performed on " an organised instrument, which has the properties of a band." As for incidental and *entr'acte* music for plays, three occasions merit attention. In 1750, Dryden's and Davenant's version of Shakespeare's *The Tempest*, with the original music by " the late Mr. Purcel," was performed in Edinburgh, a circumstance which shows that W. Barclay Squire's theory, that this version did not hold the stage later than 1745-46, is not quite correct. When Home's *Douglas* was played in 1757, " select pieces of old Scots Music " were performed between the Acts. Lastly, in 1763, during the season of Italian opera, the overtures of Abel, Jommelli, and Thomas Erskine the Sixth Earl of Kellie were programmed. Another sidelight on entr'acte music comes from Tytler, who tells us that William Corbett's *Sonatas for Two Violins and Thorough Bass* " were often played as act tunes in the Play-house."

All that has been introduced above concerns Edinburgh alone, and the dates in brackets indicate the first performance in that city. The reason for this solo acknowledgment is due to the simple fact that, outside of the capital, Thespian art had only a spasmodic existence in Scotland during the greater part of the century. When the Edinburgh company of *The Beggar's Opera* went to Glasgow in 1728, it had to play in the Weigh House. It did very poor business, much to the delight of the sanctimonious Wodrow. Indeed Glasgow's first theatre of 1752, a wooden booth, was burned down by a fanatical mob incensed by the denunciations of the revivalist George Whitfield against "the Devil's Home." Almost the same fate overtook the next Glasgow theatre, when the stage and contents were swept away by the flames of religious wrath in 1764, ere the portals of this "Satan's Temple" had opened. At Aberdeen in 1745, and again in 1751, we see the clergy successfully petitioning the magistrates to refuse "play-acting." In 1768 and in 1779, there were attempts at drama, but the first real theatre was not established there until 1780. At Dundee, a company of players, at Ramsay's instigation, found acceptance in 1734, but in the "Forties" and "Fifties" the dodge of "Vocal and Instrumental" concerts was the cover for "plays" as in Edinburgh. Yet even so late as 1784, when the stage was more or less tolerated elsewhere, the Town Council took to the law to prevent an Edinburgh company from entering Dundee. On the other hand Perth seems to have been free from clerical or magisterial interference, although it is not until 1780 that professional Thespians strut the stage, musically or otherwise.

CHAPTER 6

THE CONCERTS

" And show that music may have as good fate
In Albion's Glen as Umbria's green retreat,
And with Corelli's soft Italian song,
Mix ' Cowdenknowes ' and ' Winter nights are long.' "

ALLAN RAMSAY : *To the Music Club* (1721).

These lines were writ of Edinburgh's " Music Club," and the poet, like others, would fain have had the " Auld Scots sangs " recognized in the programmes, side by side with the works of the Italian masters which were the fashion at early concerts. This phase of the history of music in Scotland has already been specially dealt with by Dr. David Fraser Harris, in his delightful *Saint Cecilia's Hall* (Edinburgh, 1898, 1911), which treats of the Edinburgh concerts, whilst Robert A. Marr has also contributed much material in his *Music for the People* (Edinburgh, 1889). Yet nowhere have the concerts of Aberdeen and Glasgow received adequate treatment, although elsewhere (*Proceedings of the Royal Philosophical Society of Glasgow*, LXIX) I have made a contribution to the subject. Further it is necessary to distinguish between the private concerts of the classes, and the public concerts of the masses, the latter especially providing definite indices to the prevailing public taste.

We have seen that there were private concerts in Edinburgh in 1694-5 and 1705, and if we read the lines aright in Ramsay's *City of Edinburgh's Address to the Country* (1718), there was a musical society giving private concerts in that year. That the latter was flourishing in 1721, we know from the verses quoted above, and that its concerts were private seems to be confirmed by the fact that in 1720, a certain Mr. Gordon, lately " travelling in Italy," and a Signor Lorenzo Bocchi arrived in Edinburgh with proposals for " consorts." By 1725, we know quite definitely that " The Musical Society of Edinburgh " was giving private concerts at Steil's Tavern " The Cross Keys " in High Street, and three years later (1728), the society was given a proper constitution which, with seventy members, began its private concerts at St. Mary's Chapel in Niddry's Wynd, a place that remained the venue until the St. Cecilia's Hall was built in 1762.

The orchestra at these concerts comprised a number of professionals, supported by the playing amateurs of the society. In 1768, for the performance of Handel's *Alexander's Feast,* there were seventy performers, of which at least forty comprised the chorus, whilst thirty covered the instrumentalists. Arnot, in his *History of Edinburgh* (1779) gives particulars of the orchestra at that time. He says that it consisted of,—" A *maestro di capella,* an organist, two violins, two tenors, six or eight *ripienos* [amateurs], a double or *contra* base, and harpsichord ; and occasionally two French horns, besides ketteldrums, flutes, and clarinets." He does not mention violoncellos, trumpets, oboes, or bassoons, which we know from the programmes were used at some of the concerts.

The audiences at these private concerts were, naturally, confined to the members of the " Musical Society," but it was not " largely aristocratic," as the late Sir Walford Davies has said (*Grove's Dictionary of Music,* 1940), since the liberal professions and the merchant class outnumbered the aristocracy by three to one. Although no outsider could buy a ticket, " strangers and lovers of music " were accommodated when there was room, but this latter was often a serious problem, so much so that crinolined ladies were sometimes requested to attend " without hoops." At St. Cecilia's Hall, five hundred was a crowd.

The *maestro di capella,* mentioned by Arnot, was the " leader " of the orchestra, although not always a violinist. The earliest of these were Scots—Adam Craig (d. 1741) and William McGibbon (d. 1756), both before the St. Cecilia's Hall period. During the better part of the century the foreigner held sway, and among the latter were Francesco Barsanti (*fl.* 1740-50), Johann Lampe (d. 1751), Nicolo Pasquali (d. 1757), Thomas Pinto (d. 1773), Johann Schetky (d. 1824) and his brother Karl, Girolamo Stabilini (d. 1815), Wilhelm Cramer (d. 1799), Joseph Reinagle, Jr. (d. 1825), Giuseppe Puppo (d. 1827), and Johann B. Cramer (d. 1858).

Among the vocal stars were Francesco Senesino (d. *c.* 1750) who was Handel's famous *mezzo soprano*, Tenducci (d. 1827)—"a thing from Italy" as *Humphrey Clinker* saw him, Pietri Urbani (d. 1816)—"a narrow conceited creature" thought Burns, Domenico Corri (d. 1825) and his wife Miss Bacchelli, and a dozen more Italians of lesser account. The home products as instrumentalists were the organists Stephen Clarke (d. 1797), Robert Ross (d. 1808), and John Hamilton (d. 1814), whilst the British vocalists were Maria Dickons, Elizabeth Billington, Cornforth Gilson and his daughter, William Wilson, and Maxwell Shaw.

The programmes of the concerts of the Edinburgh Musical Society and its music catalogue, still extant, are eloquent testimony of the tastes of the period., Here symphonies, overtures (over 400 of these are indexed), concertos, sonatas, quartets and trios, as well as complete oratorios and similar works have their place. As George Thomson, one of the annalists of Scottish music, says, the music played was chiefly "the concertos of Corelli and Handel, and the overtures of Bach, Abel, Stamitz, Vanhall, and latterly of Haydn and Pleyel. . . . The vocal department . . . consisted of the songs of Handel, Arne, Gluck, Sarti, Jommelli, Guglielmi, Paisiello, Scottish songs, etc. ; and every year generally we had an oratorio of Handel." Needless to say, the compositions of the local foreigners, Pasquali, Lampe, and Corri, also had a hearing, as did those of Scotland's own composer, Thomas Erskine the Sixth Earl of Kellie.

These concerts deserve recognition comparable to that accorded the London institutions,—the Academy of Antient Music (1710), the Castle Society (1724), the Devil Tavern (1728), the Concert of Antient Music (1776). Yet it is only the Scots themselves who have expressed commendation of this worthy effort. Maitland (*History of Edinburgh*, 1753) gives details of the early constitution of the society. Smollett, in a letter of 1756, says,—"All the diversions of London we enjoy at Edinburgh in a small compass. Here is a well-conducted *Concert*." Samuel Richardson, who continued Defoe's *Tour through the whole of Great Britain* (1769), gives a letter of 1768 from a " gentleman of eminence in the literary world," which speaks of St. Cecilia's Hall as " one of the best calculated rooms for music that is (perhaps) to be met with in Britain." Captain Topham, in his *Letters from Edinburgh*, where he resided in the " Seventies," considered that " the band is a good one in general," but he was amazed that so much attention was given to music in Scotland. " Music," he says, " alone engrosses every idea." " In religion," he continues, " a Scotchman is grave and abstracted, in politics serious and deliberate : it is in the power of harmony alone to make him an enthusiast." He thought it a " misfortune " to Scotland that so many of its philosophers, scientists, and others should spend so much time disputing " on the merits of an Italian fiddle and the preciseness of a demi-quaver," and " couch beneath the dominion of an air or a ballad." Hugo Arnot (*History of Edinburgh*, 1779) is replete with details of the concerts of his day. " The music performed," he says, " is a proper mixture of the modern and ancient style. The former, although agreeable to the prevailing taste, is not allowed to debar . . . the old compositions."

It is only natural that Aberdeen should also play a prominent part in the renascence of music in 18th century Scotland. In the city of *Bon Accord* the reaction to the concert movement was therefore to be expected, although it was not until 1748 that the Aberdeen Musical Society was founded. At first it was a " Town and Gown " affair, i.e. its sponsors and first supporters were connected with the Town Council and the Universities, with two professional musicians as prime movers. Soon the aristocracy crowded in as members, with a goodly sprinkling of the merchant class, just as in Edinburgh. At first the Trades Hall was the venue, but in 1749 they acquired their own " Musick Room " in Huxter Row, where the weekly concerts were held.

The concerts were private, i.e. they were confined to members only, although two tickets were set aside for " country gentlemen that happened to be in the city," who would be equivalent to the " strangers " admitted to the Edinburgh concerts. The majority of the performers were amateurs *plus* hired professionals, and these latter occur in the accounts so early as 1753, but at no time did these latter number more than eight. We only know from the inventories of instruments possessed by the society and the catalogues of music, what the instrumentation of the orchestra was. In the former we read of a violin, tenor, contra bass, two German flutes, *flûte d'amour*, oboe, a set of clarionets, two French horns, and kettledrums, which reveal that, so far as " property " is concerned, the society was well equipped for the latest music. In 1784, when an attempt was made to improve the standard of the concerts, a printed circular said : " There cannot be fewer than the following hired performers, viz., A Leader of second-rate ability at least, . . . A Second Violin, an Organist, a Violoncello, and Tenor. These, with the assistance of the gentlemen [amateurs] who . . . perform at the concerts, would always make up a good band. . . . If funds would permit of it, a clarinet, oboe, and horn players should also be engaged."

There was a paid Leader, and a Mr. Roche was " First Fiddle or Conductor " in 1759, in which year he also agreed to " play occasionally on the Bassoon and Hautboy when desired." In 1768, Martini Olivieri was engaged from Edinburgh for the position, and another Italian, Alexander Dasti, from the Glasgow concerts, was Leader in 1785, but he was soon succeeded by Scotland's own violinist, Robert Mackintosh (1785-88). He was of an irascible temperament and gave offence to members and professionals alike. For a time he was moved down to Second Violin, when a Mr. Thrustans of London took his place. Two native musicians, Francis Peacock (d. 1807), a violinist, and Andrew Tait (d. 1783), who played the organ and harpsichord, as well as the latter's successor John Ross (d. 1837), were among the mainstays of the society on the professional side. Among the star *artistes* engaged as vocalists and instrumentalists were Joseph Reinagle Jr., Cornforth Gilson's daughter, Madame Giuseppe Puppo, and William Wilson whose songs were then becoming popular.

Being a private society, it is difficult to trace its printed programmes, and all that remains to indicate their nature is its music catalogues drawn up in 1749-55. From these we learn that the society possessed the overtures of Handel, Hasse, Da Vinci, Giuseppe San Martini, Barsanti, and Thomas Arne, together with the concertos and sonatas of Handel, Gluck, Corelli, Scarlatti, Hasse, Geminiani, San Martini, Barsanti, and Jommelli, as well as the works of the British composers Avison, Festing, Stanley, Humphries, and Oswald, together with Brebner's [?] *Scots Tunes*. Unlike Edinburgh, there was no choral music. Songs, and latterly catches and glees, alone found favour, although at the Coronation festivities of George III in 1761, the society gave a concert in Marischal College in which an anthem by Peacock was rendered.

Of Glasgow's earlier concerts we have the efforts of a certain Mr. Gordon, who, having already (1720) impressed Edinburgh, was invited (May, 1722) by several Glasgow gentlemen to give a " consort " in their city. If we are to believe the garrulous " Jupiter " Carlyle, Glasgow was in a poor way musically during the winters of 1743-45 according to his *Autobiography* :—

" There never was but one concert during the two winters I was in Glasgow, and that was given by Walter Scott, Esq., of Harden, who was himself an eminent performer on the violin, and his band of assistants consisted of two dancing-school fiddlers and the town waits."

Whether this gloomy picture adequately depicts musical Glasgow at this period, one cannot say for lack of complementary evidence, but it has been used by Robert A. Marr in his *Music for the People* (1889) and by *Grove's Dictionary of Music* (1940) to cover the remainder of the century. This, as I have shown elsewhere (*Proceedings of the Royal Philosophical Society of Glasgow*, LXIX), is an absolute travesty. By the year 1745 the Glasgow Music Fund was established. Precisely what it was for, we do not know, but a fund with such a title must have had a *raison d'être*. By the " Sixties " great strides had been made. In the *Glasgow Journal* (January, 1762) we are told that " vocal and instrumental music is now becoming a branch of education [in Glasgow], for which the most people of all ranks in this city . . . discover a very high regard." Senex, one of Glasgow's historians (*Glasgow, Past and Present*, 1884), speaks of the " Gentlemen's Private Concerts " in February, 1788, but to this appellation Robert Marr (*Music for the People*, 1889) objects, and calls it a misnomer, which it is not. So early as March, 1780, we have reference in the *Glasgow Mercury* to the " Gentlemen of the Music Society " assisting the orchestra at the public concerts, and in January, 1788, i.e. a month before the date given by Senex, to which Marr demurs, we see a notice of the " Gentlemen of the Private Concerts " playing at the public concerts. What appears to have misled Marr is the fact that a new series known as the " Gentlemen's Subscription Concerts " were inaugurated in December, 1799, and we read in Strang's *Glasgow and its Clubs* (1856) that these concerts had their origin in the " Club of Packers " which had met for several years at the Three Tuns Tavern which, in my paper before the *Royal Philosophical Society of Glasgow* (1945) has been amusingly printed as the " Three Nuns Tavern." It may have been this club that sponsored the earlier " Gentlemen's " efforts in this direction.

A word about the prevailing tastes in concert music would seem to be appropriate. George Thomson, speaking of the late 18th century Edinburgh concerts says :—" When the overtures and quartetts of Haydn first found their way into this country, I well remember with what coldness the former were received by most of the grave Handelians." The celebrated Dr. John Gregory, who was a prominent performer at Aberdeen's private concerts, tilted at the new music in his *State and Faculties of Man* (1766). " The present mode " he says, " is to admire a new noisy stile of composition, lately cultivated in Germany, and to despise Corelli as wanting spirit and variety. The truth is, Correlli's stile and this will not bear a comparison. Corelli's excellence consists in the chastity of his composition, and in the richness and sweetness of his harmonies. The other sometimes pleases by its spirit and a wild luxuriancy, which makes an agreeable variety in a concert, but possesses too little of the elegance and pathetic expression of music to remain long the public taste. The great merit of that nobleman's

[Thomas Erskine's] compositions, who first introduced this species of music into this country, and his own spirited performance of them, first seduced the public ear. They are certainly much superior to any of the kind we have yet heard; though, by the delicacy of the airs in his slow movements, he displays a genius capable of shining in a much superior stile of music."

Glasgow also had its views on the new tastes in music, and the opinions of a vicious reactionary is expressed by a certain Alexander Molleson in his *Melody the Soul of Music* (1798). " Those symphonies and concertos " he says, " which to gratify a depraved taste for variety, and to display the science of the composer, and the talents of the performers, sacrifice the genuine expression of good music." The writer pours out his wrath against this " corrupted taste " and the " mechanical complication of modern harmony." Yet when these contemners had gone the way of all flesh, the very music which had been an abomination to their ears had become the norm, whilst a newer school had to take all the revilings of the then older school. It was ever thus. To-day, when we can scan programmes and find that neither the Corelli of the older school, nor the Erskine of the newer school has any recognition therein, one is inclined to wonder why all this pother. Will the world never learn from the past ?

There was one phase of the art in which the public taste rarely changed, and that was in the traditional song, which continued to be a feature on the concert programmes in Edinburgh from the day (1721) when Ramsay signalized their inclusion, down to the very close of the century, as we know from George Thomson's account of these concerts which he wrote for Robert Chambers (*Traditions of Edinburgh*). At Glasgow and Aberdeen we see the " auld Scots sangs " equally favoured on the concert programmes. Indeed, in the latter city, there was a rumpus because this type of music was played at the close of the concerts when many of the audience were preoccupied with thoughts of getting homeward. As a result it was ordered that " for the future the Scots Tunes should be played in the middle . . . & not at the end . . . as formerly."

Yet it was not only the classes who had the opportunity to indulge in concerts, since the leading music teachers in both Edinburgh and Glasgow found that to widen a clientèle of pupils they had to reach the general public. Thus arose the public concerts, the programmes of which were generally quite different from those of the private concerts. The latter, as we have seen, were adapted to the tastes of the select few of the amateurs of the leisured and professional classes, whereas those of the former, being run on strictly business lines, had to attract all and sundry to make them a paying proposition. The earliest of the Edinburgh public concerts were those held in the Taylors' Hall, the Assembly Rooms, and the Canongate Concert Hall, in the second half of which a " play " was given *gratis*. We know little of their contents, save that they were " vocal and instrumental." More interesting, from a point of view of judging the public taste in music, were those concerts where there was no " play " which, after all, was the main attraction.

So, early in 1750, open-air concerts were started in Edinburgh. Emboldened by the fame of those entertainments at the Vauxhall and Ranelagh Gardens in London, where the public could sit and sup whilst listening to a concert, " Fair Edina " established a similar project in the Lauriston Gardens where " a good band of music, accompanied by two French Horns," performed. For this, *plus* coffee, tea, and tea-bread, one paid a shilling. In the following year, Lampe began concerts at Heriot's Gardens, but with the proviso—if " the weather is not unfavourable." Later in the century Domenico Corri gave similar attractions. Yet it is at the concerts given by Passerini and Pasquali in the public halls that we are able to judge the type of programme that was performed. Passerini's offerings were confined to a Handel overture, with instrumental solos and songs. They were advertised as " Spiritual Concerts after the manner of Oratorios." For these joys one had to pay 2s. 6d. or 3s. At Pasquali's concerts a more substantial fare was offered for the same prices, and here could invariably be heard a " Full piece with Trumpets, French Horns, Kettledrums " added to the usual strings. Almost all the music teachers ran public concerts in the capital,—Cornforth Gilson and Stephen Clarke among the Britishers, and Domenico Corri and Pietro Urbani among the foreigners.

In Glasgow it was precisely the same, although we do not read of public concerts until 1779. These were held in the Merchants' Hall, the Saracen's Head Hall, the old Assembly Hall, the new Assembly Hall, the Trades Hall, and the Assembly Hall in Ingram Street. The leaders of these concerts were John Banks, Joshua and James Campbell, Alexander Dasti, John Fergus, William Goold, Alexander Reinagle, and William Wilson. *Extra mural* attractions came from Edinburgh in Urbani, Domenico Corri, and Jarnovick. Yet the greatest draw was William Crotch who, as an infant prodigy, appeared at the Bridgegate Hall and the Saracen's Head Hall in 1781. At these concerts we may hazard a guess that the string section was complete since quartets were often played. On other occasions we read of the overtures being accompanied " with French Horns and Clarionets," whilst flutes and oboes also found a place. Of course, many of these concerts were confined to vocal and instrumental solos with harpsichord accompaniment, but the better programmes tell of a symphony by Haydn, overtures by Haydn, Gossec, [Johann] Stamitz, and Thomas Erskine, as well as concertos and the like by Borghi and Pfeiffer, and quartets by Pleyel and Vanhall. At the concerts of the Sacred Music Institution, founded in 1796 by John Fergus, the religious works of Handel, Arne, Greene, and Samuel Arnold held the field, and at the concerts held in the Episcopal Chapel much the same type of programme was submitted with the works of Marcello and Boyce added. Other towns also established Music Societies and concerts. Dundee had its Music Society in the mid-century, and concerts were certainly being given there in 1757. There was a Forfar Musical Society in 1792, and concerts were given at Greenock in 1793, and one programme in the latter year contained an *Overture of Lord Kelley*.

In the rise of the concert in the eighteenth century, Scotland shows herself well abreast of the times. The private concerts prove that the primary urge came from the members themselves rather than as an inducement from impresarios, a circumstance which reveals a rather high standard of appreciation among the aristocracy, the liberal professions, and the merchant class, who took to making music for themselves in preference to having it made for them by others. As for the public concerts, their programmes show that the general music-loving public were only satisfied with the best available, even in much maligned, commercially minded Glasgow (cf. Grove, sub voce). Edinburgh's contribution to the revival of music in Scotland, as revealed in her concerts, both private and public, stands unrivalled in these Islands, and the work done at St. Cecilia's Hall is comparable to that of any other city. Obviously it could not always command the services of many of the great London artistes but, as Aberdeen insisted in its turn, it would tolerate " no less than second rate." On the whole, its performances were more spontaneous, and its programmes more virile than anywhere else in the British Isles.

One other source of pleasure for the people was military music as Army bands had made considerable strides in the second half of the century. Prior to this, regiments of foot and dragoons were content with the music of hautboys which, with a curtal or bassoon, made a fair display, although their music was more generally confined to marches and divertimenti. In 1726, the Royal Company of Archers had a band of hautboys and trumpets, but in 1732 French horns were added. The Scots Greys, then the Second Dragoons, had five hautboys in 1704, but in 1777 it had two clarionets, two French horns, and two bassoons, and this combination, sometimes with a trumpet added, was usual in Scotland even so late as 1794, as we see in the scores of Fergus' Grand March (Edin., 1794) and R. Baillie's Favorite March and Quick Step (Edin., 1794).

When the flute, bugle, trombone and serpent were admitted later, the military band was able to give better results than the average concert orchestra, and it furnished the people at large with the only opportunity of hearing music of a better type which otherwise had been reserved for those who could afford the private or public concerts. Indeed, the regimental band often supplied the wind players for many of the concerts of the upper and middle class, when local performers were either unobtainable or unsuitable. We see this in Edinburgh where a Mr. Rakeman, the "Master Musician" of the Royal Welch Fusiliers, was in professional demand, and in Glasgow, where a Mr. Sippe, " Master of the Band " of the 56th Regiment was similarly employed. Sometimes we read of entire concerts being given by these bands, which were " all the rage " during the Napoleonic scare when volunteer and fencible regiments were raised in great numbers to protect these shores. Museums and other collections in Scotland have many band instruments from this source, while regimental marches exist by the score in contemporary Scottish music collections.

CHAPTER 7

THE TEACHERS

" In . . . Wales and . . . Ireland, it appears that music derived very little assistance from those precepts which it had been the endeavour of learned and ingenious men to disseminate throughout Europe ; the consequence thereof has been that . . . the music of those countries has for many centuries remained the same ; and can hardly be said to have received the least degree of improvement. In Scotland the case has been somewhat different. . . . The study of the mathematics has in these later years been cultivated in Scotland, and at the beginning of this century some faint essays were made in that country towards an investigation of the principles of music : the result of these we [in England] are strangers to."

HAWKINS : *A General History . . . of Music* (1776).

If any phase of history can be taken as a sure index of progress, one can depend on didactics to reveal this. Wherever we discern a desire to learn, the urge to teach is not far away, and in Scotland in the 18th century, the realm of didactics in music became noticeably wider because the closer cultural link with England had opened fresh vistas to the Scots which had so long been obscured by the puritanical *régime* of the previous century. In pure didactics there were two promptings for the change. Firstly, the Scots have ever been keen on mathematics, and the new outlook gave a fillip to the speculative theory of music. Secondly, the decay and gradual disappearance of the Sang Schools, which had been the sole music seminaries, offered the private teacher greater opportunities in the practical art. Unfortunately, as in the performing sphere, the foreigner reaped the best harvest on this ground, but it could scarcely have been otherwise.

Although Italian music had already penetrated Scotland *via* England, in the preceding century, as we know from Forbes' *Cantus* (1682) and contemporary manuscript sources, it was not until the vogue of Italian opera at the opening of the 18th century, that it became the fashion to look upon the Italian musician himself as superior to all others. In Edinburgh especially, which seems to have followed English modes, he reigned supreme. Here we find Barsanti, Passerini, Bocchi, Puppo, Pasquali, Corri, Stabilini, Urbani, and others, who all made comfortable livings as teachers. Their success induced further immigrants—Lampe, Schetky, and Joseph Reinagle and Sons, who came from German-speaking lands, Joseph being appointed " King's Trumpeter."

Not one of these incomers, save perhaps Corri, were any better than British teachers or performers, but the former represented the land of Corelli, Bassani, Geminiani and Paisiello, while the latter spelt J. C. Bach, Handel, Stamitz, and Abel, whose works were being continually featured on Scottish concert programmes and placarded in music shops. For this reason it was Lampe's *Method of Teaching Thorough Bass* (1737) and his *Art of Musick* (1740) that was preferred in Scotland, as was Pasquali's *Thorough-Bass made Easy* (Edin., 1757). Yet there was an admirable Scottish primer of the art in *An Introduction to the Knowledge and Practice of Thoro' Bass by A. B.* (Edin., 1717). It is an extremely rare work and the Taphouse copy had a contemporary [Scottish ?] manuscript bound up with it entitled, *The Institutions of Musick wherein are sett forth the practicall principles of Musicall Composition.* Kidson (*Grove's Dictionary*) thought that the Taphouse copy was unique, but I possessed a copy that belonged to " Sir Archibald Grant of Monymoske," which is now in Glasgow University Library. Dr. David Laing thought that " A. B." was

Alexander Baillie, but we now know that the author's name was Alexander Bayne, who was the first " governor " (1728-31) of the Musical Society of Edinburgh.

Many of the psalters of this century contained an " Introduction " on the elements of music, generally what was sufficient for those interested in psalmody. More important, although still elementary, was Robert Bremner's *Rudiments of Music* (Edin., 1756, 1762 ; Lond., 1763), the more original *Essay towards a Rational System of Music* (Glasg., 1770) by John Holden, and Christopher Lindsay's *Scheme showing the Distance of Intervals* (1793). The latter was the son of the Fifth Earl of Balcarres (d. 1768) and sister to Lady Anne Barnard (d. 1825) who wrote *Auld Robin Gray* which William Leeves impudently claimed to have set to music. Yet the works which display the Scottish mind at its best are those which deal with the speculative science of music, and it is to one of these in particular that Sir John Hawkins refers, viz., Malcolm's *Treatise of Musick* : *Speculative, Practical and Historical* (Edin., 1721 ; Lond., 1730 ; abridged, 1776 ; 1779). Alexander Malcolm was a graduate of Edinburgh University and a first-rate mathematician who was known for his *New Treatise on Arithmetic* (1718), and later even better famed for his *New System of Arithmetic* (1730). Hawkins said of the first-named book that it was " one of the most valuable treatises on the subject of theoretical and practical music to be found in any of the modern languages." It was in this work that the facts of just intonation, and the necessity for establishing equal temperament, were explained " a year before the appearance of Bach's *Wohltemperirtes Clavier*," as Fuller-Maitland pointed out (*Oxford History of Music*, iv., 346). Another such work was *An Essay upon Tune* (Edin., 1781). Although published anonymously, the author was Francis Kelly Maxwell, D.D., of Edinburgh, and in this book he sought "to free the scale of music, and the tune of instruments, from imperfections." Fétis considered it " one of the most important books on the philosophy of music " and, even in his day, was of " extreme rarity " in the book market. Maxwell's arguments were thoroughly sound and convincing, and *Grove's Dictionary* wisely dubs it " an able work."

In the field of æsthetics, the land of Hume, Hutcheson, and Adam Smith, could scarcely lag behind. Algarotti's *Saggio sopra l'Opera in Musica* (1763) appeared as *An Essay on the Opera* (Glasg., 1768), only a year after it had been issued in London. This work was " a most remarkable book " in its day, as Ernest Newman has pointed out. Almost as significant was James Beattie's *Essays on Poetry and Music* (1776), although the philosopher's book was published in London. The closing stanzas of Beattie's *The Minstrel* contain a tribute to one of his musical friends and associates in the Aberdeen Musical Society, Dr. John Gregory (d. 1773), whose admirable work *The State and Faculties of Man* (1766) reveals him as a keen musician and a discreet æsthetician. We have already observed in the case of Dr. Maxwell that some of the clergy seem to have outgrown their narrow prejudices against music in that they could become interested in the physical approach to the art, but in a work by the Rev. Dr. Thomas Robertson of Dalmeny (d. 1799) entitled *An Enquiry into the Fine Arts* (Lond., 1784) we see another clergyman who is not only prepared to express a profound appreciation of the theoretical work of Malcolm and Holden, but gives unstinted praise to the compositions of the great masters, including his own countryman Thomas Erskine the Sixth Earl of Kellie. Lastly there was John Brown (1752-81) of Edinburgh, whose thoughtful *Letters upon the Poetry and Music of the Italian Opera* (Edin., 1789) is a well-designed piece of criticism.

In the more practical domain of teaching instrumental music we see the domination of the foreigner. Early in the century in Edinburgh, Henry Crumbden taught the harpsichord, singing, and thorough-bass, as Tytler records, and gave concerts with his pupils, probably the first of their kind in Scotland. Crumbden is said to have been of German origin, as was his contemporary Beck, and these two seem to have been the forerunners of the Teutons who later became so fawned on in Edinburgh. It had not been customary to favour foreign musicians in official positions in Scotland during the

17th and early 18th centuries, and indeed, save for Louis de France and Jacques de Canton, who held burgh posts in Aberdeen, Edinburgh and Glasgow, almost all the official musicians were Scotsmen. Yet a change came with the fall of the Sang Schools in the mid-18th century.   During the first half of this period these schools still existed in the larger towns, Aberdeen, as of old, taking the lead. Here the town Sang School was directed by Alexander Coupar (1692) who had been Master of St. Machar's Sang School, Alexander Scott (1722), Charles Macklean (1736) who came from Dundee, and finally Andrew Tait (1740).   At St. Machar's Sang School, the Masters were William Crystal (1696) of Perth, William Molyson (1731) who became a minister, and James Paterson (1744).   At Haddington, the Sang School Master taught the hautboy, [common] flute, and bass viol in 1728, whilst in 1733 the singing master was the Provost.   At Dundee the masters were Alexander Keth (1656), who was succeeded by John Coupar (1713), followed by Alexander Scott (1720) who went to Aberdeen two years later. Whilst hardly entitled to fame, save in the case of Macklean and Tait, I have specially mentioned these individuals by name so that it can be appreciated how thoroughly national were these masters in the last days of the Sang Schools.   It was the falling into desuetude of these schools that gave rise to the private teacher who, no longer being an " official," had greater freedom, hence the emergence of the foreigner.

At first, these new teachers required to be licensed.   In the year 1722 we read, for instance, in Dundee, that a certain David Bruce was " permitted " to teach music in the town, and later a William Herriot and a Ferdinand Shuman were given similar authority.   The reason for these licences was not necessarily a puritanical bias against music, but rather because in many towns it had been found difficult to obtain masters for the Sang Schools and precentors for the kirks unless they could be guaranteed sole rights to teach within the burgh.   When concerts were instituted in the " Twenties " at Edinburgh, the foreign impresarios became the rage, and by the " Fifties " other strangers had taken up residence in " Auld Reekie."

Naturally, they took music teaching in their stride, and indeed it would seem to have been their staple subsistence. As a result, the native musicians were pushed into the background. Outside the capital however, the Britisher seems to have been able to hold his own, although many of the advertisements show that he had to be a " Jack of all trades " to get a living. The public notices which reveal this state of affairs are worthy of quotation. An Aberdeen newspaper of 1758 reads :

" Mr. Roche, Music Master, just arrived from Germany . . . proposes to teach the following instruments, viz., the Fiddle, the German Flute, Hautboy, Bassoon, Violoncello, French Horn, etc. He likewise teaches Singing and the Guittar."

A Glasgow advertisement of 1762 says with naïvete :

" Joshua Campbell, Musician, proposes to teach the guitar having been at some expense at Edinburgh in perfecting himself with the best masters there."

The blandishments of some teachers also deserve recording as a sidelight on contemporary musical life in Scotland. Glasgow is specially selected for these extracts because the city of St. Mungo has always been both famed and blamed for its commercial instincts. These notices belong to 1780-90 :

" Mr. Frazer, Teacher of Vocal Music from Edinburgh, who has been instructed by the best masters . . . will attend Ladies and Gentlemen at their lodgings, on moderate terms. . . . Pupils taught to sing with propriety of taste and expression."

" William Wilson . . . continues to teach vocal and instrumental music in their various branches. . . . Can make [his pupils] sing, in the space of four months, any song that may be laid before them."

" Mr. [Alexander] Reinagle respectfully informs his friends, and the public that he continues to teach the Harpsichord and Singing, on his usual terms . . . at his own lodgings at 10s. 6d. for twelve lessons, and has opened a class for singing, at 5s. a month."

" James Campbell . . . continues, as usual, to teach the Violin,

Harpsichord, German Flute, and Guitar. . . . He has lately opened a class . . . for . . . instructing young Gentlemen to Play in Concert."

Two other advertisements warrant attention because the first suggests that those desiring instruction could test the abilities of the prospective teacher beforehand, whilst the second advertiser offers his services free to the deserving poor of his congregation. Here they are :

"Mr. Cranmer, from St. Paul's Cathedral, London . . . proposes . . . to teach the Harpsichord and German Flute, likewise songs. . . . Those . . . who please to employ him, may hear him at Mr. Aird's music shop . . . and may depend on punctual attendance."

"John Fergus, Jr., . . . teaches the Harpsichord, Pianoforte, and Organ, upon reasonable terms. . . . He will teach gratis the children of parents belonging to that congregation [the English Chapel], who are unable to pay for their instruction."

The note is reminiscent of one which Pasquali inserted in the Edinburgh *Evening Courant* (27-11-1752) that he would instruct " gratis any poor girl with an extraordinary strong voice." Needless to say, the more reputable of the music teachers kept their " professorship " within reasonable bounds, limiting it to the violin and violoncello, or harpsichord and thorough bass, generally with singing attached.

Official teaching also had its place in some towns from the beginning of the half century. The decay of the Sang School had brought about an appreciable deterioration of psalmody in the kirks. The result was that the town councils were compelled, doubtless at the insistence of the church, to promote the establishment of schools, or at least classes, but these were specially designed " for improving *church* music." Both Glasgow and Edinburgh established these schools in 1755, as we have already seen in dealing with Church Music. What the particular curriculum was in this teaching may be deduced from the various " Introductions " to the psalters of those days. That " sol-fa-ing," as it was then called, played its part is well evidenced. Bremner (1755) says: "This I know to be much used, and little understood; nor is this to be wondered at, as its intricacy is very great." Finlay and McLachlan in their *Precentor* (1776) use the system, and Boyd (1793) deals at length with these "singing syllables." Seemingly, the old solmisation never really died out in Scotland, although in England it was Sarah Glover, and later John Curwen, who revived the system.

Of tutors issued in Scotland there were quite a few but, as in the performing sphere, the Italian and German products were preferred. A work which had a place "on the desk of almost every organ or harpsichord practitioner" (*The British Minstrel*, Glasg., 1845) was Pasquali's *Thorough-Bass Made Easy* (Edin., 1757) for the spinet or harpsichord, and many exemplars of this show that they were possessed by plebeian and patrician alike in Scotland, although his *Art of Fingering the Harpsichord* (Edin., 1758), Tenducci's *Collections of Lessons for the Harpsichord or Piano and Forte* (Edin., c. 1768), and Bremner's *Harpsichord or Spinnet Miscellany* (Edin., 1761) were also great favourites. The prestige of Domenico Corri was high in Scotland, and it must be admitted that his publications were not only excellently presented, but they were so framed that they suited all requirements, as we see in his book entitled *A Complete Musical Grammar, with a Concise Dictionary comprehending all the Signs, Marks & Terms necessary to the Practice of Music; The Art of Fingering; the Rules of Thorough Bass; a Prelude in every Key, and other Various Instructions, all comprehended in this Board. Invented and Arranged by D. Corri* (Edin., c. 1787). Yet the foreigners did not have it all their own way. An Edinburgh man who had settled in London named John Gunn wrote an *Essay . . . towards a more easy and scientific method of . . . the Study of the Pianoforte, with the Principles of Thorough-Bass and Musical Science* (Lond., n.d.), and a *New and General System of Music . . . Translated from the Original Italian* (Lond., 1790), both of which were valuable studies, the former especially since the exposition was so plain and simple. These latter works were well known in Scotland as were other books by this writer.

Turning to the vocal art, which was of prime interest to most Scots, we find that Cornforth Gilson's *Lessons on the Practice of Singing* (Edin., 1759) had considerable sales in its day, but Corri's now rather rare book, *The Singer's Preceptor or Corri's Treatise on Vocal Music*, later became the prevailing fashion. The first violin tutor published in Scotland appears to have been Tessarini's *Musical Grammar ... an Easy ... Method ... of Learning ... the Violin* (Edin., c. 1760), although Geminiani's *Art of Playing on the Violin* (Lond., 1751) was to be found in more than one Scottish home. Of course there were manuscript tutors in circulation, and one of the most interesting of these, which I once possessed, but is now in the National Library of Scotland, is James Gillespie's *Collection ... for the Violin* [*with*] *an Introduction ... for Playing the Violin* (Perth, 1768). I have fully described this manuscript in the *Proceedings of the Society of Antiquaries of Scotland* (Vol. LXV, 1930-31), where it is shown that the Introduction is dependent considerably on Prelleur's *Complete Tutor for the Violin* (Lond., 1750). John Gunn of Edinburgh (c. 1765-1824) wrote several works which had acceptance in Scotland, notably his *Forty Favourite Scotch Airs* (Lond., c. 1790) which contained a supplement on the " theory and practice of fingering the violoncello," which appeared in better form later as *The Theory and Practice of Fingering the Violoncello* (Lond., 1793). Two other works of his were *An Essay . . . towards . . . the Study of the Pianoforte* and *The Art of Playing the German Flute*. As for the guitar, Bremner was the first in Britain to issue a tutor for the so-called English guitar in his *Instructions for the Guitar* (Edin., 1758), and he also published Geminiani's *Art of Playing the Guitar or Cittra* (Edin., 1760). One of the most interesting didactic works of the period, since it contains an intimate view of methods, is *The Self-Taught Musician* (Edin., 1796) by Hurka de Monti (c. 1753-1823), an Austrian who settled in Glasgow. It is written in the form of a dialogue.

Edinburgh had now wrested from Aberdeen the position of being *facile princeps* in music. It had become Scotland's cultural centre once more, and her concerts, having attracted so many outsiders, made the demand for the music press grow by leaps and bounds as we have seen in dealing with the publishers. Indeed, the tutorial productions of the capital may be said to have been of some little force in the renascence of music in Scotland in the 18th century.

CHAPTER 8

THE COMPOSERS

" The Scots are all musicians. Every man you meet plays on the flute, the violin or the violoncello, and there is one nobleman [the Earl of Kellie] whose compositions are universally admired."
TOBIAS SMOLLETT : *Letter*, 8/8/1756.

Even if we allow with the author of *Humphrey Clinker* that every Scot was an instrumentalist, we must also admit that composers were not so plentiful in Scotland as they were elsewhere. At this state of affairs we need not wonder, since there was no traditional school, for this had died out with the Reformation. Secondly, didactics, so far as actual composition is concerned, was practically non-existent in the land. Thirdly, even if there had been this tutoring for creative work, there was little subsistence for the composer, as Thomas Wood had predicted in 1566, a reason that had compelled both Oswald and Bremner to emigrate. Nearly all the best work that was composed had to be published in London, since works by native composers would not have paid their way in Scotland, which was still almost wholly absorbed in the old Italian school. Men like Erskine, Reid, and Foulis, who belonged to the leisured or professional class, could afford to print their own compositions, but not so Macklean and McGibbon, who were dependent upon music for their livelihood, and had to bend the knee to patronage. Oswald was also a professional, but he turned publisher as well, as there was more money in business than in art, and he was thus able to print and publish his own compositions.

Who were the first composers to emerge in the dawning days of Scotland's musical renascence is not easy to descry. Although George F. Graham says that Thomas Erskine " was the first Scotsman who ever composed overtures," there was a certain Mr.

Clerk whose Overture was performed at the 1695 St. Cecilia's Concert in Edinburgh. His precise identity is denied us. Dr. Harry M. Willsher is of opinion that he may have been Jeremiah Clarke, an Englishman. It seems to me to be more likely that he is identical with Hugh Clerk who appears as a subscriber to Macklean's *Twelve Solos or Sonatas for a Violin* (Edin., 1737), a name also attached to " Shetchers' March " and the " Edinburgh Train Bands March " in Bremner's *Collection of Airs and Marches* (Edin., *c.* 1750). The work of another hidden composer is to be found in *Airs for the Flute* (Edin., 1735) issued by Alexander Baillie. The composer is denoted as a " Gentleman," and one is prompted to ask if this latter could have been the late Lord Colville of Ochiltree ? He had studied in Italy and, according to Tytler, " understood counterpoint well." It was to him and the Earl of Haddington that Defoe refers in his *Caledonia :*

> " The God of Musick joyns when Colville plays,
>   And all the Muses dance to Haddington's essays."

Still, nothing of Colville's creative work seems to have survived, although he amassed a huge music library which may still be tucked away somewhere in Scotland. At any rate, Baillie merely claimed to have edited the work, but he may have had a deeper hand in the affair. It is an extremely interesting collection of pleasing but rather short melodies, which are enhanced by a quaint if not original fancy in the harmonies. Incidentally, it might be remarked here that the Scottish nobility produced some other extraordinarily clever musicians. The Earl of Abercorn (d. 1744) is a further example. He studied under Pepusch and issued a *Short Treatise on Harmony* (Lond., 1730) based on his master's lessons. In the British Museum there are five catches which W. Barclay Squire attributed to him. If the assumption is correct, they do Abercorn credit. Hawkins tells us that Abercorn tried to revive the old *racket* or *cervelas*, which Stanesby made for him, but that " the whole blew up." His son was equally musical, and it was in the regiment of which he was colonel that the famous Logier served as a bandsman under Bandmaster John Willman, the father of Thomas Lindsay Willman the famous clarionettist.

In this period the first outstanding composer of Scottish birth was Charles Macklean. Because of this differently-written surname, Frank Kidson considers that he is not the " Late Chas. McLean " whose *Collection of Favourite Scots Tunes* (Edin., *c.* 1770) had great praise in its day. I have strong suspicion, as had the late W. Barclay Squire of the British Museum, that the two are identical, and that this Macklean is the Charles Maclean who was Master of the Aberdeen Sang School (1736-40), previously at Dundee. Neil Stewart's *Collection of Marches and Airs* (Edin., *c.* 1756) contains two gavottes and an air by a " Mr. McLean," whilst a " gavott " by " Chas. Maclean " is in the Gillespie MS. (1768). Perhaps he was connected with the William Maclean, dancing master of Edinburgh who, as Master of the Revels, invoked the law to prevent Beck, the German, from holding concerts in 1694. Charles Macklean's *Twelve Solos or Sonatas for a Violin* (Edin., 1737), are of a genre that appeal to the immaculate in taste, and most of them contain a distinct individual quality. The slow movements are often quite emotional whilst the allegros are extremely bright and spirited. They would repay study even to-day in spite of our modern whims although, alas, only one, the fifth, has been republished by that " Old Mortality " of violin music, Alfred Moffat, himself a Scot, in his " Old English Violin Music." One other has been edited by Dr. Ernest Bullock. It is the No. 9 of the series and, although light in texture, has an unusual freshness (See *Glasgow Herald*, Nov. 15, 1945).

His fellow was William McGibbon. He was born in the closing years of the 17th century and died in Edinburgh in 1756. His father, Matthew, played the oboe at the St. Cecilia's Concert of 1695 as described by Tytler. The latter tells us that " William was sent early to London by his father, and studied many years under Corbet[t]." When he returned to Edinburgh he became Leader of the concerts there. Tytler says that he " was considered an excellent performer," and also speaks with praise of his rendering of the works of Corelli, Geminiani, and Handel, adding that " he likewise composed a set of sonatas or trios for two violins and a bass, which were esteemed good." John Glen mentions *Six Sonatas or Solos for a German Flute or Violin* (1740) which must be identical with the *Six Sonatos* [sic] *or Solos for a German Flute or Violin, Edin.* : *R. Cooper for the author* (1740), sold at the Taphouse sale in 1905, but as I have not seen a copy of this extremely rare oblong folio, I cannot discuss it.   I did, however, possess his *Six Sonatas for Two German Flutes* (J. Simpson, Lond., *c.* 1745), and they deserve a few words of commendation.   Whilst they are somewhat formal and stilted, as the digital restrictions of the instrument did not allow of much deviation from the diatonic, they are certainly not of the flimsy type that was more marketable in those days.   The late Dr. W. Gillies Whittaker thought so well of these sonatas that he edited them just prior to his death, and it is to be hoped that they will eventually be published.   McGibbon is, unfortunately, only well known by his *Collection of Scots Tunes*, in three books (Edin., 1742, 1746, 1755), which, as Kidson says, are " of great value in the study of Scots music."   On the other hand, Simon Fraser heaps abuse on his name for his treatment of Highland airs.   Many of McGibbon's compositions are to be found scattered in the various contemporary printed and manuscript collections.   That a kindly reverence clung to his memory is visioned in the lines of the poet Robert Fergusson, although he could not have known him :

> " Macgibbon gane, a' waes my heart :
> The man in music maist expert,
> Wha could sweet melody impart,
> And tune the reed
> Wi' sic a slee and pawky art,
> But now he's dead."

Perhaps the most outstanding of the working musician composers was James Oswald (1711-1769).   Beginning life as a dancing master at Dunfermline he moved, in 1736, to Edinburgh, having won some attention by his *Collection of Minuets . . . for the Violin and Bass Viol* (1734).   Here appeared his first *Curious Collection of Scots Tunes* (1740) as well as some chamber music, and he seems to have gained appreciable recognition as a violinist and organist.   Yet the complimentary word or commendatory line did not suffice for

Oswald's material needs, and rather than submit to penury, as did the poets Robert Fergusson and Michael Bruce, he left for London in 1741, which woeful event was signalised by Allan Ramsay(?) in the *Scots Magazine*, where Edinburgh's loss and London's gain was emphatically stressed. Truly indeed did the great metropolis benefit, for Oswald became one of the musical giants in the land. John Simpson, the London music publisher, being a " canny " Scot probably, soon found that Oswald was a paying proposition, especially after his *protégé*, probably through the influence of the Earl of Bute, was patronised by royalty. It is said that he had some share in the early musical education of George III, which possibly accounted for his appointment as " Chamber Composer " to this king (1761). Oswald's songs, for which his fellow Scots, the caustic Smollett and the felicitous Thomson, supplied the words, as well as the more stagey Dodsley and Garrick, soon brought him wider appreciation. His music to *Harlequin Ranger* (1751), *The Genii* (1752), and *Fortunatus* (1753) increased his reputation, yet what stand to his lasting credit are his *Twelve Songs* (*c.* 1742), *Six Pastoral Solos for a Violin and Violoncello* (*c.* 1745), *Airs for Spring* [*Summer, Autumn, Winter*] (*c.* 1747), and *Twelve Seranatas* [*sic*] *for Two Violins and a Violoncello* (*c.* 1765), which reveal an extremely gifted musician who knew precisely what he wanted to say and could express it convincingly. All of the work of Oswald, including his editing, is praiseworthy, and every page reveals the hand of competency. His songs are delightfully melodious and vocally most effective, when in compass. Most of his concerted work shows original moods with gifts of imagination and lines of special beauty. As a harmonist he is quite skilful and even bolder than many of his contemporaries. It is a pity that such an original mind was taken up so much with publishing rather than with composing.

It is to be regretted that the winds of criticism have blown rather coldly on Oswald from one irresponsible quarter at least. David Baptie (*Musical Scotland*, 1894) says : " His compositions do not rise above mediocrity," to which rash opinion one can only reply that Baptie could not have known the works of Oswald, or at least only as much as he did of Archibald Menzies who, he said, " taught the first and second violin." Yet another Scot, the brusque Alexander Campbell, who was never prone to cast bouquets at anyone, says of Oswald: " Had he composed nothing else but *The Braes of Ballenden* and the air to *Lovely Nymph*, introduced in the burletta of *Midas*, his fame would live as long as a relish exists for genuine Scottish melody." Burns was so enamoured of Oswald's melodies that he set words to *seven* of them, which is more than the accepted authorities, Dick (*Songs of Robert Burns*) and Glen (*Early Scottish Melodies*) have acknowledged of these sources. They are all to be found in either Oswald's *Curious Collection of Scots Songs* (1740) or his *Caledonian Pocket Companion* (1745-59), although the seventh had appeared in the *Universal Harmony* (1745) before it was included in the *Caledonian Pocket Companion*. Because these facts are not widely known, even in Burnsiana, here is a list of these songs and their sources: " It is na, Jean, thy bonny face " (=*The Maid's Complaint*), " Anna, thy charms my bosom fire " (=*Bonny Mary*), "Yon wild mossy mountains" (=*Phoebe*), "If thou should ask my love " (=*Jamy Come Try Me*), " O were I on Parnassus' Hill " (=*My Love is Lost to Me*), " The lovely lass o' Inverness " (=*The Lovely Lass of Inverness*), and " Go, fetch to me a pint o' wine " (=*The Stolen Kiss* =*The Secret Kiss*). Only the last-named can be said to be well known, since the outlandish compass of most of the others precluded even reasonable popularity. Burns' " O leeze me on my spinning-wheel " was also taken from Oswald's *Sweet's the lass that loves me*, but actually it is the earlier Scottish tune *Cozen Cole's Delight*, which appeared in Playford's *Original Scotch Tunes* (1700).

Yet the composer who was lionised, and perhaps justly so, was Thomas Alexander Erskine (1732-81) the Sixth Earl of Kellie. He was the nobleman, as Smollett hinted, whose compositions were " universally admired." Johann Stamitz had been his teacher at Mannheim, and when he returned to this country he sprang into almost immediate fame as a composer. In addition to many smaller works, Erskine wrote " overtures and symphonies," as *Grove's*

Dictionary of Music and Musicians (1940) so sparingly tells us. We certainly know of *Six Overtures in Eight Parts* (*c*.1775) which Bremner published, four of which, at least, Nos. 13, 17, 25, and 28, had been issued earlier in the " Periodical Overture " series, the last mentioned being the famous *Maid of the Mill* Overture (1765). Of his symphonies, which can scarcely be distinguished in " form " from his overtures, for such was the contemporary practice, only one is actually known to us. It is to be found in No. 4 in E Flat of the *Six Simphonies in Four Parts . . . by J. Stamitz, his Pupil the Earl of Kelly, and Others* (Lond., *c.* 1765) issued by Bremner. Wind parts for this symphony of Erskine, dating from 1810, are in the present writer's possession, and they bear the name of " Lord Kelly." Further confirmation of Erskine's connection with this symphony is to be seen in Charles Kirkpatrick Sharpe's issue of Erskine's *Minuets and Songs* (1839) where the minuet movement can be identified. Another work of great merit is his *Six Sonatas for Two Violins and a Bass* (*c.* 1770) published by Welcher. His songs are characteristic of the period and one of them, *Death is now my only Treasure*, according to the late Dr. W. Gillies Whittaker, might easily have been attributed to " Haydn in his more serious moods." To those who revel in 18th century music, the frolicsome joy of his *allegros*, the exquisite mien of his *minuets*, and the alluring pathos of his *andantes*, are quite unforgettable. Yet once more, as with Oswald, one can only regret that he paid such scant heed to his compositions. As Sharpe, his biographer, has shown, Erskine was too much of a *bon vivant*, more sought and flattered as such than was good for his art. The result was that he more often than not sat down to compose as a whim and, once the work had been performed and the fleeting joy of audition had been satiated, thought no more of what he had written. Indeed, he would often write such things for an orchestra or military band on the spur of the moment and hand the work to those concerned. Thus most of his compositions have disappeared, and all that remains is what the printing press has, with good fortune, preserved. What else could have been expected of a grandson of Archibald Pitcairn (d. 1713).

Erskine possibly stands shoulders above even Oswald, and was certainly hailed with acclamation by his contemporaries. Burney said, although admittedly much was coloured by friendship, that " there was no part of theoretical or practical music in which he [Erskine] was not equally versed with the greatest professors of his time," remarking in conclusion that he " had a genius for composition." Thomas Robertson, in his *Inquiry into the Fine Arts* (1784), commented that Erskine was " the greatest secular musician in his time in the British Islands." Matched by his contemporaries, J. C. Bach, Abel, Wagensteil, and others who wrote such works, Erskine can be considered their equal. Indeed, the rubicund countenanced nobleman, whose appearance so amused Foote the actor, was a pioneer in music, in that his compositions were " a new noisy stile of composition, lately cultivated in Germany," as the philosopher John Gregory wrote in his *State and Faculties of Man* (1766). Yet the same writer was constrained to admit that Erskine's compositions were " certainly much superior to any of the kind we have yet heard." They were undoubtedly ahead of the conventional type that was accepted in the second half of this century. The melody was always satisfying, flowing gracefully, with the harmony either quite bold or less stereotyped in character, and to some extent even inspired.

Another excellent composer, although but one outstanding example of his abilities has survived, was furnished by the liberal professions. This was David Foulis (b. 1713), or at least the available evidence points to him as the composer, and here is the story. Somewhere about the year 1740, if we are to accept the British Museum date, but more likely it is slightly later, there was published in Scotland a work, without place name, or publisher's or printer's name, entitled *Six Solos for the Violin with a Bass for a Violoncello or Harpsichord, Composed by a Gentleman,* and it was " Inscribed to the Honourable Francis Charteris, Esq., of Amisfield." In the *Scots Musical Museum* (1853) we are told that " in a copy that belonged to . . . Charles Sharpe of Hoddam, the author's name is given as Foulis." In the year 1933, when I acquired the residue of the John Glen collection of Scottish music books, there came to me a copy of these *Six Solos*. They were bound up with works of other contemporary composers for the violin—Festing, Giardini, Borghi, Agus, Barbella, and Pasquali— and in the manuscript list of contents, bearing the date 1817, the composer's name is given as " Dr. Foulis." There had been a semi-anonymous " Dr. F." known in Scottish musical circles for some years, and two examples of his work, a minuet and a march, were published in Neil Stewart's *Collection of Marches and Airs* (Edin., c. 1756). A " Mr. Foulis " was also a subscriber to John Addison's *Six Sonatas . . . for Two Violins* (Edin., 1772). The absence of a forename in these several references indicates that Foulis must have been well known as a " Doctor " at this period, and the only Foulis traceable who could be thus alluded to is David Foulis, who was physician at Heriot's Hospital, Edinburgh. Quite apart from the scant productivity of Scottish composers at this period, which makes almost every item of tolerable sufficiency valuable, the *Six Solos* of Foulis have unusual interest because they scan pleasurably. Most of them are not technically difficult, and the performer is not taken beyond the 5th position. Indeed, one imagines that the composer was himself a violinist, or was well acquainted with the instrument, since the bowing is carefully marked in places. Side by side with the works of the composers with which the *Six Solos* were bound up, one is forced to confess that, in spite of occasional lapses and weak harmonic texture here and there, Foulis compares favourably. The solos are never dull and, on the whole, display good, solid, technical workmanship. One of these solos, No. 1, has been frequently given by me at concerts, and two have been broadcast. They so intrigued the late Dr. W. Gillies Whittaker that he edited the whole six for publication just prior to his death in 1944.

Next comes John Reid (1721-1807), better known as General John Reid, the founder of the Reid Chair of Music at the University of Edinburgh. As Frank Kidson has shown, Reid was one of the original members of the London " Society of the Temple of Apollo," with Oswald, Erskine, and Burney, and in those days he first became known as a composer when Bremner included " The Highland March by Capt. Reid " in his *Collection of Airs and Marches* (Edin., *c.* 1756), although it was better known as *The Garb of Old Gaul* after Sir Henry Erskine's words in *The Lark* (Edin., 1765) were set to it, a question which I have dealt with at length elsewhere (*Papers on Martial Music*). Slightly earlier, Oswald issued Reid's *Six Solos for a German Flute* (*c.* 1755), followed by a *Second Sett of Six Solos*, the composer being denominated " I.R." After the death of Oswald, this second set was re-issued about 1775 by William Randall, who had purchased many of Oswald's plates, when it was stated that this second set was really composed by Oswald and *not* by Reid, a view which Frank Kidson accepted, without warrant, as covering both sets, although W. Barclay Squire of the British Museum gives the more correct implication. With the latter point of view I am in partial agreement, but Randall's " mysterious note," as Kidson calls it, is rather suspicious. It appears that when Oswald died, Reid went, with quite understandable clannishness, to another Scot, Bremner, as his publisher, a proceeding which seems to have nettled Randall, who had purchased Oswald's plates of Reid's *Solos*. The result was the malicious canard that Randall published. Nor was Reid the only one to be attacked. Randall said the same about Burney's *Queen Mab* (1751), probably for a similar reason, since this composer had also made Bremner his publisher after Oswald's death. Seemingly there were anti-gaelicans as well as anti-gallicans in those days. Reid's flute music might appear to be, as the Scots say, " a wee bit shilpit " or wishy-washy, but we must remember the digital limitations of the instrument at that period. At any rate, measured even by the compositions for the flute by the great Bach and Handel, these works of Reid can hold their own. Other of his productions, the *Set of [Military] Marches* (*c.* 1770) and the *Minuets and Marches* (*c.* 1775), slight as they are, deserve as much recognition as the more popular *Garb of Old Gaul*.

As I have hinted in treating of the theatre, there was no attempt to develop Ramsay's pastoral opera in Scotland. Of course, most people would have hesitated at dabbling in stage productions themselves, although like good Christians, they were prepared to support others who did. As we all know, Home's *Douglas*, which became almost a fixture on the Scottish stage, was a lone production. Only one man tried to punt down Ramsay's stream and that was Andrew Shirrefs (1762 - *c.*1801), whose *Jamie and Bess* had some slight success, of which *The Overture, Airs, Songs and Duetts in the Scots Pastoral Comedy of "Jamie and Bess"* (Edin., *c.*1787) has survived in print. If we judge it by the period, it might be counted as passable in its particular genre. Better fare was provided in his earlier *Forty Pieces of Original Music* (Aberdeen, 1788). Shirrefs was a graduate of Marischal College and had edited the *Aberdeen Chronicle* and the *Caledonian Magazine* but, in 1798, being enamoured of music, he went to London to seek his fortune, but found the grave of penury instead. Burns met this " little decrepit body with some abilities " at Aberdeen in the office of James Chalmers, when he ran into Bishop Skinner, Professor John Ross and Professor John Gordon, all members of the Aberdeen Musical Society.

Among a dozen of lesser-known composers stand Hugh Montgomerie, William Cranmer, William Boyd, Alexander Campbell, John Fergus, William Wilson, George Muschet and Robert Mackintosh. Hugh Montgomerie (1739-1819) was the Twelfth Earl of Eglinton, the composer of the not unworthy *Three Duetts for Two German Flutes by an Amateur* (Lond., *c.* 1790), which we find in Glasgow University Library. He was also responsible for the more popular *New Strathspey Reels Composed by a Gentleman . . . for Nathl. Gow* (Edin., 1796), as well as some songs, one of which, *My Gentle Jean*, being set to the words of Mrs. John Hunter, the friend of Haydn and the wife of the more famous surgeon. John Turnbull edited some of Montgomerie's unpublished works in a *Selection of Songs, Marches . . .* (Glasg., *c.* 1838). Nothing of his more mature work is remembered to-day, but " the people " still clamour for *Lady Montgomery's Reel* and the *Ayrshire Lasses* when they take to the floor for an " Eightsome." It was for this music-loving earl that Arne wrote the glee *Let not Rage.*

William Cranmer, who flourished in the last quarter of the century in Edinburgh and Glasgow, was claimed by Charles Baptie as a Scot. Other than these references he is unknown to us biographically, save that he claimed to have sung at " St. Paul's, London," and that he composed a *Collection of Catches and Glees* (Edin., *c.* 1780). These catches, which are really rounds, " reveal real musicianship," said the late Dr. W. Gillies Whittaker, whilst his glees are " about as good specimens as may be met with anywhere." Thus it was said on the radio in " Music from the Scottish Past." Of William Boyd (d. 1792) we have a manuscript *Sonata for the Harpsichord*, which I programmed at a concert in Glasgow in 1934. It is a work of the old, sedate, courtly approach, with just the slightest suggestion of technical difficulty beyond what was the accepted procedure, but otherwise quite commendable. Augustus Hughes-Hughes (*Catalogue of Manuscript Music*, i, 589) thought that there were some songs " apparently " by Boyd in the British Museum, but the evidence is not too clear. As the precentor of the Methodist Chapel, John Street, Glasgow, he compiled a *Select Collection of Psalms and Hymn Tunes in Three Parts* (Glasg., 1793), published after his death " for the benefit of his widow," a line that tells the old, old story.

Alexander Campbell (1764-1824), whose story is pathetic, is better remembered for his efforts on behalf of the national song, as we have seen. From his *Collections of Scottish Songs* (Lond., 1792), and a second book (n.d.) which was arranged for the harpsichord, he shows himself to be quite a capable arranger and editor, as he does in his *Albyn's Anthology* (Edin., 1816-18). As a composer, however, if his *Twelve Songs* (Lond., 1785 ; Edin., 1790) may be taken as a criterion, he did not express much above the ordinary. Still, his memory is evergreen in Scotland because of his beautiful melody to which is sung Tannahill's *Gloomy Winter's now awa'*. The music teacher of Sir Walter Scott is in Kay's *Portraits.*

John Fergus (d. 1820-21) was made of better stuff musically. He was for many years the organist of St. Andrew's Episcopal Chapel, Glasgow, and known for his songs, glees, organ pieces, and other works, although only a song in Golding's *Feast of Apollo* (Lond., 1788) and another entitled *O'er Woodlands and Mountains* (Lond., *c.* 1790), his estimable *Three Glees* (Glasg., *c.* 1790), and a *Grand March* (in score) for a military band (Edin., *c.* 1795), have survived. Lastly comes William Wilson, who was a well-known singer and composer in Aberdeen and Glasgow during the " Eighties", and best minded for his *Twelve Original Scotch Songs . . .* Op. 3 (Lond., *c.* 1785), many of which gained further publicity in the *Aberdeen Journal* (1788), although they are not so " original " as the title page says. George Muschet flourished in the second half of the century in Edinburgh. He composed *Six Duets for Two German Flutes or Violins*, Op. 2 (Edin., 1780), which has some merit, besides a number of smaller works. Robert Mackintosh (1745-1807) was a violinist who had led the Aberdeen concerts for a time, and was the teacher of Nathaniel Gow. His *Airs, Minuets, Gavotts and Reels* (Edin., 1783) deserve passing mention because the book contains a " solo . . . intended as a specimen of a Set of Solos for the Violin, which the author proposes to publish afterwards." He does not appear to have published them, and the " high brows " who scan this solo may, with modern taste, think it just as well that he did not. Yet this work was the composer's Op. 1, and as such, it is certainly not an insignificant production. Mackintosh is better remembered by his fine dance music, the *Sixty-eight New Reels . . .* (Edin., 1792), followed by three other books (1793, 1796, *c.* 1804), the last, from London, in which city he had sought refuge from unappreciation in the North.

This mention of Mackintosh makes an easy modulation to the works of his fellow composers of reels and strathspeys. However much superior people may elevate their brows at " mere dance music," the Scottish achievement in this field reveals, in many instances, thorough musicianship, as well as virility and originality, which is lacking in some of the serious music of the period even in

England.   Robert Mackintosh himself is a good example of this, as may be heeded in his strathspeys *Miss Mariane Oliphant* and *Sir Alexander Don* with their spacious gamut.   Of the scaring, wild, abandon of the melody of " Red Rob Mackintosh " we also catch a glint in the works of his son Abraham (1769-*c*.1807), who penned many an inventive theme in his *Thirty New Strathspey Reels* (Edin., 1792) and a *Collection of Strathspeys* (Newcastle, 1805).   His reel *Kelo House* and the strathspey *Pease Bridge* are worthy examples.

Actually the first composer of reels known to us in Scotland is John Riddell (1718-95), whose *Collection of Scots Reels or Country Dances* (Edin., *c*. 1766) was a prime favourite.   The contents have a salutary freshness in comparison with the older material as shown in the collections of Bremner and Neil Stewart.   Next in importance came Daniel Dow (1732-83), who won some celebrity for his *Thirty Seven New Reells and Strathspeys* (Edin., *c*. 1775).   John Glen rightly considers that " many of his tunes are excellent," to witness *Athol House* and *Monymusk*.   That the contour of his melody was worth pilfering is evident from the depredations of Nathaniel Gow, who absorbed more than one in his collections under other titles.   Of the same ilk, as a composer, was Malcolm McDonald, and Glen also notes " that strange wild nature so characteristic of the compositions of Daniel Dow " which is to be found in McDonald's works.   He published some singular and interesting items in his *Collections of Strathspey Reels* (Edin., 1788), with later issues (1789, 1792, 1797).

Burns, who was not a bad judge of such things, thought that " the first composer of strathspeys of the age " was William Marshall (1748-1833), and we see the latter's mettle in his early *Collection of Reels* (Edin., 1781), but wider still in his *Scottish Airs, Melodies, Strathspeys, Reels* (Edin., 1822), and his *Collection of Scottish Melodies* issued posthumously.   His was a magic hand at a strathspey, not because of any divine spark of inspiration, but rather on account of the charm and elegance of sheer melody as seen in *The Marquis of Huntly* strathspey and *Mr. George Gordon* reel.   Of the composers of secondary interest are Angus Cumming, Alexander

McGlashan, and Duncan McIntyre, although their music is still " bonnie, bonnie," as Burns would say.

Naturally, one cannot ignore the famous Gow family, more especially since they are given such prominence in the annals of Scottish music, frequently out of all proportion to their merits as by Davey and Walker the historians of English music. Niel Gow (1727-1807) was the first of the family to make a name. Of him little need be said since so much is recorded of him elsewhere, for the most part fable. As a " fiddler " he stood pre-eminent in his day and his claims as a composer are considerable, although much must be accepted with reserve. John Glen, whose opinion is final in such matters, says that among eighty-seven works attributed to him, " at least a fourth are constructed from old tunes, or are plagiarised to some extent." Those which can be claimed as original are quite inferior to those of his predecessors and contemporaries mentioned above. Others were borrowed unblushingly from fellow composers without as much as a word of gratitude. His *Collection of Strathspey Reels* (Edin., 1784) was followed by two other books (1788, 1792) while his *Complete Repository of Original Scots Slow Strathspeys and Dances* (1799) appeared in four parts, two others being published later (1808, 1822). All these works, which had an enormous sale, ran into several editions. The fame of Niel Gow was trumpeted high and low, and even his portrait was sought, the great Raeburn painting it several times. His son, Nathaniel (1763-1831), became even more famous. He seems to have been a better all-round performer and musician than most of the contemporary fiddlers, but his compositions, like those of his father, do not display the great originality claimed for them, although his name is justly inseparable from the history of the reel and strathspey. His *Collection of Strathspey Reels* (Edin., 1797), the *Beauties of Niel Gow [and Sons]* (*c.* 1819), the *Select Collection of Original Dances* (Edin., *c.* 1815), and numerous other publications, reveal his enormous industry, but where he does not openly filch the produce of his contemporaries and others—and Burns pilloried him for this in Cromek's *Reliques* (1808)—he cleverly grafts his material. Although famed for *Lady Charlotte Campbell* and other strathspeys, as well as the reel *Miss H. Hunter of Blackness*, these do not compare with the strathspey *Major Molle* by Andrew Gow, or the reel *Mrs. Muir Mackenzie* by William Gow, who were his little-known brothers. In spite of all this criticism we are still grateful for Nathaniel Gow's *Caller Herrin*.

It is remarkable that the early composers of the reel and strathspey should have displayed such rhythmic and melodic originality at the very cradle of development in the Lowlands, whilst their successors produced so much that was commonplace if not dull. Was it because such names as McGlashan, Cumming, Mackintosh, McDonald and McIntyre tell of the Highlands, the fountain head of the strathspey at least ? It may be recalled that Angus Cumming claimed to follow the " profession of his forefathers, who have been for many generations musicians in Strathspey [in the Highlands]." Perhaps the cunning of digital and bow technique had lost its best exponents as the years rolled on, and that simpler and less energetic forms ensued in consequence. All this bareness and lack of inspiration in the later strathspeys and reels might easily have been due to such causes, as well as to the demands for simplicity by the Lowland public.

Finally, it must not be forgotten how many of these dance measures, old and new, are now enshrined in songs that will never die. *The Grant's Rant, Lady Macintosh's Reel, Rothiemurchie's Rant, Miss Admiral Gordon's Strathspey,* and *Sir Alexander Don* have been immortalised by Burns in " Green grows the Rashes," " A Man's a Man for a' that," "Lassie wi' the lint white Locks," "Of a' the airts the wind can blaw," and " Auld Lang Syne." John Skinner set *Carron's Reel* to " The Ewie wi' the crookit horn," whilst it was his setting of *Tullochgorum* that led Burns to say, in his open-hearted way, that it was " the best Scotch song Scotland ever saw," an appraisement which Robert Fergusson had given the tune in his *Daft Days.* Tannahill set his " Loudon's Bonnie Woods and Braes " and " Gloomy Winter's noo awa' " to the *Earl of Loudoun and Moira* and the strathspey *Rev. Mr. Patrick Macdonald.*

Lady Nairne did likewise with many of her songs, " The Fife Laird " (*The Fife Hunt*), " Cairney Burn " (*The Bog o' Bight*), and others, whilst Hector Macneill wrote his "Dinna think Bonnie Lassie " to the *Carrick Rant*. At all this there is no need for wonder in Scotland. As that " ill-fated genius " Robert Fergusson says :

> " For nought can cheer the heart sae weel
> As can a canty Highland reel."

In view of what has preceded, the summing up of Scotland's productivity in the higher creative sphere of the art in those days ought to be accomplished in a line or two. Yet a discreet assessment cannot be done without a comparative estimate. The usual taunt,—" Where are the achievements of Macklean, McGibbon, Foulis, Oswald, or Erskine to-day ?"—only touches the fringe of the question, as can be amply proved by appeal to the works of even greater men, since among those composers whose names were on the lips of all and sundry in the first half of the century, only Handel, Corelli, and Scarlatti have a place to-day, and even then, often as antiques. Indeed, one might even ask what has survived of the once applauded compositions of the then leading English musicians, Croft, Greene, Boyce, and Arne, all contemporaries of the great Handel ? Where, too, are the works of Cooke, Arnold, Attwood, Samuel Wesley, the younger Arne, and William Shield, who were so successful in the second half of the century ? Croft is only re-membered by his *Musica Sacra*, but if anyone cares to place his *Six Sonatas . . . for Two Flutes* cheek by jowl with McGibbon's work of a similar nature, the Edinburgh craftsman can smilingly stand the comparison. I would give the same verdict to Erskine's work against Greene's *Six Overtures . . . in Seven parts* or Boyce's *Eight Symphonies in Eight parts*. Nor do I consider Arne's *Seven Sonatas for Two Violins . . . [and] Harpsicord* nearly as impressive as Oswald's compositions for the same combination. Lest there may be critics prepared to urge that there is no gradation in medio-crity, let me say that I would be in full agreement, but all of the works that I have mentioned are well above the commonplace, judged by contemporary standards.

As I have shown, Scotland had no traditional school in music in which to find guidance or inspiration, since even the names of the pre-Reformation composers were but a vague memory. The result was that at the revival of music in 18th century Scotland, her incipient composers, as in Oswald and McGibbon, turned to English models, as Macklean and Foulis did to the Italian school, and Erskine to the German, or to be more precise the Bohemian. Later vocal writers were deeply influenced by Haydn. Yet these Scottish composers, who brought their creative genius into play in the dawning years of this renascence, were still able to express something of an individual character and an inspiration that are quite commendable. This is also the opinion of many who are capable of a discriminating judgment as I have shown, and it is a great pity that on occasions, when an antiquarian interest prompts a programme maker to feature a Corelli or a Scarlatti item, room could not also be found for one of these old names in " Music from the Scottish Past," as the B.B.C. did some years ago.

PART VII

THE NINETEENTH CENTURY

" Perhaps at no period in the annals of Scottish music was this art
more universally cultivated than at present. It forms a general part
of modern education, and few are to be met with who cannot sing or
play upon one instrument or another."

STARK : *Picture of Edinburgh* (1806).

IT would seem that Stark only echoes Smollett's observation of
half a century earlier, although it was doubtless just as true, but with
this difference. What the portrayer of *Humphrey Clinker* had to say
in 1756 could have only included the fashionable set with whom he
rubbed shoulders in Edinburgh. Stark, on the other hand, seems
to have been embracing the denizens from the foot of High Street,
over the brae, to the citizens of New Town. This he would be
forced to do since society no longer meant the privileged classes.
We have seen in the days before the Industrial Revolution that the
upper classes were all musicians, or at least musically minded, for
their education had been directed into this path. Much about the
same could be said of the middle classes. With the working classes,
the appreciation of music more generally found expression in the
national songs and dance tunes. All, perforce, were interested in
psalmody, which was not a negligible attraction, because it gave
the ground basis of music, even if its *gamut* was " scrimpit." Yet
with the dawn of the new era, a wider public interest in the more
abstruse forms of the art manifested itself, which estimation was
reflected in the rise of small amateur vocal, glee, and instrumental
societies with the masses, and this novelty began at precisely the
same time as similar societies began to fall into decay among the
classes.

These changes affected the concerts, as we shall see presently,
because, since the masses preferred to make their own music
rather than have it made for them, the subscription concerts run
by " professionals " had little attraction for them at first. Obviously
the same line of argument ought to apply to the classes, but it
does not at this period. With the latter, there was not the same

interest in music whether they themselves or someone else supplied it. Indeed, in both Edinburgh and Aberdeen the old Musical Societies, and their attendant concerts, had collapsed by the opening of this century as much by reason of the falling off of aristocratic patronage as anything else. Here and there a few of the noble families retained a personal interest in music, as the sale of the Hamilton Palace Library revealed, in which its vast music collection showed that a few items were acquired, or were copied, as late as 1824. Still, there were other causes that contributed to the neglect of music by the classes, and among them was the economic one. The industrial age, with its intriguing vistas, opened attractive horizons that bred new desires. The erstwhile landed and agricultural interests and aims began to take second place to those of industry and commerce, and a plutocratic outlook took the place of the old aristocratic view. In truth it was the Golden Calf that attracted most knees, and the results were apparent everywhere.

The professions became infected by the virus and in music the *impresario* and *entrepreneur* began to flourish. The musician himself felt the social and economic pressure around him, and it was only the best equipped who survived the struggle for existence. Thus music became a specialised profession in Scotland as elsewhere. In the old days, most of the aristocratic amateur class could hold their own as executants with the professional performer, but all that had changed, and it soon came to be recognised that the musical profession required a long and strict apprenticeship, against which the aristocratic or bourgeoise amateur could not possibly compete effectively, however great their love of music. The outcome of all this was not only that the position of the professional performer was enhanced, but the music itself obtained greater consideration. It could be seen in the symphonies of Mozart and Beethoven in the concert hall, and in the operas of Rossini, Weber, Bellini, Auber, and others in the theatre, where greater skill was now demanded in performance.

The very structure of the music of the old and new age reflected the change. Under the *ancien régime*, the trills, turns, and other

broderies, as the French so expressively term these musical ornaments, were the counterparts of the ruffles and lace of the apparel
of the period.   The decoration of the " good old days " was notice-
able even in the traditional music of Scotland as given by Oswald
and others, although it was not, *sui generis*, Scottish, but an affectation from the Continent via England, of which accretion we shall
have some evidence when dealing with the *auld sangs*.   It was of
this alien trait that the wise, though ill-tempered Ritson complained
in 1794, when he said that " the era of Scottish music and Scottish
song is now past.   The pastoral simplicity and natural genius of
former ages no longer exist : a total change of manners has taken
place, . . . and servile imitation [has] usurped the place of original
invention."   Needless to say, Ritson's fears were groundless, and
within a decade or two we see all this musical decoration in the old
songs, as elsewhere, making a polite exit, just as the apparel frillings
disappear in its company, both, probably, being interdependent.
On this specific question it is interesting to compare the æsthetic
outlook of two Scottish musicographers a half-century apart—
Tytler and Dauney.   Writing in 1780, dear old William Tytler of
Woodhouselee, whilst admitting that the " Scottish song admits of
no cadence," recommends " an easy shake " at " the close of a tune."
In 1838 William Dauney comments that if a young lady were to
indulge in such an affectation as a " shake " in his day, " it would
occasion nearly as much surprise as if she were to enter the room
with her grandmother's [crinoline] hoop and high-heeled shoes."

   The intimate way in which all forms of instrumental music
pervaded social life may be seen in the *genre* art of David Wilkie
(1785-1841).   It may be allowed that Wilkie was rather partial
to music and had learned the violin in his earliest studio days at
Cupar, but even this fondness for the art would scarcely account
for the many instances in which he limns an instrument.   That
they are true in technical detail, as well as in occurrence, we car
well believe from his *Blind Fiddler* (1806), *The Jews Harp* (1809),
The Bagpiper (1813) who handles a Lowland pipe, *The Reading of
the Will* (1819) in which an English guitar is displayed, *The Penny*

Wedding (1819) with a violinist (Niel Gow) and a 'cellist, and *The Gentle Shepherd* (1823) who plays a stockhorn.   Scottish auto-biographies and recollections teem with similar proof of tastes in instruments.   Sheriff Hugh Barclay, who penned the amusing although anonymous *Rambling Recollections of Glasgow* (Glasg., 1880) has some illuminating comments.   " For some years," he says, " in the early stages of the Nineteenth Century, there was for a time something like a musical mania amongst the young men of the age.   It was not deemed that education was completed without a period more or less devoted to music. . . . The violin was con-sidered rather vulgar, and not so much respected as were wind instruments.   The [German] flute, the flageolet (single and double), the pandean reed, . . . were all great favourites."   From the amount of music published for the flute in Edinburgh and Glasgow, it would seem that this instrument was a special favourite among the middle class, even more so than the pianoforte.   Indeed, Andrew Aird, in his *Glimpses of Glasgow* (Glasg., 1894), says that " little more than a generation ago [i.e. 1830-60], pianofortes were to be found only in the houses of the well-to-do ; but now [1894] there are few working-men's homes in which there is not either a pianoforte, a harmonium, or an American organ."   It was from this soil of instrumental zeal that the amateur orchestral societies sprang during the first half-century, which were to become, with the leavening of professionals, the only purveyors of orchestral music in Scotland, until the birth of the Choral Union Orchestra in 1874, as we shall see in the story of the concert in Scotland.   Yet orchestral societies were not numerous, firstly because it meant the provision of instruments, and secondly because their adequate mastery was a question of years.   With choral societies, since almost everybody had a voice, the problem was simpler, and there was no end to such organisations.

The Reformation had produced the congregational singer both good and bad.   We have already seen that psalm tunes had become part and parcel of secular life, and they had insinuated themselves as a more integral factor than most people imagine or than we have

hitherto contemplated. In the Highlands we have mentioned
how the psalm tunes had been innocently adapted to everyday
ditties, but now this seeming impiety had taken a hold in the cities.
Robert Turnbull, in his interesting *Old Musical Glasgow* (*Transactions of the Old Glasgow Club*, 1916) tells us about this devilment.
" While the clergy," he says, " were discussing the sinfulness of
organs, the people were singing to common metre tunes of the
psalms, such things as—

> " I sat me down on yonder hill—
> Dumfarmin I thocht on,
> In it there was guid yill [ale] to sell,
> But siller I had none."

Yet the people were not actually to blame for such levities because
at choir practice the Church forbade that sacred words should be
" bandied about " in mere rehearsing, and it was ordered that other
words should be introduced. The above was the result, although
it must have been considered harmless enough at the time. Much
was quite innocently done. At the same time an advertisement in
a Glasgow newspaper announced a meeting of the Sacred Music
Institution to be held in " Mrs. Lamont's Tavern " which was
surely strange surroundings for sanctity, and it prompted a profane
wit to remark that " the bottle was quite respectable in these days
if the organ was not."

Yet the real point of the above is that there was a growing secular
outlook in the glee, catch, and vocal clubs which had sprung up.
These had originally made the psalm tunes their chief items,
but a wider vision soon turned these clubs into choral societies, a
circumstance which left the glee and psalm tune behind, more
especially when the oratorio and cantata became the aim. In these
early societies it ought to be remarked that there were only male
altos, as ladies were still held to the apron-strings of the conventional and did not sing in public. Even in St. Mary's Episcopal
Church, Glasgow, where ladies first sang in its choir, they had to be
accompanied by a lay clerk on the violin to give them confidence.
In 1852, a tenor led the lady sopranos of the Glasgow Musical
Association, and Robert A. Marr says that the male alto did not

finally make his exit from choral societies until about 1860. We shall see in detail how rapidly the choral and orchestral societies, the former especially, developed in Scotland, and how much Scotland owes to them in the furtherance of public taste for the best music, although their endeavours did not meet with complete approval at first.

The dilating interest in secular music and the corresponding indifference to sacred music is the constant theme during the first half of the century, and one of the most illuminating sidelights on this question is contained in a leaflet published in Scotland about 1850 entitled *A Plea for the Cultivation of Sacred Music by the Upper Classes* which, incidentally, is quite an index to the musical taste of the period. Here is an extract which speaks for itself :

" If sacred music be neglected by those who enjoy the best advantages for the study of it,—if it be put off with a mere fraction of its claims by such as lavish time and money upon other departments of the musical art,—if proficients in vocal and instrumental execution are unable to raise a simple tune at family worship, and tones that charm the drawing-room circle are hushed into silence in the sanctuary,—if young people pass through the hands of celebrated masters, and return from fashionable boarding-schools, without ever having had a psalm tune set before them,— if no collection of Church Music is to be found in the family library, while songs and dances can be counted by the score, it needs little reasoning to discover that all this must produce a deleterious influence upon the grade of society immediately inferior. . . .

" There can be no doubt that though in recent years music has been largely cultivated among the middle and higher classes of society, these considerations [as outlined above] have been very generally overlooked. . . . Instrumental music is cultivated more than vocal, contrary to the order of nature, and secular vocal music more than sacred, contrary to the order of importance."

The Church was clearly worried about the state of affairs and suggested several remedies. " As instruction on the Pianoforte has become a common element in female education, and as that instrument is adapted to the performance of sacred music," it was recommended to teachers that sacred music should become part of the curriculum, although it was considered that " the Harmonium exhibits the powers of Sacred Music much better than the Pianoforte, and it is to be wished that it were brought into more extensive use as a family instrument."

The plea and protest did not stem the tide of appreciation of secular music, and it had but slight suasion in the revival of sacred music either in the tabernacle or tenement save that, after the organ found acceptance by the Church itself (1864), the harmonium nudged its way into the houses of the middle and working-classes, as much by reason of its cost being more reasonably within the limits of the family purse, as the propriety of its use in sacred music.

After the " Sixties " the cause of music rose to the ascendant in Scotland. Its great choral societies forged ahead with works and performances which, on the choral side, were equal to those of any other in Britain. In 1874, when the fine technique of the Hallé Orchestra had roused music lovers in Scotland to something better on their own account, the Glasgow Choral Union Orchestra was born and, strengthened by collaboration with the Edinburgh Choral Union, it became a power in the land, although the crowning triumph came when the Scottish Orchestra took its place in 1894, in which organisation a really national orchestra, in service at any rate, came into existence. Side by side with these strides came the establishment of the Glasgow Athenaeum School of Music (1890), which gave Scottish youth the opportunity to pursue a musical training in Scotland which hitherto had to be obtained elsewhere. The introduction of degrees in music at the University of Edinburgh (1893) was a complementary step. More important still was the rise of the Scottish National Group of composers, whose works during the " Eighties " and " Nineties," received early recognition in the land of their fathers, even if this enthusiasm has since cooled.

CHAPTER 1

THE NATIONAL MUSIC

" This land, classic in song and history."
HENRY WARD BEECHER : *Glasgow City Hall* (Oct. 1863)

" There is scarcely in all Scotland, from the thrifty and well-taught labourer and mechanic up to the lordliest duke, a man in whose house volumes of the noble music of his native country, as well as every scrap of national poetry or song, both in Gaelic and English, that from time to time issues from the active press of his country, may not be found."
O'CURRY : *Manners and Customs of the Ancient Irish* (1873).

In the all-absorbing processes of industrial life in 19th-century Scotland, one would have thought that much of the old fervour for the national muse would have cooled in the searing, for such a process of wear and tear is discernible elsewhere. In England, where so much good and bad music had crowded out the national song, this is quite apparent. The growth of the popular entertainment, and more especially in the latter half of the century when the Music Hall began to absorb the leisure hours of the middle and working classes, had produced a type of music that was inimical to the older traditional kind. The new tunes were simpler and more catchy, whilst the words to which they were set, although often atrocious as verse, were topical and even risky, all of which secured popularity for many an item, if only for a decade. These notorieties were not new, as many outrageous lines in the *Beggar's Opera* show, and as a few themes in the old rounds and catches display, but in this century they were given expression under more popular conditions and with more disastrous results.

In Scotland however, the influence of this ephemeral music was not so great for two reasons. The attitude of the Presbyterian Church in the early days of the century was such that it discouraged much that was permitted in England. Not that the church was solicitous of good music and abhorred the bad, but that it viewed the question rather from the old angle of forbidding indulgence in entertainments of this kind. Then there was the mighty influence of Burns, whose very name had enshrined the melodies of the past with such a halo that the popular entertainment demanded the *auld sangs.* The programmes of the concerts, whether it was at the Glasgow Musical Festivals and the Edinburgh Reid Concerts, or at the *potpourri* entertainments at the theatres and the mere " free and easy," amply testify to this preference in Scotland. Even more convincing is the output of the music publishers and music sellers, and we may be sure that the latter, with native shrewdness, would be catering for a demand.

One may rightly ask what caused this continual request for the old songs ? The answer is : Firstly, they satisfied emotionally the innermost yearnings of the people, as the very title of John Stuart Blackie's book, *Scottish Song : Its Wealth, Wisdom, and Social Significance* (1889) so pertinently displays. " In Scottish song," as William Barr has said, " love is the great burden and source of inspiration. Yet alongside of this there is a constant divergence into other phases of life and action. Songs of nature, of incident, of the avocation of rural and pastoral life, of social customs and, above all, of humour, find many embodiments in the lyric poesy of our country." Because of this the popular ballads, such as were received with satisfaction in England, did not compensate the Scot. Secondly, this particular currency in the *auld sangs* was symptomatic and indicative of the age. We see much the same thing in the graphic arts, where *genre* painting leaped into prominence at precisely this moment. Kidd's *Cobbler's Shop*, Wilkie's *Village Politicians*, and Burnet's *Tam o' Shanter*, are redolent of the atmosphere of the *auld sangs* which, in turn, are cousins-german to the scenes in Sir Walter Scott's novels from *Marmion* to *The Fair Maid of Perth*.

When the century threw open its portals, it was George Thomson's *Select Collection of Original Scottish Airs* (1793-1841), with their Haydn and Beethoven connections, that were attracting the more well-to-do purchasers, and Thomson's success prompted another Edinburgh publisher, William Whyte (1771-1858), to try a similar plan in his *Collection of Scotch Airs* (1806-7), edited by Haydn, and contributed to by Sir Walter Scott.

A Swiss harpist, who had gained some favour in Scotland, named Joseph Elouis (1752- *c.* 1817) then published a *Selection of Favourite*

Scots Songs (2nd vol., Edin., 1807) which, with Oliver's and Boyd's *Cabinet of the Scottish Muses* (Edin., 1808), seem to have had a wide sale. Of Elouis' work it can be said that he judiciously handled the pruning knife towards the " modern embellishments " in the airs, a decoration which, he said, " destroys their characteristic originality." In England too, there was a re-kindling of the somewhat cooling embers of the music of Caledonia in *Twenty-Four Original Scots Songs* (Liverpool, 1802) by Samuel Webbe, Junr., and the more celebrated *Six Admired Scotch Songs arranged as Rondos* (Lond., *c.* 1805) by Haydn, and a timely *Selection of Scottish Melodies* (Lond., 1812) by [Sir] Henry Bishop.

Even Highland music came in for special attention in the *Airs and Melodies peculiar to the Highlands* (Edin., 1815) by Simon Fraser (1773-1852), said to have been gathered 1715-45—quite an interesting period. It was an important collection because it broke some new ground, although the compiler blamed his predecessors, Oswald and McGibbon, because their editing " tended to complicate the melody." He also censured Patrick Macdonald and Alexander Campbell for their versions of Highland music, but the truth is that there were not two places in the Highlands where the same tune, handed down *viva voce*, could be found in the same form. Even in the re-issue of this work by the Gaelic Society of London (1876), Fraser's own versions were changed. The work of Alexander Campbell (1764-1824) as displayed in his *Albyn's Anthology* (Edin., 1816-18) is noteworthy, especially since it includes " Highland, Hebridean, and Lowland melodies, . . . never before published," set to modern verses by Scott, Hogg, and others. The prefatory note on the national music is critical throughout, although sometimes unbalanced. His treatment of Ritson is unmerciful, and he evidently relished tripping up the quarrelsome Englishman sfor speaking of Forbes' *Cantus* as " the first collection of Scottish song*i*." Here, too, one ought to afford passing notice to *The Jacobite Relcs of Scotland* (Edin., 1819-21) by James Hogg (1772-1835), since he was the first to deal specifically with those " airs . . . of the House of Stuart." George R. Kinloch, who issued *Ancient Scottish Ballads*

Recovered from Tradition (Edin., 1827) deserves a nod of recognition here because he was responsible for the dance tune *Kinloch of Kinloch*, to which Conolly's song *Mary Macneil* is sung, and also Andrew Park's *Hurrah for the Highlands*.

It was not until the advent of Robert A. Smith (1780-1829), when the much-admired *Scottish Minstrel* (Edin., 1821-24) was published at a reasonable price, that there was shown a really widespread demand for the national song. The popularity of this work led Finlay Dun (1795-1853) and John Thomson (1805-41) to issue the *Vocal Melodies of Scotland* (Edin., 1836, *et seq.*), in which embellishments were sedulously avoided and melodies were restored to " their true and native state." A little later John Turnbull (1804-44) edited the *Garland of Scotia* (Glasg., 1841), with Patrick Buchan contributing " descriptive and historical notes." It was these two publications, together with the *Songs of Scotland* (Lond., 1842) by John Wilson (1800-49), that were the most esteemed collections at this time, the last-named being especially popular because Wilson himself sang these songs at his lecture-recitals. Two other works of interest were : a collection of Gaelic songs *Orain na'h Albain* (Edin., 1848) edited by Finlay Dun, and *Selections from the Melodies of Scotland* (Lond., 1851) by Andrew Thomson (c.1792-1860).

Then came a collection which became, in its day, the standard one—the *Songs of Scotland* (Edin., 1848-9), with " historical, biographical and critical notices " by George F. Graham, which was re-issued, with additional notes, by John M. Wood (1805-92) in 1884. Side by side with Graham's book were the *Select Songs of Scotland* (Glasg., 1848) published by William Hamilton, the *Songs of Scotland* (Edin., 1852) by John T. Surenne (1814-78), and the *Lyric Gems of Scotland* (Edin., 1854-58) by David Jack. Graham's collection was undoubtedly the most important, and in its production he was assisted by some first-rate arrangers in T. M. Mudie, J. T. Surenne, H. E. Dibdin, Finlay Dun, and A. Laurie. On the literary side, Graham's contributions are quite valuable, although later research has proved that some of his conclusions were erroneous.

Those unseemly songs in Scotland's repertory seem to have wounded Graham's puritanic self, and he thought *The Wauking o' the Fauld* was " much too coarse for modern currency." Others of that sort were *Willie was a Wanton Wag* and *We're a' Noddin*. Graham appears to have become as " select " as old George Thomson. Even the *British Minstrel* (Glasg., 1844) had become solicitous over " the low and ribald words " of Scots songs, and lamented, although with doubtful fitness, that there is " no longer a Burns to redeem them from the base alliance to which bad taste has bound them." Obviously, the modern generation was beginning to be rather over sensitive about such indelicacies, although what was complained of was quite harmless, and was really endemic in Scotland. As Robert Chambers says in his *Robert Burns*— " The Scottish people . . . possessed a wonderful quantity of indecorous verse—not of an inflammatory character, but simply expressive of a profound sense of the ludicrous in connection with sexual affections." It was, in fact, part of local humour, and had no prurient associations. To geld these verses (and Burns tried it) as some purists have also done the old English dramatists, is to rob them of their pristine character.

The researches of William Stenhouse, and the more critical attitude of such writers as George F. Graham, William Dauney and Robert Chambers, of whom we shall read presently, as well as the arrangers mentioned above, ought to have urged editors and others to a more perspicuous outlook, but in many instances it did not, as later issues of collections of the national song reveal. In Donald Campbell's *Treatise on the Language, Poetry and Music of the Highlands* (Edin., 1862), we see the " ancient Highland airs " actually spoiled by puerile settings, and this is but one example of many. On the other hand, the arrangements of Fulcher in the *Lays and Lyrics of Scotland* (Lond., 1870) are quite praiseworthy, although the " historical epitome of Scottish song " by James Ballantine runs in the old groove. Fulcher's work in the *Beauties of Scottish Song* (Glasgow., n.d.), in conjunction with Thomas S. Gleadhill (1827-90) is also of a high character. Equally commendable at this period were the books of Colin Brown (1818-96)—the *Songs ʾcotland* (Lond., *c.* 1878) and *The Thistle* (Glasg., 1884).

After th 'here appeared the vanguard of the pioneers in independent. .carch and *viva voce* collecting, the first of whom was Dean William Christie (1817-85), whose precious *Traditional Ballad Airs* (Edin., 1876-81) were " procured in the counties of Aberdeen, Banff and Moray," some having been collected prior to 1849 by his father (*c.* 1778-1849). The work is justly praised by Frank Kidson, although he wisely observes that " it would have been much more valuable if the Dean had been content to present them [the airs] exactly as noted." Another of this class was Charles Stewart (1823-94), who was Lieut-.Colonel of the 2nd Highland Rifle Corps, but also a keen collector, as his *Killin Collection of Gaelic Songs* (Edin., 1884) shows. Further afield in gleaning went David Balfour, another military man, whose *Ancient Orkney Melodies* (Lond., 1885), some of which were " memories of voices around the kitchen fire," were worthy of the trouble of gathering. At the very edge of the century and the subject, came a most unusual study, fascinating in its way as folk-music, in *Vagabond Songs and Ballads of Scotland* (Paisley, 1899-1901) by Robert Ford. Finally there was Lucy Broadwood (d. 1929). the granddaughter of John Broadwood (1732-1812) of pianoforte fame. She was a foundation member of the English Folk Song Society (1898) and became its secretary (1904-08). She collected " largely in the Highlands " as well as elsewhere. With her can be mentioned Anne Geddes Gilchrist (1863-   ), another important worker in the same field whose contributions of Gaelic-Manx and Skye material is of great value. Returning to the conventional editors, mention must be made of Alfred Moffat (1866-   ) and his *Minstrelsy of Scotland* (Lond., 1895) and similar works, John Greig (1854-1909) with his *Scots Minstrelsie* (Edin., 1892-95), and Keith Norman MacDonald in his *Gesto Collection of Highland Music* (1895).

That the national songs stood their ground so firmly during the century is not a circumstance at which we should wonder, as two factors assured their permanance—the name of Burns and the lure of the Doric. The national dance tunes had not these props. Still, in the early century, many collections had enormous sales, especially McFayden's *Collection of Highland Strathspey Reels* (Glasg., *c.* 1802), Crosby's *Caledonian Musical Repository* (Edin., 1806, 1811), Nathaniel Gow's *Complete Repository* (1799-1822), and Davie's *Caledonian Repository* (Aberdeen, Edin., *c.*1829-30). Writing in 1852, Surenne said that fifty years earlier it was the minuet, cotillon, reel, strathspey, and country dance that were in season in Scotland. All of these, save the reel and strathspey, had disappeared by the latter date, but even these were to be pushed aside by the waltz, quadrille and mazurka. The latter, according to *Grove's Dictionary of Music*, did not reach England until " towards 1845," but Joseph Lowe (1797-1866), the famous Scottish dancing master, was certainly teaching the mazurka in Glasgow in the " Twenties " at the same time as the *gallopade*, " a new and much admired figure " as the *Glasgow Herald* of 1830 described it. It was in this wise that the music of the reel and strathspey, much of which was traditional, fell into desuetude. Yet in the " Forties " there was sufficient demand for the old dance tunes to urge Alexander Mackenzie to issue his *National Dance Music of Scotland*, which was re-edited by his son [Sir] Alexander C. Mackenzie in 1891. Joseph Lowe himself also catered for public tastes in his *Collection of Reels and Strathspeys* (Edin., 1844), as did Surenne when he produced his *Dance Music of Scotland* (Edin., 1851). Later, James Spiers Kerr (1841-83) of Glasgow, became the protector of the reel and strathspey tunes, but interest in them gradually faded with the neglect of the dances themselves. In the " Eighties " a revival of interest in the old dances and their music was shown in Edinburgh when the Highland Reel and Strathspey Society was formed (1881), which was due mainly to the lead given by James Stewart Robertson (b. 1823), who edited the *Athole Collection of the Dance Music of Scotland* (Edin., 1884), the largest collection of its kind. To the choicest of the dance tunes of the 18th century, John Glen brought his unrivalled knowledge to bear when he presented his historical and biographical survey of the subject in the *Glen Collection of Scottish Dance Music* (Edin., 1891, 1895), a work that will long remain a mine of authoritative information.

In the foregoing we get a fairly reliable picture of the continued popularity of the national music in Scotland although, as has been pointed out, the music of the dance waned in public esteem. There was of course, much more of this music published than what has been quoted—scores of cheap collections and even chap-books (in the modern connotation of the term), as well as reams of sheet music. The melodies were also issued for flute, fife and violin so as to meet the purses of the working class. Some singers made the *auld sangs* a speciality, and one of the first to do this was John Wilson (1800-49) who, despite his success in opera, found the lecture-recital in " Nights with Burns," " Jacobite Songs," and similar entertainments, much more to his taste and profit. David Kennedy (1825-86) followed the same path, even to making a reputation in America and the Colonies. Thomas H. McGhie (1845-85) successfully featured Jacobite songs, whilst Jessie McLachlan (1866-1916) attracted attention because she particularized in the old Gaelic songs.

It was during this century that the national music of Scotland drew the attention of people beyond these shores. Herder (1744-1803) had already awakened Germany to the beauty of the Scots song, and Adolf Marx (1795-1866) in his *Kunst des Gesanges* (1826) gave various examples of Scottish melodies and analyzed them saying :—" They are invaluable, and no musician, and especially no singer, should be unacquainted with them." Beginning, as we have seen, with George Thomson's enticement of Haydn, Kotzeluch, Pleyel and Beethoven to contribute arrangements to his famous collection of Scottish airs, the national music gradually extended its fascination to many other outside composers, although, as Sir Alexander C. Mackenzie once facetiously remarked, " The kilt does not become the foreigner (*British Musician*, April, 1895). Ries (op. 101), Czerny (op. 557) and Moscheles (op. 75, 80) show how *schottische Volkslieder* had deeply attracted them, just as the *schottische*, as a dance form, had persuaded their forefathers. Mendelssohn, who visited Scotland (1829), revealed the impress in *Fingal's Cave* overture, the *Scotch Symphony* and the *Scottish Sonata* (op. 28), whilst Taubert (op. 30), Dreyschock (*Airs Écossais*), Reinecke (*Schottische Volkslieder*), Max Bruch (*Schottlands Tränen, Schottische Phantasie* and *Schottische Lieder*), Niels Gade (Overture *Im Hochland*), and Sarasate (*Airs Écossais*), also fell under the spell, with Paganini, Ole Bull, and Barth featuring the old airs with their wizard hands.

In accordance with what has been recorded in previous chapters, there is still the original work of the " fiddlers " to be envisaged, although their productions may not be meat for ordinary stomachs. In spite of a falling off in the patronage of the national dances, its composers were as inclined as ever to show their mettle in producing strathspey and reel, even though but rarely with much signs of originality.   There was James Walker (d. 1840) of Dysart, who published a *Collection of New Scots Reels, Strathspeys, Jigs* . . . (Dysart, 1797), with another (Dysart, 1800).   On the more original side was John Pringle of Edinburgh, whose *Collection of Reels, Strathspeys* (Edin., 1801-2) deserves notice, one strathspey, *Lady Ann Hope*, being especially praised.   John French was also responsible for some catchy *New Strathspey Reels* (Edin., c. 1801). John Morison (1772-1848) published an interesting *Collection of New Strathpey Reels* (Edin., 1801).   He is said to have been a precentor " in St. Peter's Church, Peterhead," but on the title page of his *Marquis of Huntly's Welcome to Peterhead* he is designated " Organist of St. Peter's Chapel " although the *Ordnance Gazetteer* says that its organ was not erected until 1867.

From London came a *Set of Favourite Strathspey Reels* (c. 1810) which seems to show that the great metropolis was still in the throes of the " fling."   A *Collection of Highland Music* (Inverness, 1812) by William Morrison contains good material among the " original " compositions. A sign of freshness was displayed by John Hall (d. 1862) of Ayr in his *Selection of Strathspeys, Reels* (Ayr, 1818) and more so in his autograph *John Hall, his Music Book*, in Glasgow University Library. Donald Grant's *Collection* (Edin., 1790) also strikes a fresh note here and there, whilst the *Collection* (Edin., 1820) of William Christie (1778-1849) has an equal interest, more especially as he was the father of Dean Christie who was responsible for the *Traditional Ballads* (Edin., 1876-81). The original manuscript of Christie's *Collection* (*c.* 1818) is preserved in Aberdeen University Library. An original and distinctive producer was Duncan McKercher (d. 1873) whose two Collections, to which Daniel Menzies also contributed, reach a high water mark, as seen in his *Sir Niel Menzies* strathspey. Alas, " the Athole Paganini," as the Hon. Fox Maule called McKercher, died in poverty in the Edinburgh Royal Infirmary. When Peter Milne (b. 1824) issued a *Selection of Strathspeys* (Keith, n.d.), five editions of it saw light, which showed its evident popularity. Yet the exigency of this music began to diminish owing to the Lowland craze for the gallopade and quadrille, and nothing of any moment emerged until James Scott Skinner (1843-1927) came forward with his *Miller o' Hirn Collection* (Elgin, 1881), the *Elgin Collection* (1884) and the *Logie Collection* (Keith, 1888), in which something of the spirit of the old composers was recaptured.

Finally, a word or two must be spared for those who collected or wrote music for the bagpipe, since *piobaireachd* (piping), whether it be in the *ceòl mór* (classical art) or the *ceòl beag* (popular art), has an enduring claim on most people in the " North Countrie." South of the Border the bagpipe is looked upon as a mere folk instrument, which it gloriously is, without the qualification. That its diction is as alien to Southern ears as the Doric itself, is quite understandable. One could no more expect a crowd in the street to appreciate a Bach fugue than picture the average Southerner trying to apprehend the theme (*urlar*) and variations (*torluath, crùnluath*) in *piobaireachd*. Therefore this particular section will appeal only to the elect. The vedettes in the domain of writing for and on piping were Joseph (1739-62) and Patrick Macdonald (1729-1824), the former being the actual author, and the latter the editor, of *A Collection of Bagpipe Music* (Edin., 1803), which included a " Treatise on the Theory of the Scots Highland Bagpipe." Patrick was the author of the *Highland Vocal Airs* (1784) which has been mentioned in the previous chapter. A contemporary collector was Donald Macdonald, who compiled a *Collection of the Ancient Martial Music of Caledonia* . . . (Edin., 1831), which also contained a tutor. Then came *A Collection of Piobaireachd* (Edin., 1828) by Neil Macleod, and *A Collection of Ancient Piobaireachd* (Edin., 1838) by Angus Mackay (*c*. 1813-59), to which are added " sketches of the principal hereditary pipers and their establishments." He also issued *The Piper's Assistant, a Collection of Marches, Quicksteps, Strathspeys, Reels and Jigs* (Edin., n.d.). William Gunn compiled a similar collection entitled *The Caledonian Repository of Music* (Glasg., 4th edit., 1867). The piper to Queen Victoria, William Ross (*c*. 1815-91), issued *A Collection of Pipe Music* (1869), the second edition (1876) of which was embellished by " an essay on the bagpipe and its music by the Rev. Norman Macleod," whilst a third edition (1885) showed its continued popularity. Donald MacPhee (1841-80) of Coatbridge, was responsible for *A Selection of Music for the Highland Bagpipe* (Glasg., 1876), and *Marches, Quicksteps, Reels, and Strathspeys, and Collection of Pibrochs* (Glasg., 1879). From Edinburgh came the well-known *Collection for the Great Highland Bagpipe* (Edin., n.d.) of John Glen (1833-1904) and Robert Glen (1835-1911). Alexander Glen (1801-73) was the compiler of *The Caledonian Repository of Music for the Great Highland Bagpipe* (2nd edit., Edin., 1870), whilst his son David (b. 1850) issued *A Collection of Highland Bagpipe Music* (Edin., 1876-80), and other music for the instrument.

As I have said elsewhere (*The Art Review*, 1945), " the bagpipe has a homely attraction for the Scots. Not that the instrument is peculiar to Scotland, to repeat a Sassenach legend, but rather because Scotland is the only part of the British Isles in which this Mediaeval instrument survives with any degree of popularity,

despite spasmodic leanings towards it in Eire and Northumbria."
Naturally, it has not the appeal that it had in days of yore when, as
Robert Nicholl said :

> " In weal, as in wae—amid tears, amid wine,
> The bagpipe aye moved the bauld hearts o' lang-syne."

Yet it still has its place at the august ceremony, the martial throng,
and the cottage door.

CHAPTER 2

THE CHURCH

" The use of organs in the public worship of God is *contrary to the
law of the land*, and to the law and constitution of our Established
Church."

Glasgow Presbytery (1807).

" We are surprised at the simplicity, the beauty, the spirit which
animates Scotland's *now forgotten melodies* of former days."

MAINZER : *Standard Psalmody* (1845).

Scotland was, perhaps, the only land where the use of the organ
in public worship was considered " contrary to the law " and certainly the only country in Europe that was not proud of its old
Reformation music. Yet however strange the former may appear
to us in the 20th century, this state of affairs continued in Scotland,
so far as the established church was concerned, until 1864. The
above finding of the Glasgow Presbytery of 1807 was due to the
Lord Provost and other stern puritans seeking an injunction against
the Rev. Dr. William Ritchie of St. Andrew's Church, Glasgow,
who had dared to introduce an organ into his church service, in
spite of a warning not to do so the previous year. As the
quotation indicates, the verdict went against this progressive minister
who, thoroughly disgusted, sought freedom elsewhere, and was
" translated " to Edinburgh, eventually to become Professor of
Divinity at the University. A contemporary caricature depicts
Ritchie on his way to the capital as an organ grinder playing
I'll gang nae mair to yon toun.

The incident created great disquiet in the dovecotes of Presbyterian purity, and a war of pamphleteers ensued. The High

Priest of the opposition was the Rev. Dr. James Begg, formerly minister (1794-1801) of the Calton Chapel, Glasgow, but afterwards of New Monkland, who published a *Treatise on the use of Organs and other Instruments of Music in the Worship of God* (Glasg., 1808). The gauntlet in defence of the organ was lifted by the Rev. Alexander Fleming (1770-1845), the minister of Neilston, who replied with *Letters on the subject of the Organ which . . . was introduced into St. Andrew's Church, Glasgow : To which are added remarks on the Rev. James Begg's Treatise on the use of Organs* (Glasg., 1808) and *Answer to a Statement of the proceedings of the Presbytery of Glasgow, relative to the use of an Organ* (Glasg., 1808). The arguments of the anti-organ crowd read like something from the Middle Ages. In point of fact there is no real argument since all that we get is a " Thus saith the Lord " attitude, which is merely

> " The dark lanthorn of the spirit
> Which none can see by but those who bear it."

Reason is dispensed with and what takes its place is a text from the Bible. Yet these types of pious puerilities against the use of the organ in church went on for over half a century, being prompted, not by the laity who, as George Farquhar said in one of his plays, " paid their tithes to be kept in obscurity," but by Rev. D.D.'s who, often out of sheer venality, sought publicity.

Before this had occurred, a situation had arisen at Glasgow Cathedral which cannot be overlooked because it seems to show that by this time the Presbyterian Church was really only averse to the organ when it was considered as an accompaniment to its service. We have seen that the Sacred Music Institution, reared by the Episcopal organist John Fergus, had installed an organ in the Trades' House, where it held its meetings and concerts, but in 1798, when the Society gave a concert in the Cathedral, we are told that the vocal solos were sung " with an organ accompaniment." Since there was no such an instrument at the Cathedral at that time, we can only conclude that a portable organ, then rather common, had been brought into the Cathedral specially for the purpose.

The incident reveals that the authorities at the Cathedral could have had no animus against the organ as such. This tolerant attitude is seen to even better advantage in 1803, when the Glasgow magistrates permitted the Society to remove its organ from the Trades' House and erect it at the east end of the choir of the Inner High Church of the Cathedral in what was presumably the organ loft of pre-Reformation times, for it was within the Cathedral that the Society had been permitted to hold its gatherings. The Society was dissolved in 1805, but the organ remained in the sacred precincts until 1812 when it was sold to St. Andrew's Episcopal Chapel, where it is still in use, although considerably altered and enlarged. In view of the Ritchie perturbation outlined above, it is passing strange that some Presbyterian stalwart did not hint that there was an organ actually standing in the Inner High Kirk itself, as this part of the Cathedral was called. A century and a half earlier (1643) its very presence would certainly have been considered " scandalous."

Notwithstanding Ritchie's failure to introduce the organ in 1807, an even more determined effort was made by the Relief Church, Roxburgh Place, Edinburgh, which, in 1818, 1821, and 1823, had given the question of the use of an organ very serious consideration. This culminated in 1828, when the minister, the Rev. John Johnstone, *and his congregation*, installed an organ in their church, one argument for their action being that the Church of Scotland itself had permitted organs in churches in Calcutta and Jamaica ! The minister was called to account by the Relief Synod for this " great temerity," when it ordered him to adhere to the Church's ruling on the question or be dismissed. Rather than submit both he and his congregation severed their connection with the Synod. The instrument itself was later acquired by the Roman Catholic Chapel of St. Margaret's Convent. Once again there was strife in print. The Rev. William Anderson (1799-1872), minister of the United Presbyterian Church, Glasgow, wrote *An Apology for the Organ as an Assistance of Congregational Psalmody* (Glasg., 1829), to which the Rev. James Russel penned a counterblast " lamenting the recent innovation," saying that the organ " elevated inarticulate sound into the same level with the human voice." Other pamphlets were :—*Nugae Organicae* (Glasg., Edin., 1829), *Organs and Presbyterians* (Edin., 1829), *A new Stop to the Organ* (1829), and *Instrumental Music in Public Worship* (1829).

It is quite interesting to notice how even some of the really musical clergy sat on the fence in this conflict, and among them was the Rev. Dr. Andrew Mitchell Thomson (1778-1831). In his preface to Robert A. Smith's *Edinburgh Sacred Harmony* (Edin., 1829), at the very meridian of the heat, he averred that he " wished not to debate the question." At the same time, he made it quite clear that " in the place of a good and well-played organ " he preferred " a good and well-trained choir." That significant nod gave him a place in Russel's camp and his anti-organ party, yet as he did not want to offend the pro-organ community, he admitted that " in training and practising the choir, we should always make use of the organ . . . in order to give the singers the habit of sustaining their voices at the proper pitch."

The next onslaught by the organ enthusiasts came from a body of Independents at North College Street Church in Edinburgh, where the Rev. Dr. Lindsay Alexander (1808-84), an eminent Scottish divine of the Congregational persuasion, was minister. Since the congregation itself was its own ruler, there was no dissent when, in 1845, an organ was erected in this church. This meant that, in addition to the Episcopalians and the Roman Catholics, the Congregationalists were now using the organ. Little impressed by this, the Presbyterians maintained their attitude of forbiddance. Russel's treatise against the organ was re-issued in 1858, but Anderson's reply had reached a 3rd edition in the same year, which shows that there was even more demand for a tolerant attitude. A common-sense point of view was enunciated in a tract, *The Sacrifice of Praise* (Glasg., 1858) by " A Precentor," in which he affirmed that " an organ in church, for the celebration of God's praise, is quite in accordance with the Holy Scriptures." He saw that " the psalmody of the Presbyterian Church of Scotland has sunk to a very low ebb " and expressed the view that an organ " of fine tone, and played by a skilful performer, is certainly superior to a multitude of voices, where a large proportion are untrained and discordant."

In the year 1863, the Rev. Robert Lee of the famous Greyfriars' Church, Edinburgh, who was already known as a reformer in the Presbyterian service, introduced an *harmonium* into his church. Once again the old cry of " Popery " was heard, and " Jesuit in disguise " was hurled at the head of the innovator. Little perturbed, Dr. Lee so ably defended his case for instrumental music that the General Assembly of 1864 decided that " such innovations should only be put down when they interfered with the peace of the Church and harmony of congregations." Armed by this resolution, Dr. Lee then installed an organ at a cost of £450 which was first heard in April, 1865. The battle was won constitutionally, although there was still much opposition from congregations to be overcome, as we know from the *Glasgow Herald* of 1866, in which year St. Andrew's Church, Glasgow, once more tried to instal an organ. Indeed, William Carnie (*The Revised Northern Psalter*, 1900) says that " organs and harmoniums were few and far between " until 1873. At the Presbyterian outposts the position was still difficult. In a work entitled *Instrumental Music in the Church of Scotland* (1872), by the Minister [the Rev. David Johnston] of the United Parishes of Harray and Birsay in the Orkneys, the author thought that the organ was the sign of the anti-Christ, and pointed out that Old Greyfriars, Edinburgh, where the organ had first gained a hearing in 1863, had become " a public platform for the open dissemination of rationalism, scepticism, and infidelity."

Yet the Free Church was not disposed to capitulate without a struggle. She was still impressed by the philippics of old Dr. James Begg and the arguments of Dr. Robert S. Candlish (1806-73), the latter being the author of *The Organ Question : Statements by Dr. Ritchie and Dr. Porteous for and against* (Edin., 1856). James Begg *secundus* (1809-83) also supported the views of his father, and issued *The Use of Organs and Other Instruments of Music in Christian Worship Indefensible* (Glasg., 1866) and *Instrumental Music unwanted in the Worship of God.* Fate willed it that his son, William Begg, became the well-known actor " Walter Bentley." Among the protagonists of the instrument were the Rev. Alexander Cromar at Liverpool, who wrote *A Vindication of the Organ* (Edin., 1866) which was a reply to Dr. Candlish. In the West, the Rev. Henry Batchelor upheld the cause in his *Instrumental Music in Christian Worship* (Glasg., 1866). Opposition to the organ finally succumbed in 1872 and 1883, when the General Assemblies of the United Presbyterian Church and the Free Church of Scotland respectively withheld further opposition. To-day in Scotland most churches, whatever their denomination may be, admit the organ or other instrumental music within their walls and into their services. Thus, in some respects, we are back to where we were in pre-Reformation times. Yet only a few pages earlier we saw those same Presbyterians eschewing the " kist o' whistles," just as they did the designation " Reverend Father," as things " unscriptural " and " Papistical." Nowadays the " Organ Recital" and the appellation " Right Reverend " or " Very Reverend " are looked upon as desiderata in the Church of Scotland. The wheel of progress most certainly turns slowly yet just as surely.

That Presbyterian church music generally was in a poor way in Scotland in the early years of the century, much of it being due to the absence of a choir and organ, was everywhere unmistakably apparent. So early as 1817 the thoughtful George F. Graham pleaded for organs and choirs, but Presbyterian ears were deaf. George Hogarth, the music critic and historian, himself a Scot and deeply interested in psalmody, which was the church's only musical outlet, put his finger on the source of the trouble. In his *Musical History* (Lond., 1838) he points out that, in Scotland, " the psalms are generally sung in unison, . . . but in congregations, among whom there is some musical knowledge, an imperfect harmony is produced by the bass and other parts." Secondly, as he wisely observed, " many books of psalmody have been, and still continue to be, . . . produced by very incompetent persons, . . . filled with mean and vulgar tunes, and crude and incorrect harmonies.

The circulation of so many books of this description has tended very much to injure parochial singing, though the evil could easily be remedied by the clergymen and other persons in authority taking care that no books of psalmody were used in places of worship but such as are of known and established character."

All this was nothing new to the land. It had been going on, more or less, since the opening of the 17th century. In those days the Church was, in theory, able to control the publication of psalm books, that is to say, only those who could claim *cum privilegio* dare print them. In practice however, since the Church did not always countenance the skilled professional musician, it was unable in every case to control even the numerous typographical errors, which gave currency to wrong notes. The Church could get into high dudgeon when it espied an " objectionable " *secular song* in one of Bassandyne's psalters, but to objectional *notes*, it was quite unabashed. Yet the Roman Church took care, and still takes care, precious care, that its service books are thoroughly scanned before it appends its *imprimatur*. By the second half of the 18th century onwards to the 19th century, printers issued psalm books with little interference from those who held the licence as King's Printer. The result was that the most insignificant precentor, without any real musical qualification, issued his psalm book, with the appalling consequences of which George Hogarth complains.

In Edinburgh and the other principal towns, as Hogarth also notes, the more independent of the clergy were beginning to seek for some improvement in psalmody and its performance by producing carefully edited psalm and hymn books, as well as by forming " little choirs of trained singers to lead the congregation," although they had seen these features, *plus* the organ, in the Episcopal and Roman Churches for half a century or more. Among the first to make an effort in this direction was the Rev. Dr. Andrew Mitchell Thomson of St. George's Edinburgh who, with Robert A. Smith, issued their *Sacred Harmony for the Use of St. George's Church* (Edin., 1820). I have previously mentioned that he aimed at " a good and well-trained choir " because, as a keen musician, he wanted the best.   Yet because he was also a good Presbyterian he still hankered after congregational voices as the primary consideration.   He speaks in the preface to R. A. Smith's *Edinburgh Sacred Harmony* (1829) about " mere artists, or mere amateurs " not being equal to promoting " spiritual edification, and contributing to our purest and loftiest enjoyment," which gift, he says, is reserved only " for those whose love of music is accompanied with the heartfelt experience of that religion which lifts the soul to God and Heaven."   Unfortunately we are faced with the unpleasant truth that however near the singers whom he preferred might be to deity and the empyrean, they were still liable to sing wrong notes, whereas the " mere artists " were not so prone to err.   It looks as though Thomson realized this, since he urges that the congregation should only join in " a subdued voice," for the good man had not the courage of a James Beattie to say :—" I entreat those who sing ill, not to sing at all, at least *in the church*."

Thomson's coadjutor was Robert A. Smith (1780-1829), whose *Sacred Music . . . Tunes, Sanctuses, Doxologies* (Edin., 1825), *Sacred Harmony of the Church of Scotland* (Edin., 1828), together with his previously mentioned works, contributed to arouse the country in a demand for better church music.   Nor should the *Supplement to R. A. Smith's Sacred Harmony* by James S. Geikie, and his *Songs of the Sanctuary* be overlooked in this effort at improvement.   In Glasgow, James Steven (d. *c.* 1830), a music seller who led the psalmody at the University Hall, issued a *Selection of Psalm and Hymn Tunes* (Glasg., 1801), with subsequent works of some import.   Alexander Duncan (*c.* 1796-1863), later the precentor of the Outer High Church, Glasgow, compiled *The Choir* (Glasg., 1828) with a preface by the above cited Rev. William Anderson (1799-1872).   Choirs were being favourably received in some quarters and in 1832 a Glasgow newspaper was advocating more " bands," i.e. choirs.   In *The Psalmody of the Free Church of Scotland* (Edin., 1845) there were frowns at such things, and it was stated that " the foreign aid of instruments or of a trained band " was not required.   Even in 1852 the same church still thought the choir was " objectionable." For the Synod of Relief, the Rev. William Anderson edited *The Sacred Choir* (Glasg., 1841) and a *Selection of Psalm and Hymn Tunes* (Glasg., 1844). In the north there was John Daniel (1803-81) who edited *The National Psalmody of the Church of Scotland* (1837) and James Davie (*c.* 1783-1857), conductor of the Aberdeen Choral Society, whose *Music of the Church of Scotland* (Aberdeen, 1841) has some interesting " Remarks on Church Music." In *The People's Tune Book* (Aberdeen,1844) by William Smith (1803-78) we see how deeply ears were being attuned to Anglican ideas, although the collection was intended as " a manual of Psalmody for Scotland." In the south-east, one observes the same influence, which was strengthened by the Episcopal Church of Scotland's later music books—*A Collection of Church Music* (Edin., 1843-44) by John T. Surenne (1814-78) and Henry E. Dibdin (1813-66), and the *British Psalmody* (Edin., *c.* 1848) of Alexander Hume (1811-59).

The foregoing works reveal the growing activity of organists and precentors during this first half-century in the matter of psalters and the like, and they also indicate a mounting evil that Hogarth forgot to specify. Whilst the above books do not display the " incompetence " in editing and the " incorrect harmonies " of which he complains, they do multiply the already crowded market of *different* harmonies and arrangements which, as we shall see presently, had to be halted. Yet the adoption of harmony, whether correct or incorrect, was only to be found in a few progressive churches. This is vouched for by the *Report of the Association for the Revival of Sacred Music* (Edin., 1845) which says :—" Until within the last two years it would have been a difficult matter to have found *twenty* persons . . . singing any psalms in four parts." It has also to be regretfully noted that the neglect of the old Scottish psalms continued apace. The indifference roused no protest from the Scots themselves, and only one man seems to have tried to re-awaken interest in the treasures of the glorious past, and he was a foreigner, Joseph Mainzer (1801-51), who essayed to shame

the people out of their apathy and disregard, and this is what he
said :—

> " While the Protestants of Germany, Switzerland, Sweden,
> and Bohemia, cling with veneration and almost filial devotion
> to the psalm tunes of the Reformation, and consider them
> as a sacred trust, as a national legacy . . . the Presbyterians of
> Scotland have been taught melodies of other countries, of
> which many have not even borrowed their inspiration from
> the Church—their own psalmody, one of the most beautiful
> musical remnants of the Reformation, being allowed to perish
> unnoticed, and fall into oblivion."

The first to respond to this clarion call was an Englishman, Henry
Edward Dibdin (1813-66), who had settled in Edinburgh (1833)
and was honorary organist at Trinity Chapel there. In his *Standard
Psalm-Tune Book* (Lond., 1851), which contains six hundred
specimens, most of the old tunes from the Scottish psalter were
included. The title page claimed that they were " compiled from
the original editions," but actually many were abridged and were set
to new harmonies. Yet the chief point is that in this work, which
was intended for general purposes, the old Scottish psalm-tunes
were thought worthy of inclusion, but the Church of Scotland took
not the slightest advantage of it. Indeed, not a solitary voice
was raised in Scotland, either by way of apology or explanation, in
regard to this shameful neglect of the old psalm-tunes, until the
gracious hand of the Rev. Neil Livingston (1803-91) appeared in
protest in his historic reprint of *The Scottish Metrical Psalter of* 1635
(Glasg., 1864), whose sentiments were re-echoed by the Rev.
John West Macmeeken (*c.*1825-80) in his *History of the Scottish
Metrical Psalms* (Glasg., 1872). Who was to blame for this disgraceful unconcern ? Certainly not the precentors. In most cases
these were not skilled musicians and, as Livingston points out,
nine-tenths of them were probably quite ignorant that the old
psalms existed. Even if they had known, it was not their place to
express opinions on such matters, as more than one kirk session
records reveal. It was only the clergy that had the right to say

Yea or Nay, a sufferance which many an organist even to-day in Scotland has to endure. Of course the reason for all this is simply explained, as we read in *The Sacrifice of Praise* by " A Precentor " (Glasg., 1858),—" Few office bearers, and still fewer ministers, know anything of music."

In the second half of the century, as a step towards some regulation in the music of the Presbyterian Church, and as a dam against the ingress of the innumerable psalm books of doubtful quality, the Free Church began to gather up its trailing garments in this respect. In 1852, it issued *Practical Suggestions for the Improvement of Church Music* (Edin., 1852), wherein there were bemoanings that the universal complaint was that the practices for psalmody were so thinly attended that they were now being abandoned. A mutual improvement association to bring about a betterment was suggested, and the securing of the services of professional musicians was outlined with a recommendation that the " position of the precentor must be elevated." Church music was " surely entitled to something more than the fag-end of a man's time. . . . Our precentors must be *teachers of music*, and nothing short of this will elevate our psalmody." At the same time it was made quite clear that these improvements were not to lead to the establishment of choirs. Such things, says the pamphlet, " have been found objectionable, on the ground of their concentrating *all* the good singers, and tempting the congregation to sit and listen to them," a statement which shows that in psalmody the mind of the Church was still back in Reformation days. What was aimed at, said the leaflet, was a " Presbyterial singing " that would " eclipse the heartless choir, and rival—nay, surpass—the thunders of the organ," which latter, by the way, was still anathema to the Church.

Yet the greatest drawback to any improvement was the want of a standard psalm book. The country, it was stated, was being " deluged with tune books, . . . and new works are appearing every day," each one being harmonized differently from the one published earlier. It was admitted that part-singing was " only in its infancy " in the Free Church, but its cultivation was to be encouraged, and this could only be brought about by the adoption of a standard psalter. Such a work the Free Church had just issued under the editorship of Thomas L. Hately (1815-67) who, with Hogarth, had edited *The Psalmody of the Free Church of Scotland* (1845). This newly proposed standard book was the *Scottish Psalmody* (Edin., 1852), a work which, according to Mackmeeken (*Scottish Metrical Psalms*, 1872), created " quite an era in the modern history of music " ! In its choice of tunes the Free Church Committee was determined that " it would bind down our congregations to the use of only genuine ecclesiastical tunes, and save the infliction of the employment of jigs and rants—a distraction to Presbyterian worship, and a disgrace to Presbyterian Scotland." Yet there were things introduced into the *Scottish Psalmody* (1852) which might also be considered a disgrace. The Committee gave vent to effusions about the " noble melodies of our martyr forefathers " but, strangely enough, they ignored most of the melodies of that valiant band, and actually spurned all the harmonies of the adepts of the old Scottish psalters from 1615 to 1635.

In 1862 the Church of Scotland also began to look into its music with a view to improvement, although this only came as the result of an overture sent to the General Assembly by the Presbytery of Paisley. Yet it was only the persistence of an enthusiastic music-lover, Alexander T. Niven, that a committee on psalmody was appointed, on which the latter served, later as convener, labouring unceasingly in the cause of better psalmody until he retired in 1882 as a protest against " the funds of the Psalmody Committee being diverted . . . from their legitimate purpose in improving psalmody and raising the qualifications and status of precentors." Even the Glasgow Choral Union took a hand in this effort at " improvement in church psalmody " by giving concerts to demonstrate the class of music that was suggested as a means of improvement. Special prominence was given to the English anthem which, said the directors of the Choral Union, was " too little known in Scotland," and they recommended it because it " is always of a sound and dignified character." This expression of opinion was

contained in the Union's printed programme, which also stated that
" Italy and even Germany had degenerated " in their church music,
a statement which seems to have given umbrage to some people,
because a second printing of the same programme omits this
passage !

Even the Free Church was still not satisfied with what it had
accomplished in 1852, although a new edition of .the *Scottish
Psalmody* was published in 1856. In 1867, under the convenership
of the " Old Mortality " of psalmody, the Rev. Neil Livingston, its
Committee on Psalmody tried to introduce some of the older
psalms which contained " a much greater diversity of metre," the
opinion being held, and rightly so, that the existing psalm book
had " a large amount of literary and musical monotony, which is
fitted to diminish the interest felt in praise." Once more it was
recommended " to raise the status of precentors," a principle
strongly advocated by the Scottish Vocal Music Association in
1856. It had been pointed out by this association that even in the
days of Nehemiah (II *Chron.*, xxiii, 13) " Chenaniah, chief of the
Levites, instructed about the song, *because he was skilful*," but,
said the association, it was quite impossible to obtain " skilful "
men " on a salary of £5, £10, or, in munificent cases, £20 a year."
Yet little of material advantage accrued from all this agitation.
" A Precentor " in 1858 pleaded that " so long as the Precentor is
obliged to work as a tradesman . . . it is unreasonable to expect
him to discharge his duties in the church satisfactorily " (*The
Sacrifice of Praise*).

Hymns and their like were among other aspects of church music
that came up for consideration. Since the adoption of Scriptural
Songs or Paraphrases in 1781, the Church of Scotland now
possessed sixty-two of these sacred songs, in addition to the one
hundred and fifty psalms. Yet much more were accepted by the
Dissenters. The United Presbyterians, for instance, possessed
some four hundred and sixty hymns as well as twenty-three doxologies, and so the Church of Scotland began to extend its repertory.
In 1868 its Committee submitted a report which contained some

healthy points of view.   Some two hundred hymns were planned
for recognition in a *Scottish Hymnal*, together with the insistence
on a national outlook, and the importance of fresh metres.   In
1870 it was recommended that there be a " return to the old rule
of special music to each psalm or hymn," and the establishment of
the *Scottish Hymnal*.   In this same year the Free Church Assembly
began deliberations on Paraphrases and Hymns, and the next year
a sub-committee on the revision of Scottish Psalmody was appointed
to consider " What tunes should be omitted as bad ? . . . What
tunes are of doubtful character ?   What tunes require alteration
in melody or in harmony ? "   It sat under the vice-convener, Colin
Brown, the Euing Lecturer on Music at Anderson's College,
Glasgow.   From the report issued in October of that year, we see
that the temporary tinkering with the question was still going on,
just as it had been since the old psalter was discarded in 1650.
During the last quarter of the century the Presbyterian Church
in Scotland came to a final decision and new psalters and hymnals
were given an official *imprimatur*.   Of these were the *United
Presbyterian Hymnal* (1877), the *United Presbyterian Psalter* (1878),
the *Free Church Hymnal* (1882), the *Scottish Psalter* (1883), the
Scottish Hymnal (1885), *Psalms and Paraphrases* (1886), and the
Presbyterian Hymnal, Scripture Sentences and Chants (1886), all
published by the authority of the Synod of the United Presbyterian
Church, the General Assembly of the Church of Scotland, and the
General Assembly of the Free Church of Scotland.

   The contents of these works have been exhaustively studied by
James Love (1858-1928) in his admirable *Scottish Church Music*
(Edin., 1891), and from his careful indexing of the music we see
what little endeavour had been made to remedy the defects of two
centuries in the disregard of the old melodies.   Out of over one
thousand two hundred tunes to be found in the above books, there
are included from the old Scottish psalters—eight from the 1565
psalter, seven from that of 1615, and ten from that of 1635.   Of
18th and 19th Century Scottish composers, or tunes from Scottish
books of that period, there are fifty-five examples.   Of the latter

some remarks will be expressed in the appropriate place. Of the former, i.e. the old psalm tunes, there was some slight improvement in the numbers made available, there being twenty-five included against " some half dozen," as Livingston said, which had been previously recognized. Why there was not a more generous comprehension of the older material cannot be understood, although looking facts squarely in the face it would seem highly probable that the editors were out of touch or sympathy with the old psalters. Dr. Albert Lister Peace, who was not a Scot, was one of these. In justice to many of the old psalm tunes, more especially after comparison with some of those which squeezed them out of the newer Scottish psalters and hymnals, one is compelled to say that twenty-five, the number admitted by the new dispensation, was not enough. Even if the opinions of Livingston (1864) and Macmeeken (1872) were leavened by devotional or patriotic leanings in their appraisement of the old material, this charge will not hold good against the earlier evaluation by an outsider like Mainzer (1845), nor could this be urged against the carefully expressed sentiments of one who was without any sectarian or national bias in this matter and I refer to the late Sir Richard R. Terry, who said :—

" I think the day is coming when Scotland will return to these noble tunes, and that the future generation will atone, by its appreciation, for the unmerited oblivion to which they have too long been consigned "—(*A Forgotten Psalter*, 1929).

CHAPTER 3

THE TEACHING OF MUSIC

" In the mass of our schools music forms no part of systematic instruction ; and though in many an attempt is made at singing, the results are generally meagre and very unsatisfactory."

Scottish Music Vocal Association : *Tract* (1856).

The above picture of music in the schools of Scotland in the mid-19th Century, drawn by a certain James Valentine of Aberdeen, is limned in rather drab, grey tints, but it bears out the testimony of Andrew Aird (*Glimpses of Old Glasgow*, 1894) that " forty years ago, it might be said that the schoolmaster was abroad so far as musical education . . . was concerned." Yet perhaps this only portrays what might be termed the official attitude towards music, since we know that outside the school the fervour with which both vocal and instrumental music was prosecuted in Scotland was admitted even south of the border. Further, it must be remembered that in the old parish schools that existed before the Education Act (Scotland) of 1872, it was only the "Three R's" that really mattered. Apparently the aspect towards music teaching had worsened by 1850. Earlier in the century the state of affairs was not so bad, at least not in Glasgow and Edinburgh. In the former, in the year 1816, music was certainly not recognized in the University and High School curricula, although the latter actually owed its origin to the *Sang Schuile* of pre-Reformation days. Yet in eight of the endowed schools known as the Charity and Free Schools, vocal music was taught, which reflects rather well on the " Second City." The unofficial attitude was even better still since in every one of the ten boarding schools both vocal and instrumental music were part of the instruction, whilst of private teachers of music within the city, sixteen imparted the vocal art, and thirteen the instrumental, which shows a fair average of music teachers *per capita* in a population of 120,000. Against this view, however, is the fact that whilst vocal music stood with foreign languages in the matter of fees at 10s. 6d. and 15s. a month, instrumental music was the most expensive of all, the cost being 31s. 6d., 42s., and 52s. 6d. a month, which might be taken as evidence that the demand was greater than the supply.

Attempts at organising the teaching of music were frequent in the first half-century. In Glasgow, a Union of Precentors had been formed in 1811, but we have little knowledge of its didactic activities. We know that several precentors conducted classes, notably Andrew Thomson and John Anderson, at the John Street Relief Session House, which prompts the remark that it is passing strange how often we find dissenters in the van of progress. Indeed, it was generally the " chapels " that provided choirs at concerts. In Edinburgh a Church Music Society was established in 1810, and from its " Regulations " (1818) we see that there were classes, presumably, as in the foregoing, for church music only. Then appeared the Institution of Sacred Music in 1815, a foundation which seems to point to dissatisfaction with the preceding society. It certainly advertised for pupils who would be instructed *gratis*. These were taught by John Mather (1781-1850), a very efficient Episcopal organist, and it was for these classes that George F. Graham (1789-1867) issued his *Elements of Singing* (Edin., 1817). The Institution did not last long. The first real attempt to form a definite music school was that established by David Hamilton (1803-63), the organist of St. John's Episcopal Chapel, Edinburgh, when he founded a School of Music attached to the chapel in 1838. This school, says Robert A. Marr (*Music for the People*, 1889) did " good work " for several years, and had some teachers of repute in Edmund Edmunds (1809-1900), J. R. Durner (1810-59), and Carl Drechsler (1800-73), yet a wide cultural influence could scarcely be expected since it was an Episcopal School, a foundation not likely to be a recommendation in Presbyterian eyes. Still, in spite of the lack of public teaching of music, the psalm books of the Presbyterian Church invariably contained a fairly adequate " Introduction " on the elements of music, of which a good example is to be seen in Brown's-Robertson's *Selection of Sacred Music* (Glasg., c.1830). Indeed, it would not be too much to say that the people of Scotland were far better instructed in music than the English, a circumstance due mainly to the Presbyterian psalm books. In the schools of the north quite a high standard had been reached, as we know from *The Schoolmaster's Musical Assistant* (Aberdeen, *c.*1839), which contains hymns and songs in two, three, and four parts, specially arranged for schools.

What invariably acted as a fillip in the educational sphere was the " new system " which, ever and anon, came on the scene during the first half of the century. The earliest of these concerned the pianoforte, and it was the much-boosted " Logier System " which first showed itself in a pamphlet on the subject published in Glasgow in 1816. The next year Johann B. Logier (1777-1846) himself lectured in Edinburgh, where his teaching attracted some attention, although George F. Graham criticised it in his *General Observations . . . on Mr. Logier's System* (Edin., 1817), published anonymously. When Logier went to Glasgow, a Hungarian music teacher, resident in the city, named Hurka de Monti (*c.*1753-1823), opened a fusillade against the " new system " in a brochure entitled *Strictures on Mr. Logier's System of Musical Education* (Glasg., 1817), in which the chiroplast and the teaching involved was considered " musical quackery." On the other hand, John Donaldson (*c.* 1790-1865), later Professor of Music at Edinburgh University, had rather optimistic views and said that " instead of a little imperfect tinkling, picked up from tuition of a French or Italian valet [possibly a hit at Hurka], the pupil of ordinary capacity and ordinary industry may emulate Corelli, Handel, Haydn and Mozart." Of far greater moment in the didactic sphere was the stir created by the emergence of two outstanding pioneers of " systems," Joseph Mainzer and John Hullah.

Joseph Mainzer (1801-51) arrived in Scotland in 1842 and was so persuasive in his new teaching that a " Provisional Association for Diffusing a Knowledge of the Art of Singing among the Working Classes " was founded with strident fanfares. Classes were formed under Charles Guynemer, a pupil of Catel and Reicha at the Paris Conservatoire, and Edmund Edmunds, late of the Episcopal Music School, for whom Sir Alexander C. Mackenzie has praise in his *A Musician's Narrative*. A circular letter was then sent to the clergy begging their co-operation so that the new instruction could be introduced into the " parochial congregations." The outcome of the appeal was the establishment of the Association for the Revival of Sacred Music in Scotland (1844), a title which reveals a more restricted outlook than that which had been visualized originally. A school was opened in York Place, Edinburgh, which was so successful that more commodious headquarters were built at Randolph Place. Here Mainzer remained until 1848, when he was succeeded by B. Kreutzer and Otto Richter. Thousands of pupils passed through the portals of this school, all attracted and sustained by the clarion call of " Singing for the Million."

Whilst Edinburgh and south-east Scotland were thrilled by Mainzer's schemes, Glasgow and the south-west were hearkening to the gospel of John Hullah (1812-84). This was the " Wilhem Method," a rival teaching, which William H. Lithgow (1806-74), a favourite pupil of Hullah, was advocating in the " Second City." This also started in 1842, and it soon spread far and wide, with pupils reckoned by the thousand. As we know from George Lewis' *Observations on the Present State of Congregational Singing in Scotland* (Edin., 1851), the Wilhem Method even penetrated into Edinburgh, which was Mainzer's stronghold, where it was taught by Peter Cruickshank, whilst Lewis himself introduced it into Selkirk, and the resultant Wilhem Choral Society was the first of its kind in this town.

Although the systems and methods of Logier, Mainzer, and Hullah aroused the greatest enthusiasm in the land, the precise didactic schemes enunciated soon faded, and to-day they are known no more. This was not the fate of the teaching of their successor, John Curwen (1816-80), the author of *An Account of the Tonic Sol-fa Method* (Lond., 1854). The broad principles of solfeggio had been known in Scotland in the mid-eighteenth century, but the modifications and improvements of Curwen soon found fresh disciples following his visit in 1855, when his advocacy led to the establishment of classes under the prompting of a newly founded Scottish Vocal Music Association (1856). In Edinburgh, Thomas

L. Hately (1815-67) became Director of the Association, whilst William D. Read (1808-58) held a similar position in Glasgow. By 1858 the Association had established an " Academy of Music," and was awarding diplomas.   It conducted a graduated course for (1) Elementary, (2) Advanced, (3) Normal (for teachers), and (4) Harmony and Composition, in addition to classes for singing, pianoforte and harmonium.

The mid-century had now passed, but little was being done for the systematic instruction of music in the Parish schools, notwithstanding all the fervour of the masses for music. Wherever we look in the large cities we see that the endowed schools were fairly well provided with music teachers, especially in Edinburgh, and even the Glasgow High School, the stronghold of " classical education," had taken a singing master on its staff.   In the Normal colleges for the training of teachers, music had become part of the curriculum, the Free Church perhaps being the pioneer. In Glasgow, where Andrew D. Thomson was the teacher (1846-54), his *Training-School Song Book* (1848) was looked upon as a model, although in the Church of Scotland's Training College, Dr. James Currie (1828-86), its Rector, produced *School Songs* of a more worthy character later. The same author's *Elements of Musical Analysis* (Edin., 1858) and *A First Musical Grammar* (Edin., 1873, Lond., 1885), were also noteworthy.   It was not until the Education Act (Scotland) of 1872 brought about the School Board system that any definite progress was made in the ordinary schools. The inspectors' reports for 1872 are eloquent of the disgraceful situation of music in the curriculum.   In the four reports submitted, music is not even mentioned in the first and fourth record.   In the third, it is merely included in the list of extra standard subjects taught, whilst the second gives this statement: " In some schools the pupils sing in parts with skill, taste, and evident enjoyment . . . In others simple melodies are practised, but in probably two-thirds of the schools visited, *no singing was forthcoming* on the day of examination."   This last report covered the counties of Lanark and Renfrew.

Yet the new School Boards soon settled down to work with a worthy captain at the helm in John Hullah, who was the Musical Inspector of Training Schools for the United Kingdom. In 1873 he was appointed " to make himself acquainted with the system of musical instruction pursued in the Normal Schools " in Scotland, and by the following year the prospectus laid down a music course which included the elements of harmony. For those who already had some knowledge of the pianoforte, instruction on this instrument was also provided in one of the Edinburgh schools. There were five Normal Schools in Edinburgh and Glasgow. [Sir] Alexander C. Mackenzie taught the pianoforte in the Church of Scotland Training College in Edinburgh, whilst Joseph Geoghegan (1830-92), who was music master at several Edinburgh colleges, was responsible for " music." In the Glasgow centre, music was in the hands of William H. Lithgow (d. 1874), who was followed by William Moodie (1833-1915). The Free Church Normal School in Edinburgh had Walter Strang (1825-97) as music master. He was a pupil of Hullah and Crivelli, and was known for his *School Music* (Edin., 1853). At the Glasgow centre was John McLelland, the editor of *Patriotic Songs* (*c.* 1865), specially adapted for schools. He was succeeded by William H. Miller (1831-94), the conductor of the Sol-fa Choral Society, who then became Superintendent of Music in the Glasgow schools.

As the years rolled on, so did more liberal ideas towards " Music in the Schools " find acceptance among educationists, although the rightful place of music in the curriculum was not recognized, nor indeed does it exist to-day either in Scotland or in England. Nowhere has the Pythagorean and Platonic attitude to the art ever been understood, let alone accepted, and by that I mean the cognizance of its moral and social value. As a Chinese philosopher says, " Music is that which unifies," and there is no other subject in the school curriculum that has this power save music and its congeners— verse and action. However slow any new ideas on music in the schools were in taking shape in Scotland, the situation was better than in England, and the last decades of the century brought many changes, as we shall see in the adoption of the school cantata. Little attempt had been made in the special application of teaching music to the younger children. Ann Gunn, in her admirable *Introduction to Music* (Edin., 1803), where the elements of music were explained and taught by means of musical games, opened the door to a fresh approach, but this delectable book has been forgotten by educationists. The first treatise on the alphabet of music for children is actually to be found in an insignificant book by C. H. Bateman entitled *Sacred Melodies for Children* (Edin., 1843), although it was religion and not music *per se*, that was the object of this tiny book. There was no lack of books intended for the instruction of teachers, and school song-books were issued by the dozen, but there was little originality in any of these contributions until the last three decades of the century when, possibly among a hundred or so music books for schools which came from the Scottish printing presses, a few educationists struck a fresh note.

Although we have seen part-singing in the Aberdeen schools in 1839, two books by James Sneddon (1830-1915) Mus. B. (Cantab.), *School Songs New and Old* classified for the standards, and the *Edinburgh Song School*, which was in two- and three-part harmony, led the way in the south. In addition there were two good primers, *The Quick Reader* and *The Alto Trainer* by W. Stewart Roddie (b. 1845) of Glasgow, and *The School Choir* graded for the standards, by William H. Murray (b. 1850), who was also responsible for " Musical Drill " in *The Teacher's Aid*, whilst Robert Booth (b. 1862) wrote and arranged another school song-book, *The Mavis*, which consisted of part-songs, hymns, and anthems, in three-part harmony. More progressive was Alan S. B. Reid (b. 1853), the author of *Music for Pupil Teachers*, *School Music for the Standards*, and *Music and Motion*, the latter being one of the first books of action songs for infants. An outstanding creator of action songs, almost voluminous in his output, was W. Stewart Roddie, most of whose works are indicative, e.g. *The Handkerchief Song*, with kerchief display and movement; *The Dancing Lesson*, which features the gavotte; *The Little Witches*, with broomstick riding; *The Tambourine Song*, that needs the instrument itself for the rhythm, and quite a dozen more items of equal educational and musical value.

What particularly stands to Scotland's credit in the educational sphere is the introduction of children's cantatas and operettas into the schools. The best composer of these was John Charles Grieve (b. 1842) of Edinburgh, who will have fuller recognition among the more eminent composers. Here he calls for notice by reason of his school cantatas, *The Happy Family*, *Playmates*, *Princess Pirliwinkie*, and *The Flowers of the Forest*, so full of graceful, melodious music, and all carrying the pointed moral. His best in this *genre* is a setting of Scott's venturesome story which is here called *The Maid of Rokeby*, a lengthy (two-hours' duration) and effective work. A more prolific composer in this sphere was W. Stewart Roddie already mentioned. His work may not always display the finer musicianship of the preceding, but it certainly shows ingenious settings that admirably fit the situations. Most of these joyously simple and sometimes attractively witty cantatas are of fair dimensions, and among them are *The Sleeping Beauty*, *King of the Seasons*, *Aladdin the Wonderful Scamp*, *The Springtime Holiday*, *Flowers in Concert*, and *The Forest Rovers*. Another who deserves mention is John Murdoch (b. 1849) of Camelon, the composer of *The Holiday Concert*, which gained success so far afield as the colonies. Even more satisfying are his other cantatas *Christ on Earth* and *Rustic Life*, the latter being his best production. His *Falkirk Song Book* for schools created a furore in its day. In this " glorious company of the apostles " of school music stands Alan S. B. Reid of Arbroath, whose children's cantatas, *Friendship's Circle*, *The School Holiday*, *Who is Best?*, the operetta *The Prince and the Peasant*, and the sangspiel *Round ye Clock*, brought fresh zest to school life. Two more writers also deserve a line on this page. One is John Kerr (b. 1859) of Greenock, whose spirited cantatas, *Work and Play*, *The Sultan of Trebizond*, *Sherwood Company Ltd.*, and *The King and the Cobbler*, were great favourites. The other is Alfred Moffat (b. 1866), whose delightful miniature oratorio, *The Childhood of*

Joseph, and similar works, ought long to remain features in this class of musical activity.

Of recent years alas, there has been somewhat of a falling off in the appreciation of this type of work in school curricula, an attitude which is definitely retrograde both from the social and artistic, as well as from the purely educational point of view.   Yet the leaders of modern pedagogy have long insisted on two important principles : (1) The value of the motor factor in education ; and (2) the need for a non-sectarian approach in ethical teaching.   The action songs, such as those of Roddie already specified, go further than any others for the reason that they are not mere movements to musical strains, but illustrative actions indicative of some social activity set to appropriate music.   The school cantata, such as obtained in Scotland, enabled social and ethical ideas to be implanted in the mind of the young with greater efficacy than by the more conventional means.   The music hour has always been the favoured class in schools in Scotland, and in this the goal ought to be the cantata or operetta, for therein lies the making of a musical Scotland.   It may be proper to point out that when Dr. Samuel McBurney (b. 1847) of Glasgow went to Australia, where he eventually became Inspector of Music to the Melbourne Education Department, he took with him the Scottish innovation of cantatas in the schools, of which he himself composed many.

By the last decade of the century, Scotland might be said to have been leading the way in the British Isles in her " Music in the Schools." It was no longer left to the overburdened general teacher to impart the merest elements of the vocal art which had once been the rule.   There were now skilled teachers of music in the Board Schools, with specialists attending periodically to supervise the studies.   Andrew Aird, writing in his *Glimpses of Old Glasgow* (1894), says : " Times have changed.   Music is [now] taught, not only in Glasgow, but all over the country, on well-defined principles, and with the happiest results.   Under the School Board of Glasgow, and in a few denominational schools, upwards of 90,000 children are receiving instruction in singing, at the hands of thoroughly competent teachers ; whilst a staff of visiting masters are in regular attendance, superintending the whole. These children are taught to sing in two parts, and to read the notes at first sight ; and the public demonstrations they give occasionally show that they can do this not only correctly, but also with considerable taste and expression. Many of them are able to write down the melody of a tune on hearing it sung for the first time ; and also rhythms containing various nice divisions of a pulse ; feats that would have sorely puzzled the so-called ' teachers ' of the past generation."

CHAPTER 4

HIGHER EDUCATION

" Music . . . an art and science in which the Scots stand unrivalled by all the neighbouring nations in pastoral melody, and sweet combination of sounds."

The Will of General John Reid (1803).

The ease of Reid's calm conviction disarms all criticism. Indeed it is symptomatic of the Scots. The Greeks would have said that it was the *ethos* of the people of this land to express themselves in this emphatic way. The old general had been used to such " deeds of daring " in his campaigning days, as we see in his other self—Sir Henry Erskine—who set the lines to Reid's *Highland March* as " The Garb of Old Gaul." In the second stanza of the latter the Scots are " as tall as the oak," and it was the claymore, not the sword, that forced " old France " to sue for peace. When Reid wrote of Scotland as " unrivalled " in the " science " of music he must have had the 18th Century theorist Malcolm in his mind's eye and the delightful strains of Erskine and Oswald in his ears when he thought of the " art " of music in similar terms. His exuberance is forgivable, although at that time (1803), Scotland was not producing either theorists or composers, nor was there either a nursery or a training ground for such in Scotland. The theory of music was quite neglected in the higher studies, although in the previous centuries Bœthius was doubtless included in the *quadrivium*.

Music theory in the Scottish Universities was now outwith the liberal arts, and it remained so until 1839, when its presence was merely tolerated, although there were professorships of music at Oxford (1626), Cambridge (1684) and Dublin (1764). The reason for this neglect was obviously the shadow of the old puritanic objection to music, since the Scottish universities were, and still are, officially within the Presbyterian fold. A change of face, though not of heart, came in 1839, when upwards of £68,000 became available under the will of the late General John Reid, of whom we have read in the previous chapter, for the establishment of a Professorship of Music at Edinburgh University. The grasping *senatus*, whilst it did not care a jot for music, could scarcely do otherwise than accept such munificance, but it only gave a mere gesture of tolerance to the professorship of music. Indeed it fixed the lowest possible sum—£300 a year—as the salary of the professor, denied suitable accommodation for the lectures, and misapplied the Reid funds to the tune of many thousands of pounds to alien purposes, including higher emoluments for other professors. Further, a Faculty of Music and the conferring of Degrees in Music were not even contemplated. The first professor appointed was John Thomson (1805-41), a pupil of Schnyder von Wartensee at Leipsic, and he was nominated by General Reid's trustees. As a composer he had won some fame by his London operas *Hermann* and *The Shadow on the Wall*, as we shall see, but he was better appreciated in the north by his *Vocal Melodies of Scotland* (Edin., 1836, *et seq.*) and his lighter compositions. Despite the indifference and the parsimony of the University, although he gave no lectures, Thomson aimed at fulfilling the aims of the founder in the practical requirements and gave the first Reid Concert on the 12th February, 1841, the founder's birthday anniversary, although before many months had passed his career was cut short by his early death. It it worth remembering that the programme, or book of words for this concert, contained analytical notes which were, according to *Grove's Dictionary of Music*, " probably the first instance of such a thing." Indeed, Thomson wrote concert analyses even earlier, as may be seen in his *Brief Notices of the Music to be Performed by the Professional Society on 3rd March, 1838* (Edin., 1838) and, as the concert session was 1837-38, these notes probably occurred in the 1837 programmes.

Although two Scots, George F. Graham and John Donaldson, as well as the brilliant Samuel S. Wesley, were among the applicants for the vacant professorship, the appointment went to an Englishman [Sir] Henry R. Bishop (1786-1855), who had won wide fame by his stage works, although to-day he may only be remembered by his songs and glees. In Scotland however, he had gained favour by his music to Sir Walter Scott's works that had been dramatized, especially *Guy Mannering* (1816), *Heart of Midlothian* (1819), *The Antiquary*, *Bothwell Brig*, and *Montrose* (1820), as well as by his *Selection of Scottish Melodies* (1812), the *Select and Rare Scottish Melodies* to the words of Hogg, and his music to Burns' *Jolly Beggars* (1818), all of which would have contributed to his success with an uncritical Senate. Obviously such a gifted musician could not have been expected to remain long in a Chair where the conditions, musically and financially, were at the lowest ebb. After two years he resigned, to be precise, in December, 1843, for reasons of " ill-health." The truth is that he looked upon the position as a sinecure, did not lecture, and was not even in residence, hence the call from the Senate for his resignation.

The next holder, also from England, was Henry Hugh Pearson (1815-73), a pupil of Attwood, Tomaschek, and Reissiger. He was quite unknown to fame, although a set of six songs of his had been favourably reviewed by Schumann in Germany, but he was more preciously endowed in another way since he had the good fortune to be the son of the Dean of Salisbury who, in his turn, had been auspiciously placed as a favoured chaplain to George IV. Pearson was appointed in 1844, but he also appears to have found that the professorship would be a waste of good time in the circumstances, and resigned in 1845 without giving a lecture, save to tell the Senate of its mismanagement of the Reid Trust Fund.

Returning to Germany as Hugo Pierson, he gained deserved fame, as his *Faust* music (1854) indicates.

The applicants at the new vacancy were [Sir] Henry R. Bishop, Samuel S. Wesley, Henry J. Gauntlett, Charles Guynemer, and John Donaldson. The last named, John Donaldson, an erstwhile teacher of music, but now an Edinburgh advocate, was the successful candidate. The historian of the University, Sir Alexander Grant, gives the following as a likely explanation of the choice. He says:— " Perhaps the Senatus was disheartened by the ill success of their two appointments of eminent English composers ; [and] they now accepted a local aspirant, whose name does not appear in any book of musical biographies." That statement is not strictly correct. Pearson was *not* at that time an " eminent " English composer, and Donaldson's name *does* appear in a book of musical biographies, to wit, in David Baptie's *Musical Biography*, which Sir Alexander actually used. It is true that little is known of Donaldson's early history but he was in Glasgow as a music teacher in 1811. His name disappears from the *Directory* in 1814, yet apparently he was still in Glasgow in 1817 when Logier made his visit with his chiroplast, on which occasion Donaldson became an ardent supporter. We next find him in Edinburgh. Here, in 1824-25, the *Directory* shows a John Donaldson, Esq., at Writer's Court, but in 1827-28 we can clearly identify the later Professor John Donaldson as an Advocate at 14 Northumberland Street, and for nearly twenty years he followed this profession at various addresses in Edinburgh until 1844-45, when he is found at 12 Rutland Street, at which address the 1845-46 *Directory* dubs him " Advocate and Professor of Theory of Music in the University."

Although not one of his predecessors had lectured at the University, Donaldson was determined to do so, and endeavoured to obtain a class-room for this purpose, but so many obstacles were thrown in his path by the Senate that he appealed to the Patrons of the University, who assigned him a room and agreed to £250 being spent on necessary alterations. When this was done the Senate refused to homologate this arrangement and Donaldson was told by the latter that he would be expected to pay this cost out of his salary—£300 a year ! Donaldson, who was a lawyer, refused to allow the Senate to maladminister the Reid Trust in this high-handed fashion, and although George F. Graham and the Edinburgh and London press had already called attention to the scandal of the Reid Professorship, it was Donaldson who brought the simmering to the boil. In 1849, whilst there were upwards of 200 students enrolled in the music classes, the Senate refused to implement the will of General Reid to enable the professor to carry out his duties. The result was that the Magistrates and Council of the City of Edinburgh, as Patrons of the University, and at Donaldson's petition, instituted an action against the Senate which resulted in a lengthy litigation (1851-55), ending in the Senate being forced to disgorge. It was ordered to build a music department, increase the professor's salary, provide an organ, furnish an annual sum for the purchase of instruments and apparatus, allocate a certain sum for the Reid Concert, and reimburse the Patrons and the Professor for the sums already spent by them on the classes and concert. Yet the Senate fought every step, and even in 1858, it had not implemented a single legal requirement. It even accepted a motion by one of its members (Professor Pillans) that " the establishment of the Chair of Music as an Academical Class would be a detriment instead of an advantage to the University, as well as to the students, and would require to be abated as a nuisance." It was not until 1861 that the battle was really won, although the worry and anxiety over the litigation and the attitude of the Senate towards Professor Donaldson, brought this valiant fighter to his grave in 1865. It ought to be mentioned that in addition to his regular " course," which dealt with the philosophy of sound and the theory of music, Donaldson gave a series of other lectures which deserve mention because of the most precise Reformation period decorum which obtained. Of these lectures there was " *one* for gentlemen, and *one* exclusively for ladies." The University of Edinburgh owes it to John Donaldson that its Chair of Music was first placed on a workable basis.

At the death of Donaldson in 1865 the Chair went to [Sir] Herbert S. Oakeley (1830-1903), an Oxford graduate and a pupil of Stephen Elvey, Moscheles, J. Gottlob Schneider, and Breidenstein. His mother was a daughter of the Fourth Duke of Athole, which possibly explains much, since nepotism still obtained in the Universities. Under the new professor the annual Reid Concert became a three-day festival, which was a great uplift to music in the capital, more especially because of the wider cultivation of orchestral music by the engagement of the Hallé Orchestra (1869, *et seq.*), whilst Oakeley's own organ recitals were outstanding events of the season. In his first lecture he advised the formation of an organ class, chiefly because " on the organ the sublime thoughts, and thrilling harmonies, the towering might and unsurpassed majesty of that immortal master, Bach, are, perhaps, best appreciated." Oakeley's influence on music in Edinburgh and the East of Scotland was lasting. Indeed, his lessons on the organ and pianoforte must have been quite a novelty in professorial usage. Among Oakeley's compositions that have an associational interest are his songs in the *Students Song Book*, the *Scottish National Melodies* (op. 18) and his *Edinburgh Festal March* (Liverpool, 1874).

When he retired in 1891, John Greig, D. Mus. Oxon. (d. 1909), an extremely gifted man, was appointed *interim* Professor, but the University sniffed at a Scot in the chair and preferred to appoint an outsider in Friedrich Niecks (1845-1924) who had settled in Scotland as a viola player in [Sir] Alexander C. Mackenzie's Edinburgh Quartet. Under the guidance of Niecks, the activities of the University Musical Society were expanded, and each winter a series of Historical Concerts of the highest value and interest were held. The curriculum of the music classes was widened so as to embrace every phase of the art and practice of music. Niecks' lectures were considered a model of statement, and in 1901 he founded a Musical Education Society, on which topic he had already written a telling brochure,—*Musical Education and Culture* (Edin., 1892). It was owing to Niecks and the advocacy of the Scottish

Musical Society, as we shall see, that a Faculty of Music and the conferring of Degrees in Music were instituted in 1893, and the present high position of the Edinburgh faculty among British universities is mainly due to the seeds sown by Friedrich Niecks.

Outwith the University of Edinburgh some progress had been made in the specialized teaching of music in several institutions, notably in Glasgow. Here, at the Mechanics Institute, a working-class college founded 1822-23, a well-known teacher of music, Samuel Barr (1807-66) held classes on music. His two textbooks, *The Art of Singing at Sight* (Glasg., 1847, 1859) and his *Theory and Practice of Harmony and Composition* (Lond., 1861), show that he aimed at taking his students a fair distance towards the goal. It is claimed (*British Musical Biography*) that he was the first to have " introduced class music-teaching into the West of Scotland." A further advance in the " Second City " was made in 1866 when William Euing (1788-1874) endowed the Euing Lectureship in Music at Anderson's College, bequeathing his priceless Euing Musical Library to the same college, together with a collection of rare instruments of music. For the first two sessions the lectures were given by John Curwen (1866-67) and Henry Lambeth (1867-68), but in 1869 Colin Brown (1818-96) was appointed as the permanent lecturer. His classes had wide appreciation, but he is best remembered by his *Music in Common Things* (Glasg., 1870-76), which contained a description of his Voice Harmonium, giving perfect intonation, now in Glasgow Art Galleries and Museum. He was succeeded in 1896 by Harry Colin Miller, Mus. B., (Lond.).

Despite the creation of the English [Royal] Academy of Music (1822), the Royal Irish Academy of Music (1848), the National Training School for Music (1873) which became the Royal College of Music (1882), and the Guildhall School of Music (1880), there was no comparable institution in Scotland, although it was two Scots, George F. Graham and Sir George Clerk of Pennicuik, who first mooted the idea of the English Academy of Music. Writing in 1816, Graham said :

" If an academy of music were formed in England upon a

liberal and extensive plan, having . . . lectures upon the history, the theory, and the practice of musical composition . . . a well arranged library, . . . public concerts, . . . in which the talents of the students in performance and in composition, might be fairly brought forward, . . . the art of musical composition would rise in this Island, in a few years, to a degree of excellence sufficient to commend the respect of all the rest of Europe."
It was this advocacy that prompted Sir George Clerk of Pennicuik, "who did not think Graham's suggestion unworthy of attention," to formulate a scheme out of which issued the English [Royal] Academy of Music in 1822. Among the six original members of the Academy's foundation committee were Sir John Murray and the Hon. A. Macdonald, whilst the first list of teachers included John Mackintosh, the world-famous Scottish bassoonist. Later, many Scots found places as teachers, e.g. Frederick B. Jewson (piano) and Thomas Molleson Mudie (piano), together with its famous principals, Sir Alexander C. Mackenzie and Sir John B. McEwen, to say nothing of a worthy benefactor in Roger Rowson Ross, and its several illustrious pupils of the calibre of Learmont Drysdale, William Wallace, and others, all of whom have added laurels of glory to this institution.

Nothing was done in Scotland for a similar foundation until the "Seventies." Somewhere between 1875 and 1880 efforts were made in Edinburgh to establish a Scottish Academy of Music, and details of the scheme have been preserved by one of its prime movers, the late Sir James Donaldson, the Principal of St. Andrews University (see *The Dunedin Magazine*, vol. ii, 1913). Both Hans von Bülow and [Sir] Alexander C. Mackenzie were ardent supporters of the project, but Sir Herbert S. Oakeley, then the Reid Professor of Music in Edinburgh, looked askance at the scheme as competitive with his " course " at the University, and not only refused to associate but was openly antagonistic, more especially when Mackenzie was whispered as the likely Principal of the new Academy. In spite of this opposition, a " Scottish Musical Society " was formed to further the proposals and to keep its members *en rapport*. It embraced as office bearers the best in the country, together with a good financial backing, the Duke of Buccleuch promising £500 towards the projects, chief of which was the establishment of a Scottish Academy of Music. Robert A. Marr, the secretary of the society, put the case in these words :

" Scotland is the only nation in Europe that has no National School of Music, and, with her rich store of song and her strong musical aspiration, she stands, an anomaly in the eyes of musical Europe. She sends her children to Continental Schools of Music, and they become a credit to their masters and to their country."
That was in 1881, but for nine years little substantial progress could be claimed by the Society towards the goal. One factor which militated against success was the departure of Mackenzie from Scotland. His indifferent health, together with the deliberate and continuous hostility of *The Scotsman*, due to the personal animosity of its Music Critic, had forced the greatest composer that Scotland had produced since the Reformation to leave the land of his birth.

Yet in 1890, thanks to the energies of the insistent Marr, a decisive stroke was made which, if it did not reach its parochial aim, had the most beneficial collateral results. In this year the Society issued a Memorandum to the Scottish Universities' Commissioners which pressed for the promotion of Higher Musical Education in Scotland, and especially that the " Reid Endowment within the University of Edinburgh [which has no Faculty of Music and no Degrees in Music] . . . be put in a position to fulfil its true purposes, and thus render an independent Academy unnecesarsy." The University position, as we have seen, was remedied in 1893, and the programme for a Scottish Academy of Music was therefore shelved so far as Edinburgh was concerned but, as Sir James Donaldson said, since Glasgow was even more enthusiastic over such a project, it " has therefore a right to say something in regard to a Scottish Academy of Music," and it did.

In the Zavertal Collection in Glasgow University Library is a manuscript by Wenceslas H. Zavertal (1821-99), then resident at Helensburgh, which contains a plan for a Conservatory of Music in

Glasgow. Nothing was done however in this city until it was moved by Edinburgh's call, and in September of this year (1890) the Athenaeum School of Music opened its doors. Julius Seligmann (1817-1903) had already founded a private West of Scotland Conservatoire of Music in 1888, but it soon came to grief for want of support. The Athenaeum School of Music was more fortunate because it was a corporate body connected with an older establishment which dated from 1845. This latter was the Glasgow Commercial College, which did not, however, include music in its classes. It was not until 1847, when this college became the Glasgow Athenaeum, that music was recognized. It had its quarters at the Assembly Rooms, Ingram Street, the hall of which was the chief venue for music in the city. James Lauder, the Athenaeum's historian (*The Glasgow Athenaeum*, Glasg., 1897), tells us that " the teaching of singing was one of the first subjects included in the educational curriculum." This was taught by William H. Lithgow, who was succeeded by John Fulcher, both of whom were skilled instructors. In 1849 a Philharmonic Society was given elbow room within the walls of the Athenaeum, Thomas Macfarlane, a well-known organist, instructing the vocal department, whilst Julius Seligmann directed the instrumental. After Fulcher there came a man who considerably widened the educational scope. This was Joshua Ives, Mus. B., who introduced (*c.* 1876) classes for harmony. He became Professor of Music at Adelaide University in 1884. Three others who taught music at the old Athenaeum were David B. Johnstone of the Church of Scotland Normal School, James Pattinson, Mus. B., the organist of Maxwell Church, and William I. Robson (1853-91), the choirmaster of St. George's Free Church.

Meanwhile the old Athenaeum had moved to St. George's Place (1888), and here the new Athenaeum School of Music began its career (1890) on very much the same lines as that of the Guildhall School of Music in London. Its first Principal was Allan Macbeth (1856-1910) who had studied at Leipsic Conservatorium under E. Richter, Jadassohn, and Reinecke. He had held important organ appointments in Glasgow and was Choirmaster of the Glasgow

Choral Union (1880-87). The success of the school was instantaneous, over 800 students enrolling at the opening, and ere seven sessions had passed twice this number were enrolled. Within two years the question of accommodation became so acute that a contiguous building in Buchanan Street was erected which was opened in 1893, in which a small but fully equipped theatre was built, where for many years light opera was staged by the students. Much of the credit for the giant strides which the new seminary made was due to its Principal. Macbeth was a respectable composer, an able organist and choirmaster, but, above all, an astute organiser. Surrounding himself with about sixty teachers, including some first-class men of the character of [Sir] John B. McEwen, W. Lindsay Lamb, W. H. Cole, W. R. Wright, Mus.B., and J. Michael Diack, he was able to boast at the end of the century that he had made the school one of Scotland's brightest possessions in her realm of music.

CHAPTER 5

THE INSTRUMENTS

" In Scotland at the beginning of the 19th Century, the pianoforte had just replaced the spinet and harpsichord, and was little played. The harmonium was not played at all, for the very good reason that it was not yet invented. Fiddle and flute were probably more popular than any of the keyed instruments."

ROBERT TURNBULL : *Old Glasgow Club* (1916).

One might imagine that there can be little or nothing to be said of instruments of music in so recent an age as the 19th century because most of those to be mentioned are so familiar to us in the 20th century. Yet there was greater development in this field during this one century than in all the preceding years of history and, so far as Scotland is concerned, her instrument makers and importers tried to keep abreast of the times, even to contributing their mite to this progress which marks the era. Instruments of all sorts were common to the people at large, the harpsichord and pianoforte, and later the harmonium, with the middle-class, as well as the English and Spanish guitars, whilst the violin, flute, and flageolet, were more acceptable to the masses.

Those were what satisfied domestic needs, but there was much more. Organs had to be supplied occasionally to Episcopal, Roman Catholic, and Dissenting Churches. In the theatres and army bands, there was a market for flutes, oboes, clarionets, bassoons, key bugles and cornets, horns, trombones, ophicleides, serpents, and later the brass instruments popularized by Sax and Distin. That there were makers and inventors in the music trade in Scotland, as well as dealers, we shall attempt to show. The organ comes first for attention, and Sir John G. Dalyell (*Musical Memoirs*, 1849) shows that it had a fairly wide popularity among the middle and upper classes. "At the present day" he says, "organs of superior quality are seen in the private dwellings of some families endowed with a predilection for the higher compositions. Likewise many have been constructed in the Scottish capital both for domestic and ecclesiastical use in Scotland, and for distant places, which would be creditable to the talents of any artists." He also informs us that "much of the improvement in the detail of organ building [in Scotland] was derived from . . . Samuel Letts, a native of Ireland, who resorted hither about the year 1802-03." In 1804 he was employed by Muir & Wood, Edinburgh (founded 1796), who advertised themselves (1799) as "Musical Instrument Makers to His Majesty." Letts, who died shortly afterwards, expressed the opinion as a constructor, which is worth repeating, that the Scots and Irish preferred "softer and deeper toned organs," whilst the English liked "louder and shriller instruments," which reminds one of Handel's advice to Gluck :—" If you want to work for the English, you must give them something tumultuous, like the rattle of drum-sticks or a drum." Dalyell, in 1849, said that " organs constructed in Scotland are the more melodious."

At the same time these instruments were smaller than those used in England and many of them were portable. A fair specimen of the larger church organ may be seen in the frontispiece to James Steven's *Harmonia Sacra* (Glasg., *c.* 1820). Although pedals had been introduced into England in 1790 the device was unknown in Scotland, or at least not adopted, for half a century at least. When

Adam Hamilton (1820-1907) returned to Edinburgh from Germany in 1841 " he found that no organ in the city possessed proper pedals," and it was his brother, the famous David, who then " put pedals, of the German scale, to the organ of St. John's Episcopal Church," where Adam gave organ recitals to large audiences (see James Waddell, *History of the Edinburgh Choral Union*, 1908). Yet Henry Liston (1771-1836) of Ecclesmachan, in his patent (1810) " improvements in the construction of organs " specified pedals for his enharmonic system, described in his *Essay on Perfect Intonation* (Lond., 1812). Flight and Robson of London built one or two of these enharmonic organs. More valuable was the invention of the *pneumatic lever* for the organ, for although both Booth and Barker are credited with this, the pregnant experiment made in 1835 by David Hamilton (1803-63) with his organ at St. John's Episcopal Church, Edinburgh, which he described to the British Association in 1839, also deserves notice. It was of the utmost importance to future developments of the instrument. Dalyell avers that Hamilton was also " an expert organ builder . . . who had the benefit of instruction and information from personal knowledge acquired in several establishments on the Continent." The original model of his pneumatic lever is preserved by the Edinburgh Society of Musicians.

There was no dearth of organ builders in Scotland. Thom, the Aberdeen historian, speaks, in 1811, of the firm of Knowles and Allen of that city who had a musical instrument manufactory, established in 1808, that made organs, pianofortes, violins, guitars, etc., which supplied London as well as Scotland, although it was doing rather poor business at that particular date. In Glasgow, the very hub of Scotland's industry and commerce, there was not a solitary musical instrument maker in its directories at the opening of the century. Its first organ builder appears to have been Robert Mirrlees (1830), although the firm claimed to have been founded earlier (1811), and it was still in existence until recent years. Another (1834-64) was T. W. Gardner. Edinburgh, as we have seen, was already in the field. Muir and Wood were

certainly constructing organs in 1803, and the one that was built
for the Episcopal Chapel, Dundee, in 1812 was described as " the
largest in Scotland." James Bruce, who won the high esteem
of Dalyell in 1849, had been making organs for quite twenty years
earlier, and the latter speaks well of the " very reputable instruments
of considerable dimensions " by Bruce. The firm, Small, Bruce
& Co., had a high reputation and built the organ for the Theatre
Royal, Edinburgh, in 1828. It was James Bruce, when he was with
Muir, Wood & Co., who altered the organ of the Roman Catholic
Chapel which was lent for the Edinburgh Musical Festival of
1824, when it was specially provided with " a long movement, so
that the conductor could sit immediately in front of the band."
The same was done in 1834. As this was before the days of electric
action, it is a pity that we do not possess a specification of the
mechanism of this " long movement..' The first electro-pneumatic
organ in Scotland was installed by Hope-Jones at St. John's, Perth,
in 1894, although the earliest Scottish maker was Joseph Brook &
Co. (Glasgow).

Whilst organs were to be found in several concert halls in Scotland, as we have seen in the previous century, the idea did not find
general acceptance, possibly because of the decay of the private
concerts. At the old Assembly Rooms, Edinburgh, they still used
the Snetzler organ that had been acquired from the old St. Cecilia's
Hall (1762-1801). When the Music Hall was built in 1843,
an organ by Hill of London, the lineal business descendant of
Snetzler, was installed. Although Glasgow opened its City Hall
in 1841, an organ was not adopted until 1853, when Henry
Lambeth played a Gray and Davison instrument, on which occasion
the *Glasgow Herald* said that now " people will learn to appreciate
the solemn and severe grandeur of the world-renowned fugues of
John Sebastian Bach."

An instrument, seemingly of the organ class, was the *euhponicon*,
invented by Duncan Campbell (b. *c.* 1810), although all that we can
learn of its structure is that it was " about the size of a piccolo
pianoforte," and that it was " a wind instrument played by bellows,

which were worked by the right foot." It was first exhibited in the Monteith Rooms, Buchanan Street, Glasgow, in March, 1830, when it was played by Henry G. Nixon (1796-1849) the organist of St. Andrew's Roman Catholic Chapel (1833-39). It was also used at the consecration of St. Mary's Roman Catholic Chapel in 1842. Strange to say, in this latter year, Messrs. Cramer, Addison, and Beale of London, exhibited a *euphonikon* which was described as a combination harp and pianoforte.

When the *harmonium* was invented or improved by Debain in 1840, it displaced the older *harmonica* and *seraphine*, and Julian Adams (1824-87), then in Glasgow, is said to have introduced it. The instrument immediately became popular in Scotland, more especially by reason of its religious appeal. In a leaflet entitled *A Plea for the Cultivation of Sacred Music by the Upper Classes* (*c.*1850), it was claimed that, as " the harmonium exhibits the power of sacred music much better than the pianoforte . . . it is to be wished that it were brought into more extensive use as a family instrument." It was, and when the Scottish Vocal Music Association planned its Academy of Music in 1858, a teacher on the pianoforte and harmonium was on the syllabus. Although Wood & Co., of Edinburgh, Glasgow, and Aberdeen, had introduced an " Improved Patent Harmonium " made by Alexandre of Paris, local makers sprang up in various towns in Scotland, and among them James Gilmour & Co. of Glasgow, and A. Henry & Co. of Greenock. The Gilmour firm were outstanding and progressive manufacturers who, in 1864, patented among other things an apparatus for " softening and swelling the bass and treble divisions of the instrument independently of each other." They constructed large and powerful instruments which they called Church Harmonium-Organs in which the reeds, instead of being all in one box, were divided into different boxes, no one of which contained more than two sets of reeds. Julian Adams wrote a *Method for the Patent Harmonium* (1855).

In 1872 John Farmer (1836-1901) registered (*Pat.* 3381) a free-reed instrument which vibrated strings as well as reeds, but a more perfect contrivance, known as the *vocalion*, was patented by a Scot named James Buchanan Bailie Hamilton (b. 1837). Eventually the string complement in this instrument was abandoned, but the later developments on the reed side produced a " much better and rounder tone " than that of the ordinary harmonium. Indeed the vocalion shown at the International Inventions Exhibition (1885), as well as his American specification (U.S.A., 1885), enables us to see how much the modern *American organ* owes to Hamilton.

The *voice harmonium* of Colin Brown (1818-96) ought not perhaps to be included here, since it was essentially a scientific instrument, yet since the specification (1875) claimed for the patent certain " improvements in musical instruments having keyboards," it might well have become a practical proposition. The object of the invention was " the playing of the musical scale in any and every key with just or perfect intonation " by means of a special keyboard, which was a great improvement on the system of his fellow Scot Henry Liston in 1810, where the enharmonic changes were brought into play by pedals. Brown describes his system in part 2 of his *Music in Common Things* (Glasg., 1878), and it is dealt with at considerable length by Alexander J. Ellis in his brilliant edition of Helmholtz's *Sensations of Tone* (Lond., 1895), in which he refers to Brown's keyboard as " highly ingenious."

One other keyboard instrument deserves mention here, although it belongs, strictly speaking, to the idiophonic group. Charles Clagget (1740-*c*. 1795) had conceived an instrument which comprised tuning forks struck by hammers worked by a keyboard, yet it was not until much later that such an instrument was put to practical use. In 1865, Mustel of Paris " invented " his *typophone*, which was registered in this country in 1866. It was Clagget's idea, but with the forks placed in resonance boxes. Yet prior to this (1860), Thomas Machell (1841-1915) of Edinburgh and Glasgow, was already working on his *dulcitone* which, however, was not placed on the market until 1885. This instrument has been a great success.

The *pianoforte* also owes something to the ingenuity of the

Scots. After the improvements of John Broadwood (1732-1812), which have already been detailed in the 18th Century, his son, James (d. 1851), applied iron bars to a grand pianoforte. One of John Broadwood's pupils was Robert Stodart, who set up in business for himself about 1776. He was succeeded by his son, William, and in his employment were two young Scottish tuners, James Thom and William Allen who, in 1820, patented a compensating grand pianoforte with metal tubes and plates, the actual idea having been conceived by Allen. In 1831 the latter patented a complete cast-iron frame for the instrument which quite revolutionised pianoforte construction. Scottish makers were fairly plentiful, and Glasgow contributed not a few. During the first decade of the century there were, as we have seen, no musical instrument makers of any kind in this city, but in 1833 there were three classed as " Musical Instrument Makers," two as Organ Builders, and three as " Piano Forte Makers." The earliest pianoforte maker in Glasgow appears to have been John Allan who started business in 1825. Then came Francis and George Melville, who had a music shop in 1820, but in 1825 they separated and ran separate establishments, both starting as pianoforte makers conjointly in 1828. To the former we owe an improvement (1825) in the square piano. These were followed by Robert Allan (1830), McKellar and Robertson (1834), and Lutted and Bowman (1838). By 1850 there were thirteen pianoforte makers in Glasgow. In 1867, James Gilmour of Glasgow patented some " improvements in the construction of pianofortes," four of which were : (1) counterbalancing the strain of the wires ; (2) using tubular metal braces and iron pin blocks ; (3) making the soundboard " hollow or belly-shaped " or " double " ; (4) aiding the tuning by means of adjustable tuning slips and screw tuning pins. Those interested in the structure of the pianoforte at this period ought to turn to William Mitchison's *Few Remarks on the Pianoforte : Giving Details of the Mechanical Construction of that Instrument* (Glasg., 1845), although strange to say, he does not mention a solitary Scottish maker. Of course, Mitchison himself was primarily a dealer.

By the "seventies" pianoforte manufacture was at its peak in Scotland. In Edinburgh there were Purdie, Curle, and other well-known firms, who were as busy as they could be with orders, whilst further north, the factories of Marr, and MacBeth, supplied most wants. In Glasgow there were the older firms of Allan, Bowman, and Gilmour, as well as those of lesser repute in Mackenzie and Mackenzie, Lindsay, Findlay, and others. William Thomson of Govan Road, Glasgow, a later manufacturer, has written (*Govan Press*, Sept. 28th, 1923) about the Scottish makers and instruments. "The pianofortes, which were built in Glasgow in those days, reached a very high standard of musical and artistic excellence. They were dignified instruments, built to adorn drawing-rooms of the wealthiest families. . . . They were all made by hand, fitted with the admirable old sticker action, and were products of which the makers had every reason to be proud. . . . A period of transition came, . . . and there arose a demand for more pianofortes, but of a cheaper price. To meet this growing demand there was evolved the London-made pianoforte, in the manufacture of which machinery took a large part. . . . The cheaper London models satisfied the cravings of the new recruits to music for a moderately priced instrument, and the superior Glasgow-made pianoforte languished and ultimately passed out."

Early pianoforte instructor music and literature from Scotland have some interest as many items are quite scarce. The earliest is Ann Gunn's *Elements of Music and of Fingering the Harpsichord* (Edin., 1803), the second edition of which (1820) used the word *Pianoforte*. A tutor that was to be found in more than one household in Scotland was John Monro's *New and Complete Introduction to the Art of Playing the Pianoforte* (Lond., 1819). D. Macpherson's *Catechism of Music, Adapted for Learners on the Piano* (Edin., c. 1830) is in the form of a dialogue between master and pupil. In the mid-century came Robert McAlister's *Easy Introduction to the Keyboard of the Pianoforte or Harmonium* (Glasg., c. 1850) and [Broomfield's] *Pianoforte Preceptor* (Glasg., c. 1856).

The principle of Debain's *piano méchanique* (*ca.* 1850) was not altogether quite original since the main contrivance had already been visualized by Duncan Mackenzie in 1848 (*Pat.* 12,229), the latter having adapted Jacquard's machinery to playing instruments. Nor were the later American and French mechanical pianofortes of 1860 and 1863 respectively the first of their kind. When Alexander Bain (1818-1903), the famous moral philosopher, was a professor of natural philosophy at Anderson's University, Glasgow, he patented, in 1847 the device of " a moving perforated surface, such as paper," whose openings corresponded to notes of specific pitches and mensural values, which was the forerunner of the modern pianola. (Cf. " Bayne " *Oxford Companion to Music*).

For popularity, the violin was *facile princeps* in Scotland, " in almost every farmhouse a fiddle being within easy reach," as Sir Alexander C. Mackenzie testified. No wonder that it has been looked upon almost as the national instrument. Whatever method the professional class adopted in holding the violin in the early 19th Century, the " fiddler " of the people still followed the old mode of placing the chin on the *right* side of the tailpiece, with the head of the instrument pointing downwards. This is what we see in David Wilkie's pictures. Good violin makers were still to the fore in Scotland. David Stirrat of Edinburgh was a pupil of Matthew Hardie (1755-1826), and a worthy one, with violas and 'cellos to his credit. His labels run from 1810 to 1820. Greater still was a Glasgow craftsman, John Alexander Mann (1810-89). He came from Forfar, but settling in Glasgow began making on the Stradivari model about 1845. Honeyman says : " There may be violins made in this kingdom equal to the best of Mann's, though I have not seen them." James Gilchrist (1834-94) came from Rothesay, where many of his earlier violins were made. Later he settled in Glasgow and his total output was eighty-six instruments, including violas, violoncellos, and " celletos." In spite of the strictures of Honeyman, his best work reveals the eye and hand of a master craftsman. He introduced " bushes " to the peg-holes to lessen wearing. James Hardie, *Secundus* (1836-1916) of Glasgow was a grandson of Peter Hardie (1775-1863) of Dunkeld, and from him he learned the craft. He was one of the first to use the amber varnish that Dr. George Dickson of Edinburgh had discovered or revived, and which James Whitelaw of Glasgow put to practical use. Although Hardie made many instruments for a quick sale, his best work " will bear comparison with any living [1910] Scottish maker." Lastly one must mention George Duncan (1855-19. .). He came from Kingston-on-Spey, but established himself in Glasgow in 1875. He was a first-rate workman and at the International Inventions Exhibition (London, 1885) he was awarded the gold medal. Unfortunately for this country he emigrated to America in 1892. Among curiosities were a violin made of hardened leather by Gavin Wilson of Edinburgh which, according to the *Gentleman's Magazine* (1818) was " not inferior to any made of wood," and a double-stringed violin " invented " by Andrew Bowers of Portobello (1895), with a novel tuning device which has since found acceptance.

That the old *clarsech* or Highland harp had fallen into complete neglect by the 19th Century is evident from *An Historical Enquiry Respecting the Performance on the Harp . . . Until it was Discontinued, about the Year 1734* (Edin., 1807) by John Gunn. The same author issued a prospectus for *An Enquiry into the Antiquity of the Harp*, the final chapter of which was to have dealt with the neglect of the instrument " and of the causes which have brought on the decline of music, and prevented its cultivation, and that of musical science in Scotland." Unfortunately, especially from what was promised in his last chapter, the book was not published. The instrument which took the place of the *clarsech* was the modern *pedal harp*. Gunn refers to a " Mr. Wood, an ingenious mechanic, and a manufacturer of the harp and other musical instruments " in Edinburgh, which seems to betoken the modern harp. The names of some of the harp professors who were settled in Edinburgh during the first half of the 19th Century also prove the popularity of this instrument. Among these were such well-known performers as S. Philip Seybold, Joseph (or Jean) Elouis, and Henry E. Dibdin who lived for many years (1833-66) in the capital. Dalyell (1849) says that the instrument was favoured by the ladies. Still, when

Patrick Byrne (*c*.1784-1863) the Irish *clarsair* visited Edinburgh and Fifeshire in 1843-44 he was well received.

The flute was now a six- or eight-keyed instrument. Many British makers had made improvements but it was Malcolm Macgregor, a Scot working in London, who made the first definite step forward in his patent of 1810, which consisted of improved keys, originally furnished for a bass flute. Then came William Gordon, possibly of Scottish extraction, who made the most lasting contribution to the mechanism of the instrument (1826) when he devised a system of open holes and open keys which was perfected by Boehm in 1832. Among some early scarce items in tutors for the flute in 19th Century Scotland are John Brysson's *Compleat Tutor for the German Flute* (Edin., *c*. 1807), the *Flute Player's Pocket Companion* (Edin., 1817), and William Whyte's *Instructions for the German Flute* (Edin., *c*. 1820), which are not mentioned in Dayton C. Miller's *Catalogue of Books . . . Relating to the Flute* (Cleveland, 1835). Scotland provided one or two good makers of the instrument, notably Thomas M. Glen who began business in Edinburgh in 1826, and James Taylor of High John Street, Glasgow, who worked at instruments in wood and ivory from 1834 to 1849. The latter also made flageolets. As old Sheriff Barclay recalls, the flageolet was a great favourite in those days, and lovers of Robert L. Stevenson will remember that the delightful Scottish essayist himself played the flageolet. He was very musical, and in his *Vailima Letters* he tells us how he listened to a Samoan mill-wheel clicking with " a *schottische* movement."

Although later Scottish makers did not contribute anything fresh to the flute's development, one novelty deserves recording since it is one of the curiosities of the flute world. Its " inventor," David Hatton of Dunfermline, called it a *chamber flute-orum* [*sic*], but it was actually a bellows flute. According to a description given in the *Glasgow Mechanics' Magazine* (xxxi, 1824), accompanied by a woodcut illustration, it consisted of " (1) a German flute, of the ordinary size, which plays the tune, the fingers operating in the ordinary way ; (2) a large C flute, which sounds the key note of the tune, the tone being altered with corks which fit the finger holes, and the mouth hole of it is shut and opened by a lever valve moved by the thumb of the left hand ; (3) the bellows that fill (4), which is an air cistern, the air being pressed up the two air pipes by the pressure of the left arm [on the bellows]."

In some of the remainder of the wood-wind group, the Scots appear to have contributed some improvements. Dalyell (1849) says : " In a manuscript treatise by Mr. William Meikle, formerly master of a military band, he describes various attempts to improve the instrument [the *clarionet*] by altering the bore, employing a reed of better than the ordinary construction, and other expedients greatly ameliorating the tone and facilitating performance. . . . By his improvements, the compass of the instrument is extended from B [below the stave] to an octave above C [above the stave]." Thomas M. Glen (1804-73), the Edinburgh musical instrument maker, made clarionets in metal long before they became popular in the 20th Century. At the Glasgow Art Galleries and Museum there is a six-keyed clarionet stamped " A[rchibald] Campbell's Improved : 104 Stockwell Street, Glasgow." From its structure it would seem to date from 1810-25, but this maker is only known at this address from 1855 to 1877, and even then only as a " Music-seller."

This same William Meikle of Strathaven also invented an instrument called the *Caledonica*, now preserved in the music department of Edinburgh University, together with the original manuscript fingering chart. It is actually in C, an octave higher than the bassoon, although the inventor, as the manuscript chart tells us, intended to have two other sizes, in F and B Flat. According to Lyndesay G. Langwill of Edinburgh (*Musical Progress and Mail*, April, 1934) this instrument was the original of the *Alto Fagotto* now in the Glasgow Art Galleries and Museum which bears the stamp, " George Wood, . . . London, Invented by William Meikle." Although the latter is dated 18th Century by C. R. Day in his *Catalogue of the Musical Instruments . . . Royal Military Exhibition* (Lond., 1891), we know from the *Harmonicon* (April,

1830) that it was only " lately invented." Since it seems to have been played with a single reed similar to that of a clarionet but smaller, Meikle's invention must be considered a forerunner of the saxophone (see *The Saxophone before Sax*, by F. G. Rendall, *Musical Times*, Dec., 1932). Dalyell suggests that Meikle " added both to the quality of the tone and the compass of the *bassoon* by certain alterations on the bore, and the position and additions to the apertures."

The Glen family of Edinburgh, the founder of which, Thomas M. Glen, has already been mentioned, were famed as *bagpipe* makers. Long before the use of African blackwood and vulcanite, when all wood-wind instruments were subject to shrinkage and torsion in equatorial climes, it was Glen who introduced an inner metal tube so as to obviate infraction, and the family were the first to make a metal chanter and drones for the bagpipe. Another famous Edinburgh maker was Alexander Glen (1801-73), a brother of the preceding. There were also George Walker, who supplied the army, and D. MacDonald, who was " Pipe Maker to the Highland Society of London." In Glasgow the leading crafts-men were William Gunn (d. 1867), Donald MacPhee (d. 1880), and the successor of the latter, Peter Henderson (d. 1902). Among the accepted bagpipe tutors of the century were *A New and Complete Tutor for the Great Highland Bagpipe* (Edin., 1827) by Thomas M. Glen, the *Complete Tutor* (Edin., 1840) of William Mackay, and the *Highland Bagpipe Tutor* (Edin., 1886) by David Glen (b. 1850). As for the bellows pipe, whether Irish or Lowland, it seems to have flourished. T. Campbell of Edinburgh was making the former at the dawn of the century, and Robert Reid (1784-1837) of Newcastle supplied the latter, the form of which is well delineated by Wilkie in *The Bagpiper* (1813).

At the opening of the century all brass-wind instruments, save the trombone, were still, in principle, non-chromatic. When James Halliday patented his *key bugle* in 1810 this drawback was remedied, and the whole brass family leaped forward with this improvement, more especially when a complete choir of these instruments, with the *ophicleide* as bass, was evolved. In the Copenhagen Museum there is a key bugle of 9 keys (1832), stamped " John Mackenzie, Dundee." The key bugle itself was brought to its " highest state of perfection " by Köhler & Sons in a device of George Macfarlane, a Scottish instrumentalist in London, who added two additional keys to facilitate shakes, making ten keys in all on the instrument. On the bass side, Thomas M. Glen (d. 1873) of Edinburgh produced a wooden ophicleide which he called a *serpentcleide*.

Then came the invention of the valve and the emergence of the *cornopean* or *cornet*, which completely ousted the key bugle. With the improvements of Sax and Distin, a whole family, from a sopranino to a double bombardon, came into existence, and improvements became the order of the day, in which another Scot, James Waddell (1797-1879) of Banff, played a part. He was then the bandmaster of the 1st Life Guards, and in 1858 he patented, with George Metzler, several improvements in valve instruments. These were : (1) Instead of the abrupt turns in the tubing of brass instruments, as in the saxhorns, a " circular arrangement " was devised, seemingly as in the modern *helicon* or circular bombardon ; (2) The third valve was made part of the pitch tubing, which it raised a tone and a half; (3) The bell of the instrument [a bombardon] was turned in the same direction as the trumpet and trombone. Meanwhile George Macfarlane had added a shake key to the cornopean, but more important was his patent of 1860. His suggested third valve, according to his claim, " almost obviates the necessity for cross fingering " and " facilitates the performance of chromatic passages and shakes." He also conceived the first mute for the cornet. It was a " concave-convex " disc, with a central aperture which, fastened on a hinge in the bell of the instrument, could be used to give *crescendo* or *diminuendo* effects, whilst by closing the aperture it acted as a mute. He was the compiler of one of the earliest tutors for the instrument in his *Cornopean Instructor* (Lond., n.d.).

Among the " unconsidered trifles " as inventions, three deserve notice. James Waddell, already mentioned, patented an improvement in drums (1861) which consisted of "connecting the head of the drum to metal bars which, when the head is struck, causes the drum to emit a sound about an octave lower than a similar drum constructed in the ordinary manner." Another interesting novelty was an improved tuning fork invented by J. B. Moulds of Edinburgh, which was acknowledged by the Society for Encouragement of the Useful Arts (1837). It consisted of "a keeper clasping the arms of the fork which, sliding upwards or downwards over a graduated scale on the arm, altered the pitch at pleasure." Lastly there was James Mitchell (b. 1834) of Kilmarnock, who perfected a metronome "which not only beats the constituent units of a given bar, but also its fractional aliquot parts—halves, quarters, etc.—giving a loud click for the beat, and a softer click for the fractions." Yet we are told that there is "Nothing new under the Sun."

CHAPTER 6
THE THEATRE

"Our present theatrical season . . . made me for some time waver whether I should continue my strictures or not."
The Monthly Mirror (Edinburgh, 1800).

The theatre, as we last saw it in the 18th Century, had triumphed over the Church in so far as the legal position was concerned, but it still had to combat the intolerance of bigots and fanatics. In this latter, some rather significant measures were adopted by the Church. When Joseph Ebsworth (1788-1868) the famous *basso* received his appointment as precentor at St. Stephen's Church, Edinburgh, in 1829, it was "on the express condition of his giving up his connection with the theatre." Even to-day, actors and actresses appear to be considered beyond the pale in the eyes of the Church of Scotland. If one enters a Scottish theatre stage door, there will be found in the entrance hall two notices, issued respectively by the Actors Church Union and the Catholic Stage Guild, giving information of the church services and the names of the theatre chaplains, but these notices *only* concern the Episcopal Church of Scotland and the Roman Catholic Church.

At the opening of the 19th Century many things had gone wrong managerially with the theatre in Scotland, if we can trust the Edinburgh and Glasgow press. Although the placards sometimes blazoned " the best company out of London," both the performers and the productions could only be classed as second-rate or even at a lower category. Still, under persistent criticism, matters showed an improvement in Edinburgh, and there were a few redeeming features on the musical side, in spite of them being well-wrinkled. Michael Kelly and Elizabeth Billington appeared in *Love in a Village* (1802), whilst Linley's *Duenna* was revived (1806) together with the *Beggar's Opera* (1807) starring Mrs. Mountain (her husband conducting), and Storace's *Siege of Belgrade* which featured the brilliant Braham. Then came a flash in the pan with Italian Opera, the great Catalani being the star attraction with Spagnoletti in charge of the band.

A new era opened in 1809 at the freshly-decorated Theatre Royal in Leith Walk, which was actually Corri's Concert-rooms. The press was immensely pleased at the change of venue and even deigned to mention the theatre band, which was quite unusual, since its eyes and ears were generally only agog for the stage. *The Monthly Mirror* said that " the music, which was formerly execrable, [is] very much improved," whilst the *Courant* beamed on the overture when it espied the oboe " touched by the hand of a master," the latter being Thomas Fraser whose playing so captivated Burns. Returning to the old Theatre Royal, we see that the company still ran its musical presentation on past lines in such pieces as Bishop's *Knight of Snowdoun* (1811) and the *Miller and his Men* (1813), with Kelly's *Royal Oak* (1813). After this Edinburgh fell under the spell of plays, followed by the lure of Scott's works which had been dramatised or operatised, much of the music, mostly a hash of Scottish songs, being by Bishop, notably *Guy Mannering* (1817) with its delightful " Chough and the Crow," *The Heart of Midlothian* (1820), *The Antiquary* (1820), *The Battle of Bothwell Brig* (1823), and others. They were all mere drama with songs interspersed. John Dewar, the conductor of the theatre, did better music for *Waverley* (1823) and one or two more, whilst John Thomson supplied a real musical setting to *The House of Aspen* (1829).

In 1824 English opera, i.e. Italian opera in English, held the boards for a spell, and in the repertory was Rossini's *Barber of Seville*, probably in Bishop's arrangement, with Mary Ann Paton, a Scot, as Rosina. At the close of the year William Hawes, who had just produced Weber's *Der Freischütz* in London, came north and presented it with James Thorne and Agnes Noel as the attractions. It was the latter who so deeply affected the author of *Noctes Ambrosianae* by her singing. When the opera was revived the following year it was accompanied by a burlesque called *Der Fryshot*, a " clever travesty," as Benson Hill remarks in his delightful *Playing About*. The event shows the taste of the period, although such an audacity would not be tolerated nowadays. Real Italian opera returned in 1827 in a handful of Rossini's works, including *Il Barbiere di Siviglia*, *Il Turco in Italia*, and *La Gazza Ladra*. It is also worthy of note that John Wilson, the famous Scottish tenor, made his stage début when *Guy Mannering* (1829) was revived. This same year, when Auber's *Masaniello* had its first hearing in Scotland, Wilson took the title rôle. This, like many other continental operas produced at this time, was an adaptation by Bishop.

Meanwhile Corri's Concert-rooms, now named the Caledonian Theatre, had not been idle musically. It was here that Weber's *Oberon*, adapted by Montague Corri, was heard for the first time in Scotland (1826). In 1830, the Caledonian staged Mozart's *Figaro* and *Don Giovanni*, Rossini's *Il Barbiere*, Weber's *Der Freichütz*, in addition to Arne's *Artaxerxes* and the evergreen *Beggar's Opera*. At the old Theatre Royal were given Lampe's *Dragon of Wantley* (1832), *Love in a Village* (1833), *Barber of Seville* (1834), Dibdin's *Waterman* (1834) with George Barker, Mozart's *Figaro* (1835) " after which a comic song by Lloyd " which rather spoils the picture, Barnett's *Mountain Sylph* (1836), Weber's *Der Freichütz* (1837) with Wilson as Rudolph, Bellini's *La Sonnambula* (1838) with John Templeton and Eliza Inverarity, the famous Scottish stars, and Handel's *Acis and Galatea* (1840) by amateurs. Opera in the capital during the " Forties " was rather bare, the only outstanding items being *Masaniello* (1846) with the *Bohemian Girl* and *Maritana* (1849), although the next decade showed some improvement. In 1852, an operetta, *The Provost's Daughter*, by Alexander Mackenzie, the conductor of the theatre band, was of local moment. The same year brought a revival of interest in *opera seria* when an adaptation of Halévy's *Jewess* was sumptuously produced, which was followed by a crowd of works from the old repertory, with *Crown Diamonds* of Auber to relieve the monotony. In the company were Louisa Pyne and William Harrison playing the leads. They later married and formed (1856) the famous " English Opera Company " under their names. The next year brought John [Sims] Reeves to the capital in more opera, and each year following allowed for an opera season, *Il Trovatore* being given in 1856, but the closing of the Theatre Royal in 1859 brought its contribution to this form of art to an end.

As a result of the demolition of this old centre of theatrical life, opera languished for a time in Edinburgh, although the Pyne-Harrison combination produced Benedict's *Lily of Killarney* (1863) at the Queen's Theatre, with Louisa Pyne, Mrs. Aynsley Cook, George Perren, Charles Lyall, and J. G. Patey in the caste. Yet opera occasionally found audiences at the Princess' Theatre, the Southminster Theatre, and the Edinburgh Theatre. In the last-named appeared the Mapleson Italian Opera Company ending a season with Beethoven's *Fidelio*, Tietjens being in the title rôle. Yet rather than proceed with the story of the opera in Scotland as it developed in Edinburgh, it would seem preferable to continue its unfolding in Glasgow.

Compared with the capital, Glasgow lagged for a long time in staging opera, for the " Second City " seems to have thought that " the play's the thing," although we read of John Corri conducting Mozart's *Don Giovanni* in 1818. It was evergreens like *Guy Mannering*, and works of a similar genre, that more invariably attracted audiences. Indeed, it was not until 1845, when John

PLATE XII

Elliot & Fry.

HAMISH MACCUNN
(1868-1916)

PLATE XIII

LEARMONT DRYSDALE
(1866-1909)

[Sims] Reeves appeared at the City Theatre in the *Bohemian Girl,* creating a perfect furore, that Glasgow really awoke to opera, and when, in 1848, *La Figlia del Reggimento* and *La Sonnambula* were presented by stars of such brilliance as Jenny Lind, Lablache, and Roger, the pace was definitely set.

Picking up the thread of history from where we left it in Edinburgh we can follow the development of opera in Glasgow. Here the old Theatre Royal had been burned down in 1863, and although reopened successfully it finally closed its doors in 1868. Meantime the Colosseum had been built in the Cowcaddens (1867) for variety entertainments, and this was opened in 1869 for dramatic productions as the Theatre Royal. The " Seventies " reveal how great was the demand for opera in Glasgow, yet one can only give the merest outline of the craving for the best type of this art. In 1872 Tietjens, Colombo, Foli, and Agnesi were delighting audiences with Italian opera in Donizetti's *Don Pasquale* and *Lucretia Borgia,* Meyerbeer's *Huguenots* and *Robert le Diable,* Mozart's *Don Giovanni* and the *Magic Flute,* Beethoven's *Fidelio,* Flotow's *Marta,* and other works. The next year saw English opera in *Maritana, L'Africaine, Fra Diavolo,* and later in the same year, Bellini's *Norma,* Gounod's *Faust,* and Rossini's *Semiramide.* Light opera found expression in Offenbach's *Princess of Trebizond* and *Geneviève de Brabant,* Délibes' *Fleur de Lys,* and Hervé's *Chilpéric.*

The enthusiasm did not abate in the slightest. Italian opera in 1874 was displayed in *Oberon, Caterina* (=*Crown Diamonds*), and Balfe's *Il Talismano,* as outstanding items, featuring the old stars with Marie Roze in addition. The year 1875 brought *Der Freichütz, I Puritani, Dinorah,* and Wagner's *Lohengrin,* with Albani, Zaré Thalberg, Maurel, and Naudin in the caste, and later in the year Nilsson and Trebelli-Bettini were among the stars. Carl Rosa, himself conducting, came in 1877, supported by Santley, Lyall, J. W. Turner, and Mr. and Mrs. Aynsley Cook, the novelties being Cowen's *Pauline* and Macfarren's *Robin Hood.* Nor was light opera ignored, *La Belle Helene, La Fille de Madame Angot, La Grande Duchesse,* and others of this class, being performed. Italian opera in the following year, with Madame Lablache, Bauermeister, and Foli, brought fresh presentations in Donizetti's *Linda di Chamouni* and Marchetti's *Ruy Blas*. Carl Rosa, in 1879, had Maas, Crotty, and Georgina Burns as prominent attractions in his castes. Four of the outstanding of the Carl Rosa productions of the " Eighties " in Glasgow were Corder's *Nordissa* and Massé's *Galatea* (1887), as well as Thomas' *Mignon* and Halévy's *La Juive* (1888), with Barton McGuckin, Charles Manners and Fanny Moody, the two latter to become frequent visitors in subsequent years with their own company. In the year 1885 there was produced at the Royalty Theatre an opera *The Uhlans*, by Christina W. Bogue, with the libretto by her husband, W. McIvor Morison. In the caste was J. W. Turner. The composer was said to be the " first Scotswoman who ever wrote an opera," although Jane P. Smieton, the mother of John More Smieton, had already published a lyric opera *The Restored* (Dundee, 1874).

The last decade of the century revealed Glasgow at the peak of its appreciation of opera, thanks to Carl Rosa and J. W. Turner. The novelties were Gounod's *Romeo and Juliet* (1890), Mascagni's *L'Amico Fritz*, Donizetti's *Adina*, Bizet's *Carmen* (1892), Goring Thomas' *Golden Webb*, Bizet's *Djamileh*, Adam's *Postillion of Longumeau*, Leoncavallo's *I Pagliacci*, Mascagni's *I Rantzau* (1893), Berlioz' *Damnation of Faust*, Wagner's *Meistersinger*, Mozart's *Bastien et Bastienne*, Humperdinck's *Hänsel and Gretel*, Sullivan's *Ivanhoe*, Verdi's *Falstaff*, Massenet's *La Navarraise* (1894), and Cowen's *Signa*. Other works new to Scotland were Mendelssohn's *Son and Stranger* (1895), Hamish MacCunn's *Diarmid* (1896), and Ambroise Thomas' *Le Songe* (1898). It stands to the undying credit of Carl Rosa that he especially furthered the interests of the British composer, and it was due to him that [Sir] Alexander C. Mackenzie's *Colomba* (1883) and MacCunn's *Jeannie Deans* (1894) were first staged.

Theatre bands in Scotland, which supplied the music for the productions in those days, had considerably improved in both quality and numbers during the first half of the century. The occasional praise bestowed by the press warrants the opinion of improvement, whilst the augmentation is evident from the documents quoted by J. C. Dibdin (*Annals of the Edinburgh Stage*, 1888). At the Theatre Royal, Edinburgh, in 1810, there were twelve performers, including a flute, oboe, clarinet, bassoon, and two horns, with the usual strings. Later (1824) a trumpet was added, and in 1830 a trombone, whilst the substitution of two cornopeans for the trumpet and horns in 1847 is significant, although the horns were reinstated in 1851. Drums are not mentioned until 1844, but they were doubtless used much earlier. At the Theatre Royal (Dunlop Street), Glasgow, in 1850, there were two 1st violins, two 2nd violins, viola, 'cello, bass, two cornopeans, one flute or flageolet, and these, together with the performers, were named on the playbills with an additional line which said that " the other parts of the orchestra will be complete," whatever that may imply. Under the various managements the number of instrumentalists varied, but the greatest strength of a permanent theatre orchestra in Scotland during the century would appear to be twenty-two, as at Edinburgh in 1830. Of course, when opera or a similar musical production was staged, the band was augmented locally or by musicians toured by the particular company which, as in the case of Carl Rosa, was sometimes considerable, and included particularly fine soloists, and in this way there came to Glasgow [Sir] August Mann, later of Crystal Palace fame, and Carl Boosé, afterwards the Bandmaster of the Scots Guards and founder of *Boosé's Journal*.

Among resident theatre conductors there were no outstanding personalities, although they were generally good practical and theoretical musicians who were expected to be not only efficient " Leaders," as they were called in the early days, but also competent to compose and arrange music for the various stock productions. Rarely did they receive their deserts, although under some managements an annual Benefit Concert was accorded them in common with the leading stage players. In Edinburgh in 1810, William Penson was conductor at the Theatre Royal, where he was well known as a music publisher, having joined (before 1807) with another musician named Alexander Robertson (d. 1819) as Penson & Robertson. These two also conducted a music academy in George Street. Penson was succeeded at the theatre in 1817 by his pupil James Dewar (1793-1846), who continued in this position until his death, save for two short periods when James Wilkinson (1834-37) and Musgrave (1838-40) were the conductors. Dewar was an excellent musician, both as an organist at St. George's Episcopal Chapel (1805-35) where he was highly respected, and as leader of the Professional Society Concerts. He composed some of the music for Scott's dramas, his overture to *The Antiquary* being praised, although he was better remembered by his *Popular National Melodies* (Edin., 1826 *et seq.*) and *The Border Garland* (Edin., *c.* 1829) to Hogg's poetry. Sir Alexander C. Mackenzie thought that Dewar was " a first-rate musician," and said that manuscripts in his possession proved Dewar's " high attainments."

He was succeeded at the Theatre Royal in 1848 by Alexander Mackenzie (1819-57), who had been reared in the profession, his father John Mackenzie (1797-1852) having been conductor of the Theatre Royal, Aberdeen, and of the Philharmonic Society there, whilst his grandfather was a member of the band of the Forfarshire Militia. Alexander Mackenzie was a skilled violinist who had studied under Sainton in London and Lipinski in Dresden. Although his music to Scott's plays and his operetta *The Provost's Daughter* (1852) have long passed out of ken, his songs *Nameless Lassie* and *Linton Lowrie*, were once almost the rage in Edinburgh and the east of Scotland. More lasting was his *National Dance Music of Scotland* (*c.* 1848), a new edition of which (1889) was edited by his son, the more renowned [Sir] Alexander C. Mackenzie. His Theatre Royal Band became of such repute that it made an annual visit to London. His successor was another brilliant musician of Edinburgh, Robert Barclay Stewart (1804-85), the son of Charles Stewart (d. 1818), a violinist and composer who was well appreciated for his *Collection of Strathspey Reels* (Edin., 1799). Robert had already made a name for himself in the capital and Glasgow by his Concerts *à la Musard* (1838-43) and as the leader of other concerts after the death of Dewar in 1846. His stay at the Theatre Royal was short (1857-59) because of the pulling down of the theatre for the building of the present post office, when Stewart returned to the concert world, although we find him directing the band at the Princess' Theatre, Edinburgh, in 1863-64. When Bach's *St. Matthew's Passion* was published in 1862, the subscription list included but one name from Scotland, that of R. B. Stewart, 14 Sardinia Terrace, Glasgow. With all the great lovers of music in Scotland, not a few among them in favoured positions, it was Robert Barclay Stewart, a conductor of a theatre band, who stood alone in this Bach effort from Scotland. Is it any wonder that we are prompted to ask "*Qu'allait-il faire dans cette galère ?* "

In Glasgow, where the history of music in the theatres has been continued, there were also a few men of ability as conductors who deserve at least passing notice. Thomas H. Allwood (d. 1866) was in charge of the band at the old Theatre Royal, and is well remembered for the uproar that he and the lessee John H. Alexander created in 1845, which has been so often told in the annals of the Scottish stage (see Baynham's *The Glasgow Stage*, 1892). His son, W. Fred Allwood, conducted at the Gaiety Theatre in the " Eighties." At the Theatre Royal, Allwood was succeeded by Edwin McCann, whose band and entr'acte music became quite a feature in the " Fifties." More important was Samuel Dixon Smyth (1822-84), who was in charge from the close of the " Fifties " until fire consumed the old theatre in 1863, when he went to the Prince's Theatre. At the opening of the new Theatre Royal in 1869, William Martin Foster (d. 1872) was the conductor, and he was long remembered for his *Rob Roy* overture and his song *John o' Brent* from Scott's *Lady of the Lake*. He was followed in 1873 by John Ross, an excellent violinist from Ballater, and he was succeeded in 1876 by the old Theatre Royal conductor, Samuel Dixon Smyth, whose son Thomas was conductor of the Royalty Theatre (1879-92). During the last quarter of the century the lessees of Glasgow theatres were " dazzled by the appellations ' Herr,' ' Signor,' and ' M'sieur '," to quote the late J. A. Fuller-Maitland, as the names of such conductors as Franz Groenings, Alois Brousil, Jules Guitton, Joseph Pelzer, Claude Jaquinot, and Wilhelm Iff so pertinently reveal. However, they were all good musicians.

Salaries paid to theatrical musicians in those days had scarcely altered in a century, a statement which can be tested by comparing the details made available by Dibdin (*Annals of the Edinburgh Stage*) for 1842 with the data already given for the year 1758. At the Theatre Royal, Edinburgh, in the former year, the conductor received £3 13s. 6d. weekly, which must have been considered a good salary in those days when viewed with the £4 which Murray, the lessee and manager, allowed as his own salary. The rest of the band were paid £1 to £2 a week, which was on a par with what nearly half of the actors and actresses received. In 1885, when August Manns was in Edinburgh, he confessed—" I received in Edinburgh £3, and in Glasgow, where I took [Alexander] Mackenzie's place as leader, £4 a week." It might be considered a fair remuneration for the period. Unfortunately, musicians' salaries remained at much about this level until the last decade of the century, but with the establishment of the Amalgamated Musicians' Union (1893) an improved wage system, in place of the inclusive salary, was introduced, together with better working conditions, all of which have been beneficial to the musical profession and to music itself.

In these 20th-Century days, when the instrumentalist in the symphony orchestra is considered the acme, professionally and socially, in the public eye, many people are apt to ignore the theatrical musician. Yet the theatre band has ever been the nursery of the musical profession. In the first half of the 19th Century, when concerts were few and far between, these could not have existed but for the services of the theatrical musician, who sent his customary but professionally inferior deputy to the theatre so as to enable the concert engagement at a higher fee to be fulfilled. Nor was it only the rank and file of the concert orchestras that came from theatre bands in these days. Many of the foremost conductors and composers in the world of music graduated in the theatre band, and even Scotland's own great composer, Sir Alexander C. Mackenzie, has placed on record his experiences at " busking " in a London music hall.   At any rate, long before the foundation of the Choral Unions of Glasgow and Edinburgh, and the emergence of the Scottish Orchestra and the Reid Orchestra, when there were only the occasional celebrity concerts, it was the theatre band alone that regularly catered for those interested in good orchestral music during the entr'actes or intermissions, the latter often being a programmed feature in the 19th Century.   The probable first performance of the overture *Oberon* in Scotland was played by the band of the Theatre Royal, Edinburgh, at a benefit concert in 1827. Indeed, Sir Alexander C. Mackenzie possessed a playbill of the Theatre Royal, Edinburgh, of the year 1848, in which the band, under his father's direction, played the overtures to *William Tell, Midsummer Night's Dream, Oberon,* and *Fidelio* on the same evening.

CHAPTER 7

THE LITERATORS

" In the course of study laid down for the aspirants to academical degrees, no provision was made except here and there in the most superficial and elementary style for any historical teaching. . . . The hopeful youth of Scotland are regularly trained, according to a rigid routine, to take the highest honours in arts, without the slightest taste of native historical criticism, or the slightest breath of patriotic inspiration.   And so it has come to pass that a knowledge of the history and archæology of his own country, which ought to be the household furniture, so to speak, of every educated Scotsman, was left to be sought after by a few antiquarian specialists."

JOHN STUART BLACKIE : *Scottish Song* (1889).

As just as Blackie's denunciation may have been of Scottish university training in its neglect of the " history of the fatherland " in his day, he did not mention that the reasons for the omission were primarily and essentially political.   The Union was but a century old, and the privileged classes, who were sheltering and thriving under its beneficent protection, were strongly in agreement with this policy in university training and actually wanted more universality and less nationality. Yet what Blackie also forgot was that there was a wider world than the seats of learning, and that in spite of this palpable disregard of national themes by the Universities there was always a regiment of writers outside of the schools who were interested in the national point of view, and in music, as in other spheres, the footprints of these *extra mural* phalanxes are discernible everywhere.

Scotland, as was only to be expected of a land which produced world-famous historians from George Buchanan to David Hume, could boast of not a few in the 19th Century who wrote convincingly of the annals of music in Scotland. After the pedestrian efforts of Tytler of Woodhouselee, the first to make a study of the past of Scotland's music was William Stenhouse (1773-1827) who came from Roxburghshire. It was the national song that particularly claimed his attention, and his plan was to annotate Johnson's *Scots Musical Museum* (Edin., 1787-1803). When a fresh issue of Johnson's book was contemplated in 1820, his notes, which had originally appeared in *Blackwood's Magazine* in 1817, were printed, although they were not published until they appeared in his *Illustrations of the Lyric Poetry and Music of Scotland* (Edin., 1839), to be re-issued by David Laing in 1853. Stenhouse was venomously attacked by William Chappell (*Popular Music of the Olden Time*, 1855-59) for no sensible reason, seeing that both George F. Graham and David Laing had already rectified the mistakes of Stenhouse. Despite the arrogant and mischievous opinions of William Chappell concerning Stenhouse, many of which are quite unwarrantable, the labours of the Scottish author were quite commendable, although modern research has shown him to be wrong in many instances. Stenhouse also had an editorial hand in Hogg's *Jacobite Relics* (1819-21).

Meantime David Laing (1790-1878) of Edinburgh was busy at collateral research as shown in his *Select Remains of the Ancient Poetry of Scotland* (Edin., 1822) but invariably with an eye on the music, as we see in his additional notes to Stenhouse's *Illustrations* which he published in 1853. One other valuable contribution from his pen was *An Account of the Scottish Psalter of A.D. 1566* (Edin., 1871), which had appeared in the *Proceedings of the Society of Antiquaries of Scotland* (1868). This became a precious study for later historians of music as it revealed the precise conditions of, and the attitude of the Reformers towards music immediately after the Reformation.

Next came a writer who won his spurs in England, and he stands, for the nonce, outwith our story. This was George Hogarth (1783-1870) who was born at Oxton, Berwickshire. He married the daughter of George Thomson, the editor of the *Select Collection of Original Scottish Airs* (1793-1841), and their daughter, Catherine, married Charles Dickens. Hogarth had been joint-secretary with Graham of the Edinburgh Musical Festival (1815), a contributor to the *Harmonicon* (1830), and editor of the *Morning Chronicle* (1834) in London, in which city he finally settled. Here he devoted himself entirely to musical work and published his *Musical History* (Lond., 1835), with a second edition (1838), followed by *Memoirs of the Music Drama* (Lond., 1838), which was improved as *Memoirs of the Opera* (Lond., 1851). Meantime he became editor of the *Musical Herald* (1846-47) and music critic to the *Daily News* (1846-66). He wielded a critical but temperate pen.

Returning to Scotland we come to William Dauney (1800-43) of Aberdeen, who was the author of the well-known *Ancient Scotish Melodies* (Edin., 1838), which contained a valuable introductory enquiry into the history of early Scottish music that was beyond the bounds of what Tytler and Ritson had accomplished. It has been said of the book that " it displays much judgment and learning in the general handling of the subject." Its particular value lies in the transcription of the tablature of the Skene MS. (1615-35) into modern notation, which was executed by George F. Graham, and not by Dauney, as stated by Grove (*Dictionary of Music*). Glasgow University Library contains George F. Graham's interleaved and annotated copy of Dauney's book. All subsequent writers on music in Scotland have had to use Dauney as their sheet anchor for the simple reason that, save for the work of the next author to be mentioned, there was nobody else of any authority upon whom dependence could be placed.

This other work was the *Musical Memoirs of Scotland* (Edin., 1849) by Sir John Graham Dalyell (1776-1851) of Linlithgow, a painstaking book which must have taken many years to compile. The author seems to have noted almost everything appertaining to musical instruments in Scotland that came his way as a voracious reader. Like Shakespeare, little escaped his eyes and ears. On the instruments of music of Scotland he has gathered in his book of 300 pages treasures from all sources, including the national manuscripts. Especially valuable are his plates of instruments in sculptures at Melrose, Roslyn and elsewhere, the originals of which, by now, a hundred years later, show the devastating hand of time in weathering. It is considered a rare book nowadays and, together with the Dauney volume, ought to be republished with judicious editing.

As a continuator of the work of Stenhouse came the more eclectic and accurate George Farquhar Graham (1789-1867) of Edinburgh. We shall see later that he was a man of considerable musical ability, but here we are only concerned with his literary attainments. He not only furnished Dauney with a transcription of the Skene tablature, but contributed many critical and historical notes to the music and songs, which was his forte. This latter is seen at once in the elaborate apparatus which he added to his *Songs of Scotland adapted to their appropriate Melodies* (Edin., 1848-49). His work is, for the period, highly meritorious and, in the main, thoroughly reliable, although one must always have the book of John Glen (*Early Scottish Melodies*, 1900) at hand as a check. It was also due to Graham, who fortunately made a copy of them, that we possess most of the contents of the Straloch MS. (1627-29) and the Leyden MS. (1692). Graham was an extremely able writer on music, whether he dealt with theory, history, or æsthetics. His *Account of the First Edinburgh Musical Festival* . . . 1815 (Edin., 1816) has a wider measure than its face value suggests, as its appendices prove. The same may be said of his *General Observa-*

tions upon Music, and Remarks upon Mr. Logier's System (Edin., 1817). Of his contributions on " Music " and " Organ " to the *Encyclopædia Britannica* (7th-8th editions) I shall speak later.

Robert Chambers (1802-71) had already showed interest in Scotland's music in his *Traditions of Edinburgh* (Edin., 1824), but it was not until his *Songs of Scotland Prior to Burns* (Edin., 1862) appeared that he was able to spread himself at full length on the subject, and herein we see him revelling in fact and fable regarding the old songs to his heart's content, although not always to the more critical reader's complete satisfaction. Still, he had a genuine love of music, and his *Twelve Romantic Scottish Ballads* (Edin., 1844), printed for private distribution, show that he was well equipped musically. This book is now " extremely rare," as his brother says in his *Memoirs of Robert Chambers* (Edin., 1874).

An outstanding man of letters who contributed to this special subject was that fine, sturdy character, John Stuart Blackie (1809-95), whose *Scottish Song : Its Wealth, Wisdom and Social Significance* (Edin., 1889), written when he was nearly eighty years of age, caused many a flutter in Carlyle's " gigs of respectability " because of its outspoken tone. This priceless book ought to be reprinted so as to be available to the present generation as a perpetual reminder of its heritage in Scottish song, and as a shield against the feeble, enervating stuff that has currency to-day. When Blackie saw the modern pretentious, simpering crowd calling the national song " vulgar," it roused him to wrath, and he said : " Is it vulgar to be true to nature, to hate all affectation, and call a spade a spade roundly, as Shakespeare did, and the English Bible, and Robert Burns ? Is it vulgar to be patriotic, and love the land from which came to you your father's blood and with your mother's milk ? Is it vulgar to pour forth from the heart melody of native growth as fresh and bright and strong as the heather on the Scottish braes, . . . instead of piping forth soap-bells of shallow sentiment to tickle the ear of dreamy girls and shallow foplings in a drawing-room ? " Blackie was not only appassioned of the Scottish song, but was aversioned to the sloppy sentimental stuff that passes for the ballad.

Then there came those seekers who still went up-stream to find the source of the songs. Among them was John Muir Wood (1805-92) of Edinburgh and Glasgow. His firm attempted to revive a musical periodical for Scotland in the *Scottish Monthly Musical Times* (1876-78). Wood was keenly interested in the music of the Scottish past and re-issued George F. Graham's *Songs of Scotland* (1848-49) with revised and additional historical notes, as *The Popular Songs and Melodies of Scotland* (1884). Yet, as John Glen has shown, his emendations were not always judicious, as he placed too much reliance in the strictures of William Chappell (*Popular Music of the Olden Time*, 1855-59), many of which Glen himself demonstrated to be quite unwarranted. Wood's own annotated copy of the Skene MS. (*c*. 1615-35) and his copy of Dauney's *Ancient Scotish Melodies* (1838) annotated by Graham, are preserved in his family. Wood was also one of the contributors to the first *Grove's Dictionary of Music* (1878-79 *et seq.*), writing the article on " Scottish Music " in collaboration with Thomas Logan Stillie (1832-83) of Maybole, who was for many years the music critic of the *Glasgow Herald*, in which his articles reveal a vigorous but well-disciplined pen. Four volumes of these criticisms are to be found in the Stillie Collection which he bequeathed to Glasgow University Library.

Yet the most important of all these writers on the music of Scotland was John Glen (1833-1904) of Edinburgh. Dissatisfied with the researches of Stenhouse, Graham, Wood, and others, Glen probed the very core of the question. Having built up a huge library of old Scottish music which, through the beneficence (1927) of Lady Dorothea Ruggles-Brice, is now in the National Library of Scotland, he was well armed for the fray, and his first great work of rectification was the *Glen Collection of Scottish Dance Music . . . Containing an Introduction on Scottish Dance Music, Sketches of Musicians, and Music-sellers* (Edin., 1891, Vol. ii, 1895). To the student and historian, the bibliographer and collector, these books are invaluable. Of greater importance is his *Early Scottish Melodies* (Edin., 1900). As Glen states in the preface to this book : " The necessity for such a work will be apparent when it is understood that a considerable number of our national melodies have been claimed for England, while on the other hand many Anglo-Scottish tunes manufactured in London and elsewhere for the English market, have found admittance into our national collections, and so given rise to perplexities and misunderstandings." In this reclamation of " melodies which primarily belong to Scotland," and the renunciation of others " erroneously supposed to be Scottish productions," Glen contributed a fine piece of work, thoroughly critical and substantial, which is undoubtedly the most valuable analysis of this material that has yet been published. More especially is his work praiseworthy because it exposes the pretensions of William Chappell whose book had hitherto been considered an authoritative and unimpeachable refutation of Scottish claims.

Two other writers who deserve mention are Robert Alexander Marr (1850-1905) and David Fraser Harris (1867-1912), both of whom contributed to the story of Scotland's past in music. Marr claims our special interest because he was the secretary of the Scottish Musical Society (1878) which did work of sterling value in its day. In the literary field he put forth several books which, in spite of their titles, have much more than local interest, notably his *Music and Musicians at the Edinburgh International Exhibition, 1886* (Edin., 1887), and *Music for the People : A Retrospect of the Glasgow International Exhibition, 1888* (Edin., Glasg., 1889), the latter containing a valuable " Account of the Rise of Choral Societies in Scotland." As chairman of the Entertainments' Committee of the International Exhibition, Edinburgh, 1890, he was the organiser of the Historic Musical Collection, the first music and musical instrument loan exhibition in Scotland, consisting of nearly four hundred exhibits. He also wrote a minor work *Musical History as Shown in the International Exhibition of Music and the Drama, Vienna, 1892* (Lond., 1893). Marr amassed a rare collection of programmes, placards, books and papers concerning Scottish music.

David Fraser Harris, who was greatly indebted to Marr for assistance in his musicological work, came from Edinburgh, although he was a graduate (M.D.) of Glasgow University. He became Professor of Physiology at Dalhousie University, but in private life was keenly interested in music from the Scottish past and a prominent member of the Dunedin Association. He brought greater publicity to Scotland's early activities in music in his *Saint Cecilia's Hall in the Niddry Wynd* (Edin., 1898, 2nd edit., 1911), a delightfully chatty " chapter in the history of the music of the past in Edinburgh," and particularly that of the Edinburgh Musical Society of the 18th century, which subject has been greatly added to by the contribution of W. Forbes Gray in the *Book of the Old Edinburgh Club* (Vol. xix).

As might be expected, the Church also had its music historians, although much of their work is tucked away in periodical publications. A considerable amount of this latter is of mere parochial interest, although sometimes an item here and there illumines the more important field. For example, William Anderson (1817-75) was the author of *Remarks on Congregational Psalmody* (Aberdeen, 1855), although more useful is his *Precentors and Musical Professors . . . who Flourished in Aberdeen in the Course of the Last Hundred Years* (Aberdeen, 1876). The latter is prefaced by a memoir of the author from which we learn that he was precentor of the South Parish Church (1835) in the Granite City, but at the Disruption he went to the South Free Church (1843-71). More important was Neil Livingston (1803-1891), a Free Church clergyman at Stair, Ayrshire (1844-86). His life interest was in Scottish psalmody, and he was convener of the Committee on Psalmody of the Free Church in 1867. He compiled the *Report of the Committee on Psalmody to the General Assembly* (Edin., 1867) and the *Versions of Psalms Submitted to the General Assembly* (Edin., 1867). His monument is *The Scottish Metrical Psalter of A.D. 1635* (Glasg., 1864) which, besides being a reprint in full of the original work, has valuable additional matter and various readings in the Scottish psalters from 1565 to 1655, the whole being illustrated by dissertations, notes, and facsimiles. Livingston's work was, and still is, the most earnest and reliable contribution to the history of Scottish psalmody.

On the same lines was the *History of the Scottish Metrical Psalms* (Glasg., 1872), by John West Macmeeken (*c.*1825-80) of Lesmahagow. Indeed, many a page is borrowed verbatim from Livingston, although fresh material is offered in " an account of the paraphrases and hymns." It also contains an analysis of Thomas Wood's Psalter of 1566, with twelve facsimiles, which is, for the most part, derived from the work of David Laing in 1868-71. His son, James, published *Masonic Odes and Anthems and Hymns set to Music* (Lanark, 1909). A book " of much value and accuracy, which is particularly strong in its biographical details," as the *British Musical Biography* (1897) says, is *Scottish Church Music: Its Composers and Sources* (Edin., 1891) by James Love (1858-1928) of Dundee. The author began his career as a music teacher in Glasgow, but then became organist at the High Church, Falkirk, where he remained (1877-1928) to the end of his days. Another useful book by him is *The Music of the Church Hymnary and Psalter in Metre* (Edin., 1901).

Beyond the sphere of Scottish music itself there were several Scots who made a name in the more general literature of music. One who did much for the English madrigal was Thomas Oliphant (1799-1873) of Condie, Perthshire. He joined the London Madrigal Society in 1830, becoming its honorary secretary and eventually its president. To his pen we owe *A Brief Account of the Madrigal Society* (Lond., 1835), *Short Account of Madrigals* (Lond., 1836), and the first *Catalogue of Manuscript Music in the British Museum* (Lond., 1842). He also edited *Catches and Rounds by Old Composers* (Lond., 1835), *Ditties of the Olden Time* (Lond., 1835), *Ten Favourite Madrigals* (Lond., 1836), *German Songs* . . . (Lond., 1838-49), *La Musa Madrigalesca* (Lond., 1837), *Six Ancient Part-Songs* (Lond., 1845), and *Swedish Part-Songs* (Lond., 1860), which is not an inconsiderable display of specialised interest even for a music lover.

A remarkably able historian of music was the Edinburgh born John Frederick Rowbotham (1854-1925), despite the fact that his name does not appear in *Grove's Dictionary of Music*, although he undoubtedly deserves the fullest recognition in its ample pages. If he had made no other contribution to the world of letters than his *History of Music* (Lond., 1885-87) it would have sufficed. Yet he bestowed much more, including *How to Write Music Correctly* (1889), the *Private Life of Great Composers* (1892), and *The Troubadours* (1895), besides contributions to the periodical press. When one takes into consideration the size alone of his *History of Music,* which consists of over one thousand six hundred pages, and even with that wide expanse stops short of the Renaissance, we can appreciate the comprehensiveness of the author's treatment. Every chapter displays the erudition of a scholar and the contemplation of a philosopher, although it may be that the generality of musicians nowadays have little use for either of these gifts. No wonder that he published a more popular *History of Music* (Lond., 1893) that would be more acceptable to the Philistines.

Biographers can be counted on the fingers of one hand. Lady Maxwell Wallace (1815-78), *née* Stein, was born and bred in Edinburgh, and gained some repute in her day for her translations of the letters of famous composers—*Letters from Italy and Switzerland by Felix Mendelssohn-Bartholdy* (Lond., 1862), *Letters of Felix Mendelssohn-Bartholdy from 1833 to 1847* (Lond., 1863), *Letters of W. A. Mozart, 1769-1791* (Lond., 1865), *Beethoven's Letters, 1790-1826* (Lond., 1866), *Letters of Distinguished Musicians* (Lond., 1867), *Reminiscences of Felix Mendelssohn-Bartholdy,* [*a translation of*] ... *Elise Polko* (Lond., 1869). These works, whilst they may have certain defects in translation, were the first of their kind, and opened up fresh vistas to the music-loving public. Another translator was Robert Brown-Borthwick (1840-94) of Aberdeen, who was a clergyman of the Church of England and a church composer. He translated Barbadette's *Stephen Heller* (1876) into English (Lond., 1877). Edward Bannerman B. Ramsay (1793-1872) was a dean in the Episcopal Church of Scotland who wrote *Two Lectures on the Genius of Handel* (Edin., 1862) and an excellent book on *The Use of Organs in Christian Worship* (Edin., 1865). Of course the day was over when an apology was needed when dealing with this subject, but the

PLATE XIV

SIR JOHN McEWEN, D.Mus., LL.D.
Principal: Royal Academy of Music (1924-36).

PLATE XV

Elsmore, Glasgow.

FREDERICK LAMOND, LL.D.

dean's work was timely since it came a year after the Church of Scotland had legalised the use of the organ (1864).

Among the encyclopædic workers David Baptie (1822-1906) was one of the first to supply a cheap and handy volume for those to whom *Grove's Dictionary of Music* (Lond., 1878 *et seq.*) was too expensive and too bulky. It was a *Handbook of Musical Biography* (Lond., 1883 ; 2nd edition, 1887), which has an additional value since it contains names not to be found elsewhere in English biographical dictionaries. The same might be said of his *Musicians of all Times* (Lond., 1889). On the other hand his *Musical Scotland* (Paisley, 1894) is annoyingly inaccurate. It is true that it was a pioneer work, but he omitted to practice even elementary caution in checking his dates and facts, and this book must be used with great care by those consulting it. His *Sketches of English Glee Composers* (Lond., 1895) is better. In the British Museum is his manuscript *Descriptive Catalogue* of upwards of twenty-three thousand secular part-songs, glees, madrigals, etc., which he began compiling *c.* 1846. A painstaking and more reliable author in this field was James Duff Brown (1862-1914) of Edinburgh, who was an assistant librarian in the Mitchell Library, Glasgow (1878-88), and later (1888) librarian of Clerkenwell (=Finsbury) Public Library, London. His *Biographical Dictionary of Musicians* (Paisley, 1886) is a model of its kind and " a book of considerable value as far as facts are concerned," as the late J. A. Fuller-Maitland has testified. His *Guide to the Formation of a Music Library* (Lond., 1893) was the authoritative textbook for almost half a century, and is still of great value. With Stephen S. Stratton, he edited the much-needed *British Musical Biography* (Lond., 1897), a carefully-constructed book of reference which deserves reprinting.

A writer of outstanding ability was James Cuthbert Hadden (1861-1914) of Banchory-Ternan. He was an organist, first at Mannofield Church, Aberdeen (1882), then at St. Michael's, Crieff (1884), and finally at St. John's, Edinburgh (1889), where he was probably one of the earliest in Scotland to give musical Sunday evenings in his church. He is best known, however, in the literary world where he first made his mark with *George Frederick Handel* (Lond., 1888) and *Mendelssohn* (Lond., 1888). Nearer home was his *George Thomson : The Friend of Burns* (Edin., 1898), a most useful volume in the history of music in Scotland. After this came his *Haydn* (Lond., 1902) and *Chopin* (Lond., 1903), which were easily the best in Dent's " Master Musician Series." Later books were the *Operas of Richard Wagner* (Lond., 1908), *Master Musicians* (Lond., 1909), *Favourite Operas* (Lond., 1910), *Composers in Love and Marriage* (Lond., 1912), and *Modern Musicians* (Lond., 1913). Besides his authoritative articles in the *Dictionary of National Biography* and similar works, he contributed to the *Fortnightly*, *Nineteenth Century*, *Cornhill*, and *Century* magazines, whilst he was the editor of the *Scottish Musical Monthly* (1893 *et seq*.). As the late Dr. Robertson Nicoll wrote of Hadden, he was " equally at home in literature and in music " and could write in " a clear, deft, and business-like style, with little waste of words and with a strong grasp of facts."

The speculative theory of music continued to appeal to the Scots just as it had done in the preceding century, and we find John Macdonald (1759-1831), the son of the Scottish heroine Flora Macdonald, keenly interested in the subject. He published a *Treatise Explanatory of the Principles Constituting the Practice and Theory of the Violoncello* (Lond., 1811) and a *Treatise on the Harmonic System, arising from the Vibrations of the Notes* (Lond., 1822). The book is a curiosity in its way because, whilst it is not too sound on the mathematical side, it contains some useful suggestions, although one fails to see the utility of abolishing the tailpiece on the violin.

Another and a more scientific attempt at reform was made by Henry Liston (1771-1836) of Aberdour, the author of *An Essay on Perfect Intonation* (Lond., 1812), and the inventor of an enharmonic organ which I have mentioned in the section on instruments. It is dealt with by Alexander J. Ellis in his valuable edition of Helmholtz's *Sensations of Tone* (1895). He was the father of the famous surgeon. Robert Brown (*c.* 1789-1873) of

Rockhaven was quite a remarkable man, as his published works indicate. In his *Elements of Musical Science* (Lond., 1860) he suggested the adoption of a uniform clef, and illustrated its practibility in this book which, by the way, was dedicated to Sir John F. W. Herschel. He also wrote *Rudiments of Harmony and Counterpoint on a New Method* (Lond., 1863), and an *Introduction to Musical Arithmetic, with its Application to Temperament* (Lond., 1865). Certain modifications in the method of expressing harmonical combinations are suggested in his works. A nephew, seemingly, of the last named, was Colin Brown (1818-96) who, although born in Liverpool, came of an Argyll family. He was for many years (1868-96) the Euing Lecturer on Music at Anderson's College and was the author of *Music in Common Things* (Glasg., 1870-76) which consisted of four parts :—(1) *Analysis of a Musical Sound*; (2) *Mathematical and Musical Relations of the Scale*; (3) not published ; and (4) *Music in Speech and Speech in Music*. In the second of the above brochures he described the *voice harmonium* which he invented, an instrument which gave perfect intonation, as I have already described in the section dealing with instruments of music. Another writer on the subject was James Walker (1827-95) of Aberdeen, who published a work *On Just Intonation in Song and Speech* (Aberdeen, 1878). He presented his collection of music and books on music, including some manuscripts, to Aberdeen Public Library. Then there was John Gray McKendrick (1841-1926), the Professor of Physiology at Glasgow University (1876-1906), who was an eminent authority on physiological acoustics and experimental phonetics, and published a considerable amount of material on the subject including *Sound and Speech Waves as Revealed by the Phonograph* (Glasg., 1896, Lond., 1897) and *On the Physiological Perception of Musical Tone* (Oxford, 1899). Lastly comes William Wallace (1860-1940) of Greenock, who will have a conspicuous place among composers. He was a gifted writer and a keen investigator. As an M.B. and Ch.M. (Glasg.), he showed his analytical mind in some original ophthalmological studies, but when he abandoned medicine for music his intellectual interests found scope in the physiological and psychological aspects of the art in two most useful books :—*The Threshold of Music* (Lond., 1908) and *The Musical Faculty* (Lond., 1914), which are among the best contributions to the subject.

On the more practical side were several outstanding writers. John Gunn (1765-*c.* 1824) has already been mentioned in the previous century as a skilled writer on the violoncello and theory of music. He returned to his native city, Edinburgh, just after the opening of the century, and spent most of his remaining days in antiquarian and historical research, which showed itself in his *Historical Enquiry Respecting the Performance on the Harp in the Highlands* (Edin., 1807), and in a projected *Enquiry into the Antiquity of the Harp* which was not published. He married Anne or Ann Young, " an eminent pianist " and a most gifted woman who had published *An Introduction to Music . . . Illustrated by the Musical Games and Apparatus* (Edin., 1803), which is not to be confounded, as in *Grove's Dictionary of Music*, with her *Elements of Music* (Edin., 1803, 1820). This remarkable apparatus for games, which was entirely her own conception, may be seen in the Science and Arts Museum, Dublin. The idea deserves the attention of modern educationists because of the extreme importance of the motor factor in education. It reminds one that much later Goethe, in his *Wilhelm Meister's Wanderjahre* (1821), shows how children could acquire the art of penmanship, and conceive the high value of mensuration and arithmetic much sooner by learning the elements of music theoretically.

One of the first in the century to write on the theory of music in Scotland was James Fairbairn (*c.* 1805-1857), who may have been a school teacher, seeing that the composed some school part-songs. His book was entitled *Elements of Music*, (1) *Melody*, (2) *Harmony* (Edin., 1832), and contained an Appendix " on the nature and causes of sound, and the consonance and dissonance of intervals, as arising from one system of vibration." Next came William Grier of Aberdeen, who issued *An Essay on the First Principle of Music*

(Aberdeen, 1838), which had previously appeared in *The Musical Cyclopaedia* (Lond., 1835 ; 2nd ed., 1852).

In the north also a small book that had some acceptance was Cowie's *Catechism of Music* (Aberdeen, c.1835). Another textbook, popular in its day was an *Essay on the Theory and Practice of Musical Composition* (Edin., 1838) by George F. Graham (1789-1867) which was an enlarged reprint of his article " Music " in the *Encyclopaedia Britannica* (7th-8th editions). Another contributor of articles on music to the latter was William Dyce (1806-64) of Aberdeen, one of the founders of the Motett Society in London, and the editor of the *Book of Common Prayer . . . at the Reformation Period, with an Essay on that class of Music* (Lond., 1844). The works of Dr. James Currie (1828-86) were of paramount importance. His *Elements of Musical Analysis* (Edin., 1858) was an excellent production, and there was nothing comparable in English except the translations from Catel and Marx. His *First Musical Grammar* (Edin., 1873) was equally praiseworthy. Samuel Barr (1807-66), who taught music theory at the Mechanics' Institute, Glasgow, issued quite a good textbook on the *Theory and Practice of Harmony and Composition* (Lond, 1861). An elementary work, the *Science of Music Simplified* (Glasg., 1860) by Peter Carmichael was popular in its day. From Inverary came William R. Broomfield (1826-88), a practical music teacher, who wrote *The Principles of Ancient and Modern Music deduced from the Harmonical Numbers of Antiquity* (Aberdeen, 1863), and a *Manual of Harmony for the Use of Students in Musical Composition* (Glasg., 1872). Franklin S. Petersen (1861-1914), B.Mus.(Oxon.), was for many years a university lecturer at Edinburgh and St. Andrews, and later became Ormond Professor of Music at Melbourne University. He was the author of two first-rate books,—*Elements of Music* (Lond., 1896) and *An Introduction to the Study of Theory* (Lond., 1897).

One of the best practical works of its kind was the *Musical Educator* (Edin., Lond., 1895-1908), in five volumes, edited by John Greig, D.Mus. (1854-1909). As contributors he gathered around him a number of prominent fellow Scots whose articles were of the highest value. Among them were James Sneddon, Mus. Bac. (1833-1915) on the " Rudiments of Music " ; John Robertson, Mus. Bac. (1838-19 . .) on " Harmony " and " Counterpoint " ; John Grieve (1842-1916) on " Musical Form " and " Harmonium and American Organ " ; James Smith Anderson, Mus. Bac. (1853-1945), on the " Organ " ; James Robert Dibdin (1856-1902) on " Nationality in Music " ; and William Townsend (1849-1925) on the " Pianoforte," a very thoughtful study. The last-named was for many years at the head of his craft in Edinburgh and was considered " a pioneer in modern pianoforte technique," as his book *Balance of Arm in Pianoforte Technique* (4th ed., 1932) revealed, a work of quite a new outlook on the subject and one which certainly contributed fresh views from the angle of dynamics. Here, too, is the place for the mention of the didactic contributions of Sir John B. McEwen (b. 1868) who, in his early years (1895-98) taught the pianoforte, harmony and composition at the Glasgow Athenaeum School of Music, although he became better known at the Royal Academy of Music, London, where he taught harmony and composition (1898-1924), and followed Mackenzie as Principal (1924-36). In addition to his *Text-Book of Harmony and Counterpoint* (Lond., 1908), *Exercises on Phrasing in Pianoforte Playing* (Lond., 1908), *A Primer of Harmony* (Lond., 1911), and *Musical Composition* (Lond., 1922), he has issued three works which are out of the ordinary ; these are : *The Thought in Music* (Lond., 1912), *The Principles of Phrasing and Articulation in Music* (Lond., 1916), and an *Introduction to Beethoven's Piano Sonatas* (Lond., 1931). In these books we have the results of a life's experience in theory and practice set down by one who does not merely amass material but sifts it.

Improvements in musical notation seem to have intrigued the Scots, and the first of these novelties is to be seen in a book by John Austin (1752-1830), of Craigton, Dunbartonshire, entitled *A System of Stenographic Music* (Lond., 1820), in which one line and six characters are used to express the modern stave and notation.

Another curious " inventor " was Robert Wark (1804-84) of Glasgow, who thought out what he called " a system of ' Map ' notation " by means of coloured notes. Alexander Macdonald, who seems to be identical with a precentor at Old Greyfriars, Edinburgh (1807-17), was the author of *The Notation of Music Simplified* (Glasg., 1826), in which " the characters employed in the notation of language are applied to the notation of music," a novation which seems to have pleased William Hawes, the English musician. Then there were several novel sol-faists who had " systems." Robert McAlister (b. 1822), of Glasgow; William Brechin (b. 1824) of Brechin; John Lang (b. 1829) of Paisley; and David Colville (b. 1829) of Campbeltown. The first claimed that he had originated the " Tonic sliding scale or musical ladder." The second brought out " Brechin's Stave Sol-fa Notation " which, through Professor Halberg, was adopted in Sweden as a national system. The third stated that he was the author of the " Union Notation," in which the notes are indicated to sol-fa musicians by having the initial letter of the various notes in the sol-fa scale placed within the head of the ordinary musical characters." The fourth published a *Graduated Course of Elementary Instruction in Singing* (1864) " on the letter-note method." James Mackintosh, another concocter, published an interesting book called *The Musicmaster for Schools and Families* (Lond., Glasg., 1862), which displayed some " improvements on the sol-fa system." Meanwhile, Henry Steedman (1826-84) of Edinburgh was protesting that the " sol-faing *against* the key " was wrong, and in 1848 was already an established teacher of a method which Curwen, in a more thorough way, brought to Scotland in 1855. Here, too, one can mention the work of John Alston (1777-1846), whose bust in the Glasgow Royal Blind Asylum tells us that he printed the first bible "in raised letters" for the blind. His *Musical Catechism, with Tunes, for the Blind* (Glasg., 1838), and his *Selection of Scottish Songs, embossed for the use of the Blind* (Glasg., 1844) were " the earliest of the kind known."

In addition to the specious advice given in most of the psalm books on how to sing, or how *not* to sing, there were a goodly few books specially written on singing, which was only natural, seeing that Scotland is a land of singers. A brief survey of this field shows that George F. Graham wrote his *Elements of Singing* (Edin., 1817) for the Edinburgh Institution of Sacred Music. In the following decade Robert A. Smith's *Introduction to Singing* (Edin., 1826), and Finlay Dun's *Solfeggi and Exercises* (Lond., 1829) commanded special attention. James Davie (*c.* 1783-1857) of Aberdeen also wrote a *Compendious Introduction to the Art of Singing* (Aberdeen, *c.* 1840). Two rival books in the " Forties " were the *Art of Singing at Sight Simplified* (Glasg., 1844) by Robert McAllister, and a work with a similar title (1847, 1859) by Samuel Barr. Next came a work by an adept, *Vocal Exercises* (Lond., 1855) by Elizabeth Masson, a work that was appreciated in Scotland. Then there was a *Graduated Course of Elementary Instruction in Singing* (1864) by David Colville, but more advanced were the *Solo Singer* (Lond., 1887), the *Art of Singing* (Lond., 1892) by Matthew S. Dunn, and a *Textbook on the Natural Use of the Voice* (Lond., 1895) by William Nicholl. From one who was actually connected with the old school boards, James W. Tosh, there came a useful *Sight-singing, Voice and Ear Training for Schools* (1889). The same author had previously issued *The Musical Inspection, and How to Prepare for It* (1888).

The violin, which has even been considered Scotland's national instrument, could scarcely escape the attentions of musicographers. There were two writers who touched the fringe of the subject. One was Peter Davidson of Speyside who published *The Violin : A Concise Exposition of the General Principles of Construction* (Glasg., 1871),with a second edition (Lond., 1880) containing useful addenda. The other was Alexander Gregor Murdoch (1843-91) of Glasgow who wrote *The Fiddle in Scotland* (Lond., 1888) which dealt with " Scotch Fiddlers and Fiddle-Makers." A far greater authority was James M. Fleming (b. 1839) also of Glasgow, and a pupil of Samuel D. Smyth and Ole Bull for the violin. He contributed many articles on the violin to music journals, but was better appreciated for his books *Old Violins and their Makers* (Lond., 1883), and the *Fiddle Fancier's Guide* (Lond., 1892), both of which reveal the matured views of a skilled connoisseur. A more popular authority on the subject was William Crawford Honeyman (1845-1919) who, although born in New Zealand, was of Scottish parentage, and was reared in Edinburgh. Beginning life as a professional violinist, becoming conductor of the orchestra at Macarte's Theatre, Leith, he later abandoned the bow for the pen and gained some celebrity for his serials in the popular press, in the pages of which there first appeared his books on *The Violin : How to Master It* (1880), *Hints to Violin Players* (1885), and his more important *Scottish Violin Makers : Past and Present* (1898, 2nd edit., 1910), this latter being a reliable guide in this field, showing excellent judgment. He also compiled *The Young Violinist's Tutor and Duet Book* (1883) and the *Strathspey, Reel, and Hornpipe Tutor* (1898).

Journals devoted exclusively to music were not so plentiful in Scotland as they were in England, nor were they, with one exception, so important, although that is no reason why *Grove's Dictionary of Music* should ignore the few that did exist. A glance at the London monthly musical journal, *The Harmonicon* (1823-33), shows that even if Scotland did not possess its own periodical, there were Scots who were contributing to its pages. George F. Graham (1789-1867) and George Hogarth, (1783-1870) wrote on Scottish musical news, whilst John Thomson (1805-41), Finlay Dun (1795-1853), Charles A. Seymour (1810-75), as well as Hogarth and others, composed music for the supplements. Grove's neglect is more to be deplored because it was William Hamilton (1812-87) of Glasgow, in his *British Minstrel*, the first Scottish music journal, originally issued with music supplements in penny and twopenny numbers in 1842, who must be considered as the pioneer in cheap music, since Novello's *Musical Times* (London) did not begin until 1844. The *British Minstrel* of Glasgow, which was edited by James Manson (c. 1812-63), ran for three years (1842-45) and was bound up and issued in three volumes (I and II, 1844 ; III, 1845). When the " Fifties " came, and there was an urge for an improvement in psalmody, *The Psalmodist and Magazine of Sacred Music* (1856) was published in Edinburgh under the auspices of the Scottish Vocal Music Association. It contained some good articles and music supplements. Few people seem to have been sufficiently interested, outside of the movement, to give it adequate support, with the result that it only ran for twelve monthly issues. A similar venture from the capital was made in 1871 when the *Presbyterian Psalmodist* was launched. It was quite a virile production, and it coincided with the movement for improved psalmody, but it lasted no longer than its predecessor. Paisley also had an unsuccessful monthly *Psalmodist* in 1874. Meantime, Ernst Köhler & Son, Edinburgh, had issued the *Musical Star* (1864), also with musical supplements. John Charles Grieve (1842-1916) was its editor, and in its pages some of his books first appeared as articles. Then came the *Scottish Monthly Musical Times* (1876-78) edited by Robert McHardy for Wood & Co. After this there does not appear to have been a journal devoted to music until Edinburgh attempted a monthly in 1883-84 called *St. Cecilia's Magazine*. In 1893 the *Scottish Musical Monthly* was founded, the best journal of its kind in the country. Edited by J. Cuthbert Hadden (1861-1914), it became the mouthpiece of independent opinion and the battle ground for the thrusts of forlorn hopes, apart from the sterling work which it did for the cause of music and musicians in Scotland. It attracted some brilliant writers and critics, including G. Bernard Shaw, who contributed an amusing article *How to become a Musical Critic*, whilst the caustic editorials of Hadden and the even more maliciously pungent London Notes of J. F. Runciman, created quite a stir in musical journalism. It came to a sudden *finale* in April 1896, when it was acquired by the publishers of the *Scottish Musical Review* with which, according to the announcement, it was supposed to be incorporated. This latter journal was founded in 1894 and lasted until 1897, but although at the so-called " incorporation " it had promised " to retain some features " of the old *Scottish Musical Monthly*, originality and independence were not certainly among them.

CHAPTER 8

THE PERFORMERS

" Scotland is gaining ground. Until the last decade there were no Scotchmen possessing a musical reputation beyond that of Niel Gow, or R. A. Smith ; now we have composers, vocalists, and instrumentalists in the highest departments, and the cry is ' still they come.' "
The British Bandsman and Orchestral Times : Nov., 1890.

It is in the tail of this extract that the sting hides its venom, for one senses the feeling that the writer was not pleased with the influx of " Scotchmen." In any case, the truth is that Scotsmen as composers and instrumentalists " in the highest departments " were not plentiful, although the suggestion is admissible of singers, since some of the most dazzling of vocal stars during the first half of the century came from north of the Tweed. Nor is this to be wondered at, since the Scots are a race of singers, as are the Irish and Welsh, although, if we open our ears to Sassenach amusement we learn that the reason for the Scot's delight in vocal music is that it is cheaper than learning an instrument. In Scotland, one benefit at least accrued from the Reformation, and that was that it almost compelled all to be singers whether they wanted this virtuosity or not. So, when the 19th Century dawned with the people easing themselves from the yoke of eternal psalmody, Scotland was able to show more vocal societies to her credit than the remainder of the British Isles put together. Indeed many of the leading concert and theatrical tenors and basses had originally been church precentors, and one at least of these, John Templeton, notwithstanding his superb voice, never rid himself of the style of the psalmist and the limbus of the pew. Further, this precentorial link with the concert and stage discloses quite an interesting sidelight in the fact that almost all these erstwhile precentors came from Secession or Relief Churches or, in other words, they were Dissenters, and thereby hangs a moral, as the warning finger of the Established Church would point in triumph.

The first of these Scottish singers who brought glory to the British stage was John Sinclair (1791-1857), who began his meteoric career as a bandsman in Campbell of Shawfield's Regiment. After teaching music in Aberdeen, he appeared at the Haymarket Theatre, London, as Cheerly in *Lock and Key* (1810), and the following year triumphed as Don Carlos in Linley's *Duenna*. After this his success was assured, and even in the Provinces he created a perfect *furore*. Then Paris and Italy claimed him, which brought the opportunity of study under Pellegrini and Banderali but, above all, he had instruction from Rossini, who wrote the part of Idreno in *Semiramide* for him. After singing in all the great Italian cities, he returned to Covent Garden, the Adelphi, and Drury Lane, singing with greater charm than ever. He was " one of the most popular singers of his day," and was the creator of the tenor roles in Bishop's *Guy Mannering*, Davy's *Rob Roy*, to mention only two Scottish favourites.

Almost as great an artist was John Wilson (1800-49), a pupil of John Mather, Benjamin Gleadhill, and Finlay Dun of Edinburgh, his home town. After holding several precentorships he went to London and studied under Lanza and Crivelli, but made his stage début in Edinburgh as Bertram in *Guy Mannering* (1830). After this he went straight to London, where he appeared at Covent Garden as Don Carlos in Linley's *Duenna*. At this theatre he stayed until 1835, when he crossed over to Drury Lane and sang in Balfe's *Siege of Rochelle* and other operas, but in 1838 he went to America with Seguin. He then conceived his Scottish entertainments which were rapturously received because of their specialized *gamut*, as in his " Jacobite Songs," " A Nicht wi' Burns," " Mary Queen of Scots," and the like, all of which became attractions by reason of his book entitled *Wilson's Edition of Songs of Scotland* (1842). " One of the most successful Scottish singers " is the opinion expressed of Wilson in the *British Musical Biography* (1897).

The Templeton family of Riccarton were all singers : James (1784-1868), Robert (1790-1853), Matthew (1792-1870), Andrew (1796-1841), and John (1802-86), the majority of whom were precentors. The greatest of all was John who, " with splendid voice, graceful execution and exquisite taste " (Grove), won his way to fame. Forsaking the precentor's desk at Dr. Brown's Secession

Church, Edinburgh, he made his operatic début at Worthing (1828) in Shield's *Poor Soldier* as Dermot, but was soon at Drury Lane (1831) as Belville in *Rosina* and as Hawthorn in *Love in a Village* with another Scot, Mary Ann Paton, as Rosetta. His success was instantaneous, but greater triumphs came in 1833 when the great Malibran chose him as her tenor, a position which he retained until the prima donna's death (1836), which forms the basis of the book, *Templeton and Malibran*, by W. H. H. (Lond., 1880). He then continued as a radiant tenor star in all the great operas, playing as many as eighty different rôles, his supreme artistry being universally admitted. At the conclusion of a performance of *La Sonnambula* (1833) Bellini embraced him, and when he went to Paris with Balfe (1842) he was received with the most profound respect by Auber and the *élite* of the musical and literary *salons*. He retired in 1852 after having toured America with his " Templeton Entertainments " to the greatest *éclat*.

His contemporary was Mary Ann Paton (1802-64), an exquisite soprano with the wonderful compass. Coming of a musical family, her father being a violinist and her great-uncle one of the founders of the Aberdeen Musical Society, she was bred to music, and at the age of four played the harp, pianoforte, and violin. When only eight she made her first public appearance in Edinburgh as a singer and performer, playing Viotti's *Concerto in G* for the violin. After singing at the Bath Concerts (1820) she appeared at the Haymarket, London, as Susanna in Mozart's *Figaro* (1822), which established her reputation. For two decades she was at the peak in professional circles, both at Covent Garden and Drury Lane. Her voice was " a pure soprano, . . . powerful, sweet-toned, and brilliant " (Grove). Her sisters were also in opera, Isabella at Drury Lane (*c.* 1825) and Eliza at the Haymarket (1833).

Of subordinate interest, but still quite famous in her day, was Eliza Inverarity (1813-46), a fine soprano and a grand-niece of Robert Fergusson. Taught by Thorne and Alexander Murray of Edinburgh, her birthplace, she made her first public appearance at a concert given by Murray in 1829, but the following year was making her bow to London audiences. In 1836 she married the *basso* Charles T. Martyn, and sang with him in opera throughout the country, notably at Edinburgh in Bellini's *La Sonnambula* (1838) with John Templeton. In the United States, where she appeared in opera with her husband, she attracted attention, especially in Beethoven's *Fidelio* at New York (1839). Unfortunately she died at the early age of thirty-three. Another well-known Scot was Elizabeth Masson (1806-65), a contralto singer taught by Mrs. Henry Smart and Giuditta Pasta. She made her *début* at the Ancient Concerts, London (1831) and sang at the Aberdeen Musical Festival (1834), but became better known as a composer and teacher, as her *Vocal Exercises* (Lond., 1855) show. She was, with Mary Sarah Steele, the founder of the Royal Society of Female Musicians (1838). In her own land, Helen Drysdale Kirk (*c.* 1844-71), also a contralto, won her way into the hearts of the people by her delectable singing of Scots songs. Here too, might be mentioned, for association sake, Euphrosyne Parepa-Rosa (1836-74) who, although born in Edinburgh, was of Wallachian and English parents. She became a famous *prima donna* and was partly responsible for the formation of the opera company headed by Carl Rosa, who she married.

David Kennedy (1825-86) was the son of a Perth precentor, and himself held a similar position there and in Edinburgh, where he studied under Edmund Edmunds. In 1860 he began his concert tours as a tenor vocalist which took him to Hanover Square Rooms and the Egyptian Hall, London (1862), and to various parts of England, specializing in the " auld Scots sangs." Later he visited the United States, Canada, Australia, New Zealand, South Africa and India, winning plaudits everywhere. His daughter, Marjory Kennedy Fraser (1857-1930), widely known for her *Songs of the Hebrides* (1909, 1917, 1919), wrote an interesting work about her father entitled *David Kennedy, the Scottish Singer* (1887), and her own autobiography *My Life of Song* (1928).

Matthew Sinclair Dunn (1846-1911) began his musical career as a cornettist in the band of a Glasgow Volunteer Regiment, and then became a precentor in Ayrshire, but after studying under W. H. Cummings and Ettore Fiori at the Royal Academy of Music, London, he appeared as a concert tenor at the Crystal Palace and the Promenade Concerts with much success. Finally, he settled down at teaching, notably at Trinity College of Music, London, being widely known for his books of instruction and for his compositions. His contemporary and fellow townsman, William Nicholl (1851-1902) was also a pupil of the Royal Academy of Music (1884-45), where he secured the Parepa-Rosa Gold Medal. He became a teacher of singing at the Academy (1891) and sang at the Richter, Crystal Palace, London Ballad, and other concerts, as well as at the great provincial festivals. His *Text-book on the Natural Use of the Voice* (Lond., 1895) contained some acceptable practical hints.

Better known in Scotland was Durward Lely (1857-1944) *né* James Lyle. After pupilage at Arbroath, his home town, he studied in Milan under Lamperti and others. Returning to England he entered upon an operatic career and was the original Don José in *Carmen* when Emily Soldene produced the opera (1879). For two years he was with Carl Rosa but gained greater renown with Gilbert and Sullivan, creating many parts, notably Nanky-Poo in the *Mikado*. After that began his series of successful recitals "Scottish Song and Story," which were heard as far afield as Canada and the United States. He first appeared at the Glasgow Choral Union Concerts in 1891. In 1896 he founded his own opera company. Equally famed, in Scotland at least, was Jessie Niven MᶜLachlan (1866-1916), a delightful soprano whose Highland songs, in Gaelic, earned for her endearment throughout the land of her birth and with Scots everywhere. For several years she sang at the concerts of the Gaelic Society in London and her vogue so intrigued the late Queen Victoria that the Gaelic songstress was "commanded" to appear at Balmoral in 1892. In 1921 a memorial was erected over her grave in Cathcart Cemetery.

The repute of a contemporary soprano, Margaret Macintyre was gained in a different field and brought wider recognition. Although a Scot, she was born in India, because her father, General John Mackenzie Macintyre, was serving in that land. She was a pupil of Manuel Garcia and others in London and made her *début* at Covent Garden as Micaela in *Carmen* (1888). " Her success was emphatic," and she continued this triumph as Inez in *L'Africaine,* Mathilde in *Guglielmo Tell,* and Marguerite in *Mefistofele* and *Faust.* Her first festival appearance was at Leeds (1889), where she gained later attraction (1892, 1895), as well as at the Glasgow Choral Union concerts (1890) where she sang in the *Messiah* in a brilliant cast with Marian McKenzie, Iver McKay and Andrew Black. She was the first Rebecca in Sullivan's *Ivanhoe* (1891) and sang Senta in the *Flying Dutchman* at Covent Garden (1892). During her Russian tour she played Elizabeth in *Tannhäuser* with Battistini as Wolfram.

Lastly, among Scotland's great singers comes Andrew Black (1859-1920), who began his musical carrer as organist at Anderston United Presbyterian Church, Glasgow. Studying under Randegger and J. B. Welch in London, and with Domenico Scafati at Milan, he first appeared in London at the Crystal Palace Concerts in 1887, where his fine baritone voice won him the plaudits of the press. Although he sang in opera, both in this country and America, it was in the festival and concert that he found his *métier*. After his early appearance at Glasgow with Iver McKay in MacCunn's *Lay of the Last Minstrel* (1888), came his sensational performance in Dvořák's *Spectre's Bride* (Leeds Festival, 1892). From then onwards to his part of Judas in Elgar's *Apostles* (Birmingham Festival, 1903) he proved himself as the real successor of Santley. In 1893 he became a teacher of singing at the Manchester College of Music.

All of the aforementioned " stars " in the firmament of the art belonged to " singing," an accomplishment which, in Scotland, was considered quite distinct from, and less objectionable than " music." Yet those who followed the latter and more reprobative calling in

Scotland managed to make a name here and there, one or two at the very pinnacle. When John Broadwood (1732-1812) of Cockburns-path produced the modern pianoforte in England, he scarcely had any idea that some of his countrymen would be spreading their fingers over its keyboard, gaining as much repute as performers as he was doing as an inventor. To be sure, there were not many Scots to win such recognition, but the handful that did were not unworthy. Perhaps the first to make a name outside of Scotland was Thomas Molleson Mudie (1809-76) who, although born in London, came of Scottish parents, and spoke the Doric to his last days. He was one of the first ten pupils at the [Royal] Academy of Music, London, where he studied the pianoforte under Cipriani Potter and composition under Dr. William Crotch. His student days at the Academy (1823-32) were almost Sorbonique in duration, and, it is said, this would have continued had he not been appointed Teacher of the Pianoforte (1832-44) at the institution. Scotland then called him and, settling in the capital in 1844, made a name for himself as a distinguished teacher, the best, said Sir Alexander C. Mackenzie, that the country ever had. Yet after nearly twenty years in Edin-burgh he returned to London. Sir George A. Macfarren, who knew him in his early Academy days, wrote his biography for *Grove's Dictionary of Music*, but stressed his work as a composer rather than as a pianist.

Another and more famous pianist of Scottish parentage and education was Robena Anna Laidlaw (1819-1901). She was born at Bretton in Yorkshire, but was educated at her aunt's school in Edinburgh, and had her earliest lessons on the pianoforte from Robert Müller in that city. Following her studies later in Germany and London, she soon gained sufficient distinction to be invited to the concert platform and was engaged at Paganini's farewell concert in London (1834), at other concerts in Berlin (1836), and at the Gewandhaus Concerts, Leipsic (1837). From this period dates Schumann's *Fantasiestücke* (Op. 12), one of " that splendid set of pianoforte works of the highest excellence, on which a considerable part of his fame rests " (Spitta), which the composer dedicated to

Robena Laidlaw. After a lengthy and successful tour through Prussia, Russia, and Austria, and an appointment as pianist to the Queen of Hanover, she returned to London. In 1852 (1855) she married a fellow Scot (Thomson) and went into complete retirement.

One who found both renown and reward as a pianist at the Royal Academy of Music, London, was Frederick Bowen Jewson (1823-91) of Edinburgh. Taught first by his father, S. Jewson, a well-known musician in the capital, he came to the front almost as a child. Indeed, at the age of twelve he gave a concert in Edinburgh, on which occasion he also played one of his own compositions. According to the late Philip Halstead of Glasgow, his technique as a youth was so amazing that George F. Graham arranged that he should go to the Royal Academy of Music to study under his friend, Cipriani Potter, where, in 1837, he became King's Scholar, later to be appointed Teacher of the Pianoforte, and finally a Director of the institution. In 1866 he was appointed Musician in Ordinary to Queen Victoria. As a composer, he has a place elsewhere in these pages, but as a pianist he was considered, in his younger days, as one of the outstanding *virtuosi* in London, whilst as a teacher he was recognized as unrivalled. He claimed the friendship of Mendelssohn, Wagner, Chopin, and Moscheles.

William Townsend (1849-1925) was another Edinburgh man who went to the Royal Academy of Music (1865-8), studying the pianoforte under Sterndale Bennett and W. H. Holmes, but later at Leipsic Conservatorium under Ernst Wenzel. He became an A.R.A.M. (1870) and an examiner for the Royal College of Music (1883). There is little vital testimony of his playing, but the press received his pianoforte recitals in Scotland with the highest praise, whilst others who were intimately acquainted with him have spoken with considerable zeal of his abilities. Of greater importance was Helen Hopekirk (1856-1941), who also came from Edinburgh. Studying first at Edinburgh under G. Lichtenstein and [Sir] Alexander C. Mackenzie, she went to Leipsic Conservatorium and to Leschetitzky and Navrátil at Vienna. Making her *début* at the Gewandhaus Concerts, Leipsic (1879), she came to England the following year and appeared under [Sir] August Manns at the Crystal Palace Concerts. At the Choral Union Concerts, Glasgow (1879, 1889), under Manns and Henschel, she had a warm reception. Perhaps her greatest triumphs were gained in America (1883-84, 1886), notably at the Boston Symphony Concerts and the Philadelphia Festival. In 1886 she was winning fresh laurels at the Vienna Philharmonic Concerts and later at the Richter Concerts in London under Henschel, Nikisch, and Gericke. Contemporary criticism of her playing is quite lavish in praise, and the *Biographical Dictionary of Musicians* (1886), which can generally be trusted as registering the prevailing pulse, says : " Her style is refined, and her execution brilliant." Yet the fame of all who had gone before was dimmed by the radiance of one who stands pre-eminent among the world's *virtuosi*,—Lamond.

Frederick A. Lamond (1868-19. .) was born in Glasgow, where he found his earliest instructors in his brother David for the pianoforte, and Henry C. Cooper (1819-81) the conductor at the Gaiety Theatre, " one of the foremost of the English school of violinists." At the age of fourteen he was sent to the Raff Conservatorium, Frankfort, where he studied under Max Schwarz (pianoforte), Heermann (violin), and Anton Urspruch the pianist (composition). Later he became the envied pupil of Von Bülow and Liszt. After his first important concert appearance in Berlin (1885) at seventeen years of age, where he took the audience by storm, his position was assured on the Continent. The following year he made his concert *début* in Britain at a Glasgow recital, when the critic of the *Musical Times* said :—" I deem it no exaggeration . . . to say that he must take rank even now with the very foremost of pianoforte *virtuosi*. His *technique* is simply marvellous." When he appeared at St. James's Hall, London, in 1889, the same journal opined that " he displayed an even more remarkable purity and accuracy of *méchanisme* than when he came to us fresh from the hands of Liszt three years ago." It said further, which might well be remembered in view of subsequent neglect by this country, that Lamond " is one of the foremost pianists of the day, and in course of time this fact will surely be recognized by the English public." However, it mattered little what evaluation we placed on his abilities, since he continued to win laurels in lands where he was appreciated—Germany and Russia, until the upheaval of 1914 brought its woe. To-day he is in his native land where he is justly revered. As a composer he will have due recognition later.

Since the organ was practically confined for three-quarters of the century to the few Episcopalian and Roman Catholic Churches, it is only in the nature of things that there were so few organists of note *from* Scotland. The first outstanding man of native birth was David Hamilton (1803-63) of St. John's Episcopal Church, Edinburgh, and the inventor of the pneumatic lever action. Others were Augustus G. Jamieson (1844-88) who was at St. Paul's Episcopal Church, Edinburgh, Arthur J. Curle (1853-1906), a pupil of Reinecke and E. F. Richter at Leipsic Conservatorium, who was for years at St. Augustine's Church, Edinburgh, and Thomas Smith Drummond whose recitals at the Glasgow International Exhibition (1888) were much appreciated. Another clever organist was Daniel F. Wilson, a pupil of Peace. He took his D.Mus. (Oxon.) degree in 1894. The fame of these organists was confined to Scotland. Those who earned wider celebrity were Englishmen holding organ appointments in Scotland, such as Henry Lambeth (1822-95) and Albert Lister Peace (1844-1912). The only Scot who made a name for himself south of the border was James Kelt Strachan (1860-19..) who was born at Errol, Perthshire. Beginning his career as a chorister at St. Paul's Episcopal Church, Dundee, he became organist at St. Enoch's Church in the same city (1877). From 1880 until 1888 he was at Kelvingrove U.P. Church, Glasgow. After studying at Paris under Guilmant he returned to Scotland and in 1892 became organist at the Free College Church, Glasgow but, like most of Scotland's best he was soon attracted south where his recitals at the Albert Hall and the Bow and Bromley Institute, London, " established his reputation as one of the finest executants " of his day. Later he was at Anderston Parish Church, Glasgow.

Among violinists, only a few Scots commanded attention as performers, and even that was confined to Britain. In Edinburgh, in the opening years of the century, instead of *virtuosi* of the pose of Schetky, Stabilini and Janiewicz, there appeared men whose names reveal their land, James Dewar (1793-1846), Robert B. Stewart (1804-85), Alexander Murray (*fl.* 1800-40), Alex Mackenzie (1819-57), and William Howard (1831-77). Obviously they were not soloists of the rank of a Paganini, but they were as good probably as Spagnoletti or Loder, and often shared honours with them as leaders. Indeed, their reputation was practically confined to Scotland, although Murray was engaged at the York Musical Festival (1823) and at the Westminster Abbey Festival (1834) with Dewar.

One who did make something of a reputation as a violinist was Charles A. Seymour (1810-75) of Edinburgh. He had studied at the [Royal] Academy of Music, London, being one of the foundation students, and almost immediately sprang into eminence when he became principal violinist in Queen Adelaide's Private Band (1830). It was in Manchester however, where he settled, that Seymour made a permanent name for himself, first as leader of the Manchester Concert-Hall Orchestra (1838) and then of the Hallé Orchestra (1858). Another remarkable Edinburgh violinist was William Waddel (b. 1842). Taught at home by William Howard, and in London by Henry Blagrove, he went to Leipsic (1862) where he studied under Ferdinand David. Returning to Edinburgh he had to accept an organist's position in a church, but later founded a violin academy of his own which had great success. He was also known for his Free Musical Evenings for the People and for Mr. Waddel's Choir. Then there were the scions of " the clever Drechsler-Hamilton family," as Sir Alexander C. Mackenzie dubs his colleagues in the Edinburgh String Quartet. The first was Carl Drechsler Hamilton (1846-1900) who was " a violoncellist of great merit," and then his sister, Emmy Drechsler Hamilton, a violinist of repute, who had appeared in 1869 at the Gewandhaus Concerts, Leipsic. Indeed, Sir Alexander C. Mackenzie (1847-

1935) must be included here among Scotland's best known violinists. He was a pupil of Sainton at the Royal Academy of Music, and after his student days he toured as a solo violinist. Later, for business purposes, he practically abandoned the instrument for the piano-forte, although occasionally he took part in quartets with Joachim, Wilhelmj, Strauss and Lady Hallé.

Two Scottish exponents on the wood-wind, Fraser and Mackintosh, gained fame nationally and internationally respectively. Thomas Fraser (c. 1760-1825) was Scotland's own superb oboist. His playing enraptured Burns who, in a letter (1793) to George Thomson, enclosing the air *Saw ye Johnnie comin'*, said of Fraser:— " When he plays it slow . . . he makes it the language of despair." Burns set the words *Thou hast left me ever Jamie* to this pathetic melody. Fraser, we are told in 1820, was " the principal oboe concerto player in Edinburgh, of which city he is a native. His style of playing the melodies of Scotland is peculiarly chaste and masterly." George F. Graham, who knew Fraser well, spoke of him as an " excellent oboe player," saying that it was for him that he wrote " several passages in orchestral symphonies " which he composed for the Edinburgh " Fund Concerts." At the lower end of the *gamut* was John Mackintosh (1767-1844) the bassoonist, " famous as one of the finest performers of his day, and celebrated all over Europe for the excellent tone and style of playing." He succeeded Holmes, who held sway in London from 1784-1821, as the principal bassoonist in all the orchestras in the Metropolis (1821-35). Grove (*Dictionary of Music*) speaks of his " somewhat coarse tone," but the *British Musician* (May, 1898) refers to his " excellent tone and refined style." Fétis (*Biographie universelle des Musiciens*) writes :—" Il parait que l'exécution de cet artist était particulièrement remarquable par la netteté et la précision."

Although it may offend the snobs in music, space must be found for a few celebrated bagpipers. The first of the period was Donald Macdonald (*fl.* 1831), one of the most famous of his day. John Bain Mackenzie (d. 1864), called the " King of Pipers," was piper to the Marquis of Breadalbane for thirty-two years. " As a player he was held in the highest estimation." Then there was Donald Cameron (d. 1868) who was piper to the Earl of Seaforth. His two sons also had some repute, Colin, piper to the Duke of Fife, and Alexander, piper to the Marquis of Huntly. Two of Queen Victoria's pipers were Angus MacKay (d. 1859) and William Ross (d. 1891).

That Scotland commanded attention by her superb vocalists is only what was to be expected of the land, and even the success of her few pianists is explicable since the pianoforte was in most households of the classes after the opening of the century, where its study was considered a requisite social accomplishment. As for the organ, its sphere was narrowed by reason of the Presbyterian attitude towards it until the " Seventies " when, as Harry Colin Miller says, " the dreary winter of ecclesiastical opposition passed away " (*Euing Lectures*). That orchestral instrumentalists were not so plentiful was probably due to the lack of encouragement, *plus* the frowns of the Church on mere " fiddlers " and " pipers," and since the *infamia* covered all of such, there can be little doubt that the dearth of orchestral instruments in the hands of the Scots in the earlier days was partly due to this attitude. At the Aberdeen Musical Festival (1834), London supplied *seventeen* performers out of an orchestra of *fifty*, with Thomas Cooke of London as leader. When Willem Kes, a Dutchman, was appointed conductor of the Scottish Orchestra in 1895, the *Scottish Musical Monthly* poked fun and said :

" It should be remembered that an Englishman (or should I say a Briton ?) would be handicapped with a band composed mainly of foreigners. That is the misfortune of it. Our orchestra of ' raw Highlanders ' is no more Scottish than Hottentot. It is a pity, when our schools of music are yearly turning out numbers of competent and enthusiastic young orchestral players, that these are shoved on one side for the sake of foreigners. The question is an economic more than an artistic one. What is to become of these young people ? What is the good of our richly endowed schools if they simply turn their men into the streets when their course is completed ? "

Nor was Scotland playing *solo* in this protest. In 1897 [Sir] Granville Bantock called attention to the fact that in the Scottish Orchestra of *seventy-seven* players he could only find *thirty-four* British names, whilst the following year it was pointed out that even among the latter there were only *nine* Scots (*The British Musician*, April, 1897 ; June, 1898).

CHAPTER 9

THE AMATEUR SOCIETIES

"Eighteenth-century exclusiveness did not suit nineteenth-century reforms. The workers had to go down to the people and begin to build up a structure more suited to the requirements of the time."

ROBERT A. MARR : *Music for the People* (Edin., 1889).

Of all the arts, music alone belongs to the people. As Jules Combarieu has so well pointed out, music draws its very substance from social life, just as a plant does from the soil in which its roots are deeply embedded, and social life in the 19th-Century Scotland had a far different meaning from what it had previously. As I have attempted to show in the 18th Century, concerts played a normal part in social life in the cities. It is true that in Edinburgh, Glasgow, and Aberdeen, this type of musical activity was in the hands of the nobility and bourgeoisie, but since those infectious ideas of the French Revolution had got abroad, and the more consolidating pressure of the Industrial Revolution was being felt, a breakdown in the old system of aristocratic patronage in music had come about. Although one imagines that in some respects the rich middle class almost took the place of the latter, the masses also became largely the inheritors of what had hitherto been the possession of the privileged few.

Of course there were the reactionaries and *émigrés* (as in Edinburgh's new West End) who longed for the so-called " good old days." In 1809 the *Courant* of " Fair Edina " urged a revival of the old " Gentlemen's Concerts." There was no response. Precisely the same thing was attempted in Aberdeen in 1805, where the concerts of the classes had fizzled out in 1800-01. In Glasgow, strange as it may seem, the " Gentlemen's Concerts," which were run by the *élite* of the prosperous merchant class, were carried on until 1822, when they died of a strange complaint—a fare that was too rich. It seems that the professional musicians who were responsible for the direction of the concerts had been submitting, says Robert A. Marr, " too classical a programme," for which the gentlemen subscribers had no stomach. In 1821 an effort was made to save the situation by " popular music which the committee have resolved to select." It was too late. In this way passed the last of the societies of the *ancien régime.*

We have already had a glimpse of the participation of the masses in concerts both in Edinburgh and Glasgow, and out of this enthusiasm a wider interest in amateur societies sprang up. In the " new town " of the capital an Harmonical Society was already in existence in 1787, and in Glasgow a Sacred Music Institution had been formed in 1796. This latter was an Episcopal venture which lasted until 1805, but in spite of its title, it was actually a concert-giving amateur association run by John Fergus, the organist of St. Andrew's Episcopal Chapel. A like organisation was formed in Edinburgh in 1815 under the title of the Institution of Sacred Music, with John Mather (1781-1850) of Sheffield, the organist at St. John's Episcopal Chapel, as director of studies and organist. He was succeeded by Nicholas Swift (d. *c.* 1864), also from Sheffield, whom Mather had brought north. This was also a concert-giving society and an Episcopalian prompting, although its membership was not confined to " chapel " people. Indeed, the very titles of " Sacred " and " Church " given to these societies seem to have been adopted so as to give them a respectable countenance which would tolerate the stricter Presbyterian parents allowing the younger generation taking part in such activities. At any rate, the latter were worldly enough to demand payment for concerts on one occasion

(1818), and even went on strike to enforce it. The Institution came to an end soon after this.

It must have been quite obvious to the Presbyterians that the Episcopal Church and the Roman Catholic Church were making important contributions to music. In these " chapels," for such they were called, recitals and performances of sacred music were the order of the day. It was this, probably, that led the Glasgow Presbyterian precentors to form a Union of Precentors in 1811, which seems to have been the directing force in the concerts of sacred and secular pieces which these individuals and their *pupils* gave at this time. I have italicized the word *pupils* lest it should be implied that it meant their *choirs*, which actually did not exist in those days. Not that the Presbyterian Church fully approved of the above *extra mural* activities, as we know from what happened at the Edinburgh Musical Festival in 1824. During this period several fires had occurred in the capital, a calamity which one of the clergy attributed to the performance of sacred music at the festival (see *The Importance of Hearing the Voice of God : A Sermon* . . . by J. A. Haldane, Edinburgh, 1824). Organs were still *anathema* to the Presbyterian body as we have seen in the section devoted to the Church. Indeed, the organ used for the second Edinburgh Musical Festival of 1819 had to be borrowed from a Roman Catholic Chapel !

If the Church of Scotland did not want the organ, choir, and good music, the people of Scotland did, and these exigencies showed themselves in no timorous fashion in secular life. We have seen in the past that the psalms were being used alongside purely secular compositions in vocal organisations, and this custom was still in vogue as shown in David Wilson's *Collection of Church Tunes* (Edin., *c.* 1800), which includes catches and Scots songs. Vocal clubs and societies began to spread with astonishing rapidity. If we look at Glasgow alone we see the giant strides that were being made. At the close of the previous century there were but the Vocal Music Club (founded 1770) and the Sacred Music Institution (founded 1796), but the first decade of the era saw the Gorbals

Vocal Music Club (1802), the Glee and Madrigal Club (1805), the Union Vocal Music Club (1805), the Bridgetown Vocal Music Institution (1807), and the Concord Club (1810), all of which unmistakeably reveal the trend of affairs in that the people were responding to the enticement of music quite apart from the concerts provided by the professionals. These vocal societies, and the dozens of others which arose during three-quarters of the century, were not only musical, but strongly social, and so they must not be confused with the later type of amateur choral and orchestral societies which mainly depended on a leavening of the professional element at their public auditions. Yet before dealing with the rise of the latter, which were the pioneers of the modern concerts in Scotland, there was another phase of musical life that had its share in concert activity.

During the first half-century, concerts of sacred music were quite frequent, and these were held in the dissenting chapels which became not only the *locus* but the *focus* of early concert giving. In Edinburgh we see them at St. George's Chapel under Robert Gale (1769-1845) and James Wilkinson (*fl.* 1835-41), St. John's Chapel under John Mather (1781-50) and David Hamilton (1803-63), St. George's Church under R. Atkinson and Robert A. Smith (1780-1829), the Roman Catholic Chapel under J. Macpherson, the Hope Park Chapel under John Knott, and St. Paul's Chapel. In Glasgow, they were held at St. Andrew's Episcopal Chapel under John Fergus (d. 1820) and Thomas Macfarlane (1808-92), and St. Andrew's Roman Catholic Chapel under John Fergus *secundus* (1767-1825), Charles Hurka de Monti (*c.* 1796-1820) and Henry G. Nixon (1796-1849). The programmes at these concerts which at first were confined to Handel, Pergolesi and Haydn, soon showed wider tastes in Beethoven, Mozart, Spohr, Naumann, Neukomm, Graun, J. C. Bach and even Bishop. Professional vocalists and instrumentalists were almost invariably engaged, supported by the chapel choir or choirs, often augmented by a regimental band. These concerts were the forerunners of those which came into being after the rise of the real amateur associations, which now claim our attention.

When the Edinburgh Institution of Sacred Music petered out in 1819, the professional concert was continued, as we shall see later, by the Professional Society of Musicians which was formed in this year. Amateur interests however, were allowed to lapse, although it was in the activities of the dissenting chapels already mentioned that the amateur found scope. It was not until the " Thirties " that the types which we know to-day as amateur societies came into existence. In the capital, the old aristocratic Catch Club ceased to function about 1790. and the Edinburgh Glee Club claimed to be its " legitimate successor." This latter became the Edinburgh Harmonists' Society in 1826, with much wider aims in programme. Strangely enough, a St. Cecilia Society arose in 1834 in " an attempt to revive the society of 1728." This was an advanced group which held weekly practices, each night being spent in going through a couple of symphonies of Haydn, Mozart, or Beethoven, as well as two overtures of Mozart, Rossini, or Auber, quite like the old aristocratic Musical Society at St. Cecilia's Hall in the old days. It gave two public concerts a year, and often combined with the next society to be mentioned in concerts. This was the Edinburgh Choral Society, founded about 1830, said to be " the finest amateur choral association in Scotland," with a hundred voices, and conducted by James Wilkinson. The latter soon transferred his services to a rival society, the Edinburgh Harmonic Association, being succeeded in the first named society by John Jackson (c. 1802-46). A first-rate conductor in Robert B. Stewart (1804-85) led the newly formed (1831) Leith Philharmonic Society which, in 1833, had a choir of sixty, and when he gave a concert in 1834, its orchestra numbered forty. The Glasgow Amateur Musical Society which was both orchestral and choral, was founded in 1831, to be followed (1832) by the Glasgow Philharmonic Society (orchestral), both being conducted by Thomas Macfarlane. In 1836 the Dundee Philharmonic Society began its career and, not content with the choral works of Handel, Hadyn, Mozart,

Beethoven and Rossini, could venture on Beethoven's *Symphony in D* and Méhul's overture *Joseph*.

When the tempestuous enthusiasm for the rival gospels of Mainzer and Hullah was at its height in the " Forties," further amateur societies sprang up, and in Edinburgh there were the Wilhemian Choral Association, the Thistle Solfeggio Club, the Edinburgh Singverein, and a half-dozen more elsewhere, whose very titles bespeak their origin. That Mendelssohn's *Festgesang* (1847) and Félicien David's *Le Désert* (1850) were among their productions, shows their varied tastes. At the former were used, as at the Cologne Festival (1846), 4 trumpets, 4 horns, 4 trombones, an ophicleide and a tuba. In Aberdeen, the Haydn Society, an instrumental group, was instituted in 1840, giving weekly concerts under the direction of Robert H. Baker. This was followed (1845) by the Euterpean Society, also orchestral, conducted by William Carnie, the Aberdeen Harmonic Choir (1847) also under Carnie, and in 1849 the important Aberdeen Choral Society under James Melvin. Glasgow, which had temporarily fallen back, now moved with the times, and a " Society for the performance of the Messiah " was born in 1843, its main object being reached in 1844 when this oratorio was given in its entirety, with Sims Reeves among the soloists, and a choir and orchestra of two hundred performers conducted by Thomas Macfarlane. Out of this great effort emerged the formation (1844) of the Glasgow Musical Association, of which we shall read later.

In 1853 a rival organisation appeared in the Glasgow Harmonic Society conducted by Julian Adams (1824-87). This was an amalgamation of the Hutcheson Musical Association (1847) and the Southern Musical Association (1851). It was when the Glasgow Musical Association and the Glasgow Harmonic Society pooled their resources in 1855 that the Glasgow Choral Union was born. Other towns were equally affected by the new musical spirit that was abroad, as we see in the Paisley Musical Association (1846), the Selkirk Wilhem Choral Society (1847), the Dunfermline Harmonists' Society (1847), the Jedburgh Choral Society (1848), the

Perth Choral Society (1850) with David Kennedy the singer as its conductor, the Dundee St. Cecilia Society (1850) the Kirkcaldy Philharmonic Society (1851), the Dundee Amateur Musical Association (1855) under James Pearman, the Perth Philharmonic (1856) conducted by Edward Herbert (1830-72), the Greenock Choral Union (1857) directed by J. M. Hutcheson, the Edinburgh Choral Union (1858) under Charles John Hargitt (1833-1918), and the Stirling Choral Society (1860) conducted by James Graham. Although this recital of the leading amateur musical societies may be as tedious as counting tombstones, it is rather necessary that we should know precisely how widespread this new cultural urge was operating in Scotland.

Vocal fluency being a congregational legacy of the Reformation meant that the greater part of the amateur societies were choral. The formation of amateur orchestral societies was slower in taking root. Generally, the so-called Philharmonic societies were orchestral, although a few Choral Societies had an instrumental group attached, and almost every society of any standing engaged professional solo singers and orchestral performers for their concerts. Another reason for the tardy growth of orchestral societies was still to be attributed to Presbyterian aloofness from such things, an attitude which peeps out in the *Report of the Association for the Revival of Sacred Music in Scotland* (Edin., 1845), where it is stated that " Instrumental music . . . though it may add much to the enjoyment of private society, . . . probably never will become a national pursuit throughout." The wish was probably father to the thought, and it certainly admirably illustrates the truth of George Eliot's opinion that " prophecy is the most gratuitous form of error."

A society which played a vital part in the wider cultivation and dissemination of music was the Scottish Vocal Music Association, founded in 1856, whose professional teachers have already been mentioned, [Sir] Alexander C. Mackenzie, Thomas L. Hately (1815-67), James Heriot (*c.* 1822-66), William D. Read (1808-58), John T. Surenne (1814-78), Heinrich Küchler (1815-73) and Samuel Barr (1807-66), being among them. Under the auspices of the society was given a monster fête at the Royal Zoological Gardens Hall, Edinburgh, in 1859, in which 600 children took part. More important was its Handel Centenary Celebration at the Music Hall, Edinburgh, the same year, when Prosper Sainton conducted *Judas Maccabaeus*, the *Messiah*, and extracts from *Samson* and *Acis and Galatea*. William Howard was leader, and J. Wilbye Cooper and Willoughby Weiss were among the principal vocalists.

It is not possible to record details of the later outstanding choral and orchestral societies that contributed so largely to the musical life of Scotland, but one or two deserve mention. Mr. Lambeth's Select Choir, as it was called, was instituted in 1868 by Henry A. Lambeth (1822-95), Glasgow's city organist and conductor of the Glasgow Choral Union (1858-80). It numbered twenty-four voices and won a deserved reputation, being the first of its kind in Scotland. Henry Chorley said in *The Athenaeum* : " Good choral conductors in Europe could be counted on the fingers of one hand : Mr. Lambert is one of them." One can appreciate therefore why his Select Choir made its mark. The Glasgow Amateur Orchestral Society, instituted in 1870, which has essayed to do without professional performers during its long career, was in the " Seventies " and " Eighties " a definite part of Glasgow's concert activities. Its early conductors were M. D. Méhul (1870-73), a nephew of the great Méhul ; Ladislao Zavertal (1874-81) afterwards the famous conductor of the Royal Artillery Band ; George Montague Smith (1882-83) the University organist ; and William T. Hoeck (1883-1913). Next, in point of time, was the Kirkhope Choir, founded by John Kirkhope of Edinburgh in 1881, although its beginnings could be traced back to 1875. Its originator and teacher, as Grove says, had a " remarkable gift for choir training," and his choir had a reputation for *finesse*, as well as for the type of work performed, which sometimes included Scottish cantatas by MacCunn and Drysdale. The Moonie Choir dates from 1896, when James Anderson Moonie (1853-1923) of Edinburgh, the conductor of Hope Park Musical Association, started it on a successful path, which was carried on by his son, William B. Moonie. Yet the more important societies were those whose beginnings have already been related—the Glasgow Choral Union (1855) and the Edinburgh Choral Union (1858), both of which have been so closely associated with the professional activities of Scotland. For this reason their contributions will be acknowledged later when dealing with the rise and progress of the professional concerts.

Finally, it would not be too much to say, that the amateur effort in Scotland, which was far in advance of that in England, made a distinct and lasting contribution to the cultivation of the highest ideals in music in the land. Firstly, the amateur societies encouraged people to make music for themselves which brought a higher æsthetic appreciation of the art. Secondly, they added to the general musical social life of the community by their own concerts, often filling in gaps between those run by the professionals. Thirdly, they gave further employment to the professional musician, a circumstance which not only enhanced their own performances, but contributed indirectly to the encouragement of a better class of professional performer, since greater social security in the continuity of engagements made the profession worth while.

CHAPTER 10

THE CONCERTS

" [This festival of 1815] . . . may be followed by important consequences at a time when the hand that now attempts to describe its immediate effects, and the hearts of all who participated in its pleasures, are moulded into dust."

GEORGE F. GRAHAM : *The First Edinburgh Musical Festival* (Edin. 1816).

There is something quite pathetic, yet strangely prophetic, in these words of George Farquhar Graham, and we shall see in the unfolding of the story of the professional concert in Scotland how this particular phase of musicial activity came to occupy such an important place in Scottish social and artistic life in the 19th Century, just as Graham had not unreasonably predicted. Of course the festival, which opened the way for the professional concert, never became a permanency in Scotland in the form that it is understood in England, the land of its birth. Yet its transient adoption in the north opened the eyes of the people to the value of many things. By means of the festivals of 1815, 1819, 1821, 1823, 1824, 1828, 1834 and 1843, Scotland was able to see and hear, for the most part, large choirs and orchestras which had previously been denied her. Further, it gave her the opportunity to appreciate the performances of more adept orchestral musicians that she had hitherto heard, and to realize how much the art depended on the better type of performer. Indeed, it soon became clear that the orchestral side of the concert would gradually have to pass into the hands of skilled professionals, although this would not necessarily detract from the more spontaneous contribution of amateurs and their societies, but rather would give momentum and direction to those who were pure music lovers. As the activities of the latter have already been discerned, we can now give attention to the concerts of the professionals, although in some instances, their success is bound up with the praiseworthy efforts of amateurs.

Although the St. Cecilia's Hall at Edinburgh had closed its doors in 1798, the aristocratic Musical Society was not actually wound up until 1801. The event has been considered a catastrophe, which it was not. Edinburgh was growing. The district of the " Ancient Royalty," with its wynds and closes, was fast becoming the East End, whilst the New Town, to which the gentry and upper middle class had migrated, was now the West End. Here, in George Street, the new Assembly Rooms had been built (1787), whilst further north, at the head of Leith Walk, was Corri's Concert-Rooms (opened 1803), which had previously been the Circus (built 1790), and these two halls became the venue for concerts. The foreign professionals,—Natale Corri, Stabilini, Urbani, and Schetky, taking time by the forelock in 1799, after the collapse of the fashionable Musical Society, gave a series of eight subscription concerts at the Assembly Rooms. The next year, J. P. Salomon, who made such a stir with the symphonies of Haydn and Mozart in London, journeyed to Edinburgh and Glasgow and produced the *Military* and *Surprise* symphonies. It was a red letter day in the concert world, and it gave a temporary fillip to the Edinburgh impresarios. Continuing his concerts in 1801, Corri said that " the symphonies as well as the solo performers will be varied every night " and that, thanks to the help of Salomon, " some of the grand symphonies *in manuscript*. . . by Haydn, and which cannot be heard elsewhere out of London," would be performed. But there was a rift in the lute between Urbani and Corri. In 1803, Urbani attempted to revive Handelian oratorio, and gave *Samson* and the *Messiah* at the Assembly Rooms, but he lost heavily on the project. His rival, Corri, rather chagrined, took his concerts to his newly acquired Concert-Rooms, where he featured " Beethoven's Celebrated Symphony " among a few novelties. These latter concerts held the platform until the year 1809, the symphonies of Haydn, Mozart, and Beethoven being given, with an occasional choral or vocal touch of Pergolesi, Jomelli, Corelli, and Handel, so as to placate, seemingly, the older generation. Yet this first phase of Edinburgh's high-class concerts quietly faded out.

Schemes were put forward (1809) for a revival of the old " Gentlemen's Concerts " which, naturally, made no impression. To meet the supposed demand, John Mather gave " specially select " choral and orchestral concerts at the Assembly Rooms, with a fare made up of the usual favourites from Handel and Haydn. That was in 1812, but matters still drifted generally. Indeed it was not until Scotland viewed with slightly jaundiced eyes the success of English musical festivals that anything practical emerged for the resuscitation of the concerts. At last Edinburgh's music lovers met in conclave and decided on the first Edinburgh Musical Festival of 1815, which turned out to be " one of the greatest musical festivals of the country." Charles J. Ashley of London conducted, with Janiewicz, who had settled in Scotland, as leader of an orchestra of sixty-two, whilst Elizabeth Salmon and John Braham were among the six star vocalists, surrounded by a picked choir of fifty-eight. Since it was the first of its kind in Scotland, some of the outstanding orchestral items on the programmes of the eight concerts are worthy of notice in Beethoven's " Second " [First] *Symphony in C Major*," Mozart's *Symphony in E Flat* [K. 543], and Haydn's *Symphony No. 8 in E Flat* [Salomon set]. Among the overtures were those to Handel's *Esther, Saul* and *Samson* which Graham, one of the organising secretaries, would call *Sampson*, as though he had the Septuagint before his eyes. Other overtures were Mozart's *Die Zauberflöte*, Cherubini's *Anacreon*, and one of Graham's own overtures, " composed for the occasion."

On the choral side the outstanding items were Handel's *Messiah*, seemingly in full, and Haydn's *Creation*, save the last recitative, duet, and chorus. This dubiety concerning the full *Messiah* deserves to be probed because it has been generally assumed that no complete performance was given until 1844. (See Grove, *Dictionary of Music*, V, 241 ; Harry C. Miller, *Introductory Euing Lectures*, 1914, p. 177 ; and Robert Craig, *Short History of the Glasgow Choral Union*, 1943, p. 15). Robert Craig says : " The *Messiah* . . . had never been heard in Scotland as a complete work [until 1844]. Fragments of it may have found their way into the scheme of the Edinburgh Musical Festival of 1815, but the authentic records of these early Scottish musical celebrations have nearly all disappeared." So far as " authentic records " are concerned, we have the valuable documents of the Edinburgh Musical Society, and from these we know that " the celebrated and truly sublime musical performance, the oratorio of the *Messiah*," was performed at St. Cecilia's Hall in 1772, and there is no mention of any cuts. As for the Edinburgh Musical Festival of 1815, we have the exhaustive account of George F. Graham, so frequently mentioned in these pages, who was, with George Hogarth, one of the secretaries. The programme itself simply carries the title, *The Messiah*. That it was the complete work may be assumed from the following : (1) On the day when the *Creation* was performed, " with the exception of the last Recitative, Duet, and Chorus," as the programme distinctly states, it occupied the second half of the programme. On the day when the *Messiah* was performed, no mention of cuts is made, and it occupied the entire programme. (2) Graham, in his programme note on " the

admirable Oratorio, which constitutes this day's performance " says :
" the style of each piece is so well described by Dr. Burney, that I
need only refer to his account," and this Graham gives *in full*.
Handel's *Messiah*, with Mozart's accompaniments, was also given
at the Edinburgh Musical Festival of 1819, and again there is no
reference on the programme to a part performance, although in the
case of *The Creation* and *The Mount of Olives* it is specifically stated
that only " Parts Second and Third " of the former, and " Part
Third " of the latter were performed.

The inordinate enthusiasm evoked by the 1815 festival showed
itself in many ways in the Edinburgh concert world. A meeting was
held immediately at the City Chambers which led to the establishment of the Institution of Sacred Music already mentioned which,
under the direction of John Mather (1781-1850), soon had a choir
of nearly four hundred voices, with a " select band " of its own.
With Mather as conductor and organist, and Janiewicz as leader of
the orchestra, they gave six concerts in 1816, with four more in 1817.
During 1818 and 1819 these concerts were developed. Side by
side with these, Janiewicz himself organized professional concerts
in 1818-19, one of which deserves mention since he acknowledged
the kindness of the Philharmonic Society of London in lending
him the parts of the " celebrated characteristic *Sinfonia Pastorale* of
Beethoven." The professional concerts had now taken a firm root in
the soil, and this was helped materially by the establishment of the
Edinburgh Professional Society of Musicians in 1819, and the
second Edinburgh Musical Festival in the same year.

Shifting the scene to Glasgow, we find that Andrew Thomson
(*c.* 1792-1860) was giving concerts in the College Hall of the University in 1818, and in the following year he produced there an
oratorio, *The Intercession*, which he claimed to be " the first time
[in Glasgow ?] that an *entire* oratorio had been attempted." At the
Trades Hall, the old Glasgow Musical Fund (founded 1745) was
responsible in this year for a concert in which sixty performers took
part, and the following year another effort at the Theatre Royal
showed seventy performers. Things seemed to be improving in

the great industrial city in matters musical. In the year 1821, all former efforts were eclipsed by a four-days "festival" at the Theatre Royal, in which the orchestra alone numbered forty-five performers, the principal vocalists being Catalini, Elizabeth Salmon, John Braham, and Placci. John Dewar of Edinburgh was the conductor and Spagnoletti was the leader. At this festival no choral works were offered. In spite of its success, there was little improvement in the concert situation, and the preceding enthusiasm was but a flash in the pan. The old " Gentlemen's Subscription Concerts," which had their origin in the previous century, came to be less patronized, and its last concerts were given in the 1821-22 season. Perhaps, as Robert A. Marr has suggested, " its membership was too exclusive." Still there was another " Grand Musical Festival " in 1823, yet in truth it was but a poor affair of a miscellaneous programme character, although it lasted six days. Again there were no choral items. During 1826-27, John Dewar of Edinburgh and James May Jr., of Glasgow ran subscription concerts, but attendances showed that there was no real demand for these things. Glasgow was certainly not the " Second City " in her appreciation of music in those days. Perhaps the industrial and political events had something to do with the general apathy of the public. The reform agitation, which did not cease until the Reform Bill of 1832, brought crowds of workers parading the streets demanding employment or food. Apart from this, the government viewed Glasgow as the hub of a revolutionary movement, and when notices appeared, probably from the hands of *agents provocateurs*, calling for a revolutionary " Provisional Government," troops were hurried to the city. That was in 1820, but the unsettled situation continued until 1823, and must have had its effect on the concert as well as the theatre.

In the capital, a second musical festival was arranged for 1819, when ten programmes were submitted. Sir George Smart conducted with Janiewicz as leader of an orchestra of sixty, and among the " principals " were the Edinburgh soprano Mary Ann Paton, Catherine Stephens, and the great Braham. It was another artistic and financial success. A third festival, on much the same lines, was held in 1824. Aberdeen was next to catch the festival fever when three programmes, featuring Deborah Knyvett, Thomas Bellamy, and Thomas Vaughan, with a " full orchestra," were presented in 1828. More impressive was the Granite City's Second festival of 1834, which had a choir of sixty-six and an orchestra of fifty under the direction of Edward Taylor, the conductor of the Norwich festivals, who later became the Gresham Professor of Music. Tom Cooke of London was the leader and the vocalists included the Scottish contralto Elizabeth Masson, Margaret Stockhausen, and John W. Hobbs. The last of the great festivals in Edinburgh took place in 1843, when it ran for six days. There were one hundred and twenty-five voices and an orchestra of seventy. Loder was the leader and [Sir] Henry Bishop was the conductor. Unlike its predecessors, it resulted in a deficit.

Meanwhile Edinburgh was enjoying a fairly adequate concert life, much of the success being due to the Professional Society of Musicians which had been formed in 1819 " for the purpose of improving the state of vocal and instrumental music in the city." We know from its concert programmes that it produced " the great orchestral works of the time." It was this society that was the leavening body for more than half a century in all the concert ventures in the city. In 1835, so as to assist the Professional Society financially, the Edinburgh Musical Association was formed, and under these fresh auspices the concerts became a feature in the land, and their " Brief Notices of the Music Performed by the Professional Society " for 1837-38 contains the first published analytical programmes in the history of the concert. In addition to these professional concerts there were dozens of others run by *entrepreneurs* or societies, the latter generally backed up by the Professional Society. Among these was a type of concert which had attracted Paris and London known as the Musard Concerts, and Edinburgh soon found itself in the throes of " Concerts *à la* Musard," which were conducted by Robert B. Stewart, William Napier, and John Jackson, the father of the composer of *The Dear Little Shamrock*. They were naturally of a popular type, and the advertisement said that they aimed at providing " rational and economical *amusement*." About thirty-five concerts were given during 1838-39, and the orchestra numbered from twenty at first to thirty at the close, *plus* a regimental band on some occasions. The old Edinburgh Choral Society also appeared, whilst Agnes Noel (Mrs. Bushe) the eminent soprano, and Koenig the great cornettist were among the attractions. Stewart later introduced these Musard Concerts into Glasgow.

Better accommodation for concerts and similar demands brought the erection of new halls in the cities,—the Assembly Rooms, Aberdeen (1820), the City Hall, Glasgow (1841), the Music Hall, Edinburgh (1843) and the Queen's Rooms, Glasgow (1850). These gave wider opportunities and encouragement to choral and orchestral societies to increase their ranks, and in Glasgow it was in the new City Hall that the alleged first complete performance of the *Messiah* was given in Scotland in 1844, when Agnes Noel, Sims Reeves, Henry Phillips, and others, supported by a choir and orchestra two hundred strong, appeared on the platform. In the new Edinburgh Music Hall, the city's fourth and last musical festival was held in 1843, which was conducted by [Sir] Henry R. Bishop who was then the Reid Professor of Music at the University. These two concert halls eventually became the homes of the Glasgow Choral Union and the Edinburgh Choral Union respectively which, with their attendant orchestras, were the leading concert-giving bodies in Scotland.

Meanwhile, the first Reid Concert of the University of Edinburgh, which was provided for in the will of General John Reid, was held in the Assembly Rooms in February, 1841. On this occasion a choir of over one hundred and thirty voices was engaged which performed works by Handel, Haydn, Graun, Beethoven and Mendelssohn, under the baton of Professor John Thomson. For many years following, choral performances were a feature of the annual Reid Concert. By the " Fifties," whilst John Donaldson was Reid Professor of Music, the choral features were dropped in favour of orchestral, instrumental, and vocal items. In 1855,

Karl Anschütz, afterwards the founder of opera in America, was the conductor. Beethoven's *Prometheus* overture was on the programme, together with a *Quadruple Concerto for Four Violons* by Ludwig Maurer, two of the performers being August Manns and Alexander Mackenzie, the latter also being leader of the orchestra. Among the vocalists were Herminie Rudersdorff, Maria Caradori, and Alexander Reichardt. The following year, Josef Gung'l was one of the conductors, with Josephine Fodor and Reichardt among the star singers. Mackenzie was leader of the orchestra, which played Mendelssohn's *Symphony in A Minor* [*The Scotch*] and the *finale* of Beethoven's *Symphony No. 1*. When [Sir] Herbert Oakeley became Reid Professor (1865-91), the annual Reid Concert became a three-day festival. Then the Hallé Orchestra was first engaged (1869) and really high-class concerts became the established practice at the Reid concerts.

Naturally these were not the only professional concerts in Edinburgh and Glasgow. George Wood of Edinburgh, and his brother John Muir Wood of Glasgow, gave series of concerts for many years. Julian Adams was another. John Purdie of Edinburgh ran Monday Evening Concerts, whilst William Howard conducted Saturday Popular Concerts. " Mons " Jullien attracted huge crowds with his famous orchestra. The Distin Family of brass *virtuosi* were equally successful. Then there were the precursors of the modern Celebrity Concerts, and just as Moscheles (1828), Paganini (1831), Ole Bull (1837), Liszt (1840) and Chopin (1848) had appeared in Scotland, so the later famed instrumentalists came north for recitals. It was the same with the operatic stars who, quite apart from their appearances at the theatres, often booked, or were engaged at, the concert halls, even with a supporting company. When the choral unions of Glasgow and Edinburgh were firmly established in their concerts, all the great singers and players were featured,—Patti, Albani, Nordica, Marie Roze, Sims Reeves, Néruda, Vieuxtemps, Carrodus, Sarasate, Sauret, Joachim, Ysaÿe, Helen Hopekirk, Fanny Davies, Von Bülow, Pauer, Pachmann, Paderewski, Borwick, and Lamond. Yet the real history of the concert is not to be sought " in distinguished names which appear on the front page of the newspapers," as Dr. R. Vaughan Williams says (*National Music*), who mainly depend on curiosity mongers for their support, but rather in places where the music *per se* is the acid test of attraction, as in " the local choral societies." Thus we can modulate back to our original theme, the choral societies of Scotland's two great cities in their professional aspect.

The Glasgow Choral Union, as we have seen, was founded in 1855 out of the amalgamation of two earlier societies,—The Glasgow Musical Association (1843) and the Glasgow Harmonic Society (1853). The former had a run of good conductors in Thomas Macfarlane (1843-44), Andrew Thomson (1844-47, 1850-51), John Harkin (1849-50) and Julius Seligmann (1851-55). The latter was conducted by Julian Adams (1853-55). Seligmann was given charge of the new Glasgow Choral Union (1855-57) and was succeeded by Henry A. Lambeth (1858-80), who was followed by [Sir] August Manns (1880-87), and Joseph Bradley (1887-1908). The choir, during its history, has usually numbered around the four hundred mark and its activities, whilst mainly confined to Glasgow and the West of Scotland, were quite wide, and embraced Dundee, Perth, Stirling, Forfar, and even farther afield. Although in its earlier years it kept strictly to the path of Handel, Haydn, Mozart, Beethoven, Rossini, Mendelssohn, Spohr, Gounod, Berlioz and the remainder of the foreign masters, it was not unmindful of the claims of British composers. When the early British school emerged in Pearsall, Smart, Macfarren, Bennett, and Horsley, they were given due recognition, just as were Sullivan, Mackenzie, Parry, Corder, Stanford and MacCunn, in the later decades. Within living memory the performances and interpretation of the Glasgow Choral Union were carried out with great artistry. Two of its greatest triumphs were the Festivals of 1860 and 1873. The former was called the " First " Glasgow Festival for the simple reason that those held in the city in 1821 and 1823 were not considered such because no choral works had been programmed.

Royal Patronage was given to the 1860 festival which ran for four days in the City Hall when Mendelssohn's *Elijah*, Handel's *Messiah* and Horsley's *Gideon* were performed, the latter being expressly composed for the occasion. The City Hall now had an organ (erected 1853) and Henry Smart, who had designed the instrument, was the organist on this occasion. Henry A. Lambeth conducted (save on the day that Horsley directed his oratorio) and Henry Blagrove led an orchestra of fifty-seven and a choir of over three hundred. Among the leading vocalists were Clara Novello, Charlotte Dolby, Sims Reeves, and Willoughby H. Weiss. The first named does not breathe a word about her Glasgow visit in her entertaining *Clara Novello's Reminiscences* (1910), although she came again to the City Hall later in the year for a concert with Molique and William H. Cummings. She does however mention an Edinburgh visit in 1836, when she was taught " to sing Scotch songs in the *national* as distinguished from the *professional* style."

The " Second " Glasgow Festival in 1873 lasted five days, at which six concerts were given, Tietjens, Marie Roze, [Sarah] Edith Wynne the Nightingale of Wales, Trebelli-Bettini, Patey (her father belonged to Glasgow), Edward Lloyd, Vernon Rigby, and Santley being among the star vocalists. There was an orchestra of sixty-six and a choir of three hundred and fifty. W. T. Best was at the organ and Randegger at the pianoforte, whilst Carrodus, who came of a Scottish family originally Carruthers, was the leader, with Costa and Lambeth as conductors. The descriptive handbook, with full analytical notes, comprised 168 pages, from which we see that the *Messiah*, *Elijah*, Costa's *Eli*, Smart's *Jacob*, and Lambeth's *Bow down thine ear* were the chief choral items, whilst Beethoven's *Pastoral Symphony*, Schumann's *Symphony in B Flat* (No. 1), together with such overtures as Rossini's *William Tell*, Bennett's *Naïads*, Wagner's *Flying Dutchman*, Weber's *Oberon*, Sullivan's *Di Ballo* and Mendelssohn's *Ruy Blas* were among the more important orchestral pieces. Again Royal Patronage was extended to the festival. Seemingly, the Presbyterian conscience had still to be placated. At the 1843 Edinburgh Festival " a narrow-minded clerical section of the community " had circulated silly rumours which, in spite of denials by the *Scotsman*, killed attendances, and brought about a loss of £1,500. At the Glasgow *Messiah* venture of 1844 there were more rumours from the same circle about " worship of the Virgin Mary." One can therefore appreciate the delicious sop offered on the programme of the 1873 Festival which said that " In consequence of the character of the Work [Mendelssohn's *Elijah*], the Committee respectfully submit that there should be no applause." As a further safeguard to complete sanctity, the printer was dragged in so as to appease the over pious. Whilst the ordinary sections of the printed programme terminated with the conventional printer's ornaments, the tailpiece to the *Messiah* was the Cross entwined by the Crown of Thorns !

Although there had always been an orchestra, partly amateur, attached to the Glasgow Choral Union, which was usually announced as the " Instrumental Section of the Choral Union, assisted by Eminent Instrumentalists," it was not actually an integral part of the Union, although some of its players were known as " orchestral members," as in 1868-69 when, out of four hundred and thirty members, twenty-nine were in the " orchestral " category. Sometimes a special orchestra was engaged as in November, 1872, when De Jong's Manchester Orchestra came north for the occasion. Out of forty-nine players in this combination only fourteen were British. This we know from the programme published at the time when, probably by reason of their being foreigners, a complete list of the personnel was printed. In the December however, the Union reverted to the old orchestra, but not to the above special publicity of naming the members, although [Sir] Alexander C. Mackenzie was the leader. In May, 1873, the programme refers to " Mr. Lambeth's Orchestra," but this title also did not find repetition. In December, the practice of giving a list of the orchestral players was re-introduced which has since remained a feature, and from this first list, with Carrodus as leader, one can see that almost all the performers were British, mainly from the London Philharmonic, Covent Garden, and Drury Lane orchestras. Up to the year 1873, the orchestra was generally stated to consist of " upwards of fifty " or " about sixty," but there was soon to be a change.

Hitherto, purely orchestral items had been but sparingly admitted into the choral programmes, although sometimes a symphony was featured, generally at the beginning of the first and second parts of the programme, but there had long been a growing demand for more orchestral works, and even purely orchestral programmes. In 1865, a scheme was launched for the establishment of a Phil-harmonic Association for the West of Scotland (see *The Morning Journal*, Jan., 1865), and the Lord Provost issued a circular calling a meeting to that end. Here it was stated that the object was " to form another society [in addition to the Glasgow Choral Union] by which we may at all times command a powerful body of instru-mental performers." Manchester, with its successful Hallé Orches-tra, and its series of concerts, was pointed to as " the style now proposed for Glasgow," with a five- or six-months season. Yet in spite of the large and influential support given to the scheme at this meeting, at which the usual officers were appointed, nothing materialized, and nine years elapsed before even the slightest improvement on the old system came about.

In the year 1873 the Glasgow Choral Union began to wake up to the inadequacy of its hired orchestra. " Thirty years' experience," says Robert Craig (*Short History of the Glasgow Choral Union*, Glasg., 1843), " had now established the conviction that a large and efficient orchestra was essential for the progress of classical music in Scot-land." The real urge was as much critical comparison with other orchestras, as it was the Choral Union's own domestic experience. Hallé's Orchestra, which had been going north for years for series of concerts, had been giving superb performances of the best music of the day which simply threw the local efforts deep into the shade, and, as we have seen, it was Hallé's Orchestra that was the urge in the proposed Philharmonic Association for the West of Scotland in 1865. However, the fresh outlook brought about the establishment of a Choral Union Orchestra in 1874, and it was planned that it would give separate orchestral concerts, which proposal, by arrangement with the Edinburgh Choral Union, would be extended to the capital. The new orchestra, with John T. Carrodus as leader, naturally took the Glasgow Choral Union's chief, Henry A. Lambert, as its first conductor (1874-75), but after this the orchestra had its own conductor in [Sir] Arthur Sullivan (1875-76), Hans von Bülow (1877-78), Julius Tausch (1878-79) and [Sir] August Manns (1879-94). With the exception of Tausch, who has been described as " a brilliant failure," these conductors brought fame to Scotland's first permanent orchestra.

The new orchestra opened its season (1874-75) with a personnel of fifty performers, which rose to " about sixty " (1881), and then varied around seventy-five and eighty until 1891, when there were ninety players. During the first season the Union gave sixty-three concerts, not only in Glasgow and Edinburgh, but in Greenock, Dundee, Hamilton, Kilmarnock, Dumbarton, Helensburgh, Paisley, Stirling, Perth, Forfar, Alloa, and Tillicoultry. Thus the wider sphere of influence began. Then came a year (1891) which was one of crisis for the Choral Union. A group of music lovers who thought that the orchestral season of the Choral Union was " too short, perfunctory and uninspired," had formed a " Scottish Orchestra Co. Ltd." in opposition to the Choral Union, and set out to run a six months' season of orchestral concerts with [Sir] George Henschel as conductor. Yet Glasgow was not big enough for two concert-giving societies, and the result was that both organisations lost money over their respective seasons (1893-94). When wiser counsels had prevailed, a joint arrangement was made between the Glasgow Choral Union and the Scottish Orchestra Company, with the result that the Choral and Orchestral Union came into being (1894).

The new orchestra numbered eighty players to which, as with the preceding Choral Union Orchestra, a separate conductor was appointed in [Sir] George Henschel (1894-95). His place was taken by Willem Kes (1895-98), a Dutchman. The *Scottish Musical Monthly* registered " an energetic protest . . . against this persistent pandering to the foreigner, when we have musicians of our

own who are quite as competent as any foreigner." Yet the
clique of business men who ruled the Union were a law unto
themselves. They would excuse themselves by the old cry that
" Music is International," although in their own particular line
of business they were firm opponents of Free Trade. Three years
later another foreigner, a German, Wilhelm Bruch (1898-1900),
succeeded Kes. This time the London press joined in the
fray and much bitter criticism was engendered. It added fuel
to the flames of an existing fire of controversy which had been
raging over the continued employment of foreign leaders in Glasgow's
orchestra,—Hermann Francke (1879), Victor Buzian (1881),
Robert Heckmann (1884), Maurice Sons (1885-87, 1888-1903), and
Fernandez-Arbós (1887-88). The *Musical Times*, London, ever
the standard bearer in the fight against this " snobbery," as Dr.
Vaughan Williams terms Britain's patronizing of foreign musicians,
devoted a special article to the subject. [Sir] Frederick Cowen
had recently been appointed conductor of the Hallé Orchestra on
a " year to year " contract which, said the *Musical Times*, was
clearly " keeping the place warm " until such time as Richter,
already engaged on the Continent, was free to accept the position.
It was this same Richter who, as the music critic of *The World*
pointed out, after earning six times as much money in Britain as
he would have done in Germany, repudiated his British honorary
diplomas in 1914, selling them for the funds of the German Red
Cross. When Glasgow appointed Bruch to conduct the Scottish
Orchestra the *Musical Times* saw in this a further rebuff to the native
musician, and reasoned thus :—

> " What becomes of our boasted progress in music if
> important appointments like those of Manchester and Glasgow
> are *not* to be filled by native musicians ? Cannot we raise the
> article on our own soil ? Are we always to import it ? Would
> such a stigma be tolerated in any other European country ? "

Needless to say, most thinking people will agree with every line of
these questionings, for the truth is that the British musician seems
ever to have had the scales of justice weighed against him in this

country. As Cecil Forsyth says in his *Music and Nationalism*, the British musician is beaten "not in a foreign country . . . but by his own people in secret and murderous league with their own enemies." But to return to our major theme and its variations in Edinburgh.

Although Edinburgh is the capital and the home of the arts in Scotland, and it certainly took the lead in matters musical during the first half of the century, it found itself in the second place musically to Glasgow, during the second half of the century. This is not the boast of the great city of the west, but the open admission of the Edinburgh press. Glasgow formed its Choral Union in 1854, which was four years before the Edinburgh Choral Union was founded. Further, a comparison between the two societies from the date of their foundation to the close of the century will show that Glasgow was an easy first, not merely in size and efficiency, but in programmes and general outlook. Edinburgh's first conductor was Charles J. Hargitt (1858-62), who was succeeded by James Shaw (1862-64), William Howard (1864-66), Adam Hamilton (1866-83), and Thomas H. Collinson (1883-19..), all of whom performed good work. On special occasions the Edinburgh Choral Union has been conducted by Otto Goldschmidt, Bevignani, [Sir] Arthur Sullivan, [Sir] Michael Costa, John T. Carrodus, [Sir] Alexander C. Mackenzie, [Sir] Charles Hallé, Hamish MacCunn, [Sir] George Henschel, and Henry Dambmann. When the Union gave Haydn's *Creation* in 1861 it had a choir and orchestra of two hundred and fifty, on which occasion Goldschmidt conducted, with Henry Blagrove and William Howard as leaders, and Jenny Lind and Sims Reeves as the vocal stars. *Elijah* was done in 1862 with only one hundred and twenty in the choir, which included teams from Leeds and Bradford, although when it was repeated in 1867, with the help of the Glasgow Musical Association, there were one hundred and fifty voices. In 1865 *Elijah* was produced with two hundred and fifty singing.

Its earlier orchestra, as with Glasgow, was an amateur affair, e.g. the Edinburgh Musical Association which played for the

Union in 1860-62.   It then tried (1865) to form an orchestral section of its own, as Glasgow Choral Union had done, but it was not successful.   The employment of a professional orchestra began in 1867, which brought players mainly from the London Philharmonic Orchestra, Covent Garden, and Drury Lane, reinforced by Edinburgh professionals such as Robert B. Stewart and [Sir] Alexander C. Mackenzie, the whole led by John T. Carrodus.   In this venture, Edinburgh did better than Glasgow, and must have obtained far better results, even apart from the praise of the *Scotsman*.   This system continued until 1870 and the orchestra numbered from forty to fifty.   In the latter year the Union went back to amateurs, although we read that their playing " embarrassed the singers."   Then a Scottish Orchestral Society appeared (1870-71) which was led by Adolph Küchler, but the next year De Jong's Manchester Orchestra, led by Sainton, was engaged in the September, although in December, " a new orchestral society lately instituted " under [Agnes] Drechsler Hamilton was featured.   By 1873 a return was made to the previous system of professionals from London which brought Carrodus once more as leader.   The press was pleased at the result, and we read that " such orchestral playing has never before been heard in Edinburgh, except . . . when we have had Mr. Hallé's band."

In the year 1874 negotiations were opened with the Glasgow Choral Union, when the Choral Union Orchestra was formed, which resulted in a joint series of orchestral concerts.   At the same time, Edinburgh did not accept the Glasgow conductor for the first three years of the new arrangement, so that Adam Hamilton, the Edinburgh conductor, directed both the choral and orchestral concerts until 1877, when Hans von Bülow (1877-78), Julius Tausch (1878-79), and [Sir] August Manns (1879-87), who were the conductors of the Choral Union Orchestra, were appointed. Among its conductors for special occasions were,—[Sir] Herbert Oakeley, [Sir] Frederick Cowen, and [Sir] Villiers Stanford.   In 1887, by reason of the financial losses incurred, the arrangements with the Choral Union Orchestra lapsed.   Fortunately, Robert

Roy Paterson, of Paterson & Sons, stepped into the breach and assumed responsibility for these concerts, generally known as " Paterson's Concerts," which were continued under [Sir] August Manns until 1893-94, when the establishment of the Scottish Orchestra brought about a renewal of the old joint agreement between Glasgow and Edinburgh for orchestral concerts.

That the concert in Scotland during the second half of the century was as good as that in England, with the exception of London and Manchester, there can be little doubt. This was chiefly due to the efforts of the Glasgow Choral Union, the Edinburgh Choral Union, and the Choral Union Orchestra with its successor the Scottish Orchestra. The contribution of the Scottish orchestra to Scotland's concert life was of great merit and moment. As R. W. Greig says (*The Story of the Scottish Orchestra*), it has " added notably to the culture of Scotland, something with a noble history, something which deserves the support and appreciation of everyone interested in the inspiring influence of the great arts, something of which everyone in Scotland . . . has good reason to be proud."

CHAPTER 11

THE COMPOSERS OF THE RELAPSE

" It is clear to all who take an interest in the history of music that among European nations the English is far more ready than any other to welcome musicians from abroad."
FULLER-MAITLAND : *English Music in the XIXth Century* (1902).

In this " virulent snobbery," as Dr. R. Vaughan Williams (*National Music*, 1934) has called this British adoration of the foreigner, Scotland was as culpable as England, for when Fuller-Maitland wrote " English," he actually meant " British," a misnomer which, although committed unwittingly, has persisted since 1707, and is one of the minor blunders that have contributed to a sum-total which has had disastrous effects on the body politic, including the loss of Eire to the comity of British peoples. It is undeniably true that, at the opening of the 19th century, Scotland could not have acted otherwise, as she herself had little to supply in the way of composers and performers. In spite of the blushing promise which she offered to musical composition at the re-awakening in the 18th century, of which the works of Macklean, McGibbon, Oswald, Erskine, Reid, and Foulis were an earnest pledge, the first period of the 19th century was almost as barren as the Outer Hebrides. It is for this reason that Scotland's creative musical work in this century cannot be taken as a whole, the first eighty years being so widely different in the cultural aspect from the remaining twenty. Therefore, these two periods must be discussed separately, and first of all, let us consider the causes of this retrogression on the creative side during the first period.

After 1815, when the turmoil of war had passed, the forty years of piping peace showed that all was well with the land materially, for it was an era unparalleled in British history for commercial and industrial development. The Scots played quite an important part in this progress, as such names as James Watt, George Stephenson, James Nasmyth, and Henry Bell so loudly proclaim, and Scotland took its share in the rich benefits that accrued, as the growth of a comfortable middle class showed. With all this material prosperity one would have thought that the higher forms of art would have benefited by the auspicious circumstance, but they did not. The brush of the painter was mainly devoted to bourgeois portraiture, whilst the pen of the literator was generally steeped in politics. As for the composer, and such did exist, his output seems to show that he had no thoughts beyond what pleased the mutable many, whether among the renters of pews or the patronisers of popular entertainments, although it can be explained. With all that alleged " canny " outlook of the Scot, he was not sufficiently businesslike to jump on the crest of the wave of Sir Walter Scott's popularity in romantic literature, but allowed an Englishman, Henry Rowley Bishop, to compose music or, what was more general, hash up the national airs for *Guy Mannering* and the remainder of his works that were issued as plays. Admitted, there were James Dewar, Alexander

Mackenzie, and John Thomson who did much better than Bishop with original music for Scott's plays, but the latter, with borrowed implements, reaped the crop, leaving the stubble to the Scots. Of course there were contributory causes for this. London was the cradle of stage productions, and Bishop was in London.

Had the 18th century Scottish composers been established factors in public   em, both their names and their works might have acted as a fillip ι   hers, but they had long ceased to have a place in the repertories.   ̣utside of Erksine, their compositions belonged to chamber music which, by this time, was losing its place on the programmes. It may be admitted that Erskine's overtures and symphonies (and there was more than one of the latter) were still available in print, and they were undoubtedly better than much that was programmed in their day.   Indeed, as late as 1811 one of his symphonies was being played in London (*Music Review*, 1945, p. 159). Yet Haydn, Mozart, and Beethoven had arrived, and the works of Erskine passed from the scene in company with those of J. C. Bach, Stamitz, Abel, Wagensteil, and others. Further, society had changed.   The *habitués* of the aristocratic concerts of the *ancien régime* might have interested themselves in Erskine, Reid, Oswald, and the rest, but they were defunct, and in the new world that had dawned there were not as yet the amateur orchestral societies of the people who might have taken a kindly interest in these composers of the past. Choral music, which now took so prominent a part in programmes, had nothing to offer from the Scottish past, since 19th century Scots knew nothing of the great 16th century works of Johnson, Carver, and Douglas.

Still one must recognize that there were many obstacles in the way of likely composers. There was nothing like the benign attitude towards music that existed in England. Few Scots would wittingly have made their sons musicians, i.e. in the professional sense, since the old *infamia* towards the art still persisted among the " unco guid." As George F. Graham has pointed out, there was "the great and unnecessary apprehension entertained by most parents, respecting the effects of musical accomplishments on the morals and temporal interests of their sons, . . . [yet] they nevertheless, with very little consistency in their code of conduct, permit, and even encourage these youths to join in many of the fashionable follies and vices of the day." Even the few who defied this ban and were turning their eyes and ears either culturally or professionally to the higher realms of the art, had to go elsewhere for nurture. Not only was music unrecognized in the Scottish universities, but there was no college or academy of music in the land. Although Edinburgh University had established a Professorship in Music in 1839, one could not take a degree in music there until 1893. It was these circumstances that drove James Smith Anderson, John Greig, John Robertson, W. A. Campbell Cruickshank, Samuel McBurney, Archibald D. Arnott, Daniel F. Wilson, and others to take their degrees in music elsewhere. It was a similar circumstance that forced so many Scots to seek higher instruction in London colleges, mainly at the Royal Academy of Music, as exemplified in Frederick Jewson, Charles A. Seymour, William Townsend, Matthew Sinclair Dunn, Alexander C. Mackenzie, John B. MacEwen, Hamish McCunn, Learmont Drysdale, Charles Macpherson, J. Moir Clark, William Wallace, and the rest of their professional kin.

Then there were those who turned to Germany for instruction, and this persisted almost throughout the century, as in John Thomson, Francis Gibson, Helen Hopekirk, Adam Hamilton, Walter Hately, John Robertson, Alexander C. Mackenzie, Allan Macbeth, Frederick A. Lamond, Frederick J. Simpson, Charles Hall Woolnoth, and Alfred Moffat. The cause of this is easily explained. Quite apart from the lack of specialized teaching in this country, both Scotland and England were positive slaves in what Fuller-Maitland called the "foreign domination." This was by no means a novel craze for it had its roots in the historic past. Beginning *piano* at the Restoration (1660) this affectation expressed itself *mezzo forte* under the House of Orange (1689), surging into a forceful *crescendo* with the establishment of Hanoverian rule (1714) to reach a *forzando* by the opening of the 19th Century. Indeed, during almost the whole of the latter century, both

Edinburgh and Glasgow were the Mecca for German musicians who, as was only natural, were open advocates of Germany and its music. Even some of the Scottish music critics had a pronounced Teutonic outlook, e.g. Leonora Schmitz (Mrs. John Hunter), of the *North British Daily Mail* and the *Glasgow Herald* who had been educated at Leipsic (1857-62) under Moscheles, Plaidy, E. F. Richter and Hauptmann. Indeed, as Sir Alexander C. Mackenzie has said (*A Musician's Narrative*), " our characteristic predilection for the foreign teacher [of music] steadily increased." Actually, several Scottish musicians found it convenient to adopt German or Italian names so as to further their professional interests, and thus came into existence " Hermann Kessler," " B. Leopold," " Carlo Zotti," " Josef Meissler," " Oscar Seydel " and others, whose compositions spread like wildfire in consequence, although, in private life, they were good Scots, the last two *noms de guerre* being used by William Marshall Hutchison, the composer of *Ehren on the Rhine* and dozens of such like ballads that had an enormous sale.

This state of affairs was distinctly harmful for several reasons. Firstly, the absence of facilities for higher instruction in music, which drove so many to London and Leipsic, meant that such benefits were reserved for the privileged few who could afford it. Secondly, those who went to London often stayed there because they found wider scope for their abilities in the great metropolis and, unfortunately so, more genuine appreciation of their abilities than would be afforded them in their own land. Thirdly, the German influence had a deleterious effect in many ways. That Leipsic had outstanding teachers cannot be challenged, and also that they made a special point of favouring pupils from abroad, the best of whom were featured at the Gewandhaus Concerts. Most of these pupils returned home with not only a German training in music, but a Gernam outlook in most things, especially those who had been flattered as débutants at the Leipsic concerts. To these latter, the Germans were the chosen people in the world of music. In view of all this one can quite appreciate why so little creative work was accomplished *in* Scotland, and what did appear could not be considered, either in thought or expression, to be really *Scottish*. Further, even apart from these considerations, if anyone in Scotland did aim at composition, the likelihood of the performance of a work of serious dimensions would have been doubtful. Room might have been found for a psalm or hymn tune, or even an anthem in some advanced church, or perhaps a glee at an amateur concert, or a ballad at an occasional "sing-song," but anything of a more serious nature would have been out of the question. The concert in Scotland had such a fitful existence during the first half of the century that programme makers already had their hands full in finding room for German and Italian composers. In addition, the Scot was not considered competent in the creative sphere, at least not according to Scottish lights. In literature a Walter Scott and Thomas Carlyle, in philosophy a Thomas Brown and Alexander Bain, in painting a David Wilkie and William McTaggart, clearly showed that Scottish genius could reveal itself in an inimitable way, but in *music*, so the Scots deluded themselves, it was only the foreigner who was capable as a creator in music, a presumption which, as Sir Alexander C. Mackenzie once said, was simply " a grovelling superstition." The result was that the Scot was almost compelled to seek the humblest creative sphere for recognition, i.e. the vocal field, in which the church offered ground for tillage so long as it was for simple pasture.

In the Church, because of the conditions that had obtained for two centuries and a half, there was not much scope, although it was certainly wider than it had been. At any rate, the official psalters and hymnals of the " Seventies " and " Eighties " are fair indices of what was admissible, and one must confess at the outset that most of the contents are quite ordinary, some of it as dreary as the proverbial "twice-told tale." Only a very small amount is as good as that of the 17th Century psalter, and there is nothing approaching the old Psalms in Reports. Here we are mainly concerned with Scottish church composers of the first three-quarters of the 19th Century, and they are a mixed lot, including humble workmen like Hugh Wilson and Neil Dougall, esteemed amateurs of the standing of Bell and Ewing, and such professionals as the Hatelys and Robert A. Smith. Of course, better work is discernible outside the official psalters and hymnals, where there is a charm and certainty of expression that seems to guarantee abidance. The following are the best of the church composers of the period, approved or unapproved, in alphabetical order.

James Allan (1842-85) was a precentor at Kelvinside Free Church, Glasgow, who later became conductor of the Glasgow Select Choir (1880-85). He is best known for his hymn tune *Vevay* in the *Free Church Hymnal*. James Smith Anderson (1853-1945) was organist at St. Andrew's Parish Church, Edinburgh, and a teacher of the pianoforte at Moray House Training College. Although but one hymn tune of his, *Fingal*, is recognized in Scotland, he was well known as a contributor to such hymnals as *The Songs of Zion*, *Hymnal Companion*, the *Blackburn Tune Book*, and others. John Montgomery Bell (1837-1919) was a lawyer whose hymns, it was said, " brought him greater renown than his briefs did siller," since they were not only acceptable to Scotland but found a place in the *National Book of Hymn Tunes* (Leeds, 1885), the best known being *Grange*, *Ruthwell*, *St. Giles*, and *Renfrew*. William R. Broomfield (1826-88), famed for his *St. Kilda*, which is cut on his tombstone at Aberdeen, is remembered in the secular field as editor of the *National Songs* (Lond., n.d. ; Glasg., 1868). Robert Brown-Borthwick (1840-94), a Scottish clergyman of the Church of England, was a musician of no mean gifts, although in Scotland he has only gained recognition for his psalm tune *Aberdeen*. Yet he wrote much more, including *Twelve Kyries* and a praiseworthy anthem, *Blessed are the Dead*. As an editor he showed discrimination in his *Select Hymns for Church and Home* (Edin., 1871).

In Alexander Ewing (1830-95) Scotland produced her greatest hymn composer. Born at Aberdeen and educated at Marischal College, he became a Lieut.-Colonel (Staff Paymaster) in the army, but won greater celebrity as the composer of the hymn tune *Ewing*, better known as *Jerusalem the Golden*. There, one is pained to admit, his name and fame ends both in Scotland and England. Yet, thanks to the perspicacious outlook of the National Library of Scotland, a number of Ewing's manuscripts have been preserved which, one fervently hopes, will finally establish the place that I have assigned him. His fine anthems, *He that goeth*, *Now upon the first day*, and *There shall come a star*, as well as his deeply-moving *Deus Misereatur* and *Oh how amiable*, all composed in the " Sixties," are sufficient to increase his reputation as a church composer. His secular compositions will be treated later.

Of a more conservative character are the official tunes *Glencairn*, *Leuchars*, *Zuingle*, *Makerstoun*, and others, by Thomas Legerwood Hately (1815-67) of Greenlaw, who was a precentor at North Leith Parish Church (1836) and, at the disruption, became the leading musical authority of the Free Church, editing the *Psalmody of the Free Church of Scotland* (Edin., 1845), the *National Psalmody* (Edin., 1847), the *Scottish Psalmody* (Edin., 1852), and other similar works. His son, Walter Hately (1843-1907), was an outstanding musician in his day as we shall see later, although here he is only noted for his tunes *St. Helen* and *Inchcolm*, as well as his editorship of the *Church of Scotland Psalter and Hymnal* (Edin., 1868). George F. Graham (1789-1867) is not recognized among the elect in modern Presbyterian music books, yet his work cannot be passed over since his duet and chorus *God be Merciful* and the two doxologies in Smith's *Edinburgh Sacred Harmony* (1829) deserve mention, as does a worthy doxology by Finlay Dun (1795-1853) in the same collection. Allan Macbeth (1856-1910), the Principal of the Glasgow Athenaeum School of Music, contributed two fair anthems, *O that thou* and *He shall feed his flock*, to the *Free Church Hymnal* (1882). James Merrylees (1824-91), a pupil of John Curwen, was best known for his hymn tunes *Atlantic* and *Formosa*, although better work is seen in his anthem *For the eyes of the Lord* in the *Free Church Hymnal*.

The most outstanding composer of his day in the Presbyterian Church was Robert Archibald Smith (1780-1829). George Hogarth said that " his sacred music is uniformly excellent, possessing in a high degree the simplicity of design and solemnity of effect which this species of music requires." With that evaluation few critics would disagree, and the Church looks upon such tunes as *Morven, Selma, St. Lawrence, St. Mirren, Invocation,* the doxology *Lord bless us still,* and the scripture sentences (anthems) *Blessed be the Lord* and *How beautiful upon the mountains,* as almost part of her very structure. He was precentor of the Abbey Church, Paisley (1807) and St. George's Church, Edinburgh (1823-29). Between these dates were published his *Devotional Music* (Edin., 1810), which included original as well as selected music, some noteworthy *Anthems in Four Vocal Parts* (Edin., 1819), *Sacred Harmony* (Edin., 1820), *Sacred Music* (Edin., 1825), and *Edinburgh Sacred Harmony* (Edin., 1829), all of which opened new portals in the church music of Scotland. It was therefore with the fullest justification that James Love said (*Scottish Church Music*) that " in any history . . . of Scottish psalmody, Smith's name must ever be mentioned with profound respect." One feels, however, that Smith was much more dexterous than his church music reveals. Possibly his medium hampered his imagination and expression. His " Repeating Tunes " placed side by side with the " Tunes in Reports " of the 1635 psalter are sheer mediocrity.

Those who still remain to be mentioned are, on the whole, of much less importance, so far as the church's accepted composers are concerned. Walter Strang (1825-97), the composer of *The sun shall be no more thy light,* was precentor to the General Assembly of the Free Church (1867-89) and lecturer on music at Moray House Training College. Better was the work of Andrew Mitchell Thomson (1738-1831), the minister of St. George's, Edinburgh, from where he issued, in conjunction with Robert A. Smith, the *Sacred Harmony* (Edin., 1820). His psalm tunes *Redemption* and *St. George's Edinburgh,* had great popularity, although much more solid were his two dismissions, two sanctuses, and a doxology in Smith's *Edinburgh Sacred Harmony* (Edin., 1829). He was the father of John Thomson (1805-41), Scotland's great composer of the first half-century, and the first Reid Professor of Music at Edinburgh. A doxology, a sanctus, and a quartet and chorus of his are included in Smith's *Edinburgh Sacred Harmony* (1829). Another church composer worthy of note is John Turnbull (1804-44) who, in spite of his gifts, is only recognized by his tune *Torwood* in the *Northern Psalter* (1900). In his day his *Selection of Original Sacred Music* (Glasg., 1833), *The Sacred Harp* (Glasg., 1840), and his edition of Smith's *Devotional Music* were much in demand. Finally, there comes the Rev. Dr. W. Young of Erskine, who was one of the teachers of Robert A. Smith, and Burns was given a letter of introduction to him in 1787 by John Ramsay as " a person qualified to introduce him more extensively to Highland music." To Dr. Young we owe a few works in Smith's publications that are not negligible. Baptie (*Musical Scotland*) wrongly identifies this composer with a Perth minister, David Young (d. 1865), whereas Smith himself refers in 1829 to the *late* Rev. Dr. Young, Minister of Erskine.

This recital of the output of Scotland's church composers may be considered scarcely worth the trouble. Such a view would be hardly just for several reasons. Firstly, the church was one of the few means of expression for composers. Secondly, psalmody, with the national song, was the music of the people. Thirdly, it was through psalmody and the national song that appreciation of the higher forms of music was attained later. Indeed this century in Scotland reveals some strange anomalies and contradictions in these respects. We have seen that, in spite of the Church's disapproval of choirs and its contempt for the organ, the general love of music throughout Scotland was far greater than in England. The reason is palpable enough. It was actually the insistence of the Presbyterian Church on *congregational* singing that enhanced this general affection for music, with the result that all were singers, or imagined that they were. It was the psalm books, with the " Introduction " on the theory of music, that brought the elements of the art into almost every household, which was no small asset. With such an enriched soil can it be wondered at that the Mainzers and Hullahs attracted about 50,000 scholars to their classes in the " Forties " ? Can we be surprised that Scotland was able to produce such outstanding operatic stars in the first half of the century? When choirs and organs came to the Presbyterian Church in the second half of the century there followed a diminution of congregational interest in singing, and one naturally asks whether this did not also narrow the womb from which Scotland's great vocalists sprang?

In the purely secular field, Scottish composers were again restricted to the simpler media of ballad and glee. The concert platform being denied them, public approval of such works was confined to the home and the vocal clubs for the first half century. So far as instrumental compositions are concerned, it was only in the theatre that there was any opening for the Scottish composer, and even then the foremost exponent, John Thomson, had to go to London to have his operas performed. Any musician in Scotland who thought of making a living as a composer would need to have been a super-optimist. If he had not been blessed or cursed with independence of a livelihood, he would have been compelled to link composing with a precentorship in a church, or a position in a theatre band. Teaching, unless you were a German, was a precarious business, and had to be carried on with some other vocation. That is why in the early days of the century the modicum of Scottish composers came from the pew, the band " pit," or the armchair of the affluent.

There were even difficulties for ballad composers to obtain success. Since the national song was first in public estimation, the favourable acceptance of any new songs chiefly depended on their being set to some Scottish poet or some Scottish theme, as well as in an idiomatic style both in words and music. Only the songs that fulfilled these conditions have survived from those days, and this popularity of Scottish songs, both the new and old, was quite general, although the bourgeois amateur, as ever, clamoured for the latest operatic *arias*. In the instrumental sphere, much the same tastes prevailed. The people at large patronized *rondos* on national airs for the pianoforte, such as those which John Ross of Aberdeen turned out of his musical mill. Others were more attracted by the works of Steibelt, Kalkbrenner, Moscheles, and the rest. In spite of all this there was no lack of Scottish composers, but during the first half-century these were almost all confined to the ballad and glee for the reasons outlined, and among those who shone, either in brilliance or dulness, were a few whose work has lived to this day, if only in Scotland.

As might well be expected, the first outstanding composer was Robert A. Smith (1780-1829) who, though professionally a precentor, lived in a wider and more joyous world. As Burns would say,—" Nae *lento, largo,* in the play, But *allegretto, forte,* gay." Although his weighty contribution to church music can never be forgotten, one imagines that his secular compositions will long outlast that fame, as the well-known story of the boy at the Sabbath School prophetically indicates. Asked by his teacher " Who was Jesse ? " the lad replied : " Please, she cam frae Dumblane." The truth is that Smith's songs, *Jessie, the flow'r o' Dunblane, The Harper of Mull, Loudon's Bonnie Woods and Braes, On wi' the Tartan,* and their attractively intimate fellows, were more intriguing to the public at large than the story in I *Samuel,* xvi. How delightful too, is that duet, *Row weel, my boatie* (*c.* 1820), and how sublime the trio *Ave Sanctissima,* and so catchy that glee, *Marjory Miller.* George Hogarth, who thought the composer " a musician of sterling talent," was truly prophetic when he said that Smith " enriched the music of our country with many melodies which have deservedly become national, and will probably descend in that character from generation to generation in Scotland."

Of George Farquhar Graham (1789-1867) we have already spoken as a literator and theorist, but he deserves mention here as a composer since the *Encyclopaedia Britannica* avers that his songs were " considered excellent in their day." His first publication appears to have been a grand divertimento for the pianoforte, *The Battle of Barrosa,* Op. 3 (Edin., 1811), on the title page of which is the following piece of naïveté : " L'auteur de cette pièce ne joue pas du Piano Forte, et il compose sans l'aide d'aucun instrument de musique." Then there was the anonymous *Twelve Pieces of Vocal*

*Music with accompaniments for the Pianoforte . . . Composed and
. . . Inscribed to . . . Haydn, by a Dilettante* (Edin., 1811).
Among his best-known songs were *Ah! County Guy* (Scott), which
the poet asked him to set ; *You Never Longed nor Loved* (Goethe) ;
and *The Mariner's Song* (Cunningham). Others were *While Hours
of Bliss* and *Oh! for the Days when we were Young*, as well as a fine
glee, *A Wet Sheet and a Flowing Sea*. *Grove's Dictionary of Music*
simply says that " he composed and published some ballads,"
which may be true enough, but he did more. Mention has already
been made of his *God be Merciful* and two doxologies in Smith's
Edinburgh Sacred Harmony (1829). At the third evening concert
of the Edinburgh Musical Festival (1815) his *Overture*, " composed
for the occasion," was performed, and he himself refers to his
" orchestral symphonies . . . which were performed at the public
Edinburgh ' Fund Concerts '." The present writer once owned a
number of his autograph pianoforte and orchestral compositions
which went into the possession of Harold Reeves, Shaftesbury
Avenue, London. Similarly, *Grove's Dictionary of Music* merely
credits Graham with having furnished " historical, biographical
and critical notices " to his *Songs of Scotland* (Edin., 1848-9),
whereas he also admirably harmonized twenty-eight of the three
hundred and fifteen songs in this collection, the remainder being
set by Mudie (eighty-six), Surenne (eighty), Dun (twenty-six),
Lawrie (eight), and Dibdin (seven).

It is a great pity that we do not possess Graham's setting of
The Jolly Beggars, composed at George Thomson's request. George
Hogarth had recommended Graham to Thomson to set Burns'
poem to music, but so early as 1814, Thomson's brother James tried
to prejudice the publisher against Graham, and said that whilst the
composer " had a fine taste for the rich and varied harmony of the
German school of instrumental music," he did not think that Graham
had a good idea of " vocal style " because, he said, the latter allowed
" his desires of displaying learning" to run away with him. Graham's
music was completed by 1816 but George Thomson, whilst acknow-
ledging its " prodigious merit," thought that it was too difficult for

his public and sent the score to John Mather (1781-1850), an English organist in Edinburgh, asking him to point out where it was " too difficult," and how it could be simplified. In 1817, Thomson wrote to Graham saying : " Highly as I admire a great part of it, I now plainly perceive that the performance of it requires more talent than is to be found in the generality of those for whom my volumes are intended." The result was that Thomson resolved not to publish it, and immediately commissioned [Sir] Henry R. Bishop with the composing of fresh music. We have the result of the latter in print, and we are able to judge its value. In spite of Thomson's own opinion that it was a " masterly proof " of Bishop's talents (which it probably is), every stave reveals its tame respectability, so utterly alien to the spirit of this " puissant production " as Matthew Arnold called Burns' masterpiece.

Finlay Dun (1795-1853) belonged to Aberdeen. He was a man of remarkable gifts, a violinist and violist, singer, pianist, and composer. For the violin he had studied under the great Baillot, and had played the viola in the orchestra at the San Carlo Theatre, Naples. In singing he had lessons from Crescentini, and repeated some of the *maestro's* instruction in his *Solfeggi and Exercises* (Lond., 1829). Settling in Edinburgh as a music teacher, he gained considerable prestige. Although best known as an arranger and editor of *The Vocal Melodies of Scotland* (Edin., 1836-8) with John Thomson, and of *The Songs of Scotland* (Edin., 1848-9) with George F. Graham and others, as well as being responsible for *Orain na'h Albain* (Edin., 1848), a collection of Gaelic songs to which he added historical notes, he was quite a gifted composer, which one can detect even in his graduated *solfeggi* course mentioned above. He composed two symphonies for full orchestra, which do not appear to have survived, but his part-songs and glees obtained some recognition, notably *The Parted Spirit* (Gentlemen's Glee Club Prize, Manchester, 1831), and the fresh and sincere *She is Coming* (Novello's *Part Song Book*, 1850), whilst *June* (1851) is a melodiously expressive piece of work. Perhaps his settings of Baroness Nairne's *Lays from Strathearn* (c. 1845-47) reveal him at his best. James D.

Brown (*Biographical Dictionary of Musicians*) is quite just in his estimate when he says that " all his parts-songs are fine."

Another whose *métier* was much in the same groove was John Turnbull (1804-44). Beginning as a precentor at Ayr (1827), he went to a similar post at St. George's Church, Glasgow (1833), where he spent the remainder of his life. Although better known for his sacred music, already mentioned, and a collection of Scottish songs, *The Garland of Scotia* (Glasg., 1841), his secular compositions really showed his ability. Among these were *Six Glees for Three and Four Voices* (Glasg., c. 1842), one of which, *Hail Lovely Star*, is as exquisite as his invocation. His songs, *Jeanie Lee* and *Thistle and the Briar* were long popular. Others were, *Love and Our Ocean Home*, *Guard Ye the Passes*, and *O Blessing on Thee, Land*, which were re-issued in the *British Minstrel* (Glasg., 1844).

Then followed the greatest of the Scottish composers of the first half-century, John Thomson (1805-41) of Sprouston, Roxburgh. He was the son of the Rev. Dr. Andrew Mitchell Thomson, the minister of St. George's Church, Edinburgh. We do not know of his early instructors in music, but doubtless his father was his first teacher, and he showed an aptitude for composition quite early in a *Doxology, Sanctus, Quartet and Chorus*, later published in Robert A. Smith's *Edinburgh Sacred Harmony* (Edin., 1829), and in a *Funeral Anthem*, performed at St. George's Church in 1829, when a concert in memory of Smith, who died in the January, was given. Seemingly he completed his musical education in Germany, a circumstance due to Mendelssohn, whom he met in Edinburgh in July, 1829. The composer of the *Scotch Symphony* gave him a letter of introduction to his family in Berlin, in which he says of the budding Scottish composer :—" I know of a pretty trio of his composition and some local pieces which well please me." When Thomson went to Germany he also became friendly with Schumann, Moscheles and Schnyder von Wartensee, becoming the pupil of the last named.

Thomson's first work of importance was a *Rondo for the Pianoforte* (1828), still in manuscript at Edinburgh, a piece which is not only far better than the general run of such works, but possibly the best of the composer's output in this field, which includes an interesting *Bagatelle* (1831), written after his return from Germany, some waltzes and polonaises, and an *Adagio* and *Romance* which appeared in the *Harmonicon* (1832). From the same period comes a brilliant *Allegro Maestoso* in E Flat for flute and orchestra (Edinburgh MS.) which might profitably be programmed to-day, as well as an *Allegro maestoso and Siliciano* for flute and strings (violin, viola and 'cello) in the same library (No. 118) although wrongly catalogued by Dr. Hans Gal as a string quartet. Then there is a glittering *Cappriccio* for pianoforte and violin, which is not too technically difficult although possibly more than intricate for the drawing-room young ladies of the period.

More important are Thomson's dramatic works. His first essay in this field was music for Sir Walter Scott's *The House of Aspen*. Grove says that it was produced at the Surrey Theatre, London, 17th November, 1829, but this may be erroneous, as the music for this production seems to have been composed by Jonathan Blewitt. The *Dictionary of National Biography* gives the 27th October, 1834, as the date, which more correctly belongs to Thomson's opera *Hermann*. The incomplete manuscript score, now at Edinburgh, of the *The House of Aspen* tells us that the play with Thomson's music was produced at the Theatre Royal, Edinburgh, 19th December, 1829, although Didbin, in his *Annals of the Edinburgh Stage*, says 17th December, when the overture and vocal and instrumental music was advertised as having been composed by " an amateur." The score does not contain the overture, and all that has been registered in the score is an " Entracte," " Chorus of Victory," " The [Trooper's] Rhine Wine Song," " Gertrude's Song," and " Genevieve," of which *The Trooper's Rhine Wine Song* was published (Edin., 1861). The play ran for eight nights, but was repeated several times during the season.

Thomson's greatest work was an opera in two acts, *Hermann or The Broken Spear*, the full autograph score of which, dated August, 1834, is treasured at Edinburgh. It was produced at the English

Opera House (Lyceum Theatre), London, in October, 1834 (*cf.
Dictionary of National Biography*), where it followed Loder's
Nourjahad (July, 1834) and Barnett's *Mountain Sylph* (August,
1834). George Hogarth (*Musical History*) says that although it
was " less successful than these other pieces " (of Loder and
Barnett) it " was not inferior to them in musical merit." The
Scottish music critic gives his opinion that its unsuccess was " in
consequence of the faults of the drama, and a very defective
performance." Since we are able to consult the score itself we can
judge for ourselves the value of Hogarth's evaluation. It consists
of an overture and twenty-three numbers, almost every one of
which shows that Thomson's technical musicianship was even
better than that of Loder or Barnett. The overture, which is of
classical dimensions and treatment, is an effective piece of writing
and admirably scored. It was revived at an early Reid Concert.
The opera itself sparkles with items of outstanding merit, although
the two published numbers for voice and pianoforte :—" *O Dear!
What a Terrible Eye* (Lond., *c.* 1835) and *I Shudder at my Past
Career* (Lond., 1842), are by no means indicative of the contents
of this fine opera. Both Thomson and Barnett had Schnyder von
Wartensee of Frankfort as teacher, and yet their work, in *Hermann*
and the *Mounting Sylph* respectively, have nothing in common
technically. Comparing these two operas, one might even say that
the concerted numbers of Thomson are better than those of Barnett.
They show greater originality in ideas and treatment, and are much
more impressive. Some of Thomson's interludes are skilfully
wrought, and greatly enhance the dramatic situations. Yet Barnett,
because he was the first by a month or two, has been given all the
kudos for having broken away from the old English ballad opera
traditions. Had Thomson's opera been published in full it is
probable that greater recognition would have been accorded the
composer. Thomson's other opera, *The Shadow on the Wall*,
which was produced at the English Opera House on the 20th
April, 1835, is said (*Dictionary of National Biography* and *Grove's
Dictionary of Music*) to have had " a long run."

Of Thomson's vocal compositions, about thirty were published, exclusive of one from *The House of Aspen* and two from *Hermann*, most of which are in the British Museum. Earlier songs than these are *The Savoyard's Return* (1829), *I'll Bid this Heart be Still* (1831), *Caro Bene* (1831), and *Yes, Thou May'st Sigh* (1832), which appeared in the *Harmonicon*. Others are mentioned in the *British Musical Biography*. Baptie considered that *The Song of Harold Harfager* was " spirited and expressive," and *The Pirate's Serenade* was certainly a prime favourite with John Wilson. Grove particularizes these two songs as " original," but the best view of Thomson's vocal writing is to be seen in his *Drei Lieder von Lord Byron, Schiller u. Uhland* (Leipsic, 1838), consisting of *There be None of Beauty's Daughters, Kadowessische Todenklage*, and *Das Ständchen*, a copy of which at Edinburgh contains the inscription in Thomson's handwriting : "Dr. Felix Mendelssohn-Bartholdy, with the Author's kind regards, Leipsic, 5 Sept., 1838." Thomson's songs had wide acceptance in his day, and the *Musical World*, reviewing one of these, reveals what appears to have been the general opinion of the composer's worth when it says : " The reputation of Mr. Thomson may now, we believe, be considered as firmly and deservedly established. Much of his music is both beautiful and original."

A ballad composer who had quite an enviable popularity in his day was William Richardson Dempster (1808-71) of Keith, Banff-shire, although it was not there that he found acceptance, but in London. No less than forty-five of his songs have a place in the British Museum Catalogue. One of his early successes was *The Blind Boy* (1844), although his *Come o'er the Mountain to me* is preferable. Other favourites were *Bird of the Wilderness* (1854), *The May Queen* (1855), and *The Deserted Road* (1864). James D. Brown says of his songs that a number were " good, though not always strikingly original," but certainly his *Songs in the Idylls of the King* (1864) of Tennyson, belong to the former category. The songs of Elizabeth Masson (1806-65) were much more individual and intellectually solid, although probably not of the " drawing-room " type of the preceding composer. Some of her productions are tenderly lyrical, *Oh! Love was never yet without the Pang* (1837) and *Come off to the Moors*, but in her *Original Jacobite Songs* (1839) there is a solemn impressiveness in the settings only matched by her *Twelve Songs by Byron* (1843) which are as graceful as the lines of " the greatest talent " of the century, as Goethe wrote of Byron. George Croal (1811-1907) of Edinburgh was a music publisher who wielded a talented pen. Most of his compositions, written under the pen-name " Carlo Zotti," are mere ephemera, dance music and the like, by which he turned an honest penny. Yet in his more tranquil moods he composed one or two acceptable songs, *Away to the Woods* and *The Emigrant's Dream*, although better still was his *Centenary Souvenir : Six Songs by Sir Walter Scott* (1832), which contains a fine setting of *Soldier Rest*. Croal's *Living Memories of an Octogenarian* (Edin., 1894) tells of his hearing Paganini (1833), Liszt (1840), Moscheles, Cramer, Kalkbrenner, and others, in Edinburgh.

Tragic was the life of Alexander Hume (1811-59) of Edinburgh which, but for his indiscipline, might have been otherwise, for he was a man of original gifts. He began his career in his native city as chorus master at the Theatre Royal and tenor chorister at St. Paul's Episcopal Church. Here he was appreciated for his *English Hymn Tune Book* (Edin., n.d.), *Anthems and Sacred Songs* (Edin., n.d.), and *Gall's Psalm and Hymn Book* (Edin., 1842), which grew into *British Psalmody* (Edin., *c.* 1848), the last-named containing many of his best tunes. Later he moved to Glasgow where, abandoning his church connections (or rather the church abandoned him), he settled down to composing purely secular works, many of which are still popular, including his superbly touching *Afton Water*, the evergreen *A Guid New Year*, the pathetic *Scottish Emigrant's Farewell*, and *My Ain Dear Nell*, the words of the last two being also from his pen. Once upon a time Scotland would listen to nothing else but Hume's *Bonnie Lady Ann*, *The Lass o' Moredun*, and *Lass, gin ye wad Lo'e Me*, but they have now passed out of ken. Yet one feels that even to-day there ought to be a public for his *Six Sensible Songs*, whilst the Church might still profitably

use his *Anthems and Sacred Songs*. His part-songs too are all
" of a most tuneful and elegant description," and of such are *We
Fairies Come*, which is delightful, and the madrigal *Round a Circle*,
composed in the style of Festa's *Down in a Flow'ry Vale*.

Among a crowd of lesser-known composers of songs and glees
during the first three-quarters of the century, most of whom were
only known by two or three works, are a few who are still " minded,"
to use a good old English word still preserved by the Scots, even if
this fame may not have reached other ears than those of Caledonian
folk. You may not have heard of " blithe Jamie Barr [1781-1860]
frae St. Barchan's toun," as Tannahill limned this composer, but
he wrote *Thou Bonnie Wood o' Craigielea* to the Paisley poet's
entrancing lines, which is still in dewy freshness. His glee *Robin
Hood* may be found in the *British Harmonist* (Glasg., 1848). Then
there was John Monro (1786-1851) of Edinburgh. He settled in
London like many others because he could not get a living in his own
land. Here he composed an acceptable set of six songs entitled
Border Ballads (Lond., *c.* 1825), as well as a number of separate
songs, from *Ellen Aureen* (1817) to *Wert Thou Like Me* (1847), many
of which found a temporary home north of the border, yet all seem
to have perished. As I have said, much depended on a national
sentimental approach to assure a persistent survival. For instance,
Isabella Mary Scott (1786-1838) of Edinburgh, who became Mrs.
Patrick Gibson, gained immediate favour with her ballad *Loch-na-
gar*, not that it was better than the work of Monro, but simply
because it had a sentimental national attraction. Of far greater
merit was Peter Macleod (1797-1859), an amateur who published
four volumes of choice songs. Little of their contents may be known
to-day although his *Dowie Dens o' Yarrow* or *Our's is the Land*
may be heard once in a while. The profits that accrued from his
Original Scottish Melodies were devoted to the completion of the
Burns monument at Edinburgh.

Yet few of these composers had any significance outside of
Scotland. Recognition south of the border was only given to a
select few—John Monro for example, because he wrote in England

and for the English. John Sinclair (1791-1857) was another, but much of his success was due to the circumstance that he was an outstanding singer himself, and his *Beneath the Wave, Dunbarton's Bonnie Dell, Hey the Bonnie Breast-knots, The Mountian Maid,* and others were popular in the south because he sang them.   The success of *Put Off! Put Off!* by John Templeton (1802-86), another famous tenor, is also only explicable by the fact that the composer himself publicised it. Yet much better work was accomplished by others who were not so close to public gaze and approbation.   One in particular was the Rev. John Park (1804-65) whose gifts are well displayed in a posthumous collection, hardly known, entitled :—*Songs Composed and, in part, Written by the late Rev. John Park* (Leeds, 1876), to which Principal John C. Shairp of the United College, St. Andrews, contributed an introductory memoir.   These songs reveal outstanding musicianship and, in some cases, much individuality.   In their day, seemingly, such songs as *Mi Nian Dhu* and *Were na my Heart Licht* were prime favourites (*Transactions : Old Glasgow Club,* 1909), but there are better examples. What could be finer than Park's setting of Sir Walter Scott's *Bring the Bowl*, the intensely captivating *Under the Greenwood Tree*, or his handling of Shelley's rich piping in the *Hymn to Pan*. Yet despite this appraisement there are few who turn the pages of Park's volume nowadays, and one could repeat the same burden of complaint of the neglect of other composers.

Oftentimes we see men, who were better known in other walks of music, being only remembered to-day by a song or two. Samuel Barr (1807-66), a music teacher of repute in Glasgow, composed the winsome *Hurrah for the Highlands*, which will be sung probably long after his *Theory and Practice of Harmony and Composition* (1861) has been forgotten. It is the same with William H. Lithgow (1806-74), once famous as " Professor Lithgow," widely known for his books of sacred music now long out of memory's ken, although to-day Lithgow is still minded for his stirring *Old Scotland I Love Thee*. Nor can we omit Mary Maxwell Campbell (1812-86) of Pitlour, if only by reason of her rather overestimated *March of the*

Cameron Men. James Stewart Geikie (1811-83), the father of Sir Archibald Geikie, also deserves a line because of his part-song *How Beautiful is Night* and the song, *My Heather Hills.* I once owned a spirited *Grand March* for a military band by Geikie which had been scored by his friend George F. Graham. It went into the possession of Harold Reeves, Shaftesbury Avenue, London. Lastly comes William Jackson (1828-76), the son of John Jackson, a musician of Edinburgh. For many years he was a pianist and 'cellist at several music halls in Glasgow, notably at the " Whitebait," where he composed *The Lass o' Ballochmyle* and *The Dear Little Shamrock.* Like many of his craft, he died in poverty at Girvan whilst touring with a theatrical company. In 1913, a monument was erected over his grave by local subscription.

With the exception of John Thomson, and perhaps Robert A. Smith, Scotland's composers can only be counted among the small fry. It was fortunate, however, that the period closed with two other quite worthy names,—Jewson and Ewing, which help in lifting Scotland out of the rut of mediocrity so far as its creative work in music is concerned, although even with their contribution, it does not give the country the slight eminence on which it stood in the preceding century. To Frederick Bowen Jewson (1823-91) we have already paid tribute as an outstanding pianist and teacher in London. Yet his few quite brilliant compositions must also be acknowledged. Like other Scots, he had to go south for his final musical training, and at the Royal Academy of Music, London, he was King's Scholar (1837). As a youth of twelve he had performed one of his earliest compositions in Edinburgh, but in 1838, still in his teens, he published a *Granda Sonata* for the pianoforte which called attention to his abilities in this sphere. In 1840 there was performed his overture *Killicrankie* by the R.A.M. Orchestra, a work which, with five other overtures for the orchestra from his pen, showed that he was equal to the occasion when a more colourful palette and a wider canvas were available. In spite of this he realized that his best medium for creative work was with the pianoforte, witness his dominating *Six grandes études de concert* (op. 16, 1848) and *Douze études* (op. 23). That Scotland was still in his mind's eye is evident from a contemporary work *Caledonia ; Valse de concert* (1848). Two concertos for the pianoforte demonstrate Jewson at his best, especially the *Second Concerto* in E (op. 33), first presented at St. James's Hall, London, in June 1882. Although one never hears or sees his work in the repertories, it has both intellectual and emotional appeal, revealing the mind of a skilled craftsman. Seemingly the test for admission to the repertories is bulk. Perhaps if Jewson had written say, fifty items, he might have stood a chance of being among the elect. Like boxers, it is often the test of endurance that pays, not a mere " knock out " in one round.

With the next composer, Alexander Ewing (1830-95), there is no blame to be laid at any door for his neglect. Beyond his hymn-tune *Jerusalem the Golden*, his compositions are practically unknown in the annals of music as they never touched a printer's platen. Fortunately, the National Library of Scotland has preserved many of his autograph manuscripts. Here are to be found some perfectly exquisite part-songs. Two of these, *Gladly ring, Oh joy bells* (1865) and *The Gentle Spring* are most delightful, showing the composer in the loftiest mood. Another, *Oh doubting heart*, with a throbbing intensity, reminds one of Farnaby. Two more, worthy of appreciative ears, are *The Green Trees whisper'd* and *O'er the glad waters*, both worthy of permanence. " *From Guinevere*," for eight voices (1868), is a work of maturity, and might possibly be enduring if it were only in print. Lastly among the many works that Ewing has left is a colourful madrigal (16th century style), a superbly austere offering entitled *Life is full of trouble*. What a pity it is that such delightful music should be hidden away on musty shelves.

And so this otherwise inglorious period of creative work in music by Scotsmen came to a close with the " Sixties," although so much looked promising in the initial years. George F. Graham, writing in 1816, was looking to the establishment of an Academy of Music that would so encourage composers to such flights that this land would " command the respect of all the rest of Europe." The following year John Donaldson, afterwards Reid Professor of Music, visualized pupils emulating " Corelli, Handel, Haydn, and Mozart." It was certainly true that the sudden burst of Scottish creative genius in the previous century presaged much, but it was misleading. The facts are that the cultural conditions of the two centuries were vastly different. Whilst the people at large were more musical than ever, the art itself had become more professionalized than before. This latter, in its way, was all to the good, but it bred the *impresario* and *entrepreneur* who, as was only natural from a business point of view, always looked at the box office receipts as the primary consideration.

The craze was for foreigners, both as executants and composers, much of it being due to early Hanoverian court preferences. The British public had been weaned for so long on Handel that it felt that it could not have walked musically without leaning on Germans. Scotland can be included in this fawning on the foreigner, although in defence it has to be stated that it had to depend on London for its " star " attractions on the concert platform, and so had also to follow English tastes in its programmes. The result was that there was little opportunity for the British composer in England or Scotland, as I pointed out with facts and figures some years ago (*Music and Letters*, 1931). In England, however, there was a determined stand made against the alien domination, in which resistance both performers and composers joined hands. In the first place a series of purely British Concerts were established (1822), the programmes of which were primarily designed to be made up " entirely of the works of British composers." It only existed for a year. Then came the Vocal Society (1832), formed to " present the vocal music of the English school," but this venture also disintegrated. A much more healthy body was the Society of British Musicians (1834-65), whose prospectus contained a statement which gives at least one reason why Scots were fighting shy of making music a profession, whatever their appreciation was of the art itself. The prospectus said :

" The overwhelming preponderance of foreign compositions in all musical performances, while it can scarcely fail to
impress the public with the idea that musical genius is an alien
to this country, tends also to repress those energies, and to
extinguish that emulation in the breast of the youthful aspirant,
which alone lead to pre-eminence."

Further, the Presbyterian conscience had already prejudiced people
against music as a profession and even as a social art in Scotland,
but now, even to those who were uninfluenced by the so-called
" moral scruples," there were substantial temporal reasons for
holding aloof from the art, since who would think of embarking on
music as a career when it was most palpably clear that the best
positions in the profession and on programmes were reserved for
foreigners.

CHAPTER 12

THE COMPOSERS OF THE REVIVAL

" Cosmopolitanism has done its work with a vengeance, and left
us apparently high and dry with every indication that national
characteristics will now be no longer found in our midst."
" Nationalism in music is a factor that will have to be reckoned
with in the future."

JAMES C. DIBDIN : *The Musical Educator* (Edin., 1895, *et seq.*).

These words were expressed by an Edinburgh grandson of the
great Charles Dibdin (1745-1814), whose music is as British as
the sentiment of the words to which it was set. The works of the
latter were penned at a period of storm and stress for Britons, and
they expressed the ideas of the masses rather than the classes who,
as John Stuart Blackie once said, were generally " the least national
class of society." Yet it was ever thus, since physics and politics
are causally and inevitably bound together. I have already
emphasized the opinion that all great movements of thought
have actually been connected with government by discussion, as
evidenced in many epochs from the Mediaeval Italian Republics
to the French Revolution, as Bagehot showed many years ago.

That even art is not quite immune from this influence of government by discussion, is proved, to use a Chestertonism, by its absence in Scotland during the Reformation. The argument is just as valid in modern times. In the previous chapter, where Britain was under a middle class rule (1837-68), we saw a state of affairs in which music expressed itself in an appurtenant cosmopolitan utterance, although with the scales heavily weighted on the side of German music.   Handel dominated everywhere in Britain until the pure orchestral music of Haydn, Mozart and Beethoven shook his popularity. Then came Mendelssohn and Spohr, whose influence on the British composer was far-reaching. Indeed, so cosmopolitan had the outlook become that some people were complaining that " the world of music is at present a republic " (*The British Minstrel*, Glasg., 1844).

How this cosmopolitanism affected Scotland is shown not only in its music programmes, but in those Scots who went to Germany for their musical education or in those who, although staying at home, were still influenced by German art and teaching. One of the earliest of the German school was Adam Hamilton (1820-1900) of Edinburgh, a brother of David Hamilton, the organist. He had studied at the famous *Musikschule* of Friedrich Schneider at Dessau, whose *Elementarbuch der Harmonie* (1820) was so popular in English (1828). On his return he became conductor of the Edinburgh Harmonic Society (1847) and then the Edinburgh Choral Society (1866-83). Yet in spite of his Continental training he composed little that was noteworthy, and was known only by a few songs and part songs, although two orchestral works—an *Overture* (1878) and an *Andante* and *Turkish March* (1882) were performed at the concerts of the last-named society.

The next was John Robertson (1838-19..), also from Edinburgh. He was the pupil of John Donaldson, the Reid Professor of Music at Edinburgh University, but later he studied under Franz Schulz in Berlin. As organist at St. Andrew's Episcopal Church and New Greyfriars Church, Edinburgh, he made a reputation and graduated Mus.B. (Cantab.) in 1884. His most outstanding compositions were for the church, notably his anthems—*I was Glad* (Psalm, CXXII) for solo, chorus, orchestra, and organ, *When the Storm Rages Loud*, and *Grant the Queen a Long Life* (1887), besides two *Te Deums in F* and *C*, and a *Nunc Dimittis in F*. He also wrote some charming part-songs, especially one—*Lull ye My Love asleep*. The hand of Mendelssohn was upon him, and his contributions on Harmony and Counterpoint to Dr. John Greig's *Musical Educator* (Edin., 1895 *et seq.*), admirable as they are, reveal a similar dependence.

Walter Hately (1843-1907) of Edinburgh was first taught by his father, Thomas L. Hately (1815-67) of Greenlaw, but he spent three years (1861-64) at Leipsic Conservatorium under Plaidy, Moscheles, Reinecke, Hauptmann, E. F. Richter, and Dreyschock. On his return to Edinburgh (1865) he obtained appointments at the Church of Scotland Training College as a teacher, and at Free St. George's Church as a precentor. Here again, the training abroad did not produce any outstanding creative work. In his songs—*Row Burnie Row*, *King Winter*, *Ellorie* and others, as well as in his several pianoforte pieces, we catch the glint of the *Lieder ohne Worte*.

More officially important was Allan Macbeth (1856-1910) of Greenock. He was at Leipsic later (1875-76) under some of the above-mentioned teachers. Those of Macbeth's pupils who remember him as Principal of the Glasgow Athenæum School of Music (1890-1902) recall his Teutonic outlook. Notwithstanding his sojourn at Leipsic, his compositions do not rise above the commonplace. His most important work, an operetta *The Duke's Doctor*, is said to be his best work, but it is not available for scrutiny. He composed two cantatas *The Land of Glory* (1890) and *Silver Bells*. The former, according to the *Musical Times*, was " on orthodox lines, and entirely free from the influence of the modern school." The same can be said of his *Three Four-part Songs*, his pianoforte pieces *Valse Caprice*, *Mazurka*, and others, as well as his songs, *Old Antwerp Town*, *Voice of the Waters* and *It was but a Milkmaid*. Indeed, scarcely anything of his work is remembered save his tuneful trifle, *Forget-me-not*, although he composed and published much.

Of a different calibre was Helen Hopekirk (1856-1941) the famed Scottish pianist. She was also of the Leipsic circle, although her stay there was later than that of the preceding. Whilst her earlier *Five Songs* (1894) show a German impress, her later *Six poems by Fiona Macleod* (1907) is much more expressive of herself, by which I mean the self that we see in a *Suite for Pianoforte* (1917) and her treatment of *Seventy Scottish Songs* (1905). Of her other works, which are not at hand for comparison, are a *Concerto for Pianoforte*, a *Concertstücke* for pianoforte and orchestra produced at Henschel's Concerts, Edinburgh (1894), and a *Sonata for Pianoforte and Violin* (Chicago Exhibition, 1893). Of her *Concertstücke* the *Musical Times* wrote that it was "the most important commission she has, as yet, presented to the public," and the critic praised its "musical interest and freedom of its technical treatment."

Another of Edinburgh's sons who studied abroad was Francis Gibson (1861-19..). First taught by the Scottish pianist William Townsend (1849-1925), under whom he also studied composition, he then entered the Hoch'sche Conservatorium at Frankfort-on-Main, studying composition under Raff and the pianoforte under Karl Faelten. When he came back to his native city he soon became one of its leading music teachers. Little of his compositions have been published, although his earlier *Album of Ten Songs* (Edin., 1897) held out some promise of better things. More thorough are his works for the pianoforte, *Two Characteristic Pieces* (Lond., 1912) and *Four Characteristic Pieces* (Lond., 1915).

According to all accounts, a much greater man than any of the foregoing was Charles Hall Woolnoth (1860-1911), who belonged to Glasgow. Having studied under John Farrar Howden (1818-75) he went to Leipsic to sit at the feet of Reinecke and E. F. Ritter. On his return to the Clyde he became an active figure in the city's musical life both as a composer and pianist, and with the late Philip Edwin Halstead (1866-1940) created quite a furore in their

pianoforte work. One of his earliest publications was a rather
attractive pianoforte solo *Lisette* (1881), but his more important
compositions were a cantata *Il Penseroso*, and a choral ballad *The
Skeleton in Armour* (Glasg., 1889). Yet he composed a prodigious
amount which unfortunately has not survived. Philip Edwin
Halstead, who had been a life-long friend since their Leipsic days,
had the highest opinion of Woolnoth as a composer, who could,
even in his lighter pieces, like Heine, mix gaiety and gloom in the
one effort. Halstead and Woolnoth left Glasgow together for
London in 1891, where both were to " seek their fortunes " musically. Halstead returned to Glasgow the following year, but Woolnoth
remained in the great metropolis. According to Halstead, Woolnoth
had an original and individual gift in composition, and yet in spite
of enquiries from his family, nothing of his work appears to have
been preserved save a few published works of little importance.

From the point of view of a widening cultural horizon, the strong
German influence, especially the telling persuasion of Mndelssohn,
was undoubtedly beneficial. Neither the Scots nor the English
were producing such entrancing music as was captivating everyone, high and low, professional and amateur, whether for weal
or woe. With the Scots especially, where the *Scotch Symphony* and
the *Hebrides Overture* had flattered their national pride, the sentimental appeal of his ravishing melody went straight to their hearts.
The result of this emotional bias was amazing. The *Lieder ohne
Worte* were on everybody's pianoforte desk, and the concert and
festival programmes so persistently featured *St. Paul* and *Elijah* that
their popularity was almost neck to neck with the *Messiah*. Quite
apart from the fact that British composers were almost compelled
to write in the Mendelssohnian strain to be in the swim, the constant
reiteration of this music had almost forced them to think musically
in this language, for this art is such an infectious thing that one
is persuaded, willy-nilly, in style, cadence, treatment, and instrumentation, quite unconsciously. Mendelssohn worship can be
gauged from Rockstro's *History of Music* (1886), in which seventeen
pages are devoted to him, whilst only eight are allowed Bach and

a mere five for Beethoven.   We can appreciate therefore, why and how so many of the composers were influenced by the German school even without having been trained in Germany.

Side by side with those schooled in Germany was the home product, although this does not necessarily exclude the latter from the Mendelssohnian influence, or even that of the later Spohr and Gounod.   In their own field these composers produced better work than the former school, although they still showed preferences for the old national path of vocal writing.   The first of these was Charles John Hargitt (1833-1918) of Edinburgh, the son of Charles Hargitt (1804-80), himself a pupil of Charles Knyvett and Crotch, a circumstance worth noting because the son was first taught by his father, although later he studied under Macfarren, Hallé, and Ferdinand Hiller.   His first professional posts were as organist of St. Mary's Catholic Church, Edinburgh, and conductor of the Edinburgh Choral Union (1858-62), of which latter he was the founder.   In 1862 he removed to London where he became well known for his oratorios and concerts.   He organized the Royal Albert Hall Choral Society and acted as sub-conductor to Gounod. Although he composed an opera *Coronet or Crown*, a cantata *The Harvest Queen*, as well as orchestral music and songs, notably among the latter *The Mitherless Bairn*, his real *métier* was church music, as in a moving *Ave Maria* (1857), *O Salutaris* (1858), and a most dignified motet *Tota pulchra es Maria* (1887), all showing what is characteristically English church music at its best.

Another Edinburgh composer was John Charles Grieve (1842-1916), sometime choirmaster at Lady Yester's Church there, and lecturer on music theory at Heriot-Watt College.   He was an excellent teacher whose *Practical Harmony* (Edin., n.d.), and his chapters in Greig's *Musical Educator* (Edin., 1895 *et seq.*), were very useful in their day.   Although every lassie and laddie in Scotland knows his *Bonnie Wells o' Wearie*, he had not any considerable reputation as a composer beyond the borders of his own land, yet he produced work of a meritorious character in *Christian Songs of Praise* (Edin., 1873), as well as *The Sower and the Seed* and *The Good*

Samaritan both for soli and chorus, an oratorio *Benjamin* (Edin., 1877), a cantata *Legend of St. Swithin* (1891), as well as some good part-songs, *Stars of the Summer Night* and *Fly Away Lady-Bird*, and such songs as *Comin' Hame* and *Earth's Partings*. He was the first to make headway with school cantatas. Indeed, his *Children's Festival : A Flower Service* (1915), probably one of his last works, and twelve published songs which can be seen in the British Museum, show that his output was uniformly musicianly.

John Kinross (1848-90) also came from Edinburgh, and although his "exceptional abilities as a pianist" is stressed by the *Musical Times*, it is as a composer that he claims attention here. Beginning life in the music trade he was self-taught at first, but later received instruction from Macfarren. From about 1865 he made Dundee his home, but in 1883 he sought wider appreciation in London, where he died seven years later. It was in composition that he was chiefly interested, but since most of his days were taken up at earning a living, his works in print are not considerable, but a cantata for female voices *Songs in a Vineyard*, and other vocal writings, notably a *Psalm of Life*, as well as *Twelve Scandinavian Sketches* (op. 16), *Three Rondolettos* and a *Suite* for small hands (op. 18), have more than ordinary attraction.

"Fair Edina" also produced John Greig (1854-1909). Educated at Edinburgh University and Moray House Training College, he also graduated B.Mus. (1878) and D.Mus. (1899) at Oxford. As organist at St. Cuthbert's Free Church, Edinburgh, and as interim professor of music at the University (1891) he was very popular, but later (1900) he became organist of the Scottish National Church, London, where he died. Among his more important compositions are the exquisitely graceful *Three Part-Songs* (1887), and orchestral suite *The Three Graces* (1890), an opera *Holyrood* (Glasg., 1896) produced by Durward Lely, and an oratorio *Zion*. His part-song *Life's Gloaming* (1890) carried on the best traditions of this sort of composition. Greig also edited *Scots Minstrelsie* (Edin., 1892-95), the *Musical Educator* (Edin., 1895 *et seq.*), and *British Minstrelsie* (1899). The *Musical Times* said of his so-called

opera that it was " not by any means unattractive " and that " some
fine old Scotch melodies had been resuscitated." On the other
hand it could not be termed an opera in the modern accepted
meaning of the term, since it was rather like the old drama of
Cramond Brig interspersed with songs and interludes. Yet Greig
was a man of undoubted ability. When he left Edinburgh for
London, J. Cuthbert Hadden lamented in the *Scottish Musical
Monthly* that " it was a pity that London should swallow up our
best men." Of course it was, but Edinburgh had nothing to offer
him, and who could blame him for shaking the dust of the capital
from his feet.

One more composer worthy of mention is William Alexander C.
Cruickshank (1854-1934) of Greenlaw. He was a pupil of Thomas
Hewlett, Mus. Bac., in Edinburgh. Being born in the Lowlands
his first professional post was as music master at Loretto School,
Musselburgh (1874), then as organist of St. John's, Selkirk (1875),
next at a church at Alloa (1876), finally settling at Burnley, England
(1880), where most of his creative work was accomplished, finding
time to graduate B.Mus. (Oxon.) in 1885. Among sixty-three
entries in the British Museum Catalogue, which include anthems,
hymns, part-songs, songs, pianoforte and organ pieces, his most
meritorious work seems to be that devoted to the church, in which
we have a *Communion Service* in E Flat (1884), a *Te Deum* (1908),
a *Jubilate* (1911), a *Benedictus* (1913) and a *Magnificat* and *Nunc
Dimittis* (1918). Outside of the first named, the remainder are
quite impressive in their way, showing independence of the
evangelical school and the Gounod *clichés*. His anthems (e.g.
Praise the Lord) are thoroughly virile and are on the same level as
his part-songs, of which *My True Love* is an admirable example.

Most of the aforementioned composers lived during a period
which saw the rise of two great movements in British music,—
the British Renascence of the " Seventies," and the Scottish
National Group in the " Nineties," yet all of the above are outwith
these momentous advancements. Those of the German school
were not only temperamentally averse to the Renascence, but were

incapable of contributing work on a level with the pioneers of this movement who were as giants in comparison. The others, who were bred at home, although better fitted to help than the former, were still not advanced enough to play their part in this great urge towards independence. Many of them were precluded by their vocation from entering the ranks of those seeking the Promised Land ; others, those in the church, had not the vision.

Just as the cosmopolitan outlook on music was one of the facets of middle-class rule (1837-68), so the change of political attitude in an incipient democracy (1868-85) also brought fresh vistas for the art, one of which promised a lessening of the alien hegemony which had so long held British music in servitude, and it came about this wise. The first to break down the barriers against the British composer was one whose name was soon to become a household word in the land—[Sir] Arthur Sullivan. It may be true that he was already known in so far as he had gained a nod of approval by his *Tempest* music (1862), *L'île enchantée* and *Kenilworth* (1864), but it was his association with W. S. Gilbert the librettist in comic opera that gave him, and his music, the passport to universal recognition, and, let it not be forgotten, it was Gilbert's rather *risqué* librettos that were made possible by the *liberal political* regimen. Yet other factors played their part in dispelling the illusion of an " unmusical Britain," a figment created by the " Upper Ten " in the days of Hanoverian culture, and sustained by the *entrepreneur* who looked to this class to patronize his highly priced seats. One contributory cause of the change was that growing consciousness of " nationality " which had been pressing other nations ever since those scaring days of " *liberté, egalité, et fraternité*," and was now beginning to find its expression in Dibdin's " Tight Little Islands." It did not amount to much in Britain in comparison with the ardour evinced in other countries, but it did provide an atmosphere in which the British composer could at least breathe, even if it did not allow him to fully expand his lungs. It is not remarkable that W. S. Gilbert should himself have parodied this autochthonous pleading in *H.M.S. Pinafore*

(1878) because we must not forget that the British are often quite dangerous in respect of the things at which *they* laugh. This is one of the perils of democracy. Indeed this very prospect had its roots in the political soil, since the general theory of abstract justice enunciated by the Liberal politicians was but a coalescence of a number of specific theories of a similar nature, including justice for the British composer.

Strange as it may seem, there was no definite group or school either in England or Scotland that was urging this claim, and the Society of British Musicians (1834-65) was now defunct, and its successor, the British Orchestral Society (1872-75), had too brief an existence to accomplish much. Yet it was the ideas of these organisations, rather than their practical contributions, that helped to mould public opinion and make a renascence of British music possible. Further, as Fuller-Maitland rightly emphasises, the British orchestral instrumentalist, who had just regained his position in the world of music, was now openly championing the cause of the British composer. Indeed, when the first streaks of the dawn of British music illumined the sky in the " Seventies," everything seemed quite propitious. As already explained, there was no clique or coterie acting in concert, meeting to exchange ideas or discuss plans, and so it is difficult to describe the birth of this movement. All that can be said of the circumstance is what Topsy revealed in *Uncle Tom's Cabin* of her nativity—" I 'spect I grow'd."

The five great composers that emerged in this renascence who, for want of a better word, have been termed its " Leaders," were Mackenzie, Parry, Thomas, Cowen, and Stanford, and they are given here in the order of the date of their birth. Strange to say, Mackenzie himself (*A Musician's Narrative*) does not admit Thomas into the group. This may have been because of the obvious foreign influence in his work. Indeed Cecil Forsyth (*Music and Nationalism*) calls Thomas a " denationalized Englishman." In point of emergence however, Cowen was the first, for the simple reason that, like most of the others, he came of a comfortably situated middle-class family, and was not actually tied down to getting his living

THE COMPOSERS OF THE REVIVAL

immediately he was clear of his teens. Thus he was free to devote himself to composition quite early in life. Mackenzie was in a different predicament. He was earning his living at theatres whilst he was at the Academy, and for fourteen years after he left, the best part of his days was spent in the soul-searing drudgery of teaching, which allowed neither leisure nor energy for serious composition. Indeed, it was not until he was thirty-two, when some respite came to his tired mind and body, that he was able to make up for lost time. Still we must be thankful that Fate willed it that a Scot, Mackenzie, was to be one of the first, with a Welshman, an Englishman, a Colonial, and an Irishman, in this surge of the renascence of British music in the " Seventies " of the 19th Century.

Alexander Campbell Mackenzie (1847-1935) was the greatest of Scotland's composers since the Reformation, since he eclipsed both Thomas Erskine (d. 1781) and John Thomson (d. 1841), The son of Alexander Mackenzie (1819-57), of whom we have treated as conductor of the Theatre Royal, Edinburgh, he received his earliest training from his father, but was sent to Germany (1857) for further instruction. On his return (1862) he went to the Royal Academy of Music, having won the King's Scholarship, where he stayed three years studying under Lucas (harmony and counterpoint), Sainton (violin) his father's teacher, and Jewson (pianoforte) a fellow Scot. Settling in Edinburgh (1865) as a music teacher, he held several important appointments : Precentor of St. George's Church (1870-81), conductor of the Scottish Vocal Music Association (1873-80), and teacher at the Church of Scotland Training College (1873-79). In spite of his daily grind he found the time to compose a little chamber music, some of which was performed at the Classical Chamber Concerts (1874 *et seq.*). Although his first important work in this field, the *Pianoforte Quartet in E Flat* (Op. 11), was published at Leipsic in 1874, it was not printed in Britain until 1931, when it was issued by the Oxford University Press, a circumstance which led the composer to call attention to the fact in an autograph note on the score which he presented to the Dunedin Association. For precisely the same reason, the Renascence of British music not yet having dawned, his earliest orchestral works, *Overture to a Comedy* and the overture *Cervantes*, first received a hearing at Düsseldorf (1876) and Sondershausen (1877) respectively, although the latter was repeated by Hans von Bülow at Glasgow (1878). Meanwhile, his *Scherzo for Orchestra* was given in Glasgow (1878) followed by Manns' presentation of his *Rhapsodie Écossaise* (1880) for orchestra also at the concerts of the " Second City." Then followed *In the Scottish Highlands* for the pianoforte, and his *Burns*, the second *Rhapsodie Écossaise*, also produced at Glasgow (1881). It was in these works, as Fuller-Maitland has said, that we got a fore-taste of the qualities in which Mackenzie excelled : " Poetic and imaginative, they have not merely local colour excellently handled, but something of the hidden fire that is present in the best Scotch songs."

What really established his reputation, partly because the public have from time immemorial been worshippers at this shrine, were his cantatas and oratorios,—*The Bride* (1881), *Jason* (1882), *The Rose of Sharon* (1884), and *The Story of Sayid* (1886), all at the great *English* festivals, the most original of his works in this genre, and the one which signalized his worth as a composer, being *Sharon*. His operas, *Columba* (1883) and *The Troubadour* (1886), also belong to this period. Quite as interesting perhaps are those many works which by word or deed reveal Scotland. His ode *The New Covenant* to the words of his fellow Scot Robert Buchanan (Glasgow Exhibition, 1888), and the same poet's *Bride of Love* (1893) do not exhibit much of the Scottish idiom. More impressive was his setting of Burns' *The Cottar's Saturday Night* (1888) for chorus and orchestra, which struck a new and sublime note, although it was not performed until 1889 at Edinburgh, when the *Musical Times* said that the " characteristic [scalar] intervals and national rhythm are combined by a master hand." His suite *Pibroch* for violin and orchestra played by Sarasate (Leeds Festival, 1889), the *Highland Ballad* (1893) for the same combination, and *From the North* (1895), three of which were scored for strings, showed his continued fond-ness for the violin and the Scottish idiom. Greater still in this latter respect was his *Scottish Concerto* (1897) for pianoforte and orchestra, played by Paderewski (Philharmonic Concert). His last great work of an idiomatic character was the Scottish Rhapsody *Tam o' Shanter* (1911). Besides several smaller works on Scottish themes, such as his *Ancient Scots Tunes*, he composed incidental music to Scott's *Marmion* (Glasgow, 1889) and *Ravenswood* (Lond., 1890), as well as Barrie's *The Little Minister* (Lond., 1897).

Grove's Dictionary of Music (1940) says that Mackenzie's works of Scottish title " have sufficient reference to Scottish folk-song and other suggestions of local colour to give him a place among musical nationalists ; but his idiom was really cosmopolitan, and he did not generally handle Scottish themes with special native sensitiveness. . . . His nationality found expression in more general characteristics less easily defined, in a steadfast persistence in the pursuit of an aim, in an imagination which was not afraid of the commonplace, and, by no means least, in a buoyant sense of humour." This reference to idiom may mean anything or nothing. That Mackenzie was under the spell of Mendelssohn (and who escaped it in those days ?) may readily be admitted, if that is what " cosmopolitan " means. Yet one feels inclined to say that where Mackenzie is " commonplace " is just in so far as he is " cosmopolitan," and where he is " idiomatic " he is " imaginative." That there should be any dubiety about his most explicit national idiom, whether he " handles " it with propriety or impropriety, passes all understanding. Mackenzie himself says (*A Musician's Narrative*),—" Whether with exactness or not, it has been said that all through my efforts at composition the Scot keeps peeping out. If that be so, he obtrudes his presence either unwittingly or beyond control. When I did write in the Doric I meant it ; and must have contributed more than nineteen works to its native list." To talk, as Grove does, of " local colour " in the Scottish works of Mackenzie is, to say the least, rather inept. One does not refer to the Doric in Burns' *Cottar's Saturday Night* as " local colour " any more than one would use such a phrase of the *Rubaiyat* of Omar Khayyam, although it would be strictly correct to speak of an Oriental theme in Mackenzie's *Story of Sayid* as " local colour." Suffice it to say firstly, that Mackenzie in his idiom and otherwise, opened up a new and original path in the British renascence movement which was soon to bear luxuriant fruit, and secondly, that Mackenzie was one of the glories of this great movement which placed Britain once more in the proud position which it once held in the world of music.

In spite of the generally expressed opinion to the contrary, it was the distinctly Scottish characteristic in many of Mackenzie's contributions to the renascence of British music that was the torch that kindled the flame which burned so brightly in the Scottish National Group of composers from Hamish MacCunn to [Sir] John B. McEwen in the last two decades of the 19th Century. Although neither the pioneers of the Renascence nor the disciples of the Scottish National Group were swayed by the influence of any coterie, the latter most assuredly had one link that bound them together. In almost every one of this band an intense love of country pervaded their souls. It was not prompted by mere political creed, but was rather a deep passion that moved them to express in their art a something that was as intimate as the work of Burns, of Scott, of Burnet, of Wilkie, some at least of whose creations inspired their genius. Before the " Eighties " had dawned, Scotland was already demanding a Scottish National Academy of Music, of which Mackenzie was presaged as Principal. Sir James Donaldson of St. Andrews has recorded that although this plan did not materialize in the *institutional* sense, what did result was something just as worthy. After Mackenzie's *Rhapsodie Écossaise* (1880) had appeared, the vision of a " National School " in the *creative* sense took a firm hold on the imagination of the prescient few, and before many years had passed this reverie had become an accomplished fact in the compositions of Hamish MacCunn, Learmont Drysdale, Frederick J. Simpson, William Wallace, J. Moir Clark, Charles Macpherson and John B. McEwen.

In this brilliant lead by Mackenzie, which gave rein to the imagination of the younger generation of Scottish composers to express themselves in a national or individual idiom, the first to appear on the scene was Hamish MacCunn (1868-1916) of Greenock, and he was more definitely Scottish in his utterance than his predecessor. When barely fifteen he won a scholarship in the newly established Royal College of Music, London, where he was a pupil (1883-86) of Parry and Stanford for composition, Franklin Taylor for pianoforte, and Alfred Gibson for viola. His first important composition was the overture, *Cior Mhor* (1885) which Manns produced at the Crystal Palace, followed by three other orchestral works, all featured by Manns,—*The Land of the Mountain and Flood* (1887), *The Ship o' the Fiend* (1888) which Henschel introduced, and *The Dowie Dens o' Yarrow* (1888), most of which called forth even extravagant praise, one saying that " Scotland has produced a genius of whom she might well be proud." After this the composer was silent in the purely orchestral sphere until Manns and the Philharmonic played his *Highland Memories* (1897). Not only did MacCunn " express the poetry and romance of his native land in a way in which it had never been expressed before," but his music was coloured with expressions as endemic as the Doric itself, and less periphrastic than those of Mackenzie. Then followed, in quick succession, several triumphs in cantatas and ballads for choir and orchestra,—*Lord Ullin's Daughter* (1888) which Manns gave at the Crystal Palace, *The Lay of the Last Minstrel* (1888) commissioned and first performed by the Glasgow Choral Union, and repeated by Manns the next year at the Crystal Palace, *Bonny Kilmeny* (1888) at Paterson's Concerts, Ediriburgh, and again by Manns (1889), *The Cameronian's Dream* (1890) also at Paterson's Concerts and the Crystal Palace, and *Queen Hynde of Caledon* (1892) by the Glasgow Choral Union and Manns at the Crystal Palace. These were the days when Scotland was proud of her sons of genius and regularly gave them scope in music. Both here and in London, MacCunn's work was received with enthusiasim. *Bonny Kilmeny* was rightly considered " a masterpiece " for " its beauty appeals to both cultured and uncultured—which is the test of the highest art." The *Lay of the Last Minstrel* was deemed to contain dramatic scenes " difficult to surpass, and shows a masterful treatment of all the resources of the full orchestra."

By this time MacCunn was attracted by, or was offered greater scope in, larger canvases. He had been commissioned by the Carl Rosa Co. to write an opera, and in 1894 his *Jeanie Deans* was produced in Edinburgh, and again in London in 1896. In his native land, where it was the " first opera by a Scotsman on a Scottish subject in the capital," it had a most enthusiastic reception. The *Musical Times* said : " The Scottish flavour in the music is judiciously minute, being almost confined to two national dance tunes . . . and the dialect is fortunately no more conspicuous." Apart from the critic's prejudices, he seems to have been only capable of judging what was idiomatically Scottish in the music by a foot rule that merely indicated the *snap* and the *drone*. The next opera was *Diarmid*, which was staged at Covent Garden in 1897 by the Carl Rosa Co., and this, with *Jeanie Deans*, remained in the repertory for many years. I can recall Philip Brozel's fine characterization of the title rôle. Queen Victoria " commanded " a performance of excerpts at Balmoral in 1898.

At the turn of the century we find the composer already recognized as the principal conductor for Carl Rosa, in which his work at the Lyceum Theatre, London, was greatly appreciated, as were his services in the Moody Manners Opera Co. Later we see him with the baton at the Savoy, the Adelphi, the Lyric, and other London theatres. In the great metropolis however, he found that a more cosmopolitan outlook was necessary in his creative work, hence *The Masque of War and Peace* (1900), the opera *The Golden Girl* (1905), *The Wreck of the Hesperus* (1905) for chorus and orchestra, and *The Pageant of Darkness and Light* (1908). Still, in his later years, he returned to the old themes in four excellent ballads for chorus and orchestra, *Kinmont Willie*, *The Jolly Goshawk*, *Lambkin*, and *The Death of Parcy Reed*. Nor can we omit his *Livingstone the Pilgrim*. Over a hundred songs from his pen are in print, quite half of them being settings of Scottish poets, and a good many, as Fuller-

Maitland suggested, " sometimes approach very near genius." To pick out unique pearls in this necklace would be difficult, but *The Ash Tree* is " a little gem," and Burns' *Strathallan's Lament* and *Had I a Cave* shine with equally refulgent charm, whilst the part-song *O Mistress Mine* is a worthy setting of Shakespeare's lyric.

Since almost all of MacCunn's operas and cantatas of Scottish appeal have been published, there cannot be any excuse for amateur operatic and choral societies in ignoring these finely dramatic and highly effective works. Honorary officials of such societies in Scotland often complain of the lack of general interest in their work and aims, and yet we seem to have in these compositions of MacCunn and his compatriots the very antidote to this apathy. Quite apart from any national appeal, if we allow that music itself is a socializing factor, then this latter is surely enhanced when the music presents a more homely story, a more familiar language, and a more instinctive melody and rhythm. In the works of MacCunn, especially where he handles the folk ballad, these elements are pre-eminent.

One who was, as H. Sandiford Turner said in 1915, even " more Scottish in character " in his works than MacCunn, was the Edinburgh composer, Learmont Drysdale (1866-1909). As a young man he had been (1885) organist at Greenside Parish Church, Edinburgh, and had given recitals at the International Exhibition, Edinburgh (1886), but in 1887, like all the rest, he set out for London, having accepted an organ position at Kensington All Saints Church. The following year he entered the Royal Academy of Music, where he sat under Corder and Kuhe for composition and the pianoforte respectively. He returned to Scotland in 1904 as teacher of harmony and composition at the Glasgow Athenaeum School of Music, but relinquished the position so as to devote himself to composition. His first works belong to his Academy days, one being a ballade for orchestra, *The Spirit of the Glen* (1889), which Mackenzie conducted at the Academy concerts, the *Daily Telegraph* (Joseph Bennett) saying that it was " one of the most satisfactory works we have recently met with," adding that it was " distinctly

Scottish in character of theme." In praising the instrumental treatment it called forth the remark that "skilful handling of the orchestra seems to be an instinctive gift of Scottish composers." The next year he began the cantata *Thomas the Rhymer* (1890), the prelude to which was performed at St. James's Hall. It is a delightful work for one so young, and seems to reveal complete artistic self-expression. The *Daily News* said that it was "an admirable piece of tone painting, strongly imbued with the characteristics of Scottish music." The composer was considered "a thorough master of the art of picturesque orchestration." In this year, too, he gained the Charles Lucas Medal with an *Overture to a Comedy* (1890) afterwards known as *Through the Sound of Raasay*, which has recently been revived by Dr. Ernest Bullock in Glasgow. Then followed his setting of Burns' *Ode to Edinburgh* (1890) which has yet to be performed, and the overture *Tam o' Shanter* (1890), Drysdale's best known work. [Sir] August Manns featured this at the Crystal Palace Concerts in the November, it being repeated by Manns in Glasgow in the following January, and topped the list for the plebiscite concert overshadowing even *Tannhäuser* and *The Flying Dutchman*. Edinburgh did not hear it until 1894, when [Sir] George Henschel conducted it. London and provincial critics were loud in their praise : "Drysdale has undoubtedly a future," said one.

On the heels of these successes came the cantata *The Kelpie* (1891), but it was not given in full until 1894, when it was done by Kirkhope's Choir and the Scottish Orchestra. Then followed the overture *Herondean* (1893), given at St. James's Hall, London (1894). Scotland did not hear it for many years, at Glasgow under Cowen in 1900 and at Edinburgh under Henschel in 1903, both dates clearly demonstrating Scotland's part indifference to the best music by her own composers. In 1896 was produced *The Plague*, "a new departure in musical-dramatic art," which was staged by [Sir] J. Forbes Robertson. After this came an opera, *The Red Spider*, the libretto being by Baring Gould. It was produced in 1898 and toured the length and breadth of the land, reaching its hundredth performance at Dundee. At the request of [Sir] Henry Wood in 1904 he composed an orchestral poem *A Border Romance,* performed at Queen's Hall that year. Fuller-Maitland in the *Times* said that " the themes, thoroughly Scottish in character, are beautiful; the workmanship clean, sane, and interesting, especially in the skilful use of the strings." The year 1905 saw the birth of the cantata *Tamlane,* one of the most representative works of its kind in that quarter-century. Finally came his *Hyppolytus* (1905) music and his opera *Fionn and Tera* (1908-09). The former was sublime incidental music of an extraordinarily expressive character written for [Sir] Gilbert Murray's version of the masterpiece of Euripides produced at Glasgow. The opera, although completed in all essential details by Drysdale, was left unfinished in score, as the composer died all too early at forty-three. It was completed however by the late David Stephen, and was accepted by Oscar Hammerstein for production at the London Opera House in 1912, but the famous impresario's financial collapse shortly after that put an end to all hopes. Unfortunately much of Drysdale's best work still remains in manuscript, and for this reason it is only his *Tam o' Shanter,* *The Kelpie,* and *Tamlane* that can, at the moment, hold a place in the repertories. Scotland certainly needs a Maecenas for her composers, such as the Russians had in Belaiev. This is clear even from the experience of Mackenzie who, at the height of his fame, could find no British publisher who would accept, even as a gift, his *Scottish Concerto,* although it had been written for and was featured by Paderewski. Eventually it was accepted by a German publisher who actually purchased it !

Older than the two preceding was Frederick James Simpson (1856-19..) of Portobello, and he was in his " Thirties " ere his works saw the light of day. Yet dates do not count where a spiritual awakening is concerned, since one can be " born again " in art, as in religion, in the " Forties " as in the " Twenties." Simpson was educated at Edinburgh Academy, and later in England and Switzerland. Like the credulous many of the period he journeyed to Leipsic (1878) and studied under Alfred Richter but, returning to England, went to the National Training School for Music, which later became (1882) the Royal College of Music, where he studied under [Sir] Frederick Bridge, Prout, and Franklin Taylor. Taking the B.Mus. (Oxon.) degree in 1886, he spent another *wanderjahr*, even though he was forty-two, in Germany, this time under Ludwig Bussler at the Stern Conservatorium in Berlin. To what end all this accretion of theoretical attainments was directed is not evident from Simpson's works. Prout and Bussler are names that count in the history of the groundwork of this craft in their respective lands, although the latter was less original than the former, but there is certainly nothing new-fangled in Simpson who, on the contrary, is stability itself. His *Three-part Songs* (1888) are the earliest works that can be consulted, and these, together with his enticing *Old English Songs* (1894) for three voices, are quiescent rather than transilient. Perhaps one ought not to give judgment from such evidence, which is conditioned by both form and subject, but there is not much of his work published to enable us to appreciate judiciously. He composed a *Symphony in C*, a cantata *The Departure of Summer*, and other works of like dimensions, yet none is available. His overture, *Robert Bruce* was performed at the Crystal Palace Concerts in 1889, which the *Musical Times* thought had " promise enough to commend notice for the future works of the composer." In this work Simpson used *Hey, tuttie taitie* as a subject, although it is not heard in full until it appears as a paean of triumph in the finale. His use of *p*. passages for brass was praised. Another idiomatic work was his setting of *Coronach* (1891) from Scott's " Lady of the Lake," for solo, quartet, chorus, and orchestra, which was produced in Edinburgh in the year of its publication. Here was a work of sombre majesty although it was but little appreciated at its initial hearing.

Another to be " born again " was John More Smieton (1857-1904) of Dundee, where he lived and died, although little heeded outside Scotland. Educated at Edinburgh University, where he studied music under Oakeley, he later took instruction from Frederick Bridge, Cowen, and Henschel. Whilst he became known locally by a setting of *Psalm CXXI* for solo, chorus, and strings, an orchestral sketch *The Princess of Thule*, and an *Overture in C*, his gifts were best appreciated in " meritorious choral works " (*Musical Times*), the more important of which are *Pearl* (1882), *Ariadne* (Dundee, 1883), *King Arthur* (Broughty Ferry, 1889), *The Song and the Sower* (Lond., 1891), *The Jolly Beggars* (Glasg., 1893), *Belinda* (1896) with Basil Hood, and *Connla* (op. 28, 1900). His earlier works show no particular Scottish idiom but, under the possible influence of the National Group, he seems to have caught some of their inspiration later. According to the *Scotsman*, it was *Ariadne* that made Smieton's reputation, and within ten years it had been performed over fifty times in Scotland. *King Arthur* aroused even more interest. The *Musical Times* said that it was " graceful and melodious, . . . the work of a craftsman who is steadily making progress among contemporary composers," whilst the *Glasgow Herald* praised its " delightful choruses." In his *Jolly Beggars* the composer revelled in some of the Caledonian spirit, and it gained the Glasgow Select Choir Prize in 1893 with Prout and Niecks as judges. Whilst it is most characteristic music, it is not his best. In this sparkling work, which is poles asunder from Bishop's tamely respectable setting, the composer seizes with delicious apprehension the mordant satire of Burns, and manages to reinforce the dramatic situations with equal adeptness. One can readily agree with the statement that Smieton's music " is distinguished by masterly characterisation." At the first performance, the critic of the *Musical Times* noticed " the delightful whiffs of Scotch caller air " that pervaded the scene. Indeed his conception of those drunken " tatterdemalions," as Carlyle calls that vagrant crowd in the " Poosie Nancie," proves the truth of this. His handling of the *finale*, " So sang the bard," is admirable, and the bold setting of those challenging lines,—" A fig for those by law protected," is a perfect gem, especially that closing babel of voices in the sextet to the lilt of *The Keel Row*. Yet Smieton's best work is *Connla*, a superb setting of words by his brother James (his general librettist) to a fairy story from Joyce's *Old Celtic Romances*. Herein we find delightfully ethereal music, gossamer-like in places, and yet with strongly dramatic and emotional passages side by side. His subtle treatment of the voices and his ingenious orchestral scoring make it a work that should last so long as there are ears for really good music. Yet although the *Musical Times* said, obituary-wise, that Smieton " occupied a distinct place among contemporary Scottish composers," the fact remains that his works are but little known outside the land of his birth, and even there they are beginning to fall into the twilight.

One of the creative giants of the period was William Wallace (1860-1940) of Greenock, although he stands merely on the fringe of the National Group. He, too, was later in efflorescence than MacCunn and Drysdale, but that was due to the fact that his father, an eminent surgeon, had destined him for his own profession. Educated first at Fettes College, Edinburgh, he went to Glasgow University and graduated M.B. and Ch.M. in 1888. Music called him away from this and he entered the Royal Academy of Music in 1889, where he was a contemporary of Drysdale and Bantock, being one of the six rebels, headed by Bantock, but without Drysdale, who so vehemently protested against the prevailing musical cliques and the chilling, conservative, official outlook of the " schools." The original trend of Wallace is said to have been palpable from his early scena for baritone and orchestra *Lord of Darkness* (Lond., 1890) and again in his symphonic poem *The Passing of Beatrice* (Crystal Palace, 1892). The press, speaking of his suite of incidental music to Ibsen's *The Lady from the Sea* (Lond., 1892) patronizingly said that the work " gave the impression that the young composer has much ability." Then came his prelude to the *Eumenides* of Aeschylus (Crystal Palace, 1893) which the *Musical Times* adjudged " a work of undoubted cleverness." His overture *In Praise of Scottis Poesie* (Crystal Palace, 1894) contains just a touch of *brogue*, as perhaps it ought, since it was composed at the request of his countrymen for " something Scotch," although the *Musical Times*, with an effort of wit, thought that what the composer actually offered was " an ingenious but hardly convincing answer." At the same time its critic admitted that " the work is not wanting in a certain brilliancy of a stereotyped order, and is brilliantly scored." Of greater moment was Wallace's scena *The Rhapsody of Mary Magdalene* (Lond., 1896), his symphonic poems *Anvil or Hammer* (Crystal Palace, 1896), *Sister Helen* (ditto, 1899), *To the New Century* (Philharmonic, 1901), *Wallace A.D. 1305-1905* (Queen's Hall, 1905), and *Villon* (New Symphony Orchestra, 1909), the latter being his best known work, to which must be added his noble symphony *The Creation* (New Brighton, 1899). Works revealing a definite Scottish idiom are *A Scots Fantasy*, the *Jacobite Songs*, but more so his earlier brutally amusing *Massacre of the Macpherson* which is a risible mishmash of old Scottish themes sandwiched with snippets from *Siegfried*, *Götterdämmerung* and *Die Meistersinger*. Yet only the elect appreciated the pungent gibe.

We have already gauged the kind of mind possessed by Wallace as revealed in his books,—*The Threshold of Music* (1908) and *The Musical Faculty* (1914), a type of work which seems to have taken his thoughts away from composing music.. Yet herein we have precisely the same individual prospect and the identical freedom from convention that we find in his music. Perhaps this is, as Havelock Ellis says (*Impressions and Comments*), because all great thinkers are masters of metaphor since " all thinking of any kind must be by analogy." However much æsthetes may conceive the creative act in music in terms of " dream states " or " inspiration," the fact remains that precisely the same mechanical mental processes are involved in music as in poetry, painting, science, or philosophy. The music of Wallace is pre-eminently that of a thinker, although the composer himself would probably not have agreed with this assessment, nor even with my proposition of the identity of the " mental act " in composing with other forms of creation, since he held the view that " there is no known mental process which in any respect resembles music " (*The Threshold of Music*).

A composer, although mentioned in high places (Grove, *Dictionary of Music*), who has been quite neglected is J. Moir Clark of Aberdeen.

Doubtless this latter disregard is due to the fact that his works are not in print. He was at the Royal Academy of Music (1883-86) under Prout, who had a good opinion of his future. His first composition heard in public was *Variations on an Original Theme* (1889) played by Dora Bright at her concerts. After this and other minor works the composer went to Germany and pursued his studies at Dresden where some of his compositions were featured (1892), notably his *Quintet in F* for pianoforte and strings. The latter was repeated in London (1893) by Dora Bright, and when played again the following year the *Musical Times* said that it was " noteworthy throughout for fresh and tuneful themes " but condemned other rather original features, although the composer had already explained that these were " to secure greater variety and strength of colour than chamber music usually presents." In 1895 his *Scotch Suite* for orchestra was performed by the Stock Exchange Orchestra.

Of some importance was Archibald Davidson Arnott (b. 1870) but he has no place in *Grove's Dictionary of Music*, although he clearly deserves it. Whilst born in Glasgow he was reared in London, where he studied at the Royal College of Music under Parry and Stanford, later sitting at the feet of Corder. He then became organist at several London churches and graduated B.Mus. (Dunelm.) in 1891, being the first graduate in music by examination in that university. He does not appear to have shown his hand at composition until the " Twenties " of his career, but when he did it was to reveal considerable artistic skill and a certain originality of expression, as we know from his two cantatas, which bring him in close proximity in point of time and treatment with the Scottish National Group. These were *Young Lochinvar* (1893) for chorus and orchestra which was performed at the Crystal Palace (1895) and led the *Musical Times* to say that " it possesses the welcome quality of melodiousness, is full of spirit and vigour, and, on the whole, decidedly effective." The other was *The Ballad of Carmilhan* (1894), given at the Queen's Hall (1895), and although not a Scottish subject it has some features of the idiom. It was one of the works signalised by Fuller-Maitland in his *English Music in the XIXth Century* (1902). After this, Arnott took to higher flights and wrote two operas—*Angelo* (January, 1895) in two acts, and *Marie Ancel* (July, 1895) in four acts, neither of which has been produced. Besides these works there were three cantatas or suchlike compositions, a scena *The Stilling of the Tempest* (1894) for solo and orchestra, *The Lost Galleon* (1896), and a sacred mystery *Vita Christi* (1896). In the purely orchestral sphere he contributed two overtures, several items of chamber music, whilst for the Church he wrote a striking *Communion Service in F*, and some attractive anthems such as *O Come thou Saviour* and *I Heard a Great Voice*. In surveying his work, I have only been able to assess Arnott's position among contemporary composers from his church music and his cantatas. His *Young Lochinvar* and *The Ballad of Carmilhan*, although they belong to his earliest work, are delightfully fresh in aspect and, whilst not too strongly Scottish idiomatically, are resplendently imaginative and colourful. These cantatas alone should confirm the view that the composer merits a position with his fellow Scots who have gone before as an exponent of the best that Scotland could offer in this form from those days of the " followers of the Renascence," as Fuller-Maitland has dubbed them.

Charles Macpherson (1870-1927) was born in Edinburgh, where his father was the Burgh architect, but from his ninth year he came under English influence musically when he became a chorister at St. Paul's Cathedral, London, under [Sir] George Martin, who gave him organ lessons. In 1887 he became organist to Sir Robert Menzies, Weem, Perthshire, but in 1890 he entered the Royal Academy of Music, won the Charles Lucas prize (1892), and took A.R.A.M. (1896). Meantime (1895) he had been appointed assistant organist at St. Paul's, and in 1911, succeeded his old teacher, Sir George Martin, in the chief position. He won his first laurels as a composer when still a student (1895) by his magnificent *By the Waters of Babylon* (Psalm CXXXVII), although earlier still (1893) he had gained the prize offered by the Bristol Orpheus Glee Society with his glee for five voices *There Sits a Bird*. Another early work was his overture *Cridhe an Ghaidhil* (Crystal Palace, 1895), which places him among the National Group. The *Musical Times* said that it " shows decided poetic feeling and considerable control of orchestral resource." Others of the same urge that followed were *Three Gaelic Melodies* for strings and harp, and two orchestral suites, *Hallowe'en* and a *Highland Suite in A.* Since then almost all of his published work concerns the church in such anthems as *Look on the Fields* (1901), *The Heavens Declare* (1904), *Sing Unto God* (1918), and *O, Praise God* (1924), but not one of them reaches the austere majesty of his earlier *By the Waters of Babylon* (1895), which is quite secular in its approach. It was first performed at the Royal College of Music (1895), and the following year was given a fine rendering by Thomas H. Collinson in Edinburgh.

Alfred Moffat (b. 1866) comes from Edinburgh, but he was educated musically in Germany, studying (1882-88) under Ludwig Bussler of the Stern Conservatorium, Berlin. Although better known as an editor and arranger of music, several compositions came from his pen, especially in his early days. Like his compatriots, he showed an initial attraction for the cantata, of which *The Passing Year*, *The Dressing of the Well*, and *The Children of Samuel* were the earliest, all for female or children's voices. Among his numerous instrumental and vocal works, some of which were published in Germany, is a *Quartet for Pianoforte and Strings* (1886) which was well received in Berlin, and ought to be reissued. Whilst in Germany he worked for a few years with music publishers as an editor, and found that they could be interested in old English violin composers. He was thus able to persuade Simrock to publish a number of sonatas from the old English school. Yet, as shown by Grove, when Moffat came to England as an editor, " he had a hard fight to get anyone to believe that there had been a school of English violin composers," until he finally induced Novello to issue his *Old English Violin Music* series which, incidentally, is not wholly *English*, since it contains a sonata by the 18th Century Charles Macklean. It was the old story of Dunstable over again, since it was German savants who recognised the so-called " Father of counterpoint " long before his native land discovered him. It is primarily as an editor and arranger of music that Britain owes a debt of gratitude to Moffat, and in the purely Scottish field he has issued *The Minstrelsy of Scotland, Thirty Highland Reels, Old Scottish Folk Songs, Minstrelsy of the Scottish Highlands, Fifty Traditional Scottish Nursery Rhymes with their Traditional Tunes.* It is strange that in his own creative work Moffat shows no trace of the Scottish idiom, nor is there anything specifically German for that matter. What he has written might conceivably have been composed by the generality of British composers of his period, perhaps because, as George Eliot says in *Silas Marner,* " breed is stronger than pasture."

Although but slightly connected with the National Group, Frederick A. Lamond (b. 1868) has a place at this period. As we have already seen, this world-famous pianist completed his musical education in Germany, and his compositions bear the imprint of this teaching, as evidenced by his *Symphony in A* which was produced at Glasgow in 1889. The *Musical Times* was, seemingly, not interested in this event, and merely informed its readers that the symphony " had a place on the programme." Turning to the local press we find quite lengthy notices, which was only proper for the work of a Glaswegian. The critic of the *Glasgow Herald* was quick to detect in this work the influence of Brahms, and almost refused to believe the programme notes which spoke of the national idiom peeping out. In the second movement, however, he was constrained to admit that " the lovely *trio* . . . has that remotely national flavour which the analyst of the programme professes to have discovered in the *finale.*" This latter, said the critic, almost in protest, had " sprung from the heart rather than from the head of the composer." The symphony had a poor reception from the Glasgow audience, possibly because of an admittedly bad performance, although Manns was at the helm. When the latter repeated the symphony at the Crystal Palace in 1890, the *Musical Times* said : " The themes are bold, striking and melodious, and the working out had been completed on the best possible lines and the whole indicates the existence of a mind capable of many and perhaps great things in the future." Its critic also roundly censured Glasgow audiences for being prejudiced against the work at its initial performance in 1889.

A later work of the composer was the overture *From the Scottish Highlands*, produced by the Philharmonic in 1895, when it had " rather a cold reception." According to the *Musical Times*, this was partly due to the absence of a " programme." Seemingly, if the audience had only been given some sort of a mental picture of what was going on, all would have been well for, as Fuller-Maitland once said sneeringly of the tastes of the masses, " people like having something else to think of when they are listening to music." It so happened that Fuller-Maitland, the absolutist in music, was " hoist with his own petar[d] " in his *critique* of the concert, where we find him unconsciously " programming " Lamond's intentions in this work. This is what he said in the London *Times* of Lamond's overture. " Concert overtures professedly Scottish in character have been of late a somewhat too constant element in the pro-grammes of orchestral concerts, and apart from its German title, there seems no especial quality to distinguish . . . *Aus dem schottischen Hochlande* from among others of the same school. It is a clever and decidedly picturesque piece of work, in which the clash of arms is largely represented, as well as some pretty strains of a more peaceful character." Lamond also wrote a few earlier works,—*Eight Pieces for Pianoforte* (Op. 1), followed by a *Sonata in D* for pianoforte and violoncello and a *Trio in B Minor* for piano-forte and strings, both the latter being featured at St. James's Hall, London, in 1889, with the composer at the piano and Piatti at the 'cello. Of the *Trio* the *Musical Times* said that it showed a " rhyth-mical feeling and rugged vigour that ought not to be overlooked." Before the new century dawned, Lamond had already abandoned the composer's pen, although he acquiesced in the performance of his symphony by [Sir] Henry Wood in 1912, which occasioned the following in the *Musical Times* : " It is a genial, easily intelligible work, in a style that was not advanced at the period of its composition, which occurred in 1889." If anyone cares to turn up contemporary (1889) criticism of the first performance, it will be apparent that Lamond's work was then quite beyond the apprehension of critics and audiences, and yet in 1912 the wise ones found it quite "intelligible." *O tempora! O mores!*

John Blackwood McEwen (b. 1868) was born at Hawick in the Borderland, although the formative years of his life were spent in Glasgow, in whose university he graduated (M.A. 1888). London beckoned him in 1891, as it does most Scots who sense neglect in their own land, and in 1893 he entered the Royal Academy of Music, with Prout, Corder, and Matthay as his teachers. Returning to his motherland in 1895 he took a Church appointment at South Parish Church, Greenock, and then became teacher of the pianoforte, harmony and composition at the Glasgow Athenaeum School of Music (1896). Here he remained until 1899, when the Royal Academy of Music, London, appointed him teacher of harmony and composition, which position he held until Mackenzie's retirement, when he was appointed Principal (1924-36). Like his predecessor and other eminent Scottish composers, he was firm in advocating the wider recognition of British composers and was one of the founders and strongest pillars of the Society of British Composers (1905-18) of which he was honorary secretary.

McEwen had seen in his day the gradual yet triumphant rise of the Scottish National Group of composers, speaking an idiom that was as characteristic as that of any other national school. As he said in the *Glasgow Herald* only quite recently, these composers had "something individual to say" and were "able to say it in a way which is peculiar to their race, associations, and outlook." He himself added brilliantly to their efforts. Even before he entered the Academy he had several compositions "up his sleeve," including a symphony and part of an opera on a subject from Ossian, but it was at his musical *Alma Mater* that his works were first heard (1896) —a *String Quartet in F* (No. 6) and a *Scene from Hellas* for soprano, female chorus, and orchestra, the *Musical Times* deeming the latter "estimable music, strong, imaginative and knit with masterly command of resource." Then came an *Overture to a Comedy* which Corder conducted at a Trinity College concert, also a symphonic poem *Comala*, the former to be repeated in Glasgow shortly afterwards. The year 1898 saw the composition of his *String Quartet in A Minor*, although it was not produced until 1904, on which occasion the *Standard* (Gilbert Webb) spoke with high praise of this " interesting and scholarly composition " in which he recognised those themes " possessing character expressed in Scottish musical idiom and treated with pronounced skill." Indeed, almost all of McEwen's chamber music is redolent of Caledonia, and even the famous *Biscay* (No. 13) has a whiff, although it is doubtful whether the North Sea flows so far as the *Sinus Aquitanicus*. When the *Quartet in C Minor* (No. 11) was given at Bechstein Hall in 1910 the *Morning Post* remarked that it was one of those works " that refute the charge that Great Britain has no national school of music, for the quartet is strongly imbued with the characteristic of the composer's native country of Scotland." It is perhaps the best of his works in this genre and received the praise of German critics when it was performed in Berlin, although the generality of music lovers prefer *Biscay*. Other works of national interest are his *Six Highland Dances* (1899) for violin and pianoforte, which no violinist can afford to ignore, the *Three Scottish Dances* for string orchestra, and *Three Border Ballads* (a) *Coronach*, (b) *The Demon Lover*, (c) *Grey Galloway*, of which the first was produced at the Philharmonic Concerts under Cowen (1904), and the last at the same concerts under Chevillard (1909). More recent is his Scottish rhapsody, *Prince Charlie*, for violin and pianoforte.

Although he has composed five symphonies, only one, that in C Sharp Minor (*Solway*) is known, possibly because it is the only one that has been published. It was given its first hearing in 1922 at Dumfries, although it might just as easily have been Glasgow or Edinburgh if Scotland had only been sufficiently alive to her own interests. *Scots wha hae* seems to be a clarion call in Scotland for everything from maudlin politics to big business, but never in the interest of its music. Yet this symphony is one of which

Scotland will yet be proud. Of cantatas and their kind, once so dear to Scottish audiences, he has written nearly a dozen, and it was his *Hymn on the Morning of Christ's Nativity* which led Rutland Boughton to say of this " very beautiful choral work " that it was " a whole panorama of splendid orchestral effect and characterisation." On the instrumental side many of his published works (O.U.P.) are well known, including *Vignettes* and *Preludes* for the pianoforte, as well as his sonatas and the like for violin and pianoforte. Whenever I listen to McEwen I am invariably reminded of Peploe, the Scottish post-impressionist, with whom the composer has a vision and temperament as deeply fused. It may be that one is persuaded æsthetically by memories of his settings of Verlaine in such chaste songs as *La Lune blanche* and *Soleils couchants*, or Austin Dobson's *Love's but a dance.* However this may be, McEwen's music is for eclectic souls. As the *Musical Times* said in 1922, when his music was performed at the centenary of the R.A.M.,—" It is for those who are ready to forego excitement and take measured delight in fine quality."

The last of the national school in this century was David Stephen (1869-1946) of Dundee. Unlike his predecessors, he was not a graduate of the music academies of England or Germany and so, save for summer sessions at the Tonic Sol-fa College London, and a few lessons from W. S. Hoyte and J. Francis Barnett, he can be claimed as a home product. Indeed it has been said that whatever success he attained " was due to the force of his own individuality and perseverance." He sprang from a musical family, and after having been organist at several Dundee churches, later at Westbourne Free Church Glasgow, and conductor of choral societies at Dundee, Arbroath, and St. Andrews, he was called as musical director of the Carnegie Trust at Dunfermline (1903-27) in which position he became a weighty influence on music in Scotland.

Although this appointment demanded much of his time in administration, teaching, and organ recitals, he was still able to devote some of his leisure to the development of his early bent towards composition. In this field his first real success, apart from an interesting *Quintet in D*, was a ballad for choir and orchestra—*Sir Patrick Spens*, a work by which Stephen is best known in Scotland. Other offerings of the same genre are the cantatas *The Abbey Bell* and *The Laird o' Cockpen*, all of which reflect sincere work with some spark of originality, although they were early compositions. These, together with a *Mass* for soli, chorus and orchestra, a *Te Deum in D*, a *Festal Ode*, and some delightful part-songs, have all been published, and because of this one can assess a reasonable judgment of the composer's worth as a creative artist. If his cantatas reveal how idiomatically Scottish the composer is at times, and he is always gracefully melodious, we also discern in his *Mass*, a work of dignified grandeur, the fire of genuine inspiration, although this latter is also an early work that was not produced until 1904, when Andrew Black, a fellow Scot, was one of the soloists. Of his larger canvases one can mention a *Symphony in F Minor*, a *Sinfonietta in D*, and a *Concert Overture*, although perhaps to better purpose are his *Hebridean Rhapsody*, *Border Rhapsody*, and a symphonic poem *Glenfinlas*. Percy Gordon has acutely observed—" He was at his best when writing on Scottish subjects, and what may be called his non-national music, if less individual in quality, is always musicianly in workmanship and effective in performance." Certain it is that Stephen wielded a vigorous pen and not without some individuality, whilst his colourful orchestration was that of a master hand.

Thus we approach the close of our story of Scotland's 19th Century creative offerings at the shrine of St. Cecilia. More might have been placed at her bounteous altar, but only those oblations that have a garnish acceptable to the ears of the beneficent saint, or by whose vernacular she could recognise the origin of the votive gifts, have been proffered. Among the former who have not been acknowledged are Thomas S. Gleadhill (b. 1827), James Roy Fraser (b. 1832), William Moodie (b. 1833), Peter Sinclair Terras (b. 1839), Alexander Patterson (b. 1849), William Meston (b. 1849), James Booth (b. 1850), James Watson Lee (b. 1852), W. Neilson Smith (b. 1852), John Tannahill (b. 1854), W. Marshall Hutchison

(b. 1854), William Thomson Hoeck (b. 1859), J. Michael Diack (b. 1869), and W. Augustus Barratt (b. 1873). Whilst their works may not have been known but to the homely few in the land, they gave their mete of joy, and took their meed of praise in the day of nativity. For quite different reasons have several in the latter category been omitted, although no specifically graduated rule of measurement has been used in their exclusion. I refer to such composers as William Vincent Wallace (b. 1814) who, although he was born at Waterford, sprang from Scottish parents and certainly spoke the Doric to the end of his days. Yet whilst he had deep Scottish sympathies, neither his music nor *libretti* have the slightest connection with the land of his fathers. Precisely the same can be said of Hugh Blair (b. 1864) and Godfrey Pringle (b. 1867). Nor has Eugène d'Albert (b. 1864) any claim for inclusion. True, he was born in Glasgow, and his mother was British. Further, he was educated musically at the pre-Royal College of Music under Sullivan, Stainer, and Prout, yet, in spite of later penitence, he was German in spirit and boasted of it. Much of this alienation of d'Albert was certainly due to lack of scope and appreciation in this country as a composer, and is quite understandable, but there is nothing in him or his work, save his birth and his much-appreciated performances in the land, that truly links him with Scotland.

What is of greater importance is the work of the Scottish National Group of composers, and in closing this book a final word must be said of their particular contribution. Whatever may be the judgment of posterity, their attempt to give new tones to their musical canvases ought, at least, to stand to their credit. They not only made bold to throw off the fetters of foreign domination in utterance as earnestly as, if not more so, than the pioneers of the British renascence, but they dared to be themselves in so far as they gave expression to a distinct national idiom, which was more than the earlier British renascents,—Sullivan, Parry, Stanford, or Thomas— had done. It is true that certain influences of the " schools " are patent enough in their work,—Mendelssohn in Mackenzie and MacCunn, and Gounod in Drysdale—but their borrowed cadences are quite subsidiary to the melody and rhythm of their Doric. Yet there was no stated creed or published manifesto with the new group, nor did they even work in concert. In the former respect they were at one with the slightly earlier rebellious impressionist Glasgow School of painting, and yet they were unlike it, in that they did not ignore subject matter. Indeed they were actually "expressionists" and, if equations serve the purpose, had greater affinity with the post-impressionist school of painting, both in text and treatment, since they went, as Janey C. Drysdale says, " to their country's ballads and legends for their inspiration, and steeped in Highland, Lowland, or Border romance, have clothed their creations with their individual type of Scottish genius, not possessing, but possessed by, the national spirit." That two such independent and characteristic movements should have been born in this decade or two is truly remarkable, and one is almost tempted to seize upon a common denominator. Of course it would be sheer fallacy to point to any intrinsic connection between George Henry's *Galloway* and McEwen's *Grey Galloway*, or between W. Y. Macgreggor's richly toned landscapes and Drysdale's delightfully coloured pastoral *Herondean*, yet these photisms are intriguing and most certainly have an extrinsic identity.

The efforts of this group constitute a stirring *coda* to music in Scotland in the 19th Century. This period clearly demonstrated many facets : That Scotland was still a land, above all others, which continued to cherish her rich heritage in folk and national melodies : That she evinced a growing and sustained appreciation of classical, post-classical, and modern composers, even if not with such demonstrative enthusiasm as elsewhere : That given the opportunity, she could produce *virtuosi* of the rank of a Lamond, and *prima donne* of the quality of a Margaret Macintyre ; That her composers, at the close of the century—Mackenzie, MacCunn, Drysdale, Wallace, and McEwen, who were both heralds of, and combatants for a Scottish National School, had at least something new to say that was worthy of the hearkening.

INDEX OF PERSONS

---

* There were two of this name, (1) the bookseller brother of Andrew Melville, Master of the Sang School at Aberdeen, and (2) the brother of James Melville the theologian.